RUSH FOR RICHES

RUSH
FOR
RICHES

GOLD FEVER AND THE
MAKING OF CALIFORNIA

J. S. HOLLIDAY

OAKLAND MUSEUM OF CALIFORNIA

UNIVERSITY OF CALIFORNIA
BERKELEY LOS ANGELES LONDON

for Belinda,
without whose forbearance . . .

for Timothy,
without whose editorial generosity . . .

Copublished by the Oakland Museum of California and
the University of California Press

University of California Press
Berkeley and Los Angeles, California

University of California Press, Ltd.
London, England

©1999 by J. S. Holliday

LIBRARY OF CONGRESS CATALOGUING-IN-PUBLICATION DATA

Holliday, J. S.
  Rush for riches : gold fever and the making of California / J. S. Holliday.
    p. cm.
  Includes bibliographical references and index.
  ISBN 0-520-21401-3 (alk. paper). — ISBN 0-520-21402-1 (pbk. : alk. paper)
  1. California—Gold discoveries.   2. California—History—1846–1850.
  3. California—History—1850–1950. I. Title
F865.H689 1999
979.4'04—dc21   98-55422
                                                         CIP

Printed and bound in Italy
9 8 7 6 5 4 3 2 1

Printed on acid-free paper

Design: Gordon Chun Design

CONTENTS

FOREWORD

Some five years ago, with the 150th anniversary of the California gold discovery and gold rush approaching, there commenced a growing convergence of interest in these historical events and their impactful legacy. Perhaps no historical event was more embedded in the ethos of California than the gold rush, but mounting criticism of the old interpretations of its history by scholars and the public alike all but insured that this anniversary would not pass without needed public and scholarly debate. With more than twenty-five years of devotion to presenting and interpreting the history, art, and ecology of California, the Oakland Museum of California was poised to embrace the challenge of reopening this history of a time and of events that were steeped in legend, myth, and historical controversy. Such a project, we posited, must include both the pre-gold rush period and the post-gold rush making of California which was its legacy. And we needed to bring into the mix the finest scholars in the field.

That this burgeoning interest in the gold rush era brought together historian J. S. Holliday and the Oakland Museum of California was perhaps predictable, for indeed J. S. Holliday had served as director of the museum during its formative years in the late 1960s, and he had authored in 1981 the landmark book on the California gold rush, *The World Rushed In: The California Gold Rush Experience*, which remains in print to this day. With the good fortune of major exhibition planning support from the National Endowment for the Humanities, and J. S. Holliday as principal historical advisor, we assembled scholars and resource specialists from across California and the nation in three scholarly colloquia to debate the historical questions, issues, and perspectives that would help drive the multiple exhibitions, publications, public programs, and school curriculum materials that we determined to produce. The unreconciled perspectives of these proceedings provided a daunting challenge for the museum.

As the most ambitious and costly project the museum had ever undertaken, the gold rush project ultimately encompassed four separate traveling exhibitions, a fifth traveling exhibition produced for the California Council for the Humanities, a national gold rush symposium, a diversity of public programs, statewide education materials for the public schools, two exhibition catalogues, and a national trade book. Realization of this major project with its many public dimensions was made possible by the generous sponsorship and financial support of the National Endowment for the Humanities, the Clorox Company Foundation, the Wayne and Gladys Valley Foundation, the California Department of Education, the Oakland Museum Women's Board, the City of Oakland, the Rockefeller Foundation, Wells Fargo, Levi Strauss Foundation, Transamerica Foundation, Pacific Gas and Electric, the Bernard Osher Foundation, the Walter and Elise Haas Fund, Kaiser Permanente, the L.J. Skaggs and Mary C. Skaggs Foundation, F.E. Corder, and scores of other contributors.

On January 24, 1998, 150 years to the day that James Marshall first saw the shining specks of gold in the millrace of Sutter's sawmill on the American River, the gold rush project exhibitions and programs made their public debut at the Oakland Museum of California, with the 10,000 sq. ft. exhibition, "Gold Fever! The Lure and Legacy of the California Gold Rush," as the centerpiece. The public response to the exhibitions and programs was immediate and overwhelmingly affirmative. Some 190,000 people were drawn to the "Gold Fever!" exhibition during its six-month venue at the museum. In the summer of 1998, all of the exhibitions went on tour; two, "Art of the Gold Rush" and "Silver and Gold: Cased Images of the California Gold Rush," on a national tour, including the

Smithsonian's National Museum of American Art, and "Gold Fever!" on a California tour, to the Autry Museum of Western Heritage in Los Angeles and and in summer of 1999 to the Memorial Auditorium in Sacramento. But one key cornerstone of this national observance of the sesquicentennial of the California gold rush remained to debut: J. S. Holliday's book *Rush for Riches: Gold Fever and the Making of California*.

With the national publication of the much awaited *Rush for Riches* in Spring of 1999, the remaining cornerstone of the public sesquicentennial offerings envisioned by the museum is now in place, graced by the collaboration of the University of California Press and its director, Jim Clark, in association with author J. S. Holliday and the Oakland Museum of California. That the book has taken somewhat longer to appear than we had foreseen is due in some measure to the many other tasks the museum had asked of Jim Holliday—exhibition advisor, speaker at museum cultivation events and public programs, assistance in fundraising, and help on a myriad of other fronts. Despite his generous acceptance of what he called these "welcome distractions," we often took him from the crucial task of writing, and yet his assistance was immensely important. We are most grateful for Jim's unselfish devotion to the gold rush project as a whole.

Rush for Riches serves as a companion to the "Gold Fever!" exhibition, but more importantly it is consciously a national publication, corresponding to the historical impact on the nation and California of the gold rush itself. California was quickly etched into the nation's soul, imparting into the American Dream new individual and national aspirations from the west. *Rush for Riches* chronicles the powerful forces unharnessed by the gold rush in nineteenth-century California. Triumphs and successes beyond what anyone would have dared to dream are revealed in its chapters, along with the pain, suffering, and tragedies that were also its legacy. Holliday exposes both the unapologetic rapaciousness of this golden era and its tragic human and environmental dimensions. Success, we discover, was often at someone else's expense, and failure could be the stimulus for ultimate success. J. S. Holliday's revealing narrative of these tumultuous decades of the nineteenth century has the power of an eyewitness account. Combining hundreds of evocative images and captions, quotations, maps, and more than fifty years of scholarly immersion in the subject, Jim Holliday has brought laser-like clarity to *Rush for Riches*. It is a bold, forceful account of California's nineteenth-century emergence and its impact on the history of the nation.

The Oakland Museum of California is pleased to acknowledge the invaluable assistance of key contributors to *Rush for Riches*. Oakland Museum of California Foundation Board Chair Daryl Lillie and her husband John made generous financial contributions to help underwrite the book, and were instrumental in securing a major grant to support initial book development from American President Companies, whose maritime heritage can be traced directly back to the gold rush. The Oakland Museum Women's Board provided critical early funding to support book design and development. Museum executive director Dennis Power and chief financial officer Mark Medeiros insured the unwavering commitment of the museum to the book as a cornerstone of the museum's gold rush sesquicentennial project. "Gold Fever!" exhibition co-project director Heather Huxley and museum associate director for public programs Phil Mumma provided much valued assistance in the early planning stages for the book. Image researcher Cherie Newell was tireless in her pursuit of the right images, assisted by Diane Curry, Marianne Germann, Heather Huxley, and photography curators Marcia Eymann and Drew Johnson. Jim Henley, manager of the Sacramento Archives and Museum Collection Center, brought literally hundreds of images to our attention. Libraries, archives, museums, historical societies and private collectors across California and the nation gave J. S. Holliday and the museum unrestricted access to their visual collections, a courtesy that has enriched the book immensely through the inclusion of their evocative images. Photographers Deborah Lohrke and Catherine Buchanan skillfully captured many images for the book on film.

The gifted designer, Gordon Chun of Gordon Chun Design, assisted by his wife, Suzanne, has crafted a book of great beauty, combining ease of reading with visual delight. In Gordon Chun we were thrice blessed, for he was also the designer of the "Gold Fever!" exhibition and of the exhibition catalogue, *Art of the Gold Rush,* also published by UC Press. The University of California Press, its director Jim Clark and his staff, have given *Rush for Riches* a deserving prominence, and have been patient, loyal, and supportive partners.

To the author, J. S. Holliday, go our profound thanks and admiration for his ceaseless and unstinting years of devotion to the writing of *Rush for Riches,* and the fulfillment of his promise to complete it for the sesquicentennial observance of the California gold rush. No author has given more of his intellect, his passion, and his soul to a book than Jim Holliday to *Rush for Riches.* On a personal note, I vividly recall working for and with Jim Holliday more than thirty years ago when as director he channeled all of his prodigious energy and will into creating the then developing Oakland Museum of California. His return some twenty-five years later to play a pivotal role in the museum's gold rush sesquicentennial project—both book and exhibition—completes perhaps two important chapters in his estimable career—one, a renewed, selfless commitment to this museum, and two, the completion and publication of *Rush for Riches.* For both momentous achievements, Jim, you have my heartfelt thanks and appreciation and that of the Oakland Museum of California.

L. Thomas Frye, Director
California Gold Rush Sesquicentennial Project
Oakland Museum of California

AUTHOR'S NOTE

Having finally faced the reality that there is no more time for another revision ("this will be the last change, I promise"), I am free to enjoy the pleasure of expressing my gratitude for the assistance, guidance and innumerable improvements that have made this book more readable, more accurate, and surely more worthwhile.

Beyond those to whom *Rush for Riches* is dedicated (my wife, Belinda, and son, Timothy), I wish to start with Steven Thayer who for almost three years has assisted me in managing the constant corrections and additions to the typescript as it was sent to our wonderful typist, Tammy Jones. (Confession: I use an electric typewriter, plus pen/pencil, scissors, and scotch tape to produce each page for final typing. How these pasted sheets reappear as computer discs is a mystery I am happy not to explore.) With prodigious effort and skill, Steven finalized my source notes and bibliography; and he has worked with our cartographers, Jack and Gay Reineck (Reineck & Reineck, San Francisco) to produce the carefully researched and exactly designed maps that tie in closely with the text. In sum, the making of this book has benefited immeasurably from Steven's organizational powers and his instinctive good judgment.

The historian to whom I am most indebted is Robert L. Kelley, whose pioneering book *Gold vs. Grain: the Mining Debris Controversy* (1959) remains by far the most valuable source on the evolution of the confrontation between farmers and hydraulic miners. As well, his book provided guidance to newspaper articles and official documents that led the way to further research and understanding of this dramatic subject. In his later book, *Battling the Inland Sea* (1989), Robert Kelley developed a broader perspective on the impact of hydraulic mining. And a 1969 Ph.D. thesis (unpublished) by Thomas H. Pagenhart offered a rich deposit of details and statistical evidence relating to water use by hydraulic mining on the watersheds of the Yuba and Bear Rivers.

To gain access to the various newspapers that reported the bitter struggle between valley farmers and foothill miners, I had the assistance of Patricia Morris of Sacramento who spent many hours running through reels of microfilm of Sacramento, Marysville, Nevada City, and San Francisco newspapers, 1850s–1880s. From leads I found in *Gold vs. Grain* and the Pagenhart thesis, Pat sent me scores of eyewitness accounts, official reports, and angry editorials that have enriched my story with quotations and descriptive details. Another ally in the quest for specifics has been Frank Van Konynenburg of Modesto, an authority on the history of California agriculture. He most generously provided photocopies of pages from the *Pacific Rural Press* and from various periodicals, 1850s–1880s.

To those who have read the manuscript in its various mutations, I am profoundly grateful, not only because they provided scores of corrections and improvements but as well for their encouragement. John Allman of Los Angeles took time from meeting his own pressing deadlines to send me many useful comments and concepts. Joyce Appleby, professor of history, University of California at Los Angeles, sent encouragement that made me feel honored by her judgment. Richard Dillon commented on most of the chapters, with his renowned knowledge and attention to accuracy. George Ellis of San Diego has been indefatigable in sending me not only scores of bibliographic leads and fundamental cartographic information, he has as well read the entire manuscript and compiled lists of corrections. John Hicks, former professor of English at the University of Massachusetts at Amherst, cheerfully prepared pages of suggestions for each chapter. His perseverance nurtured my own. Mead Kibbey in Sacramento searched through his extensive photographic collection, made quality prints, and otherwise helped me find my way. Thomas H. Pagenhart most graciously allowed me to make adaptations of maps and drawings in his wonderful Ph.D. thesis. And Richard Orsi, professor of history, California State University at Hayward, shared the breadth of his knowledge and applied his editorial skills. Big-hearted scholars, all!

At the Oakland Museum of California, the Chief Curator of History Emeritus, L. Thomas Frye, has been, through three years, patiently supportive despite disappointing delays. As well, the Oakland Museum's Executive Director, Dennis Power; Chief Financial Officer Mark Medeiros; and Board President Daryl Lillie have invested the museum's resources in support of this book's development.

The person most responsible for the illustrative strengths of *Rush for Riches* is Cherie Newell, also of the Oakland Museum of California. She and her colleague, Diane Curry, spent months pursuing hundreds of potential illustrations from which I have made final selections, aided by the advice and forceful opinions of Tom Frye and, not least, Heather Huxley. The result is informatively, colorfully evident in the almost 250 daguerreotypes, photographs, paintings, drawings, sketches, and lithographs woven through the text.

There are other contributors/scholars/specialists—mining partners—who have helped make this claim productive. James Henley, Manager of the Sacramento Archives and Museum Collections Center, has responded for years with knowledge and unfailing attention to every request. Gary Kurutz, Curator of Special Collections at the California State Library at Sacramento, has helped many times to meet our special requests. James Houston read early drafts of several chapters and offered welcomed advice. Bruce Hamilton suggested the lively title for chapter two. James Lenhoff of Oroville made available a wide selection of photographs from his extensive collections and he led me to the Henry R. Mighels painting (courtesy Hirschl & Adler Galleries, NYC) which is reproduced as the opening scene for chapter five. Doris

Ober offered her always perceptive suggestions. Ed Tyson at the Searls Library in Nevada City remains a kind and valuable resource. Norman Wilson never fails to share his collections and his years of experience. Robert Chandler, Wells Fargo Historical Services, is always helpful. Joseph Silva made a special effort to provide an unpublished daguerreotype.

To augment my selection of mining scenes, the famed collector Matthew Isenburg of Hadlyme, CT invited me to his home to search through his daguerreotypes, several of which embellish the pages that follow.

Always, staff members of libraries sustain historians' research and rally at the call for help to meet deadly deadlines. Once again I am grateful to the Bancroft Library at the University of California, Berkeley; the California Historical Society; the Henry E. Huntington Library; the Society of California Pioneers; and in recent years, the Seaside Public Library which secured numerous books through inter-library loan.

Which brings me to the person whose work is most visually evident and, I am sure, most pleasing—the designer of *Rush for Riches*, Gordon Chun (with the assistance of his wife, Suzanne, at their Berkeley design office). I am grateful that my hopes for the aesthetic qualities of this book have been so richly realized by Gordon's creativity.

My good fortune has also been fortified by the University of California Press. From my first meeting with the Director, James H. Clark, I have felt his generous spirit. And the Press's editor, Monica McCormick, has strengthened me by her confident commitment to this book.

Finally, Anne Canright has copyedited the text with her unique skill. Patricia Deminna produced the index in far less time than she deserved.

All these partners have labored generously on this claim. I hope on inspecting this bit of "color" they each will feel their digging was worthwhile.

J. S. Holliday
Carmel, December 1998

British midshipman Bydges Beechey painted this watercolor of Mission San Carlos Borromeo de Carmelo in November 1827 when H.M.S. *Blossom* anchored for reprovisioning at Monterey Bay. The stone church, built on the site of an earlier adobe structure, created a sense of permanence at this headquarters of the Franciscans' twenty-one missions.

BEFORE THE WORLD RUSHED IN

Despite the limitations of such instruments as this brass astrolabe (forerunner of the sextant), the perimeter of the western hemisphere had been fairly well mapped by the end of the seventeenth century. Yet California remained the subject of rumor and imaginative cartography. For navigators of Manila galleons sailing the currents across the Pacific from the Philippines, California represented little more than a rocky, fog-shrouded hazard en route to Spain's colonial settlements further south.

CHAPTER ONE

BEFORE THE WORLD RUSHED IN

AT THE OUTER EDGE OF EXPLORATION, so far on the periphery as to be mapped in 1738 as a huge island, California eluded European colonization for over two centuries, from tentative probing by a Spanish sea captain in 1542 to belated settlement in 1769. Thereafter Spain held her Pacific outpost until 1822 when newly independent Mexico began its brief rule. Impressed by California's natural resources and "a climate like that of Italy," European visitors (geographers, naval officers, traders) judged the Spanish and Mexicans to be unworthy of such a potentially rich colony. The captain of a French frigate in 1837 expressed his astonishment that "this country, so beautiful, so fertile, and at the same time so easy to take, has not yet become the prey of the great nations of the Old World." More surprising, as late as the 1840s this salubrious land had attracted fewer than ten thousand Spanish-Mexican settlers, while the native people, so long safe from civilization, died by the scores of thousands, struck down by the epidemic diseases of the white man and his arrogant culture. Thus, neglected and depopulated, California remained a remote curiosity until the time when the United States, the newest of grasping nations, would have the ambition and the power to reach across the continent.

How lucky the Americans! Not only did they easily acquire California in 1847, they immediately discovered the vast wealth that had so long escaped the notice of their predecessors. How could gold, in great abundance when found by the Yankees, have been overlooked through many centuries by the native people and not have been discovered by the Spanish, so skilled in looting treasure from the Aztecs and Incas, and have remained hidden from the ever-needy Mexicans? Protestant preachers declared it was God's plan.

Apart from the will of a Protestant divinity, it is certain that a remarkable convergence of international rivalries, devastating epidemics, cultural conflicts, and governmental blunders contrived to preserve California for its American future. During the seventy-eight years from first Spanish settlement to United States occupation, those fateful forces so retarded California's progress that French, English, Russian, and American travel reports commonly scoffed at the "backward" Indians oppressed by the Spanish mission system and the primitive economy of the Mexican rule, symbolized as late as the 1840s by the only transport—the creaking, lumbering oxcart.

In 1841 U.S. Navy commander Charles Wilkes led an expedition that explored the San Francisco Bay area. His report reflected how little California had changed since similar descriptions written by explorers in the 1780s. "Although I was prepared for anarchy and confusion, I was surprised when I found a total absence of all government in California and even its forms and ceremonies thrown aside." Like his predecessors, Wilkes also reported to his government the impotence of what military force he could find.

Unprotected from the imperial powers that rampaged around the world, undeveloped by her Spanish and Mexican colonists, California languished until the Americans' westward expansion—they grandly called it Manifest Destiny—encompassed the Pacific shore. And what a twist of fate it was that those Americans, so impatient yet so late on the scene, should be the ones to discover vast quantities of gold that, if found earlier, might well have financed an entirely different history for this far frontier.

IN ALL THE WORLD'S QUEST FOR GOLD, ALL the conquering and cruelty driven by dreams of wealth, no nation gained so much treasure, or sought even more, so mercilessly, as did Spain. With Columbus reporting Indian tales of golden kingdoms in the New World, Spain began its searching, first rewarded in 1521 by the wonder of Aztec treasure plundered by Cortés, then in 1533 by Pizarro's looting the Incas, whose king sought to ransom himself by filling a room seventeen by twenty feet with stacks of gold. But even ships laden with treasure could not cover the immense costs of Spain's worldwide struggle with England and France. Decade by decade Madrid's need for gold increased. Each viceroy in Mexico (New Spain) knew that his king expected—demanded—new sources of gold and silver.

Stories of vast wealth in a place called El Dorado and imaginative reports of the Seven Cities of Cíbola, shining with gold, sent conquistadores into unexplored jungles and deserts. Of all those expeditions, Francisco Vázquez de Coronado led the most ambitious in 1540, to search for the Seven Cities, with their streets paved in gold, women adorned with necklaces of gold, and men wearing girdles of gold. But his long desert quest led only to mud villages (in what is now New Mexico)—no treasure, and scarcely enough maize for his starving horses. Desperate, but refusing to accept such disappointment as an omen, Coronado led his men still northward in 1541–42. He hoped to find a newly reported wonder, Quivira, where even common folk were said to drink from golden bowls; where there was so much gold it would take not just horses but wagons to carry away. Lured by this vision,

Coronado's ragged band wandered all the way to the prairies of Kansas, where at last he conceded the wreckage of his dreams.

In such a time of myth and avarice, California came to the attention of the viceroys through a widely read novel published in Seville in 1510, *Las Sergas de Esplandián* by Garcí Ordóñez de Montalvo, which pictured an island of "bold and craggy rocks . . . named California. . . . The island everywhere abounds with gold and precious stones and upon it no other metal is found. There ruled over that island of California a queen of majestic proportions . . . in the very vigor of her womanhood" whose name was Calafía.

By the 1540s the name "California" had come to identify the arid, forbidding peninsula (or was it an island?) known today as Baja California. In 1542

CABRILLO

Viceroy Antonio de Mendoza ordered an exploration of the coastline north of this craggy finger, sending three ships under the command of Juan Rodríguez Cabrillo to search for the long-sought "Strait of Anián," the wished-for passage connecting the Pacific with the Atlantic. The narrative of that expedition reported landings at San Diego Bay and on several of the Channel Islands. Cabrillo's parties explored the California coast as far north as 42 degrees (Oregon), recording many meetings with Indians. Thus for the first time Europeans visited the region we now know as California. What they saw turned them back, disillusioned by the realities of Indian poverty in a land apparently without value to their king's needs or the dreams of his greedy officers.

There remained only the hope that California could provide a haven of greenery and fresh water where surviving crews of the Manila galleons (plump with the luxuries of the East—brocades, silks, spices, musks, rubies, porcelain) could find surcease from the horrors of their six-month, scurvy-ravaged voyages across the Pacific.* The

In those days of unbridled adventure, when man was permitted to prey upon his fellow-man, and when the many-sided world was as yet but partially known to civilization, gold was the chiefest good that strange lands could yield, and hence every strange land, in the imagination or desire of its discoverer, abounded in gold. So it was that California, even before it was seen by any Spaniard, was reputed, without reason, rich in gold.

Hubert Howe Bancroft, *California Inter Pocula*

search for such a harbor—and for the still hoped for Strait of Anián—included the most notable expedition, led by Sebastián Vizcaíno, who in 1602 rediscovered San Diego and wrote glowing descriptions not only of "the best port that could be desired" (Monterey Bay) but also of a land that "is fertile, with a climate and soil like those of Castile." He found "many pines for masts and yards . . . and much wild game . . . most fertile pastures, good meadows for cattle and fertile land for growing crops."

And yet following this voyage, California was ignored, even by homebound galleons, whose captains feared the coastal fogs and storms that wrecked the *San Augustín* in 1595. So long the focus of golden dreams, this temperate region would be a place of distant memories for 167 years—until 1769.

Exhausted by her wasteful military ventures in Europe, her New World colonists too few to settle even such a fertile land, Spain could not spend her

---

*To reach Mexico from the Philippines, Spanish galleons had to sail to the North Pacific where the Japan Current and favorable winds carried them south along the coast of California and finally to their destination, Acapulco.

scarce resources to control a place that offered so little of what was needed, not even evidence of the Strait of Anián. And so California remained Spanish only through the diligence of the kings' mapmakers who showed that remote place as an island, still shrouded in mist and myth, as it had been in the fable of Queen Calafía.

During those sixteen decades while California remained beyond the grasp of Europe—from Vizcaíno's exploration in 1602 until Spain finally sent a colonizing party in 1769—other imperial powers (England, France, and Russia) might have challenged, even brushed aside, the Spanish cartographic claim. But these competitors, also strained by wars and overextended by their monarchs' excesses, chose to leave that most distant coast for later attention.

Military distraction and cartographic illusion obscured from kings and queens, viceroys and admirals, what has since been made known by modern archaeologists, anthropologists, and ethnologists. Their scholarship reveals that for many thousands of years California had nurtured a burgeoning population, that as early as 2000 B.C. some 25,000 to 30,000 people lived in the valleys and foothills of California. Increasing skills in fishing, hunting, and food storage begot larger settlements, and by A.D. 1000 the population had expanded to 100,000 to 150,000. Distinct tribes established independent territories. By the time of Spain's first colonizing effort in 1769, the Indians of California may have numbered 300,000—the most dense concentration of Native Americans north of Mexico.

From the wide-ranged oak trees the Indians gathered huge quantities of acorns, from which they shelled the bitter kernels to dry and pulverize into a thin meal, which when leached and cooked made a high-calorie mush. Where oaks were scarce, mesquite pods or pine nuts served as the staple food. Fish from streams, shellfish from coastal waters; elk, deer, rabbits, and quail; wild fruits, berries, nuts,

CHRONOLOGY (1510–1769)

1510	First use of the name California (in a Spanish novel about a mythical island)
1513	Balboa crosses Isthmus of Panama; first European to sight Pacific Ocean
1519–21	Cortés conquers Aztecs (beginning of New Spain)
1522	Magellan expedition completes first circumnavigation of the world
1535	Pizarro completes conquest of Incas in Peru
1542	Cabrillo claims San Diego and Monterey Bays for Spain
1565	First voyage between the Philippines and New Spain
1579	Drake lands in northern California during first English circumnavigation
1588	Spanish Armada defeated by England
1602	Vizcaíno visits and names Monterey Bay
1607	Jamestown settled (first permanent English settlement in the New World)
1697	First mission established by the Jesuits in Baja California
1724	Gin drinking becomes popular in Great Britain
1738	de Launay atlas still shows California as a large island
1756–63	Seven Years War (Great Britain vs. France); France driven from North America
1767	Jesuits expelled from Spanish dominions by royal decree

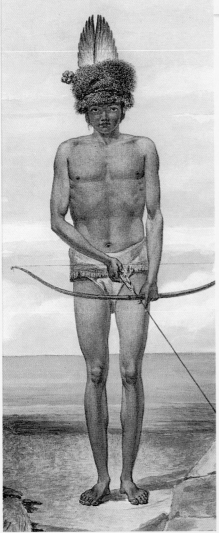

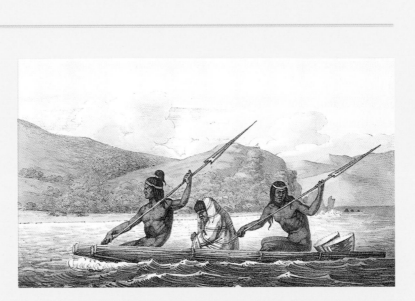

The remarkable diversity of California's native peoples—more than five hundred separate tribal groups—was reflected in their cultural distinctions and environmental adaptations. European and Russian expeditions recorded vivid evidence of Indian life, as in this 1816 painting (by Russian artist Louis Choris) of three Coast Miwoks paddling a reed balsa on San Francisco Bay. Mikhail T. Tikhanov painted this wiry Pomo hunter near Fort Ross in 1818 when his ship *Kamchatka* visited California in one of several czarist expeditions aimed at increasing Russia's share of the trade in sea otter pelts.

Lacking metal utensils, Indians learned to weave reeds and grasses into coiled baskets—like this one of the Maidu tribe—that served as watertight cooking vessels. They boiled liquids by adding heated stones to the mixture. Tribes in California's central valley fashioned tules into igloo-shaped houses—cool in the summer, easily built, and rain-resistant.

seeds, and roots—all were hunted and harvested in such abundance that most tribes never attempted to cultivate crops. The fecundity in each region provided such a dependable food supply that local populations, self-sufficient and content, seldom ventured beyond their valley-sized territories.

Millennia passed as these tribes of native Californians lived in comfortable balance with their fertile environment, at relative peace with neighboring villages, without need for leagues or conferences, alliances or governing councils. They had no wheel, no domesticated animals, little agriculture, no metal tools or weapons.

In the usually mild climate, men were naked most of the year, women skirted with skins or rushes. They built their dwellings with a framework of poles covered by reed matting or bark, and sometimes dug living spaces partly underground or in a hillside. They made bows and specialized arrows as well as wooden spears and clubs for hunting, and sometimes for fighting or war. Their baskets, tightly woven to hold water and large enough for storing acorns and other foods, were often elegantly adorned with feathers and shell beads.

Unchallenged from within and without, through uncalendared centuries, these Californians remained remarkably isolated. Tribes developed their own discrete social and ceremonial customs from region to region, often with different languages. Twenty-one "language families" have been identified, encompassing some 135 dialects, most of them mutually unintelligible.

Peaceful, comfortably divided, these three hundred thousand Indians were ill prepared to oppose the intrusion of the Spanish when they arrived on horseback, bearing iron weapons and the cross of their God. Nor would the far fewer survivors of that first devastating contact with Europeans be any more ready or able to overcome the later onslaught of goldseekers who, by the many thousands, would invade their once quiet foothills and canyons.

THE SPANISH DECADES

By 1769 Spain had conquered or acquired by treaty a hemispheric empire that extended from the tip of South America through New Spain and west from the Mississippi River to the Pacific shores of Baja and Alta California. In its relentless advance by conquest and diplomacy, Spanish success masked a deep conflict between greed and conscience—conquistadores pressing for fortune and power, Catholic priests striving to save native souls. This conundrum was perfectly expressed by a common soldier: "We came here to serve God, but also to get rich." The source of those riches—the mines, vast haciendas, and cattle herds—depended on the coerced labor of native peoples. A cruel alchemy converted human wealth into material treasure by consuming hundreds of Indian lives for every ingot of gold and silver shipped to Madrid. A holocaust of slavery, atrocities, and disease reduced New Spain's native population from eleven million at the time of Cortés to six million by 1550.

To constrain, and if possible prevent the blatant cruelties and unholy lusts of the conquistadores, and to Christianize the native peoples of the New World, the Catholic Church, with the support of the Crown, developed and established during the sixteenth century the Indian mission, "Spain's sword of the Spirit." This frontier institution was carried by the missionary orders (Jesuits, Dominicans, and Franciscans) to the farthest reaches of the empire—southern Chile, central Paraguay, along the Orinoco, through the lowlands of Guatemala, north across Mexico to Florida and Georgia, and along New Spain's northern frontier from Texas to Baja California. With a guard of only five or six soldiers, a pair of friars would advance into a new region known to have a large Indian population, sufficient water, arable land, available timber, and proximity to supply routes. There they built a simple church and outbuildings and then enticed local people to settle close around. Gardens were planted at each of these missions, and as more Indians gathered, they helped to construct new buildings, all protected by soldiers billeted at a nearby presidio.

With medieval fervor to save heathen souls for Christ, the mission padres indoctrinated their wards in Christianity and the ways of "civilized" and agricultural life. Through training and discipline they sought to prepare the "unenlightened" to become faithful Catholics, subjects of the Crown, and eventually self-sufficient settlers who would pay taxes. If such progress could be attained, the buildings, cultivated fields, and domesticated animals of each frontier community would be divided among the Christianized Indians, and the missionary fathers would move on to establish another frontier outpost. That was the plan. But human frailties—Spanish and Indian—seldom allowed its fulfillment.

Beyond the church imperative of "civilizing" Indians and saving souls for Christ, economic and practical necessity motivated Madrid and Mexico City to invest in this mission-presidio system. Because so few Spaniards were willing to emigrate to the New World to become settlers and frontiersmen, the empire could not survive without Hispanicizing the natives. At the bottom of the colonial hierarchy, the Indians provided labor for the mines and great haciendas and in such frontier towns as Santa Fe, founded in 1610, San Antonio (1718), and Tubac (Arizona, 1751). Taught to worship Christ and to speak Spanish, Indian women filled the demographic void created by the reluctance of Spanish women to leave home for the uncertainties of New Spain. Mestizos, produced by the union of Indian women and Spanish soldiers, would eventually become the dominant population of New Spain.

By the 1760s the mission system had gained a tenuous foothold even amid the rocks and thorns of Baja California, where its wards were described in 1768 as "half-fed, wholly naked, devoured by syphilis [spread by presidio soldiers]."*

---

* The native population on that peninsula declined from 24,000 in 1697 to an estimated 7,500 in 1777, that loss due principally to European diseases.

To the north of these tormented outposts of Christendom, the Indians of Alta California fished and hunted amid natural abundance, unaware of their mission future.

Much farther north, along the coast of Alaska, Russian hunters and traders gathered the pelts of sea otters. And worlds away in Madrid, the king and his advisors fretted that these Muscovites might move south and plant a colony at Monterey Bay, described so tantalizingly by Vizcaíno as a perfect port. Circumstances would now contrive to wrest California from its eons of isolation.

In a joint dispatch to the king, the viceroy and inspector general of New Spain set forth the situation as of 1768: "It is known . . . that the English, a nation that spares neither expense, diligence, nor fatigue in advancing her discoveries, and the Dutch have acquired a very particular knowledge of the ports and bays that we hold on the south coast, especially the peninsula of the Californias; so that it would be neither impossible nor indeed very difficult for one of these nations, or the Muscovites, to establish, when least expected, a colony in the port of Monterey. Wherefore, it behooves us . . . to put in force what means are possible for warding off the dangers that threaten us."

Without military or naval strength to establish bases at the two known harbors on the Alta California coast—San Diego Bay and Monterey Bay—the viceroy and inspector general turned to their only resource, the Indian mission and presidio system, even though that "sword" had fallen dull and rusty in Baja California.

In 1769 (when England's American colonies along the Atlantic coast were well on their way to declaring independence), an expedition of two ships and two overland "divisions" (cannibalized from the impoverished missions in Baja California) managed to reach San Diego Bay and to construct the beginnings of a mission and presidio. The next year similar structures were erected at Monterey Bay, "to occupy and defend the port from the atrocities of the Russians." As spiritual leader of this courageous, ill-equipped colonizing effort, Franciscan Father Junípero Serra needed all his spirit and wisdom to cope with deprivations and near starvation on that mission frontier. Supply ships from San Blas and other mainland Mexican ports—delayed by adverse winds and currents—often took three and four months to make the hazardous voyage, their crews usually skeletal victims of scurvy on reaching San Diego. Some years not one ship eased the missions' deprivations. Sorely weakened by defeats in Europe and corruption in the New World, Spain was unable to support her ambitions for California.

With only fourteen fellow Franciscans and a few Indian workers, Father Serra overcame deprivations and exasperations of every kind to erect three more log-structured missions, the fifth at San Luis Obispo in 1772. To protect these simple beginnings from the threat of Indian resistance (Mission San Gabriel suffered a brief uprising in 1771), the overworked friars had to rely on sixty-one soldiers, most of them based at the two presidios, at San Diego and four hundred miles to the north at Monterey. To strengthen this minuscule military presence, an occasional shipment of conscripts arrived from Sonora and Sinaloa—most of them drunkards, criminals, or deserters from the regular army. As these ruffians increased in number, they were housed at two new presidios, one at San Francisco Bay (1776) and the last at Santa Barbara (1782).*

The Siberia of the Spanish Empire, California could not attract even the most impoverished people of Mexico's northern states, Sonora and Sinaloa. By 1782 the province had fewer than one thousand non-Indians (Spanish, Creole, or mestizo) and some four thousand Indians at the nine missions. Determined to attract colonist-settlers, the provincial governor at Monterey developed a paternalistic plan to establish two agricultural communities, or pueblos, one at San Jose (1777) and the other at Los Angeles (1781).

Despite offering potential settlers generous grants of land with livestock and equipment for farming, these attractions failed to lure immigrants from Mexico. By 1795 San Jose had only 187 residents *(pobladores)*, and Los Angeles at the end of its first year counted 44. Both settlements produced far more trouble than crops. As much as the governor resented the colonists' failures, the Franciscans despised them even more for their gambling, drinking, and licentious behavior. One outraged friar asserted that "these people are a set of idlers. . . . They pass the day singing. Their young men wander on horseback . . . soliciting Indian women to immorality. . . . One is more likely to find in their hands a deck of cards than the spade or the plow."

When the government in Mexico City resorted to shipping convicts and vagrants to serve as colonists, Father Serra rebelled. Faced with such wastrels as husbands for his Christianized, protected Indian women, he exhorted the viceroy "not to look upon California and its missions as the China of exile. . . . Being sent here should not be a form of banishment . . . for worthless people who serve no purpose but to commit evil deeds."

Despite his contempt for lazy, drunken colonists, his frustration in watching hundreds of Indian converts flee from the missions to return to "the old delights of savagism," and his helplessness in controlling epidemics of syphilis and other diseases spread by presidio soldiers and colonists, Father Serra never wavered in his determination to bring the Catholic faith to California's pagans. Less steadfast, one Franciscan poured out his frustration: "What liberties! What excesses! What irregularities! What ignorance! What disorders! How can Christian civilization and pagan barbarity give way to one another in the same Indian?"

---

* During the summer of 1779 the captain of a supply ship from San Blas itemized in his uniquely authoritative diary what he delivered to Spain's hungry missions and presidios: rice, beans, corn, flour, and unrefined sugar. As to California's military force, he found the presidio at San Francisco Bay manned by one officer and eighteen soldiers. Of all his revelations, none more clearly exposed the province's primitive circumstances than the fact that the San Francisco presidio had no blacksmith, no forge.

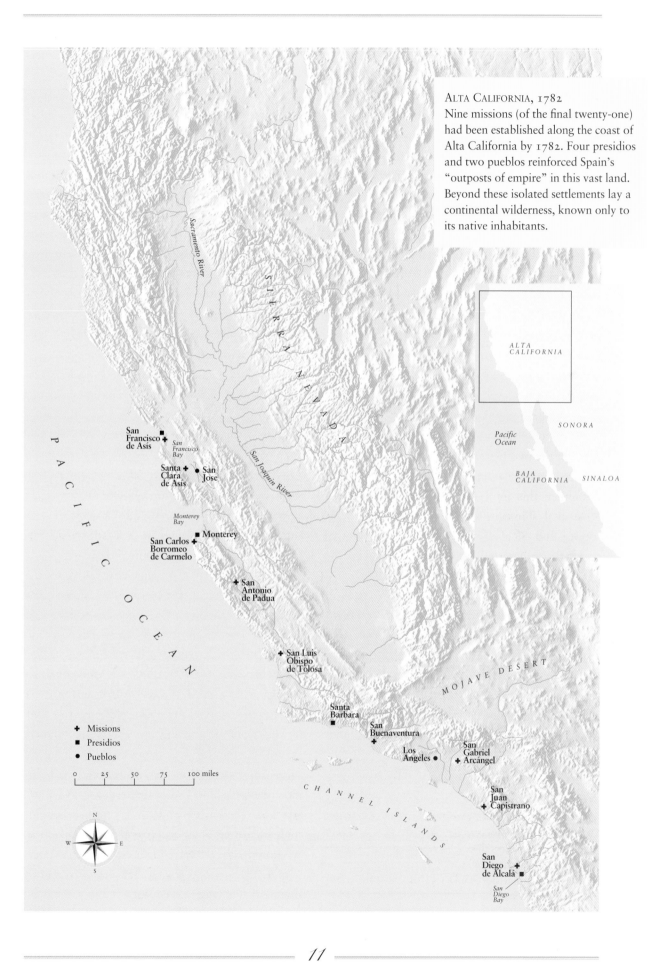

ALTA CALIFORNIA, 1782
Nine missions (of the final twenty-one) had been established along the coast of Alta California by 1782. Four presidios and two pueblos reinforced Spain's "outposts of empire" in this vast land. Beyond these isolated settlements lay a continental wilderness, known only to its native inhabitants.

ALTA CALIFORNIA

SONORA

Pacific Ocean

BAJA CALIFORNIA   SINALOA

Sacramento River

SIERRA NEVADA

San Joaquin River

PACIFIC OCEAN

San Francisco de Asís
San Francisco Bay
Santa Clara de Asís   San Jose
Monterey Bay
Monterey
San Carlos Borromeo de Carmelo
San Antonio de Padua
San Luis Obispo de Tolosa

MOJAVE DESERT

Santa Barbara
San Buenaventura
Los Angeles   San Gabriel Arcángel
San Juan Capistrano

CHANNEL ISLANDS

San Diego de Alcalá
San Diego Bay

✚ Missions
■ Presidios
● Pueblos

0   25   50   75   100 miles

N
W   E
S

Father Serra persevered, no matter the disorder and barbarities. By the time of his death at age seventy-one in 1784, he had consecrated a total of nine missions. Under his successor that number would double and by 1823 finally reach a total of twenty-one.

As the missions grew in number and their herds of free-grazing cattle, sheep, and horses multiplied over broad rangelands, the improving statistics underscored the complexity of the responsibility borne by the Franciscans as they prepared for the day when each mission's Indian "neophytes" would take over its management and operation. Most of these frontier settlements had only two friars to supervise hundreds of Indians. Some had one! Year after year these men struggled with an impossible array of ambitious tasks: to learn native languages in order to provide (twice each day) religious services and instruction; to teach Spanish to reluctant and distracted students; and to school the Indians in essential skills such as blacksmithing, carpentry, masonry, and farming. Overtaxed friars faced the additional challenge of discouraging promiscuity, homosexuality, and abortion, among other "vicious pagan practices." Meanwhile, these dedicated padres were expected to explain and promote the use of beds, chairs, kitchen utensils, and privies.

The friars believed the missions to be "enclaves of Spanish Catholicism, culture and civilization in an alien and barbaric world." Frustrated by what they saw as Indian stubbornness, friars often resorted to punishments common to the times— flogging, shackles, hobbles, confinement. In 1796 the governor of Alta California lamented that "at the rate the Indians are moving, not in ten centuries will they be out of tutelage."

Comparable pessimism, tinged more often with scorn than sympathy, marked foreigners' appraisals of Spain's theocratic colonizing effort. Whether French, British, Russian, or Spanish, most visitors belittled California's Indians for their backwardness and "animal instincts." A few Europeans saw them as victims of mission slavery. A Russian in 1816 wrote with sorrowful vividness: "I have never seen a single one look anyone in the face. I have never seen any of them laugh. They have the air of taking no notice of anything."

More than apathy, backwardness, and mistreatment sapped the strength of the mission system and Spain's colonial policy. European diseases caused appalling epidemics among the cloistered Indians. Between 1790 and 1800 the Franciscans succeeded in baptizing 16,100 neophytes, of whom 9,300 died—a 58 percent death rate. Ten years later this tragic toll reached 72 percent. In 1818, after the twentieth mission had been established at San Rafael on the northwest shore of San Francisco Bay, 86 percent of the Indians saved that year by Christianity perished from disease.

One certain and direct cause of contagion arose from the Franciscans' pious habit of confining unmarried Indian women and girls to dormitories at night to preserve their morality. These ill-ventilated chambers became breeding sites for measles, smallpox, pneumonia, and tuberculosis. Mission records listed the number of deaths, disease by disease. In 1806 an epidemic of measles killed 33 percent of all mission Indian children. Unknown to the Spanish, this epidemic also spread to the "wild" Indians of the Sacramento Valley, killing many thousands.

Not apparent in the mission necrologies, but certainly contributing to the Indians' general susceptibility to disease, must have been the drudgery of their labor, the strangeness of their new diet, and the repression of old habits—in short, culture shock, compounded by the hopelessness of their circumstances. Whether converted to Christianity by the friars or born into the Franciscan system, mission neophytes were expected to be obedient, unquestioning servants of the church, their discipline enforced by the daunting alliance of God and garrison. The Indians' misery may well explain the high incidence of abortion and infanticide, also recorded by the anguished Franciscans.

Of all the sorrows and hardships, venereal disease was certainly the most insidious, the most devastating, the most indicative of the social and moral decay of Spanish California. Foreign visitors, among them naval surgeons and other medical men, reported the prevalence of syphilis, as did the friars and their superiors. Father Ramón Abella in 1817 wrote that in his judgment the appalling decline in the mission Indian population "is chiefly due to *Mal Gálico* [syphilis], introduced among the natives by low grade soldiers recruited in Mexico." The superior of the missions, Father Vicente Sarría, declared that the Indian race was dying from syphilis.

Disease, punishment, infanticide, virtual enslavement—each contributed to a tragic failure, despite Christian idealism and Franciscan sacrifice. Perhaps more willing than any other people on the continent to submit to the white man's dominion, California's Indians in a swift thirty years were swept into a pattern of self-degradation and premature death that accelerated beyond recovery. In another fifty years only a pathetic remnant of these coastal people would survive, while the more isolated tribes of the interior suffered severe declines that would lead eventually to the same fate.

But long before the Indians' demise, the basic plan of the mission-presidio-pueblo system had failed, as evidenced by the Spanish governors' and Franciscan padres' reluctance to turn over a single mission to Indian management and ownership. Whether or not the neophytes could have fulfilled Father Serra's expectations, the missions' appalling mortality rates forced a desperate policy, decade by decade, of corralling "wild" Indians to be brought to the missions and in time baptized as replacements for those who had died or run away. These fresh recruits received training and indoctrination, and the cycle of death recurred, without one mission graduating to the status of a pueblo.

Thus the principal institution that Spain established in California waned, a perpetual disappointment, dying slowly from within—failing to Hispanicize the native people so that they could serve as settlers in this vast northern land to which so few Mexicans would immigrate. The non-Indian

1769	First mission in Alta California founded in San Diego
	Watt patents steam engine in England
1774	Anza expedition opens overland route to California missions from New Spain
1775	American Revolution begins
1776	Second Anza expedition establishes mission and presidio at San Francisco Bay
	Captain Cook trades for sea otter pelts on north coast of California, discovers Hawaiian Islands; pelts subsequently traded for great profit in Canton, China
1783	American Revolution ends
1784	Father Serra dies at Mission San Carlos in Carmel
1789	French Revolution begins
1792–94	Vancouver (Captain, British navy) visits San Francisco and Monterey Bays and publishes extensive descriptions of California
1797	Missions San Jose, San Juan Bautista, San Miguel, and San Fernando founded
1800	Spain cedes Louisiana Territory to France
1803	United States purchases Louisiana Territory from France
1805	Lewis and Clark expedition reaches mouth of Columbia River
1807	Fulton's steamboat makes first voyage on Hudson River
1808	Napoleon invades Spain
1810	Beginning of revolutions in Mexico and other colonies under Spanish rule
1812	Russians establish Fort Ross on northern California coast
1812–15	War of 1812 between United States and Great Britain
1814	Scottish seaman John Gilroy becomes first foreigner to settle in Spanish California
1815	Napoleon defeated at Waterloo

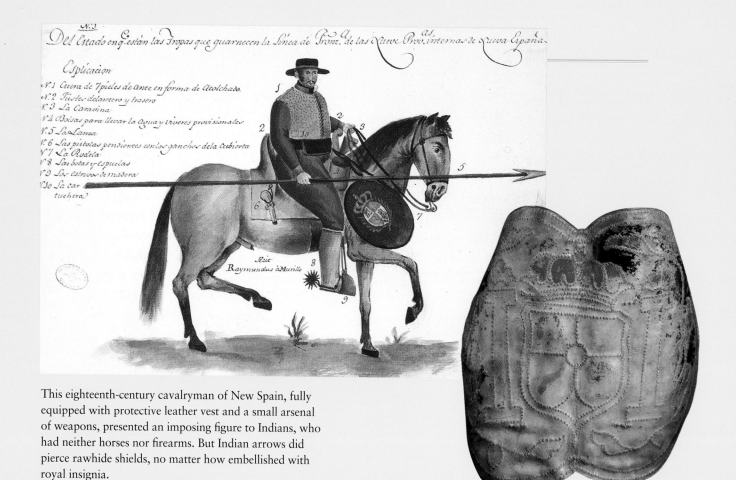

This eighteenth-century cavalryman of New Spain, fully equipped with protective leather vest and a small arsenal of weapons, presented an imposing figure to Indians, who had neither horses nor firearms. But Indian arrows did pierce rawhide shields, no matter how embellished with royal insignia.

Bronze swivel cannon (like this one made in 1631) sat on presidio walls, but their tendency to burst under the stress of firing made them more a threat to Spanish gunners than to any adversary.

This 1791 drawing shows a face-off between Costanoan archers and a Spanish dragoon. Such confrontations inevitably arose as soldiers raided Indian villages for new "converts" for the missions.

Once the Pacific coast was Spanish and British and Russian more than it was American. Yet the original European substratum was extraordinarily thin and insubstantial. There are more Basque sheepherders in the deserts of Nevada and eastern Oregon today [1965] than ever there were Spaniards in all of Spanish California. . . . The Spaniards . . . affected California less in the long run by making it Spanish than by making it ready to become American, though nothing was more remote from their expectations.

Earl Pomeroy, *The Pacific Slope: A History of California, Oregon, Washington, Idaho, Utah, and Nevada*

population (meaning those with any trace of Spanish blood) had grown only to 3,270 by 1820—and of these, 700 were soldiers.*

A failure as a colonizing agent, the mission-presidio-pueblo system fared little better at its corollary purpose, to defend against imperial rivals. In 1792 and 1793 the captain of the British sloop-of-war *Discovery*, George Vancouver, visited the presidios at San Diego, Santa Barbara, Monterey, and San Francisco, where he observed that "the only defenses against foreign attack are a few poor cannon, inconveniently placed . . . , the brass three-pounder [at San Francisco] lashed to a log instead of a gun carriage." This assessment of impotence proved sadly correct. When the cannoneers at the San Francisco presidio fired a salute to honor a new governor in 1816, one ancient weapon exploded, injuring two of its crew. On another peaceful occasion two cannon burst when the gunners lit off an

---

* In contrast to Spain's colonial situation, England's Atlantic colonies had an ever-increasing population of immigrants from the British Isles (1.6 million by 1760!) and a policy opposed to assimilating the Indians and certainly opposed to marrying them. Rather, they were to be displaced or, if need be, exterminated.

answering salute. And one indignant Russian captain wondered why his cannonade was not returned, until "an ambassador from the presidio soon solved the mystery by coming to beg so much powder as would serve to answer my courtesy."

While scoffing at military incompetence, dispatches sent by French, Russian, and English travelers shared a sense of disgust that Spanish rule had failed to develop this fertile land—no schools, no manufactures, no skilled workers, no transport. In Vancouver's words: "There is not an object to indicate the most remote connection with any European or other civilized nation."

And yet, all that foreign visitors admired and all that they scorned did belong to Spain. Her flag flew from the presidios; her many missions occupied the large regions of coastal plain and adjacent valleys. Vast herds of mission cattle, sheep, and horses roamed over a thousand hills, from San Diego to San Francisco Bay. That Spanish presence, however feebly defended, served for fifty years to divert rival claims of sovereignty northward, away from California, to the profitable fur trading coasts of Canada and Alaska.

So it was that California was held in trust, saved from effective colonization through those vulnerable years, before slipping from the fumbling grasp of Spain to the neglectful stewardship of Mexico.

BY 1800, SPAIN'S RENEWED WARS WITH FRANCE and England had drained her waning strength, both in Europe and the New World. Catastrophes climaxed in 1808, when Napoleon overthrew the Spanish sovereign, declared his own brother king of Spain, and cast the Spanish people into long and bloody years of struggle against French occupation. Across the Atlantic, colonial discontent was emboldened. Revolt erupted in Argentina and spread rapidly north. In 1810 a rebel priest, Miguel Hidalgo, ignited the struggle for Mexican independence with a challenge: "My children, . . . make the effort to recover from the h—

the lands stolen from your forefathers three hundred years ago? . . . The Spaniards . . . are about to surrender us and our country to the French. . . . Will you become Napoleon's slaves or will you as patriots defend your religion and your rights?"

For the next eleven years Mexico suffered guerrilla warfare, anarchy, and chaos, at last wresting independence in 1821, though it seemed an abstraction amid continuing years of civil war.

Through all the smoke and tumult, California remained a vague shape in the distance, ignored and deprived, a place where the *comandante* of the San Francisco presidio had to beg from the governor clothing for his family. And yet there was no revolutionary ferment among the Franciscans or the ranching families. No Hidalgo spoke up against Spain or Mexico. California drifted, her necessities and few luxuries supplied by foreign traders.

Predominantly merchant captains from Boston, these sea-roving opportunists didn't blink at sailing fourteen thousand miles around Cape Horn to reach a forbidden coastline. The first Yankee sails appeared off California in 1796, followed each year by more New England traders on their way to China, offering needed manufactured goods to Alta California's ranch families, mission padres, and the settlers of scruffy pueblos in exchange for sea otter pelts that could be sold in Canton at fortune-making prices. This trade flourished for several years, with the *bostoños* profiting gloriously and the Californios obtaining essentials and "extras" long denied by the infrequency and finally the absence of supply ships from Mexico. Though illegal under Spanish and Mexican laws, Yankee commerce was welcomed by everyone, especially Mexican officials who accepted bribes that compensated for years of unpaid salaries. As Governor José Argüello explained in a bow to Mexican pragmatism: "Necessity makes lawful that which by the law is illicit."

From 1800 through the 1830s, ships from Boston traded along the California coast, bartering for pelts and later, after the sea otters were ʰnted to near extinction, for cattle hides. The New England merchant ships brought all kinds of goods: fish hooks, cotton cloth, woolen blankets, shoes, nutmeg, pepper, and more exotic temptations (from China and Europe) such as camel's-hair shawls, painted water pitchers, porcelain plates, Brittany linens, even pianos.

Writing about these New England smugglers, one of California's last Spanish governors, José de Arrillaga, expressed his admiration for their business savvy: "Having personally witnessed the enterprise of these Americans, I do not wonder at their success. They flourish in trade and know its value. And who at present does not, except ourselves who pay for our neglect with our purse?"

While Governor Arrillaga lamented his people's indifference, the Boston sea captains expanded their control by fitting out otter-hunting parties in sea-rigged canoes rather than depending solely on the Californios for supplies of pelts. In 1806–7 one Boston ship, the *O'Cain*, gathered 4,819 otter pelts. The New Englanders gained an even greater harvest when they formed the Russian-American Fur Company with Russian hunter-traders who had for years been gathering pelts along the north coast of California.

Long feared as an imperial rival, the Russians entered California when Spanish control was too weak to prevent their illegal trade with the missions, exchanging otter pelts for the grain, potatoes, and meat desperately needed to relieve scurvy and famine at Sitka and their other suffering settlements along the Alaskan coast. To augment this vital source of food, the Russians in 1812 established two farming outposts on the California coast, one about fifty miles north of San Francisco Bay, the other farther north, which became known as Fort Ross. At this more northerly site they constructed a wooden stockade with cannon to protect a governor's residence and to shelter some one hundred Russian farmers and hunters. These end-of-the-world encampments, barely able to grow enough surplus to send to Alaska, represented the reality behind Spanish fears and Russian ambitions.

Recivimiento del Conde dela Pei Rus en la mission del Carmelo de Monterei

In 1786, Father Lasuén (Serra's successor as president of the missions) greeted the French count Jean Francois Galaup de la Pérouse at the mission in Carmel. La Pérouse and his scientific expedition were the first foreigners to visit any of the Spanish settlements in California: "We were received like lords of a parish visiting their estates for the first time." The welcoming ceremony, depicted in this copy of a painting by expedition artist Gaspard Duché de Vancy, enlivened an otherwise simple existence at this remote outpost.

Headbands (made from the quills of flickers) adorned northern Californian Indians in their ceremonial dances. Louis Choris, an artist from the Russian ship *Rurik,* painted these Costanoans in a variety of elaborate headdresses. Like most Russian visitors, Choris was strongly critical of the mission system, and that viewpoint is reflected in his 1816 painting of mounted lancers herding Indians like cattle near the presidio at San Francisco Bay.

FORT ROSS

The first foreigners to settle in Spanish California, the Russians held on at their fog-shrouded Fort Ross until 1841. They could have been evicted by order of the viceroy in Mexico City if that supposed authority had not been so distracted by more immediate concerns, like revolution and the decline of the royalist establishment. In contrast to the Russians and Spanish, the enterprising *bostoños* developed their opportunities and foresaw greater profits, all the while promoting California's prospects to the American people and their government in Washington. In 1808 one of the New England sea captains, William Shaler, published in a Philadelphia magazine an account of his lucrative foray from the *Lelia Byrd* to gather sea otter pelts—a total of 1,600—for the Canton market. More important than this impressive moneymaking, Shaler's widely read report presented the first perspective on how short-sighted and repressive the Spanish had been in managing what could have been a rich, prosperous colony. In this first phrasing of America's Manifest Destiny, Shaler asserted that the "very few white people" in California were ready for the enjoyments of liberty, property, and free trade. He deplored the backwardness and neglect of Spanish rule—not a single physician in all of California, not a single mechanized mill to grind flour from the abundant grain. In sum, "California wants nothing but a good government to rise to wealth and importance."

YANKEE TRADERS

As the slaughter of sea otters in the early 1800s drastically reduced that source of profits, the Yankee merchant captains found another seemingly inexhaustible resource for a new market, one far closer than China: cattle hides for the shoe manufacturers of New England. In developing this trade, the "Boston men" were aided by a change of government in Mexico City.

In August 1821 the royal establishment in New Spain collapsed, the viceroy resigned, and the Mexican people gained their freedom after 302 years of Spanish oppression and exploitation. Isolated and forgotten, California did not learn of this world-changing news for seven months. One of the first acts of the new government at Monterey was to remove the Spanish ban on foreign trade and to seek income from anchorage fees and import duties. But merchant captains preferred the traditional illegal operations of bribes and smuggling. Some twenty British, American, and Russian merchantmen worked the coast during 1822–23, exchanging a wide variety of manufactured goods for cattle hides. In addition, American whalers from New England (as many as thirty at one time) put into San Francisco to take on fresh water and whatever vegetables they could purchase for their three-, even four-year Pacific voyages. This ever-increasing maritime trade exemplified once again how the Spanish and the Mexicans left profitable commerce to foreigners, among whom the Americans quickly achieved dominance.

By 1823 a Boston company, Bryant and Sturgis, had gained almost total control of the California trade, muscling out their British competitors. To ensure sufficient supplies of hides for their ships— cleaned, dried, and ready to be packed into holds for the return voyage around the Horn to Boston— agreements were signed with the mission friars and ranch owners to exchange hides for merchandise. Called "California bank notes" or "leather dollars," each hide was worth from $1 to $3. Without a currency or monetary system, California remained dependent on barter for almost everything.

Moving up and down a coast unimproved by docks or wharves, the Boston ships anchored offshore while friars, ranch folk, and people from the pueblos were rowed out in the traders' launches to look in astonishment at great displays of tempting goods—cigars, stockings, jewelry, combs, paints, furniture, cooking utensils, silverware, clocks, mirrors, paper, bolts of calico, boots and shoes, tools, ready-made clothing, grindstones, casks of rum, brandy, and wine, even an occasional billiard table—everything the Californios did not have. In the confusion of cultures created by the trade, silk wraps from China became so common in Mexican California that they were thought of as Spanish shawls, and what were called "serapes" also came from Canton workrooms, delivered by Yankee seamen.

The *comandante* of the presidio at Santa Barbara, don Ignacio Martínez, had an eleven-year-old daughter who later recalled that when her father returned from visiting one of these trading ships, he brought home not only shawls and serapes, but fancy silk handkerchiefs, satin shoes, colorful bolts of silk cloth, and gleaming lacquers—all from China, more beautiful than anything they had ever seen.

The American traders, seaborne merchants, made a profit of 200 to 300 percent on the products they carried from New England, Europe, and China. At the zenith of the hide trade, 1822–46, merchant ships carried away more than a million hides and many tons of tallow. The cowhide came back to California as shoes and other leather products, earning traders a second profit from the same skins, while the tallow returned as candles and soap. But of more lasting import than commercial profit, some ship captains, company representatives, and sailors also brought home vivid descriptions of California, its resources, balmy climate, and "lazy" Spanish-Mexican inhabitants, thus creating in New England an early appreciation of that Pacific province, predisposing support for American acquisition and a future enthusiastic reception of the news of gold.

One of the laborers who helped transport the heavy, smelly hides from the beaches to the ships' holds became famous for his description of this trade and the Californios whose lives were shaped by it. Contrary to the title, Richard Henry Dana devoted two-thirds of *Two Years Before the Mast* (1840) to the sixteen months he lived on shore among a people he found wanting in "industry, frugality and enterprise." More than Shaler and other observers of these years, this educated Bostonian influenced American thinking about California with his widely read book. Echoing the opinion of sea captains like Shaler, Dana wrote: "There are no people to whom the newly invented word 'loafer' is more applicable than to the Spanish Americans." And he, too, foresaw the future: "In the hands of an enterprising people, what a country this might be!"

The Americans came to California not only by sea but through vast inland wildernesses, a feat that astonished the Californios and alarmed their government officials. The first of these overlanders, the trapper Jedediah Smith, explored a route from the Rocky Mountains across the Mojave Desert, arriving at Mission San Gabriel (east of Los Angeles) in late 1826. By spring 1827 he and his band of mountain men had trapped a bonanza of beaver in the foothill streams of the eastern San Joaquin Valley. Then they made the first known crossing of the Sierra Nevada to return to the Great Salt Lake area in July of 1827. Within ten days Smith and company were on foot again, heading back to California in an epic of trail blazing. Smith's ambition, energy, and curiosity were perfectly revealed by a casual comment in his 1828 diary. After a day's layover at a camp in northern California, he matter-of-factly noted that his band set out again because he had "become weary of rest."

In their search for beaver, Smith and other mountain men marked trails that led through the wilderness to the Sacramento Valley and would be

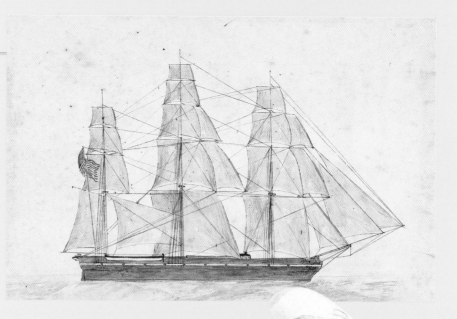

Trade between Californios and New England merchants depended on ships like the *Brookline,* one of several vessels owned by the Boston firm Bryant and Sturgis. On one journey, the *Brookline* arrived in Monterey in February 1829 and then spent eighteen months sailing the California coast, collecting hides and selling manufactured goods, before returning to Boston. Alfred Robinson, agent for Bryant and Sturgis, made this sketch of his ship.

During years-long voyages to the Pacific and back, American sailors carved images on marine animals' teeth and tusks, an art form called scrimshaw (also scrimshone, scrimshonter, and scrimshong). "We are regularly cruising with not enough to do to keep a man off a growl," one whaler wrote. "As this habit cankers the soul, I prefer to scrimshone."

The fat from hundreds of cattle slaughtered for their hides was boiled in huge iron pots, as shown in this 1847 watercolor. As the tallow cooled, Indian workers poured it into hide bags, or *botas,* for transport. Rancheros traded tallow and hides for exotic goods, such as these camphorwood chests made in China for storing laces, silks, and other finery.

followed by the emigrants of the 1840s. Some of these trappers would serve as guides for the California-bound greenhorns, while in the interim years their reports of the Mexican province added color and dash to the image forming in the American consciousness, including their provocative assessment that as the Californio men were lazy, the women were tantalizingly gracious.

IN CONTRAST TO THE AVERSION STILL FELT BY Mexicans for this isolated province, the first Americans swiftly adopted California as their home: fur trappers who welcomed a more sedentary life, sailors who deserted their ships and found wives in mission villages, and shipping agents sent to Monterey as representatives of the Boston trading companies. Year by year, the number of foreign residents increased slowly, from none in 1810 to thirteen in 1820. Amid California's non-Indian population of 4,250 in 1830, foreigners numbered only 146. That total grew to 380 by 1840, most of whom had become Mexican citizens through conversion to Catholicism, made more palatable by its animating effect upon the many Californio women, for whom there were too few bachelors of their class. In fact, California's population was still so sparse that throughout the 1820s and 1830s the Mexican government continued the old policy of shipping in convicts as settlers. The few soldiers sent to the crumbling presidios came, as before, mostly from jails.

With few exceptions the Americans easily merged into the crude but ebullient Spanish-Mexican society. Outwardly Hispanicized, in fact they began to Americanize California, not only by their entrepreneurial zeal but also by introducing the practice of selling goods on credit, thus binding the Californios economically to the Boston trading companies while stimulating new material appetites and rising expectations.

In what other country could such pushy, ambitious, impatient foreigners have been so quickly, even eagerly, welcomed to power and prestige?

Sir George Simpson, governor of the Hudson's Bay Company, visited California in 1842. Writing of the Americans' influence, he observed:

Not only from their numbers, but from their pushing and active habits and forward character, they have much influence and may be said to give law to the country.

George Simpson, letter of March 10, 1842

Within a few years they became California's strongest link with the outside world. Understanding commerce and finance, they provided credit, invested capital, and negotiated agreements with Boston companies to buy the province's exportable raw materials: cattle hides, tallow, and diminishing supplies of beaver and sea otter pelts.

In the Californio's mind, Boston became a far more important capital than Mexico City had ever been, providing for the first time a dependable source of supply for the province's necessities. As well, for the first time, California had in its midst a class of immigrants who came not as reluctant visitors, supervisors, escapees, or exiles but of their own volition. New Englanders and other Americans saw California as opportunity, not banishment. They invested not only their money but their lives. Abel Stearns of Massachusetts settled in the primitive pueblo of Los Angeles in 1830, soon prospering as its leading retail merchant. In ten years he was known as the wealthiest man in southern California, winning the hand of a daughter of the great ranchero, don Juan Bandini—the first of many marriage alliances between ambitious American immigrants and important Californio families.

Alfred Robinson, more influential than Stearns in the broader economy of California, served for many years as the shipping agent for Bryant and Sturgis. Typical of his success, in 1831 he sold over $79,000 of trading goods shipped from Boston, and a few years later supervised loading the *Alert* with the largest cargo ever collected along the California coast: 39,000 cattle hides, 31,000 horns, 709 pounds of beaver pelts, and 9 barrels of olive oil. In 1836, by then a man of influence, even power, he married the fifteen-year-old daughter of the great de la Guerra family of Santa Barbara.

Other enterprising Americans prospered through trade and marriage. William Wolfskill, from Kentucky, planted a commercial orange grove on part of his Mexican wife's vast land holdings to become the largest grower in southern California. Benjamin Wilson of Tennessee married a daughter of the Yorba family, Joseph Chapman an heiress of the Ortegas. And so it went with other Yankees whose new ties to Californio society helped to ease the region's transition to American dominance.

Of all the pioneer American settlers, Thomas Oliver Larkin had the most lasting and significant influence on California. He arrived by ship in 1832 from Charlestown, Massachusetts. Unlike most foreigners, he did not become a Mexican citizen or marry a Californio woman. Choosing a Yankee widow he had met on shipboard, Larkin settled in the Mexican capital of Alta California, Monterey, where he built the first two-story residence in the province. With foresight and an instinct for profits, he engaged in a wide range of busi-nesses—built and operated a flour mill, bakery, blacksmith shop, soap factory, lumber mill, bowling alley, and a flourishing liquor store, all the while trading with Honolulu and Mazatlán and selling imports on favorable terms of credit to local rancheros. He became California's first millionaire.

SUTTER

Johann August Sutter, the man destined to be most famous of those Californians—foreigner or Californio—came to the West Coast having abandoned his family in Switzerland. He traded in Santa Fe and traveled to Oregon, the Sandwich Islands (Hawaii), and Alaska before landing at Yerba Buena (San Francisco) in 1839. With a vision of developing an agricultural barony over which he would rule, he obtained from the Mexican governor the maximum land grant of eleven square leagues—over forty-eight thousand acres—in the barely explored Sacramento Valley, near the junction of two rivers of later fame, the Sacramento and the American. Using the labor of workers brought from the Sandwich Islands and local Indians lured with beads and cloth (and overseen by a few armed guards), Sutter directed the planting of fields and orchards and started construction of what would become Sutter's Fort. From within its eighteen-foot walls with cannon at two corners and workshops and a headquarters building, he governed a domain he named New Helvetia. In 1841 Sutter purchased from the Russians their neglected Fort Ross, promising to pay thirty thousand pesos in several annual installments of wheat from his fields. Ambitious and persuasive, Sutter planned and built for a California that would never be.

Even in its earliest, formative years, New Helvetia's advances in agriculture, architecture, and trade (not to mention plans for the future) far exceeded anything to be found at any of the hundreds of other ranchos. And along the coast the Californios were being pushed and shown "how to" by the Americans, with their many enterprises and their infiltration through marriage.

Until the 1830s, none of these outside forces had much effect on the vast, insular world of the twenty-one missions that controlled the richest pasture and most tillable land from San Diego to Sonoma. Mission San Diego encompassed some 170 square leagues, 1,200 square miles; San Juan Capistrano maybe 350 square miles; and others were measured in hundreds of thousands of acres. Working in the fields, skinning the cattle, attending Mass, the Indians labored and prayed without hope of reprieve. Orchards, vineyards, and fields of wheat, barley, corn, and beans yielded their bounty as the workers weakened and died of disease and despair. When the herds of horses grazed on too much of the pasture meant for cattle, the friars ordered their slaughter by the thousands. Fecundity, waste, and death.*

Year by year the Franciscans faced their inability to "civilize" their wards. Only the certainty of pursuit and punishment kept the Indians—even those who had been baptized—from fleeing to the wilderness. The weary friars blamed the neophytes, not the system. After forty years of devoted effort, Father-President Narcísco Durán lamented: "A slavedriver is what they ought to have."

It was a tragic grotesquerie—Indians maligned by their masters as they toiled to produce harvests from the land, all the while dying by the thousands, their ever-thinning numbers renewed by "wild" Indians, often captured by force, to be civilized-victimized within the deadly system.

DESPITE THE RAVAGES OF EPIDEMICS AND THE resistance of the survivors to the teachings of the Franciscans, the missions slowly, decade by decade, accumulated most of the assets—land and livestock—of California. By the 1830s this pastoral empire sorely tempted the Californios and the government in Mexico City. A plan evolved to secularize the twenty-one missions, to wrest them from the Catholic Church, that colonial symbol despised by so many in post-Spanish, anticlerical Mexico.

Advocates of secularization believed grants of mission land would attract, at long last, settlers from Mexico and thereby end California's dependence on the recalcitrant Indians.† In addition, the government recognized an obligation to fulfill the original purpose of the missions by providing parcels of land to the Christianized Indians. Competing with these political justifications for secularization, Californio families, retired presidial soldiers, government officials, and residents of the scruffy pueblos all greedily eyed the mission lands with private hopes and plans.

In 1834 Mexican governor José Figueroa initiated a cautious plan whereby ten missons (and six more by 1836) would be secularized, with half the property to be allocated to the mission Indians and half to be distributed to grantees by government officials. The inevitable pressure to plunder mission wealth quickly overwhelmed weak and inept government administrators. Not only were Indian rights trampled, but the provisions for opening mission lands to new settlers were quickly blocked by the influence and well-placed bribes of upper-class Californios who sought to secure vast land grants for themselves.

In a few swift years of fraud and pillage all twenty-one missions—their property and the lands once promised in trust to the Indians—were sold or given to friends and cronies of the Mexican governors. Cattle, sheep, and horses by the tens of thousands were driven away by disillusioned Indian vaqueros, cheated of their promised inheritance. Mission storerooms were looted; chaos and corruption reigned. The "freed" Indians little understood the abstraction of property ownership. Those few who did receive land often gambled it away or lost it to scheming interlopers. Bewildered, demoralized by liquor and violence, tempted by booty, or determined to seek vengeance for abuses suffered, some Indians angrily took part in the destruction of

---

* The only "farms" in California, the missions provided what food was grown. Despite the fertility of the virgin soil and the availability of Indian labor, agricultural production languished, reflecting the primitive equipment and methods of cultivation. For example, as late as 1831, annual yield in wheat came to only 63,000 bushels, corn 27,000, barley 18,000, beans 4,000, and so on, for a total of 115,000 bushels for all grains and legumes. The missions' cattle, roaming and breeding freely, numbered in 1832 some 151,000; sheep, goats, and pigs approximately 140,000; and horses 14,000.

---

† The number of Indians—men, women, and children—living at the twenty-one missions as of 1830 totaled about 18,000. As in the past, California's non-Indian population remained but a nominal presence in such a vast country, growing from 4,250 in 1830 to 5,780 in 1840 and by 1845 totaling only 7,580.

mission buildings where they had been so long confined. Unready for their homeless freedom, others sought safety as servants or field hands at the new ranchos or as laborers in the pueblos, in effect exchanging new shackles for old. Many more fled from this civilization, returning to tribes far removed from the scenes of their servitude. At Mission San José, Friar José Rubio lamented in 1840: "All is destruction, all is misery, humiliation and despair."

Thus it was that the Mexicans destroyed, in part by plan, more by plunder, the major institution they had inherited from the Spanish—but how fortunate for the United States that the missions were formally, legally dissolved under the laws of Mexico just a few years before the province would become American territory. What an embarrassing legal problem it would have been for Protestant, fervently antipapist Americans to have taken possession of a California dominated by the Catholic Church, in control of the best land, with thousands of Spanish-speaking Indians progressing toward promised ownership of all that acreage. Instead, by 1846 the missions and four presidios had, at the hands of the Mexicans, "entirely gone to ruin."

FROM MISSIONS TO RANCHOS

FROM THE RUINS OF THE MISSIONS AND THE political machinations that transferred their vast patrimony to secular suitors, another landed institution arose to dominate Mexican California: the great family ranchos. Like feudal estates, they traced their legitimacy from royal Spanish land grants, the first issued in 1784 to encourage settlement of the unpopular Pacific outpost. Spain's largesse, however, had been limited, comprising only twenty grants by the time independent Mexico took control of the near-empty province. New legislation in 1824 had offered more generous terms for obtaining large tracts, but the missions still monopolized most of the coastal property that would support cattle

ranching, the only business known to Mexican California.

Then came secularization. With the spoils of the missionary empire controlled by Mexican administrators and their allies, these insiders were besieged by hundreds of petitioners seeking grants from what had been church-held acreage. Responding to friends and bribes, careless of what few rules were known, the governors and their deputies by 1846 had given away 26 million acres to 813 applicants.* Varying in size from 4,400 to 700,000 acres, these little kingdoms became the new economic base of California, most of them provisioned with supplies and equipment from the looted missions and staffed by Indians who, like serfs, did all the hard work and tended the herds of cattle.

Though it helped to know the governor or a local official, nearly anyone could apply for and receive a land grant: veterans of presidio service, saloon-keepers in the pueblos, government officials, small landowners, and foreigners who had consented to Mexican citizenship. The best-connected petitioners, usually old families like the de la Guerras, Carrillos, Yorbas, Ortegas, Vallejos, Bandinis, and their peers, received several grants for different members of the family, thereby accumulating immense holdings, like Pío Pico's 532,000 acres.

With an abundance of fertile land and few applicants, the Mexican governors allowed a careless system to evolve. To gain a grant required submittal of a diseño, a hand-drawn picture-map, which depicted the area claimed, with boundaries marked by the most prominent features, such as hills, streams, and coastline. Without precise measurements, "survey" marks might be a clump of bushes, the point where two trails crossed, a spring, a big rock, even a large tree. Convenient in those careless, ample times, these methods would later (under Yankee scrutiny) prove controversial, often causing years,

---

* The magnitude of this Mexican giveaway may be better appreciated by realizing that 26 million acres represents 25 percent of the land in present-day California.

Finely arrayed rancheros could ride for many miles without ever leaving their vast holdings. Their land grant boundaries were described by freehand *diseños;* this one depicted a 22,000-acre rancho awarded in 1842 to Lieutenant José Rafael Gonzales, administrator of the custom house in Monterey.

As ranchos prospered, the missions decayed. This engraving of an 1839 watercolor by French navy lieutenant Francois Edmond Pârís shows the decline of the Carmel mission, its roof falling in, just five years after the secularization order.

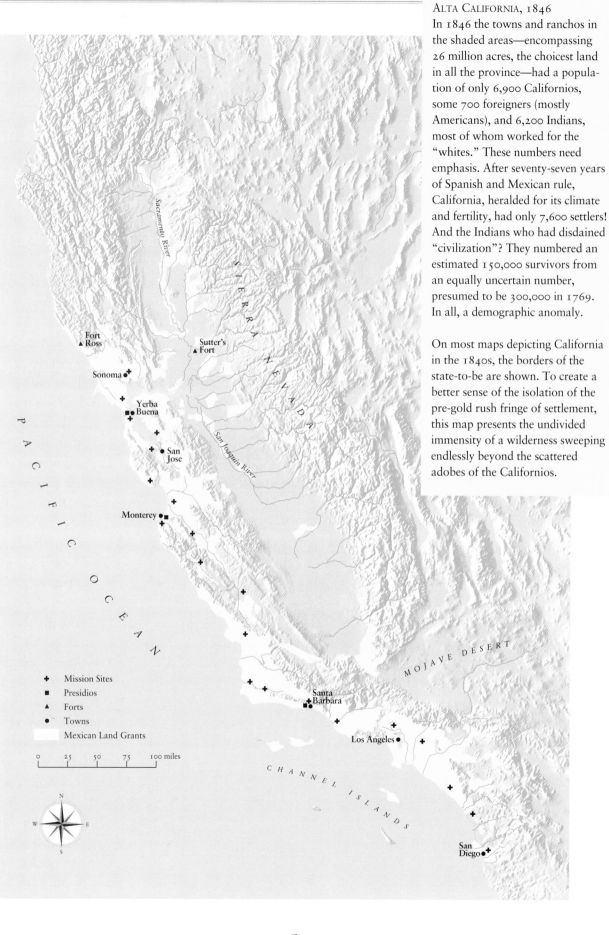

ALTA CALIFORNIA, 1846
In 1846 the towns and ranchos in the shaded areas—encompassing 26 million acres, the choicest land in all the province—had a population of only 6,900 Californios, some 700 foreigners (mostly Americans), and 6,200 Indians, most of whom worked for the "whites." These numbers need emphasis. After seventy-seven years of Spanish and Mexican rule, California, heralded for its climate and fertility, had only 7,600 settlers! And the Indians who had disdained "civilization"? They numbered an estimated 150,000 survivors from an equally uncertain number, presumed to be 300,000 in 1769. In all, a demographic anomaly.

On most maps depicting California in the 1840s, the borders of the state-to-be are shown. To create a better sense of the isolation of the pre-gold rush fringe of settlement, this map presents the undivided immensity of a wilderness sweeping endlessly beyond the scattered adobes of the Californios.

Sacramento River

Fort Ross

Sutter's Fort

SIERRA NEVADA

Sonoma

Yerba Buena

San Jose

San Joaquin River

PACIFIC OCEAN

Monterey

MOJAVE DESERT

Santa Barbara

Los Angeles

CHANNEL ISLANDS

San Diego

+   Mission Sites
■   Presidios
▲   Forts
●   Towns
    Mexican Land Grants

0   25   50   75   100 miles

N
W   E
S

The people were very fond of riding, dancing, and of shows of any kind. The young fellows took great delight in showing off their horsemanship, and would dash along, picking up a half-dollar from the ground, stop their horses in full career and turn about on the space of a bullock's hide, and their skill with the lasso was certainly wonderful. At full speed they could cast their lasso about the horns of a bull, or so throw it as to catch any particular foot. These fellows would work all day on horseback in driving cattle or catching wild-horses for a mere nothing, but all the money offered would not have hired one of them to walk a mile.

William Tecumseh Sherman, *Memoirs*

---

sometimes decades, of costly litigation and loss of ownership.

Rich with new land and increased herds, ranchero families enjoyed a simple, leisurely life, financed by *bostoños'* credit. Visitors to their ranchos described in envious detail those "happy people living without restraint or vexatious authority." But others expressed Puritan scorn: "They sleep and smoke and hum some tune of Castilian laziness, while surrounding nature is inviting them to the noblest and richest rewards of honorable toil." These and similar appraisals of the Mexican ruling class strengthened the American impression that California deserved far more energetic citizens.

Most shocking, even morally reprehensible for Americans, was the prodigal wastefulness of the rancheros. They lived surrounded by thousands of cattle, and yet very few ranchos had any milk, butter, or cheese. They slaughtered their animals for their hides, tallow, and horns, leaving thousands of carcasses to be eaten by wild animals and packs of dogs raised for that purpose. Bleached skulls and skeletons that rattled under horses' hooves, vultures that circled overhead, seemed to symbolize "a society doomed by the intemperate waste of its lavish resources."

With the disappearance of the few products formerly made at the mission workshops, the ranchos depended more than ever on New England traders, preferring the convenience and expense of imports to the rigors of self-sufficiency. Soap, candles, and blankets, even simple household implements such as brooms, now came from Boston, along with axes, ladles, strap iron, knives, and a growing variety of luxuries and foodstuffs, not to mention the shoes and boots manufactured in Massachusetts from rancho cowhides.

Easygoing, comfortably oblivious to their backwardness, the Californios had no vehicles more modern than cumbersome, creaking ox-drawn carts with wheels of solid rounds sawed from tree trunks. And no roads or bridges. No school, library, or hospital. No newspapers or books other than those delivered by the traders. And no post office. Most Californios were illiterate; they knew only how to scrawl a mark in place of signature. But they also knew how to show the Americans there was more to life than work. Like dancing, feasting, and singing in celebration of three-day weddings and religious holidays. To be condemned but also envied by many a Yankee.

Just as the ranchos remained primitive though colorful dependencies of foreign traders, failing to develop agriculture and other economic resources, so urban life faltered without any manufacturers or system of transport; indeed, town life was nearly as primitive as that of the countryside. An 1846 description of San Jose mentioned "a village of 600 to 800 inhabitants . . . with thousands of ground squirrels burrowing in the plaza." California's few other towns, all of them along the coast, survived into the 1840s without significant growth. Los Angeles (notorious for drunkenness, gambling, and frequent murders) had about 1,250 residents in 1846, the village of Yerba Buena on San Francisco

Bay could claim maybe 800, and Monterey, the province's political and social capital, had grown to an estimated 1,000.

Convergence of circumstances, fate, American luck? Whatever the cause, California drifted ever closer to acquisition by the United States, eased and even hurried by the failures of the Californios to develop agriculture, towns, commerce, or any other bulwark that might have held back or delayed the coming tide.

THE MOST VISIBLE MEXICAN INSTITUTION, THE government of Alta California, failed not only to govern minimally but even to establish provincial authority. Its ineffectiveness reflected the chaos of Mexico City, where contending factions staged coup and countercoup. Each new president of the Republic of Mexico dispatched his own governor to Monterey, and each of these interim despots found his authority enforced by a diminishing garrison, so seldom were his soldiers paid. As ever, California inspired more scorn than interest among influential *capitalinos* in Mexico City and, too, among more ordinary folk. "To speak of California was like mentioning the end of the world."

Administration succeeded administration over a subcurrent of plots, intrigues, and occasional military skirmishes. In one five-year period, 1831–36, California endured eleven governors, not counting three who were not permitted to take office. In 1836, resentment of this anarchy spawned a revolt led by native Californio Juan Bautista Alvarado, who proclaimed Alta California "a free and sovereign state" within the Republic of Mexico, with autonomy to conduct its own affairs, particularly the sale of remaining mission lands and assets (without mention of the Indian converts who were still judged unqualified for citizenship). Alvarado's regime swiftly sank into bickering and dissension, to be followed by a replacement governor sent from Mexico City at the head of band of *cholos* (scoundrels) who plundered and pillaged, ensuring

but a brief tenure for their commander. By 1845 the confusion had resolved itself into a contentious division of power, with Pío Pico as governor headquartered in Los Angeles and José Castro as *comandante general* at Monterey. They attacked each other with proclamations and *pronunciamientos.*

The internecine squabbling left but one institution that might have checked the increasing influence of the Americanos and later the thousands of fortune hunters: the patriarchal families, newly enriched by the breakup of the missions. These rancheros could have developed a sense of unity and political power, of common cause against the aggressive foreigners. Instead, family feuds, personal ambitions, and interregional rivalries preoccupied the patriarchs and their sons, preventing them from seeing the common danger ahead. Under contract to deliver thousands of cattle hides to offset their borrowings from Bryant and Sturgis, they followed their traditional lives. Many households echoed to the sounds of fifteen or more children, needy relatives, and a covey of opportunistic visitors content to accept the benefits of the rancheros' legendary hospitality—all supported by Indian servants grinding corn for tortillas, preparing meals and stoking kitchen fires, washing clothes, sewing. One rancho required the labor of six hundred Indian servants and field hands, a California cousin of the South's plantations.

Though they might themselves have lolled amid the generosity of such ranchos, typical American settlers continued to send letters "back home" that scorned the Californios for their failure to develop the land. "Wait till we Yankees take over" was their repeated message.

And Washington, too, coveted California. After a bribery-purchase scheme failed in 1835, an undaunted President Andrew Jackson authorized his diplomatic agent in Mexico City to offer $3.5 million to purchase a large part of California, with the "great object of securing the bay of San Francisco." The Mexican government indignantly rejected the secret proposal.

Californie. Rancho près du bois Rouge.

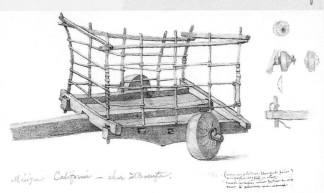

Méxique. Californie — char à Boeufs.

Although the Californios lived on thousands of acres of land and owned enormous herds of livestock, their way of life remained primitive. Dirt-floored houses and simple oxcarts served their needs with a minimum of expenditure.

Swedish adventurer G. M. Waseurtz af Sandel visited California in 1842–43 and sketched what was a novelty to him but commonplace in Mexico—women grinding cornmeal into tortillas. They ground corn on concave *metates* using round stone *manos* and patted the cakes into shape before heating them over a charcoal fire.

In April 1842, the U.S. minister to Mexico again recommended the purchase of California, "the richest, the most beautiful and the healthiest country in the world. . . . The harbor of San Francisco is capacious enough to receive the navies of the world. In addition to which California is destined to be the granary of the Pacific. . . . France and England both have had their eyes upon it. . . . The importance of the acquisition of California cannot be overestimated." President Tyler authorized the U.S. minister to attempt new negotiations with the Mexican government.

Whatever the outcome of this financial-diplomatic overture might have been, increased friction between the United States and Mexico doomed such a straightforward purchase of California. On September 1, 1842, Commodore Thomas ap Catesby Jones (he always used his full Welsh name), in command of the American naval squadron in the Pacific, received in Callao, Peru, information which he interpreted as evidence that the United States and Mexico had gone to war.*

Fearing that the British might use the conflict as a pretext for their Pacific squadron to seize California, Commodore Jones sailed north and, on October 13, 1842, brought his two warships into Monterey harbor. Under a flag of truce, he sent ashore a demand for the immediate surrender of the port. The *comandante* at the presidio considered this sudden predicament, aware that his defenses "were of no consequence, as everybody knows." Terms were quickly negotiated, with Thomas Larkin serving as impromptu interpreter. The Mexican garrison marched out of its ramshackle fort

"with music, and their colors flying." The Americans hoisted the Stars and Stripes, the ships fired a salute, and Commodore Jones issued a proclamation declaring, among other profundities, the American flag to be the "infallible emblem of civil liberty."

After two days of uneventful occupation, the commodore was shown a newspaper recently received from Mexico City that proved the rumors of war to be misleading. He ordered the flag of Mexico restored, his 150 marines and sailors returned to their ships, and a repentant salute fired in honor of the Republic of Mexico. Following an exchange of official courtesy visits between flagship and *comandante*'s office, the squadron sailed away.

Three months later, Jones and his officers attended a grand ball in their honor at Los Angeles, hosted by the governor of California and his staff, fully arrayed in glittering dress uniforms. Thus the American navy experienced the Arcadian simplicity and eager generosity of the Californios. In Mexico City, however, Commodore Jones's miscalculation outraged government ministers, and the United States lost a chance to buy "the granary of the Pacific."

Another event in 1842 might well have changed California history—the first discovery of gold. On March 9, two Californios in pursuit of stray horses stopped to rest at midday on a rancho forty miles north of Los Angeles. Using his knife to dig up some wild onions, Francisco López noticed yellow particles clinging to their roots. Digging more purposefully, he found more gleaming particles—gold, he felt certain.

The news spread quickly from the rancho to Los Angeles and beyond. Soon miners from Sonora came north to work the *placeres*, surface deposits of gold. By June, maybe a thousand goldseekers winnowed the gravel and sand in the dry creeks and gullies, some of them accumulating $2 a day in gold flakes. The miners extended the diggings and continued their work during 1843 and 1844, while the

---

* The crisis centered in Texas, where American settlers (at least twenty thousand, including their slaves) had rejected Mexican sovereignty in 1836 and declared their independence, creating the Republic of Texas. By 1842 U.S. recognition of Texas and the prospect of annexation had further antagonized Mexico, leading to rumors of war.

Mexican government sought to gain some control by appointing the owner of the rancho to collect fees from the miners and taxes from the sale of liquor and other necessities.

As the years passed, hard work gained less and less gold. By 1845 only some fifty miners remained, their once great expectations reduced to twenty-five cents per day, stingy reward for their drudgery—and a reality to be remembered when the next shouts of "Gold!" would be heard.

MANIFEST DESTINY

DURING THE 1840s CALIFORNIA ENTERED THE sphere of the most enduring, powerful force in American life: the pull of an unsettled continent beyond the frontier, the sense of what Emerson in 1844 called America's "ample geography." For many decades frontier folk had been ready to hitch up their wagons—vamoose, skedaddle, mosey on—to find rich soil and a better life farther west.

NORTH AMERICA, 1846
On the eve of the Mexican War, three powers occupied the bulk of North America: the United States, Great Britain, and Mexico. Following the admission of Texas as the twenty-eighth state, the year 1846 saw a peaceful division of Oregon Country between the United States and Great Britain and the outbreak of hostilities with Mexico in the disputed area of Texas, between the Nueces and Rio Grande Rivers. The ensuing war completed the continental expansion of the United States and began the American period of California's history.

From the Atlantic coast they had pushed into the valleys of Pennsylvania and western New York. In the nineteenth century, with their plows and axes, they settled the Ohio Valley (in 1803 Ohio became a state), and then moved on to Illinois (1818) and across the Mississippi River to settle Missouri (1821), Arkansas (1836), and Iowa (1846). To the southwest they advanced into Spanish Texas in 1821. And farm families even dared in 1835 to venture two thousand miles over fur trappers' trails to Oregon Territory, jointly claimed by Great Britain and the United States.

Letters from Oregon settlers in the Willamette Valley published in St. Louis newspapers and others farther east told of the healthy climate, mild winters, abundant crops, and the prospect that soon there would be so many Yankees that the British would have to pull out. And then Oregon could become a state. These reports created such an attractive prospect that in the summer of 1843 more than one thousand men, women, and children traveled to the Willamette Valley over what had become known as the Oregon Trail. By 1846, after only a decade of immigration, Oregon had at least six thousand American settlers—more than the number of Spaniards and Mexicans who had settled in California during the seventy-seven years since 1769.

Less attractive than Oregon because of uncertainty about ownership of land in a Mexican province, California by 1840 had fewer than four hundred American and other foreign settlers. Except for a few fur trappers, all had arrived by sea. Then in 1841 the first overland emigrant parties set out from the western states, bound for "a perfect paradise, a perpetual spring." One company of twenty-five followed the fur traders' route to Santa Fe and then, via the Old Spanish Trail, reached the remains of Mission San Gabriel near Los Angeles, thereby opening a southern route for later emigrants. A larger group, including a few women, set out that spring, following the Oregon Trail as far west as present-day Idaho; there they turned southwest and, leaving the known route, found their way

With greater candor than he might have realized, Governor Pío Pico summed up the Californios' reaction to American settlers:

We find ourselves threatened by hordes of Yankee emigrants . . . whose progress we cannot arrest. Already have the wagons of that perfidious people crossed the entire continent, scaled the almost inaccessible summits of the Sierra Nevada, and penetrated the fruitful valley of the Sacramento. . . . Already [they] are cultivating farms, establishing vineyards, erecting mills, sawing up lumber, and doing a thousand other things which seem natural to them.

Titus F. Cronise, *The Natural Wealth of California*

along the Humboldt River (Nevada), finally struggling through a pass in the Sierra Nevada to reach the promised land in November. News of this overland route reached the Missouri frontier in 1842, and each summer thereafter California attracted a small share of the westward migration—250 in 1845, compared to 3,000 settlers welcomed that year in Oregon.

With settlers in Texas, Oregon, and California sending widely published letters back to the States describing the wonders of those new frontiers, the American people and their government sensed as never before their nation's continental destiny—that the boundaries of the youthful, vigorous United States should reach from the Atlantic to the Pacific and south to the Rio Grande. In that decade of nationalistic ambitions, few leaders spoke more eloquently of America's Manifest Destiny than Missouri's senator Thomas Hart Benton. In arguing that the Republic of Texas should be annexed as the twenty-eighth state, the Great Expansionist proclaimed that "man and woman were not more formed for union by the hand of God than Texas and the United States by the hand of Nature." In his inaugural address on March 4, 1845, the newly elected president, James K. Polk, made clear that he favored annexation—which caused Mexico to lodge an immediate complaint and warn that annexation would lead to war.

For President Polk the logic of geography and the imperative of Manifest Destiny also made inevitable the inclusion of Oregon in his nation's advance across the continent. In his December 1845 message to Congress the president announced that the "patriotic pioneers" who had settled in that disputed territory must be protected. After a series of diplomatic crises leading to the threat of war with Great Britain over the "Oregon Question," a treaty was signed in June 1846 which established the Oregon-Canada boundary at the forty-ninth parallel, thus bringing Oregon Territory (including the future states of Washington, Oregon, and Idaho) into the United States.

And what about California? Even before taking office, President-elect Polk had decided to rank California's annexation as a primary goal of his administration—to be accomplished by peaceful means, if possible. That possibility, however, seemed remote in 1845 as Mexico threatened war on the Texas border. Reports received in Washington told of a British plan to acquire California by forgiving the equivalent of $50 million in debt owed Britain by Mexico. Compounding that danger, news came from California that Governor Pío Pico had approved a plan to colonize the province with ten thousand Irish settlers. And a U.S. agent in Mexico (echoing the old fear of Commodore Jones) warned that British warships in the Pacific were making ready to seize California in the event of war.

To answer these perceived dangers, Secretary of State James Buchanan in October 1845 sent a message to Thomas Oliver Larkin in Monterey, who had been serving for some time as U.S. consul. This dispatch appointed Larkin "confidential agent," with the authority "to exert the greatest vigilance" to prevent any European country from gaining control of California and to encourage the Californios

to separate from Mexico, in which endeavor they could rely on the protection of the United States. Larkin received these secret orders six months later, in April 1846, delivered by U.S. Marine Corps lieutenant Archibald Gillespie, who had traveled across Mexico disguised as an invalid.*

Pursuant to his new responsibilities, Larkin solicited the support of leading Americanos, like Abel Stearns of Los Angeles and Jacob Leese of Yerba Buena, as well as others who had married into the Californio aristocracy. With these and like-minded friends, he discussed what would be the best course for California's future. Again and again the Californios expressed their resentment of the intrigues and incompetence of the Mexican government. Annexation seemed the logical alternative—indeed, an inevitability, in the opinion of the much-respected Mariano Vallejo, one of the largest Californio landowners (238,000 acres). Even José Castro, military *comandante* for northern California, privately confided to Larkin his own plan for California's independence.

By the summer of 1846 Larkin had good reason to be hopeful that in a short time California would voluntarily petition to join the Union, like Texas. But his optimism was soon dashed by decisions in Washington, by actions on the Texas-Mexico border, and by the rashness of Captain John C. Frémont.

In Washington, President Polk's determination to acquire California had not been weakened by the distractions of Texas and Oregon. By November 1845 Polk had decided the territory might best be won by offering the bankrupt Mexican government an attractive purchase price. But circumstances in Mexico City made such an offer even less acceptable than the earlier proposals of Presidents Jackson

---

* Gillespie also carried messages (even more secret) for the famed explorer John C. Frémont, captain in the U.S. Army Corps of Topographical Engineers, who was supposed to be somewhere in northern California in command of a scientific-exploring expedition.

and Tyler. Revolution and counterrevolution, continual financial crisis, and growing hatred for the *yanquis* left the Mexicans suspicious and wary. Nonetheless, in November President Polk sent John Slidell as his "Envoy Extraordinary and Minister Plenipotentiary" to negotiate settlement of the disputed Texas border and the purchase of California. Not a timid thinker, Polk also instructed Slidell to include the vast, unmapped region then called New Mexico (present-day Arizona, New Mexico, Nevada, Utah, and part of Colorado) for an offering price of fifteen to twenty million dollars, but not to exceed forty million. Washington would buy its way to the Pacific.

News of Slidell's mission reached Mexico City as a rumor that he would offer a million-dollar bribe to President José Herrera. The believability of this story forced the harassed president to refuse even to meet the envoy extraordinary. When the report of failure reached Washington on April 7, 1846, Polk decided to turn from the carrot to the stick. The secretary of war sent orders to General Zachary Taylor to advance his troops to the Rio Grande, a provocative move the Mexicans could not ignore. On April 25, Mexican soldiers crossed the river and in their attack killed several Americans. Two weeks later President Polk read General Taylor's report of the engagement, and on May 13 the United States declared that "by the act of the Republic of Mexico a state of war exists."

Military dispatches, diplomatic instructions, and vital intelligence all traveled at the speed of the fastest horse or ship, meaning weeks and even months of uncertainty and anxiety between communiqués. Nonetheless, decisions had to be made. Intuition, or more often adherence to the last plan or reported position, served as the most prudent guide in the management of war and lesser enterprises. For Commodore John Sloat, in command of the U.S. fleet in the Pacific, the dangers of miscalculation had been painfully demonstrated by Commodore Jones in 1842. Therefore, he was carefully attentive to his orders: occupy or blockade Monterey and other California ports only when he could "ascertain beyond a doubt" that the United States had declared war against Mexico.

That certainty he finally gained on the Mexican coast at Mazatlán on June 17, whereupon he sailed for California. On July 2 his three warships entered Monterey harbor, where he and Thomas Larkin cooperated in achieving a remarkably peaceful military occupation. Commodore Sloat wrote to Larkin asking if his sailors might come ashore for liberty. "They may, as you know sailors will, make some noise in the place, but they will not do any harm and will spend 1,000 to 1,500 dollars, which will compensate for any annoyance they may occasion." Larkin agreed, and on July 4 U.S. warships off Monterey and in San Francisco Bay fired twenty-one-gun salutes, while shipboard and ashore everyone enjoyed a "great fiesta."

Not until July 7 did Commodore Sloat attend to the formality of requiring the Mexicans at Monterey to surrender. The *comandante* retired from the presidio peacefully, explaining that there were no munitions available. When U.S. sailors and marines came ashore to occupy the fort, they found no Mexican flag to be lowered—there had been no funds to buy one. It was an amicable, California-style occupation and transition, a change of command little more eventful than the ones the Californios had so often experienced. Larkin expected that with a few more ceremonies and fiestas he and his allies would be able to lead the principal rancheros to accept the inevitable and beneficial American annexation. But such a peaceful handoff, so nearly finessed, was about to be fumbled by violence from a forgotten quarter.

In December 1845 the most celebrated explorer since Lewis and Clark led a force of sixty well-armed surveyors, guides, and assistants into the Sacramento Valley. Widely heralded in the States by the title "Pathfinder," Captain John C. Frémont of the U.S. Army Corps of Topographical Engineers came to California ostensibly to continue the explorations begun in his previous two expeditions of

In depicting the American expansion westward, artists often romanticized the hardships of the grueling overland trail and the heady thrill of arrival, as did Emanuel Leutze in "Westward the Course of Empire Takes Its Way," actually painted in 1861, well after the nation had expanded across the continent.

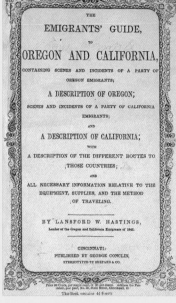

Lansford W. Hastings, an Ohio-born lawyer who followed the Oregon Trail to the Pacific in 1842, published one of the many popular overland guides in the 1840s. An enthusiastic promoter of California, he attempted to direct emigrants there instead of Oregon by way of "Hastings' Cut-off," a desert route he had never traversed that veered south of the Great Salt Lake and below the Ruby Mountains. The Donner Party heeded his advice in 1846 with calamitous results.

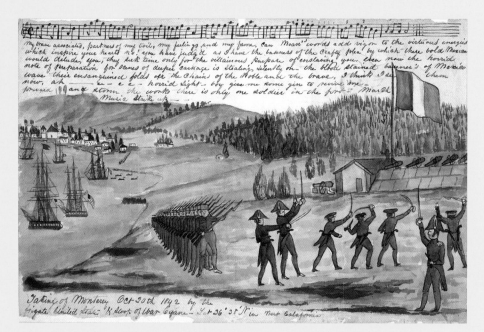

Mistakenly convinced that war with Mexico had begun, Commodore Thomas ap Catesby Jones on October 19, 1842, demanded the surrender of Monterey. The next day his marines occupied the presidio. "Although I come in arms, as a representative of a powerful nation, I come not to spread desolation," he magnanimously proclaimed. "The stars and stripes . . . now float triumphantly before you, and, henceforth and forever, will give protection and security." "Henceforth and forever" proved to be two days, and then Jones discovered his blunder. William Henry Meyers, a navy gunner aboard U.S.S. *Cyane,* depicted the attack in a tongue-in-cheek sketch—complete with a comical tune paraphrasing his commander's orders to the invading troops.

1842 and 1843–44—described in his immensely popular *Report* (which became one of the nation's first bestsellers). After resting at Sutter's Fort, Frémont met with Thomas Larkin in Monterey and then with Comandante Castro, from whom he gained permission to bivouac his party for the winter in the San Joaquin Valley. But Frémont was a restless, relentlessly ambitious young man, and impetuous too. He marched about, violated his agreement with Castro, and deeply angered that aggrieved officer. Thanks to Larkin's intercession, a confrontation was avoided. However, Castro ordered Frémont to leave California. After more bluster and expression of outrage, the Pathfinder headed north for Oregon, "slowly and growlingly," as he later wrote to his wife, the daughter of Senator Benton. Not easily constrained, along his route Frémont encouraged American settlers' scorn for Mexican authority. In his wake, he left an angry *comandante* and a confidential agent much less hopeful for a peaceful annexation.

VALLEJO

In May 1846 Lieutenant Gillespie, after delivering the Washington dispatch to Larkin, hurried after Frémont with messages from the secretary of war and news of the worsening crisis with Mexico. Whatever these dispatches conveyed (no one knows), Frémont turned his men south and headed back to California.

Emboldened by Frémont's reappearance in the Sacramento Valley in June 1846, disgruntled Americano settlers, acting with a "let's-do-something" impatience and bravado, stole a string of horses that belonged to Castro. Then, as if embarrassed not to show a higher purpose than horse rustling, these marauders decided to capture the adobe hamlet of Sonoma. Their target indicated more impulse than political intelligence, inasmuch as Sonoma was the home of General Mariano Vallejo, supporter of annexation and one of Larkin's closest allies. On the quiet Sunday morning of June 14 the unruly band

California was suffused with a knowledge that . . . its golden age had ended. No one could govern it from Mexico; no one could govern it at home. Its feudal organization, feeble at best, had broken up into cliques which lowered the standard of public honor and responsibility, enfeebled the society, and drained it alike of money and belief. An era was closing in regret; an order of mankind, a phase of society, in many ways a happy phase, was collapsing. This much the Californians knew. They felt diversely about it. . . . Some of them would welcome anything that would restore stability. . . . Some dreamed of restoring the allegiance to Mexico which had never quite existed. Some dreamed, instead, of going it alone. A good many . . . would do what they could, not much in any event, to hold together while the flood closed over them.

Bernard DeVoto, *The Year of Decision: 1846*

surrounded Vallejo's home and awakened him. He graciously invited three of their leaders into his parlor. Through an interpreter the Americanos declared the general to be their prisoner of war. Bewildered, Vallejo suggested they sit down and talk. For hours they conferred, all the while drinking from their host's decanters of brandy and wine.

Outside, the other insurrectionists grew impatient. Finally, William Ide, a farmer from Illinois, clarified their purpose: "Choose you this day what you will be! We are robbers or we must be conquerors." Preferring the sound of the latter, they scrawled a proclamation declaring California to be a republic and pieced together a makeshift flag. Cut from a petticoat and a chemise, the crude banner showed a red star opposite the indistinct shape of an animal, supposed to be a grizzly bear, and the lettering "California Republic." Thus the one-village nation found its ensign, destined to serve a future

John Charles Frémont achieved a heroic reputation through his genius for publicity and the popularity of his *Report of the Exploring Expedition . . . to Oregon and Northern California in the Years 1843–44* (Washington, D.C., 1845). His glowing descriptions of California's springlike climate and fertile soil inspired in the American people a romantic vision of California. One historian has judged his *Report* to have made a "spectacular contribution . . . to those grandiose national urges so characteristic of the times."

This photograph is the only known image of the original Bear Flag, which was destroyed in the 1906 San Francisco earthquake.

1816	Indiana becomes the nineteenth state
1820	Missouri Compromise establishes a balance between free and slave states
1822	Spanish rule ends in California; United States recognizes Mexican independence
1825	Erie Canal completed, linking New York City with the Great Lakes
1826	Thomas Jefferson and John Adams die (on the 4th of July)
	Trapper Jedediah Smith reaches California
1830	First American-built locomotive makes run on Baltimore & Ohio line
1834	McCormick patents reaper
	Secularization of California missions begins
1837	Deere begins manufacturing steel plows in Vermont
1839	Sutter arrives in California
1840	*Two Years Before the Mast* published
1842	Commodore Jones prematurely occupies Monterey
1844	Morse's telegraph put into operation (between Baltimore and Washington, D.C.)
1845	Frémont publishes widely read account of his western expeditions
	Texas annexed to United States, becomes twenty-eighth state
	Beginning of Irish Potato Famine
1846	Mormon migration to the Great Salt Lake begins
	Mexican War begins
	Sam Brannan and 238 Mormons arrive in San Francisco on the *Brooklyn*
1847	Yerba Buena renamed San Francisco
	Survivors of the Donner Party are rescued

Exasperated with American interlopers, Comandante José Castro declared before a gathering of Californios in Monterey in 1846:

These Americans are so contriving that some day they will build ladders to touch the sky, and once in the heavens they will change the whole face of the universe and even the color of the stars.

Robert Glass Cleland, "The Early Sentiment for the Annexation of California"

beyond the imaginings of even those well-liquored patriots.

Excited by their sudden power, acting without plan or concern for the consequences of their actions, the Bear Flaggers claimed as their first prisoners Vallejo and others who had been favorable to Larkin's plan for annexation. They carted them off to imprisonment at Sutter's Fort, where Sutter (believing Frémont to be the Flaggers' leader) declared himself in support of the movement. Meantime, Ide had sent a message to U.S. Navy captain John Montgomery, in command at San Francisco Bay, advising him that California was now a republic. The astonished officer refused on behalf of the United States to recognize or deal with the Bear Flaggers. In Monterey, Larkin learned with dismay of the filibuster and knew the chance for an amicable transition had been ruined. At Sonoma, Frémont, ever the opportunist, merged his troops with the armed Bear Flag men and a number of sympathetic Americano settlers, proclaiming this force the "California Battalion," with himself in command.

The Californios were outraged. Their instinct for pragmatism, so central to Larkin's calculations, did not lessen the sting of assaults on their pride. In the north, Comandante Castro exhorted Californios: "Banish from your hearts all petty resentments [i.e., put aside north-south rivalries], arise in mass,

Divine Providence will guide us to glory." In the south, Governor Pico issued his own proclamation, asserting that a "gang of North American adventurers" had taken Sonoma, just as they had stolen Texas. "Compatriots, run swiftly with me to crown your brows with the fresh laurels of unfading glory."

Tensions were heightened by rumors that Mexico had six hundred soldiers at Acapulco ready for transport to California, and campfire tales told of Castro's plans to slaughter all foreigners. When Frémont's ruffians shot and killed three unarmed Californios, northern California expected more bloodshed. Then in July came the reliable news of formal, declared war between the United States and Mexico. The hit-and-run actions of Frémont now became irrelevant, and he shifted his hopes to more significant opportunities. And most Californios accepted the reality of the Americans' superior strength, while anticipating the benefits of their rule and money. By mid-July the Stars and Stripes flew above Monterey, at the village of Yerba Buena, from the flagpole at Sonoma, and over the walls at Sutter's Fort out in the Sacramento Valley.

WHEN COMMAND OF U.S. FORCES IN CALIFORNIA passed from Commodore Sloat to newly arrived Commodore Robert Stockton on July 23, 1846, the province lay peacefully under American control from San Francisco Bay to Santa Barbara. But in Los Angeles, Pío Pico was calling upon all citizens to repel this "most unjust aggression . . . undertaken by a nation ruled by the most unheard-of ambition."

To attack the Mexicans in the south before they could organize a defense, Commodore Stockton ordered Frémont and his California Battalion by ship to San Diego. The detachment landed without opposition on July 29 and prepared to march north. A few days later, Stockton himself landed at San Pedro, on the coast near Los Angeles, with a force of sailors and marines. Faced with two advancing American columns, Governor Pico issued a final

Naval Sketches of the War in California — Meyers No. 5

In the largest engagement of the war (a bloody struggle that almost prevented his force from reaching San Diego), General Stephen Watts Kearny and his desert-weary dragoons clashed with cavalry led by André Pico at San Pasqual, December 6, 1846.

William Meyers, who had accompanied Commodore Jones during the premature capture of Monterey in 1842, was with the U.S. squadron when it returned in 1846. He painted the ships at anchor after the American flag was hoisted on July 7—this time to remain.

Naval Sketches of the War in California — Meyers No. 12

proclamation of defiance and departed for Mexico. With this, Mexican opposition sputtered out. Mounting four quarterdeck guns on creaking ox-carts, Commodore Stockton marched his two hundred men into Los Angeles on August 13. In the plaza a hastily convened military band gave forth with a make-do version of "Hail Columbia," and the Stars and Stripes were hoisted to the top of the Mexican flagpole.

As if to offer his personal assurance of California's submission, Stockton dispatched a letter to President Polk that must have given that harried leader cause for a wry smile, or maybe a frown of exasperation. The conqueror wrote: "My word is at present the law of the land. My person is more than regal. The haughty Mexican cavalier shakes hands with me with pleasure and the beautiful women look to me with joy and gladness as their friend and benefactor. In short, all of the power and luxury is spread before me, through the mysterious workings of a beneficent Providence."

STOCKTON

On his return to Monterey and Yerba Buena, Stockton enjoyed congratulations and party-going. But in Los Angeles the gladness rapidly soured. Outraged by the oppressive restrictions and tyrannical behavior of the American garrison, the Angelenos organized on September 23, 1846, an assault that forced the "despots" to flee to San Pedro. The gauntlet thrown down, Commodore Stockton interrupted his celebrating at Yerba Buena to issue a proclamation that he would return south, this time to conquer and to punish. "The Sons of Liberty are on their way . . . for fighting, not for speech making."

In their effort to fulfill Stockton's boast, reinforced American troops sallied from San Pedro on October 7 intending to recapture Los Angeles. Driven back by one hundred mounted Californios, they escaped to ships offshore. With this heady triumph over the arrogant *yanquis* the Mexican

defenders' enthusiasm for revolt spread to Santa Barbara, and for a brief time they controlled southern California. Then in November Commodore Stockton landed troops in San Diego and later sent a contingent of riflemen east to meet General Stephen Watts Kearny, in command of one hundred desert-weary dragoons who had occupied Santa Fe and then trudged a thousand miles to protect California from a possible attack by forces from Mexico. Scornful of their enemy, whether from Mexico or California, these dragoons on December 6 encountered a band of Californio cavalry at San Pasqual about thirty-five miles northeast of San Diego. In the vicious melee, General Kearny ("calm as a clock") survived two lance wounds, but eighteen of his men were killed. Sorely pressed, his battered force fought its way toward San Diego, reinforced on the fifth day by two hundred marines and sailors sent by Stockton. In the face of this new strength, the Mexicans fell back on Los Angeles. On January 10, 1847, after minor skirmishes, Stockton's and Kearny's troops entered that town, opposed only by "desperate and drunken fellows." Three days later "articles of capitulation" secured the American annexation of California.

With his usual bombast, Commodore Stockton issued a general order congratulating his troops for their "never surpassed" courage. Though their leaders had fled to Mexico, the Californios knew their gallantry and dash had convincingly refuted the *Yanquis'* earlier taunts of cowardice.

And so the sideshow to the real war in Mexico ended. Six months of proclamations, marching men, military blunders, and mercifully few casualties gained what Larkin and Vallejo might have arranged peacefully. For their foresight both men spent time in jail, the great ranchero released from Sutter's Fort on July 29 and the U.S. confidential agent set free in Los Angeles January 10, 1847, after three months' confinement by the Californios. Back in Sonoma, Vallejo returned to his rancho willing to forgive the aggressive Americanos and hoping for a new era of progress and order. In Monterey, Larkin

YERBA BUENA (SAN FRANCISCO) IN 1847

foresaw profits to be made from selling shingles as citizens stripped the last tiles from the mission at Carmel to roof their own houses and a few new buildings. Using the past to build the future, Californians took tiles and beams from the other missions, leaving them to sag and melt in the winter rains. Who cared? They represented a time that seemed long ago and very different.

In fact, the province remained little changed, as isolated as ever, an outpost between Panama and Oregon, primitive in every aspect, without a government or basic institutions, so different from mid-nineteenth-century Massachusetts and Pennsylvania as to be in another century. Vallejo and Larkin—and certainly Sutter—foresaw little change, a California that would be a frontier of cattle raising and some farming, to be slowly populated by an annual immigration of farming families arriving on the overland trails from the western states.

And so in 1847 California slipped back to its accustomed place, on the periphery—its American future to be secured by two United States armies advancing on Mexico City.

Self-consciously posed for a daguerreotypist, these miners are working a riverbank claim with pans and rockers.

FREE FOR ALL

Before the discovery of gold, California had begun to attract traditional frontier settlers. In 1841 John Bidwell led the first overland party of immigrants to the Sacramento Valley. A few years later he drew this map for Manuel Micheltorena, the last Mexican governor of California (1842–45), to show the grants made by Micheltorena and his predecessors in the delta region of the Sacramento and San Joaquin Rivers. Most prominent is the grant to John Sutter.

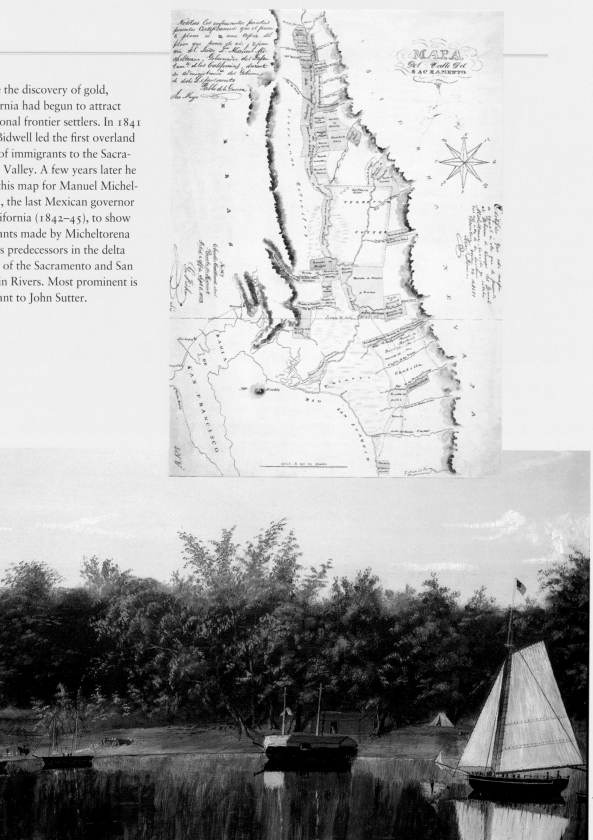

In vivid contrast to what would soon be Sacramento City's wildly commercial waterfront, this painting depicted the natural tranquillity of that site in 1848. In describing his scene, the artist wrote: "The old brig *Providence* was lying along the riverbank, dismantled with her deck housed over and a wide gangway extending from her side to a rough redwood shanty at the edge of the river. Farther upstream, two small launches were landing their goods on a sandy beach." Traders on board these ships sold supplies to miners who engaged ox teams to convey their goods to the mines.

CHAPTER TWO

FREE FOR ALL

WHEN THE WINTER RAINS OF 1847 swept in from the Pacific, soaking the Stars and Stripes atop flimsy flagpoles in the coastal villages and at Sutter's Fort, United States authority drooped and sagged as well. Discharged soldiers wandered the muddy streets of San Jose and Monterey and lazed in the plaza at Los Angeles, all of them angry that the military governor had failed to issue their long-overdue pay. American settlers, the most active and vocal residents of the province, grumbled that peace had not brought the reforms expected by the removal of the incompetent, transient Mexican governors. Scores of careless land grants, issued hurriedly by the last governor, Pío Pico, could not be challenged because there was no judicial system. Merchants had no legal recourse against debtors. Horse thieves practiced their special trade without fear. It seemed nothing had improved.

What was wrong? How could these problems persist under the sovereignty of the United States?

Of little solace to the American settlers, the answer would have to wait for a formal treaty ending the war with Mexico. Until then California would be ruled as an occupied country, under military law. What the Americans impatiently wanted was a civil government that enforced the protections provided by the Constitution. Instead, army and navy officers administered haphazardly, arriving and departing with bewildering frequency, their brief tenures of office often marred by bickering and, on one occasion, by personal confrontation. As if still a province of Mexico, California muddled along, with *alcaldes* still in power, without basic political and social institutions, and still without roads and bridges, without a library, school, hospital, or jail—little changed from the eighteenth century, still on the periphery of world, even American, affairs.

Then in January 1848 everything changed, beyond imagining. From Coloma, a quiet vale in the foothills of the Sierra Nevada, stories spread of men finding gold—and more gold. Week by week the can-it-be-believed news proved to be wonderfully true. From coastal villages and vast ranchos and family farms the people of California rushed to Sutter's Fort and on to Coloma and "the goldfields." Once at work digging along riverbanks and rocky bars, encouraged by shouts of those who had "struck it rich," none of these treasure seekers pondered the irony that the very weakness and inefficiency of the military government in Monterey, so cursed a few months earlier, made possible their heady new freedom to pocket nuggets and siftings of gold without thought of license or tax or regulation of any kind. Where else could such voracious fortune hunters have had unfettered freedom to tear open the earth and tramp about wherever their luck might lead them? They encountered no "Keep Out" signs, no armed guards. They were even free from fear of native people who might defend their homeland. California's Indians had suffered such decimation from European diseases as to have become by 1848 only a frightened remnant of their once many thousands.

Everyone who shouldered a pick or a shovel felt the gambler's thrill of fortune at hand, without fear of violating some law or being threatened by some authority—though in fact every goldseeker was trespassing on U.S. government land and taking U.S. government mineral assets. That government, so recently condemned for its distance and impotence, had no power to constrain or regulate America's first gold rush. The freedom to find and keep California's gold flourished throughout 1848, that year of plenty for all, and even through years thereafter, when the world rushed in.

As a farming frontier that had attracted an overland immigration each summer since 1841, California proved to be a fulfillment and a frustration for American settlers, 1,500 of whom made the trek west in 1846, with another 400 following in the summer of 1847. They saw about them on the coastal plain and in the Sacramento and San Joaquin Valleys a vastness of rich land, undeveloped, unfenced, the dream of every land-hungry farmer. And all that going-to-waste farmland had just been conquered by the United States Army and Navy. Why not open it up to settlement by American families?

Back in the States, the federal government had promoted westward migration for generations by offering farmers 80 to 160 acres of wilderness land. Accustomed to such grants for family farms, the newcomers to California deeply resented the Californios' immense baronial estates with their *diseños* so carelessly drawn that no one knew for sure where the boundaries ran. Adding to the insult, the U.S. military government at Monterey seemed to be more interested in protecting the Mexican land grants than in helping men and women who had braved the deserts and mountains to get to California.

The most characteristic American institution on

every frontier, the newspaper, with its booster spirit and fearless instinct to attack the ineptitudes of government, raised the cry of settlers' "rights" in California. First in the province, the *Californian* announced its presence at Monterey in August 1846, followed five months later by Sam Brannan's feisty *California Star* in San Francisco. Both these weeklies lambasted the "military despotism" at Monterey, with the *Star* arguing that the "ineffectual mongrel military government" should be replaced by a popularly elected legislature that could pass laws opening the Californios' regal land holdings to more deserving American settlers. After all, if the country were to be American, it should be ruled by American laws and customs.

But existing landowners also had reason to complain. From his 9,000-acre rancho, William Robert Garner (an Englishman who had jumped ship in 1824 and married a Californio heiress) catalogued the unsatisfactory state of affairs in February 1847: "California at this moment is in a state of anarchy. . . . There is no protection of private property. Daily complaints of robberies are made . . . but there is no jail to hold a man. . . . Vile depredators steal horses and cattle with impunity." He complained that "all things will remain in this state until the Governor, whoever he may be, shall introduce energetic measures."

KEARNY

Garner's uncertainty of the governor's identity reflected the political confusion in Monterey. Both Commodore Robert Stockton and Brigadier General Stephen Kearny claimed the dual authority of commander-in-chief and military governor. In January 1847, Stockton appointed Lieutenant Colonel John Frémont to be military governor. In that new role, he, too, refused to recognize General Kearny's superior authority. The crisis intensified. Civil war seemed to threaten. From the safety of their grassy fiefdoms, the Californios remembered the standoffs between Mexican governors and mused over the similarity.

Seldom is a conquered country in such a condition as was California in 1847. . . . The department of California was still a bit of Mexican territory, under the rule of an occupying army. Technically, therefore, the settlers were a conquered people, like all residents in any conquered province that is under military occupation. But the most active and prominent of the population were of the nation of the conquerors . . . and if the country was to be American, they naturally wished to enjoy the benefits of the conquest and to be governed after the American fashion. . . . They thought themselves free as the air and had in many cases themselves assisted in the conquest as members of Major Frémont's temporary battalion and felt a healthy contempt for all military men and for that brief authority wherein military men are too commonly puffed up.

Josiah Royce, *California: From the Conquest in 1846 to the Second Vigilance Committee in San Francisco*

Commodore succeeded commodore: the command of U.S. naval forces in California passed through five officers in six months. In May 1847 General Kearny was replaced by Colonel Richard B. Mason as military governor. Leading an overland party back to the States, Kearny took his insubordinate rival Frémont with him and on arrival at Fort Leavenworth sent the famed "Pathfinder" on to Washington to face court martial. Found guilty on all charges, including mutiny, the proud Frémont refused to accept President Polk's offer of clemency and resigned from the army.

As ever isolated by the months required for information and orders to reach the Pacific Coast, Military Governor Mason and the people of California waited through 1847 for the expected news of Mexico's defeat and the peace treaty that would allow them to petition for formal annexation to the United States, thereby freeing the province from its resented military occupation.* While waiting, the governor with remarkable patience and restraint dealt with trivial and sometimes vexatious tasks, from solemnizing marriages and granting divorces to protecting rancheros from pushy American squatters. And of no small concern, the problem of Indian horse thieves had grown more urgent. The *California Star* reported on March 28 a daring raid on a farm near San Jose in which four settlers were wounded and two hundred of their horses stolen. Without military or police resources to call on, Mason could only advise: "You may tell the people that if they catch Indians in the act of stealing their horses, they should shoot them."

Meanwhile, the governor had to concoct the means to keep his underfunded and lame-duck administration credible while holding at bay an impatient crowd of purveyors and claimants owed some $700,000 for military contracts and civilian complaints. More immediately, he needed funds to pay his soldiers and disgruntled civil officials and to meet the costs of building the first jails. One of Mason's officers lamented in a letter: "We are all supremely poor, the government having no money and no credit."

But all was not petty detail and economic legerdemain. A mood of optimism began to take root as people formed "a distant idea of what California in a very few years must become by remaining in the possession of a nation that has the will, the power, and the means to make it what it deserves to be." In Thomas Larkin's practical language, that meant California was about to be "Yankeefied."

---

* Through the summer of 1847 General Winfield Scott's army advanced from Vera Cruz to battle its way into Mexico City, where an armistice was signed on September 14. Formal end of the war came on February 2, 1848, with the Treaty of Guadalupe Hidalgo. This momentous news did not reach Governor Mason at Monterey until August.

And who better foresaw or personified the future than Larkin, that supreme businessman and the most unafraid speculator in all of California. Even with interest rates at a daunting 2 percent per month, he borrowed and bought land for development and entire ships' cargoes for resale, while in his capacity as "Navy Agent for the Territory of California" selling fifty thousand pounds of hardtack for $6,000, renting one of his warehouses for naval stores, building a wharf at Monterey, and negotiating its sale to the navy. Forecasting California's future, Larkin could little know his prescience when he proclaimed: "Business will increase astonishingly."

Real estate speculation was Larkin's special domain, even passion, though he appreciated the dangers of contested titles, of squatters and scavengers. Among many properties, in 1847 Larkin paid $2,800 for a rancho of 22,185 acres along the Feather River. This tract of wild land, well removed from the sparse settlements of the northern Sacramento Valley, would soon return him a profit more extravagant than any building project in Monterey or San Francisco. This land straddled as yet undiscovered "goldfields" and would later merit an asking price of $1 million.

Another dimension of his speculative spirit found expression in the promotion of new towns. In this, Larkin joined his old friend Mariano Vallejo, who (after his imprisonment at Sutter's Fort) felt insecure in the new world of the Yankees. The great man of Sonoma suggested to Larkin that they start a town on land he owned at Carquinez Strait, at the mouth of the Sacramento River where it flows into San Francisco Bay. An ideal site for trade, where travelers would have to cross the great river. Larkin wrote a friend that he was "trying to build a town . . . up the Sacramento. I have views and plans sufficient to amass a dozen fortunes. Time will tell. If I do nothing else I will make a bustle." What a new Californian he was, prototype of the entrepreneurial spirit soon to move California with such energy that the Spanish and Mexican eras would suddenly seem like ancient history.

MASON

When Colonel Richard B. Mason succeeded General Kearny as military governor of California in May 1847, his too-few and unpaid soldiers could not cope with a chaos of problems, including Indian raids that "carried off 200 or 300 head of stock." Mason resorted to issuing a series of proclamations, like this broadside announcing the prohibition of the sale of liquor to Indians.

In 1848 Monterey was the largest settlement in California and the major commercial center. By the summer of 1849 San Francisco claimed that primacy, leaving the old capital as a quaint reminder of the pastoral years of Mexican rule. As shown in this July 1849 scene, the town had changed but little, if any, from the quietude of pre–gold rush life.

Through complex negotiations and transfers of title, Vallejo conveyed some five square miles to Larkin and his partner, Robert B. Semple. Together these Americans carried California over the secular divide, presiding over the birth of the first town founded by promoters hoping for profit rather than by Franciscans extending the dominion of their church or by settlers seeking the redemption of a new beginning. Here in Benicia, named after Vallejo's wife, Semple devoted his time and finances, and built a ferry crossing on the strait that would prove of great value.

In Larkin's hometown, Monterey, thirty new buildings, most of them ambitious, two-story designs, were constructed during the summer of 1847, many built from adobe, lumber, and shingles supplied by Larkin's businesses. But the town that commanded his greatest attention and investment was San Francisco. Here, he predicted, "will be the busy, bustling uproar of places." He bought

LARKIN and sold lots, even several along the bay shore under six feet of tidal water.

Thomas Larkin pursued wealth and more wealth with indefatigable purposefulness. The range and energy of his activities symbolized the profound differences between the Americans' moneymaking, get-ahead impatience and the Californios' live-for-today acceptance of life as it was. As U.S. navy agent, Larkin drafted contracts that would produce profits; as land speculator, he bought large tracts, one a 17,000-acre land grant that he divided into sections and sold for profit; as lessor of land to farmers, he encouraged the cultivation of wheat and the breeding of hogs, sheep, geese, and turkeys, the bounty of which would multiply his profits; as contractor, he built houses to be sold for quick gain. Larkin epitomized the entrepreneurial ambition and avidity scorned by the Californios as Yankee greed and arrogance.

Despite all the new American bustle and energy in places like Monterey and San Francisco and Benicia, California remained a backward, primitive country. In the middle of the nineteenth century it still relied on the ubiquitous oxcart of Spanish times, creaking along California's dirt and mud tracks. U.S. Army lieutenant William Tecumseh Sherman, who landed at Monterey in February 1847, was surprised to find "not a single modern wagon to be had . . . , nothing but the old Mexican cart with wooden wheels, drawn by two or three pairs of oxen yoked by the horns."

The absence of improved transport was symptomatic of California's woeful backwardness. The nascent economy suffered from a crippling shortage of lumber, as rancher William Garner complained on October 4, 1847, in a letter sent back east. "We have fine forest trees for lumber, and yet boards are fifty dollars a thousand and difficult to get at that. Much of the sawing is done by hand. Send us out a dozen good saw mills and men to manage them."

Handsawing continued in most of California as the primary method of cutting logs into lumber. Called whipsawing, this elemental process required trunks to be dragged across a sawpit where "for endless board feet, day after weary day, month after month, a man on top pulled the long steel blade up and a man in the sawdust pit below pulled the blade down. It was unadorned, mindless drudgery." Usually the drudges were Indians.

Once cut, how to get the stacks of lumber where needed? No roads, no transport system. At best, ox teams hauled the planks a few miles for sale to a neighbor or down to a nearby beach where they could be rafted out to trading ships.

Here was California in mid-century, displaying its stubborn primitiveness, no less in an essential commodity like lumber than in most everything else. No flour mills, despite an abundance of wheat; no woolen products where thousands of sheep grazed the hillsides. William Garner explained why, in another of his 1847 letters: "California can never go ahead very fast until capitalists and manufacturers come into this country. . . . A mine of potter's clay is found and yet if we want a plate, we must wait till it comes from the United States and then pay three to four dollars for half a dozen. . . . Sheep breed regularly twice a year. Still, a rough-spun or rougher-woven blanket costs from eight to ten dollars and is rarely found even at that price. Consequently, all sorts of cloth must come from the United States, or elsewhere, woolen manufactories not being known in California. . . . Hides in California are worth only two dollars each in barter and one dollar fifty cents in cash. More than one hundred thousand, on average, have been exported from this country yearly, for many years. Still we must go barefoot or wait until some vessel brings us shoes from the United States. . . . What we require for speedy progress are machinery of all kinds, a large body of immigrants who know how to make use of them, some capitalists—and no lawyers."

As if in answer to Garner's wish, 120 Mormons, discharged from the U.S. Army in July 1847, decided to stay in California rather than trudge east to Brigham Young's settlement at Great Salt Lake. Mechanics, craftsmen, and carpenters, these industrious young men easily found jobs along the coast and at Sutter's Fort—where the good fortune that awaited them could not have been foreseen even by Joseph Smith.

ON THE EVE OF DISCOVERY

NEW RESIDENTS, NEW BUSINESSES, NEW CON-struction, and the sale of 830 city lots at $16 to $29 each gave San Francisco in August 1847 the look and sound of progress, suggestive that this sandy, overgrown village with its new name (changed in January from Yerba Buena) would become a serious competitor to Monterey as California's major commercial center. By the end of the year the town had eight hundred residents living in some 160 frame structures amid the older adobe buildings. Along the beachfronts of Broadway, Clay, and California Streets three wharves extended over the mudflats, to water deep enough for small ships to load and unload their cargo. The vessel most frequently seen

at this waterfront was the twenty-ton schooner *Sacramento,* sent by Captain Sutter from his landing on the Sacramento River to deliver produce from his fields and barrels of salted salmon to the San Francisco market. Manned by six Indians, this commercial craft made the round trip of about 250 miles in three weeks—a revealing contrast to the East Coast's extensive system of turnpikes, canals, and railroads.

Among San Francisco's citizens, no one was more impatient to promote change and progress than Sam Brannan, whose moneymaking ambition equaled that of Larkin in Monterey. Though he had been in California only one year—having landed at the Clay Street wharf in July 1846 as the leader of 238 Mormons who had sailed from New York around the Horn intent on establishing another colony far from American religious prejudice—this twenty-six-year-old entrepreneur had settled his followers on vacant lots and in abandoned buildings at Mission Dolores, sent others north to seek employment as lumbermen, and dispatched twenty more to establish an agricultural community, New Hope, on the San Joaquin River. With a printing press he had brought as part of the colony's provisions, Brannan started (January 1847) publishing the town's first newspaper, the weekly *California Star.* As a forecast of his later methods, he led off by attacking his only journalistic competition, the two owners of the weekly *Californian* in Monterey. "The one [Walter Colton] is a lying sycophant and the other [Robert Semple] an overgrown lickspittle." With the same brashness, Brannan pursued moneymaking enterprises, most of them so profitable that he would become, in the wild, disorderly years ahead, the wealthiest man in California.

Beyond San Francisco, other towns—San Diego, Los Angeles, Santa Barbara, Monterey, and San Jose—progressed at a more leisurely pace. The latter, founded in 1777, had grown to only 700 residents by 1847. California's entire population that year totaled about 7,000 Californios and probably 6,000 "foreigners," mostly Americans. Indians in

Sketched by a visitor to San Francisco in 1847, this view of the waterfront as seen from the City Hotel depicts the village simplicity of the port on the eve of the gold rush. Built in 1846 as the town's first public house, the City Hotel was mourned as a lost relic of "olden times" when destroyed in the Great Fire of September 1850.

the towns and on the ranchos numbered maybe 3,000 to 4,000, no one knew or tried to count. Out in the Central Valley and beyond in the foothills, the Indian population was simply unknown but certainly exceeded the total of all "whites."

In the Napa Valley north of San Francisco Bay—"a miniature Mediterranean"—and to the south in the Santa Clara Valley around San Jose, California's future could be seen: a fertile farming frontier where Californio rancheros and American farmers in their own ways worked the land given by Mexican governors or acquired through marriage or by purchase, despite uncertain titles. Farming families from the States planted fruit trees (evidence of their sense of permanence), thanked God for the wonder of a climate without ague or fevers, and marveled at the abundance of their wheat and corn harvests. Few of these folk knew that similar harvests had been reaped by mission Indians in California's long ago.

As if to boast of his good judgment in bringing his wife and four children to the Napa Valley, a farmer named James Reed sent a letter to his relatives back in Springfield, Illinois. Published in the *Illinois Journal* in December 1847, his report helped

to strengthen California's new image as an agricultural Eden.

"In no country can hogs be raised with less trouble, supporting themselves without expense to the owner. . . . You can go into a flock of a thousand sheep and select and kill the best for $2 each. . . . Hens lay and hatch the year round without any care. Turkeys are plenty. . . . The greatest objection to beef here is that it is too fat." On and on he reported the wonders of California farming. Seed planted in the winter rains produced "vegetables grown to perfection before the dry season. The finest pumpkins I ever saw . . . watermelons in December . . . fine cabbage and lettuce are in perfection the first of May." Potatoes, onions, corn, and beans "can be raised in great abundance and excellence," as well as apples, peaches, and grapes. Amazement at fertility was matched by gratitude for the healthy climate. "I can make a living for my little family easier here than in the States; and while I am doing this, I am certain that they are enjoying good health. . . . The globe cannot present a healthier spot than this valley."

To the south, on the banks of the San Joaquin River, the German settler Charles Weber by 1847 had laid out a "town" he called Tuleburg, not far from the struggling Mormon settlement of New Hope. Because Indian raids and horse thievery frightened potential farming families, his town languished until a few years later when it would boom as the renamed river port of Stockton. To the north, on the Calaveras, Mokelumne, and Cosumnes Rivers, Americanos and Californios lived on their thousands of acres in a vastness of fertile land. These primitive beginnings in the midst of abundant natural resources made a strong impression on the few who visited these lonely settlers. Military officers who rode horseback inland from the coast came back feeling "California mad," as one of them exclaimed. They had ridden through miles and miles of grass and wild oats so tall as to brush their shoulders, and the great oak trees seemed even more grand than those in the parks of London. And, my God! these verdant lands could be had cheap from their debt-ridden owners—$7,000 would buy a 65,000-acre rancho, if you had the cash and could trust the title and secure its transfer. What a country this could be!

For the settlers in this virgin land the nearest place for contact with the outside world was Sutter's Fort, near the confluence of the American and Sacramento Rivers. Within the walls of this famed outpost a rancher could barter with a trader from San Francisco; emigrants newly arrived on the overland trail from the States might pay a fancy price for milk or a horse; trappers from Oregon sat around ready for a game of cards. Sometimes a doctor might be found to stitch up a wound or dose a fever. Valley families gathered there for a few hours of neighborliness, wives to gossip while buying produce from the extensive gardens, husbands to share a bottle and brag about bear hunts or shooting horse thieves. And here could be purchased, or leased, an Indian boy or girl, made available by the great man himself, Captain Sutter.

His proud military rank came from self-promoting, oft-embellished stories of a commission in the Royal Swiss Guard of Charles X of France left

The fort is a parallelogram of adobe walls, 500 feet long by 150 in breadth, with loopholes and bastions at the angles, mounted with a dozen cannon that sweep the curtains. Within is a collection of granaries and warehouses, shops and stores, dwellings and outhouses, extending near and along the walls round the central building occupied by the Swiss potentate, who holds sway as patriarch and priest, judge and father....

Throughout the day the enclosure presents an animated scene of work and trafficking, by bustling laborers, diligent mechanics, and eager traders, all to the chorus clang of the smithy and reverberating strokes of the carpenters. Horsemen dash to and fro at the bidding of duty and pleasure, and an occasional wagon creaks along upon the gravelly road-bed, sure to pause for recuperating purposes before the trading store [operated by Sam Brannan and Charles Smith] where confused voices mingle with laughter and the sometimes discordant strains of drunken singers. Such is the capital of the vast interior valley pregnant with approaching importance.

Hubert Howe Bancroft, *History of California*

behind when he sailed to the United States in 1834. Sutter was one of the first California immigrants to exploit the bonus enjoyed by many thousands in later years: the freedom of anonymity. His elaborate uniforms served him best on special occasions, such as the visit in May 1847 by General Kearny when his party passed through on its way back to the States. But the rustic, local audience also admired his regalia when he ordered his private militia of one hundred Indian soldiers to parade in their remnants of blue and green uniforms which he had bought from the Russians on their departure from Fort Ross.

Resplendent in one of his military uniforms, John Sutter proudly posed for California's first portrait painter, William S. Jewett. In a letter dated April 14, 1855, Jewett boasted of this important commission. "I am up here at the Capital to dispose of a full length portrait of Capt. Sutter to the State. It is a fine picture and it is proposed I get $2,500 for it. . . . It is thought by many to be the best picture and likeness they ever saw and ALL think it is faultless."

Though daguerreotypes (the earliest form of photography) provide visual records of San Francisco, various mining camps, and the goldseekers themselves, not one such image of Sutter's Fort—or of the great man himself—is known to have survived the nineteenth century. What we know of that mecca of the gold region is preserved in drawings and engravings, such as this romantic view of the fiefdom just before the tide of goldseekers overwhelmed its bucolic serenity. In 1849 Sacramento City supplanted Sutter's headquarters as the economic and transport hub of the Sacramento Valley, and the passing wave left a mélange of broken wagons, rotting supplies, abandoned merchants' tents, and tree stumps outside these walls, soon to crumble along with Sutter's own fortunes.

Marching his amateur army indulged Sutter's delight in pomp and martial display. Such maneuvers also served to attract "wild" Indians, drawn by curiosity to the spangled hubbub and then held in service by his soldiers and by fear of gunpowder. On his first day at the site along the American River that he chose for New Helvetia, the afternoon of August 13, 1839, Sutter had ordered his several cannon to be fired "to show the Indians the effect of powder and ball." One of his men later recalled the moment the fuses were touched and sharp reports reverberated across the grassy land and into the foothills: "A large number of deer, elk, and other animals on the plains were startled, running to and fro, stopping to listen, their heads raised, full of curiosity and wonder, seemingly attracted and fascinated to the spot, while from the interior of the adjacent wood the howls of wolves and coyotes filled the air, and immense flocks of wildfowl flew wildly over the camp." Just ten years later, this wild place would be crowded with thousands of people from around the world. Here, in 1849, Sacramento City would rise to prominence and power, and Sutter would sink to despair and exile.

But in that single decade the master of New Helvetia came close to achieving his ambitious plans, his progress made possible by the labor of hundreds of Indians—just as the Franciscans' accomplishments had depended on thousands of native people lured and coerced to build and develop the twenty-one missions. Sutter paid them in cheap trade goods and snared them in a credit-and-debt system. He boasted of his success, writing: "Business increased until I had in the harvest 600 Indians and to feed them I had to kill four oxen, sometimes five daily. . . . I had at the same time twelve thousand head of cattle and two thousand horses and ten or fifteen thousand sheep. I had all the Indians I could employ." They did everything: house chores, digging drainage ditches, milling grain, laying up adobe bricks, butchering cattle, and tanning hides. Years later, Captain Sutter reflected: "My best days were just before the gold discovery."

Sutter employed his "army" in defensive patrols to fend off Indians from the foothills who came down to steal from his fields and herds. He also sent his armed soldiers to bring in "wild" Indians when they could not be lured to live at New Helvetia. Captured conscripts were locked in sheds at night to prevent them from escaping, though many did—as at the missions—through death from measles, smallpox, syphilis, and other European diseases.* In the summer of 1847 a measles epidemic swept through the valley, killing many Indian workers. Their loss required increased efforts to recruit replacements, not only for New Helvetia but also for Sutter's neighbor John Sinclair and for the great ranchos of John Bidwell on Chico Creek, the Danish trapper Peter Lassen on Deer Creek, and Pierson B. Reading on Cottonwood Creek, south of Mount Shasta.

As the labor of the mission Indians had made possible the export of hides and tallow, so the toil of Indians at New Helvetia loaded the *Sacramento* with barrels of salted salmon, bundles of dressed beaver pelts, and sacks of coarse flour for shipment to San Francisco where (like hides) they would reach distant markets. And although Captain Sutter owned the most advanced enterprise in pre–gold rush California, his Indians suffered working conditions as feudal as those suffered in Father Serra's time. An employee at New Helvetia recalled "three

---

* Though distant from missions and ranchos, the "wild" Indian tribes in the valleys and foothills were not safe from European diseases. In 1833 Canadian trappers introduced malaria to the Sacramento River and its many tributaries. That year and the next an estimated twenty thousand Indians died. An American settler wrote that entire tribes "fell before that awful pestilence . . . and disappeared as dew in the midday sun. Travelers ascending the rivers found the stench almost intolerable, and the following year heaps of whitened bones might be seen everywhere in those fertile valleys. . . . Of the thousands . . . who lived there before the pestilence, [the survivors] remained in sullen silence, like disconsolate mourners."

or four hundred wild Indians in a grain field armed, some with sickles, some with butcher knives, some with pieces of hoop iron roughly fashioned into shapes like sickles, but many having only their hands with which to gather up by small handfuls the dry and brittle grain; and as their hands would soon become sore, they resorted to willow sticks, which were split to afford a sharper edge with which to sever the straw."

That was California in 1847, an anachronism on the eve of astonishing changes.

STRAY PARTICLES, NEW VALUES

No matter how many Indians were kept at work, the ranchos and villages needed more flour than the horse-powered and hand-turned mill wheels could grind, and more lumber than native sawyers could cut in the whipsaw pits. Sutter saw opportunity in these shortages. In May 1847 he selected a site on the American River, a few miles upstream from the fort, where he planned to build a water-powered flour mill. Fortunately he was able to hire some carpenters and craftsmen, the "Saints" recently discharged from the army's Mormon battalion. By August these industrious fellows had finished the main structure and set the grinding stones. Sutter pridefully wrote to his friend Larkin that his mill "will grind what the whole Sacramento Valley will be able to produce in wheat."

To produce the planks and beams that growing towns would need, Sutter also planned a water-powered sawmill to be built under the supervision of his long-trusted employee James Marshall. On August 28, this jack-of-all-trades set out from the fort with a crew of Mormons and Indians, their tools and supplies loaded in an ox-drawn cart. With a flock of sheep for the camp larder, Marshall's party traveled some forty-five miles up the South Fork of the American River to a valley in the foothills known as Coloma, where Sutter had surveyed a fine stand of timber near the stream.

Marshall's plan called for his men to dig a channel, or headrace, to divert water from the South Fork to the mill site, where the force of the flow would turn the waterwheel. Next they would dig a tailrace to carry the water from the mill back to the river. The timbers for framing the millhouse would be cut by the Indians at a temporary whipsaw pit. In all, it would be a modest version of water-powered sawmills common on the American frontier for more than a century—but an ambitious advance and a challenge in the California of 1848.

MARSHALL

On November 28 one of the Mormon workers, Azariah Smith, confirmed their rapid progress in his journal: "The week has passed off prety bussy and the mill goes ahead at a good jog." This nineteen-year-old, soon to have more money than he could imagine, worried about his meager circumstances on December 19: "Home keeps running in my mind, and I feel somewhat lonesum especially Sundays. . . . My heart sometimes shrinks for fear that I will fail for want of means, but I keep up as good courage as I can."

By Christmas the mill was almost ready. On January 16 Marshall delivered another load of supplies to Coloma from the fort. He faced a busy week, anchoring the mill irons, inspecting the dam for damage caused by recent heavy rains, and deepening the tailrace to increase water flow under the mill wheel.

In the morning mists of January 24, 1848, James Marshall walked the tailrace to see if the night's flow had washed away stones and gravel left from the previous day's excavations. He saw a glint, a speck of color beneath the surface. He reached into the icy water and picked up a half-pea-sized particle. Gold? He looked more closely, appraising. "It made my heart thump, for I was certain it was gold," he later recalled. "Then I saw another piece in the water." More flecks and glistens of color, more grains retrieved—stray particles from an ancient geologic secret soon to be revealed and

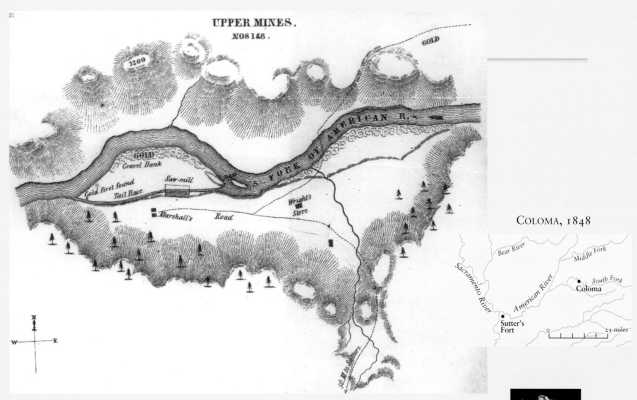

UPPER MINES.
NOS 1&8.

COLOMA, 1848

While serving as aide to Military Governor Richard B. Mason, Lieutenant William Tecumseh Sherman sketched a map of Sutter's mill and its vicinity. First published in Mason's official report (submitted to Congress in December 1848), this engraving of the original has served as the most precise record of the momentous discovery site.

The original nugget—the speck of the future—that Marshall found in the tailrace was sent to Washington in 1848 and has been preserved at the Smithsonian Institution.

James Marshall's drawing of the mill construction suggests he was far more adept with his hammer than the pencil of a draftsman. While his childlike effort has the authority of an eyewitness, a professional artist's engraving has become the ubiquitous rendering of this landmark setting create hopes that would sweep around the world.

Marshall rushed back to the mill, showing his findings to a carpenter.

"What is it?"

"Gold."

"Oh, no, that can't be."

Marshall answered this skepticism with measured judgment: "I know it to be nothing else."

As word spread through the company, his men remained dubious. Maybe it was another of their boss's notions. The momentous day ended with only Marshall sensing the import of what he had found, what more might be found come morning.

Early on the twenty-fifth Marshall was back at the tailrace. Searching carefully, he found more flakes and grains. He placed this gathering in his hat and hurried to the men at breakfast. "Boys, I believe I have found a gold mine." His excitement, the evidence in his hat—flakes and grains, some the size of a kernel of wheat—weakened their skepticism. Following Marshall back to the tailrace, they too found bits of gold. According to Azariah Smith's diary: "It is found in the raceway in small pieces. Some have been found that would weigh five dollars." Several pieces were placed on an anvil and pounded with a hammer. They flattened, not crumbling. The men boiled a grain in a soap kettle; they soaked several particles in vinegar. Each test seemed to support Marshall's assertion. Doubts dispelled, they searched with covetous eyes, no longer workers at a sawmill.

On January 28 Marshall rushed into Sutter's Fort and asked for an immediate, private meeting with the captain. Behind a locked door he pulled a cloth from his trousers in which he revealed a cluster of bright particles, some of which Sutter later recalled were "not quite as large as a pea," others "hardly the size of a pin head." They consulted a volume of the *Encyclopedia Americana,* tried what tests they could perform, pounded the specimens— and put aside their pestering doubts. They held gold in their hands.

Marshall hurried back to Coloma. Sutter fol-

lowed as soon as business could be interrupted to allow investigation of this distracting discovery. On the twenty-ninth he rode up to the mill, arriving that night. Next morning the two partners and most of the workers walked along the race looking for the newfound treasure. Sutter recalled: "I picked some up and then each of the Mormons gave me some and Marshall gave me some, too. . . . I told the people it was gold, that there was no mistake."

In their off-hours and on Sundays the workers at Coloma turned to goldseeking. Azariah Smith noted in his journal on February 14: "This past week I did not work but three and a half days. Mr. Marshall grants us the privilege of picking up gold at odd spells and Sundays, and I have gathered up considerable." A week later he added: "Today I picked up a little more of the root of all evil."

Each day they worked some of their time at completing the sawmill and more and more at searching for gold. They found "color" at greater distances from the tailrace, some by casual looking, more by digging. On February 20 one of the Mormons picked out with his knife blade an ounce of gold particles from a rock crevice half a mile from the mill. Two days later, an ounce and a half. On the twenty-eighth Marshall and one of his workers, with only their fingers, dug up a full pint of gold, some in nuggets the size of beans.

When reports of these discoveries reached the Mormon workers at the flour mill, they too turned to goldseeking. On March 2 several of them found gold in greater quantity than any yet reported, at a bend in the South Fork where the current had piled up a bank of rocks and gravel. Their luck gave this river bar its fame as the first major discovery beyond Coloma, soon to be known as Mormon Diggings or Mormon Island.

Good workers that they were, the Mormons at Coloma stayed at their tasks until the sawmill was completed on March 11. The next day Azariah Smith reported: "Today we started the mill and sawed up one log. . . . The mill cuts well, makeing beautifull plank."

What great news these inaugural planks would have been only a few weeks earlier: the first of the stout, straight boards that William Garner had dreamed would build a Yankee state. But now, amid gold hunted and ounces counted, new values pushed aside old. Gold from the tailrace, not lumber from the saw, seemed to forecast California's future. Planks should have brought great profits to Sutter and helped to build a traditional future. Instead, Providence interrupted Progress. The saw would fall silent in a few weeks, no workers to run it, a momentary advance overwhelmed by the rush of goldseekers.

In his private quarters at the fort, Sutter considered how rapidly his future had changed. He sensed danger, that his workers would leave, that his plans would be confounded. And yet, he had hopes that he could make a profit from gold, maybe more than from lumber and flour. "I have made a discovery of a gold mine, which, according to experiments we have made, is extraordinarily rich," he wrote to his old friend Mariano Vallejo.

To secure his new asset, Sutter decided that he must obtain control of the gold-bearing land in order to regulate mining and prevent opportunists from stealing his property. To that end, he and Marshall met with several leaders of the local Indians. Sutter persuaded these uncomprehending aboriginal lords to sign a treaty permitting him to lease for three years an area of ten to twelve square miles. In payment, Sutter parted with some shirts, hats, shoes, and tools. Thus he hoped to control the future, protected by a paper against rougher forces he only dimly perceived.

Seeking to have this treaty officially recorded and confirmed, Sutter sent one of his workers to deliver the document to Monterey for approval by Governor Mason, who did not yet know of the gold discovery. Nor did the treaty make reference to gold, citing only pasture land and the sawmill, with vague reference to mineral privileges. On March 5, 1848, the governor wrote to "Captain John Sutter, Sub-Indian Agent" and advised him: "I last evening received your letter of February 22, together with the lease to certain lands on the waters of the American fork, a tributary of the Sacramento, made by certain Indians of the Yalesummy tribe to yourself and Mr. James W. Marshall. The United States do not recognize the right of Indians to sell or lease lands on which they reside." Mason went on to explain why: after the war the United States might well claim all Indian lands as part of the public domain.

Not only was Sutter thwarted by Governor Mason's decision, he also learned that his messenger to Monterey had broken a promise not to tell of the discovery. Instead, the talkative fellow had bragged in both Benicia and San Francisco about the ease of gold gathering on the South Fork, and to prove his story he had shown his listeners some six ounces of Coloma's treasure. The news was out.

The first published announcement of Marshall's discovery appeared on March 15, 1848. The *Californian* (moved to San Francisco from Monterey) published on its back page a paragraph under the small heading GOLD MINE FOUND. Relying more on puffery than substance, the full account read: "In the newly made raceway of the sawmill recently erected by Captain Sutter, on the American fork, gold has been found in considerable quantities. One person brought thirty dollars' worth to New Helvetia, gathered there in a short time. California, no doubt, is rich in mineral wealth; great chances here for scientific capitalists. Gold has been found in almost every part of the country."

As if to prove himself more sophisticated than his rival publisher, who might have been taken in by the wild tales of country folk, the editor of the *California Star* on March 25 scoffed at reports of "a gold mine" on the American River, suggesting that San Francisco property owners might have a better chance of uncovering "some hidden treasure" by plowing and harrowing their own unoccupied land.

More than journalistic rivalry motivated the *Star*'s sarcasm and the doubts expressed by other skeptics. They remembered the gold discovery north of the pueblo of Los Angeles in 1842, which had produced quick rewards and then disappointment. Reports of "gold mines" in California were as old as the legend of Queen Calafía. And so in 1848, skepticism seemed to many to be temperate and appropriate.

Sutter's workers, however, week by week, were finding more flakes and nuggets in nearby riverbanks and bars. The men at the flour mill quit and headed up the American River. "The Mormons did not like to leave my mill unfinished," Sutter recalled, "but they got the gold fever like everybody else."

What could he do? Everything seemed suddenly out of kilter. Even his Indians wandered off as a growing number of curious, hopeful folk passed through the fort on their way to Coloma. Sutter complained in his diary that his entire staff had disappeared "and left me only the sick and lame behind." On April 7 he noted the arrival of a man he knew to be ambitious and shrewd, Sam Brannan. Not satisfied with owning a store and hotel and newspaper in San Francisco, Brannan had recently opened a store in rented space at the fort. And now there he was, on his way to Coloma. The next day, Sutter learned that Brannan planned to open another store, this one near the sawmill, to sell supplies to the miners in their makeshift camps. On his way back to San Francisco, Brannan also made arrangements to set up a store at the landing—the embarcadero—on the Sacramento River three miles below the fort, where river boats loaded and unloaded supplies and passengers.

BRANNAN

Unlike Sutter, who feared what seemed to lie ahead, Brannan hurried to gain advantage from the swift changes. On April 1, 1848, his *California Star* published a "Great Express Extra": six pages of descriptions extolling "The Prospects of California." With the flair of a natural promoter, Brannan

organized an overland mule-train express to carry two thousand copies of his "extra" to the Missouri frontier where he hoped they would increase emigration and thus, eventually, business at his stores. One of the more florid articles about "the mineral riches of California" was introduced by an anecdote about an Irishman who, with the help of a friend, wrote a letter to his folks in the old country. When he boasts that "in Ameriky I have beef three times a week," his friend protests: "Pat, you have it every day." "Yes, faith, but they'll never believe the likes of that."

Having prepared the reader, there followed a description of California's gold and its hard-to-believe quantity. "The Great Sacramento Valley has a mine of gold. . . . From all accounts it is immensely rich and already we learn the gold from it, collected at random and without trouble, has become an article of trade. . . . This precious metal abounds in this country."

That assessment, apparently authoritative, was read later in 1848 by hundreds of frontier folk and by thousands more when reprinted in weekly newspapers and big-city dailies farther east. Those seductive words—"collected at random and without trouble"—commanded the attention and stirred the imagination of weary farmers in Illinois and underpaid clerks in Philadelphia.

By the first weeks of May, the people of San Francisco had been reading and debating the reports of "gold mines" and "gold discoveries" for almost two months. Then they heard a voice, like a command, that swept aside the last, stubborn doubts and easy scoffing. On the afternoon of Friday, May 12, 1848, Sam Brannan walked up Montgomery Street, gathering a crowd along the way. Whether as a calculated effort to promote more customers for his businesses or in a not-to-be-suppressed burst of enthusiasm, he rushed into the Plaza flourishing above his head a bottle of golden flakes, grains, and dust, shouting, "Gold! Gold! Gold from the American River!"

There it was: proof in Sam's hand.

As if uncorked by Brannan's flamboyance, excitement spread through the streets, hotels, and saloons. The next issue of the *Californian,* Wednesday, May 17, trumpeted: "Considerable excitement exists in our midst which bids fair to become quite a gold fever." Three days later, copies of the *Star* told of "a terrible visitant we have had of late, a FEVER which has well nigh depopulated our town, a town hard pressing upon a thousand souls. And this is the GOLD FEVER."

The contagion spread. "Everybody is in the greatest state of excitement," Thomas Larkin wrote from San Jose on May 26. "We can hear of nothing but Gold, Gold, Gold! An ounce a day, two a day or three—everyone has the gold or yellow fever. . . . I think nine tenths of every store keep, mechanic or day laborer of this town and perhaps of San Francisco will leave for the Sacramento."

On May 29 the *Californian* quit publishing. "The majority of our subscribers and many of our advertising patrons have closed their doors and places of business and left town. . . . We really do believe that for the last ten days not anything in the shape of a newspaper has received five minutes' attention from any one of our citizens. . . . The field is left half planted, the house half built and everything neglected but the manufacture of shovels and pickaxes and the means of transportation to the spot where one man obtained $128 worth of the real stuff in one day's washing, and the average for all concerned is $20 per diem. . . . In consideration of this state of affairs and the degeneracy of the taste for reading . . . , it would be a useless expenditure of labor and material to continue longer the publication of our paper."

One hundred miles to the south, the capital, Monterey, had somehow remained ignorant all this time of its country's transformation. How like pre–gold rush California, that such a modest distance could have created total isolation. It wasn't until the end of May that Monterey's very intelligent and alert alcalde, Walter Colton, learned of the great doings to the north. On May 29 he wrote in his

Hubert Howe Bancroft wrote his seven-volume history of California in a style as rococo as it was authoritative. Here he described the powerful response to the news of gold discovered at Sutter's Mill:

This little scratch upon the earth to make a backwoods mill-race touched the cerebral nerve that quickened humanity and sent a thrill throughout the system. It tingled in the ear and at the finger-ends; it buzzed about the brain and tickled the stomach; it warmed the blood and swelled the heart; new fires were kindled on hearth-stones, new castles builded in the air.

Hubert Howe Bancroft, *History of California*

daily journal: "Our town was startled out of its quiet dreams today by the announcement that gold had been discovered on the American Fork. The men wondered and talked, and the women too; but neither believed." His June 5 entry reports more news about "excavating for a millrace" and "shining scales . . . that proved to be gold." To this the poetic Colton added: "Still the public incredulity remained, save here and there a glimmer of faith like the flash of a firefly at night."

Slowly, more news seeped into Monterey. On June 12 a one-ounce sample of gold was tested. "Some wanted to melt it, others to hammer it and a few were satisfied with smelling it." And then Colton noted the paradox that would be the epitaph for an era about to end: "Doubts still hovered on the minds of the great mass. They could not conceive that such a treasure could have lain there so long undiscovered. The idea seemed to convict them of stupidity."

GOLD BY THE HANDFULS

In getting ready to head for "the mines," everyone looked for a shovel, a pickax, and a hoe. The price of each rose, from one dollar to six to ten. Similarly, sloops, lighters, launches, fishing boats, and "every little cockleshell" commanded higher and higher prices to transport the hundreds of would-be miners who planned to reach the "goldfields" by sailing up the Sacramento River. Those who could not buy a boat had to compete for costly space on whatever craft promised delivery to the landing below Sutter's Fort. The owner of a typical launch carried passengers and freight from San Francisco to Sutter's Landing in two and a half to three days, using sails when he could and oars when the wind went against him. His profit: $2,500 per trip.

For the journey by land, horses and mules sold for soaring sums, as did wagons and even oxcarts. What had been free or cheap only weeks earlier now escalated in cost beyond the means of hundreds of men who set out with just a blanket or two and a few provisions, to walk the 150 miles from San Francisco Bay to their share of the gold.

Without roads or bridges to ease their advance, wagons, horsemen, and weary hikers streamed along the deepening ruts of trails leading northeast to the foothills, interrupted by muddy crossings at creeks and streams. Fortunately, Robert Semple's new ferry worked the wide stretch of water at the Carquinez Strait. Day after day, scores of wagons (as many as two hundred on one day in May) and innumerable horsemen and walkers milled about on the south landing, waiting for space on his crude ferryboat.* Some wagons carried women and children, as if on an excursion—a trip to the goldfields for a week or so, to gather nuggets. Such was the

---

*Wagons of all kinds were becoming commonplace, displacing oxcarts, not because of production in California but rather because many survived the annual overland immigration.

mood and expectation of many that summer of 1848.

For Larkin's partner, Semple, the ferry proved to be wonderfully profitable—a surrogate gold mine. But his ambition and vision could not be contained by ferriage, no matter how much money it brought in. Semple had his mind on Benicia, the hamlet taking root on the north bank of the strait. In a scolding, impatient letter to his partner on July 29, Semple argued that this town had a great future, far more promising than that of Monterey or San Francisco. The trouble was that Larkin, living in Monterey, wasn't doing his share to promote that future. "Sir, you have been trading for fifteen years with Californios and have forgotten what the Yankees can do. . . . Bet, man, bet if you expect to win. . . . Let small matters go to the devil and build a City—a big City and a reputation for your children and yourself. Here you are at the head of ship navigation, convenient by land and water to the whole people of California. Why stop in Monterey to collect a few debts of 50 to 100 dollars . . . ? Stir yourself. Get well of your Californio fever. Set yourself to work and make hay while the sun shines."

Maybe Larkin smiled as he considered the irony of Semple's reproach—in fact, he had spread "bets" in real estate and business more widely than anyone, even Brannan. Larkin saw the brightest future in San Francisco, where he had sold several lots at one hundred times what he'd paid. Beyond real estate speculation in that booming port and, too, in Benicia, he invested in shipping supplies—boots, picks, potatoes, shirts—to the mines where profits would astonish Semple.

Apart from the widening scope of his business affairs, Larkin remained mindful of his responsibility as consul to report to Washington the phenomenal rush of events in California. Sensing that his report to Secretary of State James Buchanan might be doubted, so fantastic was the news, he crowded it with facts, statistics, and careful judgments. His first letter from San Francisco, dated June 1, 1848, made clear that he believed California was experiencing nothing less than an economic revolution: "I have to report to the State Department one of the most astonishing excitements and state of affairs now existing in this country that perhaps has ever been brought to the notice of the Government. On the American Fork of the Sacramento . . . there has been discovered a placer, a vast tract of land containing gold in small particles. . . . It is now two or three weeks since men employed in these placers have appeared in this town with gold to exchange for merchandise and provisions. I presume that near $20,000 of this gold has been so exchanged. . . . I have seen several pounds of this gold and consider it very pure, worth in New York seventeen to eighteen dollars per ounce. Fourteen to sixteen dollars in merchandise is paid for it here. . . . Should this gold continue as represented, this town and others will be depopulated."

After visiting the diggings along the American River and finding them "much more than I anticipated," Larkin dispatched a second report to Secretary Buchanan on June 28. He described the simple yet effective mining methods used by the gold-seekers, and he set forth many examples of success, including fifty miners who had each accumulated a thousand dollars.

Aware that he might be judged to have been "led away by the excitement of the day," Larkin soberly assured the secretary of state: "I am not." And then he pondered the future: "If our countrymen in California as clerks, mechanics and workmen will forsake employment at from two to six dollars per day, how many more of the same class in the Atlantic states earning much less will leave for this country under such prospects?"

After wondering "how long this gathering of gold by the handfuls will continue," Larkin slipped free from the corset of official restraint: "Could Mr. Polk and yourself see California as we now see it, you would think that a few thousand people on one hundred miles square of the Sacramento Valley would yearly turn out of this river the whole price our country pays [as the cost of the war with

Mexico] for all the acquired territory. . . . A complete revolution in the ordinary state of affairs is taking place."

Even more than Larkin, California's military governor Colonel Richard Mason felt the challenge of how to explain and make credible the unprecedented circumstances that confronted him when he visited the gold regions in early July. The length of his official report (four thousand words), its abundance of descriptive detail, its eyewitness narrative and careful calculations of the ounces of gold being mined, all suggest that Mason anticipated astonishment and disbelief among his superiors back in Washington. Therefore he sent convincing evidence to support his report's veracity: 230 ounces of California gold, a small specimen of what he had seen being mined. Which is how Richard Mason became the first of many to cope with California's image being challenged by an even more astonishing reality.

Of the four thousand miners he estimated at work in the "gold district," Mason reported the stunning success of many, including:

ON WEBER CREEK	two miners in seven days took out $17,000 in gold; others from a nearby tributary, $12,000
ON THE FEATHER RIVER	six miners with fifty Indian workers took out 273 *pounds* of gold*
AT SINCLAIR'S RANCH	Sutter's neighbor, using his Indian workers, took out $16,000 in five weeks
AT SUTTER'S FORT	sales at Brannan's store totaled $36,000 during May, June, and early July

---

* 273 lbs. x 12 troy oz. = 3,276 oz. x $16 per oz. = $52,416. To translate 1848 dollars into 1998 dollars, apply the conversion factor from the appendix: $52,416 x 18.49 = $969,172.

Beyond these specific successes, Mason told of hundreds of ravines and small streams "which contain more or less gold. Those that have been worked are barely scratched and although thousands of ounces have been carried away, I do not consider that a serious impression has been made upon the whole. Every day new and rich deposits are being developed." Then, even more bold than Larkin, he dared to assert: "I have no hesitation now in saying that there is more gold in the country drained by the Sacramento and San Joaquin rivers than will pay the cost of the present war with Mexico a hundred times over." But this unexpected booty of war would not accrue to the U.S. Treasury.

Governor Mason made clear his opinion that since all the gold being mined came from land belonging to the U.S. government, "rents or fees" should be secured "for the privilege of procuring this gold." Collecting such revenue was Mason's responsibility, as it would have been for the governor of any territory or state—with the assistance of the federal government, if needed. And anywhere else, given their value, the rents would have been collected. But not by Military Governor Richard Mason that summer of 1848. With forceful brevity he explained: "Upon considering the large extent of the country, the character of the people engaged and the small, scattered force at my command, I resolved not to interfere but to permit all to work freely."

That decision has never been properly appreciated for its military and political pragmatism or for its importance in shaping California's future. Once miners were allowed "to work freely," there would later be no denying that freedom. Gold would be procured without rents or fees or sales of mining claims. It would be free for all.

THE SUMMER OF SUCCESS

THE FIRST GOLDSEEKERS FROM CALIFORNIA'S coastal villages and valley ranches (and the first outsiders who came in the fall and winter of 1848 from Oregon and the Sandwich Islands) knew nothing of mining or geology. Their farming heritage bred an instinctive sense of the wilderness as a foe to be tamed by the force of will and labor, made to submit to cultivation, planting, and home building. The idea that gravel and sand deposits might harbor sudden wealth was astonishing. Without the calluses of season-long labor, reward seemed impossible, even undeserved. American mining experience had been paltry—some gold mining in North Carolina in 1803 and Georgia in 1829–30, and more substantial lead mining near Galena, Illinois, in the 1820s and 1830s. But those local excitements were incidental to the great national agrarian culture. Unlike the Spanish, whose dreams and expectations in America had been spurred by gold, Yankee settlers shared no experience suggestive of quick and easy wealth.*

News reports from the Sierra foothills were therefore read and discussed not with the relief of vindication, of a grail finally found, but with incredulity and wonder at the windfall Nature had left for Americans to discover. She was generous in other ways as well. Not only was California's gold found in a mild climate, under accessible terrain, occupied by no claimants other than a weakened, reclusive, native people; it was as well "placer gold," freed from its ancient geologic encasement by millions of years of uplift, fracture, and erosion. Abraded and loosened from veins and fissures by

---

* Intermittent gold mining continued for thirty years in the Appalachian Mountains of North Carolina. By 1829, production—some by slave labor—was estimated at about $2,000 per week. Mining spread to northern Georgia, where gold discoveries caused a small rush in the 1830s. The average value of gold produced in this region came to less than $300,000 per year.

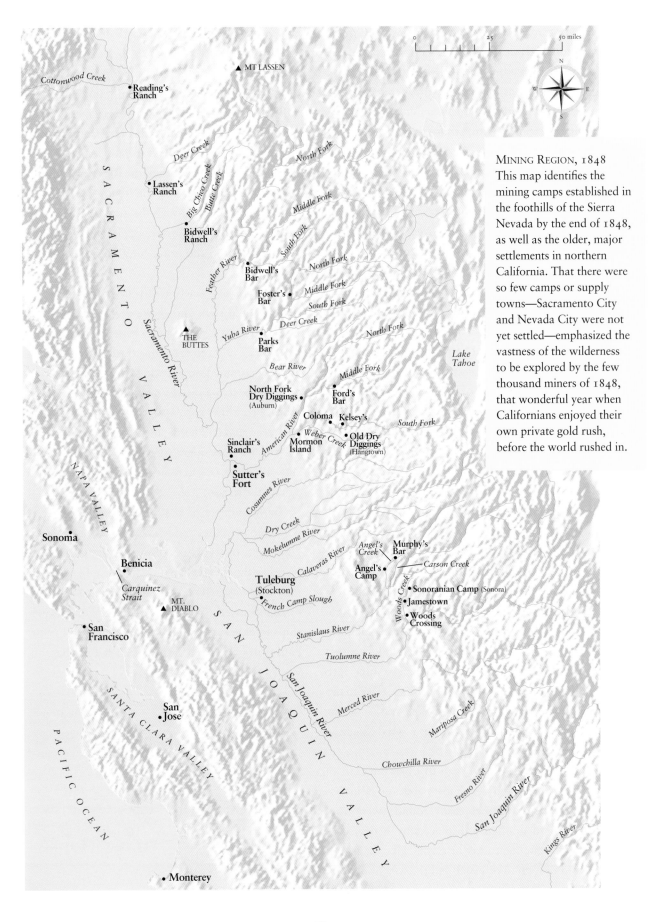

0   25   50 miles

N W E S

▲ MT LASSEN

Cottonwood Creek

● Reading's
Ranch

Deer Creek

North Fork

● Lassen's
Ranch

Big Chico Creek

Butte Creek

S A C R A M E N T O

Middle Fork

● Bidwell's
Ranch

Feather River

South Fork

Bidwell's
Bar ●

North Fork

Foster's ●
Bar

Middle Fork

South Fork

V A L L E Y

Sacramento River

Deer Creek

▲ THE
BUTTES

Yuba River

Parks
Bar ●

North Fork

Bear River

*Lake
Tahoe*

Middle Fork

North Fork ●
Dry Diggings
(Auburn)

Ford's ●
Bar

Coloma ● Kelsey's
●

South Fork

American River

Weber Creek

Sinclair's
Ranch ●

Mormon
Island ●

● Old Dry
Diggings
(Hangtown)

Sutter's
Fort ●

Cosumnes River

N A P A   V A L L E Y

● Sonoma

Dry Creek

Mokelumne River

Angel's
Creek

Murphy's
Bar ●

Benicia ●

Calaveras River

Angel's ●
Camp

── *Carson Creek*

*Carquinez
Strait*

▲ MT.
DIABLO

Tuleburg
(Stockton) ●

French Camp Slough

Woods Creek

● Sonoranian Camp (Sonora)

● Jamestown

● San
Francisco

● Woods
Crossing

Stanislaus River

S A N

Tuolumne River

S A N T A   C L A R A   V A L L E Y

San ●
Jose

J O A Q U I N

San Joaquin River

Merced River

Mariposa Creek

P A C I F I C   O C E A N

V A L L E Y

Chowchilla River

Fresno River

San Joaquin River

Kings River

● Monterey

MINING REGION, 1848
This map identifies the
mining camps established in
the foothills of the Sierra
Nevada by the end of 1848,
as well as the older, major
settlements in northern
California. That there were
so few camps or supply
towns—Sacramento City
and Nevada City were not
yet settled—emphasized the
vastness of the wilderness
to be explored by the few
thousand miners of 1848,
that wonderful year when
Californians enjoyed their
own private gold rush,
before the world rushed in.

the inexorable power of climatic forces, swept along for thousands of years in the wild torrents of prehistoric rivers cutting deep canyons and pools, these golden fragments—nineteen times heavier than water—sank among the rocks and lodged in fissures along the bottoms of those millennial rivers. Through subsequent eons lighter flakes and scales and grains finally rested downstream, where slower currents released them in quiet eddies below giant boulders and in a thousand crevices and pockets.

Many of these prehistoric rivers, thrust upward in the violent earth movements of the Pliocene period, were encountered in 1848 as water-smoothed boulders and rocks in fields of gravel and sand, far removed from flowing water. In these geologic riverbeds the '48ers and their successors found gold in what they called "dry diggings."

Occasionally as nuggets of three, or five, or even twenty ounces, more often as flakes the size of pumpkin seeds, but usually as grains and tiny granules, the placer gold was discovered north and south of Coloma in myriad hiding places—in the rocks and gravel of a bar where the Yuba River turned sharply against its canyon wall; beneath the rubble of thousands of boulders on an island exposed in July 1848 by the low water of the Stanislaus; in the crevice of an immense chunk of granite at the edge the South Fork of the Feather; in a hole dug deeply into the dry diggings not far from Hangtown.

Such surface explorations in the spring and summer of 1848 required only a knife, shovel, and pick, maybe a pry bar, and by year's end an Indian basket or a metal pan. Even a woolen blanket sufficed to hold wet sand and soil spread over its surface to dry in the sun and then to be shaken until nothing remained but the heavier particles of gold caught in the wool fibers.

As the goldseekers began to learn the craft of mining, their primitive, almost careless methods—useful where gold was easily found—were augmented and gradually displaced by a device of ancient origin, the rocker or cradle. Like the pan, it utilized the action of water and the weight of gold,

but vastly increased the volume of dirt that could be washed. Built of wood, four to six feet in length, the rocker had a removable box or hopper atop one end and on its lower level a series of parallel cleats or riffles. When gold-bearing dirt—rocks, gravel, and sand—was shoveled into the hopper and water poured over it, a perforated metal plate on the bottom of the hopper held back the rocks and much of the gravel, allowing only the lighter material and sandy water to fall through the grate and wash over the cleats and out the lower end, leaving the heavier particles, flakes, and grains of gold caught behind the cleats.

To increase the action of water and gravity, one miner would rock and shake the machine (which rested on curved supports) to better disintegrate the "pay dirt." From time to time the hopper was lifted and its accumulation of rocks and gravel dumped to one side. Several times a day the riffles were scraped clean. From this last, most important work came whatever gold had been gained by the labor of three or perhaps four men: one or two to gather and shovel the dirt, one to pour on the water, and one to agitate the rocker.

In the summer of 1848, Indians were sometimes paid with gewgaws and whiskey, maybe even a little gold dust, to work as laborers, carrying dirt and water to the rockers. In July, Larkin told of "a few men working 30 to 40 Indians and laying up 1000$ to 2000$ a week." But most miners formed partnerships to gain the manpower needed to dig for dirt, haul it in pails or canvas bags to the hopper, and

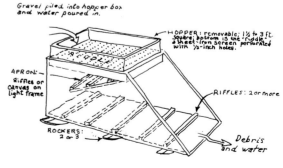

ROCKER

Made of sheet iron with a flat bottom about one foot wide and sides four inches high, rising at an angle of forty-five degrees, the pan was the indispensable companion for miners, especially prospectors who traveled light while searching for "color." Once a good location was found, larger devices, such as the rocker or long tom, could be employed to more efficiently wash for gold.

This well-worn rocker is smaller and shallower than most and lacks the riffles that once lay across its bed. The drawing of a typical rocker on the opposite page shows the several components of this essential machine.

keep plenty of water flowing and the rocker shaking. Thus mining quickly advanced from one man with the primitive pan to the joint enterprise of a machine that required some investment and teamwork.

Important as the first of many advances in the mechanization of mining, the rocker also marked the earliest evidence of a change in the social structure of the mining region—from individual miners hurrying with their pans from river bar to ravine to side canyon, each intent on his private quest, to the less mobile efforts of partners working their rockers and willing to "stay put" for a few days, maybe a week. Such cooperation and resulting stability portended the future far more than it reflected 1848.

During the summer, success came easily to a great many of the first goldseekers, almost all of them from California, several hundred by August and September from Oregon and the Sandwich Islands, and by year's end a few thousand from Sonora, Mexico. Rushing from one newly discovered digging to another expected to be even richer, they expanded the mining region week by week, from Coloma to the Middle and North Forks of the American River, where camps took names like Yankee Jim's, Ford's Bar, and Kelsey's Diggings. Farther north, John Bidwell made a famous strike on the South Fork of the Feather River at what became Bidwell's Bar. His success led to exploration of the Feather's main tributary, the Yuba, where one lucky partnership of five miners took out $75,000 ($1,386,750 in 1998 dollars) in three months. Other deposits on forks of the Yuba became known by the names of their discoverers—Long's, Foster's, and Parks Bars. And farther north, up on the Trinity River (160 miles above Sutter's Fort), the rancher Pierson B. Reading discovered a new deposit that he worked with a crew of Indians during July, taking out $80,000. Hundreds soon arrived to try their luck at Reading's Bar.

The energy and ambition of the miners pushed the limits of the known gold region southward as well, along the Cosumnes, Mokelumne, Calaveras,

Stanislaus, and to the Tuolumne River—a distance of 230 miles from Reading's Bar on the Trinity. These "southern mines" had their moments of fame at places like Murphy's Bar, Angel's Camp, Sullivan Bar (where John Sullivan, an Irish teamster, took out $26,000), Jamestown, and Woods Creek. At the latter site three miners working with only picks and knives "for some time" found $200 to $300 each day. At a digging called Arroyo Seco near the Cosumnes River, a Californio from the coastal village of San Luis Obispo dug enough gold during September to pay off his ten workers and return home with $14,000.

In this masculine world, a scattering of women and children settled at camps where supplies could be delivered by freight wagons or pack mules, and some semblance of customary society developed. But beyond these impromptu hamlets up narrow canyons and on river flats, thousands of men made do in crude, temporary shelters—tents, brush enclosures, here and there "boarding shanties," and caves. Many simply rolled into a blanket or two under sheltering pines.

All day they dug and washed, hearing on all sides the shaking of rockers and the rattle of stones thrown from hoppers. The occasional shout of triumph, of sudden success, nourished them far more than hurried meals. Slipping and sloshing over riverbed boulders and rocks, enduring icy currents of swift water pouring down from the melting Sierra snowpack, or digging in a narrow ravine where the blazing sun disappeared by three o'clock over a high ridge, the goldseekers labored and cursed, shivered and sweated, through July, August, and September. They hoped to make their fortunes before the rainy season, which might start any time after mid-September, bringing downpours that could turn streams to torrents and flood ravines.

On July 20 Thomas Larkin sent a new report to Secretary Buchanan. After citing numerous examples of success ("there are many men with tin pan and machine . . . who have taken from 300$ to 600$ in a week . . . and one who took 700$ in four hours"), Larkin summed up the realities: "200,000$ of gold was dug out in May and 400,000$ in June. I now think over a half million is the monthly estimate."

There seemed to be only one concern, not widely shared: that gold might be mined in such abundance (Governor Mason warned) that it would "seriously depreciate in value." That prediction proved accurate, for by August an ounce of gold dust purchased goods from merchants worth only $8 to $10—down from $18 in May. Some miners traded their dust at the rate of only $4 per ounce. The merchants knew they had the upper hand, and they set the price.

To feed and otherwise supply the needs of two, three, soon four thousand and more goldseekers (almost all of whom had come to the Sierra streams with provisions sufficient to stay at most a few weeks), merchants and traders set up stores— usually crude plank counters in front of wagons, with perhaps some canvas stretched overhead— where they sold flour, dried peas, bacon, coffee, salt, along with shovels, picks, and metal prospecting pans. And sometimes they had a supply of saws, hammers, and nails.

Many of these new merchants pocketed more gold than the miners, but few, if any, did as well as Sam Brannan. His store at Sutter's Fort was overwhelmed by demand for whatever he had to sell— canvas for tents, dysentery medicine, whiskey, boots. His store at Coloma, his store at the Sacramento River landing, and a fourth store at Mormon Diggings all prospered by charging the miners prices that assured him 300 to 400 percent profit.

Every box and barrel, every sack and bottle sold to the miners came from San Francisco, the burgeoning port to which the first of thousands of ships were bringing the world's merchandise. What auctioneers and merchants did not sell to meet the swelling demands of that instant city, they reloaded on a small but growing fleet of river vessels that crossed the bay and sailed slowly up the Sacramento River to the landing below Sutter's Fort. Some

In that summer of excitement and exaggeration, the official report of Military Governor Richard Mason provided an authoritative overview. From Sutter's Fort on July 5, Mason traveled east to Mormon Diggings.

The day was intensely hot, yet about two hundred men were at work washing gold, some with tin pans, some with close-woven Indian baskets, but the greater part had a rude machine known as a cradle. . . .
I was surprised to learn that crime of any kind was very unfrequent. All live in tents, bush houses, or in the open air, and men frequently have about their persons thousands of dollars worth of gold. The extent of the country is so great and the gold so abundant that for the present there is room and enough for all. . . . Unless large quantities of breadstuffs reach this country, much suffering will occur. But as each man is now able to pay a large price, it is believed that merchants will bring from Chile and Oregon a plentiful supply.

Colonel Richard Mason, Report to Adjutant General, August 17, 1848

supplies were still carried from the coast to the diggings on oxcarts or mule-drawn wagons, their progress slowed, sometimes endangered, at the muddy banks of river crossings. At several of these obstacles entrepreneurs offered dugouts and other crude craft as ferries, thereby exacting their profits in the ever-expanding complex of commerce nurtured by the needs of goldseekers.

Prices fluctuated wildly, rising as weeks passed in the absence of new shipments and dropping suddenly when a supply wagon reached a mining camp or a ship unloaded its cargo at San Francisco or the landing at Sutter's Fort. A miner might pay $300 for a horse worth only $6 the month before, ride it to

This hand-drawn map is an unusually accurate example of a miner's effort to provide the folks back home with a cartographic sense of "the diggings."

The '48ers had no intention of staying in the Sierra foothills and therefore invested minimal effort in constructing their shelter. Almost as careless and transient, miners of later years threw up the most casual lean-tos and "bush cabins," which required only a sheet of canvas suspended by a tree limb. John Woodhouse Audubon, son of the great ornithologist, sketched this tent house near Sonora in 1850. Another prospecting artist, William M'Ilvaine from Philadelphia, drew this scene of miners' tents and a brush bower at Woods Creek, also near Sonora, summer 1849.

Woods Creek

CHRONOLOGY (1848)

the next camp, and turn it loose because he could more easily scrape up enough gold to buy a new horse than take care of the first one.

In July, one of Thomas Larkin's agents wrote from San Francisco that he had been unable to buy any blankets or clothing, both in great demand. Complaining that Sam Brannan had paid almost $12,000 to buy the town's entire stock, he urged Larkin to seize the opportunity: "If you can have it done within a month, you had better have a large lot of pants made up of flannel, jeans, Osnaburg and cotton goods." But what the miners needed more than pants were boots to replace those that had rotted and worn out from daily slogging through rivers and creeks. As another agent advised Larkin in August from the Yuba mines, "There are no shoes on all the Sacramento. They are worth $10, ready sale. If you can buy some and send them up to us, we can do well with them."

As for "doing well," this same agent reported from Sutter's Fort on August 16 that two Larkin employees operating a store at the Yuba mines "say they average 500$ [profit] per day. I suppose they have 10,000$ [in gold] on hand. . . . All our goods will bring from 300 to 500 per cent profit. . . . Freight from the Fort to the Yuba is 12$ per 100 lbs. We sell very high to the Indians. Serapes from 60$ to 100$, shirts 16$, to whites 5$." Others profited from Indians by cheating them with a rigged gold scale that used a weight requiring two ounces to balance one ounce. But merchants did not confine their capitalist appetites to the sale of dry goods. One man who ran a grog shop on the Stanislaus took in over $1,000 per day for a week straight.

On August 18, Larkin's agent (still at Fort Sutter) added a postscript to one of his dispatches that reflected the swirl of uncertainty and high hopes that bedeviled the eager miners that hectic summer. "There is a great excitement here now about another placer on the Mocelomy River. It appears that the whole cause of the excitement was Dr. Cory's having been absent from his camp three or four days. Immediately after his return, he ordered his men to pack up and follow him. His leaving created a suspicion that he had found new diggings and in less than one day there was more than 500 persons leaving the dry diggings and following his trail. The general opinion is at the Fort that there are rich diggings somewhere there, but nobody knows where."

In his August report, Governor Mason told of innumerable desertions from U.S. Navy ships and Army posts, and yet he sympathized with the deserters. "Sailors desert their ships as fast as they arrive on the coast . . . ; two or three are now at anchor in San Francisco with no crews on board. Many desertions, too, have taken place from garrisons. . . . I shall spare no exertions to apprehend and punish deserters, but I believe no time in the history of our country has presented such temptations to desert as now exist in California. The danger of apprehension is small and the prospect of higher wages certain. . . . Laboring men at the mines can now earn in one day more than double a soldier's pay and allowances for a month, and even the pay of a lieutenant or captain cannot hire a servant. . . . Could any combination of affairs try a man's fidelity more than this?"

Down in Monterey, Alcalde Walter Colton chronicled in his journal the quickening pulse of local opinion. On July 18 he reported, with characteristic flair, "another bag of gold from the mines and another spasm in the community. It was brought down from the Yuba River by a sailor and contains 136 ounces. . . . It looks like the yellow scales of a dolphin passing through his rainbow hues at death. My carpenters at work on the schoolhouse, on seeing it, threw down their saws and planes, shouldered their picks and are off for the Yuba. Three seamen ran from the *Warren*, forfeiting four years' pay. A whole platoon of soldiers from the fort left only their colors behind."

On August 16, two weeks before heading for the mines himself, Colton logged in his journal exact tallies of gold brought back to Monterey by townsfolk "well known to me." They harvested their gold, he said, from deposits opened for the first time

"by the sturdy arms of the American emigrant"—a subtle slap at the Spanish and Mexicans who had failed to make the great discoveries. Among the happy citizens returning to Monterey with gold in his pockets was a boy fourteen years old who had dug gold on the Mokelumne River for fifty-four days and come home with $3,467. Colton closed his review by asking, "Is not this enough to make a man throw down his ledger and shoulder a pick?"

Gold fever spread steadily south from Monterey, stirring in turn the residents of Santa Barbara, Los Angeles, and San Diego. But these Californians were not as ready to take up Alcalde Colton's challenge as the impetuous citizens up north. Their reluctance arose less from the hindrance of distance, or the memory of southern California's lackluster gold strike back in 1842, than from the disquieting knowledge that they would be an outnumbered race in the diggings. Southern California remained largely Mexican, the stronghold of native Californios. Their welcome in the goldfields would be uncertain.

Nevertheless, through the fall of 1848 expectant hundreds from those southern towns did travel north. By winter some 1,300 Californios were prospecting and digging for gold. Kept together by language and anxiety, they showed an uncommon cooperative spirit, working in groups, sharing supplies. And as if to make up for having failed to discover the Sierra's vast treasure, their efforts produced gold in an abundance that soon became legendary. For instance, Antonio Franco Coronel with some thirty Californios, Sonorans, and Indian servants from Los Angeles set to work in August 1848 in the southern diggings. At the end of his first day Coronel reported he had "recovered about forty-five ounces of coarse gold," the next day thirty-eight ounces, the next fifty-one. On an adjoining claim his friend Valdes dug down three feet and uncovered a boulder that thousands of years earlier had blocked the flow of a river. From this pocket he took enough gold to fill a large piece of cloth. Thinking he had enough, Valdes passed his claim to another whose labor produced in eight days fifty-two *pounds* of gold. Next a Sonoran worked in the hole, digging with a spoon, piling the coarse gold onto a wooden bowl until by evening he strained to lift it out. Weary, he turned the treasure trove over to another companion who continued the cramped digging until he, too, had accumulated his fortune.* Reports of this strike, repeated as if typical of goldseeking, spread throughout the mining region and eventually to the States and overseas—an example of California's generosity.

Surrounded by what seemed to be plenty for all, there were some who missed their main chance, most prominent of these, John Sutter. An air of Shakespearean tragedy enveloped him, so dazzling had been his opportunity, so puzzling his failure. He could not cope with the revolution that transformed his domain: from wheat fields tended by obedient Indians to hundreds, even thousands of strangers trampling his land; from being in control to being pushed aside. His fort served as the center of trade for the northern mines, yet he found the swelling throngs of miners, tradesmen, and Indians, of horses, oxen, and wagons, more a threat than an opportunity. Orders not his own directed men loading and unloading crates and barrels. The bedlam of yelling, fighting, and drunken brawling left Sutter bewildered, a helpless spectator. The rents he charged for storehouses and sheds, for Brannan's store and for a two-story hotel, all increased month by month, to $1,800 in July. But he borrowed against this income, building debt on top of the money he still owed the Russians for his purchase of Fort Ross.

Crowds camped about his fort, tore down his fences for firewood, stole two hundred barrels of packed salmon. His flour mill stood unfinished, looted of beams and even its millstones. When he

---

*More than the source for this aureate anecdote, Antonio Coronel gained renown as a landowner and viticulturist and then as mayor of Los Angeles (1853) and treasurer of California (1867–71).

sold his half interest in the sawmill, the new owners soon had it running again and turning out both planks and profits.

He floundered, complained of abuses and the dishonesty of others, drank too much. He failed to keep records and to pay his bills, even spent gold dust entrusted to his safekeeping. All about him Sutter was confronted by men more aggressive, more ruthless, more ambitious than he, men driven to succeed, if not tomorrow, then the day after.

When he turned to gold mining with a large party of Indian workers and wagonloads of provisions, again the success won by others eluded the captain. After an unpromising start, he gave up on his first claim and moved to the southern mines, to a camp called Sutter Creek. But his workers spent their gold at the camp's grog shops, returning drunk or sick, unable to work. "The whole expedition proved to be a heavy loss for me," he later lamented.

He opened a store at Coloma, a booming market town, but this mercantile effort again proved Sutter's incompetence in the gold rush economy. Where others succeeded, he failed. He blamed his losses on the very source of California's new prosperity. "By this sudden discovery of gold, all my great plans were destroyed. Had I succeeded with my mills and manufactories, I should have been the richest citizen on the Pacific shore; but it had to be different. Instead of being rich, I am ruined." For Sutter, the discovery of gold was the end, not the beginning.

And so it was for the discoverer himself, James Marshall. When he and Sutter tried mining with their Indian workers, they quarreled about the treatment of the natives. Marshall drifted off alone, prospecting and digging with little success. Harassed by other goldseekers, he became morose and resentful; he told of threats to his life by miners who demanded he show them where to find gold. Lonely, broke, he lived the last years of his life not far from Coloma, something of a hermit—a famous name, a sorrowful man.

Many others, hundreds and hundreds, also failed to find their share. Some gambled and drank

Sutter and Marshall, two men who might have gained most from the discovery of gold, suffered similarly destitute fates. With his fields over-run by hundreds of goldseekers and his once impressive fort a crumbling ruin, Sutter spent the last years of his life near Washington, D.C., unsuccessfully petitioning Congress to redress his losses. Marshall, hounded by miners who presumed he knew where riches could be dug, resorted to selling autographed cards for a paltry income. He died penniless and embittered near Coloma. This daguerreotype shows someone, usually identified as James Marshall, standing in front of the sawmill in 1852 after it had been converted into living quarters. So much for monuments. Indeed, in 1853 a government surveyor reported the mill "has recently been purchased with the intention of making walking canes from its timbers."

AUTOGRAPH OF

Jas. W. Marshall

THE DISCOVERER OF GOLD IN CALIFORNIA

January 19th, 1848.

OLD SUTTER MILL

to ease the bitterness of defeat in a summer of success. Others labored with desperate energy, digging through rocks and gravel to accumulate enough pay dirt to fill their rockers. At nightfall they gulped down beans and jerky, whatever vittles could be most easily warmed in skillets. Under such strain and amid miserable, unhealthy conditions, sickness put an end to many a quest for fortune. Weakened by fever, dysentery, or scurvy, some found their way back to family care in their homes along the coast. Others, dependent on harried companions, lay in their bedrolls and hoped for recovery. Many defeated miners straggled back to Sutter's Fort to look for a job or a loan from a friend. If it could be reached, San Francisco beckoned with opportunity and allurement. Jobs were plentiful in construction and on the busy wharves. By night gaudy saloons and glittering gambling halls promised excitement and the consoling stories of others unlucky in the goldfields.

HOPES FULFILLED

On August 6, 1848, the news finally reached Monterey that the United States and Mexico had signed a peace treaty at Guadalupe Hidalgo in Mexico on February 2.* The next day Governor Mason issued a proclamation wonderfully proud and patriotic in its description of California's "new destiny." He forecast "internal tranquility . . . a firm and stable government punishing crime with the strong arm of power. . . . The labor of the agriculturalist will stimulate the earth to the most bountiful production. Americans and Californians will become a band of brothers in their common country." The people of San Francisco cared less about the future than the present opportunity to celebrate the seven-month-old news of the treaty. On August 11, the town let loose with a "grand illumination." It began with a cavalcade of citizens marching through the streets, heralded by guns firing on all sides and the thump of cannon from ships in the bay. In the

evening, windows shone with candles, while burning tar barrels and bonfires lit up the night. One of the celebrants reported that "citizens speechified and hurrahed, toasted and drank, danced and made merry. . . . Black eyes and bloody noses were occasionally visible and all the other accompaniments necessary to make the rejoicings complete."

For Military Governor Richard Mason, the news of the treaty gave hope that deliverance was at hand from his trying duties as presiding officer of an impotent military government in a land at peace. But such an agreeable resolution was not to be his fate. Back in Washington, Congress spent the rest of 1848 locked in tormented debate over the issue of slavery in California and therefore failed to pass legislation that would have conferred territorial status. California would continue its wait for a territorial governor and a civil government. That left Mason in limbo—no longer military governor under the laws of war, but not civil governor because that office had not yet been created. He would be "governor" of a de facto government, as pragmatic Secretary of State Buchanan authorized, under "the great law of necessity."

One consequence of the peace announcement was the governor's loss of authority to retain conscripts in his "army," which had dwindled to a scant fifty men. He reported his plight to Washing-

---

* By this treaty Mexico ceded California and New Mexico (the present states of Arizona, New Mexico, Nevada, and Utah) and accepted the Rio Grande as the boundary of Texas. The United States agreed to pay $15 million and to assume the adjusted claims of U.S. citizens against the Mexican government.

In the course of bombastic debate in the U.S. Senate leading to ratification of the treaty, some of the more rabid expansionists and partisans of Manifest Destiny argued in favor of taking all of Mexico. What the United States did gain by this treaty was the most extensive territorial acquisition in its history: 1.2 million square miles, compared to 828,000 square miles obtained by the Louisiana Purchase (1803) and 591,000 square miles in the purchase from Russia of Alaska in 1867.

ton: insufficient force available to repel Indian attacks on outlying ranches or to preserve orderly civilian conduct. Sending reinforcements was useless, he advised, because they would desert their $7 monthly pay and hurry off to the gold in the foothills. In another dispatch, Mason worried that without civil government there could be anarchy, murder, robbery; in short, "all sorts of crime will be committed." Finally, in November, tired and discouraged by the unending stalemate, he sent this message to Washington: "The war being over, the soldiers nearly all deserted and having now been from the States for two years, I respectfully request to be ordered home." It was an honorable request and one that Washington did not ignore. Mason would be released two months later, in January 1849.

Noble public servant though he was, Californians did not honor or miss Richard Mason. They were too occupied with the business of gold. In San Francisco the *Californian* returned to the streets with an occasional issue trumpeting new wonders in the goldfields. In August it offered the calculation that $60,000 per day was being produced in gold. On September 23, another issue reported the city's booming supply and provisioning business: "Immense quantities of merchandise have been conveyed to the mines, until it has become a matter of astonishment where so much could be disposed of. . . . Receipts here for the last eight weeks in gold dust have been $600,000."

That much gold spent in a few weeks in a small town—it was an economic orgasm. San Francisco burst forth in scores of enterprises designed to profit from the thousands of passengers and tons of freight hauled ashore from ships anchored in the bay or moored at the too-few wharves being built over the tidal mudflats. Cargoes from the world's ports piled high along the unprepared shoreline, to be auctioned before another shipment arrived that would drive down the price of sacks of potatoes (in great demand as a cure for scurvy), barrels of pickled pork, crates of boots, casks of brandy, and whatever else merchants in Baltimore and Bordeaux hoped to sell in the famous California market.

Along Montgomery Street, San Francisco's business center, new buildings rose by the dozen, some of wooden frames to be covered in canvas, a few built of brick. Carpenters, masons, and laborers demanded astronomical wages. Thomas Larkin complained that even cooks cost four to six ounces a month. He also reported that riverboats returned from Sutter's Landing each day delivering merchants and speculators from Coloma and other booming mining camps, each of them "bringing five to ten thousand dollars in gold dust to purchase goods" to be shipped upriver. He advised a business partner in Mazatlán that a cargo of Mexican goods shipped to San Francisco between August and October worth $50,000 would have "returned you over $100,000 in ninety days." One captain sold a consignment of merchandise to a merchant who overwrote the original $28,000 with an offer of $58,000. Such profits made San Francisco synonymous with the image of California. In 1848 and for decades, the boomtown remained *the* port, *the* city of El Dorado.

For many, commerce reached its most exaggerated heights in real estate speculation. One San Francisco lot bought by Larkin in 1846 for $500 sold in September 1848 for $10,000. Another lot he sold in that same month for $5,000 was resold a few weeks later for $15,000. So it went, triple and quadruple profits in the city during the fall of 1848 and for years thereafter.

While day-to-day moneymaking animated life in San Francisco no less than in the diggings, a few citizens took a longer view. Until the fifth of November, religious services had been, at best, "occasional." On that date a Protestant clergyman from Honolulu inaugurated Sunday services in the city's only schoolhouse, located amid the gambling halls on Portsmouth Square. For many the benediction of a divine spirit provided a welcome civilizing influence, but it could not make up for the absence of more secular safeguards in their frontier society.

Encouraged by the editorial voice of the *Star and Californian* (the two rivals had merged), an increasing number of San Franciscans began to agitate against "daring outrages committed of late in different parts of the country." In December, citizens gathered at several public meetings to demand genuine territorial government. They blamed the muddled authority of Colonel Mason for failing to provide "proper legal protection for the lives and property of citizens."

Not limiting their attacks to Governor Mason, numerous speakers directed a stream of invective at Washington, asserting "that Congress had been trifling with them . . . and therefore instant steps should be taken to establish a form of government for themselves," without waiting for Congress and its interminable debates. San Franciscans were shocked to learn that in August President Polk had signed legislation making Oregon—no gold there!—a bona fide territory, with a civilian governor. "Why wait any longer?" Californians asked.*

These activists called for the election of delegates to attend a meeting to be scheduled for March 1849 in San Jose "for the purpose of framing a form of constitution"—with or without Congressional approval. Once again a restive California sought to overcome the neglect of a distant and out-of-touch colonial authority.

The clamor for political reform held sway along the coast, from San Francisco to Monterey. Out in the gold country other visionaries were plotting California's commercial future. Sam Brannan looked beyond the brisk business of his supply stores and began planning a strategy to make profits from real estate development. He foresaw that, although everyone passed through the hubbub of buying and selling at Sutter's Fort, the better site for commerce and a future city would be at the landing on the banks of the Sacramento River, where riverboats from San Francisco unloaded passengers and freight and, on a lesser scale, a ferry carried overlanders and their cargoes across the broad flow of the Sacramento. At this riverfront, called the Embarcadero, these two streams of commerce converged. Sutter, however, stubbornly expected that his fort, further inland, would remain the center for future trade.

Far the shrewder businessman, Brannan decided to promote the Embarcadero's future. In October 1848 he persuaded Sutter's eldest son, John August (newly arrived from Switzerland and in charge of his father's muddled business affairs), that the landing area should be surveyed preparatory to selling lots for a city-to-be. In a move symbolic of his rising power, Brannan also convinced the younger Sutter that the future required a name other than New Helvetia. He suggested Sacramento City.

As the year closed, Brannan crafted a scheme to gain title to the key waterfront lots in the new city. His machinations would later be described as "one of the most brilliant examples of confidencemanship in the history of California."

A SEASON OF INNOCENCE

Never before had there been such a society as that in California during the summer and fall of 1848. For that brief time some five thousand men (with a few hundred women and children), virtually all from the coastal villages and valley ranches, were scattered along the rivers, streams, and dry gulches from the Trinity to the Tuolumne, a vast area over two hundred miles in length and forty to fifty miles in width. They labored each day at the same tiring work, in similar, unfamiliar surroundings, pursuing the same tantalizing dream, living the same transient, camping-out life. During those soon-to-be-

---

* Given its location, Oregon was accepted by southern senators as a free (non-slave) territory. But when President Polk recommended a territorial government for California, there followed months of bitter congressional debate. And when news of the gold discovery aroused national excitement, the issue of California's admission as a territory—free or slave—became even more contentious, leading in 1850 to a sectional debate of such intensity as to threaten disunion and civil war.

romanticized months, nearly everyone experienced moments of success, turning up at least three or four ounces every few days. Each morning nurtured fresh expectations of uncovering a rich pocket—just as happened over the ridge yesterday, and around the bend last week. Hundreds of lucky miners took out gold valued in the thousands of dollars. Others were luckier still. Envied in their camps and gossiped about nearby, they were the "millionaires," known by name, who had dug out $10,000, $20,000, even more. And scores of merchants, freighters, mule packers, and other entrepreneurs made their swift thousands, content to remain on the outer fringes of the miners' society.

Moving easily from camp to camp, sitting around the warmth of fires at night, talking about their day's rocking and washing, miners enjoyed for a time the special camaraderie of strangers thrown together by an event beyond the scope of old rules and norms. Many must have looked into the firelight and let their minds slip away to an imaginary tomorrow when they would find what everyone hoped to find—a virgin creek in an undiscovered canyon, with only the sounds of water burbling over mossy rocks and scrub jays chattering in the willows. In such a place one's pan would yield gold by the pound, and several days—maybe a week—would pass before other prospectors would show up to crowd the river bar and steal its magic.

For a few months, before news of the great treasure hunt reached Hawaii, Oregon, Mexico, and the world beyond, Californians enjoyed their season of innocence. With hopes fulfilled today or surely tomorrow, everyone felt a sense of equality. Old measures of status, like clothes and manners—even wealth—no longer mattered. Prosperity for all was at hand. Unhampered freedom prevailed, even for deserters from the U.S. Army and Navy. Miners casually left their gold in cans, bottles, and leather pouches, in their tents or beside their rockers, without concern for theft. The sense of neighborliness, of sharing the same unique experience, inspired an openhanded, plenty-for-everybody social order,

ruled only by an unspoken code of fair conduct, with no government in sight.

Among the thousands of hurrying goldseekers, a few letter writers and diary keepers sensed history in the making. One of those most aware was Lieutenant William Tecumseh Sherman, who wrote a series of letters in the fall of 1848 from the forks of the American River, where he had been sent by Governor Mason. As part of his official correspondence he described the curious human story unfolding, with its busy riverside comings and goings, its successes and expectations; he wrote of "Mrs. Eagar who won't move till she has made $20,000," and U.S. Army deserters safe from apprehension because "we have not the power, and the mines are so wide spread that the devil himself could not find one." In his final letter, dated November 14, 1848, the future scourge of Georgia allowed himself a lamentation: "Were I at liberty to continue in this vicinity this winter and next spring, I would not take $10,000 for the chance—but I must go and soon."

Too bad Sam Brannan did not pause in his moneymaking long enough to record his impressions of those months, soon to be recalled as the calm before the storm. Fortunately, Walter Colton did write regularly in his diary, and no one left a more literary yet realistic account of those evanescent times. In September, Colton described meeting a band of miners who had worked so doggedly at gold hunting that they had neglected

COLTON

provisions and were without food. Colton's group shared its grub, and these sated Jasons "took from one of their packs a large bag of gold and began to shell out a pound or two in payment. . . . This company, I afterwards ascertained, had with them over a hundred thousand dollars in grain gold. One of them had the largest lump that had yet been found; it weighed over twenty pounds. And he seemed almost ready to part with it for a mess of pottage. What is gold where there is nothing to eat?—the gilded fly of the angler in a troutless stream."

As THE SUMMER OF 1848 FADED, SO DID THE provincial simplicity, honesty, and easiness of California's backyard gold rush. Outsiders began to arrive by the hundreds and then thousands from Oregon, Hawaii, and Sonora in the first wave. Uninvited, these strangers pushed into mining camps and outlying claims, trying to find space for their first digging and washing efforts. Inevitably the Californians reacted with suspicion. With so many foreigners intruding, the "old-timers" became defensive of what they thought to be their own. Adding to their possessiveness was the pressure of late-season work carried on with heightened intensity and, each day, nervous eyes scanning the western sky. They hoped for a few more weeks of gold collecting before conceding to winter rains and swollen streams. They worried, rightly, that next season gold digging would not be the same.

With the outsiders came early harbingers of more chaotic times—more gambling and drunkenness, here and there fights, even several knifings and shootings. Good order and honesty still prevailed, but a sense of anxiety intruded like a stench on the evening breeze. In November one observer noted the changes and wondered about the future. "In the midst of all this most extraordinary prosperity, vices are creeping in and advancing by great strides. . . . Every public house, every saloon, is a den where gambling goes on night and day and where very large sums are put at risk. It is most distressing to see how general this vice has become. . . . It is to be feared there will soon result a general corruption and disorder that will be all the worse since the government, far from being able to arrest the progress of the evil, is without courts, without police, without military force, and without any means of . . . running down and punishing crimes and misdemeanors."

Those who shared this anxiety hoped that Washington would soon establish a legal, civilian government. But their hopes were dashed in December when a ship brought the news that the Congress, still locked in debate over the extension of slavery, had adjourned without passing legislation for California's provisional government. Feeling vulnerable to the threat of invading newcomers, citizens in newly founded Sacramento City attended rallies to add their voices to those in San Francisco and San Jose who had earlier called for bypassing Washington to set up a proper American government for California, to be elected by its people. Speakers at these rallies warned of the urgent need to cope with old insufficiencies and more difficult new troubles.

But who among those loud voices possessed the intellectual know-how or political experience to take the lead in establishing self-government for chaotic California? Who would care enough about the future of a society dedicated to the self-interest of fortune hunting? In a time of such turmoil, who would step forth as California's Sam Houston, much less its Thomas Jefferson? Could any of the Californios attract a political following in the midst of so many Americanos? If not the old-timers, who might rise to leadership? Governor Mason hoped to escape his frustrations as soon as his orders arrived. All the other temporary leaders had long ago sailed or marched away. In December 1848, California drifted as leaderless as it had been in 1828 or 1798.

The Hudson River steam-sailer *Hartford*
departed New York on February 20, 1849,
with fifty goldseekers aboard. Dangerously
inadequate for the arduous voyage, she
returned to New York for repairs after nearly
foundering off Bermuda. Patched up, the
Hartford again sailed for the Horn and
finally reached California ten months after
first setting forth.

WORLDWIDE CONTAGION

Labeled "Cal News," this daguerreotype reflects Americans' hunger for reports from the gold region. On February 8, 1849, the *Buffalo Morning Express* published a letter from California which announced that "gold is found pure in the native soil here . . . in the form of irregular masses. This stratum of gold is unbroken and extends over a tract 120 miles in length and 70 miles in breadth. Many men who began last June to dig for gold with capital of $50 can now show $5,000 to $15,000."

Across the nation, in cities and villages, thousands of men considered how best to reach California. Newspapers published announcements—like this one in Canajoharie, New York—of companies being organized for the overland journey.

TAKE NOTICE.
Ho! for California!

A Meeting of the Citizens of
the Village of Canajoharie and its vicinity, will be held at the house of T. W. Bingham, on

FRIDAY EVENING,

the **19th inst.**, at early candle light, for the purpose of taking into consideration the propriety of forming a company to proceed to California, and mining for **GOLD.** All who feel interested on the subject are requested to attend.
MANY CITIZENS.
Canajoharie, Jan. **16, 1849.**

CHAPTER THREE

WORLDWIDE CONTAGION

SHIPS AND PRINTING PRESSES carried the news around the world—that the abundance of California's gold was free to everyone. The wonder of it spread through the fall of 1848 and the year 1849, even more widely in 1850, to seaports and into newspaper columns, to be debated in saloons and discussed around kitchen tables. Authoritative pronouncements (the *Times,* London: "It is beyond all question that gold, in immense quantities, is being found daily") competed with instinctive uncertainty and suspicion. Readers' confidence gained strength from assurances that "there being no regulations in the mines, some time will pass before the government can control them."

Could it be true, even half of what they read? That nuggets of gold—pocketsful— could be easily found and freely brought home? In family deliberations, fathers and sons, husbands and brothers were eager to believe. Maybe California did offer the means to escape from the toil of fields, the drudgery of factories, from life as lived by fathers and grandfathers, from famine in Ireland, conscription in German duchies, boredom in Buffalo.

The first newspaper reports appeared during the summer of 1848 in Honolulu, Oregon City, Valparaíso, and Callao. From these ports hundreds of men boarded ships bound for San Francisco. From villages in the Mexican state of Sonora thousands walked north to *la abundancia.* A deluge followed in 1849: from Mexico another 6,000 *adventuristas;* from Liverpool and Dublin, Le Havre and Bordeaux, Sydney and Hobart, scores of ships carried at least 17,000 goldseekers. From the United States the westward trails were crowded with more than 42,000 '49ers, while another 25,000 reached El Dorado by sea. In April 1850 the overwhelmed harbor master at San Francisco estimated the number who had landed during the previous twelve months at over 62,000, from ports around the globe. For years thereafter, goldseekers by the hard-to-count thousands pushed ashore at California's suddenly famous city.

How could news of gold in the foothills of a distant land cause men by the scores of thousands to leave homes and families, to journey across oceans and continents, believing—indeed promising wives and parents—they would return in a few months, at most a year, with gold enough to make dreams come true? The confidence that sent them on their way was perfectly expressed by a woman in Baltimore who wrote her mother to report her husband's decision to join the rush. "Joseph has borrowed the money to go. But I am full of bright visions that never before filled my mind, because at the best of times I have never thought of much beyond a living, but now I am confident of being well off."

That confidence in Joseph's success in California was founded on trustworthy authority, the word of the president of the United States. On December 5, 1848, in his State of the Union message sent to the Thirtieth Congress, President James K. Polk officially confirmed and validated "the abundance of gold in that territory." Thereafter a contagion of confidence spread through the thirty states and around the world, encouraging many thousands like Joseph to borrow "the money to go," in defiance of the old rule of frugality. And causing wives to expect sudden success, contrary to their mother-taught dictum of patience and hard work. A few months "in the mines" would put an end to poverty and toil, to babies dying for lack of money to buy medicine.

Not only farmers, laborers, merchants, and businessmen looked to California gold as the means to obtain longed-for privileges and new social status. Even for men of wealth and position, the golden metal could assure competitive advantage and increased influence. But camouflaged by the excitement and tumult of the gold mania, there must have been a good many men who found unspoken motives for joining the exodus: a welcome chance to gain freedom from a domineering father, to shed the plight of a youngest son, to leave behind a tiresome wife. And for the lovelorn, gold might even win the hand of a beautiful woman.

That was the power of the news from California.

Beyond President Polk's endorsement of the reports and rumors, two practical considerations helped to justify leaving wives and children, jobs and parents. First, everyone understood that goldseekers would be free to take their nuggets and gold dust out of California. This miraculous opportunity stood in sharp contrast to the mineral's history, in which gold always belonged to kings and lords, or at least great landowners. But in 1848 simple folk had found California's treasure and claimed it for their own, and no one—not even the government and its army—had contested their claims to the plunder. And they had found so much gold, there would be plenty for all. If gold had been discovered in the streambeds and hillsides of North Carolina or Spain or India, the presiding governor or king or nabob would have protected his resource from trespassers with soldiers and stern laws, or at least he would have extracted official revenues through special taxes and levies. Only in California was the treasure left to be gathered and carried off by a multitude of foreigners.

The second consideration lay in the benign circumstances of California's interior. What if gold had been found in the midst of a vast desert or in the dense recesses of a jungle or in a land defended by warlike inhabitants? Such dangers would have deterred all but the most daring adventurers. And their enterprise would have been judged as rash by families and friends—not appropriate for loans, not approved for husbands and fathers.

But no such dangers were foreseen in California. Well known by 1849 for its sunny climate and scattering of easygoing Californios, the province belonged—more or less—to the United States, a nation that welcomed immigrants. And all reports placed "the goldfields" in gentle hills not far from the coast, easily reached by riverboats and trails through open country with mild winter seasons. The docility of California seemed to justify the long journey, giving it the imprimatur of "the right thing to do" for the betterment of one's family.

Thus the world's most coveted commodity beckoned from what seemed to be almost comfortable surroundings. After a few weeks' digging, or a few months' profiteering in San Francisco's booming economy, one's hoard, exempt from taxes or other inconveniences, could be safely stowed on board ship and carried home to finance a new life. Never had there been such an opportunity—for Cantonese peasants and New York City lawyers alike.

THE HAWAIIAN SCHOONER *Louise* sailed from San Francisco on May 31, 1848, dropping anchor at Honolulu June 17. A few days later the editor of the weekly *Polynesian* reported news of gold mined in such quantities that he predicted the city's merchants would soon receive payment on their California customers' long-overdue accounts. Through the summer, each issue of the newspaper told of ships sailing with every berth and all available deck space sold to expectant miners. Manifests listed potatoes, onions, oranges, bananas, and pineapples, turkeys and chickens, for the hungry San Francisco market.* In greatest demand, pickaxes and shovels were shipped from Honolulu by the thousands, along with consignments of boots and clothing. On July 15 the *Polynesian* proclaimed: "The little city of Honolulu has never before witnessed such an excitement as the gold fever has created. . . . The people of California now look upon their gold region as a bank upon which they have only to present a check, to draw what amount they wish. From this our planters and traders will doubtless reap a rich harvest."

California's thrilling news reached Oregon the first week of August, delivered by ships sailing from San Francisco to Portland. They returned with gold-seekers crammed into whatever space could be found amid stacks of lumber and barrels of flour. "Oregon is convulsed by an excitement such as never before felt here," reported the weekly *Oregon Spectator* on September 7. "What power had gold! Many excellent citizens are leaving . . . , some by sea, some by land with horses and wagons." By mid-October the paper estimated that "the gold fever has swept about 3,000 from Oregon into the

mines of California." The first overland company of 150 men and 50 wagons set out in September under the leadership of Peter H. Burnett, who in little more than a year would be California's first elected governor—another example of California being open to and governed by outsiders.

When Sam Brannan's pack mules carrying his "booster" edition of the *California Star* reached the Missouri frontier in early August, newspapers in St. Joseph and St. Louis reprinted excerpts, most frequently that beguiling report about gold being collected "at random and without trouble." Meanwhile, the first official messenger from California, U.S. Navy lieutenant Edward Beale, sailed from Monterey on July 1 carrying Larkin's report to the secretary of state and Commodore Thomas ap Catesby Jones's dispatch to the secretary of the navy, as well as public letters from Larkin and Walter Colton—and samples of California gold. After a remarkably fast journey across Mexico, Beale arrived in Washington on September 16. His gold specimens aroused great excitement. So did the publication of Larkin's and Colton's letters, the first appearing in the *New York Herald* on August 19 and the latter in New York and Philadelphia papers a few days later. To the eastern states Colton announced with his usual flourish: "Your streams have minnows, ours are paved with gold."

Some editors, foreseeing circulation gains, caught the fever and published whatever "news" they could get from California, including a letter that predicted "a Peruvian harvest of precious metals." Others sought to diminish such glittering pronouncements, warning their readers against being taken in by California's promoters, who hoped merely to increase immigration. This backlash of skepticism cooled the fever during the fall of 1848, just as editors in San Francisco and Monterey had sobered local ardor back in the spring.

But not all accounts of the gold region's bounty were easily tarnished by scoffing newspaper men. Military Governor Richard Mason's authoritative report of August 17 had been sent with an exhibit

---

* Ship arrivals at Honolulu rose from 180 in 1849 to 469 during 1850. A barrel of potatoes that sold in Hawaii for $2 brought $27 in San Francisco in 1849. That price differential soon moderated, but prices fluctuated wildly in Honolulu for several years, affected by the changing supply and demand in California.

We are quite sure that it is the duty of the newspapers to use all means in their power to repress rather than stimulate the prevailing excitement on the subject of gold in California. But we must publish all the authentic intelligence from that region, and of what avail is sedate or sage admonitory comment in the face of the glittering, dazzling news?

Editorial in *Buffalo Morning Express,*
January 26, 1849

more eye-popping than Beale's, packed in a box called a "tea caddy" and entrusted to two U.S. Army officers (double protection to ensure safe delivery): 230 ounces of raw gold nuggets and gold dust. Arriving in Washington amid November sleet, the gleaming sample of California treasure was put on display at the War Department, where it excited the imaginations of government officials and throngs of visitors. The ancient dream of the kings of Spain had come true, but for a new people and a new government.

As he prepared his final message to Congress, President Polk must have savored Mason's judgment that "there is more gold in the country drained by the Sacramento and San Joaquin rivers than will pay the cost of the present war with Mexico a hundred times over." On December 5, 1848, the president sent his State of the Union message to the Capitol. Midway through this encomium to his own wise administration, Polk finished off the naysayers who had so harshly criticized his expansionist war with Mexico, first by boasting about the acquisition of San Francisco Bay (where "a great emporium will doubtless arise on the California coast") and then (claiming hindsight as foresight) by asserting "it was known that mines of precious metals existed to a considerable extent in California at the time of its acquisition. Recent discoveries render it probable that these mines are more extensive and valuable than was anticipated."

Encouraged by Mason's temperate yet optimistic assessment, President Polk next penned language that would sweep aside all those who might still doubt the wondrous news from California: "The accounts of the abundance of gold in that territory are of such extraordinary character as would scarcely command belief were they not corroborated by the authentic reports of officers in the public service who have visited the mineral district and derived the facts which they detail from personal observation. . . . The effects produced by the discovery of these rich mineral deposits and the success which has attended the labours of those who have resorted to them have produced a surprising change in the state of affairs in California."*

POLK

There it was, a message as irrefutable as Sam Brannan's shiny bottle held aloft for ready-to-believe San Franciscans: official proof, a presidential endorsement—just what Americans needed to overcome doubts and scoffing neighbors, to persuade wives and in-laws, creditors and business partners, that a man could not stay home and ignore such an opportunity. For farmers in Massachusetts and Illinois, city workers in Cincinnati and Philadelphia, discouraged by the humdrum prospects of their daily routine; for restless veterans newly discharged from the war with Mexico; for men dreaming of escape from an empty marriage or from growing debts, the president's message seemed to offer salvation. Who was not tempted by the astonishing prospect of a quick fortune to be taken from the wondrous rivers of the Sierra Nevada?

Editorial restraint crumbled before the rush of exuberance, led by Horace Greeley, famed editor of

* Beyond validating the richness of California's "gold mines," President Polk expressed his concern that the inhabitants of California "have been left without any regularly organized government . . . to protect them from the inevitable consequences of anarchy." In urging Congress to establish a territorial government, he asserted that further delay would be "irrational."

the nationally read *New York Tribune.* He foresaw in California's abundance "the Age of Gold" and judged that "whatever else they may lack, our children will not be destitute of gold." On December 11 the rival *Herald* described the "gold mania" buzzing through New York City. Two weeks later it published the first of four special issues devoted to California, with a helpful map showing the distance from Monterey to Coloma as an easy 25 miles—135 miles short of reality.

THE WORLD RESPONDS

PRESIDENT POLK'S MESSAGE REACHED GREAT Britain via the royal steamship *Cambria* and was published in its entirety (all 15,500 words) on December 22, 1848, in London's *Times*, accompanied by reprints of "gold fever" stories from the *New York Herald* and the *Washington Union.* On January 13, 1849, an observer in Liverpool reported: "The gold excitement here and in London exceeds anything ever known or heard of. . . . Nothing is talked about but the new El Dorado. Companies are organizing in London in great numbers for the promised land. We hear it stated that not less than fourteen vessels have already been chartered and are nearly or quite filled with passengers and freight."

So it would be for months to come, a swelling stream of hopeful Britons setting out for California, among them tin and coal miners from Wales and Cornwall and several thousand Irishmen fleeing a tormented land, where blight had wiped out the potato crop. Thousands more would come in later years.

In Scotland the miseries of unemployed workers and of tenants forced off their crofts left many families desperate to find the means to escape to the New World. A ten-year-old boy in one of those scarred families remembered years later his thrill in reading descriptions of California, its beauties and gold mines. Of the moment in February 1849 when his father announced he had sold their home to pay for tickets to America, John Muir recalled his anticipation of "boundless woods full of mysterious good things and trees full of sugar, growing in ground full of gold."

Through 1848–49 innumerable young men across Europe joined the Irish, Scots, Welsh, and Cornishmen sailing west to pursue the promise of gold in a new land. Insurrections, abdications, wars of independence, and wars of dynastic restoration had released a chaos of rioting and street fighting in Paris (12,000 killed, 25,000 arrested in June 1848), demonstrations in Vienna and Prague, strikes in Berlin. Amidst such tumult, the news from California offered compelling reason to embrace an old idea: emigration to the New World, in 1849 to "the goldfields." Would-be miners boarded hundreds of ships that carried them fourteen thousand miles around Cape Horn to San Francisco, distant gateway to a new life.

More than any other country in Europe, France welcomed the news with enthusiasm. Having restored law and order, the new government in 1849 encouraged the formation of societies or associations that sold shares of stock to raise money for sending workers "to colonize California." This emigration would remove "unfortunates" and "surplus population." For this worthy purpose, the French government saw California as a land without organized government, a place that would belong to those who could get there and harvest its mineral wealth.

On February 14, 1849, an editorial in the staid Parisian newspaper *Journal des Débats* described California's "auriferous fields" as not less than eight hundred miles in length and one hundred miles wide, wherein could be found "gold dust, gold nuggets, gold ingots, weighing from one to twenty-four pounds." Then, the sober judgment: "The most remarkable development of our age in the field of material progress is beyond any contradiction the discovery and exploitation of the goldfields of California."

Promoted by such editorials, the emigration

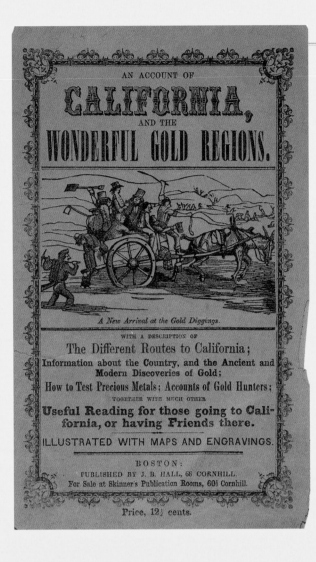

AN ACCOUNT OF

CALIFORNIA,

AND THE

WONDERFUL GOLD REGIONS.

A New Arrival at the Gold Diggings.

WITH A DESCRIPTION OF

The Different Routes to California;

Information about the Country, and the Ancient and
Modern Discoveries of Gold;

How to Test Precious Metals; Accounts of Gold Hunters;

TOGETHER WITH MUCH OTHER

Useful Reading for those going to California, or having Friends there.

ILLUSTRATED WITH MAPS AND ENGRAVINGS.

BOSTON:
PUBLISHED BY J. B. HALL, 66 CORNHILL.
For Sale at Skinner's Publication Rooms, 60½ Cornhill.

Price, 12½ cents.

California Gold.

IMPORTANT OFFICIAL REPORT.

We publish the following description of the Gold Region from the pen of Col. MASON, the Military Commandant of California, being one of the Documents accompanying the President's Message. Our readers will also see rich reports from the gold regions of Virginia:

HEADQUARTERS 10TH MILITARY DEPT.,
MONTEREY, California, Aug. 17, 1848

SIR: I have the honor to inform you that accompanied by Lieut. W. T. Sherman, 3d artillery, A. A. A. General, I started on the 12th of June last to make a tour through the northern part of California. My principal purpose, however, was to visit the newly-discovered gold "placer" in the Valley of the Sacramento. I had proceeded about forty miles, when I was overtaken by an express, bringing me intelligence of the arrival at Monterey of the U. S. ship Southampton, with important letters from Com. Shubrick and Lieut. Col. Burton. I returned at once to Monterey, and dispatched what business was most important, and on the 17th resumed my journey. We reached San Francisco on the 20th, and found that all, or nearly all, its male inhabitants had gone to the mines. The town, which a few months before was so busy and thriving, was then almost deserted.

The excitement caused by the rush for gold in California encouraged publication of numerous "guide books" and the overhaul of old schooners and abandoned hulks advertised as "first class vessels" for the voyage to El Dorado. As the primary symptom of gold fever, public gullibility flourished in many forms, not least a willingness to believe that gold deposits had been found in New Jersey and Virginia. The latter sample of fevered imagination is exhibited above in the *New York Daily Tribune*'s lead paragraph to Colonel Mason's "Official Report," published December 8, 1848.

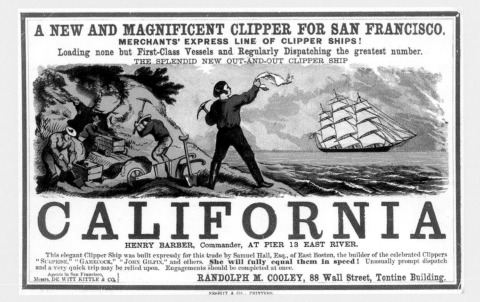

A NEW AND MAGNIFICENT CLIPPER FOR SAN FRANCISCO.
MERCHANTS' EXPRESS LINE OF CLIPPER SHIPS!
Loading none but First-Class Vessels and Regularly Dispatching the greatest number.
THE SPLENDID NEW OUT-AND-OUT CLIPPER SHIP

CALIFORNIA

HENRY BARBER, Commander, AT PIER 13 EAST RIVER.

This elegant Clipper Ship was built expressly for this trade by Samuel Hall, Esq., of East Boston, the builder of the celebrated Clippers "SURPRISE," "GAMECOCK," "JOHN GILPIN," and others. **She will fully equal them in speed!** Unusually prompt dispatch and a very quick trip may be relied upon. Engagements should be completed at once.

Agents in San Francisco,
Messrs. DE WITT KITTLE & CO.

RANDOLPH M. COOLEY, 88 Wall Street, Tontine Building.

NESBIT & CO., PRINTERS.

The high-priced San Francisco market immediately attracted the world's merchandise. Shipbuilders in Boston and New York responded with the development of the California clipper. These fast, sleek ships disdained passengers in favor of high-value cargo, shipped for as much as $1 per cubic foot from New York in a standard four months, and by 1851, in the record time of 89 days.

societies flourished. One of these, La Californienne, sent its first ship from Le Havre on November 27, 1849. During 1850 similar associations sold millions of shares using names such as La Fortune, L'Eldorado, Compagnie Universelle des Mines d'Or, and La Toison d'Or (Golden Fleece). One company modestly promised that each worker's share would increase in value fourteen times in the first year. To assure their subscribers that such returns would be attainable, the directors reminded investors that the company had utilized "all the resources provided by science" and had secured exclusive use of mining machinery invented by a university professor.

DES MILLIONS POUR UN SOU!

MINES D'OR DE LA CALIFORNIE

FRENCH BROADSIDE

The inevitable collapse of French gold rush mania came in the last months of 1850, ironically camouflaged by the rise of the government-sponsored and -managed "Loterie des Lingots d'Or." This immensely popular scheme sold over six million chances to win one of 244 gold bars *(lingots d'or)* and hundreds of smaller prizes. With the proceeds, the government shipped 3,885 emigrants to California. Other Frenchmen, not lucky enough to win subsidized passage, obtained berths with relative ease because merchants in Paris and Bordeaux regularly sent vessels to San Francisco with cargoes of wine, champagne, bottled fruit, and whatever other specialties they thought would sell in that celebratory market. By 1853 there were an estimated 28,000 Frenchmen in California.*

---

* Though every one of the eighty-three societies and associations organized to offer ordinary French citizens a share in California's gold proved to be incompetent or fraudulent, the government's strategy of encouraging emigration evolved into a great success. It has been estimated that French miners and businessmen sent home $80 million by the end of 1851, gained not only from mining but also from the wide variety of businesses they developed—vineyards, hotels, restaurants, banks, and mercantile companies.

Compared to this Gallic enthusiasm, the rest of Europe responded slowly. In Italy only a few hundred hopeful miners boarded trading ships from Genoa and other ports. From the German states some three thousand emigrated to California during 1849 and 1850, with many more thereafter. Few Spaniards joined the rush, while emigrants from Portugal exhibited their ancient mercantile heritage by favoring California's commercial potentials over the lure of its goldfields. A pamphlet published in Oporto in 1849 pointed out opportunities for profits in California's unique economy: "The innumerable throngs of people flocking into California from every quarter of the globe . . . lack even the most indispensable comforts of life, although they have plenty of gold to buy them. . . . For this reason the country will for many years be the best market for European products."

Despite its proximity and historic association, Mexico did not learn of California's latest gold rush until September or even October 1848, when news reached the northern state of Sonora. Its impact, however, was immediate. By December, according to one account, three thousand Sonorans, including some women and children, had taken to the old trails that led north into California's San Joaquin Valley. One witness to this migration as it passed through the present-day Arizona-California border area exclaimed in his diary that "Mexicans from Sonora are passing us daily on their way to the *abundancia,* the gold mines! This is all we hear, The Mines! . . . The whole state of Sonora is on the move, passing us in gangs daily. They say 'we will make our fortunes. Not a doubt of it.'"

By the summer of 1849 at least six thousand Sonorans had crowded into the southern mining region, setting up their largest camps around a settlement that became known as Sonora. And more of "their kind"—Latin foreigners—were coming from Chile and Peru. The news reached Valparaíso on August 19, 1848, when the brigantine *I.R.S.* from San Francisco anchored at that port to deliver a cargo symbolic of both California's past and its

Eastern cartoonists found easy targets in the excitement and grandiose excesses of the rush west. "California Gold," an 1849 lithograph by Nathaniel Currier, carried the tongue-in-cheek caption, "An accurate drawing of the famous hill of gold, which has been put into a scow by the owner and attached to a sperm whale towing it around the Horn." The 1849 lithograph "By Air Route" spoofed one of the many outlandish conveyances promoted to the gullible.

The great rush to California attracted the attention of international satirists as well, especially the French cartoonist known as Cham. In his weekly cartoon for a Parisian newspaper he poked fun at the spectacle of greedy California prospectors moving massive boulders of gold under human, mule, and even crocodile harness.

CROQUIS CALIFORNIENS, PAR CHAM.

Aspect général de la Californie depuis que l'on y trouve des lingots d'or de plus gros en plus gros.

future: cattle hides that sold for $7.40 per hundred pounds and gold that brought $17.50 per ounce. Seeking that future, at least one thousand Chileans had sailed for San Francisco by year's end; five thousand more Chileans and Peruvians followed in 1849 and 1850. As they and all the others rushed to California, American miners argued for control over these foreigners. But how could there be? Who could hold them back at San Francisco or in the mining camps? Three thousand passengers pushed ashore at San Francisco during one week in September 1849, most of them from ships flying foreign flags.

One of the eleven foreign vessels that sailed into San Francisco Bay on October 6, 1849, came from Sydney, Australia, where the symptoms of gold fever rivaled those in Paris. Throughout Sydney placards and broadsides displayed bold headings: "Gold. Gold in California!" Newspapers proclaimed "the extraordinary news." A shopkeeper in Hobart, Tasmania, offered a new invention called "California Gold Grease." If the purchaser covered himself with this grease and rolled down a California hill, only loose gold would adhere to him. The fever spread even more virulently when ships returned to Australia from San Francisco with reports of cargoes that had sold for prices beyond belief and of hundreds of people who, penniless a year before, now sported about with fortunes of $10,000.

By 1850 in Sydney and other Australian harbors, nearly every ship that could float was undergoing repairs or scheduled to sail for San Francisco. Berths sold quickly, and wharves piled up with barrels of nails, crates of ready-made clothes, bottled beer, woolen blankets, and bricks. There was even talk of women being attracted

FRENCH CARTOON

to California. Reports published in Sydney told of a Mrs. Farnham in the United States who planned to deliver a shipload of respectable young women "who have no prospect at home but the needle."*

In another reported strategy to tap the California marriage market, a Valparaíso merchant advertised for "two hundred young, virtuous girls" to be shipped for "honorable marriage to the thousands of North Americans who have made their fortunes in the mines." Would Australian women, already in short supply in their homeland, be tempted by this competition for rich husbands? Anxiety and anticipation proved unwarranted. Port records at San Francisco (surely accurate in this count) showed for the last six months of 1849 that only 102 women arrived from that far Pacific colony, and for all of 1850 only an additional 895. So it was in other countries. As in a war, the women waited back home.

---

* In February 1849 Mrs. Eliza Woodson Farnham (later recognized as a pioneer feminist) issued a circular from New York City which announced her belief "that the presence of women would be one of the surest checks upon the many evils that are to be apprehended in California." This widely distributed broadside further informed its readers that Mrs. Farnham planned to recruit 100 to 130 females "not under twenty-five years of age, who shall bring from their clergyman or some other authority" testimonials as to their virtue and education. Each of these "intelligent, virtuous, and efficient women" would be required to contribute $250 to defray the expenses of the voyage and to assure funding for their accommodation prior to presumed proposals of marriage. The optimistic Mrs. Farnham announced that she had "engaged the New York-built packet ship *Angelique* . . . ready to sail from New York about the 12th or 15th of April."

News of this crusade, and the prospect of a boatload of females landing in San Francisco, stimulated enthusiasm and expectations somewhat contrary to those of Mrs. Farnham. The *San Francisco Alta* irreverently reported that the redoubtable lady had searched the eastern seaboard for "Grade A spareribs" as the cargo for the bride-ship *Angelique*. To everyone's sorrow, Mrs. Farnham's high standards for rectitude and financial well-being discouraged all but three or four ladies from signing on; the others (speculated the *Alta*) "had passed the age when matrimonial alliances are sought with any degree of avidity."

FEVER IN THE STATES

From the Atlantic to the Missouri frontier, from the Great Lakes to the gulf ports, newspaper editors played up California's unfolding gold story with florid phrases and excited rhetoric. "The spirit of emigration which is carrying off thousands to California . . . increases and expands every day," the *New York Herald* trumpeted on January 11, 1849. "All classes of our citizens seem to be under the influence of this extraordinary mania [which] exceeds everything in the history of commercial adventure . . . and can only be paralleled by that which sprang up in Spain and other parts of Europe by the discovery of the mineral wealth of Mexico and Peru by the expeditions of Cortez and Pizarro."

Even more compelling than editorial fervor, what inspired the greatest expectations and challenged the fainthearted were personal letters sent back from California to Illinois and Missouri from settlers who had traveled overland prior to 1849 and had become—to their astonishment—gold miners. Their letters were eagerly sought by local newspapers, to be reprinted in turn by dailies and weeklies in distant towns and states. Written in the familiar language of neighbor and family, these personal accounts told of digging gold worth thousands of dollars by men learning as they worked, experimenting with simple, even haphazard, tools and methods.

In Jackson, Missouri, a letter from the diggings arrived at the McClellan home. "You know Bryant, the carpenter who used to work for Ebenezer Dixon, well, he has dug more gold in the last six months than a mule can pack." More of the same came to Tennessee in May 1849, when the *Memphis Eagle* published a letter from Peter Burnett, who had led Oregonians into the gold mines. "Men here are nearly crazy with the riches forced suddenly into their pockets. . . . The accounts you have seen of the gold region are not overcolored. The gold is positively inexhaustible."

This kind of exhilaration caused some skepti-

In literally every state through the winter and spring of 1849, newspapers published letters sent from California. Like germs, these reports spread the gold fever. Though more high-flown and imaginative than most, this letter from a Reverend Fulton must have raised some temperatures in Kalamazoo, Michigan:

Here the streams are paved with gold. It sparkles in the sands of the valleys, it glitters in the coronet of the steep cliffs. Send us a mint and we will startle Europe from her dreams. We have not taken California in vain, and we will vindicate the treasure she has tossed us, if you will send us that mint. I've used strong terms, but who can use weak ones? Can a man smoke his pipe under the flaming crater of Vesuvius? Or speak in whispers when an earthquake rocks?

(Kalamazoo) Michigan Gazette, March 29, 1849

cism, in one case expressed by the editor of the *Jonesborough [Tennessee] Whig and Independent Journal,* who reminded his readers that California's gold belonged to the federal government. A killjoy among the boosters, he predicted that Washington would not permit foreigners or even citizens to pocket "the public treasure with perfect impunity," but would put a stop to "this system of promiscuous, piratical plunder." Contrary to this editor's forecast, the U.S. Congress had no intent, and certainly no power, to stop the miners' gold harvest. Indeed, Governor Mason's pragmatic decision to permit all to mine freely would prevail for the next twenty-five years, until 1884.

An excited American people neither expected nor wanted their government to interfere with gold mining in California. From Maine to Texas they believed the newly acquired province offered a miraculous chance to become wealthy, not at some distant time, but as soon as a son, husband, brother, or father could get to the banks of the American, the Feather, or any one of those other rivers with strange names—the Mokelumne, Cosumnes, and Tuolumne. There would be plenty for all, a windfall for families that had never expected much more than to make a living.

Even for those who chose to stay at home, the rush created opportunities. Manufacturers of moneybelts, "complete India Rubber outfits," air pillows, bowie knives, and all manner of camping gear advertised their products as essential to surviving the trek west and to succeeding in the land of gold. Inventors attested to the infallibility of their patented mining machines, including a "hydro-centrifugal Chrysolyte or California Gold Finder" and an "Archimedes Gold Washing Machine." One especially imaginative entrepreneur announced an "aerial locomotive" (a steam-powered balloon) capable of carrying fifty to one hundred passengers from New York to California "pleasantly and safely" in three days, at a fare of $50. The advertisement advised that service would begin in April 1849 and that two hundred tickets had already been sold.

More realistic appraisals of the journey urged preparations for months of travel, cataloguing the dangers of various overland trails and the two major ocean routes. For those who lived near the Atlantic and gulf coasts, the voyage around Cape Horn or via the Isthmus of Panama seemed the easiest and safest way to reach the Golden Gate. But which to take? The 14,000-mile cape route would keep its passengers at sea five to six, even eight months, a frustrating prospect for anyone determined to get to California before the richest deposits were scooped up. The isthmus route to San Francisco was advertised to take a mere four to six weeks, but its liabilities included a trek through equatorial jungle and the risk of fever.

Forty years of Yankee trading with California had established confidence in rounding the Horn, and that uninterrupted voyage allowed passengers to take bulky mining gear and even trading goods

Mother o Mother, why do you still resist my going? My mind is made up to go. Why o why cant you let me go with a cherful heart and with a well made up mind that i will try to do well?

James Barnes, letter of October 21, 1849

for sale in San Francisco. This convinced the largest number of Argonauts to choose the cape route during the first year. On April 19, 1849, the *New York Herald* reported 14,191 embarkations from U.S. ports in 225 ships southbound to the Horn and California since December 1848. The same survey recorded 3,547 passengers who boarded 52 ships bound for the port of Chagres on the Atlantic side of the isthmus, there to commence a three- or four-day crossing to Panama City and a presumed connection with another ship to San Francisco. A third count reported 1,980 who had chosen by that April date to sail to the gulf ports of Texas and Mexico, primarily Brazos and Vera Cruz, where overland trails led—eventually—to Mazatlán, San Blas, or Acapulco and hoped-for ships to the gold coast. All together, the *Herald*'s survey tallied an impressive 19,718 goldseekers departing in 309 vessels—a rush indeed. And yet those numbers reflected only the American emigration through mid-April 1849. From May to December hundreds more ships—782 in all—reached San Francisco, many from foreign ports, each landing its complement of '49ers.

How many passengers were delivered by this vast fleet? The first surge of seaborne immigrants reached San Francisco in April of 1849. Overwhelmed by the hundreds pushing ashore day after day, the harbor master somehow came up with an estimate for the nine months of April through December 1849—31,303. Beginning in July, a more intriguing task was undertaken—to count the number of women. By year's end: 599. And for all of 1850, only 2,402!

Merchants and hucksters saw an opportunity to cash in on the hopes and fears of embarking '49ers by selling a variety of mechanical devices purported to ease the tedious labor of mining. These advertisements from newspapers in Paris and New York offered elaborate gold-washing machines and gold finders. But few such contraptions were really intended to work or even survive the rough trip to the goldfields. Their real purpose was to exploit would-be millionaires.

BRUCE'S HYDRO-CENTRIFUGAL CHRY-SOLYTE, OR CALIFORNIA GOLD-FINDER.—This machine, acknowledged by all who have witnessed its operation to be superior to anything of the kind, is now ready for exhibition.

Do not purchase of any until you have seen this. Call 167 Pearl-st. 1st floor, near Wall; or at the corner of Pike and Cherry sts. where it will be put in operation.   j16 1w*

Rufus Porter, the New England inventor who founded *Scientific American*, offered the "best route to California"—on board an "aerial locomotive," his concept of a giant balloon propelled by twin steam engines. He claimed the flight would take only seven days round trip and signed up at least two hundred passengers at $50 each before engineering realities grounded the venture.

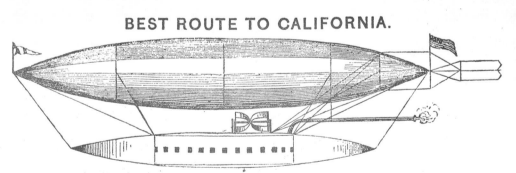

BEST ROUTE TO CALIFORNIA.

R. PORTER & CO., (office, room No. 40 in the Sun Buildings,—entrance 128 Fulton-street, New-York,) are making active progress in the construction of an Aerial Transport, for the express purpose of carrying passengers between New York and California. This transport will have a capacity to carry from 50 to 100 passengers, at a speed of 60 to 100 miles per hour. It is expected to put this machine in operation about the 1st of April, 1849. It is proposed to carry a limited number of passengers—not exceeding 300—for $50, including board, and the transport is expected to make a trip to the gold region and back in seven days. The price of passage to California is fixed at $200, with the exception above mentioned. Upwards of 200 passage tickets at $50 each have been engaged prior to Feb. 15. Books open for subscribers as above.

This broadside advertised a four-month passage to California on the packet *Apollo* in 1849. After departure from an ice-encumbered harbor in New York, passengers endured confinement between decks, "the oniony smell of which was enough to vomit a horse." By the time the owner's son marked the last position on his chart of the ship's voyage to San Francisco, eight months had elapsed.

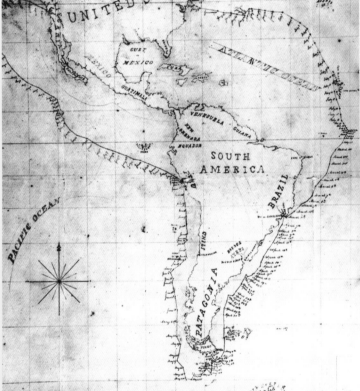

The *Apollo*'s owner decided to capitalize on the soaring property market in San Francisco by permanently mooring his ship at Central Wharf and leasing storage space in its hold. This 1850 lithograph boasts that the "Apollo Warehouses offer uncommon advantages for storage of all descriptions. They are approachable for lighters at nearly all tides, while for commodiousness, business convenience, and safety from fire and all other risks, they are truly unsurpassed."

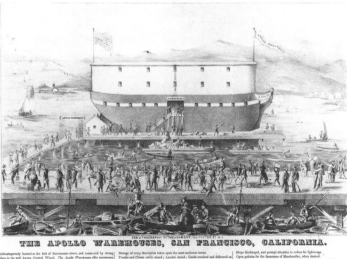

More reflective of the deluge, another estimate calculated the number of passengers for the year April 1849 through March 1850—62,000. A fantastic statistic, and even more so when translated into the reality of an invading force of impatient men, all demanding immediate accommodation of their hungers and needs: food, whiskey, shelter, entertainment, transport to the mines, doctors, medicines, and burial plots. Profits went to those quick, tough, and imaginative enough to supply those necessities amidst the confusion of San Francisco's transformation from a village to a booming city.

Around the world, the rush to California produced innumerable, unexpected needs—on a huge scale. Satisfying this demand in turn spawned opportunities for schemers, speculators, and even honest businessmen. For instance, there had never been such a sudden demand for passenger ships. The world's maritime economy was disrupted when trading companies removed their ships from established trade routes to collect fatter profits by carrying goldseekers and speculative cargoes to that sudden magnet, San Francisco. As well, old whaling ships, retired schooners at rest on mudflats, and even dismasted hulks used for floating storage were towed to repair yards, made minimally seaworthy, fitted with tiers of bunks, and advertised as first-class passenger ships. Most were quickly booked for early sailing dates.

Insatiable demand encouraged shipowners to push ticket prices to levels that shocked old tars and

banking clerks alike. In New York, Philadelphia, and other East Coast ports, cabin rates on ships "doubling the Cape" reached $350 to $450. A bunk between decks sold for $150 to $250. Adding ticket prices and the cost of personal equipment to the need for expense money (for days ashore at Rio and Valparaíso) brought a typical '49er's total to what many could raise only by borrowing. That they found willing lenders testified to the national confidence in the goldseekers' prospects. Prosperous businessmen and people too timid or old to join the rush often financed young men who signed contracts that called for sharing mining profits with their backers—the West's first grubstakers.

While many cape-bound '49ers bought tickets as individuals, others economized by joining organizations, known as joint-stock companies, which purchased berths in blocks for their members. Some of these associations bought ships and outfitted them to transport their members and speculative cargoes. Hundreds of such "companies" were formed across the United States for both the sea routes and the overland trails, in the tradition of neighbors and businessmen pooling resources to accomplish community tasks such as road building and investing in cargoes for sale in foreign markets. Their popularity was typified by the record in Massachusetts where 102 joint-stock companies sent 4,567 members to California in 1849. In contrast, 1,500 goldseekers sailed to San Francisco from Massachusetts as individuals, all of them via the cape.

Company rosters usually numbered thirty to fifty names, though the larger associations that bought ships often had as many as two hundred members. Invariably, these voluntary organizations were governed by "articles of association" or a "constitution," requiring election of officers and decisions by majority vote. Puritanical rules of conduct often prohibited swearing, alcohol, and gambling, with fines and other punishments defined. One company included a provision designed to protect its members if they gathered more gold than their ship could safely carry on her return voyage:

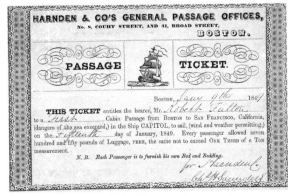

SAN FRANCISCO PASSAGE TICKET

the company's excess treasure would remain in California under proper guard until means could be arranged for returning the weighty asset to Massachusetts.

No matter how great the fortunes anticipated from mining, most seagoing associations could not forsake the opportunities for profit presented by the now famous San Francisco market, with its demand for imported goods. Such speculation delivered surprising quantities of smoked beef and writing paper, canned lobster and honey, varnish and Epsom salts. Spurred by reports of the construction boom in San Francisco, one savvy company from Beverly, Massachusetts, sailed in August 1849 with 63,000 feet of lumber, 10,000 bricks, and eight prefabricated houses.

Through 1849 and 1850, national attention was captivated by the scenes of thousands of young men grappling with trunks and gear as they left cities, villages, and farms. Under the heading "Ho! for California," local weeklies and city dailies printed long lists of "Californians" who carried with them the hopes and expectations of those who would wait at home for their return with a "pocket full of rocks." Like soldiers off to war, these "boys" waved goodbye amid the sounds and colors of bands blaring and flags waving. Speeches, editorials, and sermons offered moral admonitions and hearty wishes for their "success on the Pacific shores."

Many promised to keep diaries to record their part in what everyone knew to be a historic event. For those on ships heaving and wallowing down the Atlantic, diary keeping became a grim recital of miseries and complaints: seasickness, wretched food, quarrels with shipmates, and stench below decks; the boredom of days adrift in dead calms and in scorching heat, followed by the icy terror of shrieking winds and mountainous waves at the polar tip of South America—the infamous Horn.

Temporary escape from shipboard torments came with provisioning calls at South American ports. At Rio de Janeiro, twelve gold rush ships arrived in a single day during 1849, sending ashore

more than a thousand men, all hungry for fresh food, water, and excitement. These were the first "ugly Americans." They scoffed at what they quickly judged to be Brazil's backwardness. Some drank too much, others exhibited rampant nationalism, sometimes penalized by a stay in a dirty jail. At Valparaíso, "the great number of Americans on shore . . . seemed to nationalize the town. Yankees did just as they pleased . . . but the great California emigration has been a godsend to this place. They can well put up with the Yankee dare-devil spirit for the sake of Yankee gold."

From the west coast of South America to California the interminable voyage continued for four, five weeks, sometimes two months and longer. Sailing against prevailing winds and currents, the ships tacked laboriously west, often as far as the longitude of the Hawaiian Islands, before gaining favorable westerlies that would carry them to San Francisco. As a final torment, months of cramped and undernourished shipboard life left the passengers weak and pale when they finally came ashore, their company organizations often demoralized by sickness and quarreling. Too weak and discouraged to face the hard work of mining, many cape passengers chose to tarry in San Francisco, where it seemed possible to seek their fortunes in the easier circumstances of that booming economy.

In contrast to five or even eight months of shipboard confinement, the route via the Isthmus of Panama offered the advantage of a shorter voyage—2,000 miles from New York to Chagres and 3,500 from Panama City to San Francisco, taking an expected time of six to eight weeks. Offsetting that great advantage, lurid reports told of dangers and diseases while traveling the sixty miles across the jungled isthmus. More discouraging, there was the prospect of having to wait weeks at Panama City on the Pacific shore, in hopes of a ship to San Francisco.

Nonetheless, some 6,500 impatient goldseekers chose to gamble on the isthmus route during 1849. They landed at Chagres, a miasmal village at the

Organized by George Gordon, a wealthy New England businessman, Gordon's California Association offered safe passage, camping equipment, and mining tools for $160 a head—a bargain for an eager emigrant facing as much as $250 for just a bunk on most ships headed around the Horn. Gordon's 243-member company sailed in two ships, the first headed south to round Cape Horn and the second to the Caribbean coast of Nicaragua. With his wife and five-year-old daughter, Gordon sailed on the second ship, predicting the trip would take "50 days or 60 at the farthest," including the traverse across Nicaragua and transport up the Pacific coast on a local packet. They reached San Francisco eight months later, and Gordon's California Association, like most companies, promptly disbanded.

TO CALIFORNIA ON SHARES.

TO SAIL ON JANUARY 15th.

Entire Expense for Passage and Outfit $160.

A few persons of industrious habits and who can give undoubted references of their good moral character, can join

GORDON'S CALIFORNIA ASSOCIATION.

This Association consists of **100** members who go in a body well armed, whose object is to go safely, and comfortably fitted out and equipped.

Each member pays **$160**, for which he has passage in a fast sailing vessel, and is found with six months' provisions of the best quality.

The President of the Company, who is a practical geologist, accompanies the expedition, and for the one-fifth share in the profit provides the Association with

CAMP EQUIPMENT,

To every ten men a large tent with oil skin cover.

To every man a hammock, hammock bed, blankets and coverlid, a tin plate, dish, mug, knives and forks, &c.

To every twenty men a Field Cooking Stove, ovens, boilers and kettles. Also,

MACHINERY AND IMPLEMENTS:

Machines for washing in the gold deposits to go by horse power, force pumps, screens, seives, shovels, pick axes, axes, saws, two sets carpenters tools, set of coopers tools, set of blacksmiths tools, including forge, bellows, &c. saddlers and sailmakers tools, tinsmiths tools, &c. saddles and bridles, rifles, fowling pieces, fishing tackle, and agricultural implements.

The Association carries a complete medicine chest and a Physician.

A German assayer with chemical tests and apparatus for trying the value of minerals.

The main body of the Association go by Cape Horn, and a few go across by Mexico as pioneers, to survey locations and prepare the way for the arrival of the rest of the company.

The great object of the Association is, by combining together to make a strong party to insure the *safety* of every member, to have all the assistance that good machinery and science can give in washing for gold, and to have everything comfortable and convenient, so that the trip may be made reasonably pleasant. Good care will be taken of health, and all be brought within a small expense.

The agent of the Association is now in California and doing well.

Apply immediately and if possible personally, at the office of the Association.

A. COCHRANE'S,

143 Walnut St. 2 doors above Sixth, Phila.

The *Articles of Association* can be seen by calling upon

The California Company going from the town of York — in 1849.

Oh! Gold — Gold — the heaviest of all metals.

the following is A list of the men. R. C. Woodward. Dr. Henry Smyser. Henry Hantz. Alexander Klinefelter. George Rupp. Jacob Furney. Alexander Wentz. Alex. Stair, George Laumaster. Joseph McAllier. John Miller. Ham. Hartman. McPherson Barnitz. the above Company Arrived Save in California. & "George B Schmidt.

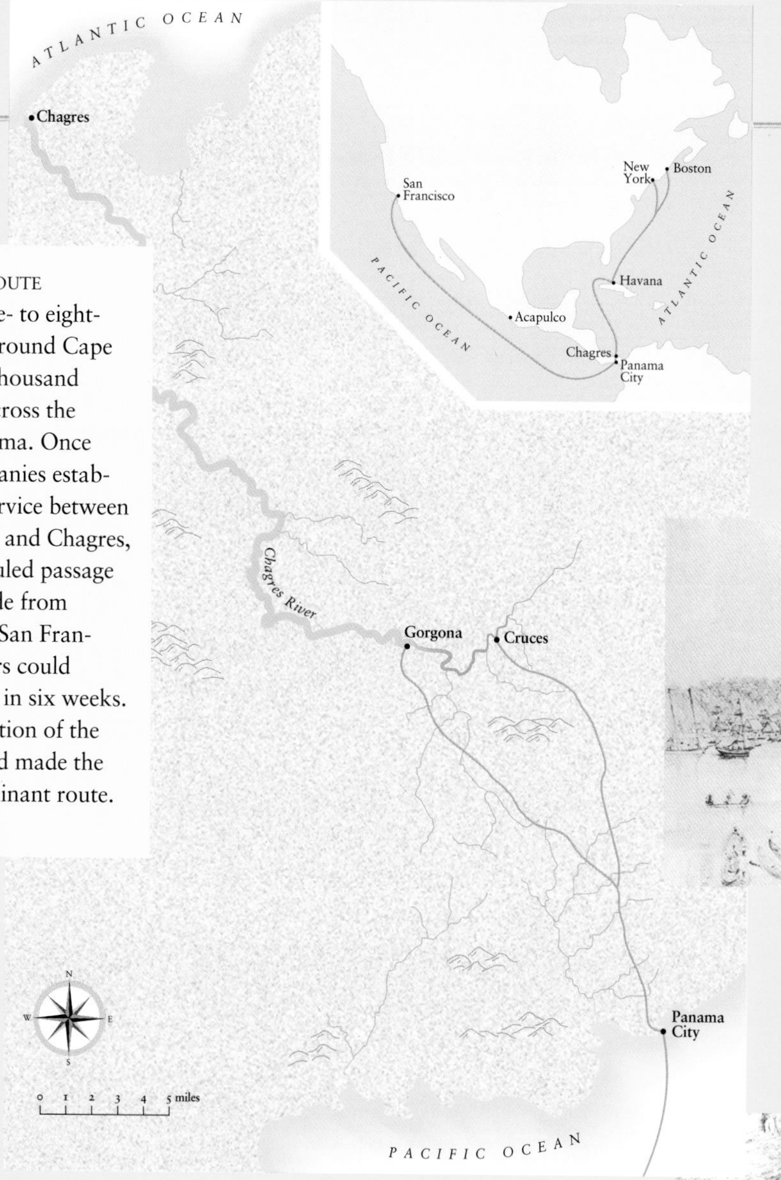

•Chagres

San
Francisco•

New
York• •Boston

PACIFIC OCEAN

•Havana

ATLANTIC OCEAN

•Acapulco

Chagres•
•Panama
City

THE ISTHMUS ROUTE

To avoid the five- to eight-month voyage around Cape Horn, over six thousand '49ers chose to cross the Isthmus of Panama. Once steamship companies established regular service between East Coast ports and Chagres, as well as scheduled passage on the Pacific side from Panama City to San Francisco, goldseekers could reach California in six weeks. In 1855, completion of the Panama Railroad made the isthmus the dominant route.

William H. Dougal, a Connecticut engraver who failed to strike it rich as a merchant in San Francisco, sailed home via Panama in November 1850. At the mouth of the Chagres River he sketched this crowd of California-bound argonauts waiting for transport to the Pacific side of the isthmus.

Chagres River

Gorgona• •Cruces

Panama
City

N
W E
S

0 1 2 3 4 5 miles

PACIFIC OCEAN

German-born Charles Nahl, the artist most often identified with the gold rush, came to California in 1851. He recalled his journey in this painting of a crude boat poled up the Chagres River. In a letter to his father, Nahl described his impressions of the jungle route: "Palms slowly waving their branches . . . full moon over the water reflecting swarming beetles and birds . . . screams of monkeys . . . Indian villages and Negro huts." Another artist, Wallace Baker from Massachusetts, sketched the memorable sight of a female traveler, trekking on mule-back through the twenty-six miles of thick jungle between the head-waters of the Chagres and Panama City at the Pacific shore.

mouth of the Chagres River, which diarists and letter writers among them described as "the very pest-house of disease. . . . The houses are all of the palm-thatched order, except for a few frame buildings. . . . The hotels, which have assumed the names of the crack [first-rate] houses in New York, as the Irving House, United States Hotel, etc., are perfect hog-holes . . . furniture, food, and everything filthy."

For the trip up the Chagres River, the Californians hired native boatmen in dugouts called *bungos* to pole them and their baggage forty miles upstream to the jungle settlement of Gorgona at mid-isthmus. "The river is exceedingly crooked," one adventurer reported. "Palms, bananas, rich vines, reeds, majestic plants, and beautiful flowers crowd upon the stream in lavish luxuriance. . . . Herons, blue and white, and vultures with white shoulders occasionally add to the diversity of the scene. . . . We see parrots swinging up on the branches, monkeys chattering among the trees with an air of impudence and self-security, alligators sunning their unwieldy carcasses on logs, and even a South American tigress."

Such was the writing of ordinary Americans with part-time schooling. What an experience, never to be forgotten, for farmers and millwrights from Michigan, clerks and preachers from Ohio, tanners and gunsmiths from Georgia, Americans in all their self-assured variety, out in the world for the first time, gawking and complaining, amazed and wondering.

When they reached Gorgona (or Cruces, farther upstream) near the river's headwaters, the sweaty travelers took to winding trails, straddling mules through twenty-six miles of dense jungle to reach Panama City and the encouraging sight of the Pacific Ocean. They were thousands of miles closer to California than the cape voyagers, but this triumph swiftly soured. Panama City's miserable hotels were overflowing with goldseekers stranded while they waited for passage to San Francisco. Hundreds camped in tents on the beaches. Frantic to buy or bribe any ticket that would deliver them to California, they waited, many for six weeks or longer, as cholera, fevers, and dysentery menaced them with sickness and death.

Adding a cruel twist to the frustration of waiting was the sight of homebound miners coming ashore when ships from San Francisco did drop anchor off Panama City. To curious and envious men waiting to sail north, many of these arrivals showed off pouches and satchels with gold from the Sierra streams. Would there be enough left when *they* finally got to California? In 1849 a diarist told of meeting "a returning Californian . . . with a box containing $22,000 in gold dust and a four pound lump in one hand. The impatience and excitement . . . already at a high pitch were greatly increased. Life and death were small matters compared with immediate departure."

The impact of so many Americans suddenly swarming into this tropical backwater, with their bluster and rude impatience, profoundly and permanently changed the economy and culture of the isthmus. Though the region belonged to the Republic of Nueva Granada (present-day Colombia) and Panama City's history reached back to 1521, the North Americans scorned the Panamanians, pushing aside local businessmen and organizing their own enterprises to provide for the needs of thousands of transients and to corner the attendant profits. A British traveler noted that "the natives appear to dislike the Americans in general. . . . The Yankees hurry them and cannot endure their slow, lingering ways." Quarreling, street fighting, and a riot were reported in Panama's two newspapers—both owned by Americans—and in San Francisco's papers as well. In October 1849 a diarist waiting on the beach forecast: "There will be serious trouble if the emigration continues. I should not be surprised at any time to hear that the Americans have taken over. . . . They are fast working themselves into the business of the place, and it will not be long before it will be monopolized by them."

Among the impatient Yankees in Panama who could not repress their mercantile appetites while waiting for passage to San Francisco was Collis P.

Whether intent on assuring his wife that his moral character remained unsullied or honestly shocked by the Panamanians and Americans in Panama City, Milo Goss from Illinois wrote home in June 1850:

Rioting, debauchery in all its different forms prevails here, in all its deformity. The Sabbath day is a day of revelry among the Spanish and of drinking and gambling with the Americans, and all kinds of sin is committed with more boldness than one performs a good act.

Milo Goss, letter of June 18, 1850

Huntington, later to become one of California's renowned "Big Four." In an early display of his shrewdness and enterprise, Huntington used his layover at Panama City to acquire a small sloop, which he sailed to local settlements, buying supplies. As he later recalled, "I filled her up with jerked beef, potatoes, rice, sugar, and syrup . . . and brought them up to Panama City and sold them"—for a profit of $3,000. Another future California tycoon, Darius Ogden Mills, also disdained the lethargy and depravity of Panama City. Responding to the obvious need for transport, he went looking for a ship, sailing on a merchantman to Callao, Peru, where he bought a schooner. He captained his prize back to Panama City, quickly sold one hundred tickets to a jostling crowd, and delivered his passengers to San Francisco—at a handsome profit.

By the summer of 1850, that kind of ambition had so improved passage across the isthmus and regularized the schedule of steamers to San Francisco that the travel time from New York to that great mecca had been set at a reliable five to six weeks. This improvement marked the end of the cape route for passage to California.*

With the isthmus the most popular water route, the tough businessmen who owned the dominant steamship line connecting Panama City and San Francisco, the Pacific Mail Steamship Company, foresaw that profits would justify the risk of building a railroad across the isthmus. Offering fast, safe passage, their railroad would monopolize transport—directly to their ships. Started in 1850, completed in 1855, this first transcontinental railroad—from the Atlantic to the Pacific, through a foreign land—exemplified San Francisco's capitalistic daring and its imperial reach. An immediate success, the Panama Railroad within six years produced $7 million in profits for its owners and created for the American people a new sense of nationalistic pride as they envisioned their steam locomotives puffing through the jungle, carrying the passengers of the world from ocean to ocean in only three hours.

Like California before, the province of Panama and its major city were slipping from the grasp of a distracted colonial chaperone (Bogotá rather than Mexico City) into the control of Yankee newcomers

*On the isthmus route, two cooperating companies (each with a subsidy from the U.S. government to carry the mails) introduced scheduled steamship service in 1849. The United States Mail Steamship Company carried passengers and mail from East Coast ports and New Orleans to Chagres. The Pacific Mail Steamship Company put three sidewheel steamers, the *California, Oregon,* and *Panama,* in service during 1849 between Panama City and San Francisco, each with accommodations designed for about two hundred passengers. By the end of 1849, the PMSC had to buy two more sidewheelers, the *Unicorn* and *Tennessee,* to help ease the crush at Panama City.

Sailing ships continued to carry many tons of freight via the cape route to San Francisco, including bulk cargoes of flour in barrels and merchandise such as "48 dozen coffee mills," iron safes, crystal chandeliers, and elaborate mahogany bars with brass foot-rails. The demand for speed hastened the development of American clipper ships, which carried high-priced items and even perishables at $1 per cubic foot and $60 to $70 per ton, delivered in 120 days, on occasion even 90 days. Built for maximum sailing performance and cargo space, the clippers could accommodate only about five passengers.

guided only by their practiced opportunism. By the end of the decade Panama would be, in effect, San Francisco's first colony, developed and exploited as the fastest route to and from Chrysopolis.*

OVERLAND CROSSINGS

A THIRD ROUTE TO CALIFORNIA ATTRACTED many thousands who judged half a year at sea or passage through a jungle in a foreign land to be a fearful or foolish risk compared to traveling a well-known trail with a wagon or pack mules in the company of neighbors. The Oregon-California Trail, the various southern routes, and the trails through Mexico publicized during the war each offered a four- to seven-month journey to the gold region. The most impatient overlanders, unwilling to wait for the spring grass on the northern prairies, could get started in January and February from Arkansas and Texas, choosing one of several trails that led some of the way through northern Mexico to reach the Gila River (in present-day southern Arizona) and then across the fearful Colorado Desert into southern California. Or these early-starters could take the other year-round trail to the old Spanish settlement at Santa Fe (described by a '49er as "a little of the hardest place I was ever in") and from there continue down the Rio Grande and on to the Gila. By these various southern trails, at least ten thousand emigrants from the States reached California during the first year, with a comparable number following in 1850.

Although they could not roll out from the jumping-off points along the Missouri frontier until late April, when spring-swollen rivers began to recede and the prairie grass stood high enough to feed oxen and mules, the largest number of overlanders throughout the gold rush years followed the Oregon-California Trail, which had been well publicized since 1841. Like all demographic statistics from those pell-mell years, estimates were imprecise as to how many guided their wagon teams across the western half of the continent via this well-rutted route. At least 32,000 made their way in 1849, probably 44,000 in 1850, and in 1851 an astonishing crest of 50,000.

Like those who went by sea, most overlanders organized volunteer associations and joint-stock companies, in which each member contributed an equal share to fund purchases of wagons, teams, and provisions. Choosing sober names like the Pittsburg and California Enterprise Company, the Illinois and California Mining Company, and the Sagamore and Sacramento Mining and Trading Company, goldseekers joined together in the spirit of ambitious businessmen, rather than mere youthful adventurers.

In Ithaca, New York, a company of fifty men, with capital of $25,000 and credit of $25,000 more at a local bank, planned to strike out from the Missouri frontier in April and reach California in June. With equal optimism they expected to "select a suitable location, erect cabins and proceed to rake in the dust." Another well-prepared company included in its equipage eleven "gold finders" and a machine for minting gold coins.

Scores of newspapers reported the preparations of overland companies, publishing their membership rosters, constitutions, and "Rules of Regulation." Letters sent back from military forts along the trail and from California's "diggings" provided news for front-page articles under headings such as "Ho! for California," "Routes to California," and "Gold Regions: Highly Important to Emigrants." Letters direct from mining camps and San Francisco offered reassuring testimonies of continuing success. "Many men who began last June [1848] to dig for

---

* John C. Frémont, in his 1848 book describing California *(Geographical Memoir of Upper California)*, originated the name Chrysopylae, or Golden Gate, to describe the entrance to San Francisco Bay, "on the same principle that the harbor of Byzantium (later Constantinople) was called Chrysoceras or Golden Horn." Hence, San Francisco came to be known, to some, as Chrysopolis.

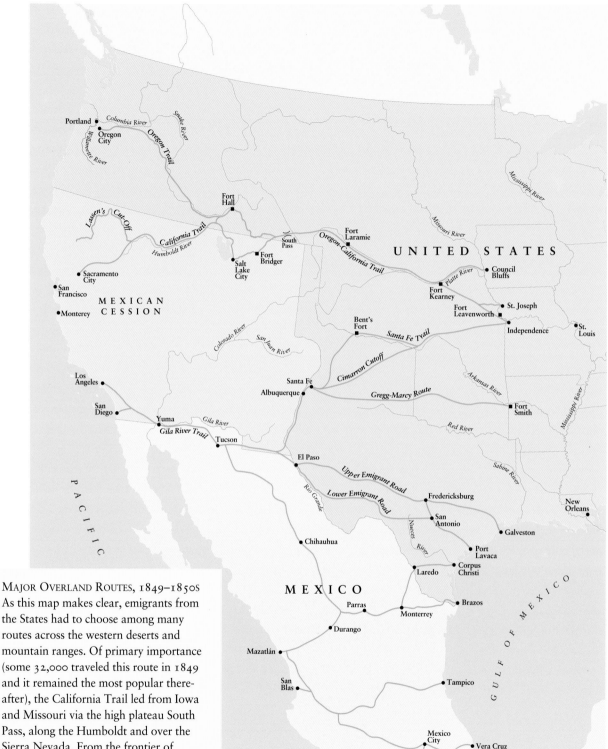

MAJOR OVERLAND ROUTES, 1849–1850S
As this map makes clear, emigrants from
the States had to choose among many
routes across the western deserts and
mountain ranges. Of primary importance
(some 32,000 traveled this route in 1849
and it remained the most popular thereafter), the California Trail led from Iowa
and Missouri via the high plateau South
Pass, along the Humboldt and over the
Sierra Nevada. From the frontier of
Missouri and Arkansas and from Texas
port towns, about 10,000 '49ers followed
routes through Texas and Mexico,
and some even dared to strike out for
Mazatlán, San Blas, or Acapulco, where,
maybe, a ship would carry them to
San Francisco.

In his farewell letter, William Pierce of Indiana assured his wife, Georgina, that he was parting from "my best friend on earth." His sense of duty sent him on his way so that

we will be slaves to none, independent of want, able to get through life with plenty & cultivate social feeling, virtue & peace without being compelled to struggle for daily bread.

William Pierce, letter of September 29, 1849

---

gold with capital of $50 can now show $5,000 to $15,000." Galvanized by that kind of news, one diarist asserted that he was "willing to brave most anything" to get his share.

Goldseekers often mortgaged or even sold their homes and farms, withdrew life savings, or borrowed from friends and fathers-in-law in order to raise the money to buy a share in an overland company or a wagon, a team of mules or oxen, and other "California fixings." The economic reverberations of this money raising caused alarm in several states where editors lamented the loss of capital withdrawn to support the sudden needs of men afflicted with the gold fever. On March 27, 1849, a newspaper in Michigan estimated that $30,000 had been taken out of Washtenaw County, with each man spending an average of $400 for his outfit and transportation to the frontier. A man in Ann Arbor sold his home for $1,200 to provide for his wife and six daughters, who would live with her parents until he returned with a "pocket full of rocks." Another wrote his wife that he had bought enough life insurance to leave her $1,250 if he should die.

Again and again the record reveals that the gold rush was far more than a distracting adventure or an outlet for the nation's adolescent restlessness. At mid-century the United States suffered the strains of its great economic transition as commercial and industrial enterprises gained momentum against the dominant, traditional agrarian society. Growing class disparities and envy of privilege began to erode the old sense of shared burdens. California fascinated the nation with its miraculous promise of wealth, sufficient to buy new status, to win freedom from "the detested sin of being poor."

Ignorant of wilderness travel, fearful of attacks by Indians, yet buoyed by their common expectations of the West as described by famous explorers, young men by the tens of thousands gathered from all the states on the western frontier, like a great volunteer army, bristling with newly bought rifles, pistols, and hunting knives. Many who came from farms and villages in Illinois, Wisconsin, Iowa, and Missouri had simply packed supplies and gear into their wagons and rolled down the nearest road leading to the Missouri River jumping-off towns. Thousands from farther east began their journeys on Ohio and Mississippi River steamboats bound for St. Louis or towns to the south, like Napoleon, Arkansas. Others stayed on board all the way south to New Orleans, there to ship out for Texas ports or Chagres. Many traveled across northern New York on the great Erie Canal or through Pennsylvania on the portage and canal system. Aboard Great Lakes steamers from Buffalo and Cleveland they often experienced their first bouts of seasickness. From East Coast cities they rode railroad cars to connect with river and canal transportation west.

Inspired by their sense of an epochal event, with the whole nation watching, a surprising number of these men kept their promises to write home. Thus began the dynamic process by which the American people became emotionally involved in the rush to California. Wives, sweethearts, parents, friends, bankers, and creditors received letters, which they shared with neighbors and local newspapers. The first of these reached home in April and May from frontier towns like St. Joseph, Missouri, where letter writers tried to describe the confusion at the ferry crossings. Pushing, shouting, and impatiently waiting, hundreds of unruly emigrants clamored to get their wagons, animals, and companions on board the crude river rafts. Day after day, from sunup till

This fierce emigrant posed at a daguerrean studio in Cincinnati to leave his family a reminder of how he had prepared to face the dangers of his odyssey. Though not all were so military as this argonaut, greenhorns who had never held a rifle, tough farmers, and everyone in between carried at least one weapon. Target shooting, buffalo hunting, and general carelessness caused innumerable accidents along the crowded trail.

To ease their homesickness, many gold rushers carried keepsakes and remembrances from their wives and families. This cased daguerreotype of a young wife and child comforted one emigrant on the trail and possibly helped him to fend off temptation in sinful California.

In commenting on a typical overland company's armament, one '49er proudly reported: "Our coats are surrounded with a belt in which are stuck two 10-inch rifle pistols and an 8-inch dirk knife, which with a United States rifle or double-barreled shotgun completes our uniform and arms and makes us appear quite formidable."

last light, the crowd swelled and roiled in confusion. The *St. Joseph Adventure* made an effort to count the cavalcade: from the earliest departures in late April to May 18, 1849, it estimated 4,350 wagons, 17,400 emigrants, and 34,500 mules, oxen, and horses had crossed at the several competing ferries.* The entrepreneurs who operated this suddenly indispensable service were the first of many along the overland trails and in the mining camps who would "strike it rich" by selling whatever the emigrants and miners most needed. The Missouri River outfitting towns forecast the wildly laissez-faire economy of California by selling everything from mules and saleratus to rifles and ferry service at whatever prices the impatient, sometimes desperate emigrants would pay.

Beyond the clamor of the river towns, the companies' wagons could be seen in an endless line stretching far to the west over "the ocean of grass." News of the emigrants' progress, their encounters with hailstorms, broken axles, and oxen and mule stampedes came in letters sent back from the U.S. Army outposts at Fort Kearny and Fort Laramie. The last place to leave a letter for anxious families was at the Mormons' embryonic city on the shores of the Great Salt Lake. Beyond that speck of civilization only the diaries recorded the story. Some overlanders persevered at their journals, but most found the task too relentless and gave up trying to find the time and a quiet place to write, to squeeze onto a small page the daily wonder and suffering of endless wilderness miles. The difficulty of reporting a story they knew to be history-in-the-making was expressed by a doctor from Michigan in an emotional

disclaimer to his wife. "It is impossible for me to give you an account of the interesting incidents that occur on this route, but when I have an opportunity I will give you enough to satisfy you that 1849 will ever be a memorable epoch in the history of our country. Neither the Crusades nor Alexander's expedition to India can equal this emigration to California."

The doctor chose the right image: an armed horde moving into the wilderness, their trail westward over the swells of the prairie and eastward back to the frontier marked by an undulating line of white-topped wagons. At night campfires flickered and glowed, nearby and in the far distance. The ancient silence of the prairies was riven by the new sounds of thousands of men laughing and singing, arguing and shouting. Hurrying westward, this army left along the fringes of its broad trail a melange of cannibalized wagons, barrels of flour and slabs of bacon, and personal possessions, all abandoned under the realities of unexpected demands and new values. Amid the detritus, shallow graves revealed the invisible, most feared companion—cholera.

In surprising contrast to their expectations of life in a vast and empty wilderness where only Indians would be seen, the thousands who so recently had been at work on farms or in cities found themselves surrounded day and night by men like themselves. As in an army on the march, they stood guard at night, in wind and rain; they ate food prepared by careless, grumbling cooks, listened to crude talk around campfires, and suffered resentments, jealousies, and irritating personal habits of companions from whom there was no escape—unless the company broke up, as often happened after arguments, fights, or disagreements over leadership.

For those who persevered with their diaries, writing offered a safe refuge for gossip and expressions of resentment, perhaps against a lazy messmate or a haughty trail boss, as well as for moral judgments against those who played cards, gambled, and ignored the Sabbath. Other diarists found

---

* Very few emigrants set out from the frontier after May 18. A later date might lead to the danger of snow in the passes of the Sierra Nevada. In competition with St. Joseph as the major jumping-off point on the frontier, the town of Independence attracted as many thousands. Lesser outfitting towns included Weston and, to the north, Council Bluffs. Emigrants bound for the southern trails made their start from Fort Smith, Arkansas, and frontier settlements in Texas.

Among the amateur artists who tried to document their never-to-be-forgotten wilderness journey, none succeeded so well as J. Goldsborough Bruff, captain of the Washington City Mining Company. On July 20, 1849, he sketched in his diary this scene of crossing the North Platte River on a makeshift ferry. On another page he recorded a great hailstorm with lightning bolts amid dark clouds that seem to tremble with thunder. Another diarist traveling nearby described the drama: "In a moment after the first hail fell, the air was literally filled with balls of ice from the size of a walnut to that of a goose egg . . . rebounding from whatever they struck, while bursts of thunder broke out in tremendous peals and forked lightning shot through the sky, streaking it with vivid lines of light."

To help his folks back in Missouri better understand the realities of the West, a young goldseeker passing through present-day southern Idaho wrote a letter to be mailed when he reached California.

Senator Benton and other big men may talk and humbug the country and you green-horns about a railroad to the Pacific, but if you and I live a thousand years, we will never see the resemblance even of such a thing. There is not timber along this route to lay the track half part of the way, and if there was, it would cost more money to build it than there is in the U.S. Men who could build a railroad to the moon perhaps could build one over these mountains, but I doubt it. You may think you have seen mountains and gone over them, but you never saw anything but a small hill compared with what I have crossed over, and it is said the worst is yet to come. But never mind. Gold lies ahead.

William Wilson, letter of August 6, 1849

Young men on the overland trails to California thought about more than gold.

The pretty Indian squaws certainly are beauties of Nature and will compare very well with some of the young ladies in the States who think themselves handsomer. . . . They are what nature designed them to be, women without stays or padding.

Andrew J. Griffith, letter of June 3, 1850

surcease from the toil and pettiness of trail life by describing the wonders near at hand and far away—the beauties of wildflowers and July snowbanks, antelope fleeing through the sage, a hailstorm that raised welts on their heads, the panorama from Independence Rock of hundreds of wagons slowly moving along the Sweetwater River in present-day Wyoming, the sense of being part of a vast migration of Americans in pursuit of a once-in-a-lifetime opportunity.

A man from Pennsylvania summed up what many others may have felt. Despite the rigors of this wilderness experience, he wrote that "it is far more pleasing to me than to sit daily locked up in a dirty office. Besides the pleasure of the thing, it gives us health and strength. I can sleep in the tent or wagon far better than I could in a bed, no roaches to disturb us at midnight and no bell to call us to breakfast." Another escapee from the routines of life back home posted a letter in June 1849 from Fort Kearny which closed with the comment: "Tell Charles that I have not been chased by a squaw nor bit by an antelope, yet!"

Such youthful exuberance found its fullest expression on July 4, the patriotic holiday most gold rush companies felt obliged to celebrate. One diarist, no doubt remembering how hot it was at home on Independence Day, told of an exotic, trailside libation. "We had a pail full of punch and cooled it with a lump of snow from a deep snow-bank. . . . Having drunk our punch and given three cheers for our Glorious Union, we resumed our march." Another company made ice cream and flavored it with wild peppermint, while another filled a barrel with explosives, buried it in a mountainside, and blew it up. Heavily armed but without Indian dangers to justify their weaponry, many companies used the Fourth as an excuse for firing their rifles and pistols. An Ohio company "fired a gun for every state in the Union and a volley for California and another for the gold diggings. In this salute one of our Rovers got his thumb shot off. The firing kept up till a late hour."

Freed from family restraints and sharing physical challenges that became a test of their manhood, they considered the dangers ahead and turned them aside with talk of California. Seeing so many on the trail, they felt an ever-increasing impatience to get to the gold mines. Sometimes their talk explored the possibility of disappointment, but such doubts were easily dismissed by recalling the reports of fortunes dug in 1848.

Most companies reached the Humboldt River (in present-day Nevada) in August. Along this "meanest, muddiest, filthiest stream," the hardships of the trail became more tormenting than anywhere else on the long journey. Walking day after day under the scorching sun, breathing gritty billows of trail dust mixed with pulverized dung, their surviving oxen and mules squealing and groaning, their messmates cursing what they knew would be more of the same tomorrow, they now encountered the danger they had forgotten and were unprepared to ward off—Indian attacks. At dawn herdsmen often found oxen and mules with arrows deep in their gaunt sides, while others had been driven off. Sometimes night sentries were mistaken for "Digger Indians" and shot by other jumpy guards. Teams killed, stolen, or felled by exhaustion forced companies to abandon wagons that had somehow held together over 1,500 miles of mountains and deserts. And the menace of "white Indians"—emigrants who stole from other emigrants—became an increasing

In another exceptional illustration of life on the trail, Bruff sketched one of many campfires where his cooks used cast-iron pots, similar to this one found in Nevada many years later. From the top of Independence Rock in July 1849, Bruff portrayed a panorama of the Sweetwater River (in present-day Wyoming) with his company's wagons circled below.

danger. Now and then, a diarist in that long train of creaking wagons scrawled a line that caught the pathos of it all. One such man recalled an evening when a messmate exclaimed: "My God, McKinstry, why do you write about this trip so you can remember it? All I hope is to get home alive as soon as possible and forget it!"

By September and October, the great majority of the 32,000 on the main California Trail had struggled into the Sacramento Valley and quickly dispersed into the diggings and mining camps. But some 8,000—the rear of the vast migration—had not reached the Humboldt until September, even late September. Fearful of Sierra snowstorms, they believed reports of a new route called Lassen's Cutoff, which promised to save many miles by leading directly west, into the gold region. Too late they realized the "cut-off" veered to the north, finally to the Oregon border—and to disaster. Caught in the first storms of winter, these cut-off victims cast away everything they had lugged across the continent and fled for their lives, most of them reduced to only a rifle and a blanket. Guided and fed by relief parties sent out from Sutter's Fort, these remnants of the great rush survived snowdrifts and attacks by Pit River Indians, finally to arrive in mid-November 1849 at Peter Lassen's dilapidated ranch in the northern Sacramento Valley. Amid the mud and filth of a refugee camp, the last stragglers collapsed on November 26. Thus ended the first year of the rush.

When sketched by John Woodhouse Audubon in April 1849, Hawkins Bar on the Tuolumne River had only these few tents and other casual structures. Like scores of other remote settings, this riverbank by September had been transformed into a noisy mining camp with a transient population of more than seven hundred.

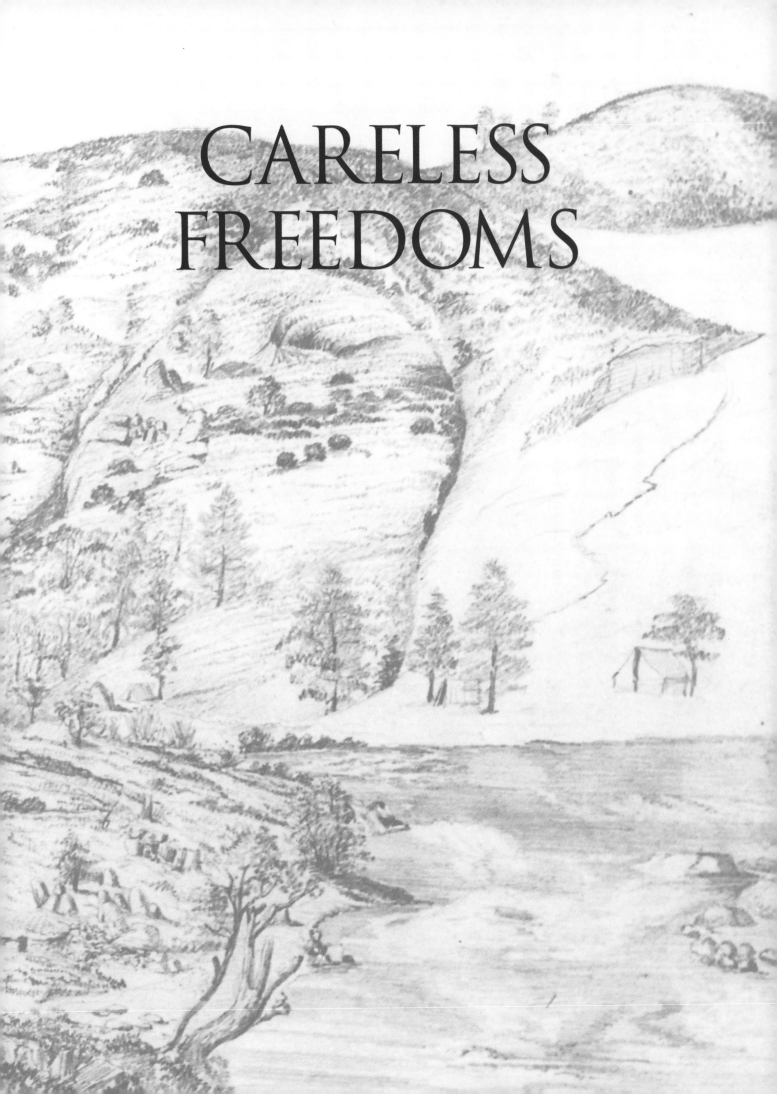

CARELESS
FREEDOMS

A daguerreotypist's portrait pleased the pride of hundreds of goldseekers. This expensive impulse could be satisfied in one of several daguerrean studios in San Francisco or by being "pictured" by a daguerreotypist who traveled to the mining camps. One of these pioneer photographers advertised that his portraits offered miners a chance "to give their friends in the States an idea of the effect which a rough and tumble life . . . has had on their appearance."

These two views illustrate the dramatic transformation of San Francisco between spring and fall 1849. In his fine pencil drawing, Daniel Coit, a Connecticut businessman who landed in April 1849, depicts Portsmouth Square and a few ships beyond, in Yerba Buena Cove. An early landmark, the gabled two-story Parker House charged rents that totaled $120,000 by year's end. As the harbor became a "forest of masts" (308 ships counted in October 1849 and 635 seven months later), San Francisco changed from a provincial port to a city of international fame.

CHAPTER FOUR

CARELESS FREEDOMS

NOT SETTLERS, NOT PIONEERS in the centuries-old tradition of America's westward migration, the goldseekers came to grab and leave, not to build and stay. They found themselves amid crowds of hustling men concerned only with how to find gold in the diggings or in the swift commerce of instant towns. The seduction of quick wealth left them indifferent to California and its future. No one knew where he would be next week: maybe headed home, maybe working a claim on the Stanislaus. Everything was temporary, changing, unfinished, unpredictable. Nothing was established, in repose, legal, familiar. No one wanted to be tied down and burdened by normal responsibilities. Like soldiers in a foreign land, the goldseekers could slough off the social codes and moral dictates that had been enforced at home by family, friends, and church. In a world of strangers, far from hometown eyes and rules, they felt liberated, as well, from polite conventions—free to grasp for fortune with shameless selfishness.

The surging currents of California's unconstrained society could lift or dash a miner or a merchant with sudden caprice, and the cry of those who sought the protections of civil institutions and public works was hard to hear over the clamor of newcomers with nothing to defend. Most of the advances that defined an American state—elected government, schools, churches, hospitals, courts, jails, paved streets, sturdy bridges—would have to wait until California's preoccupation with the present—the getting—was tempered by a growing interest in the future—the keeping.

Meanwhile, opportunists who knew how to make fast profits provided the immediate necessities: transport from San Francisco up the Sacramento and San Joaquin Rivers to inland ports near the mining camps; blankets and meals in boardinghouses and wood-plank eateries; gambling "palaces" and backroom brothels. Even out on the mountain trails, canvas shelters appeared where on-the-move miners could sleep for a night, all of it hurry-up, temporary construction. And most important for thousands of homesick Californians, the entrepreneurs found a way to deliver letters from the States to the most isolated miners and to carry back to San Francisco their finger-damaged scrawls for shipment to the isthmus and on to anxious families in Albany, New York, and Zebulon, Georgia.

Confident of a once-in-a-lifetime financial opportunity, the men to be known as '49ers came to California not as adventurers or as frontiersmen but rather as businessmen, many thousands of them greenhorns, city raised, who had never fired a rifle or raised a callus. Doctors, lawyers, clergymen, newspaper editors, undertakers, and lighthouse-keepers from every region, they joined farmers, blacksmiths, wheelwrights, millers, and coopers from across the nation to form an agglomeration of Americans—Yankee clerks and southern slave owners, Pennsylvania coal miners and Mississippi River boatmen—such as had never gathered before, dissolving in gold rush California the regional, social, and economic divisions that had so long fractured the less-than-united States.

In 1849 and for years thereafter, these impatient sojourners experienced in California a freedom of anonymity that encouraged impulses and vices beyond imagining back home (or in tradition-bound Oregon)—a careless disregard for personal hygiene and appearance; a general, even exuberant acceptance of everything scorned or forbidden in the States: swearing, sharp practices, gambling, drinking, even whoring. Joining in this wild experiment in individuality and prodigality, foreigners from around the world arrived by the many thousands to compete with possessive Yankees, each man determined to grab his main chance. The vitality and potentially explosive energies of this polyglot society were compounded by age and gender: more than half the population was between twenty and thirty years old, and virtually all the newcomers were male. Thus it was that "the dynamite of California was composed of one part vigor and one part frustration."*

As there were no societal constraints, nor any that might be considered economic (plenty of money in the form of gold dust), so there were no laws to control mining operations and opportunities. Legions of miners felt perfectly free to rip up the earth wherever their luck and perseverance led them, even to divert rivers from their ancient channels. No government regulations inhibited their rampage. The only laws the miners respected were

---

* The near absence of women—or emphasized another way, "the overwhelming presence of men of many nations and colors and creeds"—is a circumstance of central importance to understanding California during the gold rush era.

measures of their own invention designed to protect their collective self-interest, to defend individual claims and "rights," drawn up and approved by various "miners associations" and "mining districts" that formed spontaneously to safeguard the underlying right of opportunity that every miner—every *American* miner—considered his inalienable right.

Through the spring and summer of 1849 mining methods and mores remained much the same as in 1848, still animated by the excitement of easy success. Then in August the arriving thousands from ships and overland trails scrambled for their share along the rivers and dry diggings, in the instant cities and wild mining camps. Competition for claims, like competition for business profits, became intense. By September and October the great mass of overlanders—forty to fifty thousand—had crossed the Sierra and hiked up from the southern trails to crowd into the mining region, from the Trinity River in the north to Mariposa Creek in the south. By the end of the year, another great wave of forty to fifty thousand men had landed at San Francisco—in all, close to one hundred thousand new-comers intent upon grabbing their share. Still, no one that year sensed the magnitude of the immigration or the wild forces it would release on primitive but fast-changing California.

O N SEPTEMBER 29, 1849, A MIS-sourian, recently arrived in the Sacramento Valley from his over-land trip, wrote home to tell of his journey. After relating his company's struggle in getting through the Humboldt Desert and over the Sierra Nevada, he turned to the purpose of his journey: "Now I will tell you what we have done since we got here. We have worked eight days and have made $16,000. We have had extremely good luck, are on the Feather River and pretty well up at its head. . . . There are a great many in the gold diggings at work, some are making fortunes and some are spending fortunes. A man that will half work can make a great fortune in three years."

Another new arrival assured his family that "this wonderful country seems but a realization of the wild and extravagant fictions of the East. Indeed, the poor workman, as one accustomed to manual labor, has a better chance of wealth than one who has hitherto been ashamed to dig. The car-pet knights and silken striplings . . . are scarcely capable of sustaining the hardships, privations and exposure—the digging, delving and washing, by which the precious metal is obtained."

Among the many Americans who recorded their gold rush experiences during 1849, few wrote with the descriptive power or the verve and good cheer of William Perkins from Cincinnati, Ohio. For three years he kept notes (later expanded) on every aspect of life in the southern mines and his travels round and about, to Sacramento City and San Francisco. His remarkable account begins with his journey to California—down the Mississippi River on a steamer to New Orleans, by ship to the gulf port of Brazos, Texas, overland through Mexico to the west-coast port of Mazatlán, and finally by schooner to San Francisco, where he landed on May 20, 1849. Perkins and his companions then bought passage—"at an unconscionably extravagant

Apparently more intimidated by the daguerreotypist's camera than pleased with his pan's treasure, this stiff-necked miner probably sent this portrait to his folks back home, and maybe he returned with a pocketful of rocks, like these glorious nuggets spilled from a miner's poke. The promise of nuggets served to justify many a miner's delay in returning home. And while he labored to gather far fewer than promised, his dreams glistened with their color.

figure"—on a small schooner and sailed up the San Joaquin bound for Stockton. After eight days, "eating raw pork for want of fuel to cook with and losing each a pint of blood as tribute paid to the ravenous myriads of mosquitos," they landed at that depot of the southern mines, a place suddenly grown to three thousand men in tents and shanties.

From Stockton Perkins and his companions moved on to the thriving mining camp known as Sonora, fifty miles east, in the foothills on Woods Creek, a tributary of the Tuolumne. "Here were real, live miners, men who had actually dug out the shining metal and who had it in huge buckskin pouches in the pockets of their pantaloons. Men who spoke jestingly, lightly of chunks of gold weighing one, five or ten pounds! Of 'pockets' where a quarter of a bushel of gold dust had been washed from!

"These men were the awful objects of our curiosity. They were the demi-gods of the dominion. . . . Their long rough boots, red shirts, Mexican hats; their huge, uncombed beards covering half the face; the Colt's revolver attached to its belt behind; the *cuchillo* stuck into the leg of the boot—all these things were attributes belonging to another race of men than ourselves, and we looked upon them with a certain degree of respect and with a determination soon to be ourselves as little human-like in appearance as they were."

That fancy quickly faded. More pragmatists than romantics, Perkins and his partners soon decided they could best make their pile by operating a general merchandise store in Sonora. He left digging to others, marveling at their raw energy: "Along the edges of Woods Creek the ground is delved and dug and thrown up as if some gigantic and mighty Behemoth had been rooting it up with his snout! Work that would have taken hired laborers years to accomplish, the thirst for gold and the excitement of the search has consummated in a few months."

Through the first seven or eight months of that transitional year, the miners' successes and their high spirits prevailed; only the "old-timers" who had been there in 1848 recognized the threatening diminishment. Most were caught up in the enthusiasm of digging and prospecting in a land unfenced, unclaimed, and largely unexplored, searching gulches and ravines, tracing streams through canyons to their wildest, most difficult recesses, held back finally by the granite ridges and heights of the Sierra.

In this wilderness of oak-forested foothills and pine-clad lower shoulders of the great peaks, the miners threw up their tents and tree-branch shelters, here and there building wooden structures from logs or planks handsawn in whipsaw pits. Merchants set planks on barrels where they sold flour and bacon and whiskey. Gamblers offered a chance to escape the labor of digging by the turn of a card, to win gold dust worth a hundred, even a thousand dollars. At these mountain encampments, where not a single woman was ever seen—only hoped for and dreamt about—the miners dug and shoveled and washed ton after ton of rock, gravel, and sand. They gave these evanescent way stations of sweat and hope and reward names that reflected their robust energy and their freedom from the sensibilities of parents, in-laws, and preachers: Rough and Ready, Jackass Gulch, Shirt Tail Canyon, Sweet Revenge, Murderers Bar, Loafer Hill. These were concentrations of masculine life, where fifty or maybe several hundred men labored, shouted in triumph, cooked their monotonous greasy meals, went to sleep unwashed, and awakened in the same dirty clothes, ready for the fortunes of another day.

By summer of 1849 the territory of the diggings had expanded so greatly that a new terminology came into use. Mines located along the many rivers and forks flowing into the Sacramento were designated the "northern" mines—from the North Fork of the Feather River to the South Fork of the Ameri-

A SHAGGY MINER

Clothing can in great measure be dispensed with, for a pair of dungaree pants and a gray woolen shirt will last a man a year. . . . [but] one must have boots. And here it is proper that a voice should be raised in condemnation of the feeble things in the shape of boots palmed off by designing speculators upon the "honest miner." They are mere delusions, ofttimes with no more leather in their soles than honesty in the hearts of manufacturers. It is time that shoemakers here and elsewhere were disabused of the idea that the sole mission of the California miner is to wear out their worthless boots.

Prentice Mulford, *California Sketches*

can. Whatever the camps in that region needed came on freight wagons or pack mules from Sacramento City, having been shipped to that burgeoning inland port on sailing ships (later steamboats) up the Sacramento River from San Francisco.

The "southern" mines were those situated along the fewer and smaller streams and tributaries flowing into the San Joaquin—from the Cosumnes to Mariposa Creek. Their supplies arrived from San Francisco via the San Joaquin to the inland port of Stockton. From that booming commercial depot, everything from barrels of flour to billiard tables was carried overland to the scattered camps, many perched along creeks and smaller streams that dried up in May (unlike the longer-flowing northern tributaries), leaving the miners some distance from flowing water. Hence, they were called "dry diggings." Though more difficult to work, they gave up immense quantities of gold.

In prospecting along rivers and streams and in the dry diggings, many miners (especially the latest arrivals) still used the ubiquitous pan, so dominant during 1848. Imported by the thousands until production started in California in 1850, the gold pan was made of iron stamped into its familiar shape—

about eighteen inches in diameter, flat-bottomed with three- to four-inch sloping sides. This fundamental tool was invaluable when prospecting to determine if a possible claim showed enough "color" to warrant more digging. For those who used the pan to wash their pay dirt, fifty pans were judged a good day's work, though hard on legs and hands, which would be cramped and bruised by evening. In the dry diggings, the Mexicans generally used a handmade shallow wooden bowl or Indian basket.

With pan or bowl, with or without water, the process of separating gold from the gravel and sand required the same dexterous swirling motion to sweep the larger detritus over the rim. Without water, that was more difficult because the smallest particles and sand had to be blown away, either by repeated tossings into the air like wheat chaff or by lung power, slowly exposing the heavier gold. How much easier with water, which was one reason the Americans, exercising a presumed right of territorial dominion, crowded into the northern mines, leaving the dry diggings mostly to the Mexicans, Chileans, and other foreigners.

Part of the pan's persistent appeal in 1849, when gold was still being found with widely reported success, arose from the notion that its easy portability permitted a single miner to slip away from the crowd, unobserved, to search for a place not yet known to others—a new creek, a secret pool where the gold would be exclusively his own. For many, gold hunting remained a private, me-against-them effort.

"Tired of old ravines, I started one morning into the hills with the determination of finding a new place where I could labour without being disturbed by the clang of picks and shovels around me," one miner wrote in describing what became a common experience in the summer of 1849. He found a small ravine "embosomed" amid the hills and washed one panful after another, "some of them containing eight or ten dollars [in gold dust]. . . . I flattered myself that I had here at last found a quiet place, where . . . I could appropriate to myself the entire riches of the whole ravine. . . . I returned and took good care not to expose to my companions the good luck I had experienced." But the next morning, "twenty good stout fellows" arrived to work around him. "In three days the little ravine . . . was turned completely upside down. About $10,000 worth of gold dust was extracted from it, from which I realized a little over $1,000." A similar story told of an Irishman who "sank a hole about six feet deep . . . and took out the first day nearly one hundred dollars. This, of course, attracted crowds, and before a week had elapsed, nearly $15,000 had been taken."

For a single miner with a pan, or four or five partners with a rocker, the chances of hiding a promising site from the crowds of competitors persisted only in dreams or wishful talk around campfires. The more unsociable a miner became, the more he attracted interested looks from campmates and neighbors. Any nonchalant attempt to steal away down a deer path or through the trees had an effect like the Pied Piper's flute on fellow miners who suspected the wanderer of harboring secret knowledge.

With new men arriving every day, carrying shiny pans and shovels, each mining camp felt the growing pressure of competition, and even the greenest arrivals knew, at least subconsciously, that California's purse might one day be emptied. By the summer of 1849, miners committees began to form, to redress the inevitable disagreements and angry conflicts. Not ordained by the military governor (whoever, wherever he might be) or by formal legislation, but rather convened voluntarily by the miners themselves, these committees were the natural successors to the joint-stock companies that had been the '49ers' first experiments in self-government during the long journeys by sea and overland trails.

Carefully delineated mining districts appeared, promulgating scores of similar "constitutions" and "articles of association." The first principle that inspired these regulations was the conviction that each miner deserved equal opportunity, so long as he did not encroach on the rights of other miners. Therefore, the rules stated that each miner (or partnership) could claim an equal, specified area of workable ground, typically ten feet square in a highly productive placer or a larger area in poorer ground. To hold his claim, an owner had to work it at least one day each week, otherwise it was forfeited and might be claimed by anyone. To mark an area already owned, a miner left his tools in sight, a pick, shovel, or rocker. Removal of these symbols of ownership was strictly prohibited. Because miners wanted only to protect their right to extract gold, none of these rules conveyed any suggestion of permanent title.

LOOKING FOR COLOR

The discoverer of a new placer was entitled to work double the standard size of a claim. Buying and selling claims was permitted, though generally a miner could possess no more than two claims, one by discovery and one by purchase. Limits on the number of claims and the requirement of regular work were intended to prevent absentee ownership. Equally important, the miners chose to prohibit peonage: the use of gangs of Indians (as had been common in 1848) or Negro slaves. More difficult to control was the *patrón* system, whereby a wealthy Mexican would send a group of peons under supervision of a majordomo to work their own claims but pay back half or more of their earnings. Normal enough in Mexico, this system was resented by American miners, who in 1850 would resort to aggressive methods to drive out all such foreigners. But individual claim owners and partnerships were allowed to hire other miners, if they could be found, to work for wages. During the summer of 1849 few miners were so pessimistic of their own chances as to work for others, but by fall thousands of newcomers would welcome that chance.

The boundaries of each mining district, with its own code or constitution, were drawn to conform to the surrounding topography. Often they encompassed several mining camps and larger settlements that grew into towns, like Mokelumne Hill and Downieville. To keep records of claims and transfers and to render decisions in claim jumping and other disputes, these districts elected claims officers or recorders (often known as alcaldes) by majority vote. Paid by fees for their services, these officials exercised final authority, though sometimes an especially contentious or complicated argument might require five miners to interrupt their work long enough to convene as a jury.

Balancing the miners' optimistic credo that California had "room and gold enough for all" with the growing frictions of overcrowding, the self-imposed Miners' Laws sought to extend the ideal of equal opportunity (at least for Americans) and to protect the diggings from the monopolizing power of the corporations. It was a spontaneous defense of the interests of the common man—the clerk who had escaped a cramped future in St. Louis, the carpenter freed from the impenetrable class structure of Paris. Through widespread application, the rules of small-scale ownership gained the status of common law and legal precedent and became so entrenched that neither federal nor state governments would challenge or tinker with their hegemony for many years.* Corollary to their enforcement, these laws nurtured the ethos, the risk-taking mentality, that defined California's economy and image through the decades, until the 1880s when the Miner and his by-then arrogant power faced the challenge of

---

* The principles of law practiced in the mining districts were adapted through the years to various methods of mining—river mining and tunneling and hydraulic and quartz—as well as to the related issues of water rights. These codes governed the mining regions long after the state of California could have replaced them. Instead, the legislature in 1851 endorsed the local codes as common law. In 1864 the State Supreme Court upheld this judgment, as did the U.S. Supreme Court. In 1866 and again in 1872, the U.S. Congress passed legislation that in effect codified those principles so long practiced by the miners.

Often with a tone of boastfulness, diarists and letter writers reported the contrasts between "back home" and the California society in which they found themselves.

Self-protection is a necessary law . . . , consequently the miners' laws are swift and certain in their execution . . . with priest and preacher many miles away and no disposition to hunt him up. No great "criminal lawyer" is allowed to humbug . . . in this country, thereby creating a hope of escape in some would-be assassin. When caught in the act, up they go, and that's the end of it.

Charles Ross Parke, diary entry at Bidwell's Bar, Sepember 18, 1848

---

another organized group, the Farmer—and California entered a new age.

The mining codes also contained rudimentary elements of criminal law that enumerated stern punishments for offenses against private property and personal safety. But miners resented giving time for jury trials. Verdicts came quickly, punishment immediately: for theft, flogging and banishment from the district; for major larceny, the loss of an ear and a head-shaving, followed by banishment. For a second offense, the criminal was usually hanged. Stabbings, shootings, and other assaults called for heavy flogging (sometimes followed by branding) and banishment. A murder conviction required hanging. These organized but impatient inflictions of revenge were credited by everyone with keeping the robust impulses of 1849 nearly as law-abiding as those of that quaint and fading era known as '48.

Bayard Taylor, a newspaperman sent to California by Horace Greeley's *New York Tribune*, traveled through the diggings along the Mokelumne River during the summer of 1849. He expressed surprise and admiration for the "disposition to maintain order and secure the rights of all . . . throughout the mining districts. . . . Several thefts had occurred and the offending parties been severely punished after a fair trial. Some had been whipped and cropped or maimed in some other way, and one or two of them hung. . . . We met a man whose head had been shaved and his ears cut off, after receiving one hundred lashes for stealing ninety-eight pounds of gold. . . . There had been not more than twelve or fifteen executions in all, about half of which were inflicted for the crime of murder. . . . In a country without not only bolts and bars, but any effective system of law and government, this Spartan severity of discipline seemed the only security against the most frightful disorder. The camp or tent was held inviolate . . . , the canvas or pavilion of rough oak boughs as sacred as the portals of a church."

TAYLOR

Even more than the "capacity of the people for self-government," Taylor was impressed by the miners' success in finding gold. "When I first saw the men carrying heavy stones in the sun, standing nearly waist-deep in water, and grubbing with their hands in the gravel and clay, there seemed to me little virtue in gold-digging. But when the shining particles were poured out lavishly from a tin basin, I confess there was a sudden itching in my fingers to seize the heaviest crowbar and the biggest shovel." Again and again that summer he reported the diggers' success: a forenoon's work produced nearly six pounds; two day's digging, fourteen pounds. He told of "persons at work in the higher part of the gulch, searching for veins and pockets of gold, in holes which had already produced their first harvest. . . . [They] were well paid for their perseverance. There are thousands of similar gulches among the mountains, nearly all of which undoubtedly contain gold."

By fall, thousands upon thousands of newly arrived prospectors wandered about the diggings, impatient to establish claims where their own industry might yield such extravagant treasure. Their innocence and surprise when confronted with the tough realities of California were poignantly expressed by a Frenchman writing to a newspaper in Paris. "On our poor little maps of California printed in France, the San Joaquin is shown as a river flowing between the California mountains and the sea, a short distance from San Francisco, in the midst of a rich plain which its waters cover with gold dust every year. The editors had even taken the pains to gild that precious plain on their maps. . . . One could, as it were, go to the mines in the morning and return to San Francisco each evening to sleep. Alas, the same is true of the map as with almost everything that is said about California: one can find the truth only in the place itself."

Even the sinewy overlanders, toughened by months on trails, were astonished by the truth of California. After a few days in the diggings, one newcomer wrote home: "The lay of the land, the incredible difficulties and hardships attending the operations of mining are no more understood in the United States than the hieroglyphics of the pyramids. . . . The digging and washing processes are the hardest kind of work a human being ever performed. I have been in the water a week, up to my knees all day and scraping up dirt from the rocky bottom with a big spoon and with my hands. The stones and gravel have worn the nails from all my fingers, down to the quick, by scratching on the rocks and picking out stones. And in stooping constantly, it sometimes takes a minute to straighten up. . . . This is a strange world, unlike anything ever dreamed of."

CHRYSOPOLIS

For the thousands who came by sea, like the Frenchman, the strange world of California enveloped them at the wharves of San Francisco, a city so frantic, so profligate, that the passengers' letters were filled with astonishment. First they were surprised by the number of ships deserted by officers and crews: abandoned at anchor in Yerba Buena Cove, facing the town, crowded together, creaking and swaying, an estimated 150 in May 1849. By October the ghostly fleet numbered 308—a forest of masts. In June 1850 the newspapers reported an astounding number: 635 brigs, barks, schooners, and other vessels, many with their cargoes undisturbed and worthless in the glutted market. If not left to rot and sink, scores of these hulks were pulled ashore to be used for storage or for saloons and lodgings. The brig *Euphemia* served as San Francisco's first prison. Most were cannibalized for planking, canvas, cordage, and spars to supply the hurry-up construction of San Francisco.*

Even before they could get ashore, passengers encountered the competitiveness and raw economic force of life in California. Small boats hooked onto the sides of arriving ships and business agents climbed on board, eager to learn if the cargo contained merchandise in short supply in the volatile San Francisco market. A captain in luck, with, say, thousands of boots or a cargo of bricks, might receive competing bids beyond his wildest fancies. Pushing on board as well, employment agents tried to hire from among the passengers mechanics and tradesmen with sorely needed skills—carpenters, clerks, draymen, masons, blacksmiths, printers. The captain of the schooner *Alhambra*, arriving from New Orleans, reported in October 1849 that on dropping anchor off San Francisco "there was a

---

* During 1850, 1,521 ships entered San Francisco Bay—but one of many statistics supporting the judgment that San Francisco's sudden rise from an almost unknown village to a center of worldwide maritime trade "stands unprecedented in the annals of navigation."

great rush of hotel keepers and 'restaurateurs' [looking] for cooks and waiters. They bid as high as three hundred a month for my black cook."

Most of the joint-stock companies, so efficiently organized in the optimism and innocence of home-town planning, disbanded on arrival in San Francisco or within a few days of reaching the diggings. They succumbed to the inevitable antagonisms of their trying journeys, or because members quickly learned that mining in 1849 could not be conducted by an unwieldy group working under directions from a president or field officer. More disappointing, companies that came by sea had to sell their cargoes into the ebb and flow of the fast-changing market. With members anxious to get to the diggings, no one wanted to wait for advantageous prices; so they sold, hoping for the best. As with cargoes, so with their ships, once expected to serve as headquarters for mining operations. Sold into the glutted market, even the finest brigs and schooners brought only a fraction of their value in any other port. In all, a bewildering introduction to a wild world that seemed to defy all their expectations.

Eager as the passengers were to get ashore, San Francisco seemed even more eager to receive them. Across tidal mudflats the wharves of 1848 were extended in the summer of 1849 and through 1850 to reach deep water, so ships could unload passengers and cargoes without the need for small craft between ships and shore. In the race to gain profits by providing these landings, competing wharf companies used steam pile-drivers to sink timbers of Oregon fir deep into the mud. Over these supports they laid down planking thirty to sixty feet wide. Of the twelve wharves eventually built, the most prominent and successful—the Central (or Long) Wharf—gained a length of eight hundred feet by December 1849 and reached out over two thousand feet a year later.

To provide storage—at high rental fees—for the millions of dollars of imports stacked on these wharves and along the muddy shore, some companies moored storeships (taken from the ghost fleet)

With surprising skill, goldseeker-artists embellished their diaries and letters with drawings and sometimes watercolors, such as this vividly detailed scene of ships abandoned in San Francisco harbor.

Exemplifying San Francisco's bold capitalism, this handbill enumerated some of the economic forces that created California's first boomtown. Less than two years after the discovery of gold, San Francisco already presumed to compete with New York and Boston, even London and Paris.

To replace its flimsy 1846 jail, the San Francisco Town Council decided to use one of the many hulks in the harbor rather than expensive real estate ashore. In February 1850 the brig *Euphemia* was anchored amid the wharves and took in its first prisoners, as well as "any suspicious, insane, or forlorn persons found strolling about the city at night." Like the *Apollo* (prospering as a saloon and warehouse), the prison ship was soon surrounded by wharves and buildings and later buried in landfill.

along their wooden avenues, while others erected warehouses on pilings. Their competition grew so fierce that sabotage crews sometimes worked at night to pull up a competitor's newly driven pilings or to cut mooring cables.*

As aggressive waterfront construction pushed out to deeper water, San Francisco seemed to a worldly Chilean goldseeker to be "a Venice built of pine instead of marble. It is a city of ships, piers, and tides. Large ships a good distance from the beach serve as lodgings, stores, and restaurants. . . . The whole central part of the city sways noticeably because it is built on pilings the size of ships' masts, driven down into the mud."

Once ashore, the passengers entered the even more bizarre life of a boomtown given over entirely to business, speculation, and entertainment, a place hurriedly improvised to profit from its unique and powerful location as the portal to the gold regions. During July 1849 the number of men landing from ships totaled 3,565—and women, 49. They all needed shelter and food, sought in boardinghouses and hotels, eateries and saloons, recently opened in whatever structures could be quickly put together. But these businesses were already overcrowded, so most newcomers slept in temporary shelters: tents, wood-framed dormitories covered with sail canvas, wooden shanties, here and there deck cabins lifted whole from ships, and a few sheet-iron "houses" imported from the States. Using lumber from Oregon at a cost of $600 per thousand feet, businessmen intent on fast profits pushed their high-priced workers to complete frame buildings, while others, more confident of San Francisco's future, invested in two- and three-story brick buildings, all to be rented

* In the frenzy of waterfront businesses and schemes, companies and individuals could make great fortunes. Among the many ships pulled ashore and held in place with pilings to serve as storehouses, saloons, and lodgings, the 400-ton *Niantic* earned for her owners in 1849 and 1850 a monthly rental income of $20,000. A carpenter from Connecticut who specialized in driving pilings headed home in the fall of 1850 with $65,000 (a millionaire in today's dollars).

Broadcast over the plains and deserts and mountains of America and all the oceans of the world, the call to San Francisco was a clarion of opportunity, of possibility, of new beginnings and great expectations. Not all the bald, sober facts or negative reports in the world—and there were plenty, even during the rush—could dilute the strength of that message, and those who came to San Francisco came with the light of tomorrow in their eyes. Such was the conditioning that gold inspired. Great expectations—and the inevitable corollary, great disappointment— were the warp and the woof, the very fabric of San Francisco's early American life. Like some kind of hallucinogen, gold heightened, distorted, and accelerated reality, propelling spurts, bursts, and great, explosive movements. The chronicle of the years that accompanied and followed the Gold Rush is not so much a history as the record of a seismograph.

T. H. Watkins and R. R. Olmsted, *Mirror of the Dream*

at prices far beyond the most brazen avarice of landlords back east.

At the Parker House on the Plaza, a small room rented for $1,800 per month; two other rooms went for $2,400 per month. The building's annual income exceeded $150,000. For a nearby canvas tent, fifteen by twenty-five feet, called Eldorado, tenants paid $40,000 annually. Some landlords took in $50,000 *monthly.* "One's mind cannot immediately push aside its old instincts for values and ideas of business," wrote Bayard Taylor for the *New York Tribune* when he spent a few days in San Francisco in August 1849. "Men dart hither and thither, as if possessed with a never-resting spirit. You speak with an acquaintance, a merchant perhaps. He utters a few hurried words of greeting, while his

The St. Francis Hotel offered a pricey alternative to the tents and shacks that housed San Francisco's largely transient population. Journalist Bayard Taylor described the hotel's rooms as "furnished with comfort and even luxury." He must already have grown accustomed to California's spartan accommodations. Other visitors complained that the chambers were separated by "the thinnest of board partitions" or only by cloth.

A competing hostelry, the Ward House, offered a menu impressive for its prices and its variety of entrees. A band played daily from the balcony. Clearly, the rough town had its fringes of elegance.

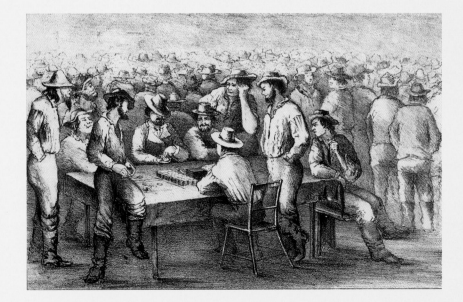

In this robust, masculine world, thousands of young men, for the first time in their lives, felt free to gamble or to watch others try their luck at the monte table, as in this scene drawn by an artist-goldseeker from Scotland. Sometimes a pistol shot scattered the onlookers.

eyes send keen glances on all sides of you. Suddenly . . . he is off, and in the next five minutes has bought up half a cargo, sold a town lot at treble the sum it cost, and taken a share in some new and imposing speculation." A boardinghouse-keeper in a letter home complained, "This place is not fit for anything but business. No one spends a minute for anything else."

Through the fall of 1849 the rush increased. During September nearly six thousand passengers landed at San Francisco, described three months later by a goldseeker from Boston as a place "the world never produced before. Crowded with . . . Yankees & the Chinaman jostling each other in the streets, while French, Germans, Sandwich Islanders, Chilians, Malays, Mexicans, &c &c in all their varieties of costume and language go to form a congrommoration of humanity." As intrigued as they were by the exotic costumes and peoples thronging San Francisco's muddy lanes, many Americans felt an instinctive resentment toward so many foreigners who had arrived with the intent of taking gold that rightfully belonged to U.S. citizens.

Of all the businesses that mined the pockets of Americans and foreigners alike, from bathhouses and billiard rooms to saloons and "dens of lewd women," none reached the prominence and profitability of gambling, offered under simple canvas tents no less than under the gilt chandeliers of elaborate "palaces." When they left home, most goldseekers had vowed to resist California's infamous temptations. Once in San Francisco, however, very few could turn away from a visit to the Parker House, the Bella Union, the Aquila d'Or, or many other gaming halls where success could be properly celebrated with the best liquor and cigars, or disappointment assuaged with friendly, understanding talk. And as everyone knew, the walls displayed life-sized paintings of naked women, while at the faro and monte tables live women—their bosoms partially, thrillingly exposed—laughed, smoked, and drank among the male patrons. In these invigorating surroundings, a few bets seemed justified—to

anticipate success in the mines, to add to winnings from hard-worked claims, or, with just a little luck, to gain at last what the diggings had capriciously withheld.

LETTERS AND LEGISLATORS

IN THEIR MOUNTAIN OUTPOSTS AND URBAN encampments, the army of goldseekers lived with two urgent desires: to "strike it rich" and to receive "tidings from home." After months at sea or on the overland trails and then weeks and months in California without letters from wives and parents, fiancées, and friends, the miners felt an increasing need for assurance of life and love from the distant world of family. In an age when few people traveled beyond their home county and seldom stayed away overnight, lonely men in their far-away bivouacs waited for news from home, indulging their worried imaginations, fearful of what a letter might report— a child or wife dead from cholera, an aged mother sick with "the fevers," a brother grievously injured in a farm accident.

Anxious waiting provoked resentment of the U.S. Post Office Department for its incompetence. In a land where there had never been a postal delivery network, the postmaster general in Washington failed miserably to cope with the surge of mail sent to California in 1849 and for years thereafter. When the first postal agent reached San Francisco in February 1849, his instructions and resources were so inadequate that mail could not be delivered beyond the single, overwhelmed San Francisco post office. And overwhelmed it was, because only two "addresses"—San Francisco and Sutter's Fort—were known to the outside world. So San Francisco received the thousands of bags of mail, and there they piled up. Under this deluge, the pygmy agency buckled.

On October 31, 1849, the Pacific Mail Steamship Company's *Panama* delivered the mails for July, August, and September—forty-five thousand letters and uncounted bushels of newspapers, all delayed at the isthmus by handling irregularities and general incompetence. When this treasure landed at the little post office on November 1, its five employees faced chaos—bulging canvas mailbags stuffed with thousands of letters to be sorted by addressee alphabetically, while outside angry men pounded on the doors and walls. By the time the windows opened—three days later—to distribute the mail, a riot threatened. Fortunately the beseechers repressed their anger and formed into lines that "extended all the way down the hill into Portsmouth Square. . . . The man at the tail of the longest line might count on spending six hours in it before he reached the window. Those who were near the goal frequently sold out their places to impatient candidates for ten and even twenty-five dollars. Indeed, several persons in want of money practiced this game daily as a means of living. Vendors of pies, cakes, and newspapers established themselves in front of the office to supply the crowd, while others did a profitable business by carrying cans of coffee up and down the lines."

San Francisco's beleaguered postmaster showed no more success in managing the larger task of opening local post offices throughout the region so that miners and merchants could pick up mail at relatively convenient locations rather than having to spend days, even weeks, making the round trip to San Francisco. Promises and announcements of local offices to be opened received acclaim, followed by outrage when the postal authorities' customary incompetence let down the many hopeful. After a second office opened at Sacramento City (Sutter's Fort) in July 1849 and was so overwhelmed that it quickly closed, the *Placer Times* (the town's first newspaper, founded as a weekly in April 1849) expostulated on August 2: "The 'Regular Mail' is a regular humbug, is stuck in the mud half the time, and might as well be the other half. . . . We understand that the Postmaster [in San Francisco] cannot afford to employ clerks."

With mud and mismanagement holding back government mail deliveries to the widely scattered miners, Yankee enterprise once again filled the gap. Individual miners gave up digging and set themselves up as one-man "express" companies. They gathered the names of several hundred miners who agreed to pay $1.00 to $2.50 to have their mail collected at the San Francisco post office and delivered to them. One expressman who operated along the forks of the Feather River boasted that he had over two thousand names on his express list.

The miners also entrusted to their expressmen the responsibility of carrying their pouches of gold dust to San Francisco (and later, Sacramento City) for deposit with a banking house, at a customary charge of 5 percent of the gold's value. As they developed their clientele and established their routes, these express companies opened offices—little more than small rooms—in towns and camps near the miners on their lists. There they kept iron safes where gold dust could be measured and held until shipped to "the City." These stockpiles of gold served the express companies as capital for loans to local businessmen and small mining companies. Thus the express companies (eventually more than two hundred of them) served both as carriers and as banks.*

---

* Reflecting the "hard money" sentiments so prevalent in the States, California's Constitution of 1849 prohibited the legislature from passing any law that would permit a "person, association, company, or corporation from . . . creating paper to circulate as money." But companies could be chartered to accept deposits of gold and silver. Thus banks could operate, but without issuing currency. The result was that for many years California did business in gold dust, coins, and on credit. Foreign coins circulated widely: Spanish, Mexican, Peruvian, and Ecuadorian doubloons; French francs, Spanish pesetas, English crowns, Dutch florins and guilders, Indian rupees, and Brazilian milreis, their valuations guessed at and heavily discounted. Everyone had gold, hence gold dust and nuggets served as money, the most common unit being a "pinch"—the amount of gold dust that could be raised between the thumb and forefinger. When a clerk was hired, the employer would ask, "How much can you raise in a pinch?" The larger the pinch, the more valued the clerk. Often a bartender or merchant would wet his thumb and forefinger before reaching into a miner's pouch.

Hoping for letters from home, fearful of the news they might contain, hundreds of men stood in line for hours (some for days, selling their up-front positions) outside the San Francisco post office. Inside, the overwhelmed staff tried to alphabetize some 45,000 letters dumped out of canvas bags received once a month, later twice a month, from the *Oregon* and other Panama mail steamers.

Back in the States, families waited for months, even a year, without response to their letters. George Swain in Youngstown, New York, north of Buffalo, sent this letter in February 1850. It reached his brother William on the South Fork of the Feather River, carried by one of many expressmen who took over mail delivery from the U.S. Postal Department. "We have not heard one word from you. . . . What the dickens is the reason you don't write, boy? If you are all dead, it would be no more than civil to send us word. . . . We have written to you every month since you left home [in April 1849]."

What it meant to receive a letter from home was described by that vivid reporter of gold rush life, William Perkins, at his store in Sonora: "There is a charm, a witchcraft in a letter from Home . . . , a man is transported at once in spirit to the scenes he has left behind. . . . My letters generally make me feel a little ashamed of finding myself in this country, leading a kind of savage life merely for the accumulation of gold." Less introspective, a miner from Wisconsin wrote to his parents: "If you could have seen us when we received our letters, you would have laughed, perhaps called us fools—such hoorahing, jumping, yelling, and screaming. . . . You will take good care and write often when I tell you that I live upon your letters, with a small sprinkling of pork and bread." For many years, and especially during the winter months when rain and snow made travel almost impossible, the arrival of the expressman came like an angel's visit for the miners on remote river bars and in sunless canyons.*

Inevitably, a business so much in demand attracted the attention of larger concerns, first among them an affiliate of Adams & Company headquartered in New York City. From its outset in December 1849, Adams & Company Express sought to dominate operations by buying pioneer express companies and taking over their offices in major mining camps. With its eastern connections, Adams & Company Express could handle the banking side of the business more directly and reliably than any other agency. Using a careful system of assays to determine the differing qualities of gold dust, the company purchased gold from the miners, paying between $14 and $16 an ounce, and trans-

ferred the appropriate value to one of its offices in the States. Thus a miner in Sonora could take his pile to the Adams office, pay a 10 percent fee, and know that his wife in Dayton, Ohio, would receive that amount of money at the Adams office in Cincinnati. How welcome that transfer, not only for his family but for the miner who could feel that he was justifying his decision to leave home.

Collecting gold throughout the diggings, Adams & Company Express became the major shipper of California's wealth, from San Francisco via the isthmus to New York. In the express and banking business, the name Adams stood for reliability and success—until the company's sudden failure in 1855, a stupefying event.†

As free enterprise improved mail deliveries and gold transfers, so it sought to cope with the many inconveniences caused by the absence of legal, standard coinage. Measuring and weighing gold dust and judging its purity in every transaction led inevitably to cheating and arguments. Coins from many countries circulated widely, but always with uncertainty as to their value. To resolve these irregularities, individuals melted gold and cast private slugs for sale, stamped with their reputed value, usually in denominations of $5 and $10. These ingots actually contained maybe $4 and $8. Nevertheless, they served as a convenient currency, and

---

* As a wonderful example of how bureaucratic thinking persists through the centuries, consider that in November 1849, when U.S. mail service continued to be decrepit and practically nonexistent, the U.S. postmaster issued an official warning that carrying letters "out of the mail" was forbidden by law and subject to "a penalty of $50." And he threatened to arrest expressmen, even though he had to admit that "multitudes send their letters . . . by these guilty parties."

---

† Wells, Fargo & Company expanded from its New York base into California in 1852. Thereafter it dominated the express business and became a major banking house after 1855.

Until the 1870s, express companies and banks thrived—and sometimes collapsed—as unregulated, private businesses. They took in deposits of gold dust for which they issued "Certificates of Deposit" to be cashed (for a fee) at any of the company's offices in California or the States—an early form of branch banking. Banks and express companies depended on public trust, the general confidence that a company could at any time refund its total deposits. Rumor to the contrary might start a "run," causing the company to close its doors, leaving economic and social chaos, among other consequences of that wildly laissez-faire era.

their manufacturers had invented a grand California business: making money by making money.

Acceptable as these and other adaptations proved to be, what merchants, speculators, bankers, and gamblers wanted were official assay offices and a trustworthy currency. In short, a government mint. But only Congress could sanction such progress, and Congress continued to ignore California's needs. Washington's legislators, locked in angry debate over the question of permitting or prohibiting slavery in the vast territories acquired in the war with Mexico, adjourned in March 1849, having failed yet again to establish a territorial government for California. Washington did manage to send out a new military governor, Brigadier General Bennet Riley, who would find in the territory's primitive affairs ample reason to burnish his reputation as a "fine, free swearer." He landed at Monterey on April 12, 1849, with orders to replace Colonel Richard Mason.* The new governor faced a populace disgusted by the travesty of a military government too weak to protect miners from hostile Indians, too poor to provide essential services, and fundamentally inappropriate in time of peace. On April 26 San Francisco's newspaper, the *Alta California* (successor to the *California Star and Californian*), proclaimed that "the present state of anarchy (we can call it nothing less) is much to be deplored." The editor's grim verdict stood as challenge to the incoming governor to try something new.

RILEY

---

* Colonel Mason sailed home on May 3, 1849, his departure unnoticed, his great contributions to California ignored in those times of confusion and self-interest. Like his predecessor General Stephen Watts Kearny, who left California unheralded and died in less than a year (October 1848), Mason died of cholera in St. Louis in July 1850. And so it was for their president and commander-in-chief, James K. Polk. He died in June 1849 (age fifty-three), only a few months after leaving the White House.

This lament from a wife in Youngstown, New York, suggests that some letters may well have caused more anguish than "hoorahing," maybe even a sense of relief not to be at home:

William, I do not want you to leave home again for the sake of leaving me to ease and comfort. My health is poor, more so I think than our folks are aware of. Not only is my back bad, but I have a pain in my chest and left side, palpitation of the heart, and dyspepsia. But do not give yourself any uneasiness about me.

Sabrina Swain, letter of July 26, 1849

Weighing congressional gridlock and the insistent demands of a self-declared legislative assembly in San Francisco, Governor Riley on June 3 issued a "Proclamation to the People of California," wherein he set forth "the means best calculated to avoid the embarrassments of our present position." Those means called for the election of delegates to a constitutional convention that would convene in Monterey in September to establish either a territorial or state government. Their document would be submitted for the approval of the people and then sent on to the Congress. California would take the initiative that Washington had ceded.

On September 1, forty-eight delegates gathered in Monterey in the only building in all of California that could accommodate such an assembly, the two-story, stone-walled Colton Hall, erected under the supervision of Walter Colton (that literary diary keeper of 1848) when he was the town's alcalde. The new lawmakers arrived by ship, on horseback, and in open wagons, most of them carrying their own blankets, knowing that accommodations would be few and primitive. Some resigned themselves to sleeping under trees. That was California in 1849. During the six weeks of debates, Thomas Oliver

Larkin (one of the delegates) each day invited to his home a fellow delegate for lunch and one for dinner, thus assuring they had at least one good meal.

The southern towns (San Diego, Los Angeles, Santa Barbara, and San Luis Obispo) sent eleven representatives, while the more populated mining districts and their adjacent commercial centers sent thirty-seven, thirteen of whom had been residents for less than a year. Age, too, reflected the vigorously nontraditional profile of that society: half of California's Founding Fathers were less than thirty-five years old.

Having experienced the consequences of depending on far-off Washington (no one remembered Madrid or Mexico City), and knowing that territorial status would continue that exasperating dependence, most delegates strongly favored California's becoming the thirty-first state. But a cautious minority, representing the great ranchers, demurred. These delegates knew that the revenue authority of a new state government would mean taxes on property—levied primarily against their thousands and thousands of acres of original land grants. And so they favored territorial status, with Washington responsible for the costs of governing California. For the miners, in contrast, property taxes were of small concern. They owned no land; they simply took the gold and moved on.

Being in the minority, the ranchers lost. The vote for statehood forecast a conflict that would torment California through the next three decades: the political power of the many goldseekers versus the interests and rights of the far fewer landowners.

With some dissent but without rancor, the delegates voted to join the Union, then turned their attention to the issue that remained so volatile in Washington: slavery. In contrast to the bitter divisions paralyzing senators and representatives in Congress, the forty-eight delegates in Monterey quickly achieved peaceful unanimity, declaring that "neither slavery nor involuntary servitude, unless for punishment of crimes, shall ever be tolerated in this State."

Why did the delegates vote unanimously for California to be "free," even though many of them and those they represented came from slave states? Because they understood and shared the values and prejudices of the miners. Almost everyone at some time had worked a claim, and as a consequence even the most callus-hardened toil had acquired respectability, a kind of dignity. Where else could the sweat of wielding a pick and shovel unearth such wealth? No one wanted this economic democracy perverted by slavery. The lament of a miner from Alabama unintentionally made the case for protecting equal opportunity in the diggings: "With twenty good Negroes and the power of managing them as at home, I could make from ten to fifteen thousand dollars per month. But here a fellow has to knock it out with his own fist, or not at all."

Determined to protect the unique opportunity of gold, especially for hard-fisted white men like themselves, the majority at Colton Hall kept the practical needs and interests of the miners uppermost in their minds as they fashioned the state's constitution. Their dominant vision of California displaced the interests of the ranchers—the men of the past—as it also ignored a new class of entrepreneurs represented by a few pioneering farmers whose profits forecast an alternative future—one that would challenge the presumption and conviction that California depended on gold.* The delegates agreed with a miner who had traveled about and concluded: "Exhaust the gold and California will no longer attract ships to its shore, [except] to carry back the poor devils who are caught here in search of El

---

* Like miners intent on striking it rich, the first farmers planted crops that could be sold for fast profits in the scurvy-threatened mining camps and gold-rich hotels and eateries. A German named Schwartz planted a crop of melons in the summer of 1849, which he sold for $30,000 in Sacramento City. Potatoes were in such demand as a cure or preventive for scurvy that there developed a "potato-growing" fever. These unheralded successes forecast the growth of farming during the 1850s.

Dorado." Another judged that the gold would be used up in five years, at which point California "will be one of the poorest states in the Union."

Meanwhile, the abundance that attracted men by the tens of thousands failed to lure what the bachelor delegates agreed the new state most needed: more women. To promote their arrival, the hopeful legislators designed the consti-tution to be the first in the nation guaranteeing that all assets owned by a wife at the time her marriage, or acquired by her thereafter, would remain her separate property. Shocking the traditionalists who argued that God had made women "frail, lovely, and dependent," proponents of this radical reform argued it would attract not only prospective wives but "women of fortune"—also in short supply. This constitutional logic won immediate approval.

The convention settled other fundamental matters, like the state's boundaries, location of the capital (in San Jose, for the time being), and rights of suffrage (Negroes and Indians excluded).* Reflecting their impatience—and their sense of California's importance—the delegates passed a resolution that authorized the new state government to take up its duties immediately after public ratification of the

---

* That the "anti-slavery" provision in the state constitution did not carry any sense of moral obligation to provide civil rights for African Americans and Native Americans was clearly evidenced by the fact that both minorities were denied not only the right to vote but also the right to testify in court cases involving whites. In 1852 the state legislature adopted a harsh fugitive slave law, in conformity with the odious federal statute. This law was overruled in 1858 in the famous Archy Lee case. As to the ban on legal testimony, after years of organized effort by blacks in California (they numbered 5,400 in 1860), the legislature removed the ban in 1863. Native Americans and Chinese gained the right to testify in 1872. In response to the U.S. Constitution's Fifteenth Amendment, the California legislature finally gave the right to vote to African Americans in 1870.

constitution, rather than await formal authorization from the Congress. Governor Riley accepted this decision, though he had "strong doubts of the legality of such a course."

As the delegates signed the constitution, ships in the harbor boomed out thirty-one salvos, the last a salute in honor of the newest state. With the sound of ceremonial cannon reverberating through the hall, delegate John Sutter excitedly jumped to his feet and exclaimed: "Gentlemen, this is the happiest day of my life. . . . This is a great day for California."

Once signed, the constitution was hurried to the only printing press in California, in the offices of the *Alta California* in San Francisco, where 1,000 copies were run off in English and 250 in Spanish—a paltry number for such a scattered electorate. On November 13, 1849, Californians for the first time voted for their own government. Although there had been a clamor in the towns to remove the military governor and the *Alta* had promoted the need for an elected government, only 12,061 votes were cast in favor of the constitution (811 against) and 6,783 for Peter Burnett as governor, out of a population estimated at 107,000. Those who cared enough to vote also selected a lieutenant governor, two representatives to the U.S. Congress, and members for the state legislature. (The two U.S. senators would be chosen by the legislature.) On December 12 General Riley proclaimed California's constitution had been "ordained and established" and would be forwarded to the Congress in Washington.

No one, however, wanted to wait for a response from that distracted authority. The transfer of power, assuming there would be some power, from General Riley to the new government moved ahead on its own. The legislature convened in San Jose on December 17. Despite complaints about inadequate accommodations for their deliberations and a vote to return the capital to the comparative comfort of Monterey, the assembled leaders conducted a proper ceremony to inaugurate California's first elected governor, Peter Burnett. With swelling pride and an equally unrestrained sense of the power of

In camps like this, few if any of the miners knew of California's constitution or of the election to determine if it would be ratified. Unaware of their sudden responsibilities as voters and unconcerned about California's future, the men in this contemporary scene busied themselves with Sunday chores and welcomed distractions—fiddle playing, card games, and a convivial saloon. This exceptionally vivid, informative drawing was entitled "Sunday at Forbes diggings, Feather River." Located on a ridge south of the South Fork of the Feather River, this camp grew into the prosperous Forbestown.

the electorate, the *Alta California* described the occasion on December 21, 1849: "Here, where but a few months since . . . civilization had scarcely deigned to pay a flying visit, were now assembled a grave legislature, empowered to put in force the machinery of a good republican government. The chief executive officer of that system . . . came alone and unattended—no pomp, no ceremony—no venal guards, no useless parade of armed men. There were with him but the people and their representatives. They were his audience and his defenders—they will be his executioners if he fails to discharge honestly and faithfully the important duties devolving upon him."

Following the inauguration, members of the Assembly and Senate attended regular sessions for the next four months, adjourning in April 1850. Though known as the "legislature of a thousand drinks" for the presumed distractions of free liquor, these first legislators succeeded in passing 146 statutes that established the functions and powers of

the new state's government. Among their accomplishments, they agreed to the creation of twenty-seven counties, which would serve as the basis for traditional municipal governments—they hoped. Twenty-one of these counties were located in the populous northern part of the state; the others encompassed the vast regions of southern California—"the cow counties"—which as of 1850 had only eight thousand non-Indian residents.

To cope with the challenge of raising revenue, the legislators resorted in April 1850 to passing an ill-considered statute recommended by the Senate Finance Committee whereby foreigners would be required to pay $20 per month for the "privilege of taking from our country the vast treasure to which they have no right." In voting for this soon-to-prove-troublesome law, the legislators naively accepted the assurance that foreign miners would "cheerfully" pay to the appointed collectors the monthly fee, though in the same legislation these "foreigners" were characterized as "the worst population of the Mexican and South American States, New South Wales [Australia], and the Southern Islands . . . [including] the convicts of Mexico, Chili, and Botany Bay who are daily turned upon our shores."

Impatient to be welcomed into the union of states, California's first assemblymen and senators selected the two men who would be sent to Washington to be on hand when the Congress—at last—voted to admit the thirty-first state: John C. Frémont, who had returned to California in early 1849 and, by the time of his election, had become one of the wealthiest men in the state;* and William M. Gwin of Tennessee, though he had been in California barely six months.

In his final proclamation, Military Governor Bennet Riley stated with obvious relief that "a new executive having been elected and installed in office . . . , the undersigned hereby resigns his power as governor of California. . . . The people have a government of their own choice."

Yes, their own choice, for the first time. During the eighty years since the first settlement in 1769, California had survived a succession of thirty-two appointed governors: eleven sent by Spain, fourteen

---

* When Frémont returned to California after a disastrous exploring expedition in the winter of 1848–49, he found that the land purchased for him by Thomas Larkin in 1847—a 45,000-acre land grant known as Las Mariposas at the south end of the southern mining region—was not the worthless tract he had thought. Its gold deposits proved far richer than he and his wife, Jessie, could ever have imagined. While in San Jose in December 1849 awaiting the election of senators, they celebrated not only John's prospects as U.S. senator but also, and even more thrilling, their new status as gold rush millionaires. Although the thought may never have occurred to Frémont, he was probably the only person in California taking gold from land he actually owned.

One of the best-known names in California history, Frémont spent only a few years of his life in the state. After his election as senator, he left for Washington, failed to gain reelection, lost Las Mariposas and his wealth, and, after a few brief visits to California, died almost forgotten in 1890.

by Mexico, and seven by the U.S. Army and Navy.

Keeping up his predecessors' tradition of transiency, California's first elected governor, Peter Burnett, resigned only thirteen months after taking office. Weary of coping with the legislators, he turned to the practice of law in San Francisco, leaving the state's leadership to Lieutenant Governor John McDougal, described by his contemporaries as "that gentlemanly drunkard." In considering his future, the new governor announced that he stood in awe of only two personages: God Almighty and Mrs. McDougal.

INSTANT CITIES AND INSTANT PROFITS

In the winter of 1849 few, if any, of the miners, merchants, shippers, speculators, and gamblers paused amid the rush and hubbub to consider the changes they had wrought in one brief year: a seaside village transformed into a world port, empty canyons and narrow gulches crowded with mining camps, a fiefdom of traditional families overrun by an unshaved society of men without women, an ignored outback proclaiming itself to be America's thirty-first state.

Indispensable to this transformation were the two great waterways—the Sacramento and San Joaquin Rivers—that linked California's seaport city to its otherwise isolated mining regions. Literally all commerce bound for the booming interior arrived via these natural highways, thousands of tons of freight and thousands of people from San Francisco's wharves to the embarcaderos at Sacramento City and Stockton. Sailing ships tacked their way through tule sloughs and winding currents, a four- to ten-day journey from the bay to the river ports, often delayed by adverse winds or becalmed amid clouds of mosquitoes. Finally making fast at their destination, the ships' crews unloaded the crates, boxes, barrels, and sacks packed with everything from nails to mirrors. Under riverbank

A "FLOATING PALACE"

sycamores, the packaged freight piled high alongside tons of bricks and lumber, some to be sold at the levee, more to be hauled by wagon and on muleback to the mining camps.

Through the summer of 1849 this inefficient transportation system persisted. Sometimes larger sailing ships that had rounded Cape Horn were coaxed upriver with passengers and freight directly to Sacramento City or Stockton, there to end their careers as storage hulks and floating wharves over which flowed the tide of the world's exports and hopeful goldseekers.

With demand and prices escalating wildly, shippers and merchants sought faster, more reliable transport. They ordered small steamboats to be disassembled in New York, shipped around the Horn, reassembled in San Francisco, and put into service on the two rivers. Launched in July and August, these side-wheelers replaced the uncertainty of sail with the dependability of steam. Overwhelmed by the demand for more cabin and cargo space and buoyed by their profits (revenue within weeks exceeded the cost of the vessels), San Francisco shippers next ordered oceangoing steamers from the East Coast. The first of these "floating palaces," the 750-ton side-wheel *Senator* from Boston, completed her round-the-Horn voyage in October and made her first trip upriver to Sacramento City on November 5, 1849, a date that marked a dramatic change in California's commercial life: a regular schedule of ten- to twelve-hour passage to Sacramento City.

Standing at the river city's embarcadero to watch the *Senator*'s arrival, a citizen burbled with enthusiasm. "All the nymphs of the ocean making their appearance in our midst would not have excited more rejoicing and excitement than did this noble floating palace. . . . She infused a vitality into our mercantile relations with San Francisco and demonstrated unequivocally the entire navigability of the beautiful river upon which our city's destiny depended . . . and imparted substantial reason for all the enthusiasm and jollification excited by her presence."

Northbound to Sacramento City one day and southbound the next to San Francisco, the *Senator* sold out consistently with passenger tickets going for $30 and cargo rates of $35 per ton. During her first twelve months of operation, the *Senator* earned over $600,000!* The powerful attraction of that astounding sum brought other paddle wheelers hurrying around South America to share in the bonanza.

From the river ports to the up-country towns and remote mining camps, all shipments depended on freight wagons and pack mules. Each day throughout the dry season (May to October or November), hundreds of mule- or ox-drawn wagons rolled out of Sacramento City and Stockton in dust so thick "it filled the air about twenty feet above the ground, so that it appeared like a fog." These freighters hauled their loads to Auburn, Hangtown, Mokelumne Hill, Sonora, and other towns that during the summer became the intermediate supply

---

* Astonishing though this frequently quoted $600,000 might be, careful calculations suggest the *Senator* earned an even more astonishing total during 1850. Running two and later three round-trips each week and carrying her capacity of 300 passengers each way and 200 tons of freight upriver, the *Senator* probably grossed $40,000 weekly and over $2 million that year. To convert to 1998 dollars, multiply by 19.23: over $38 million—for one steamboat! This emphasizes the wonder of California's gold rush economy and why such intense competition developed among steamboat owners during the 1850s, leading to monopoly.

Dismayed by the wild freedom of the place, not least by the "obscene pictures" that decorated gambling tents, a clergyman from New York City recorded his impressions of Sacramento City in June 1849:

The present of this city is under canvas and the future on paper. Everything is new except the ground and trees and stars beneath which we sleep. Quarreling and cheating form the employments, drinking and gambling the amusements, making the largest pile of gold the only ambition of the inhabitants.

Daniel B. Woods, *Sixteen Months at the Gold Diggings*

centers for the widely scattered mining camps farther up in the hills. To reach these more remote stores, hotels, eateries, and gambling saloons at the end of trails too steep and rough for wagons, supplies were transferred to pack mules (as much as 350 pounds per mule) and carried twenty to thirty miles each day, along narrow ridges and down precipitous slopes to the most isolated clusters of tents and cabins.

Once the rainy season set in, the traffic quickly bogged down in mud too deep for heavy wagons. In their place long trains of pack mules were loaded directly at the river ports and landings. In the thick of winter, sometimes even these "clipper ships of the mountains" were delayed by storms, rock slides, and snowdrifts. But at seventy-five cents per pound, profits were so irresistible that packers routinely risked extreme conditions to reach the farthest outposts.

As depots for supplies from San Francisco and base camps for new goldseekers preparing to set out, Sacramento City and Stockton boomed through the summer and winter of 1849. With their temptations and comforts, these instant cities became resorts for thousands of shaggy, bronzed miners not-so-fresh from mining camps like Steep Hollow, Fleatown, Yankee Slide, Cut Eye, Sucker Flat, Humbug Canyon, Port Wine, and Rich Gulch. Eager for a bath, a shave, a good meal, a spree in one of the gambling palaces, and a friendly woman, these many visitors spent their gold dust with a careless abandon that inspired merchants and speculators to build at an ever-faster pace. Sacramento City's first historian reported, "Every material that could be used in building tents, houses, and stores became of immense value, commanding almost instant sale at any price which might be suggested by the unscrupulous spirit of speculation. . . . Muslins, calicos, canvas, old sails, logs, boards, iron, zinc, tin, adobes, and boxes were infinitely more glittering and beautiful as building appliances than the unpolished gold scales [flakes] which were lavishly given in exchange for them."

In October a young man from Maine, newly arrived in Sacramento City and in business as a storekeeper, wrote to his sister back home. "You have no idea how this country is going ahead. Last spring there was nobody here and now people are as thick as in the city of New York. Stages run regularly to the mines, steamboats run on the river . . . , several large, handsome hotels with billiard saloons and bowling alleys and all the fixings have been put up. Even a couple of girls are around with a hand organ and tambourine. . . . Shaving is all the humbug. Nobody shaves. I am going to have my daguerreotype taken and sent home to show you how I have improved. Tomorrow I start for San Francisco on the steamer *Sacramento* and take down six thousand dollars in dust [which he sent to his uncle in Bucksport, Maine, who had financed his journey to California]. . . . This country raises gold and they have not begun to dig it up yet. I know of three men who are going home with $150,000."

On November 25 this exuberant Californian advised his sister that the "week before last we sold out of our little store $1,500 worth of goods. All cash trade in one day. Tell Joseph to beat that. It has gotten to be an old story to me. The first dust that I received, $2,800 on our selling two houses in San Francisco, made my eyes sparkle and my heart beat rather quickly as I spooned it into a two quart pail. But now, I receive it and weigh it out with as little feeling as I would so much sand."

Of the "handsome hotels" along Sacramento's filthy streets, the most prominent, the City Hotel, was built by the city's leading businessman, Sam Brannan. Since his shouts in San Francisco only a year earlier, he had prospered in all his ventures as merchant and speculator. His three-story hostelry, with its wrought-iron grillwork and spacious public rooms, brought him a monthly income of $5,000; but that was a trifle compared to the profits he earned from several stores, various investments, and the sale of real estate. He owned some five hundred prime lots in Sacramento City, obtained through his clever manipulation of befuddled Captain Sutter and his naive son. As much as any '49er, Sam was ready for the get-ahead years of the 1850s.

Other businessmen read the signs, that the booming growth of 1849 might continue for another year, maybe longer; that gold mining could sustain the wonder of it all. But who knew how long? Most optimistic were the river-steamer owners who placed orders for new and larger side-wheelers to compete in the booming San Francisco to Sacramento City and Stockton runs. Freighters and mule packers in those river ports invested in scores of new wagons and hundreds of mules, making huge profits supplying the mining camps, where the toil of thousands of gold diggers produced nothing of immediate utility—no food, no hardware, no shelter—only the gleaming yellow grains, flakes, and dust that financed everything. And there were the profits to be made—without any work—from real estate speculation, the very essence of California's risk-taking economy. In December 1849 Thomas Larkin sold nine lots in San Francisco for $300,000, giving him a gain of more than $290,000.

Another cunning old-timer, Charles Weber, who had come to California in the overland emigration of 1841, was even more successful. During the free-

CHRONOLOGY (1849)

Jan. 22	*Alta California* becomes the state's first daily newspaper
March 31	California's first postmaster lands in San Francisco
April 10	Safety pin patented
May 14	Thoreau's essay "Civil Disobedience" published
June 4	Pacific Mail Steamship Company begins scheduled service between San Francisco and Panama City
Nov. 13	California's constitution adopted by popular vote
Dec. 20	Peter Burnett takes oath as California's first elected governor
Dec. 29	San Francisco's harbormaster records 782 ship arrivals since March 26

for-all summer of 1848, Weber employed as many as one thousand Indians to work the rich diggings along what became known as Weber Creek, not far from Coloma, paying them not in gold but with colored ribbons, glass beads, and silver coins. Collecting all the gold washed by these workers, Weber added to his wealth by selling trade goods to the many other miners. By the fall of 1848, anticipating the resentments of individual miners that would lead to prohibitions of absentee ownership and gang labor, Weber closed his mining and trading operations to follow Larkin and Brannan into the gold mine of speculative real estate, setting up business in his town of Stockton, gateway to the southern mines. To this new enterprise he applied the earnings from his summer's work—a fortune of more than $400,000.

Weber built an elaborate home for his family (with a chimney of bricks imported from Massachusetts), sold lots at $3,000 to $6,000 each, purchased ships to transport supplies—and the mail—from San Francisco to Stockton, and drew fattening profits from his mercantile business. By October his town had a population of two to three thousand and offered all the pleasures "the boys" had long ago promised their families they would resolutely resist—gambling, drinking, and fast women. More appropriate for description in letters home were the eateries' California specialties—great slabs of elk steak, salmon "of astonishing size," and, most noteworthy, "the solid flesh of the grizzly bear."

THE SUMMER FADES

Writing to his fiancée back in Easton, Connecticut, a discouraged miner confessed his summerlong failure to find gold on the North Fork of the American River. Twenty-three-year-old Henry Crandall scratched out his sentences to Mary Mills, sending the news that he had decided lumber speculation offered a better chance of making the fortune he had promised. To which the spirited Mary wrote back on December 12, 1849: "Oh, Henry, I did not think you meant to stay away two whole years when you went away, and now you write . . . that you think of staying still longer. Come home. Forget the nuggets. I would rather see you than any lump in California. . . . I do not care to have the strength of my affections tested by a much longer absence."

Few wives or sweethearts wrote with Mary Mills's wry humor and forthright candor. More often they pleaded for an early return home by scrawling forlorn recitals of loneliness, in-law problems, children's illnesses, debts unpaid, and loss of confidence in the promise of California gold. Whether impelled by such calls for help or worn out by the harsh life of digging, hundreds of goldseekers, even many who had arrived in September and October, decided to quit, unwilling to wait out the winter on their lean diet of hope and envy. They crowded the steamers returning to San Francisco. There they took jobs on construction crews and in foundries to pay for the tickets to take them, via

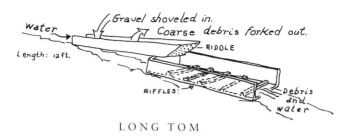

LONG TOM

Panama or Nicaragua, to the East Coast and home.

While the "backtrackers" carried stories of failure, of gold mining as a great delusion, at least forty thousand miners (by some estimates fifty thousand) continued their quest in California, buoyed by reports of the latest strikes, trumpeted in newspapers, repeated and exaggerated in saloons: $5,000 washed by two men on the Yuba; nuggets uncovered on the Stanislaus weighing 20 pounds, with one reported at 141 pounds. Everyone needed to believe these reports. They strengthened partners laboring waist deep in icy streams and livened talk around campfires. And they provided reassurance that despite the thousands of newcomers tramping up worn trails and competing for claims, the toil of digging that dulled pickaxes and bent shovels could still produce the longed-for "pocket full of rocks."

In their prospecting and digging, their impatience and yearning to strike it rich, miners continually experimented with new methods of washing and sifting the dirt on their claims. Graduating from the rocker, they "invented" the long tom. Easily constructed, this wooden trough, twelve to fifteen feet in length, required a constant flow of water entering its upper end. Two or three men shoveled in the hoped-for gold-bearing dirt, and as the force of water melted the coarse dirt, another partner stirred and cleared away the larger rocks. The muddy mix washed down to the lower end of the tom where a perforated metal sheet—the riddle— held back the coarser material, as the finer gravel and sand (with the gold) fell into a lower trough in which cleats—riffles—caught the precious particles. The longer the troughs, the more men needed and the more dirt washed.

To provide the essential flow of water, crews of

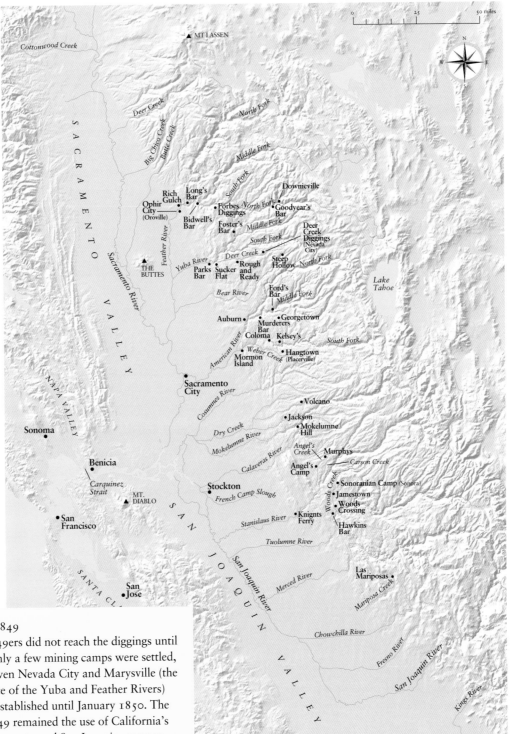

THE GOLD REGION, 1849

Because the mass of '49ers did not reach the diggings until September or later, only a few mining camps were settled, compared to 1850. Even Nevada City and Marysville (the latter at the confluence of the Yuba and Feather Rivers) did not get formally established until January 1850. The key to progress in 1849 remained the use of California's major rivers, the Sacramento and San Joaquin, as transportation routes from San Francisco to Sacramento City and Stockton. Gold rush entrepreneurs did not initially invest in building roads for slow wagon transport; rather, they paid to bring side- and stern-wheel steamboats around the Horn. Once in San Francisco, these "floating palaces" went to work making big profits by delivering freight and passengers to the inland river ports.

miners became self-taught hydrology engineers, digging ditches and constructing flumes to carry water to their long toms from streams or dammed reservoirs. This revolutionary advance—man-moved water, delivered where needed—freed the miners to stake claims in sites previously ignored because of their distance from a natural source of water. Through the next three decades as placer mining became more ambitious and aggressive, water companies engaged in ever more daring projects that rearranged nature.

Having built long toms to replace their rockers and expand their diggings, miners soon improved the tom by adding more and more interconnecting troughs with more and more riffles, thereby subjecting the gold-bearing gravel and sand to a longer washing process. These extensions caught more gold and quickly progressed to what were called sluice boxes. Wider at the upper than lower end, any number could be fitted together to form a "string," allowing a score and more men to shovel dirt over innumerable riffles. More efficient in washing a greatly increased volume of dirt, sluice boxes displaced long toms wherever a sufficient stream of water could be directed to these man-made waterways—but at considerable expense for additional lumber. To avoid this cost, miners experimented with ditches through which they directed their streams of water and into which the partners shoveled gold-bearing gravel and sand. Once again, greater length (but no greater expense) meant more "dirt" could be washed. In these lengthening "ground sluices" rocks served as riffles to catch the grains and granules of gold borne in the muddy streams. Whatever their success, miners felt cheated by the gold—how much?—carried away in the "tailings" that flowed from the ends of their sluice boxes and ground sluices. How to prevent this loss?

They turned to mercury—quicksilver—known to have a natural affinity for gold, drawing even the smallest particles into itself in the magnetic-like phenomenon of "amalgamation," while excluding foreign matter, such as sand. By placing quicksilver along riffles and at the base of rocks, the miners saved more gold, capturing—they hoped—even the elusive "float" or "flour" gold. The success of this new ally attracted widespread interest in the fall of 1849 and ever more in the years ahead when vastly increased volumes of earth—from tons, to hundreds, eventually millions of tons—would be washed by more advanced methods of mining. The more earth washed, the more gold might wash away in the tailings. Quicksilver prevented such a possible hemorrhage. Demand for this wondrous element surged in 1850 and increased for years thereafter, bringing great profits to the New Almaden Mine south of San Jose, for several years the only source of mercury in California.*

Throughout the mining region, partners with small claims and others with more ambitious projects purchased this reusable liquid metal, with which they baited thousands of riffles. On clean-up day, they stopped the flow of water and searched for the quicksilver, pregnant with gold. These lumps, known as amalgam, were placed in a retort which when heated turned the mercury to vapor, thereby releasing its burden. When cooled, the vapor condensed into its liquid state, ready to lure more passing gold.

The introduction of mercury marked the appearance of Science as a new ally in the miners'

---

*Named after the world's largest mercury mine, in Spain, this California source of cinnabar used crude kilns to heat and vaporize chunks of the ore, which condensed into mercury. To meet the ever-increasing demand, the owners of New Almaden in 1854 installed thirteen furnaces designed to "roast" increased tonnages of cinnabar, leading to a monthly production of 225,000 pounds of mercury. This invaluable ally of the gold miner was transported from New Almaden throughout the gold region in iron flasks, each containing seventy-five pounds of "quick."

If the New Almaden and other deposits of cinnabar had not made mercury available at reasonable prices, California's mining industry would have had to import that essential element from European sources—an economic burden of incalculable consequences.

This handbill announced the sale "at the large tent on the hill" of practically everything miners needed, from shovels and boots to molasses and soap, marked up to bring the trader 200–300 percent profit over San Francisco prices.

In the spring of 1849, Sacramento City was growing like a gourd in the night. By December a visitor to the riverfront found a mile-long line of ships used as storehouses. In his diary he wrote: "I was struck all aback when I saw the merchants receiving and handling gold. It is poured out and weighed almost as carelessly as rice or pepper in the States. . . . In the larger establishments the dust is dipped about in pint tin cups. In a word, it is an article of produce."

eager quest for improved technology. In the 1860s they would employ professional geologists, metallurgists, engineers, and chemists in their try-everything campaigns to extract gold from wherever new experts or old-fashioned noses might lead them.

In 1849, however, mining remained a primitive enterprise directed by the ambition and greed of farmers from Delaware, fisherman from Chile, vaqueros from Sonora, and revolutionaries from Paris, all of them quick to chase rumors of newfound treasure beyond the next ridge, up the river's farthest canyon. Looking at the rushing, tumbling waters flowing from the Sierra Nevada, peering into the deep green pools of quiet water below granite boulders, many of them imagined the gold that must have washed down through thousands of years to accumulate in submerged deposits—lodged in crevices, stored in potholes, layered in the deepest recesses, so thick as almost to be seen, wealth greater than their worn shovels could ever dig from old claims. And all of it still untouched, waiting for those with the cunning and the will to accept the rivers' challenge.

Their answer would be brute force: to turn the rivers out of their ancient channels and lay bare what beckoned beneath six, twelve, even twenty feet of rushing water. What else but the power of gold could compel weary men to move hundreds of big boulders in icy water and pile up huge earthworks of dirt to form dams; to take axes to hundreds of trees and cut them at sawpits into planks to be assembled into flumes to carry the diverted torrents to reentry points downstream—and all this bold rearrangement and destruction of Nature inflicted on land that did not belong to any one of them? Not one of the goldseekers would have conceived or countenanced such a wild scheme in the forests and hills of Indiana or Pennsylvania or France. But in California, any enterprise that promised access to gold, wherever it might be hidden, seldom encountered an opponent.

During the summer of 1849, more and more goldseekers formed partnerships and joint-stock companies to pool their labor, finances, and credit in the increasingly complex and cooperative schemes that mining demanded. Dams and flumes were now being built by small armies. The July 18 issue of the weekly *Placer Times* reported that "large companies of miners are engaged in turning the course of streams in which gold may be found. On the North Fork of the American River the stream is being turned at four points and also on the Middle Fork and at Mormon Island. The probability is that these companies will reap large rewards for their outlays, but the chances may be against them, in which case they will lose their whole summer's arduous labor."

By late August or early September, when the Sierra's snowpack had melted and the rivers flowed at their lowest volume, the companies' carpenters made one last inspection of the flumes' bracings and caulkings—and at last the rivers were diverted into their man-made channels. Then the men swarmed into the muddy, boulder-strewn riverbeds, set up their rockers and long toms, and bent to work with frantic energy to wash out their fortunes before the first rainstorm inevitably brought rising water that burst through the feeble barriers, putting an end to the season's rewards.

Because methods of damming and flume-building were hurried and experimental, most river-mining efforts in 1849 left behind as much debt as debris. But enough stories of fabulous success traveled through the diggings to nurture plans for 1850. Above Bidwell's Bar on the South Fork of the Feather, four miners from Oregon built "a small dam and took out over $9,000 each and started for home in October." A company of thirty men "turned the course of the North Fork of the American River and took out $75,000. Their greatest yield for any one day was $6,040."

Like the wiles of a temptress, these messages seduced thousands of miners to ignore their disappointments in 1849 and to believe that their river would yield in 1850.

Always ready to pose for the daguerreotypist's valued record of their toil, these miners rested their shovels, gravel rakes, and pickaxes in their long tom. The cabin suggests this was a claim worth working weeks, even months.

How amazing it was that goldseekers in 1849 and for years thereafter felt perfectly free to move a river from its natural course. At the time, no one thought to complain or to characterize their work as arrogant or destructive. Mining involved finding gold and taking it, wherever, however. The bottom of the river might prove wonderfully rewarding. So they were as ready to open up a river as a hillside or a deep shaft. Success depended on remarkable carpenters whose ingenuity, improvisational skills, and determination built— with the simplest tools: saws, hammers, axes—the flumes that carried a river's flow for hundreds or even thousands of yards. And there were inventive mechanics who rigged water-powered pumps that kept the river bottoms relatively dry so that the men with shovels and picks could dig out the gold-laden gravel for which the vast engineering project had been undertaken.

THE RAINS STARTED LATE IN 1849. WHEN THE rivers began to rise in mid-November, the miners had to choose: to stay on their claims and hope for days, perhaps weeks, when it would still be possible to work side canyons and gulches, or head for the towns and cities and accept a job until spring. Most chose to stay in the mines, though Sacramento City and San Francisco were so crowded that it seemed everyone had retreated from the high water, leaking tents, and flooded shanties. On days when creeks rose too high, partners cut down trees and whipsawed planks to improve their cabins for winter quarters. In the southern mines the winter rains were more welcome, for they turned the dusty creeks of summer and fall into flowing streams, offering—at last—plenty of water for washing stockpiled dirt.

By December, California had changed from the summer brown of drought to the rich greens of drenching rains, its roads from dust to mud. Shipments of supplies to the mining camps bogged down, leaving thousands of miners cut off until surefooted pack mules could slog through with food to stave off starvation. A miner reported on November 29, "The ground is so soft that it mires teams so deep it is impossible to get them out, and they had to be left to die or to be shot." Another passerby saw freight wagons two miles above Sacramento City with "many teams stalled to their wagon beds in the muddy road and oxen firmly mired up to their bellies. Some were being pulled out with chains around their horns by other cattle, while bundles of hay before those waiting their turns showed them to have been mired for some time."

In Sacramento City the streets became almost as impassable. A miner in mid-November reported, "They are half a leg deep in filth and mud, rendering getting around awful beyond description. . . . The city is one great cesspool of mud, offal, garbage, dead animals, and that worst of nuisances consequent upon the entire absence of outhouses." A few weeks later another diarist marveled at the "utter confusion and total disorder" in California's second city. Scattered and tumbled throughout the town, especially near the riverfront, he saw stacks of lumber, broken wagons, and "eatables" of all kinds—two hundred boxes of rotting herrings, broken barrels of pork, and moldy mounds of pilot bread, bacon, and cheese.

Surrounded by smells and outrages that even New York City would have outlawed, Sacramento City's transient miners and resident moneymakers pursued their pleasures and profits without concern for the absence of adequate levees to protect the crude but prospering town from the rising waters of the Sacramento and American Rivers. Despite heavy rains from mid-November through December, Sacramentans ignored warnings of imminent flooding. "The reckless spirit of speculation had declared an inundation as out of the question, if not physically impossible . . . and the headlong and unreflecting career of the people showed them sufficiently credulous to believe the really transparent story." In January they would look for lifeboats.

The rains produced such quagmires in the streets of San Francisco that the *New York Tribune*'s Bayard Taylor judged the mud to be "little short of fathomless." Others agreed, describing the effects in an almost boastful tone: "Not infrequently men were in danger of sinking out of sight in the mire, and it was a common occurrence to see them in up to their waists. Two horses sank so deep in the mud in Montgomery Street . . . that they were left to die; and die they did of starvation, while hundreds of merciful men would have been glad to relieve them, but could not. . . . Three men got into the mud of Montgomery Street at night, probably in a state of intoxication and were suffocated."

With a profligate inventiveness unique to California, the merchants of San Francisco found ways to assure commercial mobility. By sinking hundreds of boxes of Virginia tobacco they made several blocks of Montgomery Street passable. In other swampy streets they sank tons of wire sieve (for rockers and long toms), rolls of sheet lead, and bags of cement. At one intersection barrels of salt beef provided solid footing for several weeks. Sacks of beans that would have sold a few weeks later at great profit were used to improvise a crossing on Broadway. All these imports served as fillage because they arrived when they were in excess supply. No buyers—so, into the streets.

That careless confidence—tomorrow's profits will save us—was the source of both San Francisco's robust growth and its blindness to warnings of danger. Slapdash construction on crowded hillsides made fires, not floods, the great menace. On December 24, 1849, the first of a series of conflagrations swept through canvas hovels and elaborate gambling halls. The ubiquitous Taylor, as usual more vivid in his descriptions than other eyewitnesses, watched as "the blaze increased with fearful rapidity. . . . The roar and tumult swelled and above the clang of gongs and the cries of the populace I could hear the crackling of timbers and the smothered sound of falling roofs. . . . The canvas partitions of rooms shriveled away like paper in the breath of the flames. . . . For more than an hour there was no apparent check to the flames. A very few persons out of the thousands present did the work of arresting the flames. At the time of most extreme danger, hundreds of idle spectators refused to lend a hand unless they were paid enormous wages. One of the principal merchants . . . offered a dollar a bucket for water and made use of several thousand buckets in saving his property."

Before the embers had cooled, merchants and landlords sent in workmen to clear away the charred ruins and prepare to rebuild, while the unaffected returned to gambling, buying and selling, and new moneymaking schemes. "All over the burnt area sounded one incessant tumult of hammers, axes, and saws." Every speculator and warehouseman wanted his construction hurried because every canvas-covered storeroom, wooden shed, and sheet-iron shelter available for storage of cargoes could earn at least 10 percent per month. But the first to be rebuilt, their owners propelled by the urgency of even greater gains, were the gambling palaces at Portsmouth Square. The Parker House would rise again as a brick eminence, while the Exchange was finished for an extravagant sum in two weeks, under the penalty of $150 for every additional day. In that city even the contractors thought like gamblers.

A goldseeker newly arrived from France immediately caught the spirit of San Francisco. Watching the city's frantic rebuilding with the same materials that had fed the flames, he confided to his diary: "One calamity more or less seems to make no difference to these Californians."

THE YEAR 1849 ENCOMPASSED CALIFORNIA'S adolescence, a rambunctious, hormonal moment that would forever remain separate and legendary, more than a prologue to the get-ahead years of the 1850s. Invaded by young men to be known as '49ers, California in that year came to the end of its Spanish and Mexican eras and the beginning of its American history, with those bearded miners the Founding Fathers of a revolutionary society on the Pacific shore, and San Francisco its Mother City, more extravagant—better yet, more sinful—than Philadelphia or Boston.

In their reckless, roll-the-dice crusade for profit and wealth, the '49ers pushed America further from entwined traditions of European pedigree and New England morality toward a new ethos, unconstrained by privilege or principle and measured only by the democracy of the dollar.

The '49ers and their year created the jackpot mentality that would dominate California for decades. Profits from gold mining justified whatever machines and methods might be required to gain them. As the obstacle to those profits, Nature was to be torn asunder and rearranged to reveal her golden treasure.

From 1849 evolved the rapacious, unrestrained power and freedom of the Miner, soon to be confronted and later defeated by the Farmer, who rose to power by providing the consumer needs of his destined adversary.

Reproduced here for the first time, this painting by Henry Mighels displays the complexity of a mining company's diversion of the Feather River near Bidwell's Bar in 1853.

GET-AHEAD YEARS

This enlargement of a small section of a daguerreo-type offers an intimate exploration of these miners' domesticity—their tools of toil and hope at rest against a crude chimney braced by a tree trunk, their table askew in the cabin's one room, and beyond another open door.

The miners to the right radiate the anything-goes freedom of the 1850s and, too, their inner pleasure in knowing how their appearance will shock tradition-bound folks back home. The scene below, although posed, is so authentic that we can hear the dogs bark and smell the miners' sweat as they pause in their world of riverbank rocks, their retreat from the sun to be seen in the background, in all its architec-tural carelessness.

CHAPTER FIVE

GET-AHEAD YEARS

DURING THE DECADE OF THE 1850s, gold mining changed from a treasure hunt to an industry. While shoveling dirt into their toms and sluices, many miners could hear the steady thumping of giant stamp mills crushing gold-bearing ore dug by wage earners in underground tunnels. In contrast to partners engineering their own dams and ditches to deliver a stream of water, hydraulic mining corporations purchased millions of gallons every day from heavily capitalized water companies that delivered the vital commodity through a network of flumes, ditches, and aqueducts that by 1859 extended over 5,726 miles. And compared to the wing dams and flimsy constructions that laid bare—after massive effort—only a hundred or so yards of a riverbed, engineering skills and capital investment turned aside *twenty-five miles* of the Yuba River in 1853 and even greater lengths of the Feather and American Rivers in 1855.

These mining efforts—some stubbornly primitive, others experimentally sophisticated—employed one hundred thousand men year after year, scattered through the gold region from Shasta in the north to Mariposa three hundred miles to the south. In San Francisco and Sacramento (the word "City" was dropped in 1851) hundreds of millwrights, iron and brass founders, mechanics, and boilermakers worked in scores of foundries and machine shops. Never had there been a frontier so quickly industrialized, employing such a force of educated and skilled workers, all of them dependent on one elusive and curious commodity—as was the entire economy of California.

Letters sent back to the States (one hundred thousand a month in 1852) brimmed with descriptions of the wonders and contrasts of California—the canvas walls of gambling palaces decorated with palatial mirrors and "Frenchie" paintings; the streets knee deep in mud; the river steamboat races that killed scores when overheated boilers exploded; the rough justice of lynchings, floggings, and ear-clippings; the riots, fires, and floods; the cities crowded with thousands of men, among whom could be found only a few women, many of them prostitutes. And children? So few that when seen on the street or in a store, they were heralded as reminders and forecasts of "home."

Where else in all the world could be found thriving cities through which circulated millions of dollars in gold and international trade but without a single cathedral or museum or marbled mansion, without a uniformed police force or a public fire department? Canvas and boards, bricks and iron graced San Francisco and Sacramento, Marysville and Sonora, only here and there a structure prominent for its architectural ambition and intended longevity. With shocking frequency, conflagrations swept away city blocks, even entire towns and mining camps, cleansing by destroying, a process that in fact reinvigorated the economy by removing yesterday's thrown-together buildings to be replaced by tomorrow's rebuilding with less flammable materials and by eliminating vast quantities of stored and excess imports, thereby boosting prices and assuring profits from new shipments. Losses today would be swiftly regained, and more, tomorrow—such was the "I'll-get-mine" expectation of the 1850s.

Gold paid for everything: new methods of mining, new inventions, more daring investments. The increased production would have astonished even the most boastful '49er, the most promotional newspaper editor of 1850: $75 million in 1851, $81 million in 1852. By the end of the decade, the total came to $594 million—over $10 billion in today's dollars. California, in truth, had become the Land of Gold, a country of prodigious projects, transformed from a simple, pastoral backwater by Yankee push and ingenuity.

Certainly neither local, state, nor federal governments contributed to the astounding progress, not even by providing traditional frontier law and order. In cities the merchants, in diggings the miners, established their own forms of justice: vigilance committees to protect property from thieves and arsonists; lynch law to remove murderers and claim jumpers. As makeshift laws were judged good-enough-for-now, so were other improvisations in California's wildly free and rough capitalism, such as private fire-fighting companies, private mints turning out public currency, private mail delivery, and private toll roads and bridges—expedient, spontaneous solutions, all for profits.

The price of everything from meat and champagne to shovels and explosives depended on the needs and the successes of the miners and their ever more complex operations. Through the booms and busts of the 1850s, letters, newspapers, and magazines reported fortunes being made not only in gold mining but in more familiar endeavors as well. A hotel, restaurant, or billiard hall back home in New York or Kentucky could provide a living, but in California such enterprises gushed profits of $8,000, $10,000 a year, or more. Farmers in Ohio and Europe, laboring as had their grandfathers, read of gold miners so hungry for fresh vegetables that they paid $2 for a single watermelon. A farmer near San Jose sold his potato crop for $8,000. And women too could strike it rich. *Hunt's Merchants' Magazine* in June 1852 published news of a widow in Downieville who baked pies she sold to hungry miners. She reported sales of $18,000. Where else could so much money be made from a taken-for-granted female task? Where else could a man find a job as a waiter, drayman, deckhand, or carpenter that paid $6, $8, even $12 per day? In the States these jobs paid $1.50 for a twelve-hour day, six days a week, while farm workers earned a dollar a day for the same hours.

No wonder Oregon's population by 1860 totaled only 54,415 compared to California's 380,000, even though Oregon had been widely publicized for its agricultural riches, healthy climate, and prosperous families—and even though California lost each year an average of 25,000 men who sailed from San Francisco, headed for home.* Oregon's land versus California's gold: a life of subsistence farming in the Willamette Valley versus gold dust enough to start a new life in upstate New York.

Oregon and California—neighbors, but a world apart. One a community of church-going families with the patient tenacity of traditional farming cultures; the other a transient encampment with few churches or families and the recklessness of a gambling society. Many a miner wrote to his wife or parents to explain that he would have to stay in California another year to regain what he had lost in a failed quartz-mining venture. And merchants who supplied customers on credit for months on end went broke along with mining companies when claims failed or dams washed away. Chaotic and volatile, life in California seemed to be a great lottery. Failure was so much a part of everyday experience that it carried no shame. But the prospect of returning home having failed to keep the promise that justified leaving, of returning without one's share from a place famous for its

---

* As an example: in 1854, 21,989 men left California—and 1,033 women—as recorded by the San Francisco harbor master. Despite this exodus, through the 1850s California continued to attract immigrants, by overland routes and by sea—an annual average of 54,200.

profits and success, that sense of failure kept thousands in the mines and the cities for months, even years, longer than they had planned. So risk-taking and daring schemes became the basis for everyday decisions. Seeking swift profits, miners and merchants "were ready to change their occupation and embark on some new undertaking after two minutes consideration."

Eager to grasp a real estate deal or an opportunity in a new steamboat company, frustrated miners took longer to ponder the new talk of big money in farming, a living many remembered without nostalgia. Yet growing numbers did return to planting because they heard so many reports of massive, one-season profits. Strike-it-rich-and-head-for-home became as much the common motive in farming as in mining. And it was as easy to get into farming as mining. Get-rich-quick melon and potato growers simply planted a likely plot near a town or city and claimed the land as squatters, not bothering to buy or lease while tending their crops. One season might fulfill expectations. So it went—enterprise unguided by old rules and practices but energized by California prices.

Whatever else made money, the quest for gold—on small claims, in riverbeds, at hydraulic operations, down mine shafts—constituted the muscle and heart that powered California's economy. As the producer of gold and, no less important, the great consumer, the miner ruled the land, his ambitions and needs prevailing over all else. No law, no competing interest constrained his right to mine for gold, wherever and however. Through the 1850s that freedom flourished, as its beneficiaries took ever more boldly the liberties their self-interest required.

FAR MORE AMBITIOUS AND COSTLY THAN the summer experiments of 1849, the river-mining projects of the 1850s coordinated the engineering skills and the organized effort of scores of men. Often a hundred or more partners invested all their gold dust gained from previous mining, yet still they needed credit from local merchants and sawmill operators to obtain food and supplies during the summerlong construction of flumes and dams. On the forks of the Feather River

in 1855, seventeen companies raised $303,000 by selling stock to miners and other hopeful investors, all of that sum spent before a single ounce of gold was washed through their toms and sluices.

However extensive a partnership's labor and capital, practical ingenuity often counted most in the challenge to build a flume along steep and rocky riverbanks and a reliable dam to force the river at its lowest ebb into the man-made channel. Planks and beams needed for constructing flumes were purchased from steam-powered sawmills whose owners fed their blades with hundreds of trees cut from the pine forests that covered the Sierra foothills, trees that belonged to . . . who knew? Maybe the government, wherever it might be. No one cared. There was no government to object or to collect a fee. Like everything else in California, the trees and rivers were claimed by the miners, their imperative the de facto law of the land.

Clearing the way for a flume required removing giant boulders, felling trees, digging away protruding outcroppings, constructing timber supports and braces, and positioning heavy planks to form the "box" for its length of hundreds of yards. All this in preparation for the day when dam and flume would be joined in their crucial alliance to shift the river from its millennial course.

To build their dam, partners hefted rocks and boulders from icy currents, gathering more as needed from the shoreline, to form a double wall, the space between filled with hundreds of sacks of sand* and more rocks and then dirt or clay dug from the riverbanks. All that labor had to be carried on, week after week, despite fingers crushed, ankles sprained, legs bruised, and boots that fell apart. With a curse or a grin, these amateur engineers toiled and strained, now and then easing their pains by snuggling into a warm sandbar and tossing off a swig of whiskey. Some dams they built by felling a

giant pine and locking it in place across the river with boulders at each end. Vertical planks jammed into the river bottom and nailed into the trunk formed a curtain across the stream's width that served as backing for rocks, gravel, and dirt that were "walked out on the tree in handbarrows and tipped into the river." Thus they labored through the blistering heat of July and August, "all the while living on Hope mixed with pork and flour in sufficient quantities, trusting to the bed of the river for pay."

Here and there, miners sought simpler ways to reach the rivers' treasures. At Long's Bar on the Feather River a company employed Indians to dive into a deep pool. "They brought up in their hands from three to ten dollars in golden granules." One company invested in the use of a "submarine suit," while another tried "a diving bell" to explore the depths of the Tuolumne River. Daring and inventive, these experiments proved more frustrating than rewarding.†

On a fork of the American River, forty men completed their dam and flume and went to work in the riverbed. After several days of tempting success, these indefatigables determined that their fortunes could be made only if they removed a cluster of boulders, each weighing several tons. But they had no explosives. They improvised. From a nearby hillside, towering steeply above them, they dragged scores of dead pine trees and piled them in a great mass around and over the offending boulders. Set

---

* As another product of peculiar importance to the miners, sacks deserve some attention. The most informative statement I have seen is that of a miner on the South Fork of the Feather River, dated June 11, 1850: "Every kind of cloth is used here for sand bags to dam the river with. The quality is of no account, the only question seems to be which will make the most sand bags. The coarsest hemp sacking, common sheeting, drill, and jeans are all the same price here, six bits [75¢], and it is almost impossible to get any now in the city. The late fires have created a great demand for cloth." From this it can be deduced that the miners made their own sacks, but no one mentioned, much less described, this aspect of dam building. It is a scene to be imagined: heavy-handed, impatient miners as seamstresses.

† Exemplary of the sanguine inventiveness nurtured by the great expectations of river mining, in 1852 the San Joaquin Diving Bell Mining Company issued 250 shares of stock, selling for $100 each. The proceeds of $25,000 were "devoted exclusively and immediately to the building of two diving bells on the San Joaquin." The company had exclusive rights to use "Worster's Improved Diving Bell," for which a patent had been issued in 1849. In anticipation of the first bells' success, the stockholders were advised that the Company "shall have the privilege of constructing any number of bells." Conceived in excitement, the enterprise drowned in disappointment.

ablaze, with more and more trunks piled on day and night, a glowing mass of orange coals enveloped the boulders, heating them to the core. When the partners diverted an icy torrent from their flume to swirl and wash around the shimmering granite monoliths, they exploded, cracking and fragmenting into manageable chunks and slivers. With that obstacle removed, the goldseekers exposed "deposits that proved to be a bonanza." Letters to Michigan and Tennessee announced the miners' imminent return, in triumphant refutation of relatives who had doubted California's promise.*

Reports of success gave river companies the fortitude to carry on despite maddening difficulties. Serious trouble often erupted when rising water behind a new dam flooded claims upstream. On the South Fork of the Feather a dam backed water "over three entire claims." The injured companies took their complaints to the local miners' association. The judges ruled in favor of the dam builders, arguing they had the oldest claim. A miner upstream wrote that "everybody up this way says that the decision is grossly unjust and that the judges are fools." Nevertheless, they accepted the judgment. Less acquiescent companies sometimes attacked the offenders, destroying their dams. The formation of river-mining alliances for mutual defense or for surprise attacks resulted in bloody battles and new graves. At Shirt Tail Canyon on the Middle Fork of the American, a river-mining company "shot thirteen men who were in the act of tearing away the dam." So it was that competition for claims grew more aggressive, and the old ways of a few partners working a claim were displaced by the power of larger, better organized companies.

Damage inflicted by rivals could not compare to the devastation every river company accepted as inevitable when the rainy season set in. September was the crucial month, the last safe weeks to work the riverbeds before rainstorms might sweep through the Sierra foothills. In 1855 and 1856 that seasonal change did not come until December, making those the peak years in river mining success. Normally in October or early November a few days of cold wind and gathering clouds spurred the miners to a frantic pace, as they washed their richest dirt from sunrise into the dark of evening, hoping, laboring, to pay off their merchant creditors and have enough left for a home-stake. Some companies put their work into hauling pay dirt to safe, high ground for later washing. Others strengthened their dams and flumes to withstand the first rise from what might providentially be only a light rain. Local traders, their books crowded with summerlong credit for provisions, liquor, and boots, feared the clouds even more than the nomadic miners.

A few days of heavy rain and everyone knew what to expect. Sometimes they had time to carry to safety some, or most, of their equipment. Some miners struggled to dismantle all or part of their flumes and pumps. But often the first storm came with such fury that there was time only to climb the hillsides and watch as a chocolate surge, four, five, six feet high, roared downstream. Dams melted in the foam, sections of flumes swept past amid the lighter debris of boards, toms, pumps, and barrels. Above the din could be heard the scraping and grinding of boulders crashing against each other. Watching the destruction, the miners felt a peculiar sense of release, even satisfaction, in knowing that so many others shared the same dashing of hope and promise. At saloons and around campfires, they eased their despondency in the companionship of drinking, calculating how much more gold could have been theirs if only the rains had come a week later.

A few drinks also helped them face the task of writing home to explain how and why gold dust saved from successful claims had been lost in the latest sure-to-make-my-fortune project. Sometimes

---

* News of other big strikes that encouraged river mining included a company of twenty-one men who built a wing dam across part of the Tuolumne River and from the exposed bed took out $17,123 in thirty-three days (October–November 1850), less expenses of $3,528.

Once again an ambitious daguerreotypist has persuaded a group of miners to stop their work so he could take a picture he hoped later to sell. In this complex scene, the men posed amid boulders recently submerged beneath river water now flowing through the flume in the background. The long axle was turned by a paddle wheel in the flume to operate a pump below, removing water from a deep hole in which the miners expected to find a rich deposit of gold. It was an incongruous setting, both primitive and industrial.

Here and there giant derricks hoisted massive boulders, none too large to thwart miners determined to get to the bottom where lay, surely, treasure enough to richly compensate for crushed toes and broken fingers and hopes dashed in earlier river probings.

If its August–September volume of water could be confined to a flume, no river or stream was safe from the ambitions of river-mining companies. Nor were nearby trees spared from the ax and saw of lumbermen quick to set up steam-powered mills that turned out thousands of planks and beams for construction of the flumes that held miles—yes, miles—of river water. In the river bottoms suddenly exposed by inventive enterprise, the groans and whirrings of axles and cogs and belts competed with the rattle and click of rocks and gravel washed through sluice boxes in the riverbed.

those letters were sent with homebound partners. One of them ended: "I shall send this by Mr. Carpenter who . . . can tell you in fifteen minutes how one hundred thousand dollars worth of property was swept away better than I can describe it to you. So, I have got to stay here a while longer than I intended to get my pile."

A more desperate husband wrote to his wife: "Oh, Matilda, oft is the night when laying alone on the hard ground with a blanket under me and one over me that my thoughts go back to Ohio and I think of you and little Sis and wish myself with you. But I am willing to stand it all to make enough to get us a home and so I can be independent of some of the darned sonabitches that felt themselves above me because I was poor." Thousands more like this tormented miner faced the same dilemma: whether to return home in answer to the pleas of wives, parents, and in-laws, or to proclaim that one more year, one last partnership, would fulfill the original promise to bring home money enough for a new life.*

Everywhere beckoned the evidence of others who had persevered, in spite of failure, and finally won their "pile." A claim played out or an investment gone bust was just a detour in California. No one in the States had seen how suddenly success could strike. And who wanted to return to his old life as a laborer, a clerk, a third son? No, the best chances were in California.

That confidence motivated thousands to buy shares in new mining ventures, to invest in a new hotel, a string of pack mules, or other money-making enterprises. Promises in letters home,

justifying one more delay, pressured some to wager everything in raucous, smoky gambling dens, praying that, at monte or faro, they could win what sluices, dams, and stocks had failed to produce.

In their freedom and anonymity, miners, their suppliers, and everyone else engaged in an eager, unrestrained exploitation of California—ripping open the earth, rearranging the rivers, cutting down the forests, rebuilding what had been burned and hoping for profit before the next fire. Self-interest ruled.

POUNDING IT OUT

WHILE THOUSANDS CONTINUED TO WORK THEIR claims on river bars and up gulches, and other miners invested their labor and savings in river dams and flumes, a different method of mining (long established in Mexico) attracted increasing effort during 1851, financed by a frenzy of speculative investment. Known as quartz or hard-rock mining, this development got its start in California when miners digging through loose gravel broke off pieces of solid rock in which they could see embedded seams of gold. Further digging often produced chunks that contained pockets and fissures of gold. More often the metal spread through the rock like veins, thick in some strands, thin in others. When crushed, many samples were assayed at twenty to thirty cents per pound. Here was another of California's wonders: rock impregnated with gold and so widely distributed that excited miners judged it inexhaustible.

The news spread quickly, with John C. Frémont's mine at his Mariposa Ranch the first and most famed place of early hard-rock success. From a vein two feet wide at the surface, his workers pursued the treasure underground, sending up hundreds of buckets of broken reddish quartz, thickly streaked with gold, to be crushed and washed. For a time, Frémont and his wife, Jessie, gloried in spending their newfound wealth. Less prominent owners

---

* When to return home became the central theme in the exchange of letters through the years. A son wrote his father: "If God will forgive me and allow me to make a small pile this summer I never will trouble this country any more, but break for home. I get home often in my dreams. . . ." Striving for a moral tone, a husband promised his wife: "You can rest assured that I will not remain in this country one moment longer than I am forced from a duty to you and our little ones."

Back home wives waited, many of them tormented by months of silence. A melancholy "California widow" in Lancaster, Ohio, wrote to her husband in Downieville, hoping he would return. He never did.

I am so lonesome, tired, and discouraged, and everything. . . . You must not fail to write me when you get this. You are excusable for what you said in your last. I suppose you feel fretted sometimes as I do. . . . If you had your business arranged so you could come home, I would be glad so we could get fix to housekeep. . . . You must not think that I will forget you for I think more of you every day. . . . I remain your affectionate wife. Write soon.

Mrs. R. A. Brown, from letters of 1852 and 1855

With rare candor, James I. Maxfeld wrote to his wife in Massachusetts. From San Francisco, January 24, 1850:

I feel bad sometimes when I think of home and the comfort I am deprived of by being away. Then again, come to think of how dull it is at home, I do not want to be there.

In April 1850 he confided:

I want to be home. What is the use to have a wife in Fairhaven and be in California. Might almost as well not have one. . . . I would give anything I have got for the privilege of having a kiss from you. Then I could return it. I would hug you so that you would remember it for a year if not longer.

Manuscript letters in the collection of Matthew R. Isenburg

NEW-YORK, MONDAY, NOVEMBER 3, 1851.

New-York Daily Times.

SIXTEEN DAYS
LATER FROM CALIFORNIA.
ARRIVAL OF THE CHEROKEE.
Over Two Millions of Gold.

The steamer *Cherokee*, Capt. WINDLE, arrived at this port on Saturday afternoon, in nine days from Chagres, bringing San Francisco dates to the 1st October,—sixteen days later than previous advices, and dates from Panama to the 18th ult.

The *Cherokee* brings a California mail; but from circumstances within our knowledge, we incline to the opinion that a portion of the mails are still behind. Persons who fail to get their California correspondence to-day, may hope to receive it by the U. S. mail-steamer *Ohio*, which went into Chagres the day the *Cherokee* left, and may be looked for by to-morrow.

The steamer *Oregon*, Capt. Pearson, had arrived at Panama from San Francisco, having on board upwards of two millions of gold dust on freight, independent of large amounts in the hands of passengers.

The *Cherokee* brings *over two million dollars* of gold dust, as will be seen by the following:

Specie List.

Capt. C. Johnson	$800	Camman, Whitehouse & Co.	50,000
Mrs E. Reynolds	150	D. Hambinger & Brothers	2,560
Twombly & Lamson	1,172	H. Josephi & Co	3,570
W. W. Wakeman	6,475		
Williams, Bradford & Co.	5,500	Cashier of the Ocean Bank	3,000
Schloss Brothers	5,360	Willets & Co	6,352
W. P. Furniss	2,040	B. Levi & Co	1,993
Howland & Aspinwall	5,013	Gans, Lebermann & Co.	3,296
Simonsfield, Bach & Co	800	Isaac Wormiser	2,816
Order	79,281	W. Hoge & Co	27,600
Isaac Meyer	3,000	Newhouse & Spatz	10,000
Earp & Co	3,195	Jones & Wise	7,000
Adams & Co	553,616	Peter Naylor	2,493
Drew, Robinson & Co.	250,000	T. Brenner	2,400
American Exchange Bank	250,000	G. R. Rae	1,846
Chas. F. Toy	4,250	Adams & Co	14,400
Davis, Brooks & Co.	9,000	Moller, Sands & Riera	2,166
Minot & Hooper	9,600	Glidden & Williams	19,000
Wond & West	4,460	H. Aronson	2,528
U. S. Mint, Phila.	5,100	Case & Freeman	8,674
W. F. Burgess	1,400	F. A. Delano	10,825
Adams & Co	9,600	Rumyey Crooks	4,530
H. Dwight, Jr.	10,060	C. H. Rogers	5,500
Chambers & Heiser	18.736	Micke, Platt & Co	2,985
A. W. Canfield	9,920	A. Van Valkenberg	5,000
J. Cunningham	5,600	F. Probst	1,046
De Rham & Moore	20,000	Harbeck & Co	49,400
Brown, Bros. & Co	40,000	Dennis, Perkins & Co.	10,500
G. S. Robbins & Son	2,520	Robt. Buge	2,560
Harvey Loomis	5,120	Chambers & Heiser	4,130
Mariet & Roberts	1,204	C. W. & A. Thomas	5,000
Thomas Wattson & Sons	12,000	L. Longfeld	6,086
		J. R. Delvecchio	1,062
Collins, Cushman & Co	10,000	Beebe & Co	275,000
Soule, Wardell & Co.	5,545	S. (in diamond,) Philadelphia	4,667
A. H. Lissak	13,244	J. M. Smith & Co	4,705
Chas. King & Co	6,709	E. L. Mathews	1,000
W. Regis	9,000		
Dan'l J. Willets	3,134		$1,919,163
In hands of passengers			260,000
Total			$2,179,163

of quartz ledges envisioned their own estates and rising social status, but they needed financing to meet the costs of heavy machinery and underground tunneling. Eager financiers in San Francisco, New York, and London organized corporations and promoted sales of stock. Not only innocents in cities, but experienced miners in California were swept up in the rush to buy, at $100 per share, even $800.

Much of the money paid for elaborate machines, costing $50,000 to $100,000, that pulverized the quartz into powder and thereby "freed" its gold. To promote the sale of stock, one quartz company issued a circular that promised its machinery would crush enough quartz to produce $240 million, "a sum sufficient to revolutionize the commercial relations of the world."

Although they brought to hard-rock mining the confidence and optimism they had gained from the relative simplicity of placer mining (separating particles of gold from gravel and sand in a pan or long tom), California's miners were unprepared for the far more complex and technical processes required to extract gold from solid rock. In assembling their crushing machinery at the site of a rich outcropping, they expected the vein to continue, and maybe even widen, as they pursued its golden trail. Instead, inexplicably, with geologic and economic finality, many tantalizing veins pinched out and disappeared.

Nine of ten pioneer hard-rock companies could not pay their creditors in 1852–53. Through trial and error and continuing financial distress, the survivors struggled to cope with the basic challenges: to dig out the ore, reduce it to powder, and extract gold from that powder. Wage-laboring miners swung picks and sledgehammers, simple instruments soon augmented by handheld drills and the explosive force of black powder. Sometimes a tunnel could be cut into a hillside to follow a vein. But just as often the twists of the veins required a vertical shaft and feeder tunnels. Slow, dangerous work—and expensive for the operators. By 1852 the deepest mines reached a depth of three hundred feet and employed steam-powered winches to hoist

STAMP MILL

to the surface gold-suffused rock, as well as weary teams of miners at day's end.*

To pulverize the ore, some quartz companies abandoned their imported contraptions and turned to a device that had been in use for centuries in Europe and Mexico, the mule-driven *arrastre*. This primitive arrangement worked well enough, but too slowly for impatient Americans. They developed what became known and used world-wide, the "California stamp mill."

These giant machines pounded the quartz into powder using three, five, in later years as many as twenty heavy iron pestles ("stamps") mounted on vertical stems, or rods, lifted and dropped by the action of cams fixed on a revolving horizontal shaft, the entire mechanism bolted to massive structural beams eighteen to twenty-four inches square. Frequent improvements included rotating the stamps as they fell (to increase their crushing efficiency) and introducing quicksilver and hot water to the mix of

---

* Placer miners who had given up in disappointment and others who realized the value of regular income turned to quartz mining and received around $5 per day in 1852. By 1856 competition for these jobs reduced the daily wage to about $3—vs. $1 in the coal mines of Pennsylvania.

pulverized quartz, to save even the smallest fragments of gold.

Beyond welcomed advances in technology, greater encouragement came from the success of mining operations in the town of Grass Valley, fifty miles northeast of Sacramento. Reports from there in June 1851 told of a vein eighteen inches thick, so rich that pieces crushed by hand with a hammer yielded two and even three ounces per pound. A fourteen-pound specimen gleaming with gold attracted so much attention that promoters sent it to the first international exhibition at London's Crystal Palace, a palpable encouragement to British investors.* Suddenly famous, Grass Valley boasted "two hundred wooden houses, good hotels, stores, a sawmill, four steam crushing mills in operation, and four more in active progress of erection, and vast quantities of rock piled up ready for use."

These and other advances in quartz operations inspired pronouncements in 1851 by local observers and investors that gold digging had entered a new era, when "capital may be as safely invested in this species of mining as in railroad, factory, or bank stock, in shipping, farming, or merchandise." So wrote Alonzo Delano, a '49er from Illinois whose published mining stories under the sobriquet "Old Block" would bring him more fortune than his many mining endeavors, including his investment in the Sierra Nevada Quartz Mining Company in

Grass Valley. For a time, he spread his enthusiasm through his letters published in newspapers back East, advising readers ("God forbid that I should mislead anyone on this subject") that this company he had invested in would "do a rather snug cash business" by producing an annual net profit of $210,000.

But this time California refused to give substance to the boosterism of its exploiters. Quartz proved a less reliable shepherd of gold than the gravel and silt of riverbeds. It was hard to figure out where to dig. Most of all, the precious metal cloaked itself in the rock, diffused in concentrations too fine-grained to be seen. Tons and tons of ore, excavated at great cost, yielded less and less gold. Profits also diminished and bankruptcies increased because stamp mills could not overcome the metallurgical complexities that sent 70 and 80 percent of the gold flowing as waste into the tailings.

But as Old Block admonished, "Hope on, Hope ever." Quartz miners experimented with new techniques to save more gold from their mortars, washing the crushed ore over shaking tables and through amalgamating boxes. And they tried less scientific devices, like flushing the crush over coarse woolen blankets. The miners' inventiveness and tenacity increased expectations, profits, and the number of stamp mills. By 1858 this revival in quartz mining had encouraged investment in 279 stamp mills, built at a cost of $3,270,000—which suggests the contagious appeal of a sudden strike, of a vein two feet wide, packed with gold.

By 1859 more statistics revealed that despite immense effort and stubborn inventiveness, only 1 percent of the gold produced during the 1850s came from quartz mining—the rest from placers. But again statistics exposed only the surface facts. The gain in technical skill and engineering experience, even some understanding of geology and metallurgy, proved to be indispensable in nurturing the still greater efforts and inventions that would produce the Big Bonanza of the 1860s.

---

* In 1854 the richest piece of quartz on record—161 pounds, of which 141 were pure gold—was valued at $39,000. Innumerable lesser discoveries became the theme of competing newspaper reports through the 1850s and 1860s, many such "lumps" being described as pure gold and weighing from twenty to ninety-six pounds. Meanwhile, the newspapers continued to trumpet stories of big "raises" from placer claims. The *San Francisco Bulletin*, for example, announced in 1856 that $140,000 had been taken at Jacksonville; the *Alta* in 1853 described how a claim at Murderers Bar yielded eleven pounds daily; and the *Placer Times* of Sacramento encouraged its readers with the news of a single miner on Deer Creek at Nevada City digging out $12,000 in one day.

Most surviving views of mining towns and camps were drawn by artists and reproduced on lettersheets and invariably show neat buildings and clean streets—attractive versions of New England villages. As a rare sample of reality, this photograph presents a vivid contrast to that artistic impression. Neither this hotel's name nor its advertisement could disguise the muddy, run-down, kick-in-the-door appearance of Nevada City, which was typical of other towns and camps.

A tinderbox waiting for a spark, Placerville (Hangtown) had the good sense to rebuild after the next fire with fewer boards and logs and more bricks and iron shutters. The town thrived through the decades as the major trading center between Sacramento and the up-country mining camps.

WITHOUT CONCERN

In QUARTZ OPERATIONS AS IN RIVER MINING, companies and individual miners never hesitated to take anything and everything they needed or wanted, most importantly lumber from the vast, virgin stands of coniferous timber that grew over the western slopes of the Sierra. To construct the frameworks of stamp mills, those thundering symbols of California's advancing technology; to re-build miles of flumes each summer; to put up great trestles to support aqueducts across valleys and canyons; to erect all kinds of structures required by mining operations; and to rebuild entire cities and mining camps destroyed by recurring fires, took an astounding volume of planks, beams, and timbers cut from the abundant pines.

With forests free for the cutting (the dense slopes had not yet been surveyed, much less claimed by a government agency), the price of lumber stabilized by 1851 at $650 per thousand board feet. Fortunes were made by sawmill operators who built steam-powered mills throughout the gold region. By 1858 the whining blades of 286 mills squared and sliced the Sierra's trees, producing annually 284 million board feet—as well as incredible waste. Rampaging through forests of soaring pines that grew one hundred feet to the first limb, the loggers generally followed the rule "take three logs and leave her."*

This careless pillage amid abundance, this "savage struggle with the landscape," produced scenes of widespread devastation, such as described by a visitor to Nevada City in 1853. "The town is beautifully situated on Deer Creek and was once surrounded by a forest of magnificent pine trees which have been made to become useful instead of ornamental, and nothing now remains to show that they

ever existed but the numbers of stumps over the hillsides." In the redwood forest that covered the hills on the eastern shore of San Francisco Bay, four sawmills were at work by 1853. Year by year their owners, and others, plundered the ancient groves. By 1860 only a desolation of stumps remained.

Nature's wealth paid another expensive tribute to the gold-mining economy. The prospectors who pushed into the farthest river canyons of the Sierra foothills were the most careless, indeed presumptuous, of all explorers and pioneers. With little planning or preparation for food, supplies, and shelter, they dispersed to wherever their prospecting led them, oblivious of everything but gold, expecting that, somehow, someone would deliver essential supplies. Holed up beyond the reach of pack mules or cut off by weather, hundreds of hungry miners became impromptu hunters. Shouldering shotguns and rifles (some had only pistols), they pursued mammals and wildfowl with desperate eagerness. Living off the land like raiders, they decimated the wildlife.

To meet the demand for fresh meat, commercial hunters made fat profits from organized expeditions to shoot deer, elk, bear, and quail, hauling their slaughter by the wagonloads to hotels and butcher shops. Along the San Joaquin and Sacramento Rivers and around San Francisco Bay, professional shooters killed thousands of ducks and geese in only a few hours. With no laws in force (or even considered) for their protection, the abundant wildlife paid a heavy subsidy to California's mining and urban growth. Commercial hunting became a lucrative second career for hundreds of failed miners.

Destroyers of rivers, forests, and wildlife, the transient miners were equally blind to the plight of the native people forced to flee their homeland as refugees or to resist as its defenders. These Californians—survivors of Spanish and Mexican domination—sought to escape the horde of new invaders by retreating ever farther into the hills. But as prospectors extended their relentless searching, followed by hundreds of impatient miners, confrontations

---

* During the first years of the 1850s, before California's lumber industry achieved its capacity, ships from New England and other East Coast ports, and from Oregon, delivered millions of board feet each year to San Francisco.

were inevitable: Indians shot, miners ambushed, Indian villages raided, women raped, girls kidnapped, retaliations, more killings. As "volunteer militia," miners on occasion organized Indian-hunting expeditions, which were financed during the late 1850s with funds paid by the state government for "suppression of Indian hostilities." More permanent than the mobile miners, farmers were quick to seek vengeance when Indians—starving fugitives—stole crops and domestic animals. Indiscriminate killings and bounties for Indian scalps reflected public approval of whatever means might be used to "exterminate" California's native people.*

Ruthlessly self-centered, the miners owned neither the land they ravaged nor the shelters they so carelessly erected. By the expedient of their local mining codes, they claimed temporary possession of patches of rocky ground, stretches of rivers, and excavations of shafts and tunnels. They lived in whatever shelter the weather required and available material provided, decamping as carelessly as they had come, leaving "glory holes" ten, twenty feet deep, open and unmarked, into which the unwary might fall. A diarist near Sonora in the winter of 1851 noted that "the most common and fatal result of drunkenness is falling into some of the thousands of deep pits dug during the summer by miners and now full of water. Scarcely a week passes that two

---

* The tragic, precipitous decline in California's Indian population began in the Spanish-Mexican eras (as described in Chapter One), from an estimated 300,000 in 1769 to under 150,000 in 1848. Epidemic diseases remained the primary cause of death among the native people as syphilis, cholera, malaria, measles, smallpox, and other contagious diseases further reduced the Indian population to an estimated 30,000 in 1870. In events less horrific in statistical terms but more appalling to moral judgment, at least 4,500 Indians—men, women, and children—were killed by whites in sporadic acts of violence and campaigns of "extermination." Newspapers in the 1850s and 1860s reflected the widespread conviction, inherited from earlier frontiers, that the presence of Indians retarded progress, hence that conflict and the extinction of Indians were inevitable.

or three bodies are not fished out of these holes."

Life moved so fast that, despite its youth, California harbored ruins among its hills: deserted cabins and abandoned villages of thirty and forty shanties overgrown with vines and bushes. And everywhere, scattered along trails and in mining camps, lay the debris of thousands of hurrying men who tossed aside old boots and bent shovels, jagged cans of sardines and oysters, brandy and wine bottles, broken pickaxes, and dulled saws. No one cared. Few thought of staying in "the mines." Lucius Fairchild, future three-time governor of Wisconsin, tried to express that central fact in a letter to his family in 1851, getting a little bollixed-up by the interplay of expectation and experience. He wrote that "the greatest drawback we that came here in '49 had is that we were always going home so soon that we could not commence operations as we should have done had we known that we should have been here until next year. You understand what I mean, and it is precisely the same now." Prentice Mulford, the miners' most eloquent and thoughtful spokesman, put it more directly: "Five years at most were to be given to rifling California of her treasures, and then that country was to be thrown aside like a used-up newspaper."

Nothing better proved the miners' tour-of-duty mentality than their endurance of "the loss of female companionship." Throughout the 1850s the proportion of women to men in the mining regions seldom exceeded three in a hundred, and they were "neither maids, wives, nor widows." Letters, diaries, and newspapers year after year lamented that without the ladies' civilizing presence, California would remain an unfinished country, lawless and immoral. Yet most miners found the obvious remedy unthinkable. Almost none called for their wives, fiancées, sisters, or female relatives to come to California. No, the women belonged at home in the States, in the normal communities their men would soon rejoin. Maybe it would take longer than promised to get back, but no matter how long they labored in the Sierra, few miners ever lost the con-

The first females to come were the vicious and unchaste, who opened and presided at brilliant saloons and houses of ill-fame and sat by the gambler and assisted him in raking in his gains and paying his losses. Flaunting in their gay attire, they were civilly treated by the men, few of whom, even the most respectable and sedate, disdained to visit their houses. . . . There was little social caste or moral quality in those days. In the absence of the true, the imitation was made to answer. And so men went wild over the shadow.

Hubert Howe Bancroft, *California Inter Pocula*

viction that the gold country was a workplace, not a home. Contradictions and ironies—California offered wealth enough for a lifetime but inspired only dreams of escape.

These distant worlds—the States and California, waiting families and lonely miners—stayed in tenuous communication through letters and newspapers, coveted links which Yankee enterprise quickly turned to profit. For men unaccustomed to the task of writing, printers in San Francisco and Sacramento City ran off thousands of "pictorial letter sheets" during the 1850s and 1860s. Artists gave up mining to find unexpected success selling drawings of California to commercial lithographers and engravers, who reproduced their scenes on writing paper. Forerunners of the picture post card, the sheets had space for a written message and, when folded to form an envelope, could be sent to the States from San Francisco for the minimum postal charge of forty cents. Competing companies sold tens of thousands of these letter-sheets, illustrated with elaborate engravings of mining operations, cityscapes, natural wonders, and everything else that might seem less believable if presented only in writing. Miners could choose from more than three hundred scenes with titles such as "Bird's Eye View

of San Francisco," "View of the Steam-Boat Landing, Sacramento City," "Sonora in January, 1853," "The Mining Business in Four Pictures," "View of the Conflagration of Nevada City," and "Gambling in the Mines." The most popular of all these "picture letters" appeared in 1853 under the heading "The Miner's Ten Commandments" and within a few years sold ninety-seven thousand copies.

East Coast newspapers, especially the *New York Herald* and Horace Greeley's *Tribune*, printed special California editions. Baled and shipped by the thousands to San Francisco, their value fluctuated wildly, like all imports, dependent on the quantity unloaded from the last ship's hold. Carried by riverboats and then by pack mules and expressmen, the papers reached even the most remote river bars, where they sold for $1 or more and were passed about until in tatters. News from the outside world lessened the miners' and merchants' sense of isolation and often gave them reason to comment on what was happening in the States, as when a miner from Illinois bought an issue of the *Tribune* at Bidwell's Bar and wrote home that he was pleased to read "the important and gratifying news that Congress is becoming more sober and acting somewhat like statesmen."

What attracted the miners' greatest interest was news about California—reports that its merchants were prospering and its miners were digging gold by the pound along all the streams from the Feather River to Mariposa Creek; that millions in gold was loaded each month on steamships to Panama and thence to New York. What a shock for a tired placer miner or an interest-burdened merchant who had just written to his wife explaining why he could not come home and, just as likely, why her brother should stay there. They were amazed to read each spring that new thousands gathered at the western frontier to start yet another emigration to the goldfields. Some letters from California accused "dealers in liquor and provisions" of promoting California "to make a market for their goods." Others protested that "every description of California has been shamefully and corruptly overwrought." One cynical fellow confessed, "I really hope that no one will be deterred from coming on account of what anybody else may say. The more fools the better, the fewer to laugh when we get back home."

Although small in number, some foresighted individuals saw that the prevalent jackpot mentality was blinding the miners to California's broader potentialities. One of them protested that "a great mistake has been made by people who have emigrated to California and considered it a sort of huge goose out of which a few feathers were to be plucked and then forsaken. . . . Never was there a more egregious error in regard to the character of the country. Gold is not the only product of California. Her fertile valleys and rich prairies are capable of producing an untold store of agricultural wealth."

The fast-growing populations of San Francisco, Sacramento, Stockton, Sonora, and Marysville placed insatiable demands for food supplies on wholesalers and purveyors. Scores of thousands of miners in rough camps bought whatever was available at provision stores, eateries, and hotels, complaining regularly about the near absence of fresh food. The opportunity for profit from farming should have been apparent, especially inasmuch as many of the miners had been farmers; but it was difficult to return to a routine that so many had come to California to escape. Nevertheless, slowly through the 1850s an increasing number turned to experimental cultivation, and their widely heralded rewards encouraged others.

In the Trinity River mines near the town of Weaverville, a Mr. Howe raised a crop of potatoes that he sold in September 1852 for $16,000. Near Sacramento, an ex-miner described as "a gardener" planted an acre of onions and sold his crop for $2,100. Farmers in the Willamette Valley of Oregon exported apples to the great California market, where they sold in the mines for $1.50 each. By the mid-1850s, miners traveling from camp to camp found along the way, here and there, "good frame houses with two or three rooms, a boarded floor,

and windows, surrounded by several acres of cleared land under cultivation." Rows of cauliflower, squash, cucumbers, green beans, tomatoes, and watermelons—watered from miners' ditches or flumes—earned profits that rivaled the best in the diggings. But farming meant a commitment to stay and work the land, to make California home. For most, this required a change of thinking that came very slowly.

Though profitable and expanding, California's truck farms could provide but a small fraction of what their huge consumer market demanded. Endless tons of foodstuffs landed at San Francisco, most destined to be reshipped to the inland river ports: flour from Chile, oranges from Tahiti, rice from China, sugar from Hawaii, coffee from Java, and ice—pure pond ice cut by the ton from New England lakes and mill ponds in winter and through early spring. First shipped in 1850 and selling for eighty cents a pound (the same price as chocolate), this luxury was in such demand in saloons, gambling halls, and hotels that by 1853 the Boston and California Ice Company routinely delivered as much as nine hundred tons in its ships, to be stored in the company's icehouses in San Francisco and Sacramento. Less pristine, though no less prized, a load of cats arrived aboard a ship from Mexico and promptly sold out at $8 to $12 each, to provide hoped-for protection against the thousands of rats that destroyed quantities of perishables stored in tents and makeshift warehouses.

In Sacramento the *Placer Times* regularly listed the daily unloading of cargo along the riverfront: 3,000 pounds of butter in kegs, 5,000 pounds of cheeses in tins, 18,000 pounds of beans, and many hundreds of cases of pickled oysters, clams, lobsters, and scallops. Other cargoes included rubber tents with frames attached, 262 cases of boots, 10,000 cigars, and a large consignment of Vermont marble for tombs and headstones.

The flood of imports attested to the magnetic power of California's cash market; at the same time, it revealed something of the needs and habits of its people. In 1853 the quantities of liquor imported and presumably consumed included 20,000 barrels of whiskey, 4,000 barrels of rum, 34,000 baskets of champagne, and 156,000 cases of other wines. Beer came in 24,000 hogsheads, 13,000 barrels, and 23,000 cases, while shipments of brandy arrived variously in "9,000 casks, hogsheads and pipes; 13,000 barrels, 26,000 kegs, and 6,000 cases." And there were comparable statistics for "unspecified liquors."

Whatever such consumption said about the reduced morals of California (a subject of continuing reproach by the editors of the many newspapers), it reflected the circumstances of a society of lonely men who sought companionship in tented stand-up bars, taverns, grog shops, hotels, and gambling "palaces." In all those public places, drinking was the common bond, stimulating talk that seldom strayed from the twin themes of making money and returning home. Occasions for celebration, calling for successive rounds of drinks, ranged from a letter received after months of waiting to a decision to buy passage home. Many a miner on his last night paid for champagne and promised to carry his partners' messages to wives and sweethearts. Amid the cheering, some of those at the bar watched quietly, surprised to feel in their hearts what one of them revealed in a letter to his father: "The independence and liberality here and the excitement attending the rapid march of this country make one feel insignificant and sad at the prospect of returning to the old beaten path at home."

What a confession, that California's way of life had become so stimulating that a man might feel melancholy, in spite of himself, about the prospect of going home. Independence, opportunity, liberality, excitement—what could Home offer that was comparable? Just as gold had seemed wonderfully preferable to a piddling wage, so California's other perquisites—its freedom and anonymity—now seemed preferable to old rules and hometown gossip; its excitements superior to church sermons; its easy credit a far cry from starched bankers who said no. California more appealing than Home? The

idea made a man feel guilty. But there it was, tempering the pen as it reached each letter's closing promise. When to strike for home? The answer became more uncertain, more difficult, as California's opportunities expanded beyond gold mining. Who could resist the enticement of new stories like that of the man in Marysville whose hotel made $15,000 in six months, or the farmer near San Jose whose annual gross from selling cabbages, onions, potatoes, and tomatoes came to $175,000? New paths beckoned, none of them well worn.

GOLD ON THE HOOF

GOLD'S POWERFUL ECONOMY ALSO REACHED south, to the "cow counties," where the Californios and their Americano sons-in-law had been living in comfortable isolation, content to sell the hides of their cattle at $2 each (some years only $1.50) and leave the carcasses for the dogs and coyotes. But that simple life and its casual waste abruptly ended when the mining camps and booming cities up north began to offer big sums for fresh beef in preference to the barrels of salted meat and dry jerky that were the staple. Their demand for butchered beef drove the price of cattle to levels never before dreamed of, as high as $300 a head in 1849. Suddenly, the rancheros began taking in more gold dust than the miners. Yanked by good fortune from their insular subsistence, the "cattle barons" rapidly became some of the greatest beneficiaries of the inflated gold rush economy.

Even four years later, in November 1853, a ranchero south of Monterey sold one thousand cattle at $50 a head. Small calves brought $20 and $25. To sell at such wondrous prices, cattle by the tens of thousands were driven north along coastal trails and through the San Joaquin Valley to grazing ranges near San Francisco and Sacramento, where miners-turned-rustlers stole as many as possible. Abel Stearns, that most commercial and successful of the Americanos who had married into the ranch-

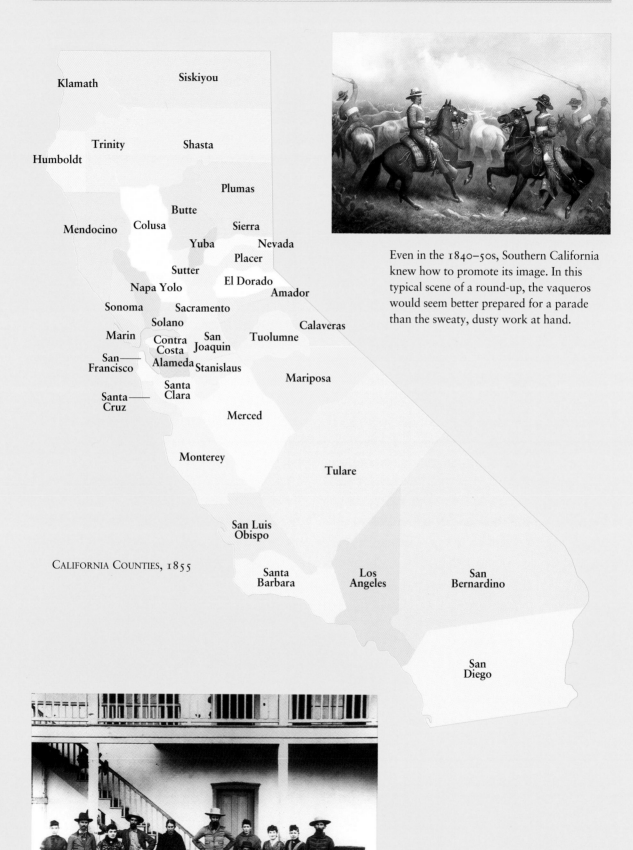

Even in the 1840–50s, Southern California knew how to promote its image. In this typical scene of a round-up, the vaqueros would seem better prepared for a parade than the sweaty, dusty work at hand.

CALIFORNIA COUNTIES, 1855

Klamath
Siskiyou
Trinity
Shasta
Humboldt
Plumas
Butte
Mendocino
Colusa
Sierra
Yuba
Nevada
Placer
Sutter
Napa Yolo
El Dorado
Amador
Sonoma
Sacramento
Solano
Calaveras
Marin
Contra
San
Tuolumne
Costa
Joaquin
San
Alameda
Stanislaus
Francisco
Mariposa
Santa
Clara
Santa
Merced
Cruz
Monterey
Tulare
San Luis
Obispo
Santa
Los
San
Barbara
Angeles
Bernardino
San
Diego

The many mining counties compared to the few "cow counties" reflected the distribution of population, even though Californio clans, like the Lugos (left) took pride in large families with twelve to eighteen children.

ing culture, estimated that during the boom years (1850–56) some 25,000 to 30,000 cattle were sold annually from the vast ranchos of southern California. In Santa Barbara County the de la Guerra family ran about 11,000 cattle on their 228,000 acres, John Wilson ran 20,000 on his wife's San Luis Obispo rancho, while uncounted thousands more grazed over other estates, like the Yorba family's in San Bernardino County, with its 213,000 acres, newly completed fifty-room house staffed by twenty-six servants, and over one hundred vaqueros to round up the cattle.

But gold seemed to work a reverse alchemy in the hands of many Californios, financing a burst of excess that led to ruin. Accustomed to the handshake credit system of a simpler day, wherein the debtor was seldom pressed, these carefree families borrowed against next year's cattle sales and, when taxes had to be paid, mortgaged their land, all the while living as grandly as ever, ignorant of the effects of compound interest. A son of Don Juan Bandini lost almost $10,000 playing cards, while the patriarch himself owed more than $12,000, carried at 4 percent each *month*. When beef prices began to drop with outside competition, this great landowner succumbed to bankruptcy in 1859. Others overwhelmed by debts included a Californio whose property taxes, lawyers' fees, and various borrowings forced him to sign a mortgage at 10 percent, payable monthly. Weekly interest of 12 percent on unsecured loans postponed the reckoning for the most desperate, while making inevitable their ultimate surrender to San Francisco bankers and lawyers. Often friends co-signed notes in a display of loyalty and honor and thus were swept under as well. Pío Pico, last of the Mexican governors and once one of California's great land barons, fell among these unhappy ranks. Deeply mired in arrears, he lost his empire and retreated to the humility of dependence on relatives.

Adding to the Californians' woes, phenomenal prices paid for beef by San Francisco and Sacramento slaughterhouses attracted stockmen from Illinois, Missouri, and other Midwest states who drove their superior breeds overland to the Sacramento and San Joaquin valleys. Sixty-one thousand head made the drive in 1854. Thousands more came from Texas and Oregon. Despite the immense numbers, "American Bullocks" ready for slaughter brought extraordinary prices, as much as $100 to $150 a head, far more than the Californios' scrawny longhorns. And unlike the casual rancheros, American cattlemen sought to improve the quality of their beef by importing purebred bulls for controlled breeding. The *San Francisco Alta* reported that "almost every steamer brings an importation of blooded stock."

The insatiable, gold-rich cities and mining camps craved not only fresh beef but mutton as well. Faraway sheepmen suffering in the Midwest from a collapse in the price of wool (sheep sold at $1 a head in 1852) learned of California's prices—$20 a head—and sent their flocks across the continent: 40,000 head in 1852. From New Mexico, even larger numbers trailed to the promised land—a total of 551,000 by 1860. These statistics for cattle and sheep suggest how California's gold reshaped economies and family fortunes at great distances from the Sierra diggings.

Even as the incomparable economics of gold attracted distant producers to their market, even as scheming Yankee lawyers filed tax liens and opportunistic bankers peddled usurious loans, Californio families still in control of their inherited fiefdoms resisted the changes and intrusions of the gringo and his money-mad cities and camps up north, a world far more distant than miles could measure. On southern California ranchos during the 1850s, husbands and wives, fathers and mothers and children, and "young gentlemen and beautiful and charming young ladies" enjoyed the pleasures of picnics, serenades, bonfires and fireworks, "feasting and hilarity," weeklong wedding fiestas, religious festivals, and always unstinting hospitality—a way of life remarkably unchanged from what Richard Henry Dana had described in the 1830s.

As the commercial center for this traditional society, Los Angeles—the Queen of the Cow Counties—prospered from the extravagant spending of the suddenly wealthy and quick-to-borrow rancheros. By 1854 its Mexican, Indian, and Americano residents numbered about five thousand, including an influx of Sonorans who had been driven from the mining camps to seek work in this more congenial, Spanish-speaking society. Though greatly outnumbered, the gringo merchants, lawyers, cattle buyers, doctors, and moneylenders dominated the primitive government and the major businesses of the town. Many merchants took Californios as partners to provide the needed language and personal connections.

So different from the world of the *yanquis* up north, Los Angeles shared with those instant camps and cities a chronic inability to cope with the epidemic of lawlessness that persisted through the 1850s and for years thereafter. Despite an array of law enforcement officers and sixteen judges with the power to hang without a jury, murderers and desperadoes virtually ruled the town from their brothels, gambling halls, and saloons. After reporting thirty-one murders in 1851, the *Los Angeles Star* asked: "Who can name *one* instance in which a murderer has been punished?" During 1854 "homicides averaged one for each day of the year."

As the law failed to pacify Los Angeles's dangerous alleyways, so it was absent in the vast ranchlands north to Santa Barbara and south to San Diego, where gangs of *bandidos* robbed stagecoach passengers, raided ranchos, rustled cattle, and did generally "about as they pleased." To pursue these Californio and Mexican outlaws, Angelenos organized a company of "Rangers" whose twenty-two hangings ("heroic measures") included those of the most notorious badmen, "Three Fingered Jack" and the legendary Joaquín Murietta.

Beyond the thugs in Los Angeles and the highwaymen in the countryside, the rancho families suffered from and resented a more distant enemy—the state legislature. That legal authority, dominated by the miners, in 1852 voted to impose on the six southern cow counties a disproportionate burden of taxes, levying against their population of 6,000 a total of $42,000 in property taxes and $4,000 for poll taxes. Taxes for the twenty northern counties, in contrast, which counted at least 250,000 residents in the mines and cities, amounted to only $21,000 and $3,500. Feeling impotent to defend their interests, the Angelenos and their allies began to advocate a division of the state, "friendly and peaceful but still complete." This sentiment strengthened, leading to a popular statewide vote in 1859 that overwhelmingly endorsed a statute (ignored by the U.S. Congress) for the establishment of a new political entity, the Territory of Colorado.

FLEDGLING GOVERNMENT

LONG BEFORE THE LEGISLATORS UP NORTH TOOK notice of the southern Californians' discontent, even willingness to secede, they grappled with a problem of more immediate concern, one that involved dignity and tradition, though neither attribute had thus far been evident in American leadership of California. Where to locate the capital of the Union's newest state? The first-chosen site, San Jose, lacked all the requisites, from an adequate meeting hall for the assembly and senate to sufficient hotels, eateries, and saloons to lodge and refresh the statesmen and their supplicants. Offers and counteroffers (even bribes, some said) came from competing towns. In a time of economic and social turmoil among its transient, rambunctious, money-mad population, California needed at least the *symbol* of stability: a capital city, the imprimatur of statehood.

That essential had become apparent after October 18, 1850, when the monthly mail steamer brought news to San Francisco that the Congress at last had voted to admit California as the thirty-first state.* To welcome the *Oregon,* her rigging festooned with flags and a huge banner proclaiming "California Is a State," San Franciscans fired off a spontaneous salute with rifles, pistols, and an old cannon. The *Oregon* answered with a thundering broadside. Summoning its irrepressible, improvising vigor (despite the devastation of a fire in September), the town organized a formal celebration described in prideful detail by the *Alta California:* an evening of "lively, gratifying jollification," and the next day (October 29th) a "triumphal procession" that crowded into Portsmouth Square to hear a lengthy oration, followed by an ode wherein California was described as "the Pride of the West." That evening bonfires on the hills, illumination on several buildings, and sky-rockets lit up the night. "The grandest public ball" climaxed the exuberance.

In Sacramento City, the *Placer Times* proclaimed its delight at "the glorious intelligence." But up in the hills, admission aroused a more jaded response. Among the scoffers, one diarist from Mississippi asserted: "To read some of the San Francisco papers and some speeches in Congress, you would think the people here were very anxious and even indignant she was not admitted sooner. Humbug! There is not one man in a hundred that cares a damn about it, one way or another. All they want is what gold they can get, and the state may go to hell, and they would vamoose for home."

---

* The debate over California's admission as a free state precipitated one of the most bitter, lengthy sectional crises in American history. Southern congressmen and senators argued that admitting California as a free state would upset the carefully maintained balance between slave and free states, thereby relegating the South to a minority position. Dissolution of the Union threatened. In late January 1850 the aging senator from Kentucky, Henry Clay, offered a series of resolutions (the Compromise of 1850), which he defended in a famous two-day speech. Congress debated the compromise for more than seven months. Finally, both houses approved the bill on September 9, 1850, admitting California to the Union.

One journalist-historian summed up the end of the crisis: "The Union is an exclusive body, but when a millionaire knocks on the door, you don't keep him waiting too long, you let him in."

Back to their tasks, the legislators convened at San Jose in January 1851 and voted to accept General Mariano Vallejo's offer of a capital city (to be called Vallejo) on his property near Carquinez Strait. But when they assembled there in 1852, the place had but one building, barely completed and unfurnished. Displeased, they considered offers from San Francisco, Benicia, Sacramento, and, most urgently, San Jose. There followed a lively interlude of political connivance and "the buying and selling of votes" as the seat of government was hawked about from town to town. Back to San Jose, then a return to Vallejo, followed almost immediately by a move to Sacramento, and then another try at Vallejo. Next Benicia induced the legislators to make that site the capital. San Jose worked to gain another chance, as did Sacramento. Finally, in 1854, the suitcase-weary legislators voted to designate Sacramento "the permanent seat of government."

Capital city, assembly, senate, yet-to-be-built capitol building—very few Californians "cared a damn" about these needs and functions of the thirty-first state. They expected very little from their new government. Where bridges, roads, and levees needed to be built, ferries put into service, firefighting companies organized and equipped, mail delivery networks established, and criminal punishment imposed, no one thought of the government. Instead, Californians set themselves to all those tasks, with an entrepreneurial sense of inventiveness and self-reliance that offset the municipal void.

The tasks that did cry out for government action suffered from continuing neglect: to establish a much-needed mint where gold dust could be sold at fixed, honest prices and coins could be made that had full value; to open post offices throughout the mining region so letters could be received and sent without the expressman's levy of a dollar or more; and to do something about the millions of acres claimed as Mexican land grants and thus denied to Americans who could make good profits by farming those "idle" ranges. But mint, post offices, and land reform all depended on action in distant Washing-

ton, not in San Jose or Vallejo, Benicia or Sacramento, or wherever the legislators sat.

However, the new state's legislators did have to cope with the consequences of the Foreign Miners' Tax, passed in April 1850 by their predecessors in the naive belief that the state could collect $200,000 each month by requiring each "foreign" miner to pay a monthly fee of $20 to dig for California's gold—or, failing to pay, face imprisonment.* If this edict had been enforced, the absence of jails would only have compounded the law's vexations. But before such practicalities arose, tax collectors encountered organized opposition among thousands of foreigners, most of them in the southern mines. In Tuolumne County, placards appeared in several camps, exhorting Frenchmen, Chileans, Peruvians, and Mexicans to unite: "Go to Sonora next Sunday, there we will try to guaranty security for us all and put a bridle in the mouths of that horde who call themselves citizens of the United States."

On Sunday, May 19, some three to five thousand foreign miners (supposedly led by "hot-headed Frenchmen of the Red Republican order") gathered in and around the town of Sonora. Reports of their speeches and rumors of "a civil war" goaded several hundred American miners from Woods Creek, Indian Gulch, Cuyota Creek, and "all the diggings on the Stanislaus and Tuolumne rivers" to rally "as the war cry rolled on from hill to dale." But the next day, a posse of five hundred Americans could not find any foreigners willing to engage them, even in

---

* The contradictions and unintended consequences of this famously controversial statute were numerous. The legislators' speeches blatantly emphasized their anti-foreign, even xenophobic motive—to use economic persecution as the means to drive out foreign miners, especially Mexicans. And yet the declared purpose of the tax was to raise desperately needed revenues. If the foreign miners could not afford to pay the tax, or if they refused, what recourse would the collectors have had? And if the foreigners obliged by fleeing, the state would lose this source of income. Receipts from the tax for 1850–51 amounted to only $29,991, and for the third year $1,003.

When the legislature convened at Vallejo in January 1852, the *Sacramento Union* chortled:

Chairs have at last reached the magnificent capital of California, and the members of the two houses are no longer compelled to sit upon nail kegs with a board placed across the open heads or upon emergency benches which now and then break under the weight of legislative dignity and let down a row of honorable gentlemen flat upon the floor, to the great hazard of the House.

Sacramento Union, January 9, 1852

camps where French, Mexican, and Chilean flags had been raised as defiant banners. Instead they found "a sullen silence, the foreigners having ceased their mining." Unable to stir up more trouble among the suddenly fearful foreigners, the Americans "flung from a tall pine the brilliant star spangled banner, saluting it with tremendous shouts of applause and vollies of small arms . . . and the furor of the foreigners was most effectively quelled."

Quelled, but at an unexpected cost. By the thousands Mexicans began to leave Sonora within a few days of the "mess." Soon American storekeepers, saloon owners, and merchants in Sonora, Stockton, and nearby camps saw their revenues collapse as their customers disappeared. More partial to the race-blind power of gold dust than to antiforeign sentiment, businessmen petitioned Governor Burnett, declaring the tax had left "incensed feelings towards the powers that be, for business has been prostrated since the [tax] collectors have been here." This and other protests persuaded the new legislature in March 1851 to repeal the xenophobic Foreign Miners' Tax, just eleven months after its passage.*

Dominating California's adolescent economy and government, merchants (many of them ex-miners) and mining companies had become mutu-

ally dependent allies. All businesses, from Sonora bathhouses to Downieville saloons, from San Francisco boilermaking shops to Marysville freight haulers, from San Joaquin River steamboats to Solano County potato farms, prospered or perished on the purchasing power of one hundred thousand miners. The dust and grains and nuggets and crush of gold gathered in the mountains translated into millions of dollars flowing into the California economy: almost $7 million each month during 1852—the equivalent of $134 million in 1998 dollars—distributed across a population that numbered approximately 255,000.

California was like a giant company town. Everyone profited from the dominant business of mining. Everyone was wedded to its continued success. The state's pragmatic senators and assemblymen could be counted on for legislative compliance. In 1851 they passed a statute that legalized the rules and regulations that miners had gradually adopted to protect their mining claims. Miners thereby gained official endorsement of their principle of "free mining," meaning no surveys, no leases, taxes, or royalties; no interference with the transfer of claims from one miner or company to another; no restrictions on placer mining, quartz operations, fluming, ditching, or tailings. Any stream could be dammed and diverted to a sluice, flume, or ditch, its water carried any distance, for any purpose. With impunity, mining companies could wash away a road, erode a farmer's most fertile fields, dig up a town's streets, even undermine buildings and homes. Occasionally claims for compensation were honored. But the payment of individual reparations did little to diminish a collective belief that what was best for the "company" was best for all.

---

* In 1852 the legislature renewed its controversial effort to raise revenue, this time imposing a less onerous tax of $3 per month. Subsequent amendments of the law and tax rate led to $6 per month in 1856, by which time Chinese miners ("Mongolians") had become the focus of virulent anti-foreign prejudice.

THE LASH AND THE NOOSE

IN THIS FREEWHEELING, LAISSEZ-FAIRE WORLD ruled by "the might of the ounce," temptations abounded. Everyone concentrated on gold, getting it by working a claim at Sullivan's Creek, operating a brothel in Oroville, investing in "water lots" in San Francisco, or resorting to the gambling table at the Big Tent in Sacramento. For some, chicanery, thievery, even violence offered the best promise to get the few thousands that could make possible a triumphant homecoming in Albany or Zebulon. So many temptations, so many disappointments, so many men desperate to win in the Great California Lottery.

Letters, diaries, and newspapers through the 1850s described brawls, knifings, robberies, and murders. Fires set by arsonists swept through mining camps, towns, and cities. In the resulting confusion and fear, looters reaped their rewards. "Brazen chaos" and "society-cankering rapacity," that's how two diarists condemned the near-anarchy. Chroniclers who looked for causes behind the lurid details usually identified gambling as the central evil. The ubiquitous tents, halls, and "palaces," with their bright chandeliers, raucous music, smiling women, and clinking bottles and glasses, lured men to risk their "pile" on the seductive turn of a card or roll of dice. Most lost to the professional gamblers, the real "nabobs of the land . . . who take their seats at their tables with all the importance of a member of Congress." Left embittered and desperate, not a few washed-up miners turned to robbery and murder. The ill-concealed bulges of pistols tucked into every belt and waistband brought heightened tension to even minor disagreements. And many succumbed to the comforts of the bottle to ease their aches and hardships. Criminals and "dregs" from cities around the world added to the social degeneracy.

California's moral laxity showed no abatement even in its better-barbered circles. The *San Francisco Evening Picayune* asserted that "there is scarce an officer entrusted with the execution of our state government, scarce a legislator chosen to frame the laws . . . , scarce a judicial officer from bench of the Supreme Court down to justice of the peace, scarce a functionary belonging to the municipal administration of our cities and incorporated towns who has not entered upon his duties and responsibilities as the means of making money enough to carry him home."

Statistics from the district attorney for San Francisco affirm the gracious amenability of sheriffs and judges to timely bribes: for 1,200 murders committed in the city between 1850 and 1853, the official legal system managed to sentence and convict only one defendant.

Most mining districts, with their thrown-together settlements of shanties, saloons, and supply stores, operated without the protections of "authorities," honest or corrupt. As criminal excesses began to fray the unwritten social contract by which most men abided, miners sought their own, self-reliant remedies, in the same hurry-up, get-it-done approach they took with so many other communal needs left untended by an impotent government.

As an unwitting spokesman for the great majority who resented the dereliction and corruption that allowed "criminals of the worst description continually to escape," William Perkins, a storekeeper in Sonora, set down the arguments for what should be done: "In a country like this, it is ridiculous to be hampered with ideas applicable to communities and societies already civilized. . . . The only means of purging this country of the dangerous villains who infest every town and settlement is to hang them. . . . We want a court that will try, sentence, and execute a man on the same day."

And so it would be. In the hands of "the mighty public," constituted in local vigilance committees, the rope efficiently dispatched scores of men accused of robbery or murder. Forty-seven were lynched in 1855, compared to only nine executed by what passed for due process.

In Perkins's town of Sonora, the sheriff dis-

Sent back to the States, lettersheets with scenes like this told the folks at home something of the catastrophes that could delay a father's or husband's return. Many a miner-turned-merchant lost his stake in fires that swept through San Francisco and virtually every other town and camp during the years of hurry-up construction with pine planks.

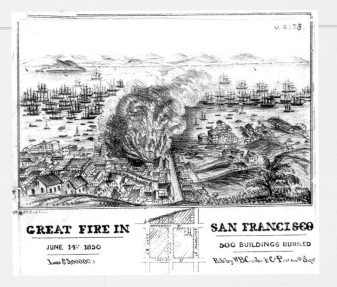

GREAT FIRE IN   **SAN FRANCISCO**

JUNE 14ᵗʰ 1850   500 BUILDINGS BURNED

Loss $300000

In their frantic efforts to hold back the conflagration of May 4, 1851, volunteer firefighters finally succeeded in saving San Francisco's waterfront of wharves, warehouses, hotels, and saloons.

covered the intensity of discontent with official justice when he wrested custody of an accused murderer from the control of an impromptu "Lynch Court." Some two hundred vigilance committee men quickly recaptured "their" prisoner and, without further deference to legal ceremony, rushed him "through a grove of pistol barrels" to an oak tree where the "guilty" man was promptly hanged, pulled high by the eager hands of "a couple score of men ranged along the rope."

On occasion, mobs toyed with a suspect, jerking him off the ground by the noose, taunting him before a final hoist. Hundreds of others apprehended for less than capital crimes received thirty to forty lashes, ear-clippings, or facial branding as vigilante punishment. Not even the state's highest authority escaped the defiance and anger of impatient vigilantes. After Governor John McDougal signed an executive pardon releasing a prisoner held by the Sacramento sheriff, the city's vigilance committee seized the reprieved man and hanged him. That night a jeering crowd turned on the governor, hooted for his resignation, and hanged and burned him in effigy. The mob's crudely wrought message sent a warning to all discredited officialdom: only popular justice could protect property and lives in such violent times.

Of all the vigilance committees to challenge lawlessness and corrupt penal authority, from Shasta to San Diego, none gained more power and notoriety than the two tribunals that took over the city of San Francisco for several months in 1851 and 1856.

Crowded and chaotic, with a population estimated at forty thousand (who could know? each day thousands of transients tramped the busy streets, some heading home via Panama and others on their way upriver to the diggings), the Pacific metropolis prospered as no other city on the continent, probably no other in the world. Wondrous profits, whether already made or expected soon,

had benumbed the citizenry to the corruptions of City Hall, its practice of buying and selling civic offices and contracts, and the everyday bribery of judges and juries. One authority declared in disgust: "There is no crime for which immunity cannot be bought."

During 1850 this distracted forbearance was sorely tested by a series of devastating conflagrations—on May 4, June 14, September 17, and December 14. Following the June fire, the city council prohibited canvas as a building material. Other inadequate fire prevention ordinances required property owners to keep six barrels of water on their premises and levied fines against those who refused to assist volunteer firemen. But it was not the volunteers' shortage of hose nor a fire's gawking spectators that most angered and frightened the city's businessmen, who were the principal victims of every blaze, losing millions in real estate and imported merchandise. Systematic pillaging by organized gangs during the confusion of each fire suggested the presence of profit-motivated arsonists. This was the menace that must be confronted. Collective self-interest required not merely barrels of water but the more effective remedy of the noose for incendiaries and the looters who employed them.

Angry newspaper editorials gave focus to public consternation. The *Alta* expressed the view, widely held by the city's merchants, that San Francisco's courts, lawyers, and police were worse than ineffective, asserting that "the city would be infinitely better off without them; they are no terror to evildoers. How many men shot or stabbed, how many thefts and arsons? . . . And where are the perpetrators?—free to reenact their outrages!"

Fed up with the perversions of official authority, the people of San Francisco looked to business leaders to force reforms. When a convicted robber escaped police custody in February 1851, a restive crowd of some five thousand gathered to hear an angry Sam Brannan speak, once again in Portsmouth Square. This time he shouted for vigilante solutions: "We are the mayor and the recorder, the

San Francisco is again in ashes. The smoke and flames are ascending from several squares of our city, as if the God of Destruction had seated himself in our midst, and was gorging himself and all his ministers of devastation upon the ruin of our doomed city and its people.

San Francisco Daily Alta California, May 4, 1851

SAN FRANCISCO'S GREAT FIRES

December 24, 1849

May 4, 1850

June 14, 1850

September 17, 1850

December 14, 1850*

May 4, 1851

June 22, 1851

*The fire was not dubbed "great" in *The Annals of San Francisco,* but did about a million dollars in damage.

The day after yet another fire, surrounded by ashes, his savings lost, one goldseeker wrote home to express the kind of stubborn optimism that put construction crews to work rebuilding before the embers cooled:

I have now only $1.50 in my pocket, but I do not care, for before many days are over, it will be without the dot in the center."

T. H. Watkins and R. R. Olmsted, *Mirror of the Dream*

hangman and the laws. . . . I want no technicalities."

But the public clamor for law and order failed to temper the boldness of the arsonists. On May 4, 1851, the anniversary of the big fire of 1850, a new blaze—later remembered as "the Great Fire"—ravaged San Francisco, sweeping away its entire business district, some 1,500 to 2,000 structures, and vast stores of imports, all valued at $10 to $12 million. "Nothing could stay the fury and progress of the united wind and flame. . . . Frame houses faded away like frost work. Thick iron shutters grew red hot, brick walls that had been so confidently relied upon crumbled in pieces before the furious flames. . . . The hollows beneath the planked streets, like great blow-pipes, stirred the fire to fearful activity. Through such strange channels, themselves as dry and flammable as tinder, the flames communicated from street to street, and in an amazingly short time the whole surface glowed, crackled, and blazed, one immense fiery field."

Only ferocious concentration by volunteer fire companies working with axes and crowbars to cut through the wooden wharves to disconnect them from the burning city saved the waterfront and dozens of ships crowded at their moorings. In nine fearful hours before the fire extinguished itself, more than twenty city blocks disappeared "in columns of smoke and flame loaded with the wealth of men and the rewards of toil and danger."

Changed but unchanging, San Francisco began to rebuild even as the embers cooled and rumors spread that arsonists might strike again in the surviving districts of the city. When an accused incendiary was arrested and indicted, a crowd gathered outside the courtroom. "Lynch the villain!" But his lawyer challenged the indictment and the suspect gained his freedom on a technicality, leaving the crowd savage with anger at yet another example of "unpunished triumphant crime."

On June 9, 1851, Sam Brannan accepted a petition from a group of businessmen to take leadership of a "Committee of Vigilance." The very next day, a looter caught with a merchant's safe became the first symbol of the committee's new kind of justice. Tried, found guilty, and delivered to Portsmouth Square, the prisoner was immediately hanged, his execution carried out by scores of men who grabbed the rope and held the corpse aloft for hours, trading off positions to give each a chance to show his approval of Brannan's shouted exhortation: "Every lover of liberty and good order, lay hold."

As more accused criminals went to the gallows in public spectacles or were deported by ship, the popularity of the committee's expedient justice grew swiftly, along with its membership. Newspaper editors defended "Vigilance" from dissenters' charges of inquisitional rule and mobocracy. The *San Francisco Evening Picayune* declared "the legal tribunals of the city and State . . . have suffered thieves, murderers, and incendiaries to live on in their guilty careers, without fear of God or man. Our people have endured this state of things . . . until patience has ceased to be a virtue. Under the force of imperative necessity . . . , they have entered upon the discharge of their self-imposed and solemn duty and will not desist until . . . the city is freed from the scoundrels who infest it."

Such was the appeal of Vigilance in the 1850s, and so efficient did it become as an instrument of popular will, that innumerable committees formed to cleanse mining camps and towns up and down the state—literally everywhere from Weaverville to Los Angeles—following San Francisco as their exemplar. Impatient, with little time for decorum and even less concern for legal procedure, these "peoples' juries" in camps like Volcano, Iowa Hill, Mariposa, and towns like Sonora and Marysville showed a fondness for the rope that led some victims to an undeserved fate. The most infamous proceeding occurred in Downieville on July 5, 1851, when a Mexican woman killed a drunken American miner—in self-defense, she insisted. Rushed through a "trial" conducted by "the hungriest, craziest, wildest mob," she was summarily hanged, her execution distinguished from others by the legendary dignity and courage she displayed on the scaffold.

By mid-decade the merchants of San Francisco found that their success in curbing violent crime was not matched by equal progress against corrupt municipal bureaucracy. Graft in city government had brought crippling new taxes, a looming municipal bankruptcy, and flagrant election frauds. One city official siphoned into his pocket as much as $800,000. (Irregularities in city hall's bookkeeping kept the exact embezzlement a convenient mystery.) Another enterprising politician won election to the Board of Supervisors from a precinct in which he was not even a candidate.

Business leaders worried that municipal chaos would irretrievably tarnish the city's image among partners and creditors back east. Vital contracts and dependable long- distance supply lines required municipal and financial stability. If eastern financiers came to view San Francisco as too wild and unstable, they might cut off credit and refuse to risk their cargoes and capital in a city judged out of control. To cleanse the city's image, allay fears, and restore confidence, businessmen in 1856 revived the Committee of Vigilance, this time under the leadership of William Coleman, one of several powerful merchants determined to end the governmental chicanery that threatened their prosperity. Their objectives sparked what would later be called "the Businessmen's Revolution."

Two assassinations launched William Coleman's revolutionary regime. On May 14, 1856, a political thug shot and severely wounded the publisher-editor of the muckraking *Daily Evening Bulletin*. In the following days angry crowds, contemptuous of official justice, shouted for the assassin's neck. His cronies slipped the culprit into the presumed safety of the city jail, where another public enemy awaited his long-postponed trial for having murdered a United States marshal.

Determined to calm the public frenzy and prevent mob rule, Coleman and his merchant allies announced on May 16 formation of the new Committee of Vigilance. They also published a constitution, which affirmed that "there is no security for

The earliest known example of California photo-journalism, this salt paper print (improvement on daguerreotypes) was taken by George R. Fardon on May 22, 1856, with the Vigilance Committee standing guard in front of its head-quarters, Fort Vigilance, as the bodies of Casey and Cora hung limply in their nooses. The presence of guards on the rooftops and of spectators standing at a distance reflects the pervasive air of crisis as the committee defied civil authority to enforce its impatient brand of justice.

The text of the lettersheet above described the scene as "the Revolution of the People, the County Jail besieged by three thousand citizen soldiers, armed and equipped." The "people" demanded the surrender of the two prisoners on May 18, 1856. The unnerved and outgunned sheriff complied, and four days later the two prisoners were hanged. Less formal and deliberate, the Vigilance Committee of June 1851 carried out the first of its four executions in the manner depicted to the left.

COLEMAN

life and property . . . under the laws as now administered." Therefore the undersigned would maintain "the peace and good order of society. . . . We are determined that no thief, burglar, incendiary, assassin, ballot-box stuffer, or other disturber of the peace shall escape punishment, either by the quibbles of the law, the insecurity of prisons, the carelessness or corruption of the police, or a laxity of those who pretend to administer justice."

This was an unprecedented attack on San Francisco's civil authority, directed not by a band of anarchists or some radical political movement but by the city's most successful businessmen. The frightened mayor appealed for help from Governor Neely Johnson, whose political blindness led him to intervene in the expectation that he could persuade Coleman to disband his committee. Far from it: by the next day more than five thousand citizens had volunteered to serve in the committee's armed companies, commanded from a Portsmouth Square headquarters fortified with sandbag ramparts and cannon, quickly named Fort Gunnybags.

On Sunday, May 18, a "citizens guard" of three thousand formed ranks in front of the jail, their cannon aimed squarely at the entrance. Challenged by such overwhelming force, the sheriff surrendered his two prisoners. Their fate was now tied to the recovery of the *Bulletin*'s publisher, attended by twenty of the city's best physicians—"surely enough to kill any man though he had not first been shot." He died on May 20, and that same day the accused were found guilty and sentenced to hang. Two days later the undertakers placed the martyred publisher in a plumed hearse, and as his cortege slowly wound its way to the hilltop cemetery, the committee let drop the gallows platform and the two assassins "fell about six feet and died almost without a struggle."

With unlimited jurisdictional authority and military power sufficient to overwhelm any counterforce short of federal troops, Coleman's executive committee went to work. It administered a rapid succession of arrests, interrogations, trials, convictions, and deportations of accused political scoundrels and thieves, all the while championed by the fevered rhetoric of San Francisco's newspapers. The *Evening Journal* proclaimed: "All pimps and street brawlers who parade our thoroughfares armed with revolvers, derringers, knives, and bludgeons must be banished from every post of official trust and power." Without the Vigilance Committee "we are lost and our city will become prey to gamblers, debaucherers, and a gang of political hell hounds that knows no law but passion and recognizes no arbiter but the assassin's knife and deadly revolver."

Faced with ever stronger popular support for the Vigilance Committee, Governor Johnson declared San Francisco a zone of insurrection and called on William Tecumseh Sherman, a major-general in the state militia, to leave his bank and gather a force to quell the insurrectionists. The angry governor also sent a dispatch to Washington requesting President Pierce to provide federal assistance against the committee's "warlike demonstrations." Among those most outspoken in support of the governor, State Supreme Court Justice David S. Terry contemptuously dismissed Coleman and his committee as "damned pork merchants."

The sense of crisis spread to Sacramento, where the *Union* cautioned the governor against the horrors of civil war, and to Nevada City, where the *Journal* coolly assessed the possibility of federal intervention. "In point of numbers and munitions of war, the governor is powerless compared with the Vigilance Committee and their supporters. . . . The president can move no number of men or arms sufficient to put down the people of this state in a shorter period than three months, and ere long that time . . . the rascals who have so long contaminated the fountain of justice will have been extirpated, and nothing will be left deserving the sword and bayonet."

A prescient forecast. By mid-August Coleman and his colleagues believed they had scoured the worst offenders and practices from San Francisco's streets and city hall. Displaying the political finesse to retire with public support and good will, the committee organized a celebration and a farewell. On August 18, through streets bright with bunting, a mammoth parade affirmed the strength and popularity of Vigilance. Four companies of artillery escorted the executive committee on horseback, followed by regiments of dragoons and infantry, with several marching bands scattered through a multitude estimated to number six thousand. Giving up overt power, the businessmen left behind an organization called the People's Party, which won city elections in November 1856 and continued thereafter to dominate San Francisco politics, preserving the reforms imposed by the "pork merchants" with such success that "the Queen of the Pacific" for a few years enjoyed a reputation for clean government and even safety in her streets.

Not easily beguiled by the blush of Vigilance cleansing, banker William Tecumseh Sherman in April 1857 sent back to his partners in St. Louis his flinty appraisal of the chastened city: "I see no signs of moral reform in California, though some vigilantes see it sticking out in every direction. My opinion is, the very nature of the country begets speculation, extravagance, failures, and rascality. . . . Nobody feels a fixed interest here, and all are ready to bolt soon as a good chance offers. Everything is chance, everything is gambling."*

ECONOMIC ARTERIES

Betting at monte and faro, speculating with a shipment of shirts or onions, investing in a hotel or warehouse that might be ashes tomorrow, working as partner on a river dam or in a shaft following a quartz vein—it was all a gamble, in a place of sudden success and sudden failure; in a time of extravagant expectations and desperate illusions. The oldest certainties and God-given rules of home could not survive the get-mine-now impatience of business in Sacramento or Rough and Ready. Even the risks at monte and faro were compounded. Some fifteen thousand decks of stamped or marked monte cards manufactured in Mexico were imported by gamblers, who routinely rigged faro boxes. Gambling operated without restrictions, like everything else in the California of the 1850s.

At the entrance to this masculine realm of Mammon, San Francisco dominated the world's image of California. Synonymous and inseparable, San Francisco and California: the one brought to mind the other, both ruled by cupidity and corrupted by vice, a veritable new Gomorrah. While moral condemna-

---

* As "banker" may seem a surprising identification for this military genius of the Civil War, so the word is inadequate to suggest the integrity of Sherman's career during 1853–58, when he was one of the most trusted and respected financial leaders in that chaotic era of unrestrained laissez-faire.

Because California's 1849 constitution explicitly prohibited the state from incorporating or chartering any banks and prohibited "creating paper to circulate as money," banks evolved as private businesses just like a store or a saloon, indeed many began under such auspices. Any individual could paint BANK on his door and welcome customers to entrust their gold dust to his iron safe. And there were no restrictions, regulations, or examinations of such indispensable operations. Banks opened, often thrived, and sometimes collapsed (as in 1855), causing commercial and social havoc. Banker Sherman so managed Turner, Lucas & Co. that when it voluntarily closed in 1858, it had a record of unusual stability and probity, including the refunding of 100 percent of its customers' deposits.

tion from press and pulpit heightened anxieties among wives and parents back home, San Franciscans scorned such jeremiads, confident that the vigilance committees' hangings and other reforms would clean up their city's reputation and dispose of the problems that most interfered with moneymaking. And for that purpose, "the City" knew no rival. On the shore of California's greatest harbor, at the mouth of its major river system, San Francisco received ships from around the world that disembarked thousands of passengers (64,640 in 1852) and unloaded vast cargoes (745,000 tons delivered by over one thousand ships in 1853). It was, in truth, "The Great Commercial Emporium of the Pacific," secure in its monopoly by the luck of geography and, more important, by the driving ambitions of its businessmen, who worked to connect their port with the vast inland mining empire, mother lode to the city's prosperity.

Because California's wealth in gold made affordable the high costs of imports and even more exorbitant charges for transshipment upriver to Sacramento, Stockton, and Marysville, as well as drayage from those river ports to the hill towns and mining camps beyond, entrepreneurs rapidly developed a transport network unique in its scope and efficiency: an interconnection of paddlewheel steamers, stagecoaches, freight wagons, pack mules, and horse-mounted expressmen. Where else but California did the cumulative costs of transport often exceed the original value of freight—barrels of flour, bales of socks, billiard tables—hauled into remote river canyons to provision and entertain hungry, lonely miners? But pay the miners did, whatever the cost, financing prosperity and development down the line. Marysville became an early beneficiary of the transport boom, burgeoning in little more than a year from a place of riverbank willows to a thriving commercial center counting more pack mules than residents.

Commerce between San Francisco and its eager-to-buy consumer market flowed over the Sacramento, San Joaquin, and Feather Rivers—

Knowing what had been reported of California's wickedness, Lucius Fairchild (future governor of Wisconsin) wrote to reassure his parents:

Gambling, drinking, and houses of ill-fame are the chief amusements of this country. Therefore, you see that we have nothing but work, reading, and writing to amuse us, as we are all nice young men and do not frequent such places.

Lucius Fairchild, letter of June 1, 1850

California's economic arteries—in side-wheel and stern-wheel steamboats. The fabulous profits that enriched the owners of the *Senator* and the *New World* emboldened other entrepreneurs to pay high prices for paddle wheelers operating on distant rivers like the Mississippi, the Hudson, and the Penobscot in Maine. The buyers ordered a number of these shallow-draft, 300- and 500-ton river steamers around the Horn in a calculated gamble with the sea. The first of these boats steamed into San Francisco in 1850–51, winning praise in the city's newspapers as "commodious floating palaces." The owners of the *Senator* and the *New World* responded by joining with several smaller steamers to form a defensive association called the People's Line, soon opposed by the Union Line, with its side-wheelers newly arrived from the East Coast. Numerous independent boats heightened the competition. New shipyards in San Francisco and Sacramento also coveted a share of the profitable business. In 1853 they launched the first steamers designed for California waterways. By the fall of 1853 eighteen steamboats competed on the Sacramento River, the fastest completing the run between San Francisco and Sacramento in six hours and twenty-five minutes.

Each year more "river palaces" joined the competition as the volume of freight soared. In 1855

Built to serve immediate needs and earn fast profits, San Francisco burned and rebuilt itself at least four times. Each rejuvenation was accomplished in a hurry, without plans or amenities. In spite of its pattern of self-destruction, the City prospered because its fortuitous location by the Golden Gate commanded a monopoly over traffic to and from California.

Until the transcontinental railroad brought overland competition in the 1870s, California imports and exports were shipped up and down the Sacramento and San Joaquin Rivers on steamers like the *New World* and *Governor Dana.*

shipments to Sacramento and Marysville totaled 320,000 tons: cases of candles, bags of coffee beans, boxes of soap, casks of sugar, barrels of pork, crates of canned oysters, bundles of shovels, millions of board feet of lumber, boots by the thousands, and a veritable flood of beer, rum, brandy, whiskey, and champagne. All this and much more to provide the staples and luxuries consumed in the growing towns and mining camps of the Sierra foothills.

In the familiar pattern, more freight shipped from San Francisco attracted more steamboats, and competition quickly sent freight rates into a dive, from $40 a ton in 1850 to just $1 in 1854. Cabin fares declined from the senatorial height of $30 per passenger to the plebeian depth of $3, with deck passage going for twenty-five cents. Some captains resorted to luring away their competitors' passengers by offers of free passage. The bar and menu in each ship's elegant mirror-walled salon were expected to help offset losses.

More than rate wars destroyed profits. Boats deliberately rammed their rivals. Lax maintenance and a craze for speed (safety laws were unknown in those robust years) caused numerous accidents. Urged on by cheering passengers, captains called for more and more steam. In one race the firemen responded by pouring tar into the furnace. The overheated boiler exploded, and sixty-seven passengers perished. Through years of rivalry and carelessness, steam pipes ruptured and blasts of steam scalded passengers; crew members shot at rival boats; and underwater snags sank steamers.*

In 1854 the river tycoons decided to end the ruinous competition. By mutual agreement they formed the California Steam Navigation Company (CSNC). Each owner turned over his boats to "the Combination" in exchange for a proportionate number of shares of stock, and all agreed to operate at a fixed schedule of rates for passengers and freight. Many boats were taken off the river and consigned to a reserve fleet.

Profits returned. And the newspapers howled. The *Sacramento Union* called the Combination a "soulless and heartless monster," and a San Francisco newspaper displayed its contempt with this headline: MAMMOTH COMPANY AND MONSTER MONOPOLY. Independent boat owners tried to operate their steamers, promoting the *Defender,* the *Surprise,* and other boats as "the Opposition." In repelling its competitors, the CSNC renewed ramming, rate wars, bribery, and shooting at rival captains. When all else failed, it simply bought those boats that were stubbornly competitive. Tenacious in their opposition, the merchants in Marysville raised enough money to build their own steamers, with which they formed the Citizens Steam Navigation Company. Bravely supporting their company, the citizens of the ambitious town voted for a $100,000 bond issue to keep their boats in competition, to the presumed advantage of local merchants. In 1858, however, Marysville finally conceded, accepting "a considerable sum" to became another buyout victim of the "Giant Monopoly."

Up in the hills thirty to forty miles or more from the river ports, miners cursed the delays caused by riverboat accidents and the inflated prices they blamed on the monopoly. But pay they would, whatever the cost, to ensure delivery of their mail, food, cigars, whiskey, and quicksilver. Between saloon-centered camps like Humbug Canyon, Lady's Crevice, and Dutch Gulch and the embarcaderos at Sacramento, Stockton, Marysville, and Red Bluff, the transport system evolved in entrepreneurial defiance of topography and weather. Freight wagons hauled supplies, and stagecoaches carried travelers from the river ports to commercial centers in the lower hills. From these transfer points pack

---

* Repairing and constructing steamboats became an important part of the iron foundering industry, which produced boilers, castings, and fittings—in addition to its primary business of making machinery for mining companies. In one of those twists of fate that shaped California's progress, the many fires in San Francisco and Sacramento left what the foundries most needed: a supply of scrap iron from ruined safes, stoves, and warped shutters and doors, even entire iron buildings.

Photographers and artists found very little beauty in California during the gold rush decades—the landscape ravaged, the towns thrown together without time for a park, a fountain, or even paint, and the people scruffy. Yet in that masculine world, the only beauty missed was that of women.

Horses and mules, freight wagons and stage-coaches, hotels and stables—outside the cities, that was California in the 1850s, even 1860s, with here and there a bathhouse or brothel to tempt the traveler. Getting gold was all that counted. Everything else could wait.

Riding "on top" was preferred to the cramped and smelly interior of a stagecoach. Come evening, what a surprise, what a relief it must have been to roll to a stop in front of a lodging like this can-it-be-real hotel at a ferry crossing on the Tuolumne River.

mules and horse-mounted expressmen followed trails that led along pine-topped ridges, down precipitous switchbacks to river bars, across rickety toll bridges, and up mountainsides to the most remote miners' camps.*

As inland transport companies hurried to connect camps to towns and towns to cities, stitching distant markets together, their aggressive expansion spawned new enterprises: the construction of thousands of wagons; the breeding and training of mules and horses (over one hundred thousand animals by 1855); the importation by ship of hundreds of expensive stagecoaches from Concord, New Hampshire; the cultivation of thousands of acres of barley and oats as draft-animal feed; the building and operation of scores of toll bridges and ferries at river crossings; and the management of innumerable roadhouses, taverns, and livery stables. Altogether, this transportation network employed at least forty thousand men by 1854 as teamsters, stage drivers, packers, muleteers, wheelwrights, and blacksmiths whose steady wages offered an alternative to the miner's pick and shovel.

At the river ports, husky laborers transferred steamboat cargoes into large freight wagons. These oversized vehicles, with great rear wheels seven and eight feet in diameter and sideboards that towered twelve feet and higher, carried two to four—sometimes six—tons of freight pulled by teams of six to eight mules. From the river port of Sacramento in the year 1852 these "land schooners" made an estimated forty thousand departures for the hill towns of Placerville, Jackson, Auburn, and Grass Valley. During 1857 more than fourteen thousand wagonloads rolled into Nevada City.

---

* In 1852 shallow-draft steamboats advanced the head of navigation on the Sacramento River as far north as Red Bluff, and that town became the staging depot from which freight wagons hauled supplies forty miles to the town of Shasta. From there pack mules outfitted Weaverville and other mining camps in northwestern California, supplying a scattered market of some ten thousand people by 1857.

From Stockton the freighters carried their cargoes east to Sonora and south to Mariposa. At the head of navigation on the Feather River, Marysville supplied the many camps on the forks of the Yuba and the expanding mining operations on North San Juan Ridge, and her freighters opened a road north to Oroville. In northern California, Red Bluff became the center for freighting after crews put through a road to Shasta in 1853. Freighters paid road builders to blast away rocky ledges and lower the steeper grades so that straining mule teams could reach new towns and extend the territory of "whoa navigation." Along the many routes, roadhouses welcomed weary teamsters with plates of beans and beefsteaks, sometimes a hearth fire, and all too often lice-infested blankets. Here and there, stables cared for injured and overworked mules and sold barley and oats.

To carry miners, merchants, gamblers, entertainers, various businessmen, and now and then a woman or two between the cities and hill towns, stagecoach companies by 1851 had established extensive service. With nine passengers cramped inside and others "on top," each coach was drawn by four to six horses under the reins of an expert driver or "whip." The "rapid locomotion" of these agile Concord coaches became so popular and profitable that inevitably competition increased until, like the riverboat companies, stage lines suffered several years of rate wars, accidents, and dangerous races. Newspaper advertisements announced service to literally hundreds of mining camps and, of course, to all the major cities. A typical ad in June 1852 listed service to sixty-four mining camps and promised that the company's "splendid coaches will pass through, by, or near all the bars, gulches, canyons, and bluffs on the Middle and South forks of the American River."

In December 1853 most of the competing companies joined to form the California Stage Company, which by 1856 operated more than two hundred coaches carrying passengers, mail, and miners' gold over a 2,000-mile network of roads maintained by the company. Though "Opposition" lines tried to compete, the company effectively monopolized this vital transportation system, which by the end of the decade extended north into Oregon and south to Los Angeles.

Stagecoaches could bump and sway over roads too rough or steep for heavy-laden freight wagons and hence could deliver passengers, mail, and small packages to mountain towns and mining camps in the more remote foothills. But coaches could not carry the tons of supplies on which every settlement depended. Where steep hills or rocky canyons confined commerce to narrow, often circuitous footpaths, surefooted pack mules took over the relay. Towns like Placerville, Sonora, and Oroville thus became secondary transfer depots, the end of the line for the big wagons and the staging ground for long trains of pack mules—"clipperships of the mountains"— awaiting their ponderous loads.

The unruly transfer from wagons to mules made a town's streets ring with the curses of teamsters unloading their high wagons and muleteers disciplining their ornery animals as they lashed down as much as four hundred pounds of boxes, crates, and sacks or a special shipment such as an iron safe or barroom fixture. In saloons, sweaty teamsters celebrated the prospect of a downhill trip, while the trail bosses outside readied for a long jaunt into the hills at the head of their strings of thirty to forty mules.

Like Sacramento, Stockton, and Red Bluff, the river port of Marysville sent out freight wagons, stagecoaches, and pack mules. And because it served the mining camps in the rough hill country along the many forks of the Yuba and Feather Rivers, this booming town became the largest of all packing centers, often loading as many as one thousand mules in one day. Estimates placed the number of mules owned by Marysville packers in excess of four thousand, a multitude that contributed greatly to the town's prosperity and its distinctive aromas. Exemplary of success in this business, one miner-turned-Marysville-packer made a net profit in three years that totaled $22,000 (1998 equivalent: $374,000).

Impressed by the always-hurrying commerce of California, a visitor to Marysville wrote home:

Yesterday a man went by here with some mules heavily loaded, at mid-day when the thermometer was three degrees from boiling. There he was, running fit to break his legs and bellowing fit to split his throat. Mules Uppe! (that is mule language) while the poor mules were galloping at the rate of six or eight miles an hour, puffing and blowing to the tune of whiskey barrels, tin pans, cigar boxes &c &c which were thumping and banging on their backs.

Sallie H. Dryden, letter of June 27, 1851

The last link in the distribution network was forged by expressmen. Many a miner with nothing more than a horse and a perceived reliability entered this business, so many that 264 of these service enterprises competed throughout the mining regions, their longevity prolonged by the U.S. Postal Department's chronic inability to manage the staggering volume of mail. Well over one million letters were posted to and from California annually (1.2 million in 1850), plus uncounted thousands of newspapers from the States, all piling into the overwhelmed post office at San Francisco.*

Employing as few as two or three riders, express companies picked up their clients' mail at the San Francisco post office, later at an annex in Sacra-

---

* In 1852 the Pacific Mail steamships delivered an estimated 60,000 letters twice each month to the post office in San Francisco—1,440,000 annually. And twice monthly, on Steamer Day, they carried away 50,000 letters bound for the Isthmus and thence to New York City. Hampered not only by this astounding volume, the postmaster had also to cope with California's unique cultural diversity. He employed clerks who understood Chinese, Russian, French, Spanish, Italian, and German.

mento when it opened in November 1850, and eventually at other U.S. postal branches closer to the mining camps. When the miners on a river bar or at the far end of a shadowed canyon hurried to the call of their expressman, he pulled from his heavy saddlebags not only mail from home but also newspapers, for sale for $1, sometimes $2, each.

With growth and prosperity, most express companies attracted buyout offers from more aggressive competitors, leading to a consolidation similar to that among the steamboat companies and stagecoach lines. Most successful in expanding its organization, Adams & Company dominated the business in both the mining regions and major cities. The company boasted in an advertisement: "From our arrangements with the steamboat companies, with upriver expresses, and our extensive interest in expresses in the Atlantic states, we can guarantee greater security and dispatch with all business entrusted to us than any other house." Adams's claim held true until the arrival in 1852 of a formidable competitor, Wells, Fargo & Company California Express, which opened several California offices and swiftly purchased the few remaining independents. The biggest profits earned by Adams and Wells, Fargo came not from carrying and delivering mail but from buying miners' gold dust at $16 to $17 an ounce in the camps and selling it for $18 at the U.S. Mint in Philadelphia.

So it was that steamboats, wagons, pack mules, Concord coaches, and solitary horsemen connected hundreds of isolated mining camps to San Francisco. From that booming port the Pacific Mail Steamship Company's side-wheelers sailed south to the isthmus twice each month, carrying hundreds of pounds of gold in their safes, letters by the tens of thousands, and a few thousand homebound miners, some with "pockets full of rocks."

However remarkable the entrepreneurial accomplishment of this vast import and distribution system, of greater significance was the fact that this network freed—or at least diverted—California from what had been the essential requirement of life on all previous frontiers: the cultivation and harvesting of crops to feed those who had settled on the periphery of civilization. California harvested at most 10 percent of its food and imported all the rest of its sustenance (and pleasures) during the years of its most rapid population growth, urban development, and economic expansion, thus unleashing the energies and inventiveness of its people to be concentrated on gold production and its many subsidiary enterprises, not least the mining of the miners. Gold paid all the bills. More gold paid for more imports, in turn stimulating more improvements to the transport system that connected San Francisco to its dependent river ports, hill towns, and mining camps, where most of the state's population lived, toiling—like no other frontiersmen—at a harvest that produced nothing of practical usefulness.

SECOND CITY

Like San Francisco, Sacramento owed its prosperity in large degree to the advantages of its location. Laid out near world-famous Sutter's Fort at the western terminus of the major overland route from the States, California's second city attracted each fall a vast influx of wayworn immigrants. An estimated fifty-two thousand overlanders reached the Sacramento Valley during September and October of 1852, and lesser numbers made the journey in later years. Thousands more greenhorns arrived by steamboat from San Francisco. While recuperating from their travels, learning the news from the diggings, and investigating what equipment to buy, many newcomers fell victim to the tender mercies of Sacramento's hotel-keepers and outfitters. And every day of the year the river city's wily merchants skimmed the pockets of miners coming down from the diggings—the sick and depressed, the strong and celebratory—looking for a doctor, for a job, for pleasure, for a hot bath, a shave, a good dinner, and clean bed: or for a ticket to San Francisco and then maybe home.

Sacramento catered to the robust appetites of the hills' 92 percent masculine population. Its busy streets offered a profusion of hotels, boarding houses, restaurants, saloons, hurdy-gurdy houses (dance halls), bowling alleys, bathhouses, gambling palaces, and not inconspicuous brothels. Public amusements ranged from Shakespearean performances at the Eagle Theater to bloody struggles between bulls and grizzly bears and contests pitting small hunting dogs against packs of rats. The disruptions of horse races through the city's streets warranted construction of a racetrack in 1855, a civic improvement welcomed by the owners of stagecoaches, freight wagons, delivery carts, and ice wagons.

In the dusty heat of summer, sprinkling carts stirred thick swarms of flies and turned the streets' horse droppings into a malodorous mire, refreshed daily by sweepings from the many livery stables. With winter rains, the streets became cesspools. Organized by Leland Stanford (he sold liquors, groceries, and miners' equipment), the merchants raised money to pay for planking over Front Street and later K Street. But the iron-rimmed wheels of heavy freighters cut through the pine planks, leaving splintered crevices that caught hooves and wagon wheels. So, merchants' profits paid for new planking, until cobblestones eventually provided a rough but more durable pavement.

While the business of attending to miners' needs and appetites brought prosperity to Sacramento's merchants, the city's greatest profits were earned at the huge supply depots that lined its teeming embarcadero, the very hub of the inland transport network. Steamboats from San Francisco crowded riverfront piers and moorings, unloading thousands of tons of foodstuffs and supplies. Some of this matériel was transferred to shallower draft steamers bound upriver to Marysville and Red Bluff. In the competition for these secondary routes, one steamboat captain boasted that his little stern-wheeler could carry freight in ten inches of water, even "anywhere there is a little damp." But the greatest

share of tonnage that crossed Sacramento's waterfront went to serve the needs of the city itself and its dependent constellation of up-country mining towns, provisioned by freight wagon caravans.

With prideful boosterism, the *Sacramento Daily Union* and other newspapers trumpeted statistics that evidenced their city's new power and wealth: for example, 162,700 tons hauled by 270 freight companies during 1854. At two cents per pound, the merchants' freight bill that year came to $6,508,000.* These charges were added to the steep bills of lading already incurred for shipment from distant places like Bordeaux, Boston, and Valparaíso, not to mention the initial cost of the imported goods. But miners' gold would pay for it all, even the fat profit margins merchants piled on. Everything depended on mining success. If a river-mining company, a sluice operation, or quartz mine failed, the reverberations shuddered through the webs of credit that led from camps and towns to Sacramento and other river ports and on to San Francisco, where unpaid bills provoked financial crisis and often bankruptcy.

Deceit compounded the risks that threatened merchants. Importers "at the Bay" often sent up-river a sudden glut of shovels, coffee, or whatever they could not sell in the San Francisco market, hoping to unload these shipments at high prices on unsuspecting Sacramento, Stockton, or Marysville buyers before news of the surplus brought an inevitable price collapse. All imports (even flour, the dominant staple) suffered "California prices," meaning wild fluctuations consequent to an actual or rumored shortage or surplus. Because East Coast

---

* Freight rates declined from $1 a pound in 1849 to an average of twenty-five cents a pound by the summer of 1852. However, each year's fall rains often pushed the charge back to $1. Improved roads allowed heavier loads by 1855, when the average charge out of Sacramento was two cents. To control rates, freight companies in 1858 formed an association, as had the steamboat and stage coach lines. But the freighters had less success with their attempts at monopoly.

merchants shipped "blind" cargoes without knowledge of the needs or wants of San Francisco and inland markets, the balance of supply and demand was forever askew, leaving California at the mercy of "adventure shipments" from all over the world. Some shippers in New York and other East Coast ports gained a sense of what was needed in California by orders received from merchants in San Francisco. They forwarded their customers' merchandise on slow-sailing vessels while sending the same products, as their own consignment, on faster ships, thus to "catch the market."

In such a world of rascality, one merchant concluded that "no calculation can be relied on. So great is our distance from sources of supply, so unequal the passage of different vessels, and so difficult it is to know, even approximately, the amount of shipments . . . that the most careful estimate is no more to be relied upon than the most arbitrary guess." No one described the unpredictable circumstances of the merchant more cogently than that tough, honest banker William Tecumseh Sherman in 1853: "Luck alone rules his destiny, the requisites of success elsewhere . . . have little to do with it here."

Compounding the merchants' dicey arithmetic, interest rates seldom fell below 3 percent *per month* and often rose as high as 10 percent. Not least among the factors provoking such usurious rates was the transience of California's population. When a promissory note came due, the borrower might be in Timbuctoo (a mining camp on the Yuba River) or, just as likely, at sea on his way to New York or London.

But good fortune could befall river city wholesalers with the same suddenness as calamity. Indeed, the one often cloaked itself in the other. When conflagrations—the scourge most common and most feared—swept through pine-board hill towns, leaving charred ruins and a sudden need for everything to be rebuilt, urgent supply orders poured in from Downieville, Sonora, Weaverville, Shasta, Columbia, and other burned-out mining centers.

No sooner rebuilt, some burned again, and reconstruction resumed with what seemed like nary a pause, driven by a contagious confidence in the power of profits yet to be made—risks be damned.

Marysville suffered two big fires in 1851, three in 1854, and another devastating blaze in 1856. Placerville rebuilt three times in 1856; Auburn swarmed with carpenters and masons after its "Great Fire" in 1855. Grass Valley burned in 1851 and was rebuilt; another fire in 1855 leveled the four-year-old business district, and rebuilding began once again. Thousands of tons of lumber, bricks, and iron shutters were ordered up from Sacramento, along with barrels of flour, salt pork, and brandy, sacks of coffee, mahogany bars, and all the other supplies that sustained life for miners, saloonkeepers, grocers, gamblers, stagecoach offices, boarding houses, express companies, and here and there a bordello. All were determined to get back in business as fast as the incoming wagons and pack mules could be unloaded.

Like its hill dependencies, Sacramento, at the confluence of two of the state's most vigorous rivers, had its own calamities to overcome. No town or city, not even San Francisco, endured so challenging a series of catastrophes. In a harbinger of the years ahead, Sacramento's several thousand residents and transients suffered two floods during its first winter, in January and again in March 1850. Severe storms brought deluges of rain as melting snow in the Sierra highlands bloated the Sacramento and American Rivers, which surged through the new town's tents and shanties and spread for miles across the surrounding floodplain—an unexpected disaster for the inhabitants, but in fact part of a timeless cycle. After the second flood, the town's businessmen recognized the terms of their predicament: either move back from the river's edge (as Sutter had done in building his fort on higher ground) or raise a levee to protect their strategic waterfront location.

Optimistic in their defiance of nature, the townspeople voted (543 to 15) to indebt themselves by the

Sprawling across the floodplain of the American and Sacramento Rivers, the capital city (shown here in 1857) suffered inevitable winter floods. Following the flood of March 1853, a determined survivor wrote to relatives back in Boston: "Hundreds have lost all they possess except their energy to earn more."

Not only floods tested the resolve of Sacramentans, major fires (as depicted to the left, November 2, 1852) destroyed large sections of the city. Months of summer heat left hotels, stables, hay yards, and hundreds of flimsy residences ready victims for what one report described as "the devouring element with its lurid fangs that fastened on the frail wooden tenements."

The first and never forgotten Great Flood of January 1850 forecast the terrible losses and the residents' fortitude of later years.

SACRAMENTO DISASTERS

January 1850	FLOOD
March 1850	FLOOD
April 1850	FIRE
August 1850	SQUATTERS' RIOTS
October 1850	CHOLERA EPIDEMIC
November 1850	FIRE
March 1852	FLOOD
November 1852	"GREAT FIRE"
December 1852	FLOOD
April 1853	FLOOD
July 1854	FIRE

The now uncontrollable enemy encircled in its resistless folds the Crescent City Hotel and in another moment the building from roof to basement was glowing like a furnace. . . . The insidious foe attacked the magnificent Overton Block, four stories high, the largest, most expensive and, as was supposed, the most thoroughly fire-proof block in the city, but it sank like a grain before the reaper's sickle. . . . Fiercely and terrifically did the raging billows hurl themselves against their powerless enemy, man and his works. . . . With but two or three exceptions, every splendid edifice in the city has gone by the board, including the Orleans Hotel and many other beautiful brick structures, the pride and ornament of the city. Fully seven-eighths of the city was destroyed. $10,000,000 will not cover the loss.

Sacramento Daily Union, November 4, 1852, describing the "Great Fire"

princely sum of $250,000 to build an earthen dike to safeguard their city against the dangers of the floodplain. This was a commitment to a long-term future unique among California settlements, made at a time when few thought beyond "next season" and investments in cheap canvas and pine planks usually sufficed to rebuild after the common loss from fire. Construction gangs unloaded thousands of wagonloads of dirt to raise a levee to a prescribed height of three feet. This first embankment would prove to be the diminutive ancestor of ever more massive projects, as Nature humbled Sacramento's early optimism, but not its resolve.

New tests of the fortitude of California's second city came in fast succession in 1850: a fire in April, squatters' riots and the shooting of both mayor and sheriff in August, an epidemic of cholera in October, another fire in November. In 1851, robberies, murders, and judicial corruption brought remedial hangings by a vigilance committee. In March 1852 spring rains and early snowmelt raised the rivers, and floodwaters breached the new levee. Once again a brown torrent surged through the city's streets, destroying buildings and vast stores of merchandise. After renewed work on the levee and more rebuilding, by the end of the summer Sacramento throbbed with business, its population grown to thirteen thousand. And then on the night of November 2, 1852, the Levee City suffered what would be remembered as the Great Fire, an inferno that left 90 percent of the city in ashes.

Among those who fought the wind-driven flames, storekeeper Collis P. Huntington (a '49er from upstate New York) tried to save his brick building on K Street, erected the previous year at a cost of $12,000. With wet blankets and sacks, he and his wife Elizabeth and several store clerks courageously battled the inferno until, as he later wrote to his brother, "the back counter was all on fire and I saw that no effort of mine could save it, and then I wrapped a wet blanket around me . . . and left the store through a sheet of flames and saw the earnings of years consumed even to the last dollar." His loss was estimated by a local newspaper at $50,000. Next door another merchant, Mark Hopkins, also lost his store. The dry goods and clothing business owned by Charles Crocker burned to the ground. Miraculously, the nearby shop of (Leland) Stanford & Brothers escaped unscathed.

With indefatigable élan and optimism, Sacramento rebuilt, this time aided by scores of wooden buildings dismantled in San Francisco and shipped upriver for reassembly. Huntington, Hopkins, Crocker, and hundreds more skimped and borrowed to put up new stores, hotels, liveries, warehouses, and all the other businesses whose handsome profits had been suspended by the disaster of November 2. By the first week of December 1852 the *Daily Union* reported "trade pours its tributes through all the usual avenues and gives promise to a more flourishing condition of things than before." That promise, however, was to be delayed by yet another catastrophe.

In mid-December the rains expected since October finally came, but in torrents: nineteen inches by New Year's Eve. Again the levee failed, and stalwart residents moved about in skiffs and rowboats. By January 1853 only a few hills and ridges, crowded with cattle, refugees, and stacks of soggy merchandise, interrupted the dismal expanse of an inland sea. Steamboats unloaded east of the embarcadero at a temporary town that sprawled on a hillside. From this muddy refuge, pack mules struggled to carry desperately needed supplies to the mountain settlements.

And then the sun returned; the Sacramento River receded. A citizen's army cleaned up the muck and rot while businessmen sent new orders to San Francisco. By mid-February mule teams strained to pull their great freight wagons through thick mud, heading once again for the hill towns with high-priced foodstuffs, including the miners' favorite, canned oysters. Along the levee, squads of city-paid workers labored to raise the earthen fortification high enough to hold back the relentless enemy.

California is the last spot . . . in which a croaker should show his despicable face. This is the land of enterprise, of energy, of hope, of high-tensioned nerves; not the land of mewling, pewling, fearful, tearful croakers. Our watchwords are EXCELSIOR! and GO AHEAD WITH A RUSH! and the croaker, who essays to throw cold water upon the glorious flame of enterprise, deserves death by the common hangman.

Marysville Herald, October 21, 1854

But Nature would not concede Sacramento its arrogant site. On March 29, 1853, endless hours of rain drowned the city's confidence as citizens watched the river rise twelve feet in twenty-four hours and surge once more through their streets. This time the city remained submerged for six weeks.

Refusing to despair, determined to control the river that was at once the source of their wealth and the threat to their future, the citizens in 1854 gamely endorsed another bond issue—this one for $350,000 to rebuild and raise their levee. As an additional incentive for this brave expenditure, the city's leaders sought to secure Sacramento as the final destination for the itinerant state capital. That long-sought distinction lost some of its luster when yet another fire, on July 14, 1854, leveled to ashes the business district, including the newly completed courthouse given to the state legislature as its permanent home.

No matter how destructive and often bankrupting the recurring fires might be, their damage was limited by the increasingly effective efforts of Sacramento's volunteer fire companies, which numbered eleven by 1856. Even though their ostentatious firehouses, complete with balconies, columns, and cupolas, testified to their owners' social pretensions more than to their fire-fighting skills, those private organizations did invest in constructing underground cisterns from which their manually operated fire engines could pump water to hold back the spread of flames.

In contrast to the controllable damage from fires, the devastation from floods continued to threaten the entire city, even its very existence. Despite years of expense and confidence invested in their defensive levees, Sacramentans knew each winter they might be inundated once again by filthy brown water swirling through their stores, warehouses, and homes, for days and even weeks. And worse, shipments into and out of the city would be halted, merchandise ruined, and interest rates increased—chaos that would lead to destitution.

Raise the levee higher, yes. But what else could be done to prevent the recurring submergence of the city? Sacramento's spirited answer wonderfully conveyed the robust "Stand Back!" attitude of the 1850s: raise all the buildings, hoist them high enough to stand above floodwaters. Through the cooperation of the local government and private enterprise, the entire city would be elevated to a height of safety.

This Herculean task Sacramentans undertook beginning in 1854 and carried on intermittently into the 1860s. Thousands of wagons streamed into town, delivering dirt and gravel by countless tons that graders then spread over the grid of streets, some higher than others. Many lesser buildings had their first floors converted into basements by the rising streets. Important structures were laboriously lifted from their foundations by phalanxes of jack screws until they stood many feet above their original elevation, sometimes for months, while wagons dumped dirt and backfilled around them and masons built new foundations. A hotel 160 feet in length creaked and groaned, sagged and straightened, as 250 jack screws raised it eight feet to a presumed level of safety.

A hodgepodge of ambition and confusion, Sacramento's "high-grading" continued for years, until a final plan enforced uniformity—but only after the worst flood ever left the Levee City submerged, from December 1861 to January 1862.

During that catastrophe, the *San Francisco Morning Call* ordained that "it is simply an act of folly for the people of the town of Sacramento to endeavor to maintain their city on its present location." In smirking agreement, the *Stockton Independent* pronounced: "Since the state capital is once more afloat, we suggest that Stockton be its next resting place." With seemingly genuine regret, the *Nevada City Transcript* concluded: "Sacramento is a doomed city."

PLANTING PROFITS

Propelled by these unique circumstances to instant wealth and urbanization, California's population by 1853 had more money per capita and in circulation than anywhere else in the world. Yet in that same year, San Francisco wholesalers imported six thousand tons of hardtack, evidence that many miners still lived on the meager hand-to-mouth fare that had been common among the '49ers. Tasteless subsistence rations shipped across two oceans at exorbitant cost tempted some ex-miners to turn to farming, to planting vegetables that could not be imported at any price, greens and fruits that prevented the ubiquitous scurvy and would sell at fortune-making prices. The *Sacramento Transcript*, as early as November 1850, assured its readers that the lucky few who went into farming "have been more universally fortunate than those who have engaged in mining."

Exemplary of that success, ex-miner John Horner and a partner worked 130 acres near San Jose, where, in Horner's words, "we flourished perhaps as no farmers ever flourished before in America, in so short a time." They grew potatoes, onions, tomatoes, and cabbages and grossed $150,000 between the spring and fall of 1850. Emboldened by his remarkable profits and by the entrepreneurial spirit of the time, farmer Horner in 1851 paid cash for his own steamboat and hired a captain and crew to deliver his harvest (expanded to include turnips and watermelons) more quickly to the San Francisco and Sacramento markets. He grossed $270,000 that year (over $5 million in 1998 dollars).

Spurred by rumors and well-publicized reports of comparable success, other miners turned to cultivating vegetables, confident of fast profits that would soon free them to head for home with their "pile." Barley and hay offered rich rewards as feed for the scores of thousands of draft animals. Enterprising bottomland farmers cleared trees, grew vegetables, and ran dairy cows along the Sacramento and San Joaquin Rivers, where they built landings to provision passing steamboats that paused long enough to take on supplies of milk, butter, produce, and—even more essential and high priced—cords of firewood for their boilers.*

Never had there been such a pay-any-price market, such a stimulus to agriculture, such a contrast to the ancient tradition of farming as a family-oriented, rural way of life. In the 1850s California farming became another hurry-up commercial enterprise, its practitioners speculative businessmen more than patient cultivators, its profits a forecast of dramatic change and challenge.

One of the most successful commercial farmers, George C. Briggs, a '49er from Ohio, gave up mining early. After several months in the freighting business, he turned to farming on the fertile bottomland along the Yuba River just north of Marysville. From his first crop of watermelons in 1851 he "cleaned up about $5,000." The next year he

planted twenty-six acres of melons and made a profit of $20,000. With such reason for optimism, Briggs chose to make an unusual long-term commitment to California. He went back to Ohio to return with his wife and fifty peach tree seedlings for his Yuba River farm. During 1853 his trees "made splendid growth," and two years later they bore their first harvest, which he sold for $2,800.

Briggs was on his way to become California's preeminent orchardist. He ordered from East Coast nurseries fruit trees by the many thousands, specially packed and shipped via Panama and delivered to San Francisco within thirty-four days. Each year he planted more trees in his four orchards along the Yuba, Feather, and Sacramento Rivers. By the summer of 1858 he had a thousand acres of peach, pear, plum, apple, nectarine, cherry, and apricot trees, their fruit so abundant that much of it could not be transported to market. Perhaps inspired by John Horner's inventive use of a steamboat to hurry his vegetables to market, Briggs boldly set up a series of relay stations with fresh mule teams to pull his wagons of carefully packed fruit over sixty miles and more to hill towns like Rough and Ready, Nevada City, and Downieville, where rock-bruised hands eagerly pressed overripe fruit to bearded faces.

By his mule teams and by shipments sent on steamboats to Sacramento, Stockton, and San Francisco, Briggs grossed in 1859 more than $100,000 and netted $70,000—proof that the alluvial bottomlands along the Yuba and other streams could yield even richer harvests than mining claims in gulches, ravines, and shafts. Each year through the 1850s, newspaper stories about successful farmers tempted disillusioned newcomers and stubborn old-timers to wonder why they toiled amid rocks and gravel for damnably elusive particles of gold when so much fertile soil would produce crops for big profits.

Miners and farmers, though interdependent, were yet fated to become antagonists when their enterprises overlapped. The state legislature and the federal government had recognized the right of

---

* Around San Francisco Bay, dairy farmers prospered from their sales to the growing metropolis. By 1860 butter had become a significant local product, and yet that year importation remained high: 5.3 million pounds delivered by clipper ship from around the Horn—enough to provide 14 pounds for every Californian. This was but one of many examples of shipments to the great consumer market that created volatility in prices and delayed agricultural progress. A more remarkable example: one clipper ship delivered 10,000 dozen eggs, a quantity that sold at wholesale for $10,000.

miners to stake their claims and dig for gold wherever they chose, generally up in the hills, in a world of rocks and forests and steep trails, far from land suitable for farming. But on the lower reaches of Sierra streams, where the hills sprawled in gentler undulations, farmers found good soil in meadows and bottomlands—and there they sometimes came into conflict with miners.

In July 1851 a farmer, Jerrod Sheldon, built a dam on the Middle Fork of the Cosumnes River to divert water for irrigation to his fields. A rise in the water level behind the dam caused the overflow of several mining claims upriver. The miners protested, angrily asserting the priority of their rights. Faced with some forty antagonists, Sheldon rallied a few farming friends. When the miners advanced with axes and rifles, he warned them off as trespassers. In answer, a rifle shot dropped one of the farmers. A subsequent exchange of gunfire killed Sheldon, while two other defenders suffered wounds. The miners demolished the dam.

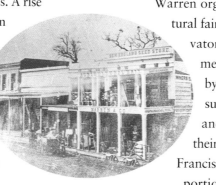

WARREN & COMPANY

Near Grass Valley two farmers found a meadow where they planned to mow two crops of grass in the summer of 1851. With hay selling at $80 a ton, they foresaw $400 per acre that year. They piled brush around several acres to keep out grazing cattle. A few weeks later a prospector pushed his way through their barrier and dug a prospect hole. He struck pay dirt. Other miners hurried in the next day, staked their claims, and soon destroyed the meadow. The farmers watched, helpless, knowing that custom and law gave the intruders superior right to use the land for mining.

Buffeted by the arrogant power of the miners, California's farmers found an able defender and champion in an ex-miner who helped to guide agriculture through its "hazardous infancy as the stepchild of ranching and mining." James Warren, from Massachusetts, had joined the 1849 rush at the exceptional age of forty-four. After operating an express company for four hundred subscribers along the forks of the American River, Warren in 1850 opened a general store in Sacramento, specializing in horticultural tools, fruit trees, seeds, and journals for farmers. By 1852 Warren & Company's Seed Store and Agricultural Warehouse offered a large assortment of seedlings "raised and put up expressly for us in the States and imported by express in hermetically sealed cases."

Warren organized the state's first agricultural fair at his store, inviting all "Cultivators of the Soil" to learn the new methods of planting necessitated by California's unfamiliar rainless summer. The next year, 1853, he and his son held a second fair in their "Horticultural Rooms" in San Francisco, where the extravagant proportions of the vegetables on display—squashes that weighed 265 pounds, beets and cabbages of 50 pounds, tomatoes and onions more than two feet in circumference—gave newspapers reason to hail California's unequaled fecundity.

Proselytizing to a society not readily distracted from its fixation on gold, Warren turned to a miner-dominated state legislature, seeking official recognition for a California Agricultural Society. In 1854 a sympathetic legislator warned Warren of the obstacles to his petition: "The representation from the agricultural counties . . . compared to that from the mining counties is very insignificant. . . . Men who are themselves birds of passage give little to the establishment of permanent institutions, and unfortunately for California we have a very large number of this class." Undaunted, Warren campaigned with zeal. He wrote letters, reports, and circulars arguing that an advanced and scientific agriculture would best secure California's economic and social stability. He condemned as an absurdity the continued expenditure of "the immense sum of twenty-five millions of dollars annually" on imported foods, including such basic staples as flour, five hundred thousand barrels of which had been imported in 1853.

Lobbied and prodded by Warren in 1854, the legislators consented to pass an act establishing the California State Agricultural Society. Through its annual fairs and year-round publications, this pioneering society would promote farming as preferable to mining, as a more reliable and more moral enterprise on which to build the state's future, embracing not only the promise of cornucopia but the values of hearth and home and man allied with nature.

Year by year the society's evangelical message warned against the transiency of miners and their destruction of the landscape. At the third annual fair in 1856 the society's lead speaker asserted that "the abundance of gold withdraws the attention of people from agriculture and mechanical arts; it leads to extravagance and idleness, tends to corrupt the public morals and fosters a spirit of reckless gambling and feverish speculation in trade. . . . It is time we had begun to feed and clothe ourselves . . . , to rely on the bounteous fruits of the earth to be drawn forth by honest labor."

And then, as if he had not yet thrown down the gauntlet, this farmer dared to speak heresy. "If the mines should suddenly fail . . . , we would not only be a happier and better people but in a few years richer and stronger in all elements of wealth and power. . . . The gamblers and loafers would instantly take their flight to Australia or Chile or Mexico. . . . In short, we might anticipate a perfect stampede amongst all that class of people . . . and there would remain here the men of character and substance, of sagacity and prudence. . . . With such a population as this, devoted to the peaceful pursuit of agriculture, California would quickly become the garden spot of the world."

So that was the farmer's vision for California: a prudent, peaceful, agrarian garden. Quite a change from the risks-be-damned, fiercely exploitive world of the miner.

But not so fast. For all their talk about character and sagacity, the farmers in the 1850s pursued profits with no less avidity than the miners and merchants—and with the ironic consequences of rotting abundance. From shortage to surplus in only three years. John Horner's fields in 1853 yielded 400,000 bushels of potatoes. His zealous production combined with the abundance of others to glut the market. Prices collapsed—and not just for potatoes. "All the large farmers . . . whose names are synonymous with . . . turnips as big as a bushel, cabbages as large as an oak tree, and onions too large for human belief are all actually failed or failing." That's what William Tecumseh Sherman reported in 1854 from his Montgomery Street bank in San Francisco. Marveling at the swift currents of change that swept through this strange new world, he added: "California is a perfect paradox, a mystery. The various ups and downs are enough to frighten any prudent person."

The Agricultural Society knew full well the consequences of overproduction. George Briggs and other fruit growers year after year had left two-thirds of their crop unpicked (a windfall for jays and magpies), yet the society's annual reports were regularly more boastful than admonishing. Its 1856 survey of farms, orchards, nurseries, and vineyards offered forty pages dense with examples of "remarkable quantity and size" (pears and apples fifteen inches in circumference) and "rapid growth" (nurseries with 40,000 peach trees, 16,000 plum, 100,000 apple; fields of barley that yielded seventy bushels per acre; ever-swelling harvests of grapes).*

Not until the Agricultural Society's 1856 report did such prodigality inspire the belated warning that

---

* Driven by the profit-seeking mentality of the 1850s, grape-growing and wine-making developed rapidly: 320,000 vines were planted in 1855 and 4 million in 1858. Haphazardly made, wine was hurried to market, much of it "vile stuff" that sold for twenty cents a gallon to profit from California's insatiable thirst. Meanwhile, imports continued at their remarkable volume. With 1 percent of the U.S. population, California consumed 25 percent of the brandy, 50 percent of the cordials, and comparable percentages of other imported alcoholic beverages.

California's farmers had outgrown their "internal market." And so, the solution? The society proposed that "if now a railroad were opened across the continent, many of our products would find a market . . . and our prices would not be ruined, as now, by a little excess of production . . . and the present hazards of agriculture, which are greater than the hazards of mining, would be effectively removed."

Beyond whining about hazards and even declaring that California's farmers had "a right" to demand a transcontinental railroad to open new markets, the Agricultural Society directed its efforts to promoting the consumption of flour milled from home-grown wheat: it was time to stop importing the staff of life from Chile and Virginia at an annual cost of up to $10 million. This argument reflected the rapid increase in the number of farmers attracted to profits to be made from this latest bonanza crop.

Planting wheat on a small scale started in 1850 and gained powerful impetus in 1853, when—despite massive imports—flour sold in many mining camps at $1, even $3, per pound. Such prices promised major profits, and wheat offered a great advantage over perishable fruits and vegetables. Hard and dry, the grain could be packed in hundred-pound sacks (centals) and shipped on riverboats to the increasing number of flour mills in Sacramento, Stockton, and San Francisco. By 1855 wheat had become the ideal crop for new immigrants and ex-miners whom the *San Francisco Alta* described as "too impatient to plant fruit trees and vines. They can hardly think of waiting for them to grow. No! they must get their returns immediately. They came to California for a fortune, and if they are not making it rapidly, they are discontented and eager to try something else."

How like the miners wheat growers were, quick to grab the main chance, using land they did not own, with only profits in mind. Hundreds of farmer-speculators hurried onto vacant bottomlands where the Feather, Yuba, Bear, and American

Rivers flowed from the Sierra foothills. Often with no more experience in farming than the '49ers brought to mining, but with equal impatience to make their pile, would-be wheat growers sowed seed across thousands of acres. Harvests by 1858 began to produce more than enough wheat to meet California's needs, true to a now predictable pattern. But unlike peaches and potatoes, this surplus could be exported in the holds of sailing ships, primarily to Great Britain—550,000 centals of raw wheat shipped out annually by 1860. Also by that time, shippers were dispatching increasing amounts of milled flour to satisfy the insatiable market in China. Here was another wonder of California's entrepreneurialism. By the late 1860s and through the 1870s—"when wheat was gold"—a fleet of specially designed ships (as many as 550 in a single season) sailed through the Golden Gate, laden with millions of centals, bound for the wharves at Liverpool and Hong Kong, thousands of miles distant.*

As California wheat became a staple in the world market, its cultivation spread widely and wildly, little hindered by the murky question of land title and property rights. Most would-be farmers knew of the Mexican land grants, those persistent reminders of a vanquished sovereignty, which encompassed a dominion of twelve to fourteen million acres, mostly in the coastal valleys and in southern California—none up in the hills where gold was mined. John Sutter claimed a grant of 48,000 acres that included land in and around the city of Sacramento. A score of Californios and American speculators claimed grants along the bottomlands of the Sacramento and San Joaquin Rivers. Would the U.S. government, as the Treaty of Guadalupe Hidalgo required, declare the Mexican titles to those and other vast holdings to be legally enforceable? It did not seem right that American

---

* Statistics define the magnitude of California's astonishing enterprise and productivity: more than one hundred flour mills in operation by the early 1860s and 5 million centals of wheat exported annually by 1867—15 million by 1881.

Architectural anarchy prevailed in the outposts of the Sierra foothills. Shacks, false-fronts, and lean-to stables pressed against more ambitious structures, some with columns and balconies. Main streets varied in width from ample to squeezed and their surfaces from planks to manured dirt. Pine framing and siding dominated, with bricks coming into general use by the mid-1850s, as well as iron doors and shutters to hold back the inevitable flames. Here and there a building received a coat of paint, always white, like a gesture of defiance against the surrounding grime and mud.

Unlike the art of lithography, the lens of the camera did not remove the hard truths about mining camps. In the daguerreotype at the top, Forbestown has a certain rough charm, but in the background looms another ugly hillside stripped of its trees. In the scene above (taken in the southern mines), the bleak and toiling life of gold mining is nakedly revealed. In cool contrast, Downieville was presented in this lithographic view as a quaint row of tidy buildings hugging the bank of the North Fork of the Yuba River.

citizens should be prohibited from planting and harvesting crops on virgin ranges unmarked by boundaries, fences, or any other evidence of ownership or productivity, save an occasional herd of cattle, roaming wild. And whoever heard of owning 200,000, or 300,000 acres?

Whatever land did not belong within the ill-defined Mexican grants, or was otherwise not privately titled certainly did belong to the United States government as custodian of the "public domain." But how was a new farmer, contemplating the empty reaches of grassland, to distinguish between the private and public land? That distinction, however, meant the difference between trespassing and exercising one's right as a citizen to settle on and claim ownership of 160 acres of public land. That right derived from the long-established frontier custom of preemption, which guaranteed that settlers—"squatters"—could acquire title to "160" at the minimal price of $1.25 per acre after the government had surveyed a district and tendered quarter sections for sale.*

Distracted, negligent, and cash poor, the federal government in faraway Washington offered no guidance to California's impatient new agrarians. Dilatory federal officials did not appoint a surveyor general for California until 1853, and not a single acre of public land was sold until 1857. Further, the U.S. Land Commission did not commence its lugubrious investigations to determine the legality of individual Mexican land grants until 1852. And

its rulings were often appealed to the U.S. District Court, where deliberations moved no faster, with the result that final decisions confirming or denying land grant titles required an average of seventeen years.

Even if Washington's cogs and wheels had turned in seventeen *months*, it would have been too slow for California. Hundreds, eventually thousands, of newly arrived immigrants and disappointed miners refused to wait for help from a government seemingly as phantom as the absentee landlords. The newcomers believed the land should be used by those who knew how to make it productive, whether miners up in the hills, lumbermen in the forests, or merchants in the towns—all of them digging, logging, or building on land not legally their own. As miners set up their toms and ran their sluices on whatever terrain showed promise of "color," so the new farmers felt no constraint in seeding any land along rivers and streams and in coastal valleys where they found good soil.

The opportunity to cash in on burgeoning demand for both wheat and barley made California's early agriculturalists both impatient and defiant. If farmers learned that a ranchero family claimed the acreage they wanted to plant (or had already planted), they usually stood ready to resist eviction, often in concert. The first or second season's harvest typically earned these squatters enough profit to move on, long before legal action might threaten. With gold in their purses, they bought land that had secure titles or tried the high life in Sacramento or San Francisco, or bought a ticket for home. Others, more disposed to farming life, stayed in increasing numbers on the undeveloped, unbounded grants of the "land monopolists." Fifteen hundred squatters were reported in 1854 to have occupied one grant. Thirty-five masked men fought off a sheriff's posse sent to evict squatters from another grant.

Year after year, forged documents, bribery, and "litigious misery" sparked violent quarrels. "Land pirates" roamed the countryside, burning crops and

---

* Following fifty years of agitation by "squatters" for reform of the varying federal policies disposing of public land, the Congress in 1841 passed the Preemption Act, which established one principle for selecting among conflicting claims: "First in time, first in right." By this rule the first arrival had first chance to buy, which was a triumph for the small homesteader over the big speculator. A settler could secure in advance of government survey a specific claim of 160 acres (a quarter section) and all his improvements thereon, at a price—$1.25 per acre—to be paid after the survey. In 1843 an amendment prohibited more than one preemption claim per settler.

killing livestock. Juries and judges were threatened, surveyors attacked, legislators and governors tormented by the opposing forces. An angry convention of "antimonopolists" met in Sacramento in 1855 to demand laws more favorable to "settlers' rights." Through the years of turmoil, hundreds of land grant claimants endured not only the damage and indignity of squatters, but also the crippling drain of taxes, court charges, high interest on loans, and—always—lawyers' fees. More than a few families of California's old landed class suffered foreclosure, their vast estates taken by conniving attorneys as settlement for unpaid bills. It was said in the 1860s that no other place in the world counted so many lawyers among its biggest landowners.

Certainly no other state endured an adolescence as orphaned from the steadying hand of enlightened leadership as California. The lawyers who skillfully maneuvered uncomprehending rancheros out of their grants symbolized the narrow ambition and greed that ruled the time. Before he departed for New York in 1857, William Tecumseh Sherman observed acidly, "I have no respect for the Law and the Lawyers here."

Still, few men could be expected to follow a higher purpose than self-interest when speculation and instant wealth abounded, in a place untempered by the influence of churches and schools or firesides and families. California did not inspire political idealism, like that of Stephen Austin and Sam Houston of Texas. In the fortune-making mentality of the 1850s, statecraft seemed a pestering distraction.

Few of the businessmen in San Francisco and Sacramento who attained prominence had interest in political power. Not Sam Brannan, busy steering his many enterprises through the obstacles of fire, flood, and wildly fluctuating prices; not William Coleman, who stepped into the leadership of San Francisco's vigilance crusade mainly to safeguard his own portfolio of businesses; not Thomas Larkin, content to enjoy a luxurious exile in New York City before returning to San Francisco, where he died in 1858.

California's forgettable political bosses expended their energies bickering over the spoils of office. Neither governors nor state legislatures nor distant Congresses made decisions that addressed the problems of erratic growth and rogue moneymaking during those adolescent years. In Sacramento, party rivalries became so divisive that for two years, 1857–58, the legislature could agree on only one senator to send to Washington. Even California's debt of $3 million was ruled by the state supreme court in 1856 to be unconstitutional (though it was later legalized). A Sacramento newspaper dismissed the political leaders of the 1850s as "that delectable crowd of brandy-drinking, pistol-shooting, swearing, swaggering gentry who turn up their noses at all honest work."

In the absence of effective civil authority, Californians did what they always did: they improvised. Disorder and violence in the hills they restrained through miners' lynch laws; arson, thievery, and corruption in the cities they controlled with merchants' vigilance committees; inconvenient land claims in the countryside they ignored and subverted by "squatterism." Swift, pragmatic solutions answered for long-term reform because almost everyone envisioned his own future far from California. It was the determination of these transient Californians to leave with some of the gold from the riverbeds, mineshafts, and sluices—or from a surefire business scheme—that kept them in that wild and promising place.

DEAD RIVERS

So many ways to make money—that was the wonder and attraction of California. In an age of rigid social barriers, when ambitious young men unblessed by inheritance or position grew up to discover that the shackles of class immobility often made folly of their dreams, California beckoned with a unique invitation: the freedom to pursue profit and even wealth without constraint or limit, save for the reach of cunning, energy, and luck.

Few succeeded more robustly in this take-all-you-can arena than the men who saw gold in the verdant forests of the Sierra foothills, the San Francisco Bay area, and the northern redwood coast. The lumber barons' profits accumulated as swiftly as the drifts of sawdust that spewed from their steam-powered blades. With their crews cutting towering sugar pines, ponderosas, and redwoods without any thought given to the question of ownership, the lumbermen sold millions of board feet and still they could not meet demand. Towns and cities, swept by fire, were rebuilt and rebuilt again. Each summer, river mining companies put up wider and longer runs of wooden flumes. Underground mining operations used thousands of beams to brace their tunnels. Water companies placed orders for vast quantities of structural lumber and planking to build new miles of flumes. The Sacramento Valley Railroad (California's first) ordered thousands of ties to lay twenty-two miles of track, completed in 1856. Lumbermen profited handsomely as well by selling massive timbers to other entrepreneurs whose bridges spanned swift-flowing streams in the Sierra foothills.

In the absence of state or county public works, private toll bridges, ferries, and roads ("among the best paying investments in the state") enabled stagecoaches, wagons, and mule trains to carry passengers and freight throughout the mining region, from Weaverville on the Trinity River three hundred miles south to the arid hills of Mariposa, southernmost of the major mining camps.

Within that vastness of narrow canyons and forested slopes, sandy creek beds and rocky flats, the enterprise of thousands of miners depended on one resource more essential even than lumber. That resource was water, the sine qua non of mining, soon to become the next commodity of entrepreneurial speculation—and a new source of profits.

Access to water, enough to lubricate the wasteful processes of placer mining, became ever more competitive by the mid-1850s. Veteran miners whose claims had played out and chastened newcomers looking for a place to start found every watercourse and adjacent gulch crowded with claims, many of them for sale. The most discouraged accepted wages for work; others prospected higher and higher into the hills. On slopes, ridges, and steep banks, some of these dispossessed placer miners discovered outcroppings of gravel that showed color, sometimes enough to promise rich rewards.

These auriferous gravels, millions of years old, were surviving segments from the beds of immense rivers that had been thrust upward when the Sierra Nevada itself rose and tilted westward. Through subsequent geologic ages, new streams rushed down the young mountains' western slopes, cutting canyons across the "dead rivers" and washing from their ancient gravels the treasure that had enriched so many goldseekers in the years since 1848. Now, in the mid and late 1850s, miners forced by overcrowding to look for gold well away from living streams found those primordial riverbeds on ridges, hilltops, and plateaus between the modern canyons, with some gravels exposed as outcroppings on the surface and others visible as strata in cliffs or steep hillsides, buried by geologic debris deposited by earthquakes, volcanic flows, and glaciers.

The first miners to work such river gravels found surface evidence in the hills north of Nevada City. As in all placer mining, they knew that the richest ore would be found at the lowest level: at the bottom of the ancient riverbeds, under the conglomerations of sand, pebbles, gravel, and rocks

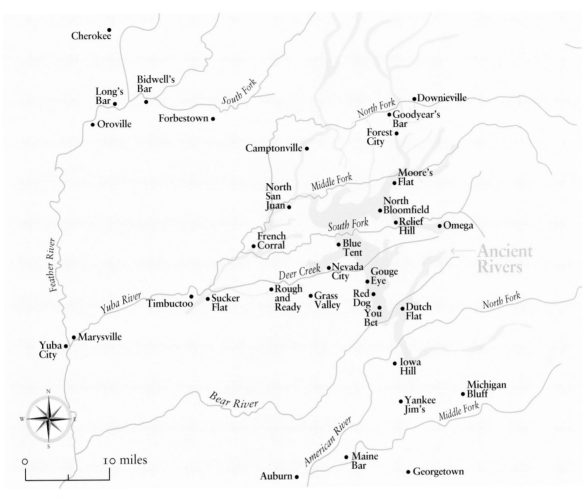

ANCIENT RIVERS

deposited by the flow of water many eons ago. They dug vertical shafts (called "coyote holes") through the surface gravels, down toward pay dirt, a single man in each pit, toiling with shovel and pick, filling bucket after bucket with gravel and rock, hoisted to the surface by partners turning a windlass. Slow work for weeks on end. Where gold proved most rich, miners dug horizontal tunnels to reach farther into the promising gravel beds. As the excavations lengthened, more men went down and more pay dirt came up, to be carried to the nearest stream where rockers and toms could wash free whatever profit there might be. But the need to haul buckets and sacks of gravel often long distances limited the profitability of these new diggings. What was

needed was a way to bring water directly to dry hillside claims, a challenge soon to be met by profit-seeking water companies.

Somewhat easier than "coyotoeing," another operation, known as drift mining, involved digging a horizontal tunnel straight into a hillside or bank where exposed traces of gravel offered hope of leading to a larger part of the buried riverbed. If that hunch proved lucky, the miners dug side tunnels—drifts—that allowed them to remove an increasing amount of gold-bearing gravel, sent out through the main tunnel in hopper carts rolling on narrow rails.

Miners digging in coyote holes or in drift mines endured grim working conditions. Just getting to pay dirt exacted weeks of intense labor, described by a drift miner in 1854: "Our drift is four feet wide and five and a half high, just large enough to allow a man to work. We worked two at a time, that is one stands up and picks with all his might as long as he can stand it, generally from eight to ten minutes. He then lays down and the next goes through the same operation by which time the other is recruited." Toiling thus with pick and crowbar, in dank air, able to see only by the dim flicker of candlelight, always in danger of a sudden cave-in, hundreds of goldseekers probed ever deeper for the hidden treasure. To cut through solid rock and compacted gravel, miners turned to the blasting force of black powder. This dangerous ally required handheld chisels driven by hammer blows to cut borings into which the miners packed explosive charges. Fuses burned slowly, allowing the men to retreat from the face of the tunnel but not always far enough to escape flying shards of rock from the powerful concussions.

No matter the accidents, drift mining expanded. By 1856 several hundred drift mines explored the hills outside Nevada City, searching for the golden gravels, each tunnel advanced by the toil of miners consigned to a dark world far from the sunshine and success of earlier placer years. At Iowa Hill, above the North Fork of the American River, ninety tunnels, some of them more than a thousand feet in length, testified to high hopes, but only thirty-two yielded profits. To reach pay dirt in the gravels inside Table Mountain, near Sonora, and at Spanish Hill, south of Placerville, tunnels were driven more than two thousand feet, several hundred of that distance blasted through rock. What sustained those intrepid and costly efforts (even more than the reward of gold itself) was the news of someone else's greater success, that potent tonic to which all were addicted.

While envy and hope animated the swing of their picks, the miners' profits depended on enough

water to wash their pay dirt, so laboriously brought to the surface. Once again risk-takers grasped a new opportunity, this time to deliver the essential commodity to the coyote and drift-mining sites. Without permit or license, without concern for anyone downstream, these water entrepreneurs organized companies that hired hundreds of laborers (many of them ex-miners, later Chinese immigrants) to dam streams, build reservoirs in the high country, and construct miles of flumes and aqueducts to carry water for sale at dry hillside claims. With pickax and shovel these work gangs dug four- and five-foot-wide ditches along the contours of hillsides, following surveyors' marks that insured sufficient fall for gravity to deliver the welcomed flow where needed. Topographic obstacles often necessitated construction of a wooden aqueduct to transport the water across a ravine or even a valley. One of these "wonders of carpentry" carried a stream of water 206 feet above a ravine for a length of 1,500 feet. The construction crews, in their haste and opportunism, simply decapitated towering pine trees growing under their projected route and laid the flume's bottom planks from trunk to trunk. This "remarkably ingenious construction," explained an impressed reporter, "rests at its center on a tower built from the bed of the valley, while at intervals of about one hundred feet stand tall trees the tops of which being cut away contribute to the permanency of the structure. Thus by means of scarcely perceivable agency, an artificial channel is formed through which 7,560,000 gallons of water pass daily. . . . Works like this in many portions of the mining region are a most striking evidence of the capacity for adaptation . . . and reflect much credit upon their enterprising proprietors."

Men who, back home, had been cabinet makers, grocers, tinsmiths, and farmers learned as they labored, becoming adept at preparing topographic

Uniquely charming for its backyard simplicities—saplings to support a simple aqueduct to deliver water to a long sluice box and wobbly poles to hold up canvas sunshades—this scene suggests the boys-at-play circumstances that here and there could be seen in the otherwise crude and rough world of gold mining.

Flume on the Ophir Ditch, Butte County, 1857

This flume, built with engineering audacity across a steep, rocky slope and supported by a trestle where it bridged a canyon, attested to the extreme measures required by many claims to obtain a flow of water.

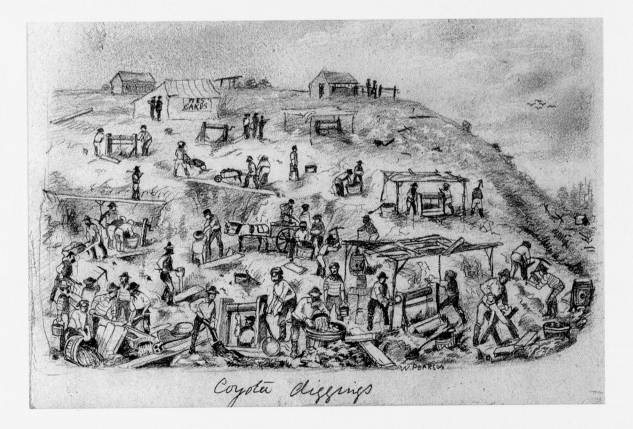

Coyota diggings

surveys, designing cantilevers and curves for soaring aqueducts, and blasting tunnels. As new "ditch enterprises" took in fresh capital, these costly water networks expanded. The Tuolumne Water Company completed its flume to the famous mines at Columbia, from a source twenty miles distant, for an investment of $200,000. Among other ditch companies, the Middle Yuba Canal and Water Company's thirty-five-mile delivery network cost $373,000 when completed in 1856. Suggesting how profitable these enterprises might be, this company's annual income by 1858 totaled $174,000, earned by selling its water for the price of thirty cents per "miner's inch," the arcane unit by which water volume was measured and sold.*

In the hurry-up tempo of that get-ahead decade, enterprising profiteers put together a delivery system more daring in execution, more extensive in reach, than California's elaborate government-financed network of man-made rivers of the following century. By 1859 the water companies had built 5,726 miles of ditches and flumes, trestles and aqueducts, that fanned out across the gold region like capillaries, bringing swift-flowing water to the most remote dry claims.

No government authority subsidized or regulated the price of water delivered to customers whose toms and sluices depended on those miner's inches. Impatient to recoup high construction costs, often answerable to syndicates of investors, water companies chared the steepest prices they could exact, causing miners' protests and even occasional

---

*The standard measure of usage, the miner's inch was commonly defined as "the quantity of water that will flow from an orifice one inch square through a two inch plank, with still water standing to a depth of six inches above the top of the orifice." On average, a miner's inch released 17,000 gallons in twenty-four hours. To accommodate the volume actually needed—often hundreds of thousands or even millions of gallons in a twelve-hour period—the orifice varied in size. Each mining operation paid its ditch company according to the size of the orifice and the hours water flowed through its feeder flume from the main channel.

Men grow older faster in this country than any place I ever saw. I think it is exposure and hardship that they have to encounter. Boys have mens' faces, and men of thirty look like men at home of forty. There is none of the quiet happiness here like you find in some new countries where farming is the main pursuit.

Ephraim Thompson, letter of June 18, 1854

sabotage to flumes and aqueducts. But howls that city-financed "water monopolists" were exploiting hardworking mountain men contradicted the laissez-faire standard by which all lived or died in California, as well as the miners' own increasingly complex financial dependencies. The very availability of water by ditch and flume so broadened mining opportunities that everywhere new joint-stock companies and miners' syndicates took in fresh capital. From San Francisco to New York and London investors bought shares in new drift mines, in water companies, in river-mining operations, even in once-questionable quartz mines.

Thanks to what one report described as "the investment of heavy capital and the employment of costly machinery," the revived interest in quartz or hard-rock mining pushed the number of stamp mills in operation to 279 by 1858. Among them, three mills in the town of Sutter Creek belonged to the Eureka Mine, property of Alvinza Hayward, who, by 1872, would be one of the richest men in California. A visitor to his Eureka operation in 1859 described riding an iron barrel (attached by rope to a windlass) down the mine's 420-foot main shaft. Clutching a lighted candle in one hand, the nervous greenhorn "bade adieu to daylight. Within the first one hundred feet the candle was extinguished by the falling drops of water and all was darkness. On and on that old iron barrel rumbled and jumbled down the steep declivity." At the bottom, he vaguely made

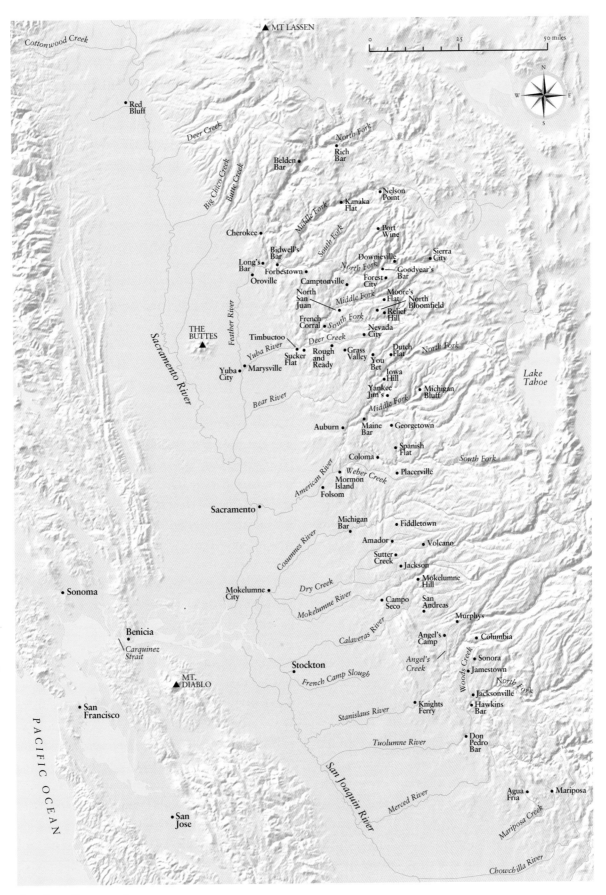

Cottonwood Creek

▲ MT LASSEN

0   25   50 miles

N
W   E
S

Deer Creek

Red
Bluff

North Fork

Rich
Bar

Belden
Bar

Nelson
Point

Big Chico Creek

Butte Creek

Kanaka
Flat

Middle Fork

Cherokee

Port
Wine

South Fork

Bidwell's
Bar

Downieville

Sierra
City

Long's
Bar

Forbestown

North Fork

Goodyear's
Bar

Oroville

Camptonville

Forest
City

Feather River

North
San
Juan

Middle Fork

Moore's
Flat

North
Bloomfield

French
Corral

South Fork

Relief
Hill

THE
BUTTES
▲

Timbuctoo

Deer Creek

Nevada
City

Sacramento River

Yuba River

Rough
and
Ready

Grass
Valley

Dutch
Flat

North Fork

Sucker
Flat

You
Bet

Yuba
City

Marysville

Iowa
Hill

Lake
Tahoe

Bear River

Yankee
Jim's

Michigan
Bluff

Middle Fork

Auburn

Maine
Bar

Georgetown

Spanish
Flat

Coloma

American River

Weber Creek

Placerville

South Fork

Mormon
Island

Folsom

Sacramento

Fiddletown

Michigan
Bar

Amador

Volcano

Cosumnes River

Sutter
Creek

Jackson

Sonoma

Mokelumne
Hill

Mokelumne
City

Dry Creek

Campo
Seco

San
Andreas

Mokelumne River

Murphys

Benicia

Calaveras River

Angel's
Camp

Columbia

Carquinez
Strait

Sonora

Angel's
Creek

Jamestown

MT.
DIABLO
▲

Stockton

North Fork

Woods Creek

Jacksonville

San
Francisco

French Camp Slough

Hawkins
Bar

Knights
Ferry

Stanislaus River

Don
Pedro
Bar

PACIFIC OCEAN

Tuolumne River

San Joaquin River

Agua
Fria

Mariposa

San
Jose

Merced River

Mariposa Creek

Chowchilla River

out the ghostly figures of miners in the gloom, wielding picks at a quartz vein twenty-five feet wide, while other miners loaded barrels with gold-bearing pieces of rock and sent them to the surface.

Up in his office, Mr. Hayward wrote a statement to promote his company, declaring that his three stamp mills (sixty-eight stamps) crushed 116 "tuns" per day, from which "I take out from $25,000 to $30,000 monthly, against expenses about $12,000 . . . employing ninety men." To allay any skeptics, he added: "This is no puff, but fact!"

Also bolstered by new investor capital, river-mining syndicates showed revived activity as well. Improved flume-building techniques and growing engineering confidence made possible ambitious plans to divert longer stretches of rivers into larger, stronger flumes. With swift enrichment everyone's purpose, no one objected to rivers turned asunder, to fish eradicated, or to once-green riverbanks left a stubble of stumps. The river miners' new ingenuity and optimism showed most famously at the Cape Claim on the Feather River near Oroville. Here in 1857 they constructed a wooden box 3,800 feet long and a sweeping 40 feet wide. Through its yawning breadth the entire river flowed for more than a month. As the summer faded, 260 miners worked furiously in the rocky riverbed, digging gravel and washing it through an array of long toms and sluice boxes. For thirty-five glorious days, before the rains came, the company's quicksilver retorts collected a daily average of $7,000 in gold. After the magnificent flume and all its appurtenances were, as expected, swept away, the company calculated its gold sales at $251,725, against expenses of $176,985, leaving a profit of $74,740— $1,283,286 in 1998 dollars. "No puff!"

To watch swollen rivers sweep away even the most heavily braced and timbered flumes must have kindled imaginations among sharp-eyed miners always seeking better and more efficient ways to reach gold. While they knew how to exploit the mountains' resources, miners had not sought to bend the *forces* of nature to their campaigns. If they could devise a means to harness the erosive power of water to supplement—or supplant—inefficient picks and shovels in digging, how much faster they might all go home rich. There in the turgid torrents that carried boulders, silt, and flotsam downstream swirled a challenge and an answer.

The first to experiment with waterpower were drift miners on hillside claims who sought to put the swift currents flowing down the water companies' flumes to work at an unorthodox task: to wash away layers of overburden where surface evidence suggested buried river gravels. Instead of laboring at traditional drift tunnels to reach the gravels, these inventive miners dug shallow channels down likely hillsides and then diverted streams of water from feeder flumes into those trenches.

The practice became known as ground sluicing. Using shovels and picks, a party of miners would broaden and deepen their artificial watercourse as it cut through the overburden and began to work down toward buried gravels. When water volume was increased, a thick, muddy cascade—loud with the clicking and rattling of rocks awash in its current—carried away layers deposited over the millennia. Once the lower strata of gravels were reached, the miners channeled their turgid stream into a series of sluice boxes where hundreds of riffles, each baited with quicksilver, captured the loosened flakes and particles of gold. Every few days they shut off the water in order to collect, with a gentleness uncustomary for such rough and callused hands, the gold amalgam accumulated at each riffle.

As the popularity of ground sluicing grew, the cost of water and the masses of earth and gravel that had to be washed away proved daunting to many miners with smaller claims. Some sold to well-capitalized companies that bought up and consolidated claims, hiring wage laborers to work the gravels. One big ground-sluicing operation in Nevada County paid for a flume to deliver water to the brink of a high bank or cliff within which lay buried some eighty feet of gravel. As water cascaded down the face, earth and gravel crumbled and fell into sluices below, where workers with shovels and sluice forks scrambled to remove rocks and break up compacted gravel that obstructed a steady flow into the riffles. The men moved larger boulders by block and tackle, with many a mishap—crushed legs and arms—as they slipped and struggled in the muck. And sometimes when large chunks of sodden earth crashed from above, the mass buried those too slow to escape. Working ten hours a day amid such dangers, men who had come to California to make a fortune settled for a wage.

GROUND SLUICING

In spite of its risks and the water companies' big bills, ground sluicing rapidly became the preferred mining method wherever water could be delivered. Its superiority was vividly illustrated in 1856 at a sluice operation where a few years earlier drift miners had abandoned their tunnels. After the sluices carried away the overburden, the laborers cut deeper and deeper into layers of gravel until gradually "old drifts and timbers, originally fifty and seventy-five feet below the surface, were laid bare, and many places were found to pay immensely."

No wonder ground sluicing attracted so many miners. With ample water delivered to their deep gravel claims, they could wash more auriferous earth than ever before—than ever dreamed of. More water, more profit: that was all that mattered. No one cared that this new advance destroyed hills and trees, clogged creeks, and spread a smothering surge of mud and rocks. To ditch companies and miners, like merchants and freighters, only profits counted; nothing else commanded their energies and their hopes. California itself, heralded for its sweep and grandeur, possessed for them but one virtue: its gold, in the ground or across the counter.

Ruthless in their ambition, the miners had no better allies than their own ingenuity and improvisation. In April 1852, while working his claim seven miles outside Nevada City, a French Canadian sailmaker, Antoine Chabot, found signs of buried river gravel on a hillside beyond the reach of the nearest water company's flume. Hoping to avoid the cost and labor of digging a long feeder ditch, he cast about for an easier means to move water where needed. He cut up some surplus saddlebags, then stitched together the strips of heavy canvas to make a hundred-foot length of six-inch hose, which he attached with a leaky collar to the end of the nearest flume—and there it was, a gushing fount of water that could be placed wherever its dissolving force would most effectively break up the gravel and hurry its flow through the riffle box. The success of Chabot's improvisation encouraged other miners in the neighborhood to make their own hose with whatever canvas they could find or from rawhide "with the hair on the outside." To replace such leaky, hand-made hose, businessmen in nearby towns quickly profited by using machines to sew vast lengths of heavy canvas hose, which soon appeared at many mining sites, wiggling and writhing "like immensely long sea serpents."

And then, in March 1853, came the "invention" that truly revolutionized placer mining. A Connecticut '49er, who had initially despaired of mining but nonetheless stayed in California, was the first to see the untapped potential in Chabot's hose. Edward Matteson had returned to mining after quitting a job with a pack mule company. With four partners and eight hired men he worked a ground-sluicing claim outside Nevada City, buying water from the Rock Creek Water Company. With their picks and shovels, they undercut the base of a high bank of gravel to hasten its collapse so that a hose could be laid out to wash the mass through their sluice box. Following a near escape from a mass of falling gravel, Matteson wondered if a stream of water from his hose might not be made to do the dangerous work of undercutting, instead of manpower. He and his partners fashioned sheet metal into a three-foot tapered funnel that narrowed to an inch-and-a-half opening, with the wider intake end clamped to their canvas hose. When they released the water from the flume into the hose, a stream shot from the crude nozzle with surprising force, quickly loosening new masses of gravel from the bank. Seemingly unimpressed by the magnitude of his innovation, Matteson reported without elaboration: "Our water bill was $153 per week and for quite awhile our claim yielded four partners $50 each per day."

Matteson's technique for harnessing the power of water attracted gawkers from Nevada City and more distant mining camps who showed more enthusiasm than the laconic inventor. Many of them quickly purchased whatever hose was available and nozzles, some of them shaped from wood. A contagion of excitement, reminiscent of the jubilant expectations of earlier years, spread from the hills down to Sacramento and on to San Francisco, where in June 1853 the *Daily Alta* hailed "the wonderful celerity of a new method of mining," boasting that the new power of water made the ore-bearing hillsides "melt like ice under the midsummer sun." Even the more knowledgeable and tough-minded reporters of the *Sacramento Weekly Union* expressed amazement. In July 1854 a *Union* correspondent described the new technology (he called it "hydraulicking") at Iowa Hill: "Ten men who own a claim are enabled . . . by directing streams of water against the base of a high bank [120 feet] to cut away such an extent as to cause immense slides of earth which often bring with them large trees and heavy boulders. . . . After these immense masses are undermined and brought down . . . those same streams are turned upon the tons of fallen earth which melt away before them and are carried away through the sluices with almost as much rapidity as if they were a bank of snow." He concluded with a sweeping but not intemperate judgment: "No such labor-saving power has ever been introduced to assist the miner in his operations."

Judged at the time and by historians to be of revolutionary importance (California's "greatest and most famous contribution to the world-wide science of extracting wealth from the earth"), hydraulicking proved wonderfully profitable in Nevada County and other areas with large deposits of deep gravels and networks of ditches and flumes that could deliver the prodigious quantities of water demanded by the new technology—fifty times more water than used in ground sluicing, by the 1860s a hundred times more, and thereafter even higher multiples.

Men who endured the drudgery of pick and shovel in drift mining and ground sluicing marveled at the new power of water to dissolve the masses they toiled against so doggedly. The speed and efficiency of hydraulic mining promised more gold in less time for less work—a formula of compelling attraction. As converts thronged to the new industry, resilient suppliers raced to produce the new equipment the miners needed: pressure-resistant canvas hose, stronger and bigger nozzles, and better couplings and collars. But the most urgent demand was for more water. As rapidly as the ditch companies expanded their capacity to deliver water, hydraulic-mining operations sought more. In June 1858 one company on the ridge between the south and middle forks of the Yuba operated three nozzles that used an average of 175 miner's inches—1,240,000 gallons—every ten-hour workday. To undercut a gravel bank one hundred feet high, another company operated two large nozzles that expended 1,700,000 gallons each day, at a cost of $1,800 per month paid to the Middle Yuba Canal and Water Company. When this operation cleaned up its riffles, the reported monthly yield came to about $20,000, less expenses for water and for the labor of six men, at $4 each per day, leaving a profit of $17,624.

More than the new power of water, what gave hydraulic mining its revolutionary impact was the economic wonder of profits from gravel that contained an average of only three cents in gold per cubic foot. A claim in Sierra County made its miners a profit of $2,340 in six days from gravel that averaged just 1.2 cents per cubic foot. What a bonanza:

A revolution, nothing less. That was the power of hydraulic mining. These hoses and nozzles, even in their primitive development by the late 1850s, could wash millions of tons of rock, gravel, and sand into sluice boxes—more work than hundreds of men could accomplish in weeks. That sense of power could make a man feel—well, almost erotic, as exhibited by the hydraulicker in the scene above. But hydraulicking was by no means the major force, not yet. Thousands of miners still tore up the earth by ground sluicing and with picks and shovels, as they had—below—near Nevada City.

seemingly limitless deposits of gold-bearing gravels available for hydraulicking, and none of it encumbered by supervision or regulation, the need for permit or license.*

In 1857 the *Nevada [City] Journal* offered its assessment of the advantages of hydraulic mining: "Now water is used as the laboring agent and only men enough to keep the machinery [i.e., the nozzles] properly directed are required. Thus banks of earth that would have kept a hundred men employed for months in their removal will now be removed by three or four men in two weeks." Even as it promised the boldest advance yet in the extraction of gold, hydraulicking introduced the specter of technological unemployment, an unforeseen side effect that would soon bring widespread dislocation to many of California's miners.

In the late 1850s, however, few looked beyond next week. There were claims to be staked out and hoses and nozzles to be set up. Nimble suppliers in Marysville and Sacramento already had stronger hose for sale and bigger nozzles designed to release more powerful jets of water. Newspapers lavished attention on the juvenile technology because it brought visual drama to gold mining. No longer all rocks and mud, now there were great arching plumes of water and crashing hillsides. Moneymaking had about it a renewed excitement. The *San Francisco Daily Alta* reflected the mood in an 1856 report sent by an awestruck correspondent: "At the end of the hose stand the noble miners . . . directing the streams of water upon the face of the moun-

tain. . . . I am at a loss for words to illustrate the tremendous force with which the water is projected from the pipes. The miners assert that they can throw a stream *four hundred* feet into the air. . . . Those streams directed upon an ordinary wooden building would speedily unroof and demolish it."

The roar of hurtling water, the rumble of collapsing gravel banks, echoed across the pine-clad ridges and plateaus above the vast watersheds of the Feather, Yuba, Bear, and American Rivers. Merchants and hoteliers, never far behind the miners, hired carpenters to put up plank-sided supply stores, bachelor barracks, and stagecoach offices close to the hydraulic operations. (More ambitious construction was usually reserved for the gambling halls and saloons that soon followed.) These rough hamlets took names as unvarnished as their architecture: Yankee Jim's and Gold Run above the North Fork of the American; Dutch Flat, You Bet, Red Dog, and Gouge Eye above the Bear. More camps sprang to life on the ridges between the many forks of the Yuba: Blue Tent, Omega, North San Juan, and Relief Hill. And where the Yuba flowed out of the hills, muddy hydraulickers plunked down their gold in the saloons and hotels of Timbuctoo and Smartsville. Along the Feather River to the north the crude settlements of Cherokee and Oroville, like all the others, prospered by satisfying the needs and pleasures of hydraulic miners whose powerful water cannons were revolutionizing placer mining as swiftly as they were washing away the Sierra hillsides.

---

* As mining technology advanced and requirements for capital investment increased, the miners relaxed their ad hoc limitations on the size of claims, originally imposed to ensure access to the diggings for everyone. By the mid-1850s hydraulic mining districts allowed larger and larger claims, with maximum limits increasing to one hundred and two hundred feet along a hillside. A more important change allowed a miner or association to own an unlimited number of claims by purchase. This latter leniency in time led to the consolidation of many claims and the exclusion of the individual miner.

DISTANT PROSPECTS

Mining's transformation from streamside panning by peripatetic prospectors of the "old days" to the industrial operations of the late 1850s depended as much on miners who were willing to stay in one place and work for a daily wage as on technological advances and capital investments. Many wage-earning miners felt trapped by industrialization, their vivid dreams of sudden wealth displaced by the reality of four dollars per day—a good wage, far better than back home, but shorn of the pan's possibility of a heart-stopping flash of color. Thousands promised themselves that their condescension to day labor would be but a temporary resort, a necessary interlude, to build a stake for a fresh try at bringing in a rich claim. Other thousands gave up mining, hopeful of better luck in one of the booming supply or service enterprises. And each month hundreds, often thousands, sailed from San Francisco wharves, some in final flight from creditors, others with gold enough for a triumphant homecoming, all bound for Panama City and on to the States or other home countries.

Offsetting this exodus, thousands of new immigrants continued to arrive by crowded passenger ships and overland trails, most of them attracted less by the promise of gold than by California's new image as a place of burgeoning business and farming opportunities and as a sanctuary of social freedom. Among these thousands came hundreds of men who knew the journey well, having quit California a year or so earlier to return to their homes and families where, as one second-timer put it, they felt "nailed down to a life of picayunes," feeding slops to pigs on a farm in North Carolina or stoking a boiler in a factory in Pittsburg. Remembering the ease of obtaining credit, the freedom of anonymity, the double-time pace and bustle of life in San Francisco and even in California's small towns and camps, they saw home with new eyes and resented old-fashioned rules and malignant curiosity and gossip. During dreary winter days and pious Sunday

No one recreated the sound and fury, the hormonal forces of the gold miners' world more vividly than Mark Twain:

It was the only population of the kind that the world has ever seen . . . , stalwart, muscular, dauntless young braves, brimful of push and energy. . . . No women, no children, no gray and stooping veterans, none but erect, bright-eyed, quick-moving, strong-handed young giants—the strangest population, the finest population, the most gallant host that ever trooped down the startled solitude of an unpeopled land. . . . They fairly revelled in gold, whiskey, fights, and fandangoes. . . . They cooked their own bacon and beans, sewed on their own buttons, washed their own shirts—blue woolen ones. . . . It was a wild, free, disorderly, grotesque society. Men—only swarming hosts of stalwart men—nothing juvenile, nothing feminine, visible anywhere.

Mark Twain, *Roughing It*

sermons, California beckoned again, dangerous and unforgiving, yes, but never routine. Hundreds packed up, some with wives and children this time, and bought tickets via Panama to sail again through the Golden Gate.

But those returnees were few compared to the many thousands California-bound for the first time, from the States, from Europe, and beginning in 1852, from southern China. That year at least 20,000 from Hong Kong (among them only 14 women) landed in San Francisco, to be followed by 27,000 more before 1860. Fleeing the turmoil of clan warfare, feuds, and bloody rebellion, men from the region around Canton sailed for the "Golden Hills" of California, usually paying their passage by indenturing themselves to Chinese merchants who operated a credit-ticket system that delivered these peasants to secret societies, or "tongs," in San Francisco and to "district companies" in the diggings. While an increasing number worked in laundries and kitchens in San Francisco and Sacramento, most of these unwelcome "Mongolians" were sent to the mining region, where they dug a meager living under the control of their Chinese bosses, reworking claims abandoned or sold by Americans and Europeans. Oppressed and ostracized, living in strictly regimented companies at some distance from "the whites," these forlorn miners numbered some 26,000 by 1860, a number that sustained California's mining population at around 100,000 throughout the decade of the fifties.

While the Chinese stoically accepted their cruel lot, many whites expressed a growing frustration that the prosperity so evident around them seemed increasingly difficult to grasp. A new mood tempered California's exuberance, a sense that the best days had past, that not only the rich merchants and clever gamblers were taking their fat share, as they had since '49, but now mine owners, ditch companies, stamp mill operators, and soft-handed investors were cashing in as well, crowding out the men who did the work, took the true risks, and not long ago had made the decisions. The contagion of optimism, the old confidence that each day could be THE day, seemed to be fading. When miners paused in the shade to gulp a drink and share news, when they sprawled wearily by evening firelight, it was the talk of a new discovery, of someone's success up-canyon, that rallied their spirits and fortified their resolve not to join the ranks of men laboring for wages in quartz mines, drift mines, and at hydraulic sites. But the heartening reports did not come as frequently anymore. When twenty-one partners shared $140,000 they had washed from their claim on the Tuolumne River, when a lonely prospector near French Gulch dug up "a lump of gold" that weighed twenty-three pounds, their stories flashed through the hills as fast as by telegraph, more urgent in the retelling because so reassuring.

What everyone hoped for, felt impatient to hear,

was a reliable report of a new El Dorado, a discovery up in the mountains, along a distant river, where yellow colored every shovelful. In mining camps and towns thousands were "ready to go anywhere if there was a reasonable hope of rich diggings, rather than submit to live without the high pay and excitement which they had enjoyed for years in the Sacramento placers."

The first rush to a new El Dorado swept the camps in the spring of 1855 when newspapers in San Francisco and Sacramento trumpeted reports of rich gold deposits along the Kern River, 150 miles south of Mariposa, where "the mines are much richer than any ever yet discovered in California." By summer five thousand eager miners were tramping to that distant river beyond any trails or transport, but not beyond the willingness of restless men to believe. Within weeks, before new thousands could join the stampede, sober eyewitness accounts deflated the hysteria and the Kern River receded, a chimera whose imagined treasure only sharpened the miners' longing.

In March 1858 news raced through California of rich diggings along the banks of the Fraser River in British Columbia, one thousand miles north of San Francisco and reached by ocean steamer through the town of Victoria. With newsboys on Montgomery Street shouting, "Latest from Fraser River: gold by the bushel," and hill towns "in spasms about the excitement," thousands of Californians succumbed to the Fraser fever. In June a San Francisco newspaper excitedly reported "the Fraser River is turning California upside down. . . . Our hotels are full of people on their way to the new El Dorado. . . . Steamers from Sacramento to this city are loaded every day. The traders and boarding-house-keepers and farmers of the mining districts are losing their debtors and customers. The stagecoaches and river steamers have raised their prices and though extraordinary stages and boats are running, they still cannot carry all who would go. . . . Many quartz mills have stopped . . . and empty cabins are to be seen on many claims. This exodus of white miners is looked upon by the Chinamen as particularly fortunate for them, for they go right into possession of deserted cabins, claims, and tools."

In San Francisco the "Fraser fever fellows" dipped into their gold pouches or took out loans, to spend freely on rain gear and boots, mining equipment and steamer tickets to Victoria, $60 one way. Through the spring and summer of 1858 the rush carried 24,153 men from California in 112 ships. But the entrancing gleam of distant gold proved as evanescent as the mists that shrouded the Canadian forests. In late August the first discouraged miners returned to San Francisco, bringing news of gold hard to find, rain and more rain in the wilds of the Fraser Valley, and exasperating restrictions imposed by the British authorities. The boom collapsed.

How different British Columbia was from California. There the governor issued a proclamation declaring that all minerals found on provincial territory, specifically precious metals, belonged to the Crown. Each miner was required to buy a mining license that, among other provisions, limited him to four hundred pounds of supplies. As miners boarded the packet steamers that carried them 175 miles upriver to the mining district, each man's dunnage was weighed, and anyone exceeding the limit paid a surcharge for his overage. The provincial gold commissioners even imposed licenses for selling liquor and attempted to enforce standards of "respectable" behavior.

Beyond the shock of British regulations and supervision, taken as an affront by miners accustomed to complete freedom of operation, what fully cured them of Fraser fever was the uncooperative river itself, which failed to recede even by September and into October, preventing the miners from working its bars and side channels. In November 1858 a depressed Californian wrote that "the miners are now leaving here very fast." By year's end almost all had returned to San Francisco, leaving at most three thousand stubborn souls who dared to winter along the Fraser's icy banks.

Years later, looking back on the rush to British Columbia, J. S. Hittell, renowned economic historian of California, perfectly distilled the enduring theme of the 1850s: "Californians are a fast people. They will attempt to outrun Old Time himself, and if they succeed once, it pays them for a dozen failures. They may lament their misfortunes and be loud in their wail about Fraser River, but if a new one were to turn up today, they would not wait to let anybody else get ahead of them. The cautious bump . . . is small on the crania of Californians."

Optimism, even recklessness—take another chance, that was the spirit of California. With so many ways to succeed, and no license needed, why pay heed to old rules or inhibiting fears? In the twelve years since James Marshall (now long forgotten) found that speck of California's future, the state had become a place of astonishing realities and extravagant expectations. More than that, it offered an escape from the nineteenth century.

Before the fearsome force and destruction of their monitors, pipers appear as Lilliputians in the pit of the Malakoff Mine.

ASTOUNDING ENTERPRISES

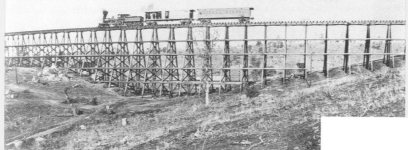

Using an abundance of timber without constraint, the Central Pacific Railroad's engineers built trestles across the valleys of the Sierra foothills. Lumber mills sold millions of board feet for construction of wharves along the San Francisco waterfront and the riverfronts at Sacramento, Stockton, and Marysville. Between these ports, side-wheel steamers—elegantly fashioned from fir and pine—carried the commerce of California, until in the 1870s these "floating palaces" faced competition from the expanding railroad system.

To extract profits from the complex ores of the Comstock mines, a vast industry evolved in Virginia City. The chemical stew stirred by these mullers yielded gold and silver in the final stage of a process housed in vast mills built of beams and planks cut from the forests of the Sierra Nevada. Back in California, timbers of immense size were used to erect aqueducts that delivered water to hydraulic mining operations. Railroads, steamboats, mills, and water networks all depended on an abundance of wood—and the skill of carpenters.

CHAPTER SIX

ASTOUNDING ENTERPRISES

LIKE A RICH, OUTLANDISH UNCLE, envied for his wealth and even more for his free and easy ways, California in its second and third decades continued to reinvent its society, as different from the other states as, indeed, from any nation. Magazine and newspaper articles and numerous books exclaimed over its wonders and excesses. No one characterized its spirit more accurately than not-yet-famous Sam Clemens, newly arrived in 1864. "It was a driving, vigorous, restless population . . . that gave to California a name for getting up astounding enterprises and rushing them through with a magnificent dash and daring and recklessness of cost or consequence."

In those new decades of exuberance, sustained by California's seemingly limitless fecundity, who cared to question the success and wealth produced by miners, merchants, and other risk-takers? Who cared about forests destroyed, hills washed away, rivers diverted into flumes or clogged with gravel and silt? Who cared about native people driven from their ancient homeland, those "devils in the forest" who were hunted and shot if they did not flee? Why find fault when everyone hoped to profit from one of those astounding enterprises? No time for scruple about tomorrow's consequences, for moral judgments, for empathy with Mexican land grant families whose vast ranchos were lost to Americans with new laws and crafty lawyers. As in the past, so in the sixties and seventies: legislators in Sacramento remained petty, needy men, easily "got at," while judges and city and county officials were as responsive as ever to an illicit envelope. So stand back, make way for the hydraulickers, wheat ranchers, railroad builders, stockbrokers, and tycoons of commerce.

What mattered were profits booked and more expected. *More,* that was the guiding principle—and with California's outrageous luck, more began to seem like a universal right. Not only more gold from hydraulic mining but silver too, discovered in a phenomenally rich vein known as the Comstock Lode on the eastern slope of the Sierra Nevada. Californians rushed to this remote site where in 1860 they put up a town called Virginia City, at first as wild as any other bivouac of tents and shacks, but soon more pretentious and far more rich. In torrid tunnels as deep as three thousand feet beneath its streets, wage-earning miners drilled, blasted, and hoisted to the surface ore worth $300 million during the years 1860 to 1880, a bounty even greater than the $170 million extracted from California's hydraulic and quartz mines in the same decades.

So much wealth, so many presumed opportunities attracted new thousands each year from around the world. By 1870, 39 percent of California's population was foreign born: 218,400 out of 560,000. Where else but in this unique society would Irish and Chinese compete (sometimes fighting in the streets) for jobs, as they did in San Francisco in 1877? Of course, immigrants from the eastern states continued to arrive by ship via Panama, and many more would come by transcontinental railroad (175,000 in three years, 1873–75) after California's entrepreneurs dared to conquer the heights of the Sierra to tie the Pacific state by iron to the federal union.

Even the state's most fanciful boosters of the 1850s could not have forecast the wonders of these decades: that wives and children in the cities (even in a few mining camps) would outnumber bartenders and prostitutes; that San Francisco would have more millionaires than Boston or New York; that four local dry-goods merchants in Sacramento would muster the ambition and know-how to direct construction of the railroad that ended California's timeless isolation in 1869. That mining corporations, some owned by London investors, would build a vast network of Sierra reservoirs and ditches and iron pipes to carry billions of gallons of water to giant nozzles that washed away entire mountainsides. That after decades of profiting from his dominating freedom, the Miner would be challenged, even constrained, by the rising outrage of the Farmer, leading to an "irrepressible conflict" in the 1880s.

What a booster proclaimed for California in 1850 proved to be even more true twenty-five years later: "Our state is a marvel to ourselves and a miracle to the world."

ORE MOB THAN CROWD, SCORES OF men—pushing and elbowing, their curses mixed with pleas—tried to force their way across the splintered planks of Montgomery Street and into the big room of the San Francisco Stock and Exchange Board. Those nearest the open door could hear the gong at eleven o'clock signaling the start of the day's trading. Inside, hundreds of yelling, gesticulating, frantic brokers and speculators bought and sold shares of stock in the famous companies that took gold and silver worth millions of dollars from the mines in the Comstock Lode, that geologic phenomenon in the newly formed Territory of Nevada, better known as Washoe. Everyone knew the names of those stocks that back in 1860 had sold for a few dollars per share—Ophir, Gould & Curry, Hale & Norcross, Chollar, and a few others. Now in 1863 those same mines commanded fabulous prices: Ophir, $2,700; Gould & Curry, $6,300—for a single share. Pushing, swearing, impatient to get inside, the men in the street hoped to buy lesser stocks, "wildcat" mines, like Uncle Sam, North America, and Overman, selling for a few dollars but promising to be worth thousands when deposits of silver mixed with gold were brought up from their tunnels and drifts. Then there would be a stampede for those shares. Think of the fortunes to be made.

Beyond the daily bedlam at the exchange, stock prices were posted on street bulletin boards each day and talked about in saloons and hotels, amid whispered "tips" and boasts of fat gains. Buying and selling "Comstocks," that was the new way to wealth. For the first time the glorious rewards of mining opened to those without pick and shovel, dam and flume, or hose and nozzle. Indeed, the managers of the exchange set aside a special section where tightly laced ladies from Nob Hill and others of more suspect silks and satins could place their orders with the harried brokers.

How different from the fifties. Now thousands—it seemed everyone—owned mining shares

and studied each day's prices, sent by telegraph from Virginia City to San Francisco, beginning in October 1861. Unlike the scattered placer and quartz operations in California, mines on the Comstock Lode were confined to a single vein just two miles long and a dozen to a hundred feet wide. And the ore hauled up from the first probing shafts yielded gold worth $867 per ton. More astounding, the assayers reported silver at $3,000 per ton. This pay-attention news in 1860 swept through California's camps and towns, saloons and hotels, through Sacramento, and overnight to San Francisco. Excitement and wild imaginings. Wondrous new profits to be made. This was no Fraser River. This was the biggest strike since 1849. Quickly the reports gained color and dimension. "Silver—solid, pure SILVER! Beds of it ten thousand feet deep! Acres of it, miles of it! Hundreds of millions of dollars poking their backs up out of the earth ready to be pocketed." Such was the hyperbole from Virginia City, the newest outpost of wealth and wildness.

COMSTOCK MINER

And the reality? None of it poked above ground. All the ore had to be found hundreds and then thousands of feet down in the geologic complexity of the earth and blasted free and hauled to the surface and crushed and chemically treated, a process that industrialized mining as never before and yielded millionaire-making profits for capitalists and speculators and $4-per-shift wages for miners toiling in the depths.

More than any mining venture in California, the deep mines of the Comstock depended on an array of complex, steam-powered machinery, not only crushing mills to pulverize the ore (some with as many as sixty stamps) and giant Cornish pumps to suck up scalding water from the dark depths but also more arcane devices like amalgamating pans, mullers, agitators, separators, and strainers. All of it purchased at immense expense by mine owners whose willingness to pay any price nurtured new industries and made rich new entrepreneurs.

To raise the millions needed, the San Francisco Stock and Exchange Board offered an efficient, seductive marketplace to attract cash and borrowed money from all levels of society—from saloon-keepers, stagecoach "whips," and boardinghouse maids to sophisticated businessmen. It was so easy to buy shares in one of those magical names, with their prices chalked up fresh each morning; easy to be seduced by talk of the latest individual to rise from a menial job to elegant wealth because of a well-timed purchase. And buying stock became even more tempting when stimulated by inside information—bait for the innocent—direct from sources in Virginia City, Silver City, or Gold Hill. Not so well reported amid all the newsmongering were the machinations of certain ruthless mine owners, unconstrained by laws or mores.

These "mining imposters" gained control of worthless mines in order to "bull and bear" the shares for their own gain, most often by issuing false reports of rich discoveries to drive up prices and then by selling to buyers deceived as much by their own hopefulness as the swindlers' trickery. To further prey on the public's mania for "Comstocks," the exchange operators in one year—1863—offered for sale shares in 2,467 newly created mining companies. Many such paper companies levied monthly assessments on stockholders, ostensibly to develop claims but more often to profit fraudulent promoters. A later report on "stock-jobbing" concluded: "It is within the experience of almost every citizen of California that in the purchase of mining shares he takes a greater risk upon the honesty of the management of the corporations than he does upon the product and profits of the mines. Indeed, it is notorious that most of them are manipulated more with a view to making money out of the public than out of the mines." With shameless rascality and remarkable ease, mine owners and corporate directors paid off judges and bribed witnesses ("hired liars") in

innumerable lawsuits contesting the boundaries of rival company claims two and three thousand feet beneath Virginia City.*

Sustaining this orgy of speculation and maleficence, the Comstock Lode yielded silver and gold in astounding abundance: $16 million in 1864 and more than $300 million by 1880. The entire network of deep tunnels and shafts, the massive pumps and mills and smelters, and every subsidiary asset from lumber mills to iron foundries was owned by California banks and California stock companies. The Washoe belonged to the Territory of Nevada, but in fact it served as a colony to be exploited by greed and litigation.

A vast industrial complex more dependent on machines than men, the Comstock mines employed only three thousand workers, even at the height of production in the late seventies. Two thousand men labored in the miles of tunnels, drifts, stopes, and winzes; above ground seldom more than one thousand tended the machinery and other tasks. Industrialization brought an elaborate hierarchy of superintendents, shift bosses, engineers, amalgamators, retorters, pumpmen, tankmen, battery men, firemen, melters, wire-rope inspectors, oilers, carmen, bulkheaders, pickmen, and miners. Those who toiled in the hot vitals beneath Virginia City earned $4 for a ten-hour shift, improved in 1866 to eight hours. Above ground, wages ranged around $5 per day. At least one mine superintendent was paid the munificent salary of $40,000.

Owners and speculators in times of bonanza often made millions, concentrating wealth and power to a degree unknown in the 1850s, when California's placer mining had spread the rewards of labor and luck so widely that it seemed almost

---

* To profit from the amazing proliferation of mining companies and the sale of their stock, the San Francisco Exchange moved to larger quarters three times by 1877. Two competitors—the California Stock and Exchange Board (1872) and the Pacific Stock Exchange (1875)—shared in the bonanza. By 1872 the sale of shares surpassed $200 million.

everyone was well off, or felt confident he would be next week. But in the sixties, and more painfully in the seventies, that confidence faded. Making a living became more urgent than making a fortune. The promise of wealth, of striking it rich, was slipping away from the man with a shovel in his hand. Kid gloves rather than calluses were the new mark of risk taking and fortune hunting.

Earning a wage demanded more of miners in the Comstock than in California's quartz and hydraulic mines. In heat of 110, 120 degrees, at depths of two thousand, even three thousand feet, they blasted out ore with newly invented explosives (nitroglycerin came into use in 1868), suffering the dangers of miscalculations with charges, fuses, and timing, as well as cave-ins, lethal fumes, and raging fires that consumed the heavy support timbers, often burning beyond control for weeks. Jets of scalding water sometimes burst from seams in the rock. In candle-lit gloom, in air fouled by sweat, rotting food, and human excrement, miners toiled in a Dantesque world, finding only meager relief where blower tubes delivered somewhat fresher air into the depths.

When shifts ended and men laid down their drills and shovels to climb onto shaft cages that hoisted them at high speed to the surface, even while thus on their way back to the familiar world, they risked their lives. The cages had no sides. Legs and arms caught between the cage platform and the shaft walls were instantly scraped and mangled. In July 1867 a misunderstood signal in the Crown Point Mine caused a cage to lurch upward, throwing off balance the first man on board. His head struck the passing wall of jagged rock. Moments later at the top, he staggered into the daylight, a horror to behold. His nose and cheeks, torn from the bone, hung in a bleeding mass over his jaw; his front teeth ripped out; his lower jaw shattered; part of his tongue severed.

No compensation allowed: all accidents on the Comstock were judged to be part of the miner's assumed risk, understood and accepted by those who chose to work for the high wage of $4. Nonetheless, hundreds applied, willing to descend to darkness and danger.*

A miner's life was regimented by seven eight-hour shifts each week, marked by a timekeeper who shouted his name at the start and end of each turn of labor. To escape their daily descent into the torrid tunnels, some miners applied for jobs "on top" or—hoping for permanent escape—bought mining stocks, thinking they knew enough not to be misled by rumors and false reports. When they could, they shared inside information, perhaps about a new pocket of rich ore not yet known to the owners. When talk spread of the latest miner whose stock sale brought him more money than months of wages, others were all the more tempted to buy from one of the many brokers in Virginia City.

Unlike most of these "investors," an old-timer named James Galloway (he had come to California from Iowa in 1853) kept a diary in which he reported his gains and losses. While working in the Consolidated Virginia Mine in the spring of 1875, he recorded a series of stock trades. "Bought 10 shares of Overman at $66." A month later: "Sold my Overman at $75." After several more successful trades, he reported, "Stocks booming," and later that year, "Great rise in stocks." But in 1876 his luck changed. "Dealing in stocks, losing all the time. . . . Have lost $300 out of $800 in stocks in ten days." Like many other miners, Galloway swore to save his money rather than risk it. But soon he noted: "Lady Bryan excitement, $4 a share." Three days later: "Lady Bryan 15 cents—infamous swindle."

Unlike city speculators and owners, miners like Galloway had more than stocks to worry about when their luck changed. While working at the 2,700-foot level, Galloway brushed against a belt

---

* Back in the States, coal miners' daily wages (1870s) ranged from $1.61 to $2.37. Other non-farm laborers' wages: shoe factories, $1.73; and iron mills, $2.01. Farm workers in Germany by the turn of the century earned "maybe forty cents a day."

Hats and mustaches completed the uniform of those who toiled in the depths of the Comstock. To pierce the darkness, they carried lanterns and hung candles, like those in this miner's blackened, bruised hands.

In digging out gold- and silver-bearing ores, Comstock miners opened huge caverns that required special support. In 1861 a German mining engineer devised a system of timbering known as "square sets" that provided extraordinary strength and rigidity by interlocking massive beams eighteen by eighteen inches and larger. Though extremely vulnerable to fire and to the more insidious consequences of dry rot, these immense honeycombs remained indispensable in the ever-larger underground excavations of the Comstock mines.

Working in torrid tunnels at depths of two and three thousand feet; dominated by the demands of machines; exposed to constant danger and discomfort—these men had little reason to smile for the camera.

that operated a huge blower. His sleeve caught. In a fierce struggle to free his arm, he was drawn into the fan and mangled. One more fatal accident not reflected in the price of Consolidated Virginia.

Above ground the industrial smells and sounds—smoke, steam, and gases, the ceaseless thumping of stamp mills, the shriek of steam whistles—could not entirely obscure many aspects of life in Virginia City and its satellite towns that recalled earlier years in California. Murders, corruption, and incompetent government mixed inevitably with the wild life of saloons, gambling, hotels, and women in dance halls and brothels. From distant farms and towns, wagons and mules delivered food, equipment, and even heavy machinery. And when the fire bell sounded, volunteers tried to slow the flames. In 1875 "pillars and volleys of flame" swept through Virginia City, destroying two thousand buildings, including hoisting works and mills. Some $10 million reduced to ashes, and again rebuilding began before the embers cooled.

There were other similarities to "old times." Miners' dreams of sudden wealth persisted stubbornly, luring many to far places of promise. In 1864 hundreds rushed from the Comstock to new discoveries around Boise, in Idaho Territory, where reports insisted that a man could work for himself—as in 1849—and make a fortune. Gold and silver deposits in the Nevada desert to the east, in Aurora and Treasure City, attracted their share of escapees from wage labor.

But most of these and other rushes proved illusory for the average miner. Ores in the new mines, like those beneath Virginia City, lay deep and held their gold and silver in complex mineral formations far more challenging than the simple Sierra placers. To extract precious metals, even from rich deposits, required the resources of syndicates willing to invest vast sums of money. At the Comstock's famous Gould & Curry Mine, stamp mills, smelters, chemical processes, miles of tunnels, and an array of related machinery cost stockholders $900,000. Nearly all such investments had to go in before the first ore-bearing rock came out (if there was any), leaving a period of great insecurity in the price of shares before the confirmation of assays and shareholders' hopes would send stocks soaring—or plummeting in the presence of barren rock.

Mine owners never ceased to pressure their superintendents to increase the tonnage of ore, no matter the expense or risk. To explain this prodigal wastefulness and the intemperate expectations of Comstock owners and stockholders, a thoughtful Virginia City reporter suggested that "California pioneers who had lived for years where fortunes were made and lost . . . by the stroke of a pick could hardly be expected to appreciate the need for thrift. . . . Their experience had made them inveterate gamblers. . . . They did not call for increased profits through reduction of expenses but through an augmented production of bullion. If their dividends could be temporarily doubled, they did not care how large a proportion of profits was lost by over-rapid and careless reduction [of the ore]. . . . Every large stockholder of a productive mine counted himself a nabob and scattered his money . . . like a prince bestowing largesses."

Not only mine owners, engineers, lawyers, and stockholders exploited the bonanza. As they had in California mines, freighters and packers charged big prices for hauling thousands of tons of supplies over the Sierra passes. To this new destination specially designed "Washoe wagons," built in Stockton and Placerville, delivered every pound of food, every barrel of whiskey, every machine and pump, all the thousands of flasks of quicksilver, the laces and corsets for the ladies on "the line"—everything that wild world on the barren slopes of Mount Davidson needed or wanted, day or night. All of it came over two toll roads, one from Placerville, the other from Nevada City. Both those towns skimmed big profits as transfer points from San Francisco and Sacramento, where wholesalers in their turn had taken a fat share. And on those two roads the private companies that each owned and maintained a stretch of the hundred-mile routes charged ample fees at their toll gates. On the Placerville road, one gatekeeper collected from $40,000 to $70,000 each year.

Like muscle beneath fancy clothes, the provisioning of Virginia City and its mines attracted little attention compared to the flamboyance of San Francisco's stock exchange. But it was a powerfully profitable business, collecting millions of dollars annually in freight charges, using 12,000 draught animals on the roads and employing 2,000 teamsters and hostlers. In 1863 the Pioneer Stage Line carried 11,103 passengers from Placerville to Virginia City and 8,430 westward, at $27 each way, for revenue of $527,390. Receipts for all three competing stage lines were estimated to exceed $1 million.*

So many ways to make money, as in California. Within a network of new businesses, lumbering again prospered. The Comstock mines consumed gargantuan quantities of firewood—more than 250,000 cords each year—to generate steam to drive their hoisting works, stamp mills, pumps, blowers, sawmills, and other machinery. They paid lumber companies between $10 and $30 per cord, even $50 in the severe winter of 1866–67. To meet the additional demand for fuel by residents and businesses in Virginia City and surrounding settlements, Chinese "gleaners" followed American woodcutters into every ravine and over every hillside, pulling up brush, stumps, and roots.

Of greater importance, construction of mills, smelters, ancillary structures, and commercial buildings in Virginia City required millions of board feet of lumber, a huge demand made still greater, as in California, by the need to rebuild after fires. Thousands of once-soaring pines disappeared into many miles of tunnels and ore chambers to serve as

---

* Once again, statistics clarify and astonish. Freight hauled over the Placerville road (101 miles) during the years 1863–70 ranged from 45,000 to 75,000 tons annually. At the average rate of $100 per ton, freightage on 50,000 tons cost $5 million. Tolls collected by the several gatekeepers from freight wagons alone averaged $639,000 annually.

In 1863 a traveler described the toll road from Placerville to Virginia City:

Sometimes three thousand teams with twenty-five thousand animals are at work at one time. We passed hundreds of freight wagons with from six to ten horses or mules each. . . . Hotels and stables abound, even at the very summit where the snow falls to an immense depth every winter. . . . But what of that? Where money is to be made . . . , there will be a man to get it.

William H. Brewer, *Up and Down California in 1860–1864*

---

massive square-cut support beams. This vast framework of wooden props required constant renewal because of cave-ins, shifting footings, and rot induced by intense heat and moisture. When by carelessness or accident a fire got started in this subterranean tinderbox, flames and gases spread irresistibly. Such infernos were sometimes quelled by flooding, a costly remedy because the tons of water poured in had to be laboriously pumped out before carpentry crews could begin to replace thousands of charred beams. By one estimate, more than 600 million feet of these timbers were interred in the Comstock's depths.

By the early seventies, having denuded the eastern slopes of the Sierra, the lumber barons cut through thousands of acres across the heights and over on the California side, leaving another desolation of stumps. On slopes too steep for teams of oxen and mules to maneuver the logs to sawmills, the loggers constructed steep V-shaped chutes down which thousands of great trunks rumbled in a trail of smoke, to plunge into mill ponds loud with the sound of giant blades slicing through earlier arrivals. As clear-cutting ranged over greater distances, mountain streams were diverted into flumes to carry lumber through valleys and along moun-

MINING THE FOREST

tainsides and finally down to the planing mills near Virginia City.

Reflecting on the ancient groves that disappeared in only a few years, a visitor to Washoe lamented: "The Comstock Lode may truthfully be said to be the tomb of the forests of the Sierra."

In that era of capricious power and corporate manipulation, when the production of millions in silver and gold each month encouraged a "recklessness of cost and consequence," the owners of Comstock mines counted their personal profits first, as contemptuous of their workers as of their stockholders. When a company opened a rich new deposit of ore, its miners might be confined at their work sites for several shifts to prevent the good news from escaping until owners had time to buy more of the soon-to-rise stock. After a discovery in 1868, Hale & Norcross miners were locked in for three days; when they were finally released and the news became known, the stock soared in one day from $1,300 to $2,200. Bad news was similarly controlled. Following a disastrous cave-in, flood, or fire in the tunnels and cross-cuts, a company's surviving miners often found themselves confined "on top," to give owners time to sell before the mine's stock suffered from the calamitous news.

As in factories on the East Coast, Americans increasingly took the safer and more advantageous jobs on the Comstock, leaving to foreigners the heavy labor in the steamy depths. By 1880, 2,000 of the Comstock's 2,770 miners came from Europe, most of them from Ireland and Cornwall. But no Chinese allowed. When the miners organized a protective association in 1863, it worked to secure the $4-per-shift wage and to prevent the hiring of "Orientals." The association gained little else, leaving the miners at the mercy of absentee owners, men they scorned as "courtroom miners" and manipulators with "icicles in their handshakes." No wonder the earlier years in California took on a romantic aura, nostalgically remembered as a time when every ounce dug belonged to the man who labored for it, not to some millionaire in San Francisco.

And there were now plenty of them, a score or more, potentates as famous for the extravagant ways they spent their wealth and wielded their power as for the Comstock mines they controlled. That was another change from the fifties. Back then no one was "famous" for his wealth or power. Maybe Sam Brannan, that enduring personality. But who else? Fruit farmer George Briggs? Few knew his name. But in the sixties there were colorful power brokers, like William Ralston, whose Bank of California controlled—for a time—most of the Comstock mines and mills. Newspapers in San Francisco and Virginia City made others famous, like mine owner John Mackay whose stock in the Kentuck Mine spurted in 1863 to more than $5,000 a share. Reports told of stockholders who received dividends of $10,000 every month. And there were Comstock lawyers—men like William Stewart, none more wily. He took his fees in sums seldom less than $100,000. And his bulk matched his wealth: "The man moved like a cathedral."

The rich and the millionaire rich spent their fortunes with lavish liberality, some in Virginia City. One mountain magnate commissioned a walnut headboard for his mansion bedroom to reach from floor to fourteen-foot ceiling; another ordered a water tank filled with the most expensive French champagne at his wedding feast, to be dispensed to his guests through silver taps. But most preferred to make their mark in the larger arena of San Francisco. That metropolis of bold investments and lucky speculations boomed as never before, grown by 1863 to 115,000 residents, more than 25 percent of the state's total population. New construction included sumptuous hotels, castlelike mansions, and wharves that reached ever farther into the bay. Giant steam shovels cut into sand hills to provide fill along the shore for new city blocks in the expanding financial and commercial districts with their marble-clad banks and brokerage houses and multistoried brick buildings crowded with offices for steamship, stagecoach, and freight companies. In warehouse workrooms, craftsmen built elegant carriages; silversmiths and goldsmiths turned out gilt doorknobs, hinges, water faucets, and mirror frames. Wealth awakened appetites not easily satiated.

San Francisco dominated California and, too, Nevada. "Not an ounce of gold dug, a pound of ore smelted, a field gleaned, or a tree felled . . . but must add to her wealth." That was the judgment of Henry George, journalist and soon to be severe critic of that city-state's concentration of wealth and power. Another observer, Lord James Bryce from London, a few years later described the City as the "commercial and intellectual centre and source of influence for the surrounding regions, more powerful over them than is any Eastern city over its neighborhood. It is a New York which has got no Boston on one side of it and no shrewd and orderly rural population on the other to keep it in order."

San Francisco's businessmen (many of whom now had wives and families) held nearly all the reins of power. They controlled the Pacific Mail steamships that connected California to Hong Kong and to the Panama Railroad that bridged the isthmus; they owned the paddle wheelers of the California Steam Navigation Company that carried freight and passengers up and down the rivers; they owned the California Stage Company, the Sacramento Valley Railroad, and the San Francisco and San Jose Railroad. They owned iron foundries, machine shops, and metal-casting plants where men worked around the clock to fill orders from the Comstock mines for hoisting engines, crushing machinery, boilers, compressors, newly invented wire rope, and always more and bigger pumps. To harvest vast fields of wheat (one "farm" planted 60,000 acres), San Francisco (and Sacramento and Stockton) manufacturers invented "gang plows" and steam-powered threshing and harvesting machines, as well as milling machines for producing flour. Others turned out burlap sacks by the countless thousands to contain the centals of wheat exported by shiploads to Liverpool. Breweries, distilleries, woolen mills, box and barrel factories, and the new-to-California technology of canning fruits and vegetables all brought ever-quick entrepreneurs a new diversity of profits. And this growth and maturing were financed with local capital, not with loans from Boston or New York or London. Like a rich, independent nation, California and its world-famous city had their own sources of wealth—gold from the Sierra foothills, silver from the colony in Washoe.

California in her second decade as a state remained powerfully attractive to hundreds of thousands of emigrants from around the world, their expectations fed by newspaper and magazine articles and books that heralded and exaggerated California's wonders, from moneymaking to social freedoms—a country so different that its distance had to be measured not in thousands of miles but in thousands of dollars, its society not by traditions but by innovations.

And different, too, because it escaped the agonies of the Civil War. While that ghastly conflict wrought devastation and killed over six hundred thousand, California prospered, its economy booming, its population increasing. With the eastern states' productivity fully committed to the war, California's nascent industries grew up safe from the competition of imports. Not satisfied with this good fortune, the state government refused to accept the new paper currency issued by Washington to finance the war. Commonly known as "greenbacks" and reviled by the *Alta California* as "dirty shin-plasters," the federal paper that filtered into the state quickly depreciated against gold coins, its value fluctuating with the victories and defeats of the Northern armies. At their lowest level, greenbacks were discounted to thirty-five cents. Announcements in San Francisco newspapers during the war years listed the names of individuals who tried to force federal paper on unwilling creditors. Most Californians reserved greenbacks to pay their taxes to Washington.

Thanks to that distant government's minimal enforcement powers, Californians (and Oregonians) escaped the military drafts that in all other loyal states replenished the ravaged ranks of the Union armies. The Lincoln administration decided that chasing draft dodgers and deserters would be too difficult and expensive in the far west. In part for that reason, war emigrants by the thousands traveled to California between 1861 and 1864, while only five hundred volunteers in the California Battalion faced the Confederates in eastern battles and another force of Californians reclaimed the territories of Arizona and New Mexico from southern control. Except for these skirmishes, men from eastern states fought the Civil War while California prospered and, in the words of the *Los Angeles Star*, served as a "shelter for all who may flee the storm." More generous with money than manpower, California contributed $1.25 million to the Sanitary Fund (the Red Cross of the time), far more than any other state but only a pittance of the immense wealth at hand and thus more token than substance at a time of mortal danger for the Union.

THE MOST MAGNIFICENT PROJECT

So WEALTHY AS TO BE SELF-RELIANT, SO ISOLATED as to be self-centered, California nonetheless had to deal with Washington to gain what it most wanted: a transcontinental railroad to end the delays and dangers of overland and ocean travel.* Such a monumental ambition—"joining the two oceans with bands of iron"—had tested the oratorical imagery of Congressmen through the 1850s, when they had, without restraint, doled out public lands and government loans for their favorite local railroads. But the much acclaimed Pacific Railroad remained a vision, its reality denied by the North-South sec-

---

* Passage on paddle-wheel steamers from San Francisco via the Panama Railroad to New York took about thirty-three days, reduced by 1866 to twenty-one days. well publicized were the risks of shipwrecks, fires, tropical diseases, and shipboard cholera. In 1862 the *Golden Gate* burned off the west coast of Mexico with the loss of 223 passengers out of 338. Almost as shocking, the ship went down with $1,400,000 in gold assigned to banks and families "back home." Even more tragic, on the Atlantic leg of the seaborne connection to the "states," the *Central America* sank in a hurricane off the North Carolina coast in 1857, with a death toll of 435 out of 596 passengers and the loss of gold worth $1,600,000.

Other overland links to the eastern states prior to the railroad: a government subsidized mail contract helped to establish in 1858 the stagecoach operations of the Butterfield Overland Mail Company which carried mail and passengers both east and west between Tipton, Missouri (via Texas and Los Angeles) and San Francisco: 2,800 miles in twenty-five days. This expensive enterprise closed in mid-1861 following the secession of the southern states. More famous, the Pony Express (eighty riders, four hundred fast horses) was operated as a private enterprise by a St. Louis freighting company to carry mail ($5 per ounce) east and west between St. Joseph, Missouri and Sacramento, in ten and sometimes eight days. Service started in April 1860 but could not compete with the federally subsidized telegraph line, completed in October 1861, from Omaha via Salt Lake City and Virginia City to Sacramento and San Francisco.

tional rivalry. Locked in angry debate, Congress in 1860 could not agree on a route across two thousand miles of western wilderness to reach the nation's treasure-rich Pacific state. When the southern states seceded in 1861 and the war's first battles brought stunning Union army defeats, the crisis that occupied Washington might well have sidelined the transcontinental railroad if not for the inventive lobbying and determination of a young construction engineer and the risk-taking and conniving of four Sacramento merchants.

JUDAH

By 1860 Theodore Judah had earned prominence as the engineer who surveyed and promoted California's first railroad, completed in 1856: twenty-two miles of track that eliminated the delays of muddy wagon roads from Sacramento northeast to the foothill town of Folsom, a new distribution center that supplied the many mining camps along the forks of the American River. The Sacramento Valley Railroad's original investors intended to advance their tracks east to Placerville and north to Marysville and even to Nevada City and thereby rake in big profits by hurrying supplies to the entire northern mining region. But the first investors, mostly Sacramento businessmen who had hired Judah, lost control of their railroad to financier William Ralston and his acquisitive San Francisco allies. Remaining only twenty-two miles in length, the railroad nevertheless became a profitable link in their transportation system, netting $90,000 in 1858.

In contrast to his new employers' fixation on profits, Theodore Judah envisioned what he called "the most magnificent project ever conceived," a Pacific railroad that would surmount the heights, the chasms, the perils of the Sierra Nevada and reach across the desert to connect with an eastern railroad, thus binding California to its sister states. In 1859 Judah went to Washington to seek congressional support for his transcontinental ambition.

Rebuffed by the sectional antagonisms that divided Congress, he returned via Panama in July 1860, convinced that the California end of his "magnificent project" must be advanced from promotional talk to realistic plans. That meant finding a practical route through the Sierra and incorporating a company backed by local financiers.

That fall he searched for and found a promising route, from Sacramento along a wagon road to the mining town of Dutch Flat, from there on a gradually rising ridge to the western summit of the Sierra and then through the Truckee River canyon to within twenty miles of the boomtown of Virginia City, where merchants would pay for faster delivery of thousands of tons of supplies. That prospect helped Judah gain pledges from investors in Dutch Flat and other camps along the proposed route to buy stock in the company he called the Central Pacific Railroad. To incorporate under California law and become eligible to sell shares, a railroad needed to show capital on account equal to $1,000 for each mile of proposed track. Since Judah estimated 115 miles from the Sacramento River to the Nevada border, he would need to raise $115,000. The optimistic engineer felt confident he could obtain the bulk of the capital from William Ralston and other wealthy leaders in San Francisco.

In fact, the City's great entrepreneurs—who controlled highly profitable steamship lines, riverboats, freighting, stagecoach, and express companies, and the Sacramento Valley Railroad—regarded Judah's plans for a transcontinental railroad as a direct threat to their ocean-oriented transportation monopoly. Beyond their self-interest, Ralston and his associates doubted that a railroad could operate through the snowdrifts of the Sierra passes. Better to invest their profits in Comstock mines and extend their own Sacramento Valley Railroad.

Dismayed by their rebuff, Judah told his wife: "I shall never talk nor labor any more with them." He added, with remarkable prescience: "Not two years will go over their heads . . . but they would give all

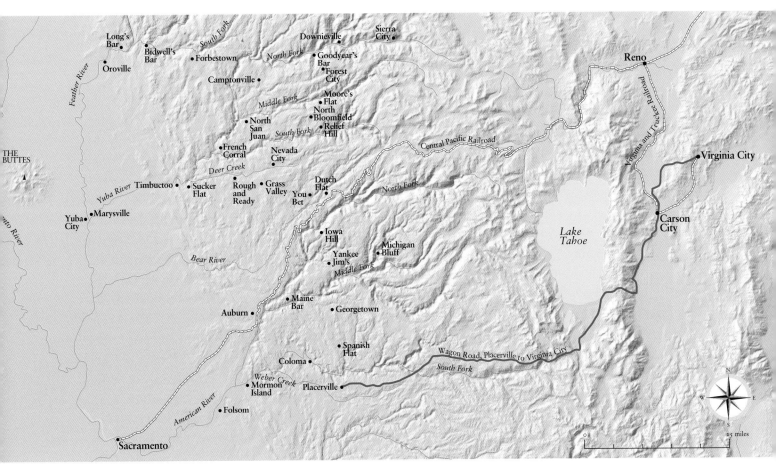

RAIL AND WAGON ROUTES ACROSS THE SIERRA NEVADA

they hope to have from their present enterprises to have what they put away tonight."

Leaving the Queen of the Pacific, Judah retreated to Sacramento where businessmen had long resented their city's secondary role as merely a transshipment center in a system owned by their domineering rival. In late November 1860 the engineer met with four storekeepers, small-time entrepreneurs compared to the millionaires by the Bay. But they, too, epitomized the ambitious, opportunistic spirit of California: Collis Huntington and Mark Hopkins (both '49ers), partners in a hardware business that sold shovels, blasting powder, and other mining supplies; Charles Crocker (arrived 1850), retailer in boots, carpets, and clothing; and Leland Stanford (1852), lawyer turned tradesman, selling groceries, liquor, and grain. Each a risk-taker, they had defied floods and fires and survived the wild fluctuations of sudden surpluses and shortages. And they were soon—and forever—to be famous as the Big Four.

When they met with Judah they had heard the news (delivered by Pony Express) that the Republican candidate, Abraham Lincoln, had been elected president. Secession by the southern states would open the way for an undivided Congress, at last, to pass legislation in support of a transcontinental railroad. Judah emphasized to these merchants (not yet familiar with the powers and largess of the national government) that such legislation, properly crafted, would provide subsidies to pay the costs of constructing their Central Pacific Railroad (CPRR). *Subsidies*—here was a word to awaken hopeful calculations. And might not additional subsidies be obtained from the California legislature, right there in Sacramento?

Interested, tempted by visions of profits unattainable in hardware, clothing, and groceries, the four men (they called themselves "the associates") agreed to invest in Judah's plan and to find others who would join to raise the money needed to incorporate the railroad company. With an instinctive skill they would later use in manipulating the government in Washington, the associates swiftly

The business of California is conducted boldly. Men make money rapidly, spend it freely and hastily. Changes in occupations are frequent and in wealth rapid. Hazardous speculation is the body of our commercial system. Most of our businessmen are young, and they are still under the influence of the feverish times of '49. Hereditary wealth is unknown. Our rich men all came to California poor, and they are prominent advertisements of the victories that may be achieved by enterprise and bold speculation. . . . It is no uncommon thing to see men who have been wealthy on three or four occasions and then poor again. "A fire . . . an unfortunate speculation in merchandise . . . an unlucky investment in a flume," these are the phrases used every day to explain the fact that this or that man though once rich is now poor. When men fail, they do not despair . . . , they hope to be rich again.

J. S. Hittell, *The Resources of California*

transcontinental railroad, the Union Pacific.

On July 1, 1862, President Lincoln signed the Pacific Railroad Act, authorizing construction of the most ambitious project of the century, hailed in later years as "The Work of the Age" and undertaken even as the nation fought the ferocious battles of its bloody civil war. Far from the death and anguish, Governor Stanford received a telegram that evening from Washington: "The President has signed the railroad bill. Let California rejoice." The news sent crowds into the streets of Sacramento, rejoicing with shouts and liquor, their enthusiasm finally organized into a parade, described by the *Sacramento Daily Union* as "the most brilliant affair of its kind that has ever taken place in this city. The procession was a mile long and the route was one blaze of torches and fireworks. . . . There were over one hundred mottoes, all of them appropriate and pithy."

But when a copy of the railroad bill reached the officers of the Central Pacific, they found little to celebrate. Forty miles of track had to be laid before the government would release subsidies (actually loans) of $16,000 for each mile of track from Sacramento across the valley to the foothills of the Sierra, then $48,000 for each mile through the fearsome terrain of the Sierra, and in Nevada $32,000 per eastward mile across the desert. How to raise the hundreds of thousands to pay for those first crucial forty miles? Initially the associates tried to sell stock in their railroad, but against the far greater attraction of Comstock shares their issue languished. In the state's great financial center only fourteen shares could be sold. San Francisco businessmen not only refused to support a company that threatened their interests, they spread rumors of the Central Pacific's likely demise.

Desperate, in December 1862 Huntington went east, to the Boston office of the Ames Shovel Company, manufacturer of more shovels than any other company in the nation and a highly profitable business through the 1850s when California's miners had bought shovels by the scores of thousands, a

arranged matters in California to their advantage. In quick succession Stanford was nominated Republican candidate for governor of California on June 18, 1861, then appointed by his partners as president of the Central Pacific Railroad, which received its papers of incorporation ten days later. In September 1861 their president was elected governor, ready and able—without scruple—to help his company gain support from the state legislature. In October Judah sailed for Washington, where he distributed Central Pacific Railroad Company stock among key congressmen. He arranged to have himself appointed clerk to both the House and the Senate committees responsible for Pacific railroad legislation. From those inside posts he helped draft the final bills, providing subsidies for the Central Pacific and for the eastern half of the hoped-for great many of them sold at Huntington and Hopkins's hardware store. Foreseeing that construction of the transcontinental railroad would require shovels by the endless thousands, the Ames brothers agreed to consider a loan of nearly $200,000, with Central Pacific bonds as collateral—if Huntington personally guaranteed the bonds' interest payments. Thus this small-time hardware merchant risked everything he owned and hoped to own—an act of remarkable daring, agreed to by the Ames brothers only because they knew that Huntington had paid every bill through good years and bad, on time and in full, an exceptional record in those wild years when men and businesses so often simply disappeared.

With the Ames loan and letters of introduction as evidence of his creditworthiness, Huntington sought out the equipment his railroad would need from eastern manufacturers, paying frightful wartime prices and using heavily discounted Central Pacific bonds as his principal currency. But the priority demands of the Union armies strained every mill and forge, leaving Huntington hard-pressed to obtain spikes, rails, and locomotives at any price. He persevered, eventually filling his requisitions and ordering the material shipped to California, the most urgent via the high-cost Panama route, the rest around the Horn.

Having signed his name as guarantor, Huntington was relieved to learn by telegram in April 1863 that Governor Stanford had prodded the state legislature to subsidize construction with a grant of $500,000 and to authorize three counties to purchase $550,000 in CPRR stock. But once again San Francisco intervened, this time with one taxpayer lawsuit to hold back county funds and another before the state Supreme Court to prohibit state financial aid to the CPRR. Governor Stanford promptly responded by appointing the railroad's chief legal counsel to serve (concurrently) as chief justice of the California Supreme Court.

More than that, the governor asked the state geologist to identify the location of the western base of the Sierra Nevada. This geologic definition was of great financial importance to the railroad because federal loans would be disbursed at the rate of $48,000 for each mile of track laid in the mountains and only $16,000 for track laid across the Sacramento Valley. Prior to the governor's request, geologists had agreed that the mountains began their rise at an outcropping twenty-two level miles east of Sacramento. Fortuitously, the state geologist now determined the Sierra Nevada's western base to be located at Arcade Creek, just seven miles from Sacramento. By their power to move mountains, the associates gained fifteen miles at the preferred rate of $48,000—but not payable until they could grade a roadbed and lay track for the first forty miles.

HUNTINGTON

By the fall of 1863 Theodore Judah's moral objections to these manipulations had thoroughly irritated Huntington, who had returned to California in June. The two men had "a big row," and Judah was forced to withdraw from the corporation. His dream undimmed by this reversal, in October Judah sailed for "the States," determined to raise enough money in New York to buy out his ex-partners. While crossing the isthmus, through the jungles of Panama on the first transcontinental railroad (which his would displace), Judah was stricken with yellow fever. He died on November 3, 1863, two days after landing in New York; he was thirty-seven.

Without any expression of sorrow for his death or of gratitude for Judah's indispensable guidance, but acutely aware that their company's treasury retained only $7,000, the associates decided to seek immediate financial aid from Washington, even though that government staggered under the burdens of a seemingly interminable war. Once again they sent their skilled lobbyist, Collis Huntington. He sailed for Panama on November 21, 1863, determined to cajole, persuade, and, if need be, buy congressional support for new legislation more favorable to the needs of the Central Pacific.

Though he had spent a decade in Sacramento and knew well the effectiveness of political payoffs, Huntington was dismayed by the "shoddy contractors and swarms of official leeches" crowding the halls of the Capitol and the bar of the Willard Hotel, "a maelstrom of political bargaining and sale, a place where the noisy, cumbersome machine of politics was oiled and greased." Working with the investors who controlled the Union Pacific, Huntington helped push through Congress—in a "tempest of wildest disorder"—a second Pacific Railroad Act, signed by President Lincoln on July 2, 1864.

So generous to the railroads that its opponents condemned it as "the greatest legislative crime in history," the bill contained a maze of land grants, first and second mortgages, government bonds, sinking funds, forfeiture penalties, devious deals, and profligate payoffs, crafted by wily lobbyists and approved by compliant representatives and senators. Amid its welter of provisions and amendments, Huntington gained what he most wanted for the CPRR: release of government subsidies at twenty miles of track laid rather than forty. Because his partners had already managed, by stubborn effort and burdensome borrowing, to push their iron rails thirty-one miles east from Sacramento, the new law allowed their overextended company to receive a government subsidy of $1,264,000*—if those first miles passed inspection by not-yet-appointed federal

engineers. New uncertainties, more delays, more weeks of appeasing creditors with heavily discounted CPRR stock.

Then there was good news. Sam Brannan, that ubiquitous chance-taker, flush with profits from his bank, vineyards, and distillery, chose to invest in Central Pacific stock and bonds in the fall of 1864, once again sensing a propitious moment with uncanny accuracy. By allying himself with the Sacramento associates, Brannan became a symbolic defector from the San Francisco camp that opposed them. As if his investment offered encouragement, local courts soon approved county purchases of CPRR stock and the California Supreme Court upheld the legality of state aid. Helpful as these new funding sources were, the associates still did not have enough money to build the railroad across the mountains, where projected costs ran from $100,000 to as much as $150,000 per mile for one hundred grueling miles before reaching the Nevada border and the comparative ease of the flat desert beyond. They faced a daunting prospect: to build bridges, trestles, and retaining walls; to cut away mountainsides and fill in canyons; to drive tunnels through solid granite—all this to be attempted with implements no more sophisticated than saws and hammers, picks and shovels, and (until 1867) explosives no more powerful than black powder, in the hands of thousands of men, all of whom had to be managed, fed, and housed in a dangerous wilderness at elevations of six and seven thousand feet, where snowdrifts did not melt until mid-July. This stupendous campaign would cost far more money than anyone calculated.

Once again Huntington used his presence in Washington to cajole important friends, satchelful of crisp Central Pacific stock certificates helping to influence congressional committees. Congress soon approved a third Pacific railroad bill, providing another package of long-term loans, incentives, and land grants to ease the cost of constructing the two railroads as the Central Pacific and the Union Pacific moved haltingly toward one another. President

---

* The government subsidies came in the form of federal bonds, $16,000 granted for each mile of flat terrain (thus for seven miles: $112,000) and $48,000 in the Sierra (twenty-four miles: $1,152,000), for a total of $1,264,000. To turn those bonds into cash, the CPRR had to sell them for greenbacks, a currency California treated with contempt. Greenbacks often brought no more than a third of what gold dollars could obtain. Thus, a painful series of discounts, from federal bonds to greenbacks and, in California, from greenback to gold coin, meant that the railroad made due with millions less in buying power than the apparent face value of the controversial sums bequeted by Congress during the construction years.

Lincoln signed the legislation on March 3, 1865, the eve of his second inauguration. For the four Sacramento merchants the date marked the fourth year they had continued to sustain their immense and audacious gamble by manipulating funds from county, state, and federal governments. Yet they still needed more. In the spring of 1866 Huntington, the master lobbyist, dared to woo Congress one last time. Whatever his means, he worked with the Union Pacific to gain a new set of generous amendments, signed on July 3, 1866, by President Andrew Johnson.

Bold and determined (a newspaperman said he was as "ruthless as a crocodile"), Huntington used the same wiles in his New York purchasing office that he applied in Washington, simultaneously directing negotiations to acquire thousands of tons of iron rails, locomotives, freight cars, and an array of other railroad equipment available only from eastern mills and factories, at high wartime prices. He chartered transport ships, as many as thirty at a time, to carry the heavy cargoes around Cape Horn to San Francisco where the vital supplies were transferred to river boats before finally landing at the docks in Sacramento. All this Huntington managed by himself, pausing to reflect in a letter, "I am loading iron on ships as fast as possible, working night and day. . . . I think sometimes I have too much to do, but I guess not. Men don't wear out."

Certainly Huntington showed no signs of wearing out, nor did his associate Charles Crocker, who, detesting account books and offices, applied his boundless energy as construction boss of the railroad. No partnership ever benefited from a more advantageous pairing of opposite skills and personalities. While Huntington manipulated the levers of politics and finance, Crocker thrived in the stress and tumult of the field, amid hundreds of graders shouting and straining, teams of horses and mules pulling scrapers and hauling wagonloads of dirt, scores of carpenters erecting bridges and spidery trestles, groups of powdermen blasting passes through ridges—all laboring to advance the

roadbed for the tracklayers. Surrounding forests yielded the trees that the CPRR's twenty-five sawmills sliced into timbers and railroad ties beyond counting. It was a world of monumental and dangerous effort, of pushing ahead no matter the obstacles, driven by the same "dedicated fury" that earlier drove the construction of great river-mining flumes and water company aqueducts. Whatever the job needed, take it. Whatever blocked the way, cut it down, blast it away, build across it. Those principles ruled the world of mining, and Crocker's orders applied them with a new impatience to building the Central Pacific.

CROCKER

Faced in the spring of 1865 with too few laborers willing to work for his railroad (many of them hung around for a payday or two and then lit out for the more compelling prospects at Virginia City), Crocker resorted to hiring Chinese—"the dregs of Asia"—from San Francisco and the mining regions. Marginalized by discrimination, the Chinese proved so willing to work and so industrious that Crocker decided to engage labor contractors to hire thousands of young men from the regions around Canton. They came as indentured laborers, ruled by Chinese bosses who meted out discipline and distributed wages and food. Their subservient toil so pleased Crocker and his superintendents that he had put more than 6,000 "celestials" on the payroll by mid-1866, along with some 2,500 Irish immigrants and numerous American workers in supervisory jobs. Together this racial polygot formed what a newspaperman from the *New York Tribune* described as "a great army laying siege to Nature in her strongest citadel . . . , shoveling, wheeling, carting, drilling, and blasting earth and rock."

Judah's route for the railroad, staked out by surveyors, followed a ridge west of Dutch Flat to an unavoidable obstacle: a massive promontory dubbed Cape Horn. To blast out a preliminary ledge and then gradually carve a roadbed along the face of this sheer wall rising 1,400 feet above the

American River, hundreds of Chinese workers, using only hammers, handheld drills, and kegs of black powder, drove holes, charged them with powder, set fuses, and crept back along narrow footholds to escape the explosions that sent chunks of rock cascading into the river far below. In spite of inevitable falls and injuries and the vertigo that menaced work at such precarious heights, the stalwart Chinese persevered. By their defiance of nature's citadel, the railroad advanced slowly into the Sierra, toward new challenges even more demanding of ingenuity and perseverance.

No mining enterprise, not even the deepest excavations of the Comstock, and no railroad yet built had confronted such formidable obstacles as those awaiting Crocker's army at the summit of the Sierra Nevada: blizzards that heaped snowdrifts thirty, even sixty feet deep; avalanches that swept away trestles and workers' camps; "mountain piled on mountain" through which fifteen tunnels had to be driven; and granite so hard that powder blasts spurted back through the drill holes. One of the forty-four snowstorms in the winter of 1866–67 swirled and howled without letup for two weeks. Twenty Chinese workers disappeared in a snowslide. When the CPRR's behemoth snowplow, pushed by ten locomotives, could not clear the track, more than two thousand men with shovels and picks attacked the frozen drifts to open a fifteen-mile pathway for delivery of supplies on ox-pulled sleds. But the snow

CPRR SNOWPLOW

drifted too fast for the shovelers; the oxen foundered, too exhausted to move. Desperate teamsters twisted their tails until the tormented creatures thrashed forward a few hundred yards and collapsed again. More twisting, more bellowing; several oxen were abandoned, their tails twisted off. But enough sleds got through with food and supplies (kegs of black powder being the most valuable) to keep thousands of Chinese blasters at work inside

the several tunnels, safe from snow but never far from explosions that shattered only eight to twelve inches of rock during each working day of three eight-hour shifts. To improve progress cutting through the solid granite of the summit tunnel, at 1,659 feet the longest of the tunnels, Crocker ordered a shaft sunk at midpoint so that his crews could work simultaneously at four faces. In early 1867 he experimented with the newly invented, frighteningly dangerous explosive known as nitroglycerin. This "blasting oil" concentrated eight times the power of black powder, yet its force only doubled the crews' progress through the steel-hard granite each twenty-four hours, to about two feet. When the summit tunnel opened in November 1867, Crocker put away the volatile "nitro" and returned exclusively to black powder, sending in as much as five hundred kegs each day.

By the summer of 1868 the Central Pacific's work force exceeded 15,000 men, some still clearing the tunnels, more laboring as graders and tracklayers down the eastern slope of the Sierra, while others were already at work in Nevada along the Humboldt River, behind surveyors staking out the rail route farther east, into Utah. Crocker drove all of them and was himself exhorted by a telegram from Huntington: "Work on as though Heaven was before you and Hell was behind you." But he could not yet deploy all his resources on the advance eastward to meet the Union Pacific. To protect the new trans-Sierra track from the destructive menace of winter avalanches and snowdrifts, the four associates agreed that snowsheds must be built to cover the most endangered miles of track, although the cost would be appalling.

That summer Crocker's superintendent in charge of bridge building gathered carpenters and other suitable workers—in all, about 2,500—to construct nearly forty miles of sheds and retaining walls. Even in July, drifts of "ice-cemented" snow hampered their work. More exasperating, crews had to clear equipment and material from the track several times each day for freight trains rattling east

Though their names would soon be known nationally as symbols of California wealth and power, the owners of this hardware emporium were not to be distinguished during the 1850s from scores of other ambitious Sacramento merchants who survived the town's fires and floods.

Cut through solid granite with hand-held drills and blasting powder, twelve tunnels opened the way for the Central Pacific Railroad through the heights of the Sierra Nevada. Forty miles of snowsheds protected the tracks from blizzards and avalanches. Such works of indomitable labor enabled steam engines like the *Conness* to deliver thousands of passengers (none so proud as these railroad officials) to Chicago and other destinations now only six days distant from Sacramento.

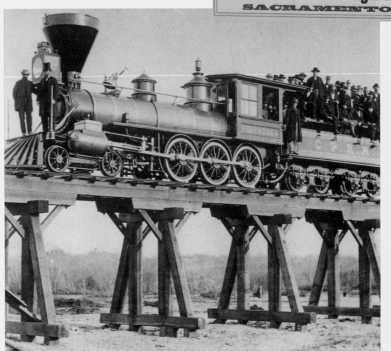

with tons of rails, ties, and hardware for the Nevada railhead, where Crocker promised Huntington he would lay "a mile of track for every working day." Demand for beams and massive planks to frame and cover the sheds and the unending plea for more railroad ties strained the CPRR's sawmills, whose overworked lumbermen freely cut whatever trees were accessible in the ravaged forests. When completed, the snow sheds alone consumed 65 million feet of timber.

Just as the development of placer mining had spawned scores of wildly robust camps and towns, the millions spent by the Central Pacific fathered lusty settlements along its route. The most important was Reno, born in 1868 as a marshaling yard and supply depot for the railroad's advance into the Nevada desert. Its influence quickly grew with the completion of a rail extension to Virginia City, built to fulfill the associates' plan to displace Sierra toll roads with a superior supply line to the rich Washoe market. Like other masculine gathering places, Reno gained a reputation for exuberance, chronicled in part by its newspaper, the *Crescent*. A December 1868 editor's note advised, "For the past two weeks Reno has been enlivened with any number of fights. An attempt to record them has proved a total failure, so we have concluded to content ourselves with a summary of the killed and wounded at the end of the season."

Of all the trackside shanty towns, none garnered more lasting recognition than Promontory, Utah, 690 miles east of Sacramento and 1,086 miles from the Union Pacific's eastern terminus at Omaha, Nebraska. At this miserable assemblage of shacks and tents, on the tenth day of May 1869, several thousand odorous laborers, various silk-hatted railroad dignitaries, and newspapermen from California and eastern states gathered to celebrate the wedding of the rails, an event of symbolic importance likened by some to the landing of the Pilgrim Fathers.

To complete the joining of the Central Pacific and the Union Pacific rails, Leland Stanford held a maul with which to drive the last spike, cast from California gold. He swung and missed. But who cared? Locomotive whistles shrieked, laborers cheered. ("We all yelled like to bust.") In contrast to the self-important speakers ("completion of a work so magnificent in contemplation, so marvelous in execution"), the telegrapher tapped out a terse message to the waiting nation: "Done." In Washington crowds shouted a thunderous approval in front of the Capitol, in New York a hundred cannon roared, in Philadelphia cheers echoed against the walls of Independence Hall. Chicago, Omaha, and Salt Lake City exulted with processional parades and pistols firing salutes.

For the people of Sacramento, the news from Promontory justified more than a spontaneous celebration. A proud front-page editorial in the *Daily Union* expressed the city's deep sense of vindication that, unlike San Francisco's timid moguls, its merchants "were bold enough to plan and take the lead in building the greatest enterprise of modern times." After lyrical passages affirming "patriotism, enterprise, courage, and pride," the *Daily Union* remembered that "when the financiers of New York and San Francisco were perfectly confident that the money could *not* be raised," it was Sacramento's businessmen who bought the railroad's stock and bonds and Sacramento's risk-takers "whose mining, packing, staging, grading, and teaming experience; whose brave triumphs over Nature had qualified them . . . to take the lead in building this great highway of the nation."

Moved only by self-interest and not immune to the misjudgments of hubris, San Francisco's magnates by 1868 had begun to ponder how the changed environment of a soon-to-be-completed transcontinental railroad might benefit them. If it threatened their monopoly on ocean commerce, it opened new opportunities as well. By the time Stanford missed his stroke at Promontory, they had largely embraced the Central Pacific Railroad and its anticipated connection with their busy wharves. They foresaw new prosperity from trade with the

Orient, with San Francisco serving as transfer point for eastbound goods sent along with California's grain and gold across the continent in only seven days. Thrilled by the prospect, San Franciscans reveled in their city's continued primacy. One parade banner proclaimed: "San Francisco annexes the United States."

In fact, the new era would prove harshly different than San Francisco's sanguine editors, bankers, merchants, stockbrokers, industrialists, and real estate speculators forecast. Their confidence in a boom in trade with China and India ignored the inauguration of another great engineering conquest of nature in that same year: the opening of the Suez Canal. Far eastern shipping bound for Europe would use that passage rather than San Francisco and the transcontinental railroad. The city's business leaders also overlooked the competition that the railroad would bring to the state's long-protected homegrown industries. Factories in Chicago, St. Louis, and even New York would soon ship their products to California on westbound trains, glutting its once isolated market with merchandise and commodities that undersold local producers. One wholesaler later recalled the shock of an "avalanche of goods . . . at prices our local men could not meet. Many firms failed, some consolidated, some retired from business. Rents dropped like lead, real estate values shriveled."

Compounding the economic torments so suddenly on the loose, Charles Crocker released some 12,000 Chinese construction workers following completion of the railroad. They drifted back to Sacramento and San Francisco, to mines and farms, ready to work for wages scoffed at by thousands of unemployed whites. Adding to the pressures, the new railroad brought thousands of hopeful workers from eastern states each month—more men for too few jobs. Lured by California's still-vivid image as the land of gold and opportunities (and by the ease of rail travel), they came in growing numbers— 140,000 in four years (1870–1873), and as many as 75,000 in one year (1875)—most of them soon dis-

appointed, many angry. The CPRR seemed to bring prosperity principally to itself, collecting fares from unwelcome immigrants, importing freight that put California companies out of business. It was a perverse reward for a gamble funded largely with government money and promoted by the rhetoric of the common good. And a foretaste of the decade to come.*

THE POWER OF MONEY

The owners of the Central Pacific Railroad, like the owners of the Comstock mining companies, drove their enterprises with an avarice and careless ambition sanctioned by laissez-faire economics, unconstrained since 1849. Constraint, even reform, would come in time, but not yet. Who was there to call "unfair"? Not the state government, which for a time had the president of the railroad in the governor's residence; not county and city administrators financially dependent on income from railroad bonds and Comstock prosperity; not the state Supreme Court whose chief justice had for a time served as legal counsel to the railroad. It was a rough world of manipulation and monopoly, a time when a few men gained wealth beyond imagining.

In November 1870 the superintendent of the Crown Point Mine on the Comstock Lode discovered promising indications of rich ore along ex-

---

* The ease and safety of rail travel compared to the old Panama route attracted an annual migration "home," including many husbands who planned to bring their wives back to California. The railroad carried 22,000 eastward in 1871 and a comparable number most years thereafter. The Central Pacific also shipped agricultural products east, fulfilling expectations of farmers and orchardists that the railroad's speed might bring eastern markets within their reach. Charles Wesley Reed, who operated a large orchard and nursery across the river from Sacramento, exemplified these beneficiaries. In July 1869 he accompanied his first shipment of Bartlett pears to Chicago, where he triumphantly reported their safe arrival on July 29, after a week's travel.

ploratory tunnels at the 1,100-foot level. He shared this important news not with his employers but with his brother-in-law, Alvinza Hayward, who had made his pile at his Eureka Mine back in the Sierra foothills. Purchasing Crown Point stock at $2 a share, Hayward guarded news of the rich deposit until he accumulated a controlling interest in the mine. Then reports of the discovery were released and Crown Point shares soared on the San Francisco Exchange, reaching the dizzying price of $1,825 in 1872. For his deft timing, Hayward collected $25 million; his informant, $10 million.

So it went for others, like John Mackay and James Fair, both mine superintendents, and James Flood and William O'Brien, owners of a popular saloon in San Francisco. After Fair's careful exploration of the Consolidated Virginia and an adjacent mine, these four partners bought enough stock (spending less than $100,000) to control both mines. In 1874 one of their tunnels struck a vast concentration of silver and gold, three to four hundred feet wide, described by the *Mining and Scientific Press* as a "body of ore absolutely immense and . . . superior in every respect to anything ever before seen on the Comstock Lode." Within a few years the "Big Bonanza" produced $105 million, most of that wealth paid in dividends to the four partners, soon famous as the Silver Kings.* Their prodigal extravagances ranged from Flood's construction of an elegant stone mansion on Nob Hill to Fair's wholesale purchase of votes in the Nevada legislature to secure a seat in the United States Senate, outbidding another Comstock millionaire for the privilege.

---

*The rise in Consolidated Virginia stock from $4 to $700 sparked a new frenzy of bidding for mining stocks. In January 1875 the value of stocks listed on the several San Francisco exchanges totaled $284 million. Californians by the thousands risked their savings, sold assets, and borrowed funds to buy mining shares. Many made fortunes of tens of thousands of dollars. Many more suffered ruin, deceived by stories of new discoveries designed to lure the innocent and by reported stock sales that never happened.

No more regulated or constrained than Comstock miners and speculators, the Big Four—Huntington, Crocker, Stanford, and Hopkins—amassed greater wealth and power during the 1870s than even the Silver Kings. By issuing new shares of CPRR stock with which to acquire local rail lines, by using ruthless financial manipulations to eliminate potential competitors, by applying political influence, and by finagling federal land grants to offset the expense of laying costly miles of track, these men (only a decade earlier obscure storekeepers in Sacramento) contrived to create a monopoly of transportation across California.

First, they extended the Central Pacific's track from Sacramento across the Central Valley to San Jose and from there sent one branch north to Oakland with another to San Francisco, thus encircling the Bay and controlling California's major seaports. To exclude competitive shipping in the Bay and on the navigable waters of the Sacramento and San Joaquin Rivers, they purchased the California Steam Navigation Company. Next the monopolists advanced their railroad up the Sacramento Valley (eventually all the way to Portland, Oregon) and south through the San Joaquin Valley, forcing towns along each route to pay special subsidies or find themselves bypassed by the main line. Even the largest town in southern California, Los Angeles (population 6,000) succumbed to this "legalized blackmail" by paying $610,000 and turning over to the CPRR a local line that ran to the seaport of San Pedro.

To protect the monopoly from a competing transcontinental railroad, the Southern Pacific Railroad—the name of the empire grown from the CPRR—preempted the route from Los Angeles to New Orleans, with Huntington once again in Washington to nurture helpful subsidies. Still not content, the Big Four completed their dominance by taking control of ocean traffic through their alliance with the Pacific Mail Steamship Company.

For thousands of businessmen and factory owners, ranchers and farmers along the Southern Paci-

STANFORD'S LIVING ROOM

fic's ever-lengthening rail lines, the conglomerate's rising freight rates determined costs, profits, and, in many cases, survival. As the railroad raised those rates year by year, the once longed for "iron horse" became an "octopus" that made the Big Four more wealthy than any other California millionaires— and more hated. One small-town newspaper reviled them as "cold-hearted, selfish, sordid men . . . their wealth accumulated in utter selfishness."

Far from apologetic, Huntington and his partners dismissed their critics, whether antagonistic reporters or investigating committees, as envious, malicious complainers. Survival of the fittest, that was the first law of economics and of Nature. Had they not survived the wild years of the 1850s and risked everything to build their railroad? Now they would manage that railroad as a private business, like any other, its property their property, its profits their just reward for risks taken. Whiners and jealous antagonists be damned.

As if to flaunt their defiance as much as their wealth, three of the Big Four (Crocker, Stanford, and Hopkins) turned from the provincial society and simple ways of Sacramento and moved the railroad's headquarters to San Francisco, where each built on Nob Hill an awesome mansion, described in later years as "ponderous palaces . . . , the most

In no other region of the United States did a railroad enjoy such a freedom from competition. Thus entrenched, the Big Four were free to adopt a system of setting freight rates according to the highest charge that the traffic would bear without completely bankrupting the shipper. . . . Often the [Southern Pacific's] agents would demand to examine the shipper's books and then set the rate according to what they thought the shipper could afford to pay. . . . The Big Four firmly believed that in selling transportation they should act just as they would in selling anything else. When Huntington had sold shovels or when Stanford had sold barrels of flour in Sacramento in the 1850s, they had charged as much as they could get. . . . They operated the Southern Pacific according to the ethical principles and economic ideas of a Yankee trader in the gold rush.

James L. Rawls, *California: An Interpretive History*

sensational residence lots, probably, in the nation." Huntington winced at such ostentation, both because it agitated his frugal nature and because his partners' turrets and carved granite offered lush evidence of what their enemies decried as ill-gotten profits. In contrast, Huntington lived in relative simplicity in New York City, managing the railroad's complex financial affairs and commuting to Washington to fend off its political opponents.

Supremely ambitious, ruthlessly expedient, the Big Four reflected the gold rush values that ruled California, the same values that eastern preachers, educators, and editorial writers had decried for years as they watched Americans head for that land of temptation and selfish abandon. None of these jeremiahs condemned California more vehemently than Henry David Thoreau. "The rush to California . . . makes God to be a moneyed gentleman who scatters a handful of pennies in order to see

Like a persistent contagion, optimism survived disappointment among river miners. Through the decades, companies invested hundreds of thousands of dollars each summer to build new flumes, few so long as this wonderful example of ambitious engineering which opened the bed of the Middle Fork of the American River at Maine Bar.

The most elegant, admired, and profitable of the many river steamers, the *Chrysopolis* delivered passengers and freight in six hours from San Francisco to these docks at Sacramento. From the Central Pacific's depot, freight was distributed to local merchants or shipped by rail and wagon to foothill towns and to that most profitable market, Virginia City.

Charles Crocker's castle at the top of Nob Hill had several nearby rivals in size and osten-tation, but far below, across the sprawl of San Francisco, nothing compared to the immensity, the self-importance of the Palace, the largest hotel in the world—eight hundred rooms—when it opened in 1875.

mankind scramble for them . . . the world's raffle."

Deaf to such moralizing, men—and more women than ever—continued the rush to California. In that land of gaudy freedom and unrestrained self-seeking, neither old-timers nor new arrivals paused to consider similar admonitions delivered by minister or editor. Among the few such brave messengers, none felt a greater concern than a young Unitarian preacher, Thomas Starr King, who landed in San Francisco in 1860 determined to help lay a moral foundation for California after "huddling so closely around the cosy stove of civilization" in Boston. Having warned from his pulpit against the contagion of selfish ambition, King set off on a tour of the diggings where for so many years others had seen fit to hail California's progress and profits. At hydraulic operations near Nevada City he was appalled by the sight before him, the crude nozzles "tearing all the beauty out of the landscape and setting up 'the abomination of desolation' in its place." He offered a portentous warning: "If the hydraulic mining method is to be infinitely used, without restraint, upon all the surface that will yield a good return, then California of the future will be a waste . . . more repulsive than any denounced in prophecy as the doom of a guilty race."

Warnings of doom and guilt, even frettings about the loss of beauty—who but a newly arrived minister from Boston would give vent to such emotional explorations? California's spectacular success had been achieved by pushing ahead with whatever it took to find and extract more gold, wonderfully augmented through the 1860s and 1870s by multiple millions in silver from the Comstock. Mewling about the beauty of the landscape, what was that all about? The riches of Nature, whether gold and silver or water and trees, were there to be used for profit, not left for the musings of preachers and poets. Americans—Californians—admired and envied *enterprise, pluck, endurance*. These were the qualities that rebuilt cities after fires, that inspired the people of Sacramento to bring in millions of tons of dirt to raise their streets and building sites above floodwaters rather than seek safety in the hills, that advanced the Central Pacific Railroad through the citadel of Nature. Look at the companies that took water from Sierra streams and lakes and delivered it through hundreds of miles of ditches, flumes, and aqueducts to be sold for handsome profits. And at the hydraulickers who used that water: their powerful jets washed entire hills and bluffs into miles of sluices where the "police duty" of quicksilver captured millions in gold. That was the kind of "get-aheadiveness" that made California famous as a place of opportunity and success, of astounding progress—because men had the ambition and freedom to defy Nature, to use whatever new invention would increase gold production. That's what counted, that's what brought new immigrants to California, not some concept of beauty to be protected, of landscape as "God's fingerprint."

THE POWER OF WATER

THE DRIVE TO WITHDRAW WEALTH FROM NATURE, to open its vaults and make it pay, nowhere showed more dramatic results, in both wealth and destruction, than at the end of the aqueducts and flumes that channeled millions of gallons of water every day to the hydraulic mines. Of all the tools the miners developed to move earth, none made more rapid progress than the metal and canvas inventions of the hydraulickers. They continually experimented with stronger hoses that could withstand greater pressures so that the force of water from their nozzles would have increased power to tear into the earth. By 1860 an inventor in Nevada City had patented a machine to produce canvas hose four layers thick, "sewn with four seams, thirty yards per hour." Subsequent improvement came with the reinforcement of closely spaced metal bands wrapping the canvas and secured with a tight rope netting. Known as "crinoline" hose, this advance allowed flexibility yet sustained so much water pressure that four, even six men were needed to hold the nozzle. The high-pressure jets produced powerful results. Entire hillsides dissolved in a rumble of falling rocks and chunks of earth. From the broken masses the nozzle men washed slurries "thick as mush" into sluice boxes, where riffles and other devices arrested most of the gold particles while a turgid current of mud and gravel flowed into nearby creeks or ravines.

As their operations and ambitions expanded, hydraulickers purchased sixteen- and twenty-inch iron pipe to increase the volume of water they could deliver to their claims. Shipped upriver as sheets of iron, the pipe was curved and riveted by blacksmiths in Sacramento and Marysville. Fabricators in Nevada City and other mining towns soon began ordering iron sheets and turning out their own lengths of pipe. Once again the need of miners—California's great economic catalyst—spawned new businesses and new opportunities for profit.

Assembling sections of pipe proved far easier and less costly than digging ditches or building flumes, and pipe could be disconnected, moved, and rejoined. Using pipe, hydraulic companies found they could deliver water from the nearest ditch or flume to previously inaccessible mining sites. At the junction where a pipe connected to a ditch or flume, a stout wooden "pressure box" or "bulkhead" enabled a water company to measure the number of miner's inches flowing each twenty-four hours to a particular mining site. One chamber in the box served to clean out sand, dirt, sticks, and other debris, while a "stilling well" removed air bubbles before the water flowed into a pipe.

From the pressure box, the pipe carried water down steep hillsides and bluffs to the "distributor," a cast-iron box designed to serve as a hydrant with valves that divided the rushing volume into two or more smaller sheet-iron pipes, each tapering to a short length of crinoline hose attached to a nozzle. Thus more than one part of a gravel bank could be hydraulicked simultaneously. By the mid-sixties the increased water pressures sometimes exceeded the strength of even the best reinforced hose. The crino-

line burst, leaving havoc. If only the nozzles could be connected directly to the iron pipe, eliminating the canvas's weak link. But how to do so without losing the flexibility to aim the nozzle where its hurtling stream would be most effective in cutting the bank? Until the answer came in 1870 (after years of inventive experimenting with "goosenecks" and ball-joint sockets), hydraulickers coped with hoses that burst, nozzles that tore free, accidents that killed workers. Yet faulty equipment and dangerous mishaps never slowed the washing of millions and millions of tons of earth as, year by year, the jets cut into the Sierra mountainsides to reach gold-bearing gravels.

The steady improvement of hydraulic technology—bigger pipes, stronger hose, tighter junctions—vastly expanded the demand for water, not only for the larger, more numerous nozzles but even more for removal of the large masses of collapsed earth. That was the crucial challenge: to move the entire overburden and the auriferous gravel (down to bedrock) into the sluices where minuscule particles of gold could be separated and captured by riffles, quicksilver, and ever more sophisticated traps. These colossal earthmoving operations along ridges between the Feather, Yuba, Bear, and American Rivers depended, above all else, on the reliable delivery of hundreds of millions of gallons of water every day.

Stimulated by the opportunity to pocket enviable new profits, water companies began to divert virtually the entire flow of mountain creeks and streams into their ditches and flumes. They appropriated lakes in the high elevations of the Sierra and built massive dams to hold back the abundant runoff from winter rains and spring snowmelt in reservoirs thus to have ample supplies through the dry summer months. By the 1870s the water companies (many owned by San Francisco capitalists) had created an immense system of lakes and reservoirs that fed into hundreds of miles of ditches, aqueducts, and flumes. Their engineers and carpenters even suspended some flumes—wooden chan-

Iron pipes and other supplies were shipped as far as giant freight wagons could be pulled by teams of horses or mules. At hectic transfer stations, teamsters unloaded their wagons and the freight was packed on the backs of mules for transport over rougher trails to the more remote outposts.

Most improvements in mining equipment gained their start from the primary rule, "let's see if it will work." This pressure box clearly required further refinement.

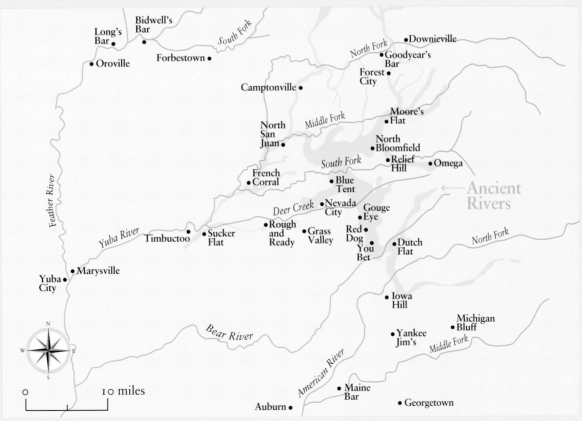

PRIMARY HYDRAULIC MINING REGION

nels of swift-flowing water—along sheer canyon walls above green threads of rivers far below.*

As water company work crews labored to build dams for reservoirs and miles of ditches and flumes through forests and along steep ridges, scores of teamsters guided loaded wagons over rough terrain to deliver planks and posts, picks and shovels, nails and lengths of pipe. Like determined army quartermasters, they reached even remote workers in places like Red Dog, Blue Tent, Moore's Flat, and You Bet to deliver, as well, flour and whiskey, beans and bacon, even an occasional billiard table. And they supplied the hydraulickers' crude camps with crinoline hose, nozzles, couplings, and valves.

Every day except Sunday, everyone could hear throughout those foothills the hissing roar of powerful jets as they cut deeper, excavating massive pits from which stretched long lines of sluice boxes, which added their own peculiar clatter of gravel and rocks rolling across the riffles, pushed along by torrents of reddish brown water. At the end of those sluices (some a thousand feet and longer), the debris-laden water discharged across hillsides and into creeks and ravines. There the rocks and gravel, mud and sand accumulated and overflowed,

---

* As water companies merged and consolidated, several became so large that they not only bought out their competitors but also acquired their own hydraulic operations. As of December 1865, one mammoth water-and-mining corporation—the Eureka Lake and Yuba Canal Company, Consolidated—had developed a reservoir system capable of supplying 85 million gallons every twenty-four hours to its extensive hydraulic sites, which yielded some $2 million annually.

In building many miles of flumes and scores of dams, water companies took timber as a free resource, without concern for ownership or payment, a practice encouraged in 1873 by advice from the U.S. commissioner of mining statistics: "Should much fluming be necessary and a great quantity of lumber have to be used for such purpose, the mountain slopes which flank the streams of California afford an inexhaustible supply of pine timber. . . . A portable sawmill could be established at any convenient point and would furnish all the necessary lumber."

sprawling and oozing into every declivity. Each year winter rains washed vast mounds of those tailings from clogged upland creeks down to the forks of the main rivers, which in turn carried the growing masses into the main channels of the Feather, Yuba, Bear, and American. And these tributaries disgorged their burdens into the Sacramento River.

In March 1860 the *Marysville Daily Appeal* described the Yuba as "that turgid vehicle of sediment." By summer the newspaper lamented: "Below its junction with the Yuba, the Feather is now a channel of muddy impurity, chocolate colored, narrow and shallow. Along its course great bars of sand are formed and forming, shifting their locality continually. In some places it is so narrow that a steamboat can barely pass."

As the discharge of debris filled channels and forced rivers out of their banks, the high water from winter rains caused floods more devastating than ever remembered. Heavy storms in November 1861 left deep snowdrifts in the Sierra. December and January brought warm tropical rains that deluged the mountains and foothills, causing a massive upstream runoff. When the surge hit Marysville, levees collapsed and over six feet of muddy water swept through the town, filling basements and ground floors with muck and sand. Hotels and numerous other large buildings crumbled as their foundations washed away. During the January flood, a steamboat churned its way through the downtown streets, unloading provisions on rooftops. In Sacramento another steamer swept through a break in a levee and grounded in an orchard at 23rd and B Streets. The force of floodwaters left ridges of sand and silt as much as eight feet deep in the capital city.

In the countryside, farm dwellings were swept away. Cattle by the tens of thousands drowned. When the water receded, some enterprising "silverliners" made big money by skinning hides from hundreds of carcasses. Few others could find reason to smile. The flood had scoured out a large part of the hydraulic tailings piled up in the mountain canyons, washing down millions of cubic yards of silt to settle over the flatlands. The editor of the *Daily Appeal* in late January 1862 described a desolate waste, a once fertile land plastered for miles with a heavy layer of muddy sand—slickens—two to seven feet in depth, "destroying all hopes of vegetation."

For George Briggs, that pioneer orchardist who had proved that farmers could make as much money as miners, the biblical disaster of January 1862 delivered an avalanche of mud three feet deep through his orchard of fifty-eight thousand fruit trees along the Yuba River above Marysville. He decided to give up. He moved to Santa Barbara, "where floods and slickens would not reach."

Briggs was luckier than others. Few farmers possessed the wealth to abandon their orchards and fields, buy new acreage somewhere safe from floods, and start anew. Even if they could move away, the very act of retreat would distance them from the profitable markets of hydraulickers, railroad workers, and the free-spending silver miners in Virginia City. What a perplexity. River bottomlands offered rich soil for growing fruit trees and vegetables and crops of wheat, barley, and hay, close to mining camps and towns, convenient to paddle-wheel transport to the urban markets at Sacramento and San Francisco. For farmers, it had been a profitable combination: fecundity and nearby customers.

But it was all changing. Orchards and fields disappeared each year under new layers of mining debris swept loose by the great jets that could melt gravel cliffs two hundred feet high. The farmers faced an untenable problem: their best customers were ruining their land.

Not only farmers felt the torment. The brown sludge threatened steamboat navigation as well. On October 28, 1862, the *Daily Appeal* complained that sand and gravel had accumulated in the Sacramento River "in a manner as to puzzle the most skillful and experienced of captains. The cause of this obstruction, at first confined to that portion of the mining streams lying within or near the

Up here in the mountains where we are all directly or indirectly connected with the business of gold mining . . . , we need no better laws and ask no better laws than those which our own experience and wisdom have enacted and sanctioned. . . . Our California miners wish to be let alone— by our legislators and by the federal government—and be permitted to manage their own affairs in their own way. A "masterly inactivity" in all that regards mining and mining interests is what miners ask of the legislators, and it is to be hoped that what is so modestly asked may not be churlishly denied.

Mining and Scientific Press, December 21, 1860

foothills, has been gradually pushing farther and farther down, with a motion something like that of alpine graciers till, accelerated by the great floods of last winter, it has found and choked the currents of the Sacramento River." By the mid-sixties, sand bars endangered stern- and side-wheelers' approach to the docks at Sacramento, and those river palaces scraped bottom or stuck fast on shoals of silt as far south as sixty miles from the capital city. No river captain showed more indignation than Enoch Fouratt of the *New World*. While ashore in Sacramento and San Francisco he growled to editors and local leaders his abhorrence of hydraulic mining. Loud and persistent, he warned that the life of his river was being choked by the miners' slickens, "an evil to be stopped at once, either by law or gunfire." In the years to come, both would be allies of rivermen and farmers in their desperate struggle to shut down what Thomas Starr King called California's "cash factories."

Yet through the decade of the 1860s even the Agricultural Society reflexively accepted the near-universal judgment that California's gold mines must retain their special, almost sacred status. In an 1865 answer to farmers who dared to propose restrictions on the hydraulickers, the society published a warning in its journal *Transactions:* "When you touch the mines with the hand of oppression, you oppress every other interest, and when you encourage and stimulate the development of the mines, you encourage and stimulate every other pursuit. In this respect, if not in actual investment of money, we are all miners and all cultivators of the soil." In an economy traditionally dependent on "yellow profits" from the mining industry, who would listen to the protests of a few farmers and riverboat captains? If not the Agricultural Society, then certainly not the legislators in Sacramento, who had little motivation to curtail the freedoms of an enterprise that put money in the pockets of everyone from San Francisco millionaires to Oroville blacksmiths.*

Many might nod in sympathy with Captain Fouratt, or with a farmer like Claude Chana, the hapless Bear River wheat grower whose farm by

---

* Hydraulic mining produced 90 percent of California's gold, even during the 1870s when money and expertise from the Comstock reinvigorated quartz mining at its primary centers around the towns of Grass Valley and Sutter Creek (in Amador County, to the south). Deeper shafts, longer tunnels, improved machinery (amalgamators, ore feeders), metallurgy, and chemistry contributed to increased profits. Reliable, long-lasting jobs in these mines and in related businesses—iron foundries, lumber mills, machine shops—established a degree of economic stability and even domesticity (miners brought their wives, children attended schools), that was most unusual in the Sierra foothills.

Though inconsequential in its importance to California's economy, a third source of gold had a considerable impact on the state's national, even worldwide image. Scattered along the western slopes of the Sierra throughout the 1860s and 1870s and in lesser numbers thereafter, uncounted hundreds of miners eked out their livelihoods from long toms and sluice boxes on remote claims at the end of winding mule trails. It was this fraternity of shaggy characters that Bret Harte made famous in his short stories, the first entitled "The Luck of Roaring Camp," published in 1868.

1875 lay smothered under twenty feet of slickens, but few would dare to challenge the hydraulickers directly. Scores of other farmers along the Bear, the Yuba, and the Feather watched floodwaters cover their dark topsoil with what the *Daily Appeal* in April 1862 described as "a slimey deposit." After the water receded, they found a crust "so deep that it cannot be plowed in, and bakes as hard as adobe and can only be turned up in huge chunks." Those who managed to till the new surface reported that land which once produced thirty to forty bushels of wheat per acre now grew no more than five, and potatoes, corn, and beans had "scarcely any yield" because their roots could not reach the nutrients in the now buried loam.

No matter the plight of the farmers, every effort of the miners was directed to increasing the daily volume of dirt washed through their sluices. Where jets encountered a bank of gravel so compacted— "cemented"—that it could not be disintegrated by the force of water, or where a bank had been cut away to a height so great that the nozzles could not be brought close enough to be effective without endangering the "pipers," hydraulickers resorted to "bank-blasting." Having driven a tunnel into the base of the bank a distance proportionate to its height and then extended cross-drifts parallel to the face of the bank (thus forming a T-shaped excavation), the miners placed a carefully calculated number of twenty-five-pound kegs of black powder inside the drifts. With the entry tunnel tightly closed, the fuse was lit, setting off an explosion of massive force. Among many blastings celebrated for their earthquake effect, one at Sucker Flat in December 1870 exploded two thousand powder kegs. Another detonation near Forest Hill raised an immense gravel bank "four or five feet, and the face was thrown forward," leaving a shattered mass of what had been cemented gravel, estimated at 500,000 cubic yards, ready to be washed by an array of nozzles.

As the new techniques brought down greater volumes of gravel, the hydraulickers harvested more

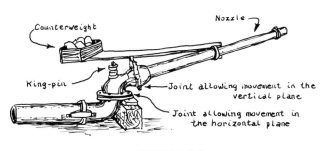

MONITOR

gold from their sluices and, inevitably, dumped more tailings into canyons and creeks. But even in towns blighted by the detritus, mining profits lavishly spent brought public acquiescence. The people of Oroville (on the Feather River thirty miles north of Marysville) lived with ditches cut through their streets, to carry debris from the mines in the nearby bluffs to the river.

In 1866 the editor of the local weekly welcomed completion of a new flume to deliver more water so hydraulickers could wash a "vast extent of land . . . to bedrock, yielding good pay." And when a new, "amazingly colossal" mine started washing in a steep ravine north of town, the same editor proudly described the effect of the great plumes of water: "The earth melts away and even the bed rock is torn up and thrown high in the air, shivered to atoms and whirled away" in a sluice four feet wide and a *mile* long that discharged the mine's mud, sand, and gravel directly into the Feather River. The same newspaper noted the consequences in November 1873: "Mining operations have so filled the bed of the river, both at the upper and lower end of town, that it is difficult to tell where the channel will be after another such flood as that of '62." Undeterred, mining continued, with more ditches, larger iron pipe, and higher water pressure melting ever more earth to clog the downstream arteries.*

Most important, the miners sought to increase the power of what one reporter called "this lance-thrust of water against the bank." Year by year their inventive tinkering yielded incremental improvements in the performance of hydraulic nozzles. Some variations leaked, others caused the nozzle "to fly around in a contrary direction," but each advance brought more durable connections between the nozzle and the water-delivering iron pipe, minimizing the use of weaker crinoline hose. In Dutch Flat in the spring of 1870, a miner named Richard Hoskins perfected and patented a joint that was not only pressure- and leak-proof but that permitted the free and controllable movement of the nozzle so that its "tremendous spout" could be directed easily in any direction. First called "Hoskins Dictator," the final evolution displaced all older inventions and quickly achieved general use as "Hoskins New Hydraulic Giant," soon shortened to "giant" or "monitor." Nine feet long, tapered to a muzzle diameter of four to nine inches, this cast-iron behemoth shot a stream of water "as hard to the touch as a bar of steel, retaining its cylindrical and solid shape till it strikes the gravel bank [two to three hundred feet distant]. At first shock, a thou-

---

* As the new technologies of hydraulic mining required larger areas within which to operate, the miners' local codes—"customary laws"—that had been operative since the 1850s (and had been legalized by the federal mining law of 1866) proved to be too restrictive. In 1872 Congress passed a general mining law that recognized all existing claims in the public domain and authorized increased size for new placer claims: 20 acres per person and 160 acres for a single association of at least eight persons.

Federal law also allowed the free appropriation and development of water rights on public land, thus greatly enhancing the progress of hydraulic mining. In effect, these laws reflected governmental and public acceptance, even endorsement, of resource exploitation by private interests.

Few sluice lines matched the industrial complexity of this one at Cherokee Flat, above the Feather River. From the uppermost overflows and grizzlies down to the two broad undercurrents in the foreground, the debris washed by the monitors flowed through a total of twenty-four undercurrents, each designed with myriad interstices (baited with quicksilver) to catch the last few particles of gold.

Having ravaged the hillside in the background, these pipers turned their monitor's tight shaft of power onto another target on the watershed of Amador Creek in the early 1870s.

The iron pipe (right) carried millions of gallons of water to the pressure box at the end of the rise, from which several smaller pipes delivered water to the company's monitors. The photograph below reveals more perfectly than almost any other the hot, sweaty, rip-it-up, what-the-hell enthusiasm and carelessness of those years when men created waterfalls and hooked up pipes and monitors to wash away hills, in the great business of hydraulic mining.

sand rays of water fly in all directions; a little later, the lance has buried itself deep in the bosom of the bank."

With such concentrated power, these giants collapsed even the most compacted bluffs and mountainsides more swiftly and cheaply than bank blasting, producing vast mounds of crumbled earth. Through muddy mists, the pipers directed their streams on the fallen masses of mud, sand, clay, and gravel, driving to the sides rocks two feet or more in diameter while always moving the main mass into the sluices. Hydraulic derricks moved larger boulders; in those that were too heavy, workers drilled holes for explosive charges that blasted them into manageable pieces, to be hauled away with trees and brush fallen from what had been their habitat atop the ever diminishing bank.

The same scene of orderly destruction unfolded day after day, sunup to sunset, at scores of hydraulic pits through the 1870s. Beneath the ceaseless cannonade, wet and muddy men operated derricks, exploded boulders, and grappled with debris, always conscious that a slip or fall could pin them under moving banks of gravel and rock. Below their battlefields, scores more labored at the sluice boxes, managing the alchemy that drew gold from mud. With their new power to rip open the earth (some companies operated four or five monitors simultaneously), the miners washed stupendous volumes of tailings into creeks and canyons that fed into the larger waterways. North of Oroville, the Spring Valley Mining Company expanded its operations (more water from a ditch company, more miners to direct the monitors) and emptied its sluices directly into Dry Creek, which in the winter of 1871–72 flooded grain fields and orchards. When the slickens killed A. J. Crum's peach trees eight miles downstream from the mine, he and his neighbors resolved to turn from angry talk to direct action. Crum filed a lawsuit against the company, demanding $2,000 in damages and an injunction to close the mine—the first skirmish in the coming conflict.

A jury of farmers and miners listened to strenu-ous defensive arguments of the sort that would be presented in future courtroom contests: it was impossible to know the source of the mud that killed Crum's fruit trees, since many companies had worked the deposits around Table Mountain; shutting down Spring Valley's giants would neither diminish the debris already spread along Dry Creek nor hold back more accumulations upstream; and the profits from just one day of mining exceeded the worth of all the farms damaged. In February 1873 the jury rejected the farmers' claim. Crum and his colleagues returned to their farms and cursed in bitter resignation when the muddy waters of Dry Creek next flooded their roads and fields, spreading new slickens.

In Sutter County on the west side of the Feather River a similar feeling of futility in April caused the *Weekly Sutter Banner* to predict doom: "The bed of the Yuba at Marysville is already some sixteen feet higher than it was twenty years ago. . . . The worst is yet to come. In less than two years the amount of washings will be double what it is now." Yet the townsfolk would not confront the hydraulickers; trade with the mining towns produced too much revenue. Instead citizens voted to pay more taxes to raise the town's protective levees. When a group of farmers in August 1874 called for a public meeting to protest the miners' debris, only a few discouraged orchardists came to the hall.

Unbeknownst to the victims of the slickens, their tormentors up in the hills were struggling with difficulties and expenses. As the hydraulickers' jets tore loose new masses of gravel from the towering cliffs, those thousands of tons of debris had to be constantly moved into the gold-catching sluice boxes, otherwise the accumulating mounds of rock, gravel, sand, and clay would pile up and smother the monitors. At those sites where the natural topography provided a slope from the base of the cliff, the force of water directed from the monitors, aided by gravity, could move the mass. But many pits were situated lower than the surrounding terrain, and channels had to be cut to carry the muddy flow to a point where the sluice boxes could be set up with the needed grade. In still less favorable locations the solution required the massive effort and expense of digging and blasting a vertical drain shaft into which all the debris could be washed, down to a tunnel cut through bedrock that led to a distant outfall where the tailings, having washed through a sluice on the floor of the tunnel, could be dumped into a canyon or ravine, out of the miners' way—and forgotten until they reached the farmers.

What a marvel it was, a water system of immense scope, embracing an impressive complexity and sophistication of engineering. The hydraulickers' vast network of dams and reservoirs, ditches, flumes, aqueducts, and iron pipes carried hundreds of millions of gallons of water along mountain ridges, across ravines, through tunnels to wilderness excavations where giant monitors the size of siege guns washed mountains into miles of sluices.* The single purpose of this audacious, nature-conquering enterprise was deceptively humble: to extract from prehistoric river gravels scatterings of gold dispersed in unpredictable concentrations, worth as little as two cents, or as much as fifteen dollars, a cubic yard. At the heart of that sprawling system, the sluice was all-important—its power to filter and retain those hidden particles determined the fate of every operation.

Planks, posts, braces, and sills by the millions of board feet were delivered from nearby sawmills for the construction of many miles of sluices, built according to the general principle that greater length always ensured "more perfect disintegration of the gravels and consequently a greater yield of gold."

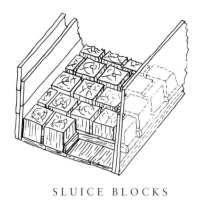

S L U I C E   B L O C K S

Extended length also served the need to carry the tailings as far from the hydraulic site as possible, to a distant dump, out of the way. The imperative of a steady fall over a long distance dictated how the sluice was constructed: laid on the ground where sloping terrain allowed, cut through topographic obstacles to maintain grade, or raised on trestles to span a ravine or creek. The steeper the grade, the more rapidly the volume of debris could be moved through the sluice box. However, a swift current would not release the finest "flour" gold. To form pockets of still water (as in a natural stream) where the tiniest particles of gold could settle, miners devised various kinds of riffles, using cobblestones or railroad rails or, most commonly, blocks of wood. A profitable product for sawmills, these pine blocks—cut as squares, or as rounds directly from trees—were spaced along the bottom of the sluice to provide quiet interstices and baited with quicksilver to catch and hold the gold. The constant abrasion of passing gravel rapidly wore down these blocks, necessitating replacement every week or two. Most mining companies burned their old blocks to release the tiny particles of gold lodged in the rough grain, often salvaging from the ashes enough gold to pay the sawmill for replacements.

Where the grade accommodated, carpenters built "drops," causing the muddy flow to fall from an upper to a lower sluice, thereby increasing disintegration of compacted clods. To remove some of the coarse and cumbersome gravel and rocks that would wear and tear the sides and bottom of the

---

* The water company supplying the North Bloomfield Gravel and Mining Company had eleven principal reservoirs that contained over two billion cubic feet, a resource none too great given the calculation that its customer's hydraulic operations consumed thirty-five cubic feet of water to move one cubic foot of gravel. Reservoir capacity of all water companies serving the primary hydraulic mining area—the Yuba, Bear, Feather, and American River region—exceeded 6.4 billion cubic feet.

If the debris pours into our rivers, it will find a place to fill—and it will keep on filling, filling and filling as it comes down upon us. . . . The time has come to act in self-defense or surrender the entire valley as a hydraulic dump.

Marysville Daily Appeal, February 23 and 24, 1878

sluice, a grate of iron bars—known as a "grizzly"—diverted this heavier debris to a dump on one side as the main flow fell through to a lower, continuing sluice. Where the terrain allowed, another screening refinement, the "undercurrent," provided a much wider (twenty to fifty feet) and more shallow auxiliary sluice into which a portion of the flow could be diverted, to pass more slowly over a specially designed grid of riffles. In these large, calmer platforms or "boxes," the elusive flour gold could more easily settle into the maze of interstices charged with quicksilver. At the end of the undercurrent, the gold-lightened flow returned to the main sluice, to be carried possibly to more undercurrents or directly to the final dump in a canyon or river.

Despite their elaborate systems for entrapping waterborne flecks of gold, the miners knew that at least 12 to 15 percent of their elusive quarry escaped, washed away in the opaque torrent, a loss they regretted far more than the suffering their slickens inflicted on the farmers and townspeople far below.*

---

* Not only finer particles of gold were lost, but significant quantities of quicksilver—mercury—flowed through the sluices and finally into the rivers. At the North Bloomfield Mine, for example, in the year ending November 1875 that company lost 1,242 pounds of quicksilver through the main sluice. The following year that loss increased to 2,556 pounds. Each of the major hydraulic operations released their corresponding share of mercury into the state's river system.

CONFRONTATION

To SHIELD THEIR HOMES, FIELDS, AND TOWNS FROM the miners' debris, farmers and local governments along the lower reaches of the rivers strengthened old levees and built new ones. They pursued these earthmoving projects without any coordination. Each farmer, each town raised embankments as money and equipment allowed, not pausing to plan collective action in the face of a collective danger. They built levees as they thought would best hold back the muck, even when construction of earthworks in one place made neighbors more vulnerable on the far side of a river or downstream. As mountain loggers cut any tree and water companies diverted any stream and hydraulickers destroyed any hill, constrained only by their reach, so in the valley, farmers and townspeople protected themselves from the anarchy upstream by building levees and berms just as haphazardly, subject to no flood control agency, guided only by their self-interest.

With horse-drawn scrapers, Ames shovels, and strong backs, farmers and townsfolk raised their ramparts. Even though the levees protecting Sacramento had repeatedly failed, what other practical recourse was there? Yuba City and Marysville, on opposite sides of the Feather River, built competing defenses, like suspicious feudal principalities. But the steady onslaught of debris flowing from the hills continued to raise the riverbeds. The main road north of Marysville, the route of commerce to the gold mining towns, flooded in 1866 and again in 1867. Its protection required an added tax to pay for a three-foot berm running seven and a half miles. When the December 1867 flood washed out a crucial embankment in Yuba City, the battered town began to question the practicality and cost of fending off the miners' unending flow of sand and stone.

At public meetings, in newspaper editorials and published letters, the valley folk debated their best defense. Some argued that only an extensive system of higher levees could protect them from the rising rivers. Other voices reflected a growing sense of despair: if silted riverbeds did not stop rising, the work of levee building would never end. George Ohleyer, an outspoken farmer familiar with mining, pushed his neighbors to admit what many tormented themselves to deny: their customers had become their enemy.

Like other farmers, George Ohleyer had ample reason to resent the hydrualickers. He had worked in the mines in 1852 and later bought land along the Yuba River where he planted an orchard. When the great flood of December 1861–January 1862 devastated his trees, Ohleyer reestablished himself on new land three miles west of Yuba City. By the 1870s he was farming several hundred productive acres. Not an unusual story, but Ohleyer showed more foresight and combativeness than others who would not look beyond the security of a levee. In a letter to the *Weekly Sutter Banner* printed on February 24, 1874, Ohleyer declared mining debris to be "an evil only palliated by levees, but not cured," and he warned that the security of levees "is delusive."

And then—the catastrophic flood of '75. Following a weeklong deluge, the brown waters of the Yuba River slapped against the top of Marysville's levees. At seven in the morning of January 20, 1875, the firehouse bell tolled its warning, sending a hundred volunteers racing to the levee. Despite frantic efforts, a crevasse opened near the cemetery north of town and the river's surge swept over the headstones and into the streets, washing through Thompson and Sons' broom factory and swirling into the hospital. Across the river, Yuba City's levee failed at about eleven o'clock, and that town was soon submerged. The next day water in Marysville's streets rose to eight feet. Overturned outhouses floated about; a little boy drowned. Men on rafts polling down F Street "maintained the best of spirits by frequent potions of something from black bottles," reported the *Daily Appeal.*

Weeks after the waters receded, citizens in both towns still toiled to dig out mud and gravel from streets, stores, and homes. A hard new layer of slick-

CHRONOLOGY (1860–1879)

1860	Abraham Lincoln elected president
1861	Civil War begins
	Transcontinental telegraph line completed
1862	Morrill Act establishes land-grant colleges
1863	Battle of Gettysburg
1865	Lee surrenders at Appomattox
	President Lincoln assassinated
1867	First oil wells drilled in California, at Ojai
	U.S. acquires Alaska ("Seward's Folly")
1869	Transcontinental railroad completed
	Suez Canal opens
1870	Rockefeller forms Standard Oil Company
	Franco-Prussian War
	Italy unified
1871	Germany unified
1872	Yellowstone Park created
1873	Big Bonanza strike in the Comstock
	University of California moves to Berkeley
1874	Barbed wire invented
1876	Bell patents telephone
	Southern Pacific Railroad extended south to Los Angeles
1877	Reconstruction ends; last federal troops withdrawn from the South
1879	California ratifies new constitution

ens overwhelmed any hope of restoration on many farms. The tragedy validated George Ohleyer's warning. Even the mining country's leading newspaper, the *Nevada City Daily Transcript*, reflected on the flood with surprising concern: "There is no doubt but a large share of the lands adjoining the rivers which carry the water from the mountains to the ocean have been flooded and irreparable damage has been the result. It is evident that no system of damming can prevent an overflow when such a freshet as the last occurs. What are the owners of farms to do? It is evident mining can never be stopped. It is an industry the whole world desires to foster. The government will encourage it, notwithstanding agriculture may suffer. . . . Each year adds to the amount of sediment deposited in the valleys. Fifty years hence the whole surface of the country will be raised much above its present level by the accumulation of dirt washed down from above. . . . So, the question becomes one of serious import. . . . What relief can be afforded we can not apprehend."

Like an apologetic manifesto, the paper's declaration foretold nothing but devastation for farmers—victims of the confident, indifferent hydraulickers.

What to do? How many would abandon their farms, like George Briggs, and simply move away? Most farmers had come to California as miners; they knew the pulse of gold fever and had shared the dreams of the men in the mountains. Back in '49 they had got California started, back when mining was mining, before millionaires and corporations in San Francisco hired men for a few dollars a day to work their hissing, roaring giants that sent slickens down to ruin other men. It was hard to be tolerant of a ruthless, heartless force that threatened thousands in order to make profits for a very damned few.

Another series of floods came in the fall of 1875; levees once again sagged beneath the swell of rising rivers. Angry farmers, now joined by town lawyers and businessmen, gathered at the city hall in Yuba City. They talked and listened and some shouted.

California state government, never a glorious achievement of probity and efficiency, sank in the 1870s to the nadir of disreputableness. San Francisco officials reverted to the roguery of the early fifties, while at Sacramento the manifestations of corruption were equally prominent. No branch of government seemed to be exempt, neither the courts, the tax assessors, nor the executive officers; yet it was the legislature that seemed to be guilty of the most flagrant abuses . . . engendered through the . . . precedents of vigilante days, the prevalence of speculative enterprise, the prominence of the nouveaux riches, and . . . the machinations of the railroad.

John Walton Caughey, *California*

George Ohleyer proposed that they petition the state legislature to regulate the practices of the hydraulickers "as may be just to all and benefit the greatest number." Many in the crowd cheered, but others felt the tug of trade with the mining communities and hung back. The debate continued in Marysville's city hall, where several more speakers argued for reliance on levees rather than a call to shut down the mines.

The crowds began to polarize between men who would take action and those who feared its consequences. A farmer named James Keyes stood in one meeting to tell of an experience that many in the audience, like George Ohleyer, knew intimately. After mining near Nevada City he bought two hundred acres on the Bear River—which were crusted by the slickens of 1862. Worse came in the fall of '75, when sand and mud three feet deep smothering his fields. Before neighbors and grave-faced men from nearby towns, Keyes concluded: "I have no objection to the miners digging out all the gold they can find, but I don't want them to send the whole side of a hill down on my ranch and bury me and all I have. And that is just what they have done and are doing. I want to be left alone. I don't know much about law and don't want to. If it is the law that one man shall use his property so as not to injure his neighbor, I should like to see that law put in force."

Despite the forcefulness of Ohleyer and Keyes, who represented those demanding an end to hydraulic mining, the crowd could agree only to appoint a committee to ask the state legislature to investigate the entire problem and another to urge the government in Washington to keep navigation open on the Sacramento River.

The debate continued in the press. Up in Nevada City the fiery editor of the *Daily Transcript* felt no sympathy for the country folk. "Supposing some one out of a dozen ranchers in Yuba County do have a half dozen acres of land covered with a coat of good mountain soil once in a while. Suppose a few sloughs are filled up above the level of a fever-breeding altitude, it won't hurt much. . . . Those ranchers depend upon the mountains to consume their produce and furnish them with coin, and we think they don't treat their customers well to try to kick up such a muss about a little matter."

In his Christmas Eve 1875 editorial, the editor of the *Sacramento Record-Union* worried about the future of navigation on the great river, and then set down the conundrum that perplexed everyone: "Of course there can be no question of stopping the development of the mines, but there is a strong question of the right of miners to destroy the valley lands in the way now proceeding. . . . The city of Sacramento is deeply involved, for disaster awaits her commerce and safety."

Back and forth it went. In San Francisco, the *Mining and Scientific Press* in January 1876 admitted to a certain ambivalence. "We confess we do not see any way out of the difficulty. . . . It is unjust to . . . yearly destroy crops, but it is also unjust to expect the miners to close their cabins. The miners were there first and claim the first right."

As the problem was "well ventilated" by the opposing editors, so it was vigorously debated in the state legislature, leading to a critical vote in March 1876. The farmers' faction supported a bill that would establish a commission to investigate the contentious issues, but the miners' allies, backed by the influence of San Francisco's capitalists, defeated the plan. One assemblyman warned that without a fair and open study "there would be riot and bloodshed between the parties contesting for their rights."

Shut out of the political forum, impatient farmers like Keyes and Ohleyer looked for a new recourse. They decided to talk to a lawyer. On the recommendation of a friend in the capital, they visited the office of a respected Sacramento attorney, George Cadwalader. One more of those remarkable, robust men who rushed to California in 1849, Cadwalader had arrived in the mines from Ohio at age nineteen and "panned out his share of gold." He later studied law, and in 1856 won his first case. Well known and successful by 1876, Cadwalader possessed an imposing figure "of giant stature. He creates the impression of immense strength. . . . He starts a case with caution, forecasts with prudence and moves forward with wide vision and firm purpose."

Unafraid of the farmers' powerful antagonists, Cadwalader encouraged Keyes to seek action through the courts as a more direct and possibly more rewarding strategy than contending against politicians. Heartened by this advice, Keyes and his allies decided to ask this courtroom master to accept their meager resources and their case. This proved a fateful expression of trust. In the coming struggle, George Cadwalader would dominate the field against counsel better paid and better pedigreed. Cheered by the farmers, hated by the miners, at the weary end he would emerge as the catalyst whose dogged campaign brought to account the forces contending for California's future.

In April 1876 Cadwalader sent an agent (disguised as a potential investor) into the hills to establish the ownership of the hydraulic mines that sent their tailings into the Bear River and its tributary

To catch particles of gold in their interstices, thousands of rounds cut from tree trunks were used to line the bottoms of sluice boxes. These laborers unloaded one of many wagons delivering rounds destined for the sluices that emptied into the Yuba River.

Two jets, two pipes, and two sluice lines formed a tracery across the rocky floor of the Malakoff Mine.

creeks and hollows. He returned with a list of nineteen names, including London investors, San Francisco capitalists, and a few local residents. Cadwalader needed these identities because he intended to sue each and all, together, in order to avoid the legal pitfall that had sunk the farmers' case against the Spring Valley Mining Company. He filed the case of *James Keyes vs. Little York Gold and Water Company et al.* on July 29, 1876, naming all those who dumped debris into the Bear River as collectively responsible and liable for the sprawling mass of gravelly muck that flowed from their pits into the valley. The court would be asked to grant a perpetual injunction against their further dumping of debris. And Cadwalader would petition for damages of $10,000 to recompense Keyes for the silting of his farm.*

Seeing this legal action against nineteen companies as a serious threat to their industry, mine owners, partners, and superintendents not just from the defendant companies but from operations all over the northern Sierra foothills traveled to San Francisco in September to meet with the capitalists who had invested millions in the water systems and hydraulic operations. After careful consultations (which contrasted sharply with the farmers raucous meetings), the miners and their financiers formed a protective alliance they called the Hydraulic Miners Association. As a mutual defense league, the association would challenge any lawsuit that sought to limit a member's right to dispose of mining debris.

The association would also seek to prevent passage of any state or federal law which might "interfere with or embarrass the operations of hydraulic mining in California." Within a few weeks, every important company in the business—a total of ninety, most of them in Nevada County—had signed the association's Articles of Agreement.

With their adversary building strong defenses and far better funded, the farmers received more dismaying news. In November on the opening day in court, the miners' attorneys, over Cadwalader's objections, obtained a change of venue, moving *Keyes vs. Little York et al.* from the state to the U.S. district court, where the more ponderous federal system would thwart a quick verdict and favor the defense because of its slower, more expensive legal process and layers of appeal, which could lead as far as the United States Supreme Court.

The mild winter of 1876–77 gave the farmers a season free from floods, and that summer the Sacramento Valley prospered with bountiful crops. Profits encouraged amity, which found expression in the farmers joining several mining companies (which put up $30,000) to pay for new levees to safeguard thousands of acres of rich bottom lands. Marysville and Yuba City spent tax monies to strengthen their surrounding barriers. Farmers planted wheat in lowlands they had feared must be abandoned. The future looked more secure, more hopeful.

But the peace and hopes of 1877 were washed away by fierce storms in January 1878. The Sacramento River rose higher than anyone could remember, in part because of the confining levees (as Ohleyer had forecast) and also because its bed was filled with debris. In February the muddy waters overwhelmed the levees to the west and south of the capital. Then the Bear River broke free, submerging vast areas of the countryside. The Feather and Yuba swelled and sprawled, as did the American—all the rivers where the hydraulickers had been most active. Protected by their newly buttressed levees, the cities of Sacramento, Marysville, and Yuba City seemed

---

*While the major hydraulic operations were concentrated on the watersheds of the Feather, Yuba, Bear, and American Rivers, other hydraulickers worked lesser ancient river channels to the south, primarily above the Cosumnes River in Amador County. And there, too, the farmers suffered from slickens. In an 1876 lawsuit they sued the Sacramento and Amador Canal Company for damages. In February 1877 the court ruled in favor of the farmers and awarded them $4,000. On appeal the decision was reversed but without resolving any of the primary issues of farmers' and miners' rights.

to float like islands in a brown sea. Hundreds of livestock stood forlornly on surviving sections of levees. The forks and limbs of trees held drowned or starved rabbits and wild hogs.

In the mountains, the miners welcomed "their" weather with its drenching rains that kept reservoirs bulging, ditches and flumes running full, monitors smashing their jets against mountainsides, and sluices gorged with ore-bearing gravel.

From the deck of a river steamer in early March, a reporter for the *San Francisco Daily Evening Bulletin* looked out at the "wild waste of waters, broken levees, rows of earth bags, fences peeping out of the water, and houses in the water. . . . The beautiful orchards were either in the water or covered with slime. . . . During the recent flood the population along the river fought the floods as men never fought anything else since the world began, but all in vain."

Feeling duped by the miners and by their own hopes, the valley folk raged at their tormentors. Surveying the flood damage, the *Sacramento Record-Union* set restraint aside. "All pretense that the miners are adding to the wealth of the state by their operations is mere moonshine." And in Marysville, the *Daily Appeal* warned: "We say it is a question of life or death between [the two] interests. One must quit. If the debris is to come, the agriculturists must pack up and go."

Equally angry, the miners' voice shouted back. Having condemned the farmers' "sophistical reasonings," the *Nevada City Daily Transcript* scoffed at the "long-winded imprecations hurled against the very industry that alone of all other agencies has been the means of placing California where it now stands."

Preoccupied by the winter's disasters, most people in the valley were unaware of the United States Supreme Court's decision in January 1878 that *Keyes vs. Little York et al.* should be heard not in the federal court system but rather in the local state court. That news put Cadwalader to work through the spring of 1878 preparing the farmers' case for

TAILINGS

trial in Yuba City before District Judge Phil Keyser. Mining company attorneys on the defense team visited farms along the Bear River to assess evidence, and they closely studied the Spring Valley Mining Company case of 1873.

In mid-July, sweltering heat did not keep scores of out-of-towners—reporters, witnesses, attorneys and their assistants, as well as curious farmers and miners—from crowding the hotels, saloons, and eateries of Yuba City and Marysville. On July 25, 1878, Judge Keyser called for order in his courtroom, and the long-awaited trial got under way.

The first witness, James Keyes, testified to the long record of destruction, beginning with the floods of 1861–62 and continuing through those of the winter just past. He described the Bear River as running "promiscuously all over the bottoms, shifting around and overflowing land formerly high. . . . In front of my place in 1856 the river ran clear, over a gravely bottom, with abrupt banks about twelve feet high. The old channel filled entirely in the winter of 1867–68. . . . Some of my land was filled above the fences. . . . In the last three years my land has suffered from damaging overflows four times. The deposits destroyed my land's productiveness. I formerly raised fifty to sixty bushels of barley and thirty to forty of wheat to the acre. Last year I raised less than ten of wheat and this year not over five. . . . I have made an effort to protect my land by spending $15,000 in leveeing, but I will probably be overflowed next winter and my entire levee destroyed."

Through the days that followed, farmer after farmer told of once rich land "entirely destroyed," of homes deep in mud, of summer dust and grit blown from slickens. With sorrowful nostalgia, one witness recalled the Bear River in the 1850s "when I saw hundreds of salmon and I killed seventeen in an hour with my shotgun. During the last sixteen years I have not seen any at all."

Arguments for the defense reemphasized long-established contentions: that shutting down the monitors would not prevent further flows of debris from the vast accumulations in canyons and creekbeds; that the value of mines far exceeded the value of farms. Some defense witnesses insisted that the debris added rich soil to the farmers' fields. Above all else, the miners' attorneys asserted their clients' right to discharge debris because they had gained that right by prescription, meaning by long and continued practice before the farmers started their complaints. Expert witnesses affirmed that "the custom of dumping tailings in the ravines and streams is the only way these mines can be worked to advantage and profit." Mine owners were appalled that consideration could be given to shutting down an industry that employed 5,000 men, supported Nevada County's population of 25,000 to 30,000, that had invested in its equipment and tunnels and facilities many millions of dollars, $2 million by the North Bloomfield Company alone. As to gold production, they boasted of $12 to $14 million annually. And most important, the miners emphasized that not one tenth of the gold-bearing gravels had yet been washed. All this present and future wealth would be destroyed if the farmers prevailed.

For two weeks Cadwalader and his opponents questioned and cross-examined witnesses. Each day reporters sent their editors dispatches describing in surprising detail—sometimes verbatim—the often arcane evidence. In column after column, thousands of words, the trial's progress was followed in the

Mining and Scientific Press, the *Pacific Rural Press,* the *Alta,* the *Record-Union,* and most avidly in the *Daily Appeal* and its rival the *Daily Transcript.* Many other newspapers gave extensive coverage because, as the *Stockton Independent* explained, everyone recognized the paramount importance of this first challenge to the gold miners whose success had for so long been the very success of California. Nonetheless, the length of the trial wearied even the *Daily Appeal* which complained about the paid, professional witnesses, "the professors who testify ad nauseam."

On August 9 Judge Keyser closed the testimony and retired to contemplate his verdict. Tense months would pass before he handed down his decision. Meantime, the arguments continued in the newspapers, more vociferous than ever and read with growing anxiety by the mutually distrustful populations of the valley and the mountains, who were warned of an "irrepressible conflict."

Worried by newspaper reports that San Francisco's capitalists had richly financed the Hydraulic Miners Association, and discouraged by the delays and expenses of the legal system, the farmers decided they too must organize and raise money for the months ahead. At a Yuba City meeting on Saturday afternoon, August 24, 1878, James Keyes quieted the crowd gathered in the courthouse. Farmers and businessmen from as far as Sacramento listened to speeches—"it is absolutely necessary to unite and organize the agriculturalists to successfully combat the capital arrayed against us"—and then passed a motion to create their own defense league, to be known as the Anti-Debris Association of the Sacramento Valley.

More populist than their rivals, the farmers opened their association to anyone who would sign its articles. Under the guidance of five directors, elected by the membership, the association would prosecute to a final decision the *Keyes vs. Little York et al.* lawsuit and initiate and prosecute any other legal action judged necessary to halt the miners' use of the region's rivers as dumping grounds.

Beneath a tin horse suspended by wires from rooftops (to advertise a livery stable), citizens paused for a photographer's image of Mill Street, Grass Valley, in the early 1870s. Shaded sidewalks, street planking, and a general air of prosperity reflected the town's importance as the center of hard-rock mining in the northern gold region.

In 1870 Marysville was still the third largest city in California. Within its high levees, the streets—like this section of Second Street—were lined with thriving stores. The business directory for the state in 1867 listed 279 commercial enterprises in Marysville, compared to 130 for Los Angeles. Most photographers of California towns sought to record a view that hid, or at least minimized, the bleak and run-down aspects of the place. In vivid, almost painful contrast, the photograph below presents a view of the mining town Dutch Flat in all its cut- over, hydraulicked, no-one-cares ugliness.

*To ride from Marysville eastward along the
Yuba is one of the saddest journeys imagin-
able. Here, on both sides of the river, were
once wide bottoms of fertile soil, farmed and
used for grain, fruit, and vegetables and
considered safe from overflow. Now this
lower bench of land is overflowed at each
slight rise. It is a swamp of willows, cotton-
woods, and vines; a malarial and pestilential
waste where bars of white sand and pools of
slimey water glisten through the saplings.
. . . The first Briggs orchard . . . , once the
most valuable orchard in the state, is now a
tangled mass of willows and a waste of
white sand and yellow slickens. . . . As we
ride eastward along the river, every farmer
has the same story to tell. The lost Eden of
these beautiful bottom lands seems to haunt
the people forever. Ghostly, too, along the
verges of the willows are the brown, rain-
beaten, decaying houses and barns, long ago
deserted.*

San Francisco Daily Evening Bulletin, July 2, 1879

To raise money, the association assessed its members a fee proportional to their assets, taking in an
impressive initial subscription of $170,000. Thus
organized and armed, the farmers looked to Judge
Keyser for the vindication they believed a fair decision would bring, and they expressed to Cadwalader their resolution to continue the fight come
what may.

Keyser did not disappoint them. On March 10,
1879, he found in favor of the farmers, ruling that
the miners had "not acquired any right to use the
bed of Bear River nor the beds of its tributaries as a
place of deposit of their mining tailings, nor to
choke and fill with such tailings the channels of Bear
River nor to flow or overflow plaintiff's lands with
such tailings"; that hydraulic mining as practiced

constituted a nuisance and an obstruction to the free
use of the plaintiff's lands and that the defendants
(he cited thirty-three Bear River companies) were
"perpetually enjoined and restrained from fouling
and corrupting the water of the Bear River and its
tributaries with tailings or debris"; and finally that
Keyes was entitled to recover the costs of his
lawsuit.

A magnificent victory. Congratulations to
George Cadwalader. Glorious celebrations in Yuba
City and Marysville and farm houses throughout
the Sacramento Valley. All this for a few hours.
Then came the shock of legal obstructions: the min-
ers' attorneys would file an appeal.

From Yuba City the case moved to the California Supreme Court in Sacramento and dragged
through new months of legal maneuvering. In spite
of Judge Keyser's stern admonitions, the monitors
and sluices never ceased their destructive work and
the rivers continued to run brown. How would the
high court rule? The *Nevada City Daily Transcript*
boldly offered the answer: "Common justice
demands that hydraulic mining be permitted to go
on undisturbed. We cannot believe the Supreme
court will sustain Keyser's decision."

Rather than wait for that fateful verdict, the
farmers accepted George Cadwalader's advice that
they seek for the Yuba River the same remedy they
hoped to gain for the Bear. Therefore, the Anti-
Debris Association and the city of Marysville
decided to take on the largest and most powerful of
all the hydraulic operators. On September 15, 1879,
Cadwalader filed suit in the Yuba County Court:
*The City of Marysville vs. The North Bloomfield
Gravel Mining Company et al.* Among the charges,
he asserted that the city had lost its clear water, its
harbor, most of its water commerce, much of its
taxable property, its system of drainage, and
$300,000 spent on levees that failed to protect its
residents. In a final flourish of confidence, he asked
not for damages but for a permanent injunction
against dumping debris in the rivers.

After Cadwalader served papers on the North

Bloomfield Company and other Yuba River hydraulickers, the *Nevada City Daily Transcript* on November 6 scoffed: "Miners will for the present at least pay about as much attention to these writs as they do to the blowing of the winds." But to everyone's surprise, the Hydraulic Miners Association offered the city $30,000 or more to pay for half the cost of building higher protective levees.

As if to provide more pressure, the *Daily Transcript* printed a threat, not even veiled. "If Marysville were to win her suit, she would still perish from . . . the certain loss of trade with the mining counties, out of which she has prospered and supported herself. . . . If she will now come forward, dismiss all thoughts of coercion and ask the aid and cooperation of the miners to withstand the threatened injury she complains of, our word for it and she will be met half way . . . and she can retain the friendship of the miners, as well as their trade."

Threatened or not, the Marysville city council sensed victory in the court and refused the Miners Association attempts at settlement, seeing them as confirmation of the strength of the city's case.

The miners' appeal of the Keyes case still awaited the Supreme Court's decision. That verdict would show whether the farmers' new confidence had merit. On November 17 waiting reporters, farmers, and miners at the court heard the announcement: the Supreme Court ruled against the farmers. Its reasoning followed the decision in the Spring Valley case, applying the argument that just as a single mining company could not be traced to an undivided mass of debris, so a group of mining companies could not be held liable for damage caused by debris impossible to assign specifically to any one of the companies. In essence, the court said liability could be established only when a plaintiff could prove which mine sent down the debris that ruined a particular farm or city property—knowledge that could not be devined. For Cadwalader and the farmers the news meant defeat—total and costly. As the *Daily Transcript* chortled, "The decision . . . knocks Marysville's suit into a cocked hat."

VICTORY!

The Supreme Court Gets Down to its Knitting !

And Fires the Slickens Case out of the Window !

How the News was Received—
Flying Flags and Booming
Bells, Crashing Cannons,
Blowing of Steam
Whistles, etc.

DAILY TRANSCRIPT,
NOVEMBER 18, 1879

In the mountains the miners celebrated with wonderful exuberance. In Nevada City at three o'clock one hundred cannons fired, church bells rang, "bombs exploded and steam whistles on the mining works blew. It was one of the biggest jubilees Nevada City has ever had. Men were going up and down the streets adding to the racket by hurrahing like mad." Miners in Grass Valley filled the streets, shouting and congratulating each other. The population of Rough and Ready turned out en masse and fired one hundred guns. In addition to these excitements, the *Daily Transcript* reported, "at Little York giant powder burned and the citizens yelled themselves hoarse. But the boss blowout was over at Dutch Flat. The Flatters turned themselves loose and with guns, bells, brass bands, dinner horns, tin pans, and everything else that would make a noise created enough racket to waken the dead. There was also a procession and fireworks. Phil Nichols, the banker, went to the various saloons and left orders to set up everything the boys called for and send their bills to him."

Flush with victory and liquor, the miners knew that gold still ruled California. How could it be otherwise?

In contrast to the destructive forces of hydraulic mining, wheat farming could be romanticized, as in this painting of harvesting in the San Joaquin Valley, by William Hahn.

VICTIMS OF
SUCCESS

Admired as an example of engineering skill, the English Dam was built in the Sierra Nevada to form a reservoir from which ditches and flumes carried water to distant hydraulic operations.

Standing amid a supply of sluice blocks, the man at the lower left provides a sense of scale in this scene of devastation wrought by the force of a monitor.

Water companies invested many thousands of dollars in the construction of flumes, like these that dominated the town of North San Juan, near the Malakoff Mine.

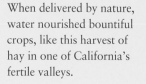

When delivered by nature, water nourished bountiful crops, like this harvest of hay in one of California's fertile valleys.

CHAPTER SEVEN

VICTIMS OF SUCCESS

At the polished rosewood bar of the Palace Hotel in San Francisco and in private dining rooms foggy with cigar smoke, officers and principal investors of hydraulic mining companies savored bright prospects for the 1880s and beyond. Years of robust experimentation, failed plans, and staggering investments (estimates: $30–$50 million) were about to reap their full reward. Through vast systems of reservoirs, flumes, monitors, sluices, and bedrock tunnels, the hydraulickers controlled an industrial process capable of recovering millions of ounces of gold. For the years ahead, mining profits would be far more dependable than the gamble of river mining or the blind chance of hard-rock tunneling, and a far cry from the primitive days of long toms and ground sluicing.

Geologists and mining superintendents confirmed vast reserves of ore-bearing gravel within reach of the mining companies' monitors—700 million cubic yards between the middle and south forks of the Yuba River and as much more beyond. Estimates varied, but calculations offered good reason to expect steady profits for at least fifty years. Never had California's miners contemplated anything comparable. San Francisco newspapers and New York magazines sent correspondents to the watersheds of the northern tributaries of the Sacramento River to describe the awesome sight of hydraulic mines at work. Their accounts affirmed that California's alchemy had not failed: thirty-one years after the gold rush began, inventive and risk-taking miners were still extracting millions in gold from gravel and mud.

While silk-hatted capitalists toasted their prospects with champagne, California's entrepreneurial farmers also anticipated healthy profits in the decade ahead. In the Sacramento and San Joaquin Valleys wheat ranchers had developed an industry that extracted a new kind of gold from the soil: wheat, harvested by the millions of bushels and exported to world markets (57 million bushels in 1884). One wheat baron banked $800,000 from his 1880 harvest of the golden grain. Using giant machines specially built for planting and harvesting across "ranches" as large as 60,000 acres, these wheat growers defied the traditions of farming and mined California's soil with an avarice equal to that of the hydraulickers.

River valley fruit and vegetable growers also looked forward to prospects that brightened their future. They saw in the transcontinental reach of the Central Pacific Railroad the opening of new markets for their perishable produce, thereby freeing them from the limitations of local demand. California inventiveness and entrepreneurial risk-taking developed ice-cooled ventilation for railroad freight cars and by the mid-1880s offered ever more dependable refrigeration for shipment of fresh produce to midwestern cities and beyond. But would the growers' orchards and fields survive the reality of floods and slickens to enjoy the promise of new markets?

Generous with its abundance, in the 1880s California would falter in its role as sustainer and patron of the ambitions and dreams of all of its wealth-seekers. The happenstance of geography placed miners and farmers so close that inevitably the destructive processes of the one interfered with the productive cycles of the other.

The hydraulickers had buried thousands of acres of rich bottomland beneath the alluvium that spewed from their sluices. Annual floods drove hundreds of farm families from their homes and forced towns to cower behind protective levees of uncertain endurance. The miners' slickens had so shoaled the Sacramento River that Marysville was closed to steamboats and Sacramento looked to be next. Vital connections to markets and suppliers would be interrupted. And all this just as growers anticipated opportunities to sell their bounty in far-distant cities.

The issue at stake was nothing less than the fundamental concept of property. A resolution in May 1882 by an Anti-Debris Convention in Sacramento called on the sate attorney general "to test the right of one man in pursuit of wealth to destroy the property of another."

The hydraulickers felt protected by gold mining's legacy as the dominant economic force in California, the engine of progress. They claimed privilege, not only because miners had arrived first, but because their economic contributions meant more to the state than those of anyone else. They did not know, or would not acknowledge, that by the 1880s the value of the state's agricultural production had surpassed the output of mining.

Seeking to mediate, the governor of California in 1881 supported a "compromise" plan alleged to protect both miners and farmers, but its bias in favor of the traditional power of gold revealed his true allegiance. In their frustration, the farmers and their allies turned once again to the courts to seek new injunctions that would stop the surges of slickens. In 1884, as if plotted by a dramatist, the circling antagonists came together in a final showdown. In the federal courtroom of a pensive jurist who had come to California as a '49er, a fifteen-month legal confrontation would produce a decision neither side could ignore. For goldseekers, thirty-five years of unrestrained freedom hung in the balance.

The entrepreneurial spirit that the '49ers brought to California had infused every other activity in the state and nurtured in agriculture ambitions and technologies as aggressive and original as those of the miners. Like an impatient second generation that proclaims "It's our turn," the growers and their allies would not let the miners' success eclipse their own.

BUILT OF HEAVY, INTERLOCKING TIMBERS, the main dam of the Milton Mining and Water Company, 400 feet wide and 125 feet high, loomed above the channel of the Middle Yuba River. At daybreak on June 18, 1883, key supports in the dam's upper structure suddenly gave way and 650 million cubic feet of water began to move. As the dam collapsed, water thundered through a widening gap for an hour and a half, an immense wave that tumbled ten-ton boulders, smashed through two lower dams, flooded a drift mine, brushed aside Freeman's toll bridge, scattered cabins and barns, and broke through a levee sixty miles to the west, above Marysville. The avalanche of water claimed two lives and wiped out the Milton Company's operations for the season.

Within hours miners began to spread a report that "the dam was blown up by powder." The Milton Company offered a $5,000 reward for evidence leading to the arrest of "the wreckers" of its great English Dam (so named because of its original British ownership). The *Nevada City Daily Transcript* repeated the rapidly spreading accusation that

"anti-miners" had sabotaged the reservoir. A few days later that newspaper mocked its rivals: "The Sacramento Bee, Marysville Appeal, and all the other anti-mining papers have struck it big by the breaking of the English Dam. They had about exhausted their supply of subject matter to misrepresent the miners." And later came the sneering question: "Must millions of dollars worth of property in the mountains be destroyed . . . to save a few sections of bug-eaten soil in the lower country?"

On August 24 the *Daily Transcript* reported that hydraulic mining companies, alarmed by the "wanton destruction of the English dam," had hired "men armed with repeating rifles to patrol the reservoirs and to send to their reckoning any property-wrecking powder-fiends who may try to emulate the deed of the dastardly wretches who did such effective work a few weeks ago."*

---

* No arrests came and no evidence corroborated the miners' accusations. No other dam suffered similar structural failure.

Immense as it was, the English Dam did not compare to the largest reservoirs in the networks of other hydraulic companies. Seven years earlier the North Bloomfield Gravel and Mining Company had enlarged its Bowman Dam, on a tributary of the South Yuba River, to retain up to one billion cubic feet of water. From the reservoir behind that stone structure, ditches and flumes delivered water across fifty-five miles of mountain terrain to the big monitors at North Bloomfield's principal operation, the Malakoff Mine. Three other company reservoirs held a total of 820 million cubic feet. By the time of the English Dam's collapse, eleven reservoirs built by the North Bloomfield Company provided a capacity of 2.2 billion cubic feet of water (16.5 billion gallons) for its growing network of ditches and flumes. Costing the company's investors over $4 million, this water empire served the Malakoff pit where the cast-iron monitors each shot out 35 to 40 million gallons every twenty-four hours as they cut into the gravel bank estimated to measure 4,000 feet in width by 175 to 600 feet in depth, a mass said to contain 348 million cubic yards of ore-bearing gravel. "Enough to wash for the next fifty years," the company's investors were advised.*

How much gold might there be in that vast mountain of boulders, rocks, gravel, sand, and clay, some of it loose, some of it compacted, most of it auriferous? North Bloomfield's superintendent-engineer, Hamilton Smith Jr., estimated the yield would range from a few cents per cubic yard in the upper strata to $5.40 in the rich gravel near bedrock. He projected the total value of the Malakoff's gold at almost $70 million. This was the number that moved the mine owners to invest millions in North Bloomfield, confident of the hydraulickers' old shibboleth, "The more dirt washed, the more gold saved"—348 million cubic yards to yield $70 million.

By the decade of the eighties, both friend and foe agreed that North Bloomfield had come to symbolize the hydraulic industry. One contemporary Nevada County historian observed: "As an example of a mammoth hydraulic enterprise, this company is unequaled." Mining engineers admired its reservoirs, water systems, tunnels, and sluice lines. Investors envied its financial strength and rich prospects for profits. Editors cited its daring vision and efficient practices as exemplary of California's prowess. Farmers and townsfolk feared North Bloomfield as the embodiment of the miners' arrogant carelessness. And for the general public, the company represented all that was either superlative or reprehensible about modern placer mining.

Consuming ever more water and employing more powerful jets to cut into their cliffs of gravel, hydraulic companies struggled with the mounting problem of moving thousands of tons of accumulated gravel away from the cliff base and into their sluices. Endless washing often wore a swale in front of the cliffs, thus requiring the pipers to waste water and time pushing the mass uphill and into the sluices. Equally troublesome, the tailings at the end of some sluices buried creeks and ravines, thus preventing further dumping. Without adequate dumps, some mines, as early as the 1870s, had to shut down. Others relocated their sluices, at great expense.

To move the gravel quickly from the cliffs, the best-capitalized companies invested in vertical shafts dropping into bedrock tunnels that carried the debris over a system of sluices and undercurrents, finally to a distant dumping site that offered long-term capacity. To secure such an outlet, the North Bloomfield Company undertook one of the most ambitious engineering projects in the history of California mining.

By sinking a small prospecting shaft to probe the

---

*The state mineralogist in 1882 emphasized the hydraulic industry's appetite for vast water resources by reporting the consumption figures for the North Bloomfield Gravel and Mining Company during a ten-month period: 18.5 billion gallons used to wash 4.77 million cubic yards of gravel, each yard yielding gold worth 5.6 cents. Thus the company used 69,250 gallons of water for each dollar of gold collected from its sluices.

After spring runoffs, the reservoir behind the Bowman Dam held as much as one billion cubic feet of water to supply the North Bloomfield Gravel and Mining Company's operations at its Malakoff Mine.

The intricacies, the precision, the expense evident in this aqueduct of the Miocene Mining Company (near Oroville) suggest profits for sawmills and wages for carpenters—and decimation for nearby forests.

Giant monitors used the power of water as never before imagined. These fifteen-foot nozzles turned mountain stream water into a blasting agent of immense power. And the spent water carried gold to the waiting sluices. No black powder could do that.

The operation of washing down the banks is called by the miners "piping.". . . It requires both skill and judgment to be a good pipeman. The water must be used without clogging the channels. The term "goosing" is used to express the driving of the debris before the stream, and "drawing" when the stream is thrown beyond and causes the debris to flow toward the nozzle. . . . No person who has not seen them in operation can have an idea of the force of these streams. If a giant nozzle should be set in front of the strongest building in San Francisco and a stream turned on it, the walls would melt away in a few minutes.

Second Report of the State Mineralogist, 1882

substrata, Superintendent Smith discovered that the gravel beneath his nozzles extended down 208 feet to bedrock. The most profitable ore in that mass, as always, lay at the bottom. Known as "blue gravel" (the objective of all hydraulickers), this deposit was 130 feet thick, resting on metamorphic slate. Smith set his workers to the task of opening a larger shaft, framed with heavy planking, down through the gravel and then down another seventy-five feet into the slate. At the bottom of this access shaft, his men started drilling and blasting a tunnel that would reach over a mile and a half through the bedrock to its planned outlet above Humbug Creek, which flowed into the deep canyon of the South Yuba River—an ideal place to dump tailings, forever.

Pressed by the North Bloomfield owners to complete this vital outlet as quickly as possible, Smith hired 175 men in April 1872 to sink seven more shafts along the line he had surveyed for the route of the tunnel.* Dug by hand labor and by the blasting force of newly introduced "Giant Powder" (an early form of dynamite), each shaft was excavated to the depth of the tunnel-to-be, and at that level the

workers at the bottom of each shaft began digging horizontally in both directions. This double-time tactic required close calculations by Engineer Smith to ensure that the separate segments of the tunnel would line up as the tunnelers dug through the hard slate toward one another.

The Malakoff tunnel drivers bored powder holes using the same hand-held drills that had been employed in the high Sierra by the Central Pacific Railroad builders, wresting the same slow progress of a foot or so at each face during three eight-hour shifts, always in danger, always laboring in the dim light of flickering candles. In 1873 a newly invented drilling machine, driven by water pressure and armed with a diamond-pointed bit, came into use, dramatically increasing the tunnelers' progress. Finally in November 1874 the eight sections were cut through and joined, to form a single tunnel 7,874 feet long—"an operation of the most stupendous character," boasted the *Daily Transcript.* And so it was, even in those years of nothing-is-impossible ambition.

Despite that tunnel's cost of $550,000, the owners of the North Bloomfield company directed their engineers to open five branch tunnels—a total of 20,000 feet through bedrock—each connected to a vertical shaft into which monitors could wash millions of cubic yards of gravel from the cliffs of the Malakoff pit. These shafts had two or three terraces or steps. As the mass of rocks, gravel, and sand fell twenty feet or more from one level to the next, each impact helped disintegrate compacted chunks before the torrent flowed into the sluices and over their riffles through the length of the tunnel. At the end of the Malakoff's main tunnel, the thick

---

* Newspaper reports and official records vary in their estimates as to the number of men employed in driving the North Bloomfield tunnel. Some said as many as four hundred. And some mentioned, as if reluctant, that many Chinese worked in the tunnel, as indeed would seem probable, for they could have brought to that toilsome, dangerous task their experience from tunneling in the Sierra for the Central Pacific Railroad.

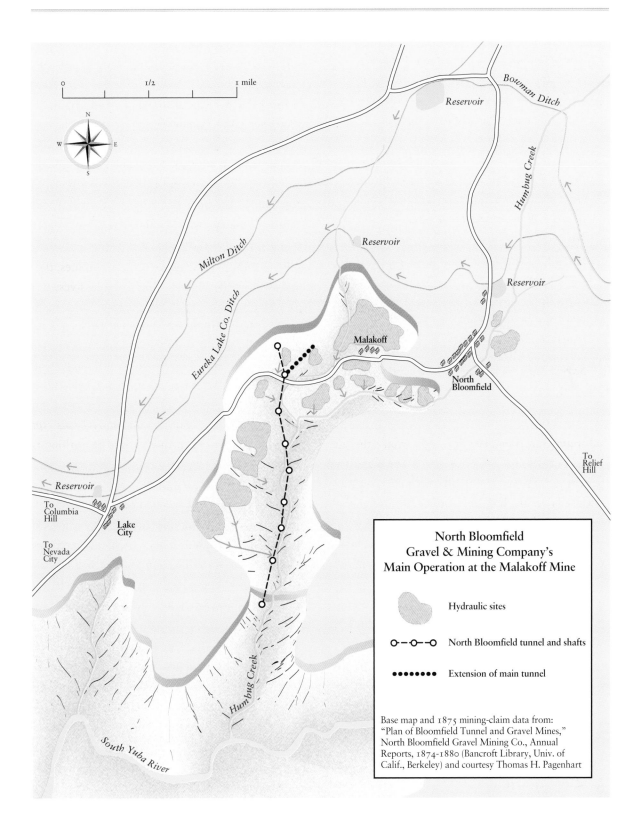

North Bloomfield
Gravel & Mining Company's
Main Operation at the Malakoff Mine

Hydraulic sites

North Bloomfield tunnel and shafts

Extension of main tunnel

Base map and 1875 mining-claim data from:
"Plan of Bloomfield Tunnel and Gravel Mines,"
North Bloomfield Gravel Mining Co., Annual
Reports, 1874-1880 (Bancroft Library, Univ. of
Calif., Berkeley) and courtesy Thomas H. Pagenhart

current received a final sifting as it passed over a descending series of undercurrents before plunging to Humbug Creek where the tailings piled up until swept by winter runoffs into the canyon of the South Yuba River.

Though no operation matched the North Bloomfield in size and expense, scores of other hydraulic companies—some with tunnels, all with sluice lines—emptied their tailings, week after week, into their nearby streams and canyons. A few hydraulickers worked gravel banks above the Cosumnes and as far south as the Tuolumne. But the great majority of the hydraulic operations, big and small, aimed their nozzles into the most extensive ancient riverbeds, those above the Feather, Yuba, Bear, and American Rivers.* Their workers lived in towns and camps scattered along miles of forested ridges. A map published in 1877 identified sixty-six of these

---

* After the North Bloomfield, the largest hydraulic companies included Gold Run Ditch and Mining Company, started in 1870 by local men around Dutch Flat who owned large claims near the headwaters of the North Fork of the American River; Excelsior Water and Mining Company, publicly owned through sale of stock, which had purchased most of the important mines around Smartsville by 1877; Birdseye Creek Mining Company, owned by British investors, and holding extensive claims between You Bet and Red Dog on the north side of the Bear River; Polar Star and Southern Cross Company, owned by San Francisco capitalists (including Alvinza Hayward, enriched by his Comstock winnings), with large claims that tailed into the Bear River; Milton Mining and Water Company, British owned, which by 1875 had purchased many mines between North San Juan and French Corral; and to the north, above Oroville on the North Fork of the Feather River, Spring Valley Mining Company, which controlled a massive gravel deposit at Cherokee where the cliff faces rose 450 feet above the monitors.

As for the North Bloomfield Gravel and Mining Company's corporate history, it was owned by thirty San Francisco capitalists, under the leadership of Lester L. Robinson. By 1880 the company had purchased the Union Gravel Mining Company and a controlling interest in the Milton Water and Mining Company. It had no equal.

settlements, some improved in appearance and civility by the presence of wives and children, even churches and schools.

The intensity and inventiveness of hydraulicking, the magnitude of its financial gambles and engineering feats, almost overwhelmed the government officials responsible for keeping annual mining records. The state mineralogist and the U.S. commissioner of mining statistics each year produced hundreds of pages of closely set type that catalogued, in never-slackening detail, the locations, finances, and ore tonnages of scores of mines; their consumption of miner's inches, explosives, and quicksilver; costs of wages, lumber, and pipe. Graphs, charts, and footnotes crowded more pages, all picturing an industry hell-bent on expansion: longer tunnels and larger nozzles; more ditches, flumes, and pipes; bigger dams and reservoirs. Forests fell and mountains disappeared under the onslaught. Never had the mining industry exploited California's natural resources so voraciously.

For investors in San Francisco and London and workers in Timbuctoo and Blue Bluffs, hydraulic mining by the 1880s seemed headed for a new era, a time when new technologies and years of investments and acquisitions would reward investors and miners with bigger profits and higher wages. In his 1879 year-end review, the president of the North Bloomfield Company confidently reported reservoirs brim-full of water for the summer of 1880 and a new system of "electric light of 12,000 candle intensity . . . to facilitate mining operations at night better than the pitch bonfires heretofore used." He also announced installation of a telephone line with twenty-two stations between French Corral and the guards at the reservoirs. With gold production sharply increased for the year just ended ($331,760), he concluded: "The mine is now in excellent order for future work, and a larger bullion production than in any previous year is confidently anticipated for 1880."

Newspapers in San Francisco and Sacramento ran excerpts of the report, exclaiming as they had for thirty years over the wondrous news of wealth flowing from the gold regions. Their message still captivated the nation. In 1883 *Century Magazine* in New York City published a lengthy illustrated article entitled "Hydraulic Mining in California," which concluded with the astounding estimate that "the great gravel deposits . . . contain not less than $6,000,000,000 in gold."

There was something about hydraulic mining even more attention-catching, more intriguing, than its huge profit potential. Hydraulicking had about it a drama, a sense of something threatening, a force that might not be under control—those lances of water pounding against immense cliffs of ancient gravels. In their imaginations, readers could see and hear the water released under tremendous pressure from eight- and ten-inch nozzles—the roaring, hissing, trembling power; the towering layers of gravel and rock and sand that might suddenly come thundering down, possibly burying a piper and his assistant. It was all fascinating, another California story to amaze those who stayed home and to lure those who wanted to live in a place where a fortune could be made by washing millions of cubic yards of gravel.

In 1882 the *Mining and Scientific Press* published a lengthy description of the North Bloomfield's huge mountain reservoirs, declaring them to be "among the greatest marvels of engineering skill the world can boast of." The article went on to describe the water delivery network: "In ditches winding along the backbones of sharp ridges, in wood flumes that are suspended by chains along straight-faced crags three hundred feet above the base, and in iron pipes across threadlike trestles as high as the tops of giant trees, water rushes from the fastnesses of the Sierra down to the foothills of this country where it is used in washing from the dead river channels the countless millions of gold, the harvesting of which for the world's enrichment has but just begun."

The *San Francisco Daily Evening Bulletin* sent a reporter up to the Malakoff Mine for a first-hand account. His dispatch reflected astonishment and admiration. "There is a real pleasure, very distinct but hard to describe, about this gigantic force tearing down the cliff. . . . If men will put their money into such ventures, there should be no one foolish enough to howl and curse at capital which pays the wages, does the planning, takes the risks."

Downstream from the Malakoff's effluent tunnel and the dumping grounds of more than ninety other hydraulic operations, ruined orchards and embattled towns surrounded by levees disproved the claim that mining financiers bore all the risks. But miners turned a blind eye to the sufferings and losses of hundreds of farmers and many more townsfolk. Their contempt for the valley's complaints was best expressed by the *Nevada City Daily Transcript*, always the hydraulickers' most ardent voice: "It is an open question whether the existence of a half dozen villages like the city of Marysville is of as much importance to the State of California and the country at large as the existence of hydraulic mining. . . . The idea of Marysville bringing suits to abate the hydraulic mining companies on the Yuba and its branches as a nuisance is preposterous; to do so would simply be the confiscation of millions of dollars of property."

From the miner's point of view, the orchardists, vegetable growers, town merchants, freighters, mule packers, and steamboat owners made their livings and fattened their savings by selling produce and services to the mining communities—as they had done since the 1850s. Such secondary enterprises had no practical right to threaten the great engine of commerce that even San Francisco depended on. With the mines prepared to distribute new millions in wealth and economic stimulus, what did the agricultural interests and their allies offer as a comparable contribution to the state's well-being?

What could cause such devastation?—not the impact of a meteor but rather the power of water serving the ambitions of man.

Silhouetted by the great arcs streaming from the muzzles of their monitors, these pipers in the Malakoff pit look fragile against the dangerous force they so casually controlled.

THE GROWERS' GOLD

By the 1880s a subtle but portentous change in the economic balance of the state was well under way, one for which mining could not claim credit. Miners might be excused for their hubris, with new millions in gold eagerly awaited after a legacy of triumphs, but the rest of California was growing too, spurred by the get-mine-now ethic the miners had instilled.

Men looking for new resources to mine turned to California's arable land. Across a succession of gentle valleys the state was blessed with millions of acres of rich loam. Not only fruit and vegetable growers sought to exploit its commercial potential; entrepreneurs with ambitions beyond the limited markets of San Francisco, Sacramento, and the mining districts also were searching for a crop that could be grown on a vast scale with limited labor, could survive the rough handling and the delays of export (as beef and produce could not), and would attract ready buyers in distant markets.

In wheat they found their new gold. With almost careless ease, large-scale production had developed in the 1860s. Sown after the rains of October or November softened the sun-baked soil, the seeds germinated and the plants grew through the mild, wet winter months and matured by May. The crop could then be left in the fields through the summer, the kernels drying and hardening. Through this cycle wheat needed no care. The cost of labor was confined to three or four weeks, for fall plowing and seeding and late-summer harvesting. Even the first year's planting usually yielded a good profit. The hard, dry quality of California wheat made it ideal for export. In 1873 more than 29 million bushels were shipped from San Francisco around the Horn to Liverpool. Four million acres of wheat fields—covering two-thirds of all land cultivated in California—yielded a harvest in 1881 that sold on the world market for $34 million, almost twice the value of gold produced that year by hydraulic and quartz mining. Behind the distracting

By the second week of June the wheat

had turned from pale yellow to golden yellow and from that to brown. Like a gigantic carpet, it spread itself over all the land. There was nothing else to be seen but the limitless sea of wheat as far as the eye could reach, dry, rustling, crisp and harsh in the rare breaths of hot wind out of the southeast.

Frank Norris, *The Octopus*

camouflage of old assumptions, uncelebrated commercial farmers were exploiting the diversity of California's resources and pocketing profits to be envied by the owners of gold mines.

Throughout the vastness of the Central Valley, from Red Bluff to the delta and south through the flat solitudes to the village of Fresno, wheat was planted across private fiefdoms measured by the tens and scores of thousands of acres. Comparable in their expanse to the Mexican land grants they replaced, these ranches produced a swelling abundance. Wheat exports in 1882 filled the cargo holds of 559 sailing ships, at a cost to shippers of $16 million—awesome statistics comparable to those that once measured the dimensions of gold mining.

Speculation in wheat futures brought shouting, gesticulating traders to the floor of the San Francisco Produce Exchange, recalling the frenzy over Comstock mining shares. Brokers bought and sold contracts, shipping agents competed for cargoes and manipulated freight charges, local millers sought their share of the year's crop. Shiploads of grain were bought and sold in transit, sometimes only hours before reaching the docks at Liverpool or Antwerp.

As they preferred the comforts of the city to the sweat and solitude of their ranches, so the wheat barons paid no attention to the agrarian ideals promoted by the California Agricultural Society. Like

The vast scale of California wheat ranches—30,000 to 60,000 acres, producing seventy-eight bushels per acre—required mechanization. Flat land, dry summers allowed combined harvester-threshers to cut swaths twenty feet wide and gather, thresh, and sack the wheat in one process. Thirty-three horses pulled this combine.

In agriculture as in mining, improvisation and invention produced new kinds of machinery to do the work in a labor-short economy. In this field, a steam engine drove a belt connected to a derrick that hoisted and stacked sacks of wheat. Machine shops like the Empire Brass and Iron Foundry in Marysville (ca. 1882) prospered by putting together combines and "traction engines."

To avoid the cost of feeding hundreds of horses or mules used to pull gang plows in the spring and combines in the summer, wheat ranchers invested in steam power. Proudly named and decorated, this hulking mechanism offered its buyer the promise of plowing deeply and broadly with its array of plowshares.

mine owners, they were quick to invest in new machines invented and manufactured to hasten the exploitation of the land. From the Stockton gang plow evolved a giant mechanism capable of plowing, seeding, and harrowing as it was pulled by long teams of mules across vast tracts of the valley. Similar adaptations and improvisations from machine shops in Stockton, Sacramento, and Marysville produced "combines" that could reap (with cutting bars as long as twenty-eight feet), thresh, and sack in a continuous process. The harvest advanced with such rapidity that within hours "the grain that was waving in the morning breeze may be sacked and ready for shipment to Liverpool." In the 1880s, steam-powered combines brought even greater efficiency, if also more accidents. One of these leviathans filled 2,784 sacks of wheat in one day. Its proud owner named it "the Monitor."

During the few weeks of summer harvest, work gangs carried sacks of grain from the fields to wagons, which hauled their loads to riverbanks and rail heads. On ranches with river frontage, bargemen might load eight to ten thousand sacks at each of many landings. As the Central Pacific pushed its rail lines farther into the valleys, freight cars carried tens of thousands of sacks to the loading docks on San Francisco Bay. In 1882, Colusa County alone shipped 2,560,000 bushels for export. It was a bonanza industry, in which the producers were not so much farmers as new miners of the soil. Certainly their vast and mechanized operations shared little with the traditional routines of family farming back in the States.

In comparison, the orchards and vegetable fields along the embattled river valleys seemed much closer to traditional images of agrarian virtue. Behind the levees, well-tended rows of fruit trees, leafy vegetable plots, and clapboard homes won praise in the *California Farmer* and the *Pacific Rural Press* as examples of a way of life more attractive to immigrant families than the rough bachelor world of Sierra mining camps. The Agricultural Society preached the same message, that the future lay with the stability and wholesomeness of farming.

But this impression of the local farmers as disciples of old-fashioned rural ideals obscured their California-trained mercantile impulses. In the escalating battle between mountain and valley newspapers, the Agricultural Society's own promotions of agrarian values worked against the farmers' cause. It was easy for thousands of miners, many of them farmers from Illinois or Pennsylvania, to scorn the impression that small-time growers would take on the great mining industry in defense of a way of life more easily pursued by *staying* in Illinois or Pennsylvania.

In fact, produce farming in California had grown up under the same gold rush mentality that encouraged the hydraulickers to build daring water networks and wheat ranchers to exploit the great expanses. Many a grower in the 1880s still envied the farmers like John Horner, who pocketed a fortune by selling a summer's crop of melons or onions, and orchardists like George Briggs, who became famously rich by shipping his abundance to mountain and city markets. Those memories and their own successes had made it difficult for farmers and city merchants to support the Anti-Debris Association, which antagonized their customers in the foothills. This reluctance suggested that the battle was as much about profits as it was about property rights.

Unlike wheat, the perishability of fruits and vegetables left growers entirely dependent on the demands of the local markets. Fortunately, California's capacity to consume grew rapidly. By 1880 San Francisco's population exceeded that of Oregon State and Washington Territory combined. Every year, the growers' dependence on their original customers in the mountain camps and supply centers diminished.

Nonetheless, productivity outpaced demand. To protect profit margins, rich harvests of apples, peaches, onions, and potatoes had to be left in the orchards and fields. And despite the devastation from the slickens, productivity could always be increased by planting on safer land. Expansion awaited access to new markets.

The Central Pacific's refrigerated freight cars—yet another testimony to California's inventiveness—heralded stunning new possibilities: markets in Denver, Chicago, and beyond. In 1880 as many as 130 freight cars with salted ice and improved ventilation delivered profitable quantities of fresh fruit. Better yet, through the decade orchardists grew prunes, which needed no refrigeration for export, and by 1886 California had more than a million of these profitable trees. From southern California, new citrus orchards added orange and yellow to the flow of growers' gold.

The miners had misjudged the strength of their adversaries. Their confidence in an almost hereditary authority over the course of California's future might have been checked if they had known one telling statistic: in the 1870s more men made their living in the broader geography and economy of farming—48,000—than in all the mines of the Sierra foothills—36,000. But given the antagonism fed by years of slickens and floods, court battles and angry editorials, it was too late for logic to lead to a truce. Editorials like that of James McClatchy, owner and editor of the *Sacramento Bee*, stripped away the last illusions. "The public will soon be compelled to consider the now apparently irrepressible conflict between the miners and the farmers. The miners are rushing down on the latter millions of tons annually of detritus, sand, clay, alluvium, or whatever it may be, filling the rivers, covering the farms, and forcing the cultivators to build higher and broader levees." Convinced that the hydraulickers would destroy navigation on the Sacramento River, and sympathetic to the agriculturists whose prosperity would secure California's future, McClatchy used his paper to attack the hydraulickers throughout the ensuing struggle.

Equally partisan on the miners' side, the *Nevada City Daily Transcript* pressed the hydraulickers' case, championing the rights of the industry's wage earners and their role as California's true pioneers,

while the big San Francisco papers glorified the capitalists and engineers. Though the *Bee* and the *Marysville Daily Appeal* steadfastly countered with the views of the valley folk—augmented by the voice of the *Pacific Rural Press* from its brave outpost in San Francisco—in 1881 the Anti-Debris Association decided that the farmers should have their own newspaper to carry agriculture's message.* With George Ohleyer as editor, the first issue of the *Sutter County Farmer*, dated April 22, expressed its objective: "The purpose of this new paper is to stop debris. . . . Hence, we consider it the duty of all to force our rulers [the state legislators] to recognize this evil and abate it."

OHLEYER

Far from ruling, the men in the capitol in Sacramento had floundered for years, unable to find their way through a swamp of payoffs to the high ground of public interest. After thirty years of rushing ahead without leadership from these soiled solons, after relying on vigilance committees and the balm of gold and silver, Californians in the 1880s had no experience in using legislation to advance their well-being or to resolve their problems.

And problems they had aplenty, which tormented far beyond the reach of the slickens. By 1880 many of the Comstock's great mines—those

---

* The first newspaper published for farmers, *California Farmer*, started in 1854 by James Warren, focused on serving the farmers' needs for information on research and new agricultural techniques. Equally important for those educational purposes, the *Pacific Rural Press* also reported extensively on the long battle with the hydraulic mining industry. The *Press*'s editor for forty-eight years (1875–1923), Edward James Wickson, played a vital role in helping California's farmers and ranchers, not only through his newspaper—advertised as "the Leading Agricultural Home Newspaper and Standard Authority on all Branches of California Agriculture"—but also through his books, including his widely used *California Fruits and How to Grow Them*, published in 1889.

At river landings like this one near Colusa on the Sacramento River, thousands of sacks of wheat were loaded onto barges towed by river steamers to the docks that lined the shore on the north end of San Francisco Bay, there to be transferred to sailing ships bound for Liverpool.

Far from the dangers of slickens and the burden of taxes for levees, this family—working with children and neighbors—prepared a field for a crop of potatoes.

On hillsides safe from monitors, farmers in Sacramento and other counties cared for millions of vines that produced grapes to be dried as raisins or pressed for wine.

At county fairs sponsored by the State Agricultural Society, farmers displayed the abundance from their orchards and fields. By 1880 California had more apple trees than all other fruits combined. Even more than improvements in the canning of fruits, sulphur and sun drying increased sales of fruit in the 1880s.

once-soaring names familiar to everyone—had run into barren rock, and the value of their shares had collapsed by as much as $150 million in a few months, wiping out hopes and savings. The continued immigration of workers from China (20 percent of San Francisco's population was Chinese) caused deep resentment—"anti-coolie clubs," mob violence—as white workers blamed "Mongolians" for taking their jobs by working for "slave wages."

Widespread discontent found an outlet in the crowds of workers (many of them unemployed) that gathered in San Francisco's vacant lots to cheer angry speakers who condemned "robber capitalists" and called for "a little judicious hanging."* These riotous meetings in January 1878 coalesced public frustrations into the formation of the Workingmen's Party, which promised: "We will send the Chinese home . . . , tax the millionaires . . . , and elevate the poor." Suddenly popular, this new party

---

* Most prominent among the demagogues, a drayman named Denis Kearney gained an enthusiastic following for his tirades against corporations and monopolists and his denunciation of Chinese immigration. Frightened by "Kearneyism" and distrustful of city government, San Francisco businessmen organized a vigilance committee (as in 1851 and 1856), this time discreetly called the Committee of Safety. Led by the experienced William T. Coleman (leader in 1856), this "merchants' militia" quickly attracted a thousand and more volunteers, many of them armed with pickax handles originally destined for miners in the foothills. When a mob threatened to burn the docks of the Pacific Mail Steamship Company—hated for importing thousands of Chinese "coolies"—the handle-wielders imposed order, though a lumberyard burned and four men were killed in the melee. With public safety restored, the committee disbanded. But this oppression by "the rich" aroused greater resentment among Kearney's supporters, who organized their Workingmen's Party with Kearney as their leader. This new political force so dominated municipal elections from San Francisco and Sacramento to Santa Barbara and Los Angeles that Republicans and Democrats feared these "rabble rousers" might control the constitutional convention. They did make up a potent minority that allied with the farmers to promote agrarian interests.

challenged the Republicans and Democrats and succeeded in electing a large number of delegates to a constitutional convention that met in Sacramento from late September 1878 to early March 1879. From those months of raucous speeches and rowdy behavior, the state's new leaders produced a new constitution crowded with rules and codes and agencies to regulate the stock exchanges and the corporations (particularly the Southern Pacific), to reduce taxes on farmlands, to prohibit employment of Chinese workers on public projects, and many more provisions that testified to a time of transition for California, when the dominance of San Francisco and the mining companies would be challenged by the rising power of the Sacramento Valley and its farmers.

In May 1879 the voters approved the new constitution. In November they elected a new governor, assembly, and senate to lead California into its fourth decade.

GRAVE DANGERS

In his inaugural address to the first session of the new legislature, Governor George C. Perkins praised agriculture and mining as "the principal sources of our prosperity and wealth." He urged promotion of "scientific farming." But then he reverted to the traditional assessment, that the importance of mining "to the state and the nation cannot be overestimated or gainsaid; and it is not without pride that we point to the fact that since the discovery of gold here, California alone has produced over one thousand two hundred and fifty million dollars, a sum that exceeds the aggregate productions of all the rest of the United States." That boast foretold the governor's position in the hydraulic mining controversy—caused, he said, by "the debris washed down by the rivers." Having thus avoided placing responsibility, he told the legislators that this "delicate question should be settled upon some broad and comprehensive basis."

To guide them in that difficult task, the governor recommended a report prepared by the state engineer, William Hammond Hall. This massive document described in shocking detail the destruction of the watersheds of the Yuba, Bear, and American Rivers, their canyons choked—mile after mile—with an immense accumulation of mining debris, in some places a hundred feet deep. For forty miles downstream from Oroville, the Feather River channel was filled with rocks, gravel, and sand. Miles of once-fertile farming countryside lay under thick layers of hardened slickens "to such depths that orchards, gardens, fields, and dwellings are buried from sight. . . . Over these, the stream now spreads at will in many shifting channels . . . confined between levees set long distances apart, generally on the ridges of highland that formerly marked the boundary of the more fertile bottoms."

HALL

Following this description, Engineer Hall turned to statistics "to convey some conception of the enormous dimensions of this phenomenon." He estimated that 143 million cubic yards of debris had accumulated in the Yuba River, 148 million in the Bear, 40 million in the Feather, and 100 million in the Sacramento.* To forecast the future, he calculated the amount of ore-bearing gravel—just in the area between the Middle and South Forks of the Yuba River—to be 700 million cubic yards, "still available to be washed by the hydraulic process."

Faced with their professional engineer's appalling statistics, the governor and legislature could no longer acquiesce to the power and plunder of the mining industry. After thirty years as spectators, they were forced by a crisis of revelation to move from passivity to bold action. Similarly, Engineer Hall's report gave new power to the farmers, river boat captains, and residents of the valley towns: at last they had irrefutable evidence to support their years of complaints and lawsuits. The hydraulickers could no longer accuse their victims of exaggerating the damage done by the slickens. Nor could the miners' newspapers ever again haughtily assert that the layers of slickens enriched the farmers' fields, like the annual inundations of the Nile.

Engineer Hall's report established the evidence in the great debate, farmers vs. miners. No matter how much gold the great monitors could unearth, their owners' present and predicted profits could no longer obscure the devastation inflicted on homes, river navigation, and farms. But neither Governor Perkins nor the legislators were ready to restrict the producers of gold, and they were certainly not ready to prohibit the hydraulickers' vast operations. Rather they believed that science, technology, and engineering—those agents of nineteenth-century progress—could now be employed to devise ways to hold back the miners' debris, safely and permanently.

They listened to and placed their confidence in Engineer Hall's concluding judgment, set forth in his report: "The study of this subject has brought me to a sense of the absolute necessity for . . . the State to take charge of the drainage ways [rivers] and the drainage works [levees and dams] and exercise such control over them as will regulate their use." He proposed to replace the here-and-there, privately built embankments with a coordinated system of well-planned levees, incorporating the safety valve of several diversion outlets that would release floodwaters into swampland basins. Above all he urged the construction of large debris dams to "immobilize" the massive, threatening deposits that continued to build in upstream canyons.

Confident in the judgment of the engineering profession and anxious to prevent future floods, the legislators in February 1880 considered an "Act to Promote Drainage," whereby an independent public

---

* Later studies showed the total cubic yardage of gravel washed by the hydraulickers to be far greater: on the watershed of the Yuba, 684 million; the American, 257 million; the Bear, 254 million; and the upper Feather, 100 million. Covered by slickens: 39,000 acres.

authority, the Board of State Drainage Commissioners, would be empowered to construct and manage a comprehensive flood control system in the Sacramento Valley. Newspapers in San Francisco praised the bill. At public meetings proponents of the bill pointed to the findings of civil engineers who held college degrees, men who had proved their skills by building fortifications and fieldworks that helped the Union armies win the Civil War. When both the *Marysville Daily Appeal* and the *Nevada City Daily Transcript* endorsed the bill it seemed that, at last, an accord between the valley and the mountains had been attained.

But many farmers remained suspicious. At public gatherings George Cadwalader and George Ohleyer warned against trusting the strength of debris dams. And they warned that valley people would be made to pay taxes to finance a system that allowed the hydraulickers (financed by owners in San Francisco) to continue their destructive operations. And more, they argued that the levee system could not hold back floodwaters. As long as the miners were allowed to dump their debris in the creeks and rivers, no engineering works could provide safety. Genuine, long-lasting security could be won only by shutting down, permanently, the "diabolical" hydraulickers.

The farmers gained unexpected allies among Californians far removed from the danger of debris. Residents in Santa Cruz and Los Angeles argued that they should not be taxed to save or reclaim private land in another part of the state. The *Los Angeles Herald* complained that it "would be just as logical to tax the whole state to pay for a failure of the crops and fleece which have been ruined by drought in the southern counties as to levy a tax to repair the ravages of the debris of mines."

Through February and March 1880 speakers coped with hecklers at public meetings; in the capitol, legislators passed a series of amendments; in newspaper offices, editors took sides; in San Francisco, "capitalists" were accused of bribery to gain votes for the Drainage Act. Finally, on April 9,

1880, the Senate, weary from debate and intrigue, passed the bill, by a margin of five votes, sowing resentment and distrust in a political compromise that seemed to have more enemies than defenders.

Work got started immediately on building levees and on the complex task of placing brush dams across the sprawling riverbeds of the Yuba and Bear Rivers. Hurried by fear that the coming of winter storms would release a new avalanche of rocks and gravel, the engineers in August hired more than a thousand workers (no Chinese) to cut trunks of willow trees and brush from the dense growth in the riverbeds, to be wired and woven together to form the barriers. In early November the *Sacramento Record-Union* sent a reporter up the Yuba to describe the work. First, though, the writer turned his attention to the "demoralized stream, a shallow and muddy sheet of water that wanders aimlessly over the shining bed of sand and yellow cement, from one to two miles in width. . . . Passing on up the river bed . . . , the visitor walks over spots where far below are the ruins of houses, where are buried orchards that once dropped their fruity wealth upon the alluvial soil, over pasture lands now twenty feet below the mining detritus and over rich bottom lands now buried in the ever-lasting gravel of a sandy avalanche."

Farther upstream, some nine miles above Marysville, this same newspaper reporter came to a recently completed brush dam, built with "engineering science." Estimating its length to be more than two miles, he reported the dam's "down-stream face presents a perpendicular front . . . of jagged butt ends of countless saplings, small trees, and logs, with alternating layers of logs like stringers and rafters. On the upriver side it presents a face of gentle slope from the top to the river bed, composed of alternate layers of young willow trees cut in full foliage, laid top down and very thickly and interspersed by horizontal layers of heavy logs. On top of these is a layer of long logs. . . . The base of the dam is from sixty-five to seventy feet wide."

Through the autumn of 1880, state engineers

Designed to hold back coarse slickens—rocks and heavier gravel—this about-to-be-overwhelmed debris dam gave towns and farmers reason to condemn the claims of hydraulickers that such barriers would "immobilize" the flow of slickens.

Dumped into the Yuba River, millions of tons of debris filled the once-deep bed and left the river to flow in a wandering course through an ever-deepening, -widening sprawl of sand and gravel. With winter rains, the river flooded, leaving a broader desert of desolation.

As idealized in this lithograph, George Ohleyer's farm near Yuba City, Sutter County, typified the fertility of river-bottom lands threatened by hydraulic-caused floods. And the scene presented a contrast between the Victorian values of farming and the rough, wasteful ways of mining.

supervised the cutting, wiring, and interlacing that slowly gave shape to this brush embankment. At the same time they directed other work crews constructing levees on both sides of the Yuba River, from the foothills to its junction with the Feather River and then seven miles farther, to a terminus well below Marysville. Similar efforts raised a brush dam and levees for the Bear River and several miles of additional levees along the Sacramento River. By year's end, the huge project was finished, at a cost of $463,153. The construction crews disbanded, confident that winter rains would no longer menace the valley's farmers.

While William Hall and his engineers completed these defensive bulwarks, opponents of the Drainage Act stubbornly lobbied for the law's repeal. Many farmers, led by Cadwalader and Ohleyer, saw the act as an insurance policy for the miners, perpetuating and legalizing the very cause of the floods. And tax haters all over the state simply wanted to reverse what they saw as a special-interest assessment that benefited someone else. When the legislature convened in January 1881, the repealers arrived with noisy support from both camps. Governor Perkins weighed in with a "Special Message on the Debris Question" meant to head off a new confrontation by arguing that only the Drainage Act offered a fair and practical balance of the competing interests. After lamenting the loss of thousands of acres of agricultural lands—valued at $6 million—"buried under the mining detritus or slickens," the governor estimated the value of future gold production—$150 million—from "the practically unlimited extent of gravel-bearing claims."

Faced with untenable alternatives—"the stoppage of hydraulic mining or the abandonment of the rivers and agricultural lands and valley towns to the flow of the advancing wave of debris"—Perkins endorsed the compromise of the Drainage Act and defended reliance on the recently completed dams and levees.

Through the first weeks of January 1881, passionate debate tied up the Senate as its members pre-

If gold is the only needful thing, then let the Supreme Court tell us so and let every man alike be at liberty to secure it in the speediest possible manner, even should he be obliged to trespass on his neighbor.

Pacific Rural Press, March 25, 1882

pared to vote for or against repeal of the Drainage Act. Then suddenly, the repealers' case was made for them. During the night of January 27, a great storm swept across the valley and into the Sierra. Six inches of rain pounded Marysville. The rivers began to rise. Farmers and townspeople, distrustful of Engineer Hall's bulwarks, hurried once again to move possessions and livestock to whatever site offered hoped-for safety. By the twenty-ninth the Feather, Yuba, Bear, and American had all breached their levees and overwhelmed the brush dams. Flood levels exceeded even those of 1862 and 1875, all the way south to Stockton. Only the capital city's levees held, with a scant foot of protection from the lapping brown current. Refugees and livestock huddled on isolated levee-tops, awaiting rescue by steamboats and small craft that carried them to hillsides. The flood took nearly a month to recede, leaving incalculable damage to farmlands, towns, and levees. Everything was covered with slickens, a glistening, viscous mass that dried hard and dusty.

The Senate did not need to wait for the murky waters to dissipate to make up its mind. On February 8 the chamber passed the bill that repealed the Drainage Act and sent it to the Assembly, where an exhaustive filibuster held off a vote. In spite of the dramatic failure of the theory that debris and slickens could be safely contained, the mining interests went to work on susceptible legislators, offering clandestine inducements. When six San Francisco assemblymen suddenly shifted allegiance to the miners, the repeal bill was doomed. The Drainage Act survived. An assemblyman summed up his colleagues' feelings: "Things are busted now."

RISING TEMPERS

Stymied by the byzantine machinations of the legislature, the frustrated leaders of the Anti-Debris Association decided to return to the courts. First George Cadwalader filed a suit to have the Drainage Act declared unconstitutional. Then on

CADWALADER

May 10 he revived the dormant 1879 Marysville lawsuit against the North Bloomfield Gravel and Mining Company and twenty-five other defendants, asking that the hydraulickers "be perpetually enjoined from depositing tailings and debris from their respective mining claims in the channel of the Yuba or its tributaries."

The legal system responded with an alacrity that made up for the legislature's paralytic indecision. On May 21, 1881, Judge Phil W. Keyser at the district court in Yuba City fulfilled the farmers' highest hopes. He issued an injunction against all the defendants. At last Marysville and its farmer allies could celebrate victory. For the first time in thirty years the monitors and sluices would have to shut down. Hurrah for Judge Keyser!

Along the ridges above the forks of the Yuba, from Ousley's Bar to Moore's Flat, an unaccustomed silence fell over the pits as companies turned the valves that cut off the water supply. Never before: gold mines closed by law. Pipers and sluice tenders cursed and wondered that a mere writ could keep miners from the very work that had built California. How could Marysville take away a man's livelihood? Through days of restless idleness, angry miners congregated in bars and meeting halls, feeling betrayed by the city with which they had traded for so many years. They talked of a boycott—make those merchants down in Marysville pay a price for their injunction.

Editorials in the *Nevada City Daily Transcript* accused Marysville of following "a pack of fee-seeking lawyers and demagogical politicians. Their course is one that will result in an eternal hate being engendered between the mountains and the valley." Under a column headed "The Miners' Embargo," the newspaper urged citizens to refuse to buy from valley merchants. "No more Marysville or Wheatland goods of any kind. . . . Send back the fish, fruit, and vegetable peddlers. . . . Many of our merchants are buying their flour from Red Bluff."

The *Daily Transcript* exhorted miners to attend a mass rally in Nevada City on Saturday night, June 18, 1881, to support the boycott and raise money for the Miners Association. Though somber in purpose, this gathering of miners from across the northern Sierra served as an occasion for reunions and entertainment. Overnight guests and the change of routine sent a stir of excitement through the town. Two brass bands competed with church bells, firebells, and "the booming of giant powder charges." At eight o'clock the crowded streets emptied as miners filed into the city's theater, with ladies taking the balcony. Out-of-work miners thundered approval at the orators' familiar message: "Mining is the parent industry of the Pacific coast, by which every other interest has been vitalized and built up. . . . We have an implacable foe, not the farmers but the evil genius [George Cadwalader] who is leading them. . . . It illy becomes the people of Marysville and vicinity who have fattened upon profits of commercial intercourse with us to yield to the selfish schemes of a few political factionists and greedy attorneys for whom ephemeral notoriety and fees are a sufficient reason for plunging us into protracted and exhausting litigation." The loudest cheers arose for the speaker who declared: "I conjure you as American citizens to stand shoulder to shoulder and by the grace of God the miners' cause will prevail. *No one can stop hydraulic mining!*"

At a protest meeting in Columbia Hill, miners drank ten gallons of beer and fired "a cannon ball that cut in two a straw effigy of Judge Keyser. The remnants were cremated in a bonfire."

As the Miners Association rallied its supporters with speeches and shenanigans, the farmers and townsmen gathered at meetings in Marysville, Wheatland, Colusa, Butte City, and as far north as Chico, where speakers condemned the Drainage Act and its taxes that paid for "worthless" brush dams. Local committees of the Anti-Debris Association were elected, funds raised, and support for George Cadwalader loudly affirmed. The leading speaker at Chico declared that protection of navigation on the rivers should be of concern to the entire state and called for statewide opposition to hydraulic mining. Striking a tone of reluctant determination, he concluded: "The farmers don't wish to injure the miners, but they must protect their land and also the rivers which they wish to use as a means of transportation. The farmers are willing to do almost anything to avoid injuring the mining interests, except to give up their farms and homes."

In September, the Drainage Act, after surviving the seesaw battles in the Assembly, fell before the State Supreme Court, which found the law unconstitutional on several counts, among them that the legislature had no power to tax everyone for the benefit of a few. But that ruling won only half the battle. By October the farmers realized that the hydraulickers along the Yuba were ignoring Judge Keyser's injunction. After a few weeks of grudging shutdown, the great system had started up again. Water flowed through ditches and flumes; the long-snouted giants sent jets cutting into tumbling banks of gravel; sluice boxes again ran full, day and night; mining camps and towns bustled back to life; and debris and muddy effluent once again spewed from tunnels into upstream river canyons. Owners and other officials of mining companies hid from sheriffs who sought to serve legal papers, thus frustrating enforcement of the injunction. Beyond keeping outside the legal net, the defiant company officers encouraged their workers to continue hydraulic operations, in the confident belief that the court could not pursue and prosecute hundreds of individual offenders. The miners (as reported in the *Mining and Scientific Press*) willingly joined in the plot, asserting that they would be better off in jail than

out of work. In any case, "at Marysville they cannot find room to put 1,400 men in jail, and if that does come to pass, some good accommodations must be made for so many men and good grub provided."

In rooms like that over A. A. Smith's drugstore in the town of North Bloomfield, where in happier times the Knights of Pythias had held their fraternal meetings, anxious miners now gathered to talk and ponder, as they did in every saloon. Many expressed astonishment that *they*, creators of so much wealth, they who had built California since 1849, now faced hostile challengers, other Californians seriously intent on stopping their great work, the engine of commerce and prosperity. Appalled, disbelieving, these shaggy men slapped one another on the back and swore defiance. Observing their resolve, a reporter from California's oldest newspaper, the *Alta* of San Francisco, dared speculate what next week, next month, might bring. "When it shall reach the point of ordering the Gatling guns to the mountains to enforce upon the miners the choice of sitting still and starving or abandoning their little homes and everything they have in the world to become tramps and scatter over the Coast, the time will have come for California to pause and ponder the problem more seriously than she has yet done."

The *Nevada City Daily Transcript* best knew the miners and their mood. Its angry, unvarnished reporting served as the hydraulickers' declaration of purpose. "The people of Nevada County are neither cowards nor babes. They know what they are about and are ready to defend their action to the bitter end. It is not a war of their own making. . . . The miners have been forced to adopt the only alternative that remains—which means that they will no longer be the playthings of Judge Keyser and his eggers-on. No threats of invading armies can terrorize them, no constabulary forces can drive them from their strongholds. . . . Men with empty larders and hungry families know but one law, and that is the first law of Nature."

Worried by the rising tempers and by the loss of the Drainage Act as an operative compromise, the

There was a Grand-Canyon-majesty to be seen in the vast pit of the Malakoff Mine—if the viewer did not know that the extent of erosion was man-made in less than twenty years and destined to cut its way ever wider.

This brush dam, overwhelmed by a mass of slickens, offered dramatic evidence of why the Yuba River bed had risen some thirty feet in twenty years, by the 1880s.

Used as an illustration for a lengthy article praising hydraulic mining (published in *Century Magazine*, New York, 1883), this drawing depicted both the nonchalance of sluice-tenders and the daring of engineers who built sluice boxes and undercurrents to empty their final washings into the canyon of Humbug Creek.

San Francisco Board of Trade decided to send a "Debris Investigating Committee" to mediate between the Anti-Debris Association and the Miners Association. On October 17, 1881, at the Western House in Marysville, the San Francisco businessmen met with George Ohleyer and his colleagues in the Anti-Debris Association and with local farmers and merchants. The main speaker of the evening, a man who had mined and farmed along the Yuba since 1849, warned that "the danger from debris is more imminent and greater than many of the most extreme agitators have ever claimed. . . . If hydraulic mining should continue, Sutter County will be absolutely destroyed and in a few years more, the Sacramento River will be obliterated."

The next day Marysville's mayor led the San Franciscans on a tour of the Bear River Valley. Along the way farmers pointed to where their homes had been, now lost beneath the slickens. At the location of an old graveyard only the tops of the tallest monuments could be seen. When they came to the site of James Keyes's farm (he had died in 1880), neighbors told how he had raised his house, first four feet and then six feet more, before finally abandoning his land. Now the visitors could kick the peak of the farmhouse roof, poking above eighteen feet of gray slickens. Further on, they passed through dry brush that proved to be the top branches of an orchard.

One of the newspaper men on the tour wrote sympathetically of the farmers' plight. "This locality was once the garden of the state. Its rich soil produced grain and fruit in almost unlimited quantities. It attracted the most enterprising agriculturists. . . . Farms were divided into grain fields, fruit orchards, pasturage, vegetable crops, and forest. But it is of no use now to look for enterprise or pluck in the face of such an impending calamity. Slickens and back water are things a man cannot fight. As the tide advances, he can only vacate his home."

On October 19, as the committeemen traveled up the Yuba Valley, a strong wind blew sand and small pebbles across their levee-top road and over a

This question which is now before us in this state is a great one for which there is no precedent. The two interests of farming and mining have never before in any land come against each other, and the decision which must be made sooner or later will of necessity be an original one.

Sacramento Record-Union, October 18, 1881

desolate sprawl below "of sandy desert, white and glistening and sterile," with here and there clumps of straggly willows. Where the Bear River broke free of the foothills, several miners joined the group and explained how a high dam in the canyon could impound all the debris upriver, but it would not be built until the farmers withdrew their injunctions.

When the businessmen traveled along San Juan Ridge, they came to the great Malakoff pit, where they watched three plumes of water sweep masses of gravel into outlet shafts that connected, they were told, with the famous bedrock tunnel that emptied into Humbug Creek and the South Yuba. Proud miners explained the operations as their amazed visitors strained to hear above the roar of the great jets. In a mighty voice conditioned by the constant din, the mining superintendent told how, day and night, the power of water moved thousands of tons of gold-bearing earth through the tunnel's sluice boxes, where thousands of crevices charged with quicksilver caught the gold that ultimately was cast into gleaming bars of bullion bound for the United States Mint in San Francisco. To businessmen from the City, the Malakoff Mine seemed a triumph of man's ingenuity: gargantuan, dynamic, efficient. And it was so wonderfully profitable!

The tour ended on October 23 at Grass Valley where an evening banquet ("wine was brought in") gained a celebratory tone. Each member of the committee spoke; several declared the controversy to be "a national issue and Congress ought to assist." George Ohleyer expressed his hope for an early remedy. Good cheer prevailed. The next morning when the visitors climbed aboard their train for San Francisco, they promised to prepare a balanced report to sustain the welcomed amity.

But behind the diplomatic smiles, the old hostilities still simmered. The leaders of the Anti-Debris Association for months had resented the hydrau-lickers' refusal to shut down their operations as required by the Marysville injunction issued back in May. It was too much to bear that the North Bloomfield Company had boastfully shown off their monitors at the Malakoff Mine when everyone knew they were operating illegally. To show that the anti-debris coalition would not accept such a sham, George Cadwalader filed a complaint and asked for reinforcement of the injunction. The court responded by threatening to fine the defendants for contempt and issued an order to the Nevada County sheriff to shut off the hydraulic companies' water supply. In response, the North Bloomfield Company obtained an injunction from the Nevada County Superior Court that restrained the sheriff from trespassing on the company's property. This exchange delighted the *Daily Transcript,* which hailed the miners' victory in the "injunction game."

For the farmers, nothing seemed to work as the tense dispute edged closer to violence—not the legis-lative process, not injunctions from the courts, not orders from sheriffs. Even the promised "balance" of the San Francisco Board of Trade's advisory re-port proved spurious when it was issued in Novem-ber. Beginning with a dramatic forecast that mining debris, if left unchecked, would "render sterile and barren that entire section of the country, . . . like a lava stream," the report then reviewed the vast economic benefit of hydraulic mining throughout California and praised its vital supply of gold. Beguiled by the power and habit of gold, the board recommended construction of a new series of stone and brush dams to hold back old and future mining debris. Thus the San Franciscans endorsed the already-tried policy of the Drainage Act and ignored the lessons of the recent floods. They even urged the

farmers to withdraw their injunctions, arguing that these legal efforts caused animosity among the miners. And finally, these objective businessmen rec-ommended that rather than restrict hydraulic min-ing as a means to preserve navigation on the rivers, the federal government should pay for dredging and thereby assume maintenance of the rivers. To the farmers, the message of this document was clear: their lands and livelihoods should be sacrificed for what San Francisco judged to be the greater good of the state.

During the summer of 1881 the state attorney general received dozens of petitions and complaints from counties "injuriously affected by the flow of mining debris." In his response to a petition from Sacramento County, the attorney general stated his wish to avoid "a wholesale resort to litigation that . . . might seriously endanger the peace and pros-perity of the State." Therefore, he would seek "a speedy determination" of the great controversy by allowing attorneys for all the petitioners to join in one legal complaint to be filed against one of the county's worst offenders, the Gold Run Ditch and Mining Company. After acquiescing to the miners making their own laws since 1849, the time had come for "the People" to consider what their inter-ests might be.

The case opened November 15, 1881, in Sacra-mento County Superior Court, Judge Jackson Tem-ple presiding. The attorney general opened with a lengthy complaint that the Gold Run Company had been for years depositing its tailings in the North Fork of the American River, which carried them into the Sacramento River, causing that river to be "filled up some thirty-five feet and thus the dangers of inundation have been increased and the navi-gability of the Sacramento River impaired." He further charged that "the debris deposits have de-stroyed homes, covered up houses and trees, and that in evidence of this, a barge which once lay on the bank of the river is now thirty feet beneath the silt. . . . All these things constitute a public nuisance of a continuously recurring nature."

As if witness to the threat and a measure of its size, a lone figure stood before a bank of "travel sand" that encroached on the remaining flow of the Yuba River.

When the time came to present evidence in the courtrooms, farmers and townsfolk used photographs that showed the failure of debris dams, as in this scene of a brush dam and the accumulation of rocks and gravel that the dam failed to contain.

More visual evidence of destruction in the Yuba River Valley was provided by this view of a levee that separated the breadth of the debris-filled river from orchards and fields on the left, owned by a Dr. Teegarden, soon to be ruined by slickens.

The *Sacramento Record-Union* declared that "no trial in California has ever brought forward such an array of talented engineers, chemists, physicians, and gentlemen of high scientific attainments." They testified at times in the presence of Governor Perkins and always before a crowd of leading journalists and various state, city, and county officials. For months the wearying "intricate examinations" of witnesses were quoted in endless columns of the rival newspapers, enlivened by equally indefatigable editorial attacks and counterattacks.

Finally, on June 12, 1882, Judge Temple handed down his decision, which many newspapers published in its entirety in long columns of small type. The *Pacific Rural Press* needed four extra pages to report all the details of "A Victory for the Valley." And so it seemed, for the judge ruled against the miners on twenty-two "findings" ranging from their claimed protection under the statute of limitations to their claimed right to use rivers for their tailings. In the final decree the Gold Run Company was perpetually enjoined and restrained from dumping what the judge defined as "coarse" debris. As the news spread, valley folk celebrated, their rejoicing in Marysville described by the *Daily Appeal*: "The streets are full of people exchanging congratulations. The city is illuminated by bonfires, and a brass band is playing. All the bells in town are ringing." In somber contrast, up in the hills, "the working miner regards the decision as a death blow, a decree whereby he is declared a criminal, and he sees only want and starvation for him and his."

In their first emotional responses, the opposing sides mistakenly assumed that Judge Temple's prohibition of dumping meant nothing less than a prohibition of hydraulic mining. The Gold Run Company would have to close, setting a portentous precedent for the rest of the industry. In fact, though, within his lengthy decision the judge stated that the hydraulickers could resume their work if they built dams that would "impound, detain, and hold back" the heavier—"coarse"—debris. In explaining this at first overlooked aspect of his decision, Judge Temple admitted: "Perhaps I am somewhat moved to this by the consideration that otherwise mining can never be prosecuted at all. . . . I confess I shrink from a consequence so far-reaching."

For the farmers, then, a ruling received as a laurel of victory proved, on more careful consideration, a sorrowful disappointment. They knew from hard experience that debris dams not only collapsed but, if they held, leaked mud and sand that silted rivers and made water unfit for irrigation and domestic use. Yet that leakage would be legally acceptable under Judge Temple's closely read verdict. For the miners, prospects brightened, revived by the judge's loophole. The companies pledged to build a dam at the Narrows of the Yuba River and others at major control points. But such commitments would not be fulfilled unless Marysville and the Anti-Debris Association agreed to cease their litigation.

GLORIOUS NEWS

A TRIUMPH FOR THE PEOPLE!

The Decision in the Gold Run Case.

A PERPETUAL INJUNCTION PUT UPON THE MINES!

Judge Temple's Decision.

SACRAMENTO, June 12th.—Judge Temple has decided the Gold Run case in favor of the valley. He sustains the injunction.

(SECOND DISPATCH.)

SACRAMENTO, June 12th.—Judge Temple decides in favor of the plaintiff in the case of the People vs. the Gold Run mine, and perpetually enjoins the defendant. The decision is eight columns long.

(THIRD DISPATCH.)

SACRAMENTO, Cal., June 12th.—The decision of Judge Temple in the Gold Run case came up to-night and was opened by the County Clerk. A perpetual injunction is granted, subject to certain conditions. This is the decision:

Now therefore, by reason of the premises, and of the last, it is considered by the Court and it is ordered, adjudged and decreed, that said defendant and all the officers, superintendents, foremen, agents and employes thereof be perpetually enjoined and restrained from discharging or dumping into the North Fork of the American river, or into any stream tributary thereto, and especially into Canyon Creek, any bowlders, cobble stones or gravel or sand from

DAILY APPEAL,
JUNE 13, 1882

Marysville could not accept such a compromise. Indeed, the *Daily Appeal* declared outright that "compromise is treason." On June 26, 1882, urged by George Cadwalader, the Anti-Debris Association sent a demand to every mine on the Yuba River watershed: stop dumping within fifteen days or lawsuits would be filed against each and every offender. Scornful and bitter, the *Nevada City Daily Transcript* grumped: "The hell-born and hellbound wretches will never see the day that hydraulic mining will be stopped." Equally defiant, the weekly

Tribune in Forest City taunted: "The mines are not going to close down, and again we ask our enemies: What will you do about it?"

What they did was instruct George Cadwalader to broaden the attack and sue every mine on the Bear River. In Yuba County, the Board of Supervisors secured a court-ordered injunction that shut down the monitors at the great Excelsior pit outside Smartsville. New injunctions followed that closed the Eureka Lake and Blue Tent mines in October. The Anti-Debris Association opened headquarters in Sacramento and sent out a call for young men to join an "Anti-Debris Guard." Seventy volunteers received uniforms with blue sashes that symbolized the demand that the valley's water must once again run pure and blue, unsullied by sediment. In a speech to the guards, George Cadwalader offered the assurance that if the need arose "to take up arms in defense of their natural and lawful rights," they would be the first called. In September 1882 Marysville rallied its own Young Men's Anti-Debris Club to welcome delegates to an Anti-Debris Convention. George Cadwalader and other speakers brought the crowd to its feet with rousing renditions of familiar dogmas, not least that construction of debris dams would only serve to encourage and prolong hydraulic mining. The greatest enthusiasm erupted over a proposal that the legislature pay for a patrol of state police to shut down mines operating in violation of the injunctions.

But speeches and legal challenges and threats did little to slow the hydraulickers through the summer and fall of 1882. In fact, the ominous stirrings in the valley drove the miners to work faster than ever, day and night. Efforts to shut them down spurred the hydraulickers to wash their mountains of gravel and harvest the golden amalgam from their sluice boxes with the appetite of hungry men about to be pulled away from a feast. No matter that the farmers had papered them with writs and stays, the mines were booming. In evening conversations in saloons and boarding houses—and in homes with wives—men talked of their work, and many swore

to the truth of the widely read editorial in the *Daily Transcript*, September 28, that praised the miners for keeping the monitors roaring despite the injunctions: "Is it reasonable to suppose that the miners are willing to sit with their hands folded and a smile of sweet submission on their faces while the farmer courts let their fates hang in the balance for months because of the dictates of greedy lawyers who stand ready to sacrifice the very existence of whole counties of people in order to feather their own nests?"

What an irony, that farming—a livelihood many had fled because of its shackle to a cycle that neither ingenuity nor ambition could affect—should now threaten the miners' freedoms, so long taken for granted.

One man's freedom, however, was another man's encroachment. Farmers had plenty of evidence that their property rights, their livelihoods, were threatened, indeed, for many, destroyed. And yet their legal victories could not be enforced. The hydraulickers simply ignored court injunctions.

SAWYER'S DECISION

Furious and frustrated, the Anti-Debris Association leaders sought a more certain weapon to use against their enemy. George Cadwalader recommended the federal court. Surely the United States government would enforce any injunction its own judiciary might hand down. Let the hydraulic companies face the power and prestige, maybe the anger, of a federal judge.

For this most important case, George Cadwalader chose as claimant Colonel Edwards Woodruff, owner of the thrice-flooded Woodruff Block in Marysville and two tracts of crusted land in Yuba County. As a legal resident of New York State, Woodruff was entitled to federal jurisdiction. On September 19, 1882, Cadwalader filed suit in the Ninth United States District Court in San Francisco, asking for a perpetual injunction against the North Bloomfield Gravel and Mining Company and all

CHRONOLOGY (1880–1899)

1880	Edison patents incandescent lamp
	California's population: 864,694
1881	President Garfield assassinated
	Southern Pacific Railroad begins service, Los Angeles to New Orleans
1883	Brooklyn Bridge opens
1884	*Huckleberry Finn* published
1885	Completion of Santa Fe Railroad, Kansas City to Los Angeles
	First trainload of oranges shipped from Los Angeles to East Coast
1886	Statue of Liberty dedicated
1887	Queen Victoria's Golden Jubilee
	William Randolph Hearst takes control of the *San Francisco Examiner*
1889	Oklahoma land rush: two million acres of former Indian territory
1890	Yosemite and Sequoia National Parks established
1891	Edison patents motion picture camera
	Stanford University opens
1892	Duryea perfects first American automobile
	Sierra Club founded
	Cholera vaccine developed
1895	Marconi invents radio telegraph
	Oil boom in Los Angeles: 700,000 barrels
1898	California celebrates 50th anniversary of gold discovery

other hydraulic companies on the Yuba River watershed.

For the miners, the federal case presented a new threat, but perhaps, as well, their best chance to stop the farmers' relentless legal attacks. Many believed a fair-minded federal judge would validate the miners' claim to prior right, established before the farmers arrived to plant and develop their downstream fields. And beyond that obvious consideration, the fact remained that the farmers could find plenty of land elsewhere for their plantings. The common sense of these and other often-repeated arguments gave the miners optimism that their harassment might soon end. Most comforting, they reminded each other, was the news that the federal district judge who would preside, Judge Lorenzo Sawyer, had come to California as a '49er. He had prospected with pan and shovel along the Sierra streams; he knew the miners' cause, their decades-long investment of labor and capital—millions and millions—risked to dig out the gold that had built California. Their confidence suffused a report in the *Nevada City Daily Transcript* on September 24: "He is one of the most distinguished jurists in the State and the miners are well satisfied to rest their case in his hands."

For the farmers, this would be their Rubicon. On the far side lay victory and an end to the slickens—or defeat and abandonment of the valley. In a San Francisco courtroom crowded with reporters, numerous attorneys, their witnesses, and a lucky few spectators, the case of *Edwards Woodruff vs. North Bloomfield Gravel and Mining Co. et al.* opened on September 19, 1882.

Through the many weeks that followed, Judge Sawyer listened to every argument with an intensity of concentration that everyone knew reflected the weighty decision he would make, a decision that would determine the future of mining in California. To see the farms and the mines—the site of the conflict—the judge conducted inspection trips accompanied by leaders he selected from both sides, men like James McClatchy of the *Sacramento Bee;*

Certainly by no other means does man more completely change the face of nature than by this method of hydraulic mining. Hills melt away and disappear . . . being distributed in the river beds below . . . whole valleys are filled with clean-washed boulders and other rocks left behind in the general debacle. . . . The desolation which remains is remediless and appalling.

Henry G. Hanks, *Second Report of the State Mineralogist . . . 1882*

SAWYER

L. S. Calkins, editor of the *Nevada City Daily Transcript*; George Ohleyer and other members of the Anti-Debris Association; Lester L. Robinson, principal investor in the North Bloomfield Company; and others, all of them quick to offer their opinion and to point to what they hoped would impress the silent jurist. They traveled across despoiled farmland and up into the foothills, along rivers, and to the hydraulic pits. As he observed and listened, Lorenzo Sawyer must have recalled his youthful days along those streams and in those mining camps, when no one paused for a moment to challenge the workings of the miners, back when California belonged to hurrying young men with only gold on their minds.

Now, in January 1883, the judge paused for hours as he studied the brush dams in which engineers and mining companies had placed so much faith. He found these barriers overwhelmed, buried beneath the annual surges of debris. And in Humbug Creek, the well-built timber dam so confidently erected by the North Bloomfield Company now gaped open, unable to hold back the clattering torrent of rocks and gravel cascading from the mouth of the great tunnel above.

The mining companies' chief lawyer, J. K. Byrne, constructed his defense on the basis of old arguments that had thwarted the farmers in earlier confrontations. He filed a motion to dismiss the entire case on the old ground that because no one could trace to any specific mine the slickens that damaged Colonel Woodruff's property, there could be no way fairly to apportion blame. In April Judge Sawyer denied Byrne's motion, stating: "I am entirely satisfied . . . that there is no misjoinder of defendants. They all pour their mining debris into several streams, which they know must, by the force of currents, be carried down into the main river where they commingle into an indistinguishable mass before they reach the point where the nuisances complained of are committed. . . . The final injury is a single one . . . and all defendants cooperate in fact in producing it."

This ruling dealt a serious defeat to the miners because it confirmed in federal court the legal basis for the farmers' earlier lawsuits and resulting injunctions against collective groups of mining companies on the Yuba and Bear Rivers. Whatever Judge Sawyer's final verdict, in the future the farmers and the state would have a powerful precedent for one lawsuit against many mining companies—an ominous prospect for the hydraulickers.

Of far greater and immediate impact, the collapse of the North Bloomfield Company's great English Dam at daybreak on June 18, 1883, struck a devastating blow to the credibility of the defendant's fundamental claim before Judge Sawyer: that dams—brush, timber, and stone—could be relied on to protect the farmers from the miners' accumulating deposits of debris.

In July of that fateful summer Judge Sawyer sought to hurry up the North Bloomfield trial by appointing a special panel of commissioners to cope with witnesses who had not yet testified. By the end of September they numbered over two hundred and the record of the trial covered twenty thousand pages. Finally, in October, the attorneys presented their closing arguments. The mining companies' litigators added a late surprise by contending that because their clients had discharged tailings on Woodruff's property each year for ten years, the companies had acquired prescriptive rights to the land. They owned it, not Woodruff. Seething with outrage, the *Marysville Daily Appeal* reviewed the miners' arguments and concluded: "They won't even let Woodruff have the debris! Can legal fiction any farther go?"

On his last trip to the hills in early October Judge Sawyer traveled up the Yuba Valley and visited the massive brush dam built by the state under the Drainage Act in 1880. Only the barrier's outer edges were still visible above the ever-rising level of debris.

Returning to San Francisco, the judge retired to his chambers to review the thousands of pages of depositions, testimony, and argument. From elegant hotels along Market Street to plank and canvas boardinghouses in Downieville, owners and workers felt the weight of an impending decision. Farmers busy with winter preparations and dry goods merchants in Marysville and Sacramento waited anxiously for the first news. An old-timer, a '49er, would decide their future. His judgment would carry the full power of the federal government. Expectations of either a new beginning or a climactic ending colored conversations and inner thoughts.

More than the usual number of loafers and curious passersby loitered near telegraph offices during November and December, hoping to be the first to catch the news from San Francisco's federal court. But silence from Judge Sawyer's chambers prevailed through Christmas. On January 6, 1884, the San Francisco telegraph office reported that Judge Sawyer would release his decision the following day.

On Friday, January 7, at 11:00 A.M., Lorenzo Sawyer emerged from his office carrying a thick document in the swirl of his black robe. Before the quiet courtroom he settled in his chair and opened the weighty folder. For the next three and a half hours the meticulous jurist read aloud his 225-page decision, determined to share his evaluation of all the evidence before revealing the verdict. After sixteen months of waiting, the people could wait a few hours more.

Encompassing far more than a legal opinion, his deliberate pace and careful detail showed a mind rigorously committed to impartial analysis. In long passages he expressed his respect for the achievements of the hydraulic mining companies: "The boldness with which capitalists, especially these defendants, have invested large amounts of capital; the perfection to which those engaged in hydraulic mining have brought machines and appliances for successful mining; the vast enterprises they have undertaken and successfully carried out; the energy, perseverance, great engineering and mining skill displayed in pursuing these enterprises, excite wonder and unbounded admiration."

Through a monotone of detail and statistics, Judge Sawyer considered the scope of the problem, that hydraulic mining was but in its infancy and its past offered only a hint of what its future would be. "Deducting liberally from the portion already worked, there remain not less than fourteen miles of gravel channel available for washing. At Columbia Hill, [the channel's] surface width varies from three thousand to eight thousand feet, and it is from three hundred to six hundred feet deep. At North Bloomfield it is opened to the bedrock, showing a depth of more than three hundred feet. After allowing for the amount still remaining to be worked at Smartsville, 700 million cubic yards may be assumed to represent the amount of gravel remaining to be worked by the hydraulic process . . . with its debris to be deposited in the water courses." And this calculation applied only to the watershed of the Yuba River.

Slowly, deliberately, the judge read on, constructing the foundation of his opinion with the blocks of evidence gleaned from twenty thousand pages of testimony and his own field trips. Describing the state of the Yuba Valley, he wrote: "Dr. Teegarden's lands afford a very striking example of individual injuries inflicted by this mining debris. . . . He owned 1,275 acres on the Yuba bottoms, some three or four miles above Marysville. All except 75 acres have been buried from three to five feet deep with sand and gravel and utterly destroyed for farming purposes, for which injuries he has received no remuneration. Dr. Teegarden now lives in a small house . . . which is liable to be swept away should the levee break. He testifies that the land on the river side of the levee is five or six feet higher with sand and sediment than on the outside where he lives."

On and on he read, piling up evidence. Mining debris had so raised the bed of the Sacramento River that navigation in Steamboat Slough, its main channel, was now impossible. Impounding dams were so buried "that now debris passes over the dam without obstruction, as though no dam at all existed at that point." Complainant Woodruff's Empire Block had been seriously damaged in the flood of 1875, with one building's foundation washed out and its roof fallen in. Like hundreds of others in Marysville, Woodruff had had to pay his repair costs of $3,000 from his own savings. And then, in an even more measured voice, now edged with his own impatience, Judge Sawyer emphasized that these acts "constitute a grievous and far-reaching public nuisance . . . , a nuisance destructive, continuous, increasing, and threatening to continue, increase, and be still more destructive." Miners and financiers in the audience shifted in their chairs.

There was more and still more, including a devastating dismissal of the defendants' argument that impounding dams would protect the valley from future debris. Methodically Judge Sawyer took apart the hydraulickers' defense with overwhelming evidence and logic, revealing his personal shock at the ruin and devastation tolerated through decades of unrestrained, continuous hydraulic mining. Finally, he delivered his verdict. Like a reluctant executioner, he announced: "After an examination of the great questions involved, as careful and thorough as we are capable of giving them, with a painfully anxious appreciation of the responsibilities resting upon us, and of the disastrous consequences to the defendants, we can come to no other conclusion than that the complainant is entitled to a perpetual injunction."

There it was at last: all hydraulic companies on the tributaries of the Yuba River must cease operations. No tailings could be dumped into stream courses. The mines would face the enforcement powers of the federal government if they attempted to use their equipment and water.

Telegraphers in San Francisco tapped out the message to scores of offices throughout the state, broadcasting the news to hopeful yet fearful thousands: to the valley towns, victory; to the Sierra foothills, calamity.

From Stockton all the way to Red Bluff, the quiet and anxiety that held through midday and into afternoon suddenly broke in a cacophony of steam whistles, gunshots, and church bells. More than any other town, Marysville let loose with wild abandon. Crowds hurrahed. From saloons, bottles circulated along the streets. "Some of the most sober-minded and steady-going men caught the infection and announced they didn't care if they did make fools of themselves." Balconies and hotels quickly sported bunting and flags. A telegraph sent by George Cadwalader brought a jubilant confirmation: "You can have a big time. Success attends us at every point."

That night Marysville was illuminated by a twenty-foot-high pile of crates, boxes, and barrels filled with straw and fifty cases of tar and kerosene

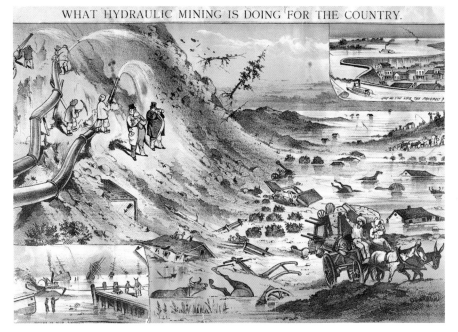

WHAT HYDRAULIC MINING IS DOING FOR THE COUNTRY.

SACRAMENTO BEE ANTI-HYDRAULIC CARTOON

which blazed like a volcano's eruption in Cortez Square. A band paraded through the streets and fireworks flashed in the night sky, cheered by hundreds of citizens confident that after so many false promises the Sawyer decision would put an end to the danger that came from the hills. Carried away by the excitement, few, if any, of the town's merchants pondered a future without those thousands of miners who had so reliably filled their order books over the years.

Celebrants in Sacramento also crowded the streets late into the night. A thirty-five-gun salute called for another round of refreshments. Congratulatory telegrams arrived at the Anti-Debris Association headquarters from all over the Central Valley, from Red Bluff south through Stockton and Merced and as far away as Bakersfield.

Long before dark, by contrast, heavy gloom had settled over the mining counties. Grass Valley expressed "profound sorrow." In Nevada City and along San Juan Ridge down to Smartsville, miners felt stunned, betrayed, disbelieving. At Dutch Flat a bitter hydraulicker spoke for many: "Most of us will pack our gripsacks."

Always more taker than giver, and opportunistic enough never to show exclusive loyalty to any enterprise, San Francisco could consider the momentous decision with some detachment. The *Daily Evening Bulletin* reflected on January 8, 1884, that perhaps Judge Sawyer had hurried an inevitable change, from the exploitive carelessness of mining to the seasonal reliability and reproduction of farming. "The wheat field produces year after year, and wine and oil and wool are perennial." Why lament if California's future growth would come not from what was ripped and washed from the earth but rather from what was planted and harvested? — not only from the annual abundance of golden grain from the Central Valley but soon a new abundance of fruit from hundreds of foothill orchards brought to blossom with water delivered from ditches and flumes that once quenched the thirsty monitors. Heirs to the indomitable spirit no less than the infrastructure of their vanquished adversaries, the farmers learned to exploit the water resources and political power of California, to build a Mesopotamian empire of reservoirs and aqueducts that would dwarf the works of the goldseekers who first gave meaning to sobriquet "Golden State."

EPILOGUE

Oɴ Jᴀɴᴜᴀʀʏ 24, 1898, California celebrated the fiftieth anniversary of the discovery of gold. Towns and cities across the state indulged in a day of pomp, parades, and pontification to commemorate what the *Sacramento Record-Union* declared to be "an event that by the very magnitude of its results amazed the world." Bedazzled by the significance of the anniversary, the newspaper urged "retrospection on the gathering of a half hundred ripened years into the sheaf of time since the discovery of gold in the Pactolean streams of El Dorado's hills." Mayors, important personages, and the governor unleashed equally billowy rhetoric in salute to that moment at Sutter's Mill "that changed the destinies of nations." Even if their Golden State lacked the maturity and prestige that Massachusetts or Virginia had earned from longevity, California's dramatic beginnings had garnered far greater fame. Its rush for riches had made the sheaf of time curl and dry more swiftly than in more mundane places.

In the city by the Golden Gate, delegations of '49ers—now described as "grand old Argonauts" and "pioneers touched with gray"—marched with younger members of the California Miners Association behind floats led by a model of Sutter's Fort "that symbolized the dawn of California's greatness." After this Grand Jubilee procession, the venerated veterans and the even more elderly "companions of James Marshall" took seats of honor at banquets and grand balls hosted by Native Sons and the Society of Pioneers. The finale of a week of festivities brought crowds to an exhibition of mining machinery in the Mechanic's Pavillion. When President McKinley sent a telegraphic signal from the White House, the machines' great wheels turned and stamps pounded, symbolizing the inventive use of technology as the cornerstone of mining and the pursuit of wealth in the Golden State.

In Sacramento, the *Bee* reported special observances that "perpetuated the memory of great men . . . in the Days of Old, Days of Gold, Days of '49." Even Los Angeles organized a parade and banquet and drowsed through ponderous speeches appropriate for the commemoration of an event from ancient history.

Far more perceiving than the orators in the crowded hotels and meeting halls that celebratory day, the state's great historian Hubert Howe Bancroft ten years earlier described the unique society that had evolved from those gold rush years. "There is nothing around us older than ourselves. All that we see has grown up under our eyes. . . . We lack the associations running back for generations, the old homesteads, the grandfather and grandmother, and uncles and aunts." As if responding to this judgment, one visitor to an almost deserted mining town suggested that the surviving '49ers "ought to be gently preserved as historic specimens . . . to remind this youthful country of its past. They are altogether harmless, possessing the peculiar charm of lions with drawn teeth."

While it was Judge Sawyer's 1884 decision that tamed the hydraulickers, those lions had not submitted to the cage of injunctions and contempt citations without growling and clawing. For ten years and more after his momentous ruling, clandestine monitors continued to wash mountainsides, as they had after prior injunctions. Not until the 1890s did a combination of new injunctions and more aggressive enforcement drive all but the most fugitive renegades to concede their fate.

After the mighty monitors shut down and the sounds of nature returned to the foothills and, slowly, the rivers began to run clear, no law could expunge the knowledge that vast riches in gold remained buried in those ancient gravels. Irresistibly tempted, placer miners once again turned to new technology, this time a system called dredging, designed to work within the confines of new legal restraints. Digging in ponds opened by their own excavations, dredges used an endless chain of cast-iron scoops or buckets to reach the richest ore near bedrock. Like huge beasts, these floating mechanisms chewed their way through alluvial basins, dumping their tailings behind, safely distant from streams and rivers. Ever more efficient, dredging continued for decades, into the 1940s. Hard-rock mining at Grass Valley and Jackson and other quartz deposits also persisted, with new inventions and old perseverance enabling modern miners to reach deeper veins of gold—some still profitable in 1998.

* * *

GOLD RUSH WEALTH GAVE CALIFORNIA an adolescence unique among all states and nations. Although the orators on that anniversary day in 1898 sought to dignify California's raucous past, their state's growing power sprang from its very freedom from any past, its absence of tradition. Gold had been the catalyst that caused men by the hundreds of thousands to discard status quo for chance, to exchange security for risk, to abolish all the old rules in pursuit of a new future. The worldly Rudyard Kipling felt the thrill of this robust sentiment in 1889 when he visited San Francisco and wrote: "Recklessness is in the air. I can't explain where it comes from, but there it is. The roaring winds off the Pacific make you drunk with it. . . . The young men are experienced in business and embark on vast enterprises, take partners as experienced as themselves and go to pieces with as much splendor as their neighbors. . . . As far as regards certain tough virtues, they are the pick of the earth. The inept or weakly died on route or went under in the days of construction."

Kipling might have predicted that neither the Sawyer decision nor the shifting currents of California's economy could quell a spirit thus born. Even with gold on the wane, one merchant wrote home to say his return would be delayed: "The independence and liberality here and the excitement attending the rapid march of this country make one feel insignificant and sad at the prospect of returning to the old beaten paths at home." Scores of thousands of letters through the decades carried messages like that, contrasting life in California with the old rules of Cincinnati or Hamburg and dreading what another new Californian called "the picayunes of life back east."

With gold mining more symbol of California's past than contributor to its wealth in the 1890s, California's men of ambition and daring tackled new enterprises, with no evidence of despair or fear that the feast was over. They used the miners' old reservoirs, flumes, and ditches to irrigate vast new orchards and shipped trainloads of golden fruit to eastern states. They drilled oil wells that gushed "black gold" in the very center of Los Angeles. With an imperial reach, they controlled fisheries in Alaska and sugar plantations in Hawaii. Beneficiaries of the seductive power of imagery and dreams, they experimented with motion pictures.

But California's most valuable commodity has not been gold or agricultural produce, barrels of oil, Hollywood movies, or computer chips. More than these emblems of wealth and success, the gold rush experiment bequeathed the idea of California as a place where the impossible is possible. This optimism continues to make the Golden State "America, only more so."

———◆———

NOTES

Without changing the meaning or fundamental tone of any quotation, I have frequently altered punctuation, occasionally changed the tense of verbs, and here and there rearranged the sequence of words, all to the purpose of increasing the readability and coherence of each quotation.

Although many quotations are not reproduced exactly as in their original form, all quotations remain true to their original language and context. Beyond the obvious need to cite the source of quotations, I have made a special effort to acknowledge the source of an idea or concept, even a phrase that I have adapted. This book is a collaborative effort, whereby I have benefited from the labor and insights of the many writers listed in these notes.

C H A P T E R   1   *(Before the World Rushed In)*

page 3

1738 California map: Carolo Ludovico de Launay, double-hemisphered map from his atlas (Augsburg, 1738), reproduced in Dora Beale Polk, *The Island of California: A History of the Myth* (Lincoln: University of Nebraska Press, 1991), plate 47.

"a climate like that of Italy": Francis Guillemard Simkinson, *H.M.S. Sulphur at California, 1837 and 1838: Being the Accounts of Midshipman Francis Guillemard Simkinson and Captain Edward Belcher*, ed. Richard A. Pierce and John H. Winslow (1969); quoted in James J. Rawls, *Indians of California: The Changing Image* (Norman: University of Oklahoma Press, 1984), 27.

"this country, so beautiful, so fertile . . . ": Cyrille Pierre La Place, quoted in George Verne Blue, "The Report of Captain La Place on His Voyage to the Northwest Coast and California in 1839," *California Historical Society Quarterly* 18, no. 4 (1939): 319; quoted in Rawls, *Indians of California*, 27.

Fewer than ten thousand Spanish-Mexican settlers: Hubert Howe Bancroft, *History of California*, vol. 4 (San Francisco: History Co., 1886), 649.

Native people, diseases: Sherburne F. Cook, *The Population of the California Indians, 1769–1970* (Berkeley: University of California Press, 1976), 43–44.

Divine intervention as explanation for delayed gold discovery: Edward Beecher, *The Papal Conspiracy Exposed, and Protestantism Defended, in the Light of Reason, History, and Scripture* (1855; reprint, New York: Arno Press, 1977), 397.

page 4

"Although I was prepared for anarchy . . . ": Charles Wilkes, *Narrative of the United States Exploring Expedition During the Years 1838, 1839, 1840, 1841, 1842*, vol. 5 (Philadelphia: C. Sherman, 1844), 162.

Description of Quivira: George G. Daniels, ed., *The Spanish West* (New York: Time-Life Books, 1976), 41.

page 5

Wreckage of his dreams: T. H. Watkins, *Gold and Silver in the West* (Palo Alto, Calif.: American West Publishing, 1971), 19.

"bold and craggy rocks . . . ": translated from Garci Rodríguez Ordóñez de Montalvo, *Las sergas de Esplandián* (c. 1510), in *California Heritage: An Anthology of History and Literature*, ed. John Caughey and Laree Caughey (Los Angeles: Ward Ritchee Press, 1962), 48–49.

Inset quotation ("In those days of unbridled adventure . . . "): Hubert Howe Bancroft, *California Inter Pocula* (San Francisco: History Co., 1888), 25.

Sebastián Vizcaíno's description of California: quoted from "Vizcaíno's diary" in *Readings in California History*, ed. N. Ray Gilmore and Gladys Gilmore (New York: Thomas Y. Crowell, 1966), 10.

page 6

Prehistoric population figures: Joseph L. Chartkoff and Kerry Kona Chartkoff, "The Pacific Period," in New *Directions in California History: A Book of Readings*, ed. James L. Rawls (New York: McGraw-Hill, 1988), 7.

1769 Indian population: Cook, *Population of California Indians*, 43.

page 8

Without need for leagues, conferences, alliances, etc.: William Brandon, *The American Heritage Book of Indians* (New York: American Heritage, 1961), 301.

Twenty-one "language families": Walton Bean and James J. Rawls, *California: An Interpretive History*, 5th ed. (New York: McGraw-Hill, 1988), 7.

"We came here to serve God . . . ": Bernal Diaz del Castillo, quoted in Brandon, *Book of Indians*, 131.

Indian population reduced, eleven million to six million: Sherburne F. Cook, *The Population of Central Mexico in the Sixteenth Century* (Berkeley: University of California Press, 1948), 31.

"Spain's sword of the Spirit": Irving Berdine Richman, *California Under Spain and Mexico* (Boston: Houghton Mifflin, 1911), 62.

page 9

"half-fed, wholly naked . . . ": ibid., 66.

Footnote (decline in native population): W. Michael Mathes to J. S. Holliday, July 8, 1997.

"It is known . . . ": Richman, *California*, 65.

"to occupy and defend . . . ": William Brandon, *The Last Americans* (New York: McGraw-Hill, 1974), 337.

page 10

Sixty-one soldiers: John Walton Caughey, *California*, 2d ed. (Englewood Cliffs, N.J.: Prentice-Hall, 1953), 113.

Footnote (observations of ship captain): Esteban José, Martinez, diary of 1779 voyage of Frigate *Santiago* (MS, Bancroft Library, University of California, Berkeley), described in *Bancroftiana* 110 (March 1997), 5–6.

Number of non-Indians and mission Indians: Richman, *California*, 226, 452 n. 40.

"these people are a set of idlers . . . ": Isidiro Alanso Salazar to Viceroy Branciforte, May 1716, quoted ibid., 171.

"not to look upon . . . ": Junípero Serra to Antonio María de Bucareli, June 11, 1773, quoted in Daniel J. Garr, "A Rare and Desolate Land: Population and Race in Hispanic California," *Western Historical Quarterly* 6, no. 2 (1975): 134.

"the old delights of savagism": Hubert Howe Bancroft, *History of California,* vol. 1 (San Francisco: History Co., 1886), 387.

"What liberties! . . . ": Francis F. Guest, "The Franciscan World View," in Rawls, *New Directions,* 30.

page 12

Duties of friars: ibid., 28–29.

"vicious pagan practices . . . ": ibid., 29.

"enclaves of Spanish Catholicism . . . ": ibid., 31.

"at the rate the Indians are moving . . . ": Diego de Borica to Pedro de Alberni, August 3, 1796, quoted in Richman, *California,* 177.

"I have never seen . . . ": Louis Choris, quoted in Brandon, *Last Americans,* 339.

Baptisms and death rate, 1790–1800: Bancroft, *History of California,* 1:577.

1810 death rate: Richman, *California,* 226–27.

1818 death rate: ibid., 227.

Condition of female quarters: ibid., 454 n. 46.

1806 measles epidemic: Sherburne F. Cook, *Population Trends Among the California Indians,* vol. 17 in *Ibero-Americana,* ed. C. O. Sauer, A. L. Kroeber, and L. B. Simpson (Berkeley: University of California Press, 1940), 26.

page 13

"is chiefly due to *Mal Gálico* . . . ": Zephyrin Engelhardt, San Francisco or Mission Dolores (Chicago: Franciscan Herald Press, 1924), 162.

Dying from syphilis: Father Sarría to Governor Solá, June 28, 1815, cited ibid., 163.

Forced replacement of Indian labor: Sherburne F. Cook, *The Conflict Between the California Indians and White Civilization* (1943), cited in Patricia Nelson Limerick, *Legacy of Conquest: The Unbroken Past of the American West* (New York: W. W. Norton, 1987), 256.

page 15

Inset quotation ("Once the Pacific coast was Spanish . . . "): Earl Pomeroy, *The Pacific Slope: A History of California, Oregon, Washington, Idaho, Utah, and Nevada* (New York: Alfred A. Knopf, 1965), 6.

Non-Indian population in 1820: Richman, *California,* 226.

Footnote (British immigrants): Howard Zinn, *A People's History of the United States, 1492–Present,* rev. and updated ed. (New York: Harper Perennial, 1995), 49.

"the only defenses against foreign attack . . . ": Captain George Vancouver, quoted in Andrew J. Rolle, *California: A History* (New York: Thomas Y. Crowell, 1963), 99.

"the brass three-pounder . . . ": George Vancouver, *A Voyage of Discovery to the North Pacific Ocean* (1798), in Caughey and Caughey, *California Heritage,* 87.

Cannon incidents: Kevin Starr, *Americans and the California Dream, 1850–1915* (New York: Oxford University Press, 1973), 5.

"an ambassador . . . ": Robert Ryal Miller, *Captain Richardson* (Berkeley: La Loma Press, 1995), 19.

"There is not an object . . . ": George Vancouver, in Caughey and Caughey, *California Heritage,* 86.

"My children . . . ": Miguel Hidalgo, speech, September 16, 1810 ("el grito de Dolores"), quoted in T. H. Watkins, "Outline of Contents for Docent Training Program, California History" (TS, n.d.), 22.

page 16

"Necessity makes lawful . . . ": José Argüello, quoted in Richman, *California,* 207.

List of commodities: Richman, *California,* 205.

"Having personally witnessed . . . ": José de Arrillaga to Viceroy, January 2, 1806, quoted ibid., 202.

Spanish fail to develop otter pelt trade: Bancroft, *History of California,* 1:440 n. 21. Opposite view: Robert Glass Cleland, *From Wilderness to Empire,* ed. Glenn S. Dumke (New York: Alfred A. Knopf, 1959), 55.

4,819 pelts: Adele Ogden, *The California Sea Otter Trade, 1784–1848* (Berkeley: University of California Press, 1941), 140.

Russians at Fort Ross: Cleland, *From Wilderness to Empire,* 58–59.

page 17

"We were received like lords . . . ": Jean Francois Galaup de la Pérouse, *Voyage autour du Monde* (Paris, 1798), quoted in Bancroft, *History of California,* 1:431.

page 18

1,600 pelts by Shaler: Hubert Howe Bancroft, *History of California,* vol. 2 (San Francisco: History Co., 1886), 11.

"very few white people": William Shaler, "Journal of a Voyage from China to the Northwestern Coast of America Made in 1804," in Caughey and Caughey, *California Heritage,* 106.

"California wants nothing . . . ": ibid., 107.

California hears about Mexican independence: Bancroft, *History of California,* 2:451.

Twenty merchantmen traded: ibid., 473–74.

Whalers in San Francisco Bay: Ray Allen Billington, *Westward Expansion* (New York: Macmillan, 1963), 554.

page 19

List of merchandise bartered: Miller, *Captain Richardson,* 15; Cleland, *From Wilderness to Empire,* 70; Richard Henry Dana, *Two Years Before the Mast* (1840; reprint, New York: New American Library, 1964), 75.

Recollections of *comandante*'s daughter: Richman, *California,* 337.

200 to 300 percent profit: Miller, *Captain Richardson,* 14; Dana, *Two Years,* 75.

Hide and tallow trade: Miller, *Captain Richardson,* 15.

Wanting in "industry, frugality and enterprise": Richard Henry Dana, quoted in James D. Hart, *American Images of Spanish California* (Berkeley: Friends of the University of California, 1960), 19.

"There are no people . . . ": ibid.

"In the hands of an enterprising people . . . ": Dana, *Two Years,* 163.

"become weary of rest": Jedediah Smith, quoted in Starr, *Americans,* 35.

page 21

Number of foreigners, 1810 etc.: Neal Harlow, *California Conquered: War and Peace on the Pacific, 1846–1850* (Berkeley: University of California Press, 1982), 15.

Non-Indian population in 1830: Hubert Howe Bancroft, *History of California,* vol. 3 (San Francisco: History Co., 1886), 699.

Convicts as settlers and soldiers: Harlow, *California Conquered,* 22.

Inset quotation ("Not only from their numbers . . . "): George Simpson to John H. Pelly, March 10, 1842, in "Letters of Sir George Simpson, 1841–1843," ed. Joseph Schafer, *American Historical Review* 14, no. 1 (1908): 89.

Cargo worth $79,000: Adele Ogden, "Alfred Robinson: New England Merchant in Mexican California," *California Historical Society Quarterly* 23, no. 3 (1944): 196.

page 22

Alert's cargo: ibid., 199.

First two-story residence: Harold Kirker, *California's Architectural Frontier: Style and Tradition in the Nineteenth Century* (San Marino, Calif.: Huntington Library, 1960; reprint, Santa Barbara, Calif.: Peregrine Smith, 1973), 13.

Enterprise of Larkin: Harlan Hague and David J. Langum, *Thomas O. Larkin: A Life of Patriotism and Profit in Old California* (Norman: University of Oklahoma Press, 1990), 59–62.

Purchase of Fort Ross: Bancroft, *History of California,* 4:179–81.

Size of mission lands: Robert Glass Cleland, *The Cattle on a Thousand Hills: Southern California, 1850–1880* (San Marino, Calif.: Huntington Library, 1951), 21.

page 23

Footnote (mission agriculture): Forbes's *California,* cited in Robert Glass Cleland and Osgood Hardy, *March of Industry* (Los Angeles: Powell Publishing, 1929), 10; Zephyrin Engelhardt, *The Missions and Missionaries of California,* vol. 3 (San Francisco: James H. Barry, 1913), app. J.

"A slavedriver . . . ": Narciso Durán, quoted in David J. Weber, "The Collapse of the Missions," in Rawls, *New Directions,* 50.

Secularization plan: Weber, "Collapse," 53.

Footnote (population figures): Bancroft, *History of California,* 3:649, 699.

page 24

"All is destruction . . . ": José Rubio, quoted by Weber in "Collapse," 54.

"entirely gone to ruin": William Hartnell, quoted in "California in 1844 as Hartnell Saw It," ed. Lauro de Rojas, *California Historical Society Quarterly* 17, no. 1 (1938): 24.

Twenty Spanish land grants: Richman, *California,* 347.

26 million acres: Claude B. Hutchinson, ed., *California Agriculture* (Berkeley: University of California Press, 1946), 25.

813 Mexican land grant applicants: Ogden Hoffman, *Report of Land Cases Determined in the United States District Court for the Northern California District of California* (1862), cited in Paul W. Gates, ed., *California Ranchos and Farms, 1846–1862* (Madison: State Historical Society of Wisconsin, 1967), 7–8.

Grants of 4,400 to 700,000 acres: Gates, *California Ranchos and Farms,* 8–9; Leonard Pitt, *The Decline of the Californios: A Social History of the Spanish-Speaking Californians, 1846–1890* (Berkeley: University of California Press, 1970), 10.

"Surveying" methods: Cleland, *From Wilderness to Empire,* 66–67. This system of granting land, "simple, vague and useful for the purposes of a pastoral people scattered over a vast territory" (Josiah Royce, *California: From the Conquest in 1846 to the Second Vigilance Committee in San Francisco: A Study in American Character* [1886; reprint, New York: Alfred A. Knopf, 1948], 38), became the most important and contentious legacy of Spanish and Mexican rule.

page 27

Inset quotation ("The people were very fond of riding . . ."): William Tecumseh Sherman, *Memoirs* (New York: Literary Classics of the United States, 1990), 45.

"happy people . . . ": John C. Frémont, quoted in Hart, *American Images,* 22.

"They sleep and smoke . . . ": Thomas Jefferson Farnham, quoted ibid., 13.

Lack of milk, cheese, butter: Alfred Robinson, *Life in California: During a Residence of Several Years in That Territory* (1846; reprint, New York: Da Capo Press, 1969), 220.

Carcasses cleaned by dogs: Richman, *California,* 349.

Skulls, skeletons, and vultures: Starr, *Americans,* 17.

"a society doomed . . . ": ibid.

Few literate: Bean and Rawls, *California,* 54.

"a village of 600 to 800 inhabitants . . . ": Richman, *California,* 285.

City populations: Richman, *California,* 286; Hubert Howe Bancroft, *History of California,* vol. 6 (San Francisco: History Co., 1888), 6; Sherman, *Memoirs,* 45.

page 28

"To speak of California . . . ": Agustín Janssens, quoted in Pitt, *Decline of the Californios,* 6.

Eleven governors, 1831–36: Bean and Rawls, *California,* 45.

Alvarado's revolt: Harlow, *California Conquered,* 27.

Band of *cholos:* T. H. Watkins, *California: An Illustrated History* (New York: American Legacy Press, 1983), 51.

Family as a potentially powerful institution: Pitt, *Decline of the Californios,* 11.

Rancho with six hundred Indian workers: Gates, *California Ranchos and Farms,* 7.

President Jackson's attempt to purchase California: Caughey, *California,* 220; Harlow, *California Conquered,* 4.

page 30

"the richest, the most beautiful . . . ": Waddy Thompson, quoted in Thomas A. Bailey, *A Diplomatic History of the American People,* 4th ed. (New York: Appleton-Century-Crofts, 1950), 265.

Footnote (twenty thousand settlers in Texas): Billington, *Westward Expansion,* 491.

"were of no consequence, as everybody knows": Bancroft, *History of California,* 4:307.

"with music, and their colors flying": ibid., 308.

"infallible emblem of civil liberty": ibid., 309 n. 19.

Gold discovery in San Fernando hills: ibid., 296–7, 630–31 n. (for 1842). The story of California's "first gold discovery" is developed in considerable detail in Emil T. H. Bunje and James C. Kean, *Pre-Marshall Gold in California,* vol. 2: *Discoveries and Near-Discoveries, 1840–1848* (Sacramento: Historic California Press, 1983), 7–19.

page 31

America's "ample geography": Ralph Waldo Emerson, quoted in Alexis Doster III, Joe Goodwin, and Robert C. Post, eds., *The American Land* (New York: W. W. Norton, 1979), 46.

page 32

Oregon immigration numbers: Billington, *Westward Expansion,* 526, 528.

California immigration, 1841–45: Caughey, *California,* 212–16.

Inset quotation ("We find ourselves threatened . . . "): Pío Pico, quoted in Titus F. Cronise, *The Natural Wealth of California* (San Francisco: H. H. Bancroft, 1868), 51.

"man and woman . . . ": Thomas Hart Benton, quoted in John A. Hawgood, "Manifest Destiny," in *British Essays in American History,* ed. H. C. Allen and C. P. Hall (n.p., n.d.), 136.

page 33

"patriotic pioneers": T. Bailey, *Diplomatic History,* 238.

Crisis with Mexico: T. Bailey, *Diplomatic History,* 262–72; Billington, *Westward Expansion,* 568–71; Caughey, California, 165–72; Robert Glass Cleland, *A History of California* (New York: Macmillan, 1922), 165–72; Bernard DeVoto, *The Year of Decision: 1846* (Boston: Houghton Mifflin, 1943), 13–17; Harlow, *California Conquered,* 51–58, 116.

"to exert the greatest vigilance": Billington, *Westward Expansion,* 570.

Vallejo's holdings: Daniels, *Spanish West,* 181.

page 34

Slidell's mission: DeVoto, *Year of Decision,* 28; Caughey, *California,* 226.

"by the act of the Republic of Mexico . . . ": James K. Polk in proclamation, May 13, 1846, quoted in Harlow, *California Conquered,* 116.

"ascertain beyond a doubt": Harlow, *California Conquered,* 116–17.

"They may, as you know sailors will . . . ": Reuben L. Underhill, *From Cowhides to Golden Fleece* (Stanford: Stanford University Press, 1939), 119.

Gun salutes and fiesta: Harlow, *California Conquered,* 119.

Surrender of Monterey: ibid., 121.

No Mexican flag: Underhill, *Cowhides to Golden Fleece,* 118.

page 35

"Although I come in arms . . . ": Thomas ap Catesby Jones, quoted in Bancroft, *History of California,* 4:309 n. 19.

page 36

"slowly and growlingly": John C. Frémont to Jessie Frémont, April 1, 1846, quoted in Hubert Howe Bancroft, *History of California,* vol. 5 (San Francisco: History Co., 1886), 21.

Beginning of Bear Flag Revolt: DeVoto, *Year of Decision,* 224–25; Harlow, *California Conquered,* 98–102.

Inset quotation ("California was suffused . . ."): DeVoto, *Year of Decision,* 127.

"Choose you this day . . . ": William Ide, quoted in Royce, *California,* 57; and Harlow, California Conquered, 102.

Making the flag: DeVoto, *Year of Decision,* 225.

One-village nation: ibid.

page 37

"spectacular contribution . . . ": William H. Goetzman, *Army Exploration in the American West, 1803–1863* (New Haven: Yale University Press, 1959), 103.

page 38

Inset quotation ("These Americans are so contriving . . ."): José Castro, quoted in Robert Glass Cleland, "The Early Sentiment for the Annexation of California: An Account of the Growth of American Interest in California, 1835–1846," *Southwestern Historical Quarterly* 18, no. 2 (1914): 151.

"Banish from your hearts . . . ": José Castro, proclamation, June 17, 1846, quoted in Harlow, *California Conquered,* 106.

"gang of North American adventurers": Pío Pico, proclamation, June 23, 1846, quoted in Harlow, *California Conquered,* 108.

"Compatriots, run swiftly . . . ": Pío Pico, quoted in Cleland, *History of California,* 204.

Six hundred soldiers at Acapulco: Harlow, *California Conquered,* 270–71.

Three unarmed Californios shot: ibid., 110.

"most unjust aggression . . . ": Pío Pico, quoted in Bancroft, *History of California,* 5:263 n. 9.

page 40

"My word is at present . . .": Robert F. Stockton to James K. Polk, August 26, 1846, quoted in Harlow, *California Conquered,* 152–53.

"The Sons of Liberty . . .": Robert F. Stockton, quoted in Harlow, *California Conquered,* 157.

Vicious melee at San Pasqual: Pitt, *Decline of the Californios,* 34.

"calm as a clock": Edward F. Beale, quoted in Dwight L. Clarke, *Stephen Watts Kearny: Soldier of the West* (Norman: University of Oklahoma Press, 1961), 214.

"desperate and drunken fellows": William H. Emory, *Notes of a Military Reconnoissance from Fort Leavenworth, in Missouri, to San Diego, in California,* 30th Cong., 1st sess., H. Ex. Doc. 41 (1848), quoted in Harlow, *California Conquered,* 217.

CHAPTER 2 *(Free For All)*

page 44

"The old brig *Providence* . . .": C.A.M. Taber, reminiscences, in *Sacramento Record-Union,* July 1, 1900.

page 47

"military despotism": *Californian,* June 5, 1847, quoted in Royce, *California,* 166 n. 27.

"ineffectual mongrel military government": William Henry Ellison, *A Self-Governing Dominion: California, 1849–1860* (Berkeley: University of California Press, 1950), 12.

"California at this moment is in a state of anarchy . . .": William Robert Garner, *Letters from California, 1846–1847,* ed. Donald Munro Craig (Berkeley: University of California Press, 1970), 185–86.

Inset quotation ("Seldom is a conquered country . . . "): Royce, *California,* 157–58.

page 48

Footnote (news of the Treaty of Guadalupe Hidalgo): Harlow, *California Conquered,* 303.

Solemnizing marriages and granting divorces: Royce, *California,* 167.

Daring raid on a farm near San Jose: *California Star,* March 28, 1847, quoted in Edwin Bryant, *What I Saw in California* (1848; reprint, Santa Ana, Calif.: Fine Arts Press, 1936), 422.

"You may tell the people . . . ": Richard B. Mason, quoted in Harlow, *California Conquered,* 295.

Mason's underfunded administration: Harlow, *California Conquered,* 296–97.

"We are all supremely poor": Philip St. George Cooke, quoted ibid., 296.

"a distant idea . . . ": Garner, *Letters,* 179.

"Yankeefied": Thomas O. Larkin to Faxon D. Atherton, August 14, 1847, quoted in Hague and Langum, *Thomas O. Larkin,* 176.

Fifty thousand pounds of hardtack for $6,000: Hague and Langum, *Thomas O. Larkin,* 159.

"Business will increase astonishingly": Thomas O. Larkin to William M. Rogers, July 24, 1846, quoted ibid.

A rancho along the Feather River: Hague and Langum, *Thomas O. Larkin,* 186.

"trying to build a town . . . ": Thomas O. Larkin to Samuel J. Hastings, November 16, 1846, in *The Larkin Papers: Personal, Business, and Official Correspondence of Thomas Oliver Larkin, Merchant and United States Consul in California,* ed. George P. Hammond, 10 vols. (Berkeley: University of California Press, 1951–64), 5:280.

page 50

"will be the busy, bustling uproar of places": Thomas O. Larkin to Samuel J. Hastings, November 16, 1846, ibid., 279.

Larkin sought profits: Hague and Langum, *Thomas O. Larkin,* 182–85.

"not a single modern wagon . . . ": Sherman, *Memoirs,* 44.

"We have fine forest trees for lumber . . . ": Garner, *Letters,* 201.

"for endless board feet . . . ": Donald Munro Craig, biographical introduction to Garner, *Letters,* 20.

"California can never go ahead very fast . . . " Garner, *Letters,* 197, 204–5.

page 51

Sale of 830 lots in San Francisco: John S. Hittell, *A History of the City of San Francisco and Incidentally of the State of California* (San Francisco: A. L. Bancroft, 1878), 116.

Eight hundred residents; 160 structures; wharves: Bancroft, *History of California,* 6:6, 7 n. 6, 7.

Twenty-ton schooner *Sacramento*: Hittell, *History of San Francisco,* 118–19; Oscar Lewis, *Sutter's Fort: Gateway to the Gold Fields* (Englewood Cliffs, N.J.: Prentice-Hall, 1966), 56, 181.

"The one is a lying sycophant . . . ": Samuel Brannan, quoted in Reva Scott, *Samuel Brannan and the Golden Fleece* (New York: Macmillan, 1944), 154.

San Jose population: Bancroft, *History of California,* 6:4.

California population: ibid., 5:643, 6:3.

page 52

"a miniature Mediterranean": Garner, *Letters,* 191 n. 1.

James Reed's description of California agriculture: James Reed to Gersham Keyes, July 2, 1847, in Dale Morgan, ed., *Overland in 1846: Diaries and Letters of the California-Oregon Trail,* 2 vols. (Georgetown, Calif: Talisman Press, 1963), 1:301–4.

page 53

"California mad": Captain Dupont to Mrs. Dupont, March 17, 1847, quoted in Harlow, *California Conquered,* 290.

$7,000 for a 65,000-acre rancho: ibid.

Sale of Indian children: Albert L. Hurtado, "John A. Sutter and the Indian Business," in *John A. Sutter and a Wider West,* ed. Kenneth M. Owens (Lincoln: University of Nebraska Press, 1994), 65.

Inset quotation ("The fort is a parallelogram . . ."): Bancroft, *History of California*, 6:13–14.

Indians in uniforms: Hurtado, "John A. Sutter," 62.

---

page 54

"I am up here at the Capital . . .": William S. Jewett, letter of April 14, 1855, in "Some Letters of William S. Jewett, California Artist," ed. Elliot Evans, *California Historical Society Quarterly* 23, no. 3 (1944): 227.

---

page 55

"to show the Indians the effect of powder and ball": John A. Sutter, quoted in Hurtado, "John A. Sutter," 59.

"A large number of deer, elk . . .": William Heath Davis, quoted ibid.

Reflections on success: John A. Sutter, quoted ibid., 61.

Use of Sutter's "army": Hurtado, "John A. Sutter," 62–63.

Footnote (epidemic of 1833): Edith Pitti, "Earthmaker's People" (Sacramento, Calif.: Sacramento Museum, n.d., photocopy), 14–15. The following statement sums up the tragedy: "Decimated by disease, overrun by a larger and better armed population, confronted by enterprises which denied them access to their traditional livelihoods as well as opportunities to participate in the new monetary economy, Native Americans struggled to survive. From a pre-contact population of over 76,000 in the Sacramento Valley, the population dropped to less than a tenth of that by 1860. . . . Thus, the three decades between 1830 and 1860 almost destroyed a way of life that had existed for 5,000 years" (ibid., 2:22–23).

Effect of European diseases on the Indians: Hurtado, "John A. Sutter," 66. For further information on Indian loss of life, see Joe Pitti et al., "Research Document," pt. 1 (Sacramento: Sacramento History Center, n.d., photocopy), 124–29.

"three or four hundred wild Indians . . . ": John Bidwell, quoted in Lewis, *Sutter's Fort*, 111–12.

---

page 56

"will grind what the whole Sacramento Valley . . . ": John A. Sutter to Thomas O. Larkin, quoted ibid., 143.

"The week has passed off prety bussy . . . ": Azariah Smith, "A Journal or History, of Azariah Smith; his travail &c in the Mormon Battalion, in the service of the United States, to California; And from there to Salt Lake valley," in *The California Gold Discovery: Sources, Documents, Accounts, and Memoirs Relating to the Discovery of Gold at Sutter's Mill*, ed. Rodman W. Paul (Georgetown, Calif.: Talisman Press, 1966), 65–66.

"Home keeps running in my mind . . . ": ibid., 66.

James Marshall's week of January 16: Paul, *California Gold Discovery*, 32.

"It made my heart thump . . . ": Charles B. Gillespie, "Marshall's Own Account of the Gold Discovery" (1891), in Paul, *California Gold Discovery*, 199.

---

page 58

Conversation between Marshall and worker: James L. Marshall and John A. Sutter, "The Discovery of Gold in California" (1857), in Paul, ed., *California Gold Discovery*, 118.

"Boys, I believe I have found a gold mine": Bancroft, *History of California*, 6:33.

"It is found in the raceway . . . ": Azariah Smith, journal entry for January 30, 1848, in Paul, *California Gold Discovery*, 67.

Sutter's statements about gold discovery: Lewis, *Sutter's Fort*, 147.

Statements of Azariah Smith on collecting gold: Smith's journal entries for February 14 and 20, 1848, in Paul, *California Gold Discovery*, 67.

February and March finds: Bancroft, *History of California*, 6:47–49.

"Today we started the mill . . . ": Azariah Smith, journal entry for March 12, 1848, in Paul, *California Gold Discovery*, 67.

---

page 59

"I have made a discovery . . . ": Bancroft, *History of California*, 6:43.

Lease with Indians: ibid., 41, 43. Note that David Allan Comstock, *Gold Diggers and Camp Followers: The Nevada County Chronicles, 1845–1851* (Grass Valley, Calif.: Comstock Bonanza Press, 1982), 106–7, says it was a twenty-year lease. Richard Dillon, *Fool's Gold: The Decline and Fall of Captain John Sutter of California* (New York: Coward-McCann, 1967; reprint, Santa Cruz, Calif.: Western Tanager Press, 1981), 285, says it was for three years.

"I last evening received your letter . . . ": Richard B. Mason to John A. Sutter, March 5, 1848, in Paul, *California Gold Discovery*, 81; also see Sherman, Memoirs, 64–65.

"In the newly made raceway . . . ": *Californian*, March 15, 1848, quoted in Bancroft, *History of California*, 6:54 n. 2.

"some hidden treasure": *California Star*, March 25, 1848, quoted in Bancroft, *History of California*, 6:54 n. 3; see also Paul, *California Gold Discovery*, 70.

---

page 60

"The Mormons did not like to leave . . . ": John A. Sutter to J. M. Hutchings, in *Hutchings Illustrated California Magazine* 2, no. 5 (1857): 194–98; reprinted in California Division of Mines, *The Elephant as They Saw It: A Collection of Contemporary Pictures and Statements on Gold Mining in California* (Sacramento: Office of State Printing, 1949), 36.

"and left me only the sick and the lame behind": John A. Sutter, *The Diary of Johann August Sutter* (San Francisco: Grabhorn Press, 1932), 45, entry for March 7, 1848.

Arrival of Sam Brannan: John A. Sutter, *New Helvetia Diary: A Record of Events Kept by John A. Sutter and His Clerks at New Helvetia, California, from September 9, 1845, to May 25, 1848* (San Francisco: Grabhorn Press, 1939), 128, entry for April 7, 1848.

"in Ameriky I have beef three times a week . . .": quoted in Douglas S. Watson, "The Great Express Extra of the *California Star* of April 1, 1848," *California Historical Society Quarterly* 11, no. 2 (1932): 137.

"The Great Sacramento Valley has a mine of gold . . . ": *California Star*, April 1, 1848, quoted in Bancroft, *History of California*, 6:54 n. 4.

"Gold! . . . from the American River!": Samuel Brannan, quoted in Bancroft, *History of California*, 6:56.

page 61

"Considerable excitement exists in our midst . . . ": *Californian*, May 17, 1848, quoted in Paul, *California Gold Discovery*, 70–71.

"a terrible visitant we have had of late . . . ": *California Star*, May 20, 1848, quoted ibid., 79.

"Everybody is in the greatest state of excitement . . .": Thomas O. Larkin to Richard B. Mason, May 26, 1848, quoted ibid., 84.

"The majority of our subscribers . . . ": *Californian*, May 29, 1848, quoted ibid., 71–72.

Inset quotation ("This little scratch . . . "): Bancroft, *History of California*, 6:52.

"Our town was startled out of its quiet dreams . . .": Walter Colton, *Three Years in California* (1850; New York: Arno Press, 1976), 242, journal entry for May 29, 1848.

Colton's June 5, 1848, journal entry: ibid., 213.

Colton's June 12, 1848, journal entry: ibid., 245.

page 62

Rising price of digging tools: ibid., Bancroft, *History of California*, 6:59.

"every little cockleshell": Miller, *Captain Richardson*, 140.

$2,500 per trip: ibid., 141.

Two hundred wagons at Carquinez ferry: Bancroft, *History of California*, 6:58.

"Sir, you have been trading for fifteen years with Californios": Robert B. Semple to Thomas O. Larkin, July, 29, 1848, in *Larkin Papers*, 7:326.

page 63

"I have to report to the State Department . . . ": Thomas O. Larkin to James Buchanan, June 1, 1848, in Paul, *California Gold Discovery*, 84–86.

Larkin's June 28 report: Thomas O. Larkin to James Buchanan, June 28, 1848, ibid., 86–90.

Shipment of gold sample: Sherman, *Memoirs*, 81; Bancroft, *History of California*, 6:115 n. 10.

Mason's report on the gold region: Richard B. Mason to Roger Jones, August 17, 1848, in Paul, *California Gold Discovery*, 93–97.

page 64

Footnote (Appalachian gold mining): Watkins, *Gold and Silver*, 21–23.

page 66

"a few men working . . . ": Thomas O. Larkin to James Buchanan, July 20, 1848, in *Larkin Papers*, 7:320.

page 68

$75,000 in three months: Bancroft, *History of California*, 6:72.

P. B. Reading's $80,000 fortune: "Pierson B. Reading: A Brief Biography," *Quarterly of the Society of California Pioneers* 7, no. 3 (1930): 137.

$26,000 at Sullivan Bar: Bancroft, *History of California*, 6:89 n.12.

$200 to $300 each day: ibid., 77.

$14,000 in September: ibid.

Larkin's July 20 report: Thomas O. Larkin to James Buchanan, July 20, 1848, in *Larkin Papers*, 7:321–22.

page 69

"seriously depreciate in value": Richard B. Mason to Roger Jones, August 17, 1848, in Paul, *California Gold Discovery*, 94.

Price of gold by August: Bancroft, *History of California*, 6:91.

300 to 400 percent profit at Brannan's store: William Tecumseh Sherman, letter of October 28, 1848, in *The California Gold Fields in 1848: Two Letters from Lt. W. T. Sherman, U.S.A.* (privately published for Frederick W. Beinecke, 1964), n.p.

Inset quotation ("The day was intensely hot . . ."): Richard B. Mason to Roger Jones, August 17, 1848, in Paul, *California Gold Discovery*, 91, 95–96.

$300 for a horse: Bancroft, *History of California*, 6:93.

page 71

Need for blankets and clothes: Charles B. Sterling to Thomas O. Larkin, July, 14, 1848, in *Larkin Papers*, 7:316.

"There are no shoes on all the Sacramento . . . ": Moses Schallenberger to Talbot H. Green, August 18, 1848, ibid., 341.

Agent's August 16 report: Moses Schallenberger to Thomas O. Larkin, August 16, 1848, ibid., 338–39.

Profits at grog shop: Dale L. Morgan and James R. Scobie, introduction to William Perkins, *Three Years in California: William Perkins' Journal of Life at Sonora, 1849–1852* (Berkeley: University of California Press, 1964), 18.

Agent's August 18 report: Moses Schallenberger to Talbot H. Green, August 18, 1848, in *Larkin Papers*, 7:342.

page 72

"Sailors desert their ships . . . ": Richard B. Mason to Roger Jones, August 17, 1848, in Paul, *California Gold Discovery*, 96–97.

"another bag of gold . . .": Colton, *Three Years in California*, 248–49.

Colton's August 16 journal entry: ibid., 252–53.

1,300 Californio goldseekers: Pitt, *Decline of the Californios*, 50.

Coronel story: Morgan and Scobie, introduction to Perkins, *Three Years*, 21–25; Bancroft, *History of California*, 6:78–81.

page 73

Scene at Sutter's Fort: Bancroft, *History of California*, 6:94–95.

$1,800 monthly rent: Dillon, *Fool's Gold*, 295.

Theft of packed salmon: ibid., 297.

Stolen millstones: Bancroft, *History of California*, 6:103 n. 28.

Sale of sawmill: Marshall and Sutter, "Discovery of Gold," in Paul, *California Gold Discovery*, 119.

Sutter's workers drawn to grog shops: ibid., 132; Dillon, *Fool's Gold*, 295.

"The whole expedition . . . ": Marshall and Sutter, "Discovery of Gold," in Paul, *California Gold Discovery*, 132.

"By this sudden discovery . . . ": ibid., 133.

Marshall and Sutter fail at mining: Bancroft, *History of California*, 6:100.

---

page 74

"has recently been purchased . . . ": R. S. Williamson, *Report of Exploration in California for Railroad Routes . . . ,* vol. 5 (Washington, D.C., 1853), 271.

---

page 75

Footnote (Treaty of Guadalupe Hidalgo): John M. Blum et al., *The National Experience: A History of the United States* (New York: Harcourt, Brace & World, 1963), 167, 274; Howard R. Lamar, ed., *The Reader's Encyclopedia of the American West* (New York: Thomas Y. Crowell, 1977), 23, 474.

Governor Mason's proclamation: quoted in Bancroft, *History of California*, 5:591–92.

San Francisco's "grand illumination": Frank Soulé, John H. Gihon, and James Nisbet, *The Annals of San Francisco* (New York: D. Appleton, 1855), 205.

"citizens speechified and hurrahed . . . ": ibid., 194.

"Black eyes and bloody noses . . .": letter signed "Watchman," August 24, 1848, in the *Polynesian* (Honolulu), September 23, 1848.

"the great law of necesssity": Harlow, *California Conquered*, 307.

Fifty-man army: ibid., 304.

---

page 76

"all sorts of crime . . . ": ibid., 314.

"The war being over . . . ": ibid, 315.

$60,000-per-day gold production: *Californian*, August 14, 1848, in Paul, *California Gold Discovery*, 73.

"Immense quantities of merchandise . . . ": *Californian*, September 23, 1848, quoted ibid., 75.

Cook's wages: Thomas O. Larkin to James Buchanan, November 16, 1848, in *Larkin Papers*, 8:39.

Larkin's report of San Francisco profits: Thomas O. Larkin to Mott Talbot and Company, December 26, 1848, in *Larkin Papers*, 8:78.

"Occasional" religious services: Soulé, Gihon, and Nisbet, *Annals of San Francisco*, 207.

---

page 77

"daring outrages . . . ": ibid., 208.

Sentiment for territorial government: ibid.

Footnote (fate of territorial legislation): Ellison, *Self-Governing Dominion*, 17; ("one of the most bitter sectional debates . . . "): Blum et al., *National Experience*, 278.

"one of the most brilliant examples of confidencemanship . . . ": Dillon, *Fool's Gold*, 308.

Population of the gold region: Richard B. Mason to Roger Jones, August 17, 1848, in Paul, *California Gold Discovery*, 92; Thomas O. Larkin to James Buchanan, July 20, 1848, in *Larkin Papers*, 7:320.

---

page 78

"Mrs. Eagar who won't move . . . ": letter of William Tecumseh Sherman, November 14, 1848, in Sherman, *California Gold Fields*, n.p.

"we have not the power . . . ": letter of William Tecumseh Sherman, October 28, 1848, ibid.

"Were I at liberty . . . ": letter of William Tecumseh Sherman, November 14, 1848, ibid.

"took from one of their packs . . . ": Colton, *Three Years in California*, 272.

---

page 79

"In the midst of all this extraordinary prosperity . . . ": Jacques Antoine Moerenhout, *The Inside Story of the Gold Rush*, trans. and ed. Abraham P. Nasatir (San Francisco: California Historical Society, 1935), 45.

CHAPTER 3 *(Worldwide Contagion)*

---

page 83

"It is beyond all question . . . ": *Times* (London), December 14, 1848.

"there being no regulations . . . ": *Polynesian* (Honolulu), June 24, 1848.

1849 overland immigration: The 6,000 figure for Mexican immigration comes from Morgan and Scobie, introduction to W. Perkins, *Three Years*, 30. The 42,000 figure for American overlanders is a combination of the 10,000 who took the southern trails (Ferol Egan, *The El Dorado Trail: The Story of the Gold Rush Routes Across Mexico* [New York: McGraw-Hill, 1970], 280) and the 32,000 who took various routes through South Pass (J. S. Holliday, *The World Rushed In: The California Gold Rush Experience* [New York: Simon & Schuster, 1981], 470–71, note on overland emigration).

1849 seaborne immigration: The figure of 17,000 foreign arrivals is obtained by subtracting Bancroft's figure for American seaborne immigrants (25,000 in *History of California*, 6:159) from a total seaborne immigration of 42,000, which in turn is obtained by adjusting Bancroft's total of 39,000 (ibid.) to reflect the estimate for deserters by Soulé, Gihon, and Nisbet (*Annals of San Francisco*, 243). The harbor master's count of 62,000 arrivals between April 1849 and April 1850 is cited in James P. Delgado, *To California by Sea: A Maritime History of the California Gold Rush* (Columbia: University of South Carolina Press, 1990), x.

page 84

"Joseph has borrowed . . .": shopkeeper's wife, quoted in Oscar Lewis, *Sea Routes to the Gold Fields: The Migration by Water to California in 1849–1852* (New York:Alfred A. Knopf, 1949), 10.

page 86

Gold fever in Honolulu: Bancroft, *History of California*, 6:111–12 n. 2.

Footnote (Hawaiian commerce): Theodore Morgan, *Hawaii: A Century of Economic Change, 1778–1876* (Cambridge: Harvard University Press, 1948), 154–56.

"The little city of Honolulu . . . ": Polynesian (Honolulu), July 15, 1848.

"The people of California . . . ": *Polynesian* (Honolulu), September 23, 1848.

"From this our planters and traders . . . ": *Polynesian* (Honolulu), July 15, 1848.

"Oregon is convulsed . . . ": *Oregon Spectator* (Oregon City), September 7, 1848.

"The gold fever . . . ": *Oregon Spectator* (Oregon City), October 12, 1848.

150 men/50 wagons: Bancroft, *History of California*, 6:113 n. 4.

"Your streams have minnows . . . ": Walter Colton, quoted in John Walton Caughey, *Gold Is the Cornerstone* (Berkeley: University of California Press, 1948), 40.

"a Peruvian harvest of precious metals": *New York Herald*, August 19, 1848.

Mason's gold report/shipment: Bancroft, *History of California*, 6:115 n. 10.

page 87

"there is more gold in the country . . . ": Richard B. Mason to Roger Jones, August 17, 1848; in Paul, *California Gold Discovery*, 97.

Presidential confirmation: James K. Polk, December 5, 1848, message to Congress, H. Ex. Doc. 1, serial 37, 30th Congress, 2d Sess.

page 88

"whatever else they may lack . . . ": Horace Greeley, quoted in Donald Dale Jackson, *Gold Dust* (New York: Alfred A. Knopf, 1980), 65.

"The gold excitement here . . . ": quoted from Daniel Walton, *The Book Needed for the Times, Containing the Latest Well-Authenticated Facts from the Gold Regions . . .* (1849), quoted in Doris Wright, "The Making of Cosmopolitan California: An Analysis of Immigration, 1848–1870, pt. 2: Immigration from European Countries," *California Historical Society Quarterly* 20, no. 1 (1941): 66.

"boundless woods . . .": John Muir, quoted in Frederick Turner, *Rediscovering America: John Muir in His Times and Ours* (San Francisco: Sierra Club Books, 1987), 30.

12,000 killed/25,000 arrested: Gilbert Chinard, *When the French Came to California* (San Francisco: California Historical Society, 1944), 3.

French reaction to gold discovery: ibid., passim.

page 90

3,885 French emigrants: A. P. Nasatir, trans., "Alexander Dumas fils and the Lottery of the Golden Ingots," *California Historical Society Quarterly* 33, no. 2 (1954): 129–30.

French in California in 1853: Daniel Lévy, *Les Francais en Californie* (San Francisco, 1884), cited in Wright, "Cosmopolitan California, pt. 2," 78 n. 61.

Footnote ($80 million): Howard R. Lamar, introduction to Jean-Nicolas Perlot, *Gold Seeker: Adventures of a Belgian Argonaut During the Gold Rush Years*, trans. Helen Harding Bretnor, ed. Howard R. Lamar (New Haven: Yale University Press, 1985), xxx. Lamar's figure of 400 million francs (p. 47) is converted to $80 million using the exchange rate of 20 cents per franc.

German/Spanish emigration: J.D.B. DeBow, *Statistical View of the United States . . . Being a Compendium of the Seventh Census . . .* (1854), cited in Doris Wright, "The Making of Cosmopolitan California: An Analysis of Immigration, 1848–1870," *California Historical Society Quarterly* 19, no. 4 (1940): 340.

"The innumerable throngs . . . ": quoted in Celestino Soares, *California and the Portuguese: How the Portuguese Helped to Build Up California* (Lisbon: S P N Books, 1939), 59.

Three thousand Sonorans in 1848: This estimate is based on the figure of 4,000 to 6,000 for October 1848 to March 1849 provided in José Francisco Velasco, *Noticias estadísticas del estado de Sonora acompañadas de ligeras reflexiones, deducidas de algunos documentos y conocimientos prácticos adquiridos en muchos años . . .* (1850), cited in Wright, "Cosmopolitan California," 324.

"Mexicans from Sonora are passing us daily . . . ": Cave Johnson Couts, *Hepah California! The Journal of Cave Johnson Couts from Monterey, Nuevo León, Mexico, to Los Angeles, California, During the Years 1848–1849*, ed. Henry F. Dobyns (Tucson: Arizona Pioneers' Historical Society, 1961), 86–88, entries for December 1 and 17.

At least six thousand Sonorans by the summer of 1849: Bancroft, *History of California*, 6:113; Ralph J. Roske, "The World Impact of the California Gold Rush 1849–1857," *Arizona and the West* 5, no. 3 (1963): 198; Susan Lee Johnson, " 'The gold she gathered': Difference, Domination, and California's Southern Mines, 1848–1853" (Ph.D. diss., Yale University, 1993), 76.

Arrival of brig I.R.S.: Roberto Hernandez Cornejo, *Los Chilenos en San Francisco de California* (Valparaíso, Chile, 1930), cited in Wright, "Cosmopolitan California," 326.

page 92

Cattle hides/gold: Faxon Dean Atherton to Thomas O. Larkin, September 10, 1848, in *Larkin Papers*, 7:352.

Chilean/Peruvian emigration: Wright, "Cosmopolitan California," 326. For a most informative report on Chileans in the gold rush, see the introduction to Edwin A. Beilharz and Carlos U. Lopes, eds. and trans., *We Were 49ers: Chilean Accounts of the*

California Gold Rush (Pasadena: Ward Ritchie Press, 1976); the entire book is valuable, with rich details.

Three thousand passengers in one week: Jay Monaghan, *Australians and the Gold Rush* (Berkeley: University of California Press, 1966), 70.

October 6 arrival from Sydney: *Alta California*, November 1, 1849, cited ibid., 70.

"California Gold Grease": *Hobart Daily Courier,* July 11, 1849, cited ibid., 55.

Shipped merchandise: Monaghan, *Australians,* 103.

"who have no prospect at home but the needle": *Hobart Town Advertiser,* December 29, 1849, cited ibid., 119.

Footnote (Eliza Farnham): David Magee, ed., *Eliza Farnham's Bride Ship: An 1849 Circular Inviting Young Women of the East to Go to California,* no. 3 in *Attention Pioneers!* series (San Francisco: Book Club of California, 1952), passim.

"two hundred young, virtuous girls": *Hobart Town Advertiser,* December 25, 1849, cited in Monaghan, *Australians,* 119.

Australian women immigrants: Willard B. Farwell, "Cape Horn and Cooperative Mining in '49," *Century Magazine* 42 (August 1891): 593.

---

page 93

"You know Bryant, the carpenter . . . ": M. T. McClellan, letter of October 28, 1848, in the *(St. Louis) Missouri Republican,* April 16, 1849.

"Men here are nearly crazy with the riches . . . ": letter from Peter H. Burnett, February 2, 1849, in *Memphis Daily Eagle,* May 22, 1849, quoted in Walter T. Durham, *Volunteer Forty-Niners: Tennesseans and the California Gold Rush* (Nashville: Vanderbilt University Press, 1997), 6.

Skeptical editorial: *Jonesborough Whig and Independent Journal,* January 17, 1849, quoted in Durham, *Volunteer Forty-Niners,* 11.

---

page 94

Aerial locomotive: Rufus Porter, *Aerial Navigation: The Practicability of Traveling Pleasantly and Safely from New York to California in Three Days* (1849; reprint, San Francisco: Lawton R. Kennedy, 1935), 12, front and back covers.

Inset quotation ("Mother o Mother . . . "): James S. Barnes, letter of October 21, 1849, quoted in Malcolm J. Rohrbough, *Days of Gold: The California Gold Rush and the American Nation* (Berkeley: University of California Press, 1997), 37.

Sailings in early 1849: Dale L. Morgan, introduction to William M'Collum, *California as I Saw It: Pencillings by the Way of its Gold and Gold Diggers! And Incidents of Travel by Land and Water,* ed. Dale L. Morgan (Los Gatos, Calif.: Talisman Press, 1960), 44.

---

page 96

"the oniony smell of which . . . ": *Apollo* log, quoted in Delgado, *To California By Sea,* 33.

---

page 97

Passenger arrivals April 1849 to March 1850: *San Francisco 1852 City Directory,* cited in Delgado, *To California by Sea,* x.

Price of shipboard accommodations: Lewis, *Sea Routes,* 14, 239.

Massachusetts joint-stock companies/emigration: Octavius Thorndike Howe, *Argonauts of '49: History and Adventures of the Emigrant Companies from Massachusetts, 1849–1850* (Cambridge: Harvard University Press, 1923), 171–75.

---

page 98

Lumber, brick, and prefabricated homes: Lewis, *Sea Routes,* 25.

Ship arrivals in Rio de Janeiro: ibid., 133.

"the great number of Americans on shore . . .": Capt. George Coffin, quoted ibid., 148–49.

6,500 goldseekers cross the isthmus: John Haskell Kemble, *The Panama Route, 1849–1869,* University of California Publications in History, vol. 29 (Berkeley: University of California Press, 1943), 254. The estimates vary on the number coming to California in 1849 by this route. Kemble uses San Francisco Custom House records for his figure of 6,489. A study done by J. Coolidge of the San Francisco Merchants' Exchange (cited in Bancroft, *History of California,* 6:159 n. 24) reckoned the total at 6,000. Given the uncertainties of the time, both figures are probably conservative.

---

page 100

"Palms slowly waving their branches . . . ": Charles Nahl to his parents, February 3, 1852, in Moreland L. Stevens, *Charles Christian Nahl: Artist of the Gold Rush, 1818–1878* (Sacramento: E. B. Crocker Art Gallery, 1976), 34.

---

page 101

"the very pest-house of disease . . . ": E.H.N. Patterson, diary of October 1850–January 1851, published in *Oquawka (Ill.) Spectator,* March–July 1851, extract for December 1850, pt. 11.

"The houses are all of the palm-thatched order . . . ": ibid.

"The hotels, which have assumed the names . . . ": Daniel Horn, letter of June 1850, in "Across the Isthmus in 1850: The Journey of Daniel A. Horn," ed. James P. Jones and William W. Rogers, *Hispanic American Historical Review* 41 (1961): 535–36.

"The river is exceedingly crooked . . . ": J. Goldsborough Bruff, *Gold Rush: The Journals Drawings, and Other Papers of J. Goldsborough Bruff . . . April 2, 1849–July 20, 1851,* vol. 2, *Bruff's Camp to Washington City,* ed. Georgia Willis Read and Ruth Gaines (New York: Columbia University Press, 1944), 987–88.

"We see parrots . . . ": Patterson, diary, extract for December 1850, pt. 11.

Terminus on Chagres River: Gorgona was used during the dry season (December–April), but during the wet season it was possible to travel 4.5 miles farther upstream to Cruces; Kemble, *Panama Route,* 169.

"a returning Californian . . . ": Bayard Taylor, *Eldorado, or Adventures in the Path of Empire, Comprising a Voyage to California, via Panama; Life in San Francisco and Monterey;*

Pictures of the Gold Region; and Experiences of Mexican Travel (1850; reprint, New York: Alfred A. Knopf, 1949), 11.

"the natives appear to dislike the Americans . . .": Emmeline Stuart Wortley, *Travels in the United States, 1849–1850* (London, 1851), 2:319.

"There will be serious trouble . . . ": L. I. Fish, diary (MS, Huntington Library, San Marino, Calif.), entry for October 21, 1849.

page 102

Inset quotation ("Rioting, debauchery . . . "): Milo Goss, letter of June 18, 1850, quoted in Rohrbough, *Days of Gold*, 59.

"I filled her up with jerked beef . . . ": David Lavender, *The Great Persuader* (New York: Doubleday, 1970), 16–17.

Enterprise of Darius Ogden Mills: from the galley proof of an undated bibliographical sketch of Mills that was prepared for but not used in *Chronicles of the Builders* (Bancroft Library, University of California, Berkeley), n.p.

Transit time via Panama (New York to Chagres, 8–12 days; isthmus crossing/wait for connection, 1–2 weeks; Panama to San Francisco, 2–3 weeks): Bancroft, *History of California*, 6:138; Lewis, *Sea Routes*, 176; Kemble, *Panama Route*, 42–43, 147–48; Roske, "World Impact," 203.

Footnote (PMSC/clipper ships): Delgado, *To California by Sea*, 48–50, 44–45.

Panama Railroad profits: David McCullough, *The Path Between the Seas: The Creation of the Panama Canal, 1870–1914* (New York: Simon & Schuster, 1977), 35.

page 103

"a little of the hardest place I was ever in": J. S. Holliday, introduction to *Gold Rush Desert Trails to San Diego and Los Angeles in 1849*, ed. George M. Ellis, Brand Book Series, no. 9 (San Diego: San Diego Corral of the Westerners, 1995), xi.

Emigration on southern trails: Egan, *El Dorado Trail*, 280.

Emigration on Oregon-California Trail, 1849–52: Holliday, *World Rushed In*, 471; John D. Unruh, *The Plains Across: The Overland Emigrants and the Trans-Mississippi West, 1840–60* (Urbana: University of Illinois Press, 1979), 120, table 2.

"select a suitable location . . . ": *Ithaca Journal*, March 21, 1849.

"Many men who began last June . . . ": letter published in *Buffalo Morning Express*, January 26, 1849.

page 105

Inset quotation ("my best friend . . . "): William Pierce, letter of September 28, 1849, quoted in Rohrbough, *Days of Gold*, 52.

"willing to brave most anything": Elisha Perkins, *Gold Rush Diary: Being the Journal . . . on the Overland Trail*, ed. Thomas D. Clark (Lexington, University of Kentucky Press, 1967), 13.

Ann Arbor newspaper report: Russell E. Bidlack, *Letters Home: The Story of Ann Arbor's Forty-Niners* (Ann Arbor, 1960), 12–13.

Home sold for $1,200: *Detroit Daily Advertiser*, April 16, 1849.

Husband's insurance policy: William Gill, *California Letters*, ed. Eva T. Clark (New York, 1922), 10.

"the detested sin of being poor": Charles E. Boyle, diary entry for April 2, 1849, published in *Columbus (Ohio) Sunday Dispatch*, October 2, 1949, quoted in Unruh, *Plains Across*, 96.

page 106

"our coats are surrounded . . .": Samuel Plimpton to Vernon Plimpton, April 14/18, quoted in Winifred Corbett, *Following Samuel Plimpton: A Search for My Great Uncle* (n.p., 1994), 6.

page 107

"It is impossible for me . . .": letter from C. N. Ormsby, July 24, 1849, in Bidlack, *Letters Home*, 29.

page 108

"In a moment after the first hail . . .": William Swain, diary (MS, Beinecke Rare Book and Manuscript Library, Yale University), entry for June 20, 1849.

Inset quotation ("Senator Benton and other big men . . ."): William Wilson, letter of August 6, 1849 (MS, Beinecke Rare Book and Manuscript Library, Yale University).

page 109

Inset quotation ("The pretty Indian squaws . . ."): Andrew J. Griffith, diary (MS, David L. Hill, Baltimore), entry for June 3, 1849.

"it is far more pleasing . . . ": Frederic W. Barnard, letter of May 6, 1849 (MS, Beinecke Rare Book and Manuscript Library, Yale University).

"Tell Charles . . . ": letter of May 17, 1849, published in *Oquawka (Ill.) Spectator*, June 13, 1849.

"We had a pail full of punch . . .": Eleazer Ingalls, *Journal of a Trip to California by the Overland Route Across the Plains . . .* (Waukegan, Ill., 1852), entry for July 4, 1850.

"fired a gun for every state . . .": William B. Lorton, diary (MS, Bancroft Library, University of California, Berkeley), entry for July 4, 1849.

page 111

"My God, McKinstry . . .": Byron N. McKinstry, *The California Gold Rush Overland Diary . . .*, ed. Bruce L. McKinstry (Glendale, Calif., 1975), entry for August 21, 1850.

CHAPTER 4 *(Careless Freedoms)*

page 116

"the dynamite of California . . . ": Franklin Walker, *San Francisco's Literary Frontier* (New York: Alfred A. Knopf, 1939), 9.

Footnote ("the overwhelming presence of men . . . "): from Susan Johnson's richly revealing study of gender and many other issues in "Difference, Domination," 59.

page 117

"Now I will tell you . . . ": Robert and Charles Springer to S. W. Springer, September 29, 1849, published in *St. Joseph Adven-*

ture, February 1, 1850; reprinted in Walker D. Wyman, ed., *California Emigrant Letters* (New York: Bookman Associates, 1952), 78–79.

"this wonderful country . . . ": letter from "V.J.F." of April 6, 1849, published in *Missouri Republican,* June 22, 1849; reprinted in Wyman, *California Emigrant Letters,* 29.

"at an unconscionably extravagant figure": W. Perkins, *Three Years,* 90.

page 119

"eating raw pork . . . ": ibid., 92.

"Here were real, live miners . . . ": ibid.

"Along the edges of Woods Creek . . . ": ibid., 101.

page 120

Inset quotation ("Clothing can in great measure . . ."): Prentice Mulford, *California Sketches,* ed. Franklin Walker (San Francisco: Book Club of California, 1935), 32.

Concentration of foreigners in southern mines: S. Johnson, "Difference, Domination," 11 n. 12.

"Tired of old ravines . . . ," description of successful prospecting and subsequent crowds: E. Gould Buffum, *Six Months in the Gold Mines: From a Journal of Three Years' Residence in Upper and Lower California, 1847-8-9,* ed. John W. Caughey ([Los Angeles]: Ward Ritchie Press, 1959), 71–72.

page 122

Footnote (mining law): John Umbeck, "The California Gold Rush: A Study of Emerging Property Rights," *Explorations in Economic History* 14, no. 3 (1977): passim.

Inset quotation ("Self-protection is a necessary law . . ."): Charles Ross Parke, *Dreams to Dust: A Diary of the California Gold Rush, 1849-50,* ed. James E. Davis (Lincoln: University of Nebraska Press, 1989), 85, entry for September 18, 1848.

page 123

Journalist's description of law and order in the diggings: Taylor, *Eldorado,* 71, 77–78.

"When I first saw . . . ": ibid., 65–66.

"persons at work . . . ": ibid., 69.

"On our poor little maps . . . ": Etienne Derbec, *A French Journalist in the California Gold Rush,* ed. Abraham P. Nasatir (Georgetown, Calif.: Talisman Press, 1964), 97–98.

"The lay of the land . . . ": Jonas Winchester, letter of August 6, 1849 (MS, California State Library, Sacramento).

page 124

ships at anchor: W. Perkins, *Three Years,* 86; *San Francisco Daily Alta California,* October 30, 1849, cited in Delgado, *To California by Sea,* 78; Soulé, Gihon, and Nisbet, *Annals of San Francisco,* 281. For extensive statistical information on San Francisco as a port, see Bancroft, *History of California,* vol. 7 (San Francisco: History Co., 1890), 122–26.

Footnote (1850 shipping): *San Francisco Daily Herald,* January 1854, cited in Delgado, *To California by Sea,* 80.

"there was a great rush . . . ": George Coffin, quoted in Lewis, *Sea Routes,* 273.

Long Wharf: Bancroft, *History of California,* 6:177–78 n. 20.

page 125

"any suspicious, insane, or forlorn persons . . . ": Stuart A. Brody, "Hospitalization of the Mentally Ill During California's Early Years, 1849–53," in *Psychiatric Quarterly Supplement,* pt. 2 (1964); quoted in James P. Delgado, "Gold Rush Jail: The Prison Ship *Euphremia,*" *California History* (Summer 1981): 138.

page 126

Piling removal, cable cutting: *San Francisco Daily Alta California,* August 31, 1890, cited in Delgado, *To California by Sea,* 84.

Footnote (*Niantic*/piling carpenter): Morgan, introduction to M'Collum, *California,* 75; D. W. Coit to Mrs. Coit, September 15, 1850, in *Digging for Gold Without a Shovel: The Letters of Daniel Wadsworth Coit from Mexico City to San Francisco, 1840-1851,* ed. George P. Hammond (San Francisco: Old West Publishing, 1967), 94.

"a Venice built of pine . . .": Benjamin Vicuña MacKenna, *Páginas de mi diario durante tres años de viaje;* in Beilharz and López, *We Were '49ers,* 194.

3,565 men and 49 women: *Alta California,* November 11, 1849.

Parker house rents: letter from *New York Weekly Tribune* correspondent of June 20, 1849, published August 18, 1849, cited in W. Perkins, *Three Years,* 87.

Inset quotation ("Broadcast over the plains . . ."): T. H. Watkins and R. R. Olmsted, *Mirror of the Dream: An Illustrated History of San Francisco* (San Francisco: Scrimshaw Press, 1976), 29.

Eldorado rent: Taylor, *Eldorado,* 44.

$50,000 income: ibid., 45.

"One's mind cannot . . . ": ibid., 44.

"Men dart hither and thither . . . ": ibid., 87.

page 127

"furnished with comfort . . . ": Taylor, *Eldorado,* 228.

"the thinest of board partitions . . . ": Soulé, Gihon, and Nisbet, *Annals of San Francisco,* 648.

page 128

"This place is not fit for anything but business. . . .": Jackson, *Gold Dust,* 210.

"the world never produced before . . . ": Rinaldo Taylor to his wife, December 30, 1849, quoted in Rohrbough, *Days of Gold,* 66.

Forty-five thousand letters: Taylor, *Eldorado,* 156.

page 129

"extended all the way down . . . ": ibid., 158.

July 1849 opening of the Sacramento City Post Office: H. E. Salley, *History of California Post Offices*, 2d. ed., ed. Edward L. Patera (Lake Grove, Ore., 1991), 185. Following its initial failure, the Sacramento City Post Office remained only a promise until June 1850 when (according to the *Placer Times,* June 6) mail from San Francisco was carried up the Sacramento River on a regular schedule by the steamboat *Senator.*

Over two thousand names on express list: Alexander H. Todd, quoted in Wiltsee, *The Pioneer Miner and the Pack Mule Express* (San Francisco, 1931), 34.

More than two hundred express companies: ibid., 24.

Footnote ("hard money" sentiments): Bancroft, *History of California*, 6:297; Dwight L. Clarke, *William Tecumseh Sherman: Gold Rush Banker* (San Francisco: California Historical Society, 1969), 5, 77–78; Ira B. Cross, "Californians and Hard Money," *California Folklore Quarterly* 4, no. 3 (1945): 271, 275.

page 130

"we have not heard from you . . . ": George Swain to William Swain, February 9, 1850, in William Swain, diary and letters (MS, Beinecke Rare Book and Manuscript Library, Yale University).

page 131

"There is a charm, a witchcraft . . . ": W. Perkins, *Three Years,* 263–64.

"If you could have seen us . . . ": Lucius Fairchild to J. C. Fairchild and Family, January 1, 1850, in *The California Letters of Lucius Fairchild*, ed. Joseph Schafer (Madison: State Historical Society of Wisconsin, 1931), 59.

Footnote (postmaster warning): printed under the heading of "California Correspondence" in *Boston Cultivator,* November 24, 1849.

Adams & Company Express: Wiltsee, *Pioneer Miner,* 59.

Overvalued gold slugs: Watkins and Olmsted, *Mirror,* 32.

page 132

"fine, free swearer": Bancroft, *History of California,* 6:275.

Inset quotation ("William, I do not want . . . "): Sabrina Swain to William Swain, July 26, 1849, in Swain, diary and letters.

"the means best calculated . . . ": Governor Riley's "Proclamation to the People of California," June 3, 1849 (original in Sacramento Archives and Museum Collection Center).

Sleeping under trees: Pamela Herr, *Jessie Benton Frémont* (New York: Franklin Watts, 1987), 207.

page 133

Larkin's hospitality: Royce, *California,* 205.

Age of California's Founding Fathers: Bancroft, *History of California,* 6:288.

Miners' opposition to slavery: The prevailing attitude was well summarized by Walter Colton in a diary entry on June 20, 1848: "All here are diggers, and free white diggers won't dig with slaves. They know they must dig themselves: they have come out here for that purpose, and they wont degrade their calling by associating it with slave-labor: self-preservation is the first law of nature"; Colton, *Three Years in California,* 374.

"With twenty good Negroes . . . ": John T. Milner, letter of August 15, 1850, in "John T. Milner's Trip to California, Letters to the Family," *Alabama Historical Quarterly* 20, no. 3 (1958): 538.

Footnote (early agricultural successes): Theodore H. Hittell, *History of California*, vol. 3 (San Francisco: N. J. Stone, 1898), 866.

"Exhaust the gold . . . ": Alonzo Delano, letter of March 2, 1850, in *Alonzo Delano's California Correspondence,* ed. Irving McKee (Sacramento: Sacramento Book Collectors Club, 1952), 44.

page 134

"will be one of the poorest states in the Union . . .": William Swain to George Swain, April 1850, in Swain, diary and letters.

"frail, lovely and dependent": Charles T. Botts, quoted in Harlow, *California Conquered,* 344.

"women of fortune": Henry W. Halleck, quoted in Ellison, *Self-Governing Dominion,* 39.

Footnote (African American, Native American, and Chinese rights): Bean and Rawls, *California,* 143.

"strong doubts of the legality . . . ": Bennet Riley, quoted in Harlow, *California Conquered,* 350.

"Gentlemen, this is the happiest day . . . ": John A. Sutter, quoted in Ellison, *Self-Governing Dominion,* 44.

Printing of the constitution: Harlow, *California Conquered,* 351.

vote for constitution/governor: ibid.

"ordained and established": Bennet Riley proclamation of December 12, 1849, cited ibid.

page 135

"Here, where but a few months since . . .": *Alta California,* December 21, 1849, in Mae Hélène Bacon Boggs, *My Playhouse Was a Concord Coach* (Oakland: Howell-North Press, 1942), 37.

Creation of twenty-seven counties: Bancroft, *History of California,* 6:317.

Non-Indian population of six southern counties: *The Seventh Census of the United States: 1850* (Washington, D.C., 1853), 969, table I, cited in Cleland, *Cattle,* 4.

Foreign Miners' Tax: "Report of California Senate Finance Committee," March 20, 1850, cited by Morgan and Scobie, introduction to W. Perkins, *Three Years,* 35.

page 136

"a new executive . . .": Bennet Riley to R. Jones, December 20, 1849, cited in Harlow, *California Conquered,* 352.

"that gentlemanly drunkard": Royce D. Delmatier, Clarence F. McIntosh, and Earl G. Waters, eds., *The Rumble of California Politics* (New York: John Wiley & Sons, 1970), 14.

In awe of God and Mrs. McDougal: John McDougal, cited ibid.

Sailing time to Sacramento: John F. Morse, *The Sacramento Directory for the Year 1853–54 . . . Together with a History of Sacramento* (Sacramento: Samuel Colville, 1853; reprint, Sacramento: California State Library Foundation, 1997), 5.

page 137

Arrival of the *Senator*: Joseph Aloysius McGowan, "Freighting to the Mines in California, 1849–1859" (Ph.D. diss., University of California, Berkeley, 1949), 30.

"All the nymphs . . . ": Morse, *History of Sacramento,* 18.

Senator's profit of $600,000: Roger W. Lotchin, *San Francisco, 1846–1856: From Hamlet to City* (New York: Oxford University Press, 1974; Lincoln: University of Nebraska Press, 1979), 68.

Footnote (*Senator*'s schedule/earnings): McGowan, "Freighting," 30–36; Bancroft, *History of California,* 6:451.

"it filled the air . . .": *The Life of Stephen Palmer Blake from His Journals,* ed. Elizabeth Hurst Ellwood (Franklin, N.C.: Genealogy Publishing Service, 1995), 61.

page 138

Inset quotation ("the present of this city . . "): Daniel B. Woods, *Sixteen Months at the Gold Diggings* (New York: Harper & Bros., 1851), 47.

350 lbs., twenty to thirty miles a day: R. R. Olmsted, ed., *Scenes of Wonder and Curiosity from Hutchings' California Magazine 1856–1861* (Berkeley: Howell-North Press, 1962), 114.

"Every material . . . ": Morse, *History of Sacramento,* 5.

"You have no idea . . . ": Three letters from Franklin A. Buck to Mary Sewell Bradley, October–November 1849, in *A Yankee Trader in the Gold Rush: The Letters of Franklin A. Buck,* comp. Katherine A. White (Boston: Houghton Mifflin, 1930), 50–53, 54, 56–57.

page 139

Brannan's hotel income and five hundred Sacramento lots: Morse, *History of Sacramento,* 5, 3.

Larkin's sale of lots: Hague and Langum, *Thomas O. Larkin,* 196.

Weber's employment of one thousand Indians; summer profit of $400,000; bricks; lots for sale: George P. Hammond, *The Weber Era in Stockton History* (Berkeley: Friends of the Bancroft Library, 1982), 88.

page 140

Elk steak, salmon, and grizzly bear: Taylor, *Eldorado,* 166.

"Oh, Henry . . . ": Mary C. Mills to Henry S. Crandall, December 16, 1849, in Roland D. Crandall, ed., *Love and Nuggets* (Old Greenwich, Conn.: Stable Books, 1967), 50.

$5,000 on the Yuba: A. Dunn, postscript to letter of November 4, 1849, published in *Kalamazoo Gazette,* February 1, 1850.

page 142

Footnote (New Almaden mine): William H. Brewer, *Up and Down California in 1860–1864: The Journal of William H. Brewer,* ed. Francis P. Farquhar (New Haven: Yale University Press, 1930), 159; Milton Lanyon and Laurence Bulmore, *Cinnabar Hills: The Quicksilver Days of New Almaden* (Los Gatos, Calif.: Village Printers, 1967), 12–16; Otis E. Young Jr., *Western Mining: An Informal Account of Precious-Metals Prospecting, Placering, Lode Mining, and Milling on the American Frontier from Spanish Times to 1893* (Norman: University of Oklahoma Press, 1970), 118; Richard B. Mason to Roger Jones, August 17, 1848, in Paul, *California Gold Discovery,* 98–99.

page 143

"I was struck all aback . . . " Isaac Lord, diary (MS, Huntington Library, San Marino, Calif.), entry for December 26, 1849.

page 144

"a small dam . . . ": Simon Doyle, letter of January 20, 1849 (MS, Beinecke Rare Book and Manuscript Library, Yale University).

"turned the course . . . ": John A. Johnson, "Letters from the California Gold Mines," in *Pioneering on the Plains* (Kaukauna, Wis., 1924), letter of November 20, 1849.

page 146

"The ground is so soft . . . ": Austin A. Hover, letter of November 29, 1849 (TS, California State Library, Sacramento).

"many teams stalled . . . ": Joseph A. Stuart, diary entry for November 13, 1849, in *My Roving Life,* vol. 1 (Auburn, Calif., 1895).

Difficulties of hauling and packing/consequent increase in prices: Alonzo Delano, letters of October 12 and November 19, 1849, in *Correspondence,* 25, 34; Jacob D. B. Stillman, letter of November 19, 1849, in *The Gold Rush Letters . . . ,* ed. Kenneth Johnson (Palo Alto, Calif., 1967); Lucius Fairchild to J. C. Fairchild and Family, December 8, 1849, in *California Letters,* 46; Edwin G. Hall, letter of November 25, 1849 (TS, California State Library, Sacramento).

"They are half a leg deep . . .": Jonas Winchester, letter of November 19, 1849 (MS, California State Library, Sacramento).

"utter confusion and total disorder" and description of street debris: Israel Shipman Pelton Lord, *"At the Extremity of Civilization": An Illinois Physician's Journey to California in 1849,* ed. Necia Dixon Liles (Jefferson, N.C.: McFarland, 1985), 192, 195.

"The reckless spirit of speculation . . . ": Morse, *History of Sacramento,* 19.

"little short of fathomless": Taylor, *Eldorado,* 229.

"Not infrequently men were in danger . . . ": Hittell, *History of San Francisco,* 154.

makeshift street fillage: Bancroft, *History of California,* 6:198; Soulé Gihon, and Nisbet, *Annals of San Francisco,* 245.

page 147

"the blaze increased . . . "; "all over the burnt area . . . "; $150 penalty: Taylor, *Eldorado*, 239–41.

"One calamity more or less . . . ": Ernest de Massey, *A Frenchman in the Gold Rush: The Journal of Ernest de Massey, Argonaut of 1849*, trans. Marguerite Eyer Wilbur (San Francisco: California Historical Society, 1927), 30.

CHAPTER 5 *(Get-Ahead Years)*

page 151

"treasure hunt to industry": This is an idea drawn from Pomeroy, *Pacific Slope*, 53; and Rodman W. Paul, *California Gold: The Beginning of Mining in the Far West* (Cambridge: Harvard University Press, 1947), chap. 5, passim.

5,726 miles of ditches/flumes and twenty-five miles of Yuba River: Paul, *California Gold*, 164.

One hundred thousand miners: Bancroft, *History of California*, 6:423 n. 23.

One hundred thousand letters a month: Bancroft, *California Inter Pocula*, 279.

page 152

Gold production ('51, '52, '60): Paul, *California Gold*, 118.

page 153

Success of farmer near San Jose: reminiscences of John M. Horner, in *Pacific Rural Press*, June 24, 1899.

$18,000 from pie sales: *Hunt's Merchants' Magazine* 26 (January–June 1852): 777.

$6 to $12 per day vs. $1.50 and $1.00 per day: Rohrbough, *Days of Gold*, 3, 186.

Average annual exodus of 25,000: Wright, "Cosmopolitan California," 341.

page 154

"were ready to change their occupation . . . ": Peter R. Decker, *Fortunes and Failures* (Cambridge: Harvard University Press, 1978), 64.

$303,000 in stock sales: Paul, *California Gold*, 127.

page 155

Use of sandbags in dams: Alonzo Delano, letter of April 4, 1850, in Delano, *Correspondence*, 61.

Footnote ("Every kind of cloth . . ."): Lord, *Extremity of Civilization*, 259, diary entry for June 11, 1850.

"walked out on the tree . . . ": Charles Main, diary (MS, Bancroft Library, University of California, Berkeley), entry for March 28, 1850.

"all the while living . . . ": Isaac Baker, diary (MS, Bancroft Library, University of California, Berkeley), entry for June 1850.

"They brought up in their hands . . . ": *Placer Times*, April 25, 1850

"submarine suit": Woods, *Sixteen Months*, 186.

"a diving bell": S. W. Carnahan, letter of July 29, 1850 (TS, Missouri Historical Society).

Footnote (San Joaquin Diving Bell Mining Company): San Joaquin Diving Bell Mining Company stock certificate (Henry Clifford Collection, Huntington Library, San Marino, Calif.).

page 156

Cracking boulders with thermal shock: Andrew Curtis Ferris, "How We Mined Gold in the Early Days of California," *Pioneer and Historical Review* (November 1898), 3 (photocopy of transcript made from records at the California Historical Society in San Francisco).

Footnote (profit from wing dam): Woods, *Sixteen Months*, 157–58.

"over three entire claims" and "everybody up this way . . .": Lord, *Extremity of Civilization*, 266–67, diary entry for July 16, 1850.

Conflict over dams: Rohrbough, *Days of Gold*, 200.

"shot thirteen men . . . ": John Banks, diary entry of August 25, 1850, in *The Buckeye Rovers*, ed. Howard L. Scamehorn (Athens: Ohio University Press, 1965), 135.

Peak years for river mining: Paul, *California Gold*, 129.

Description of river rising and damage: J. D. Borthwick, *Three Years in California* (1857; reprint, Oakland, Calif.: Biobooks, 1948), 219–20; Mulford, *California Sketches*, 396; Lucius Fairchild to J. C. Fairchild and family, October 18, 1850, in Fairchild, *California Letters*, 86; Derbec, *French Journalist*, 150; Woods, *Sixteen Months*, 152.

page 158

"I shall send this . . .": John R. Fitch, letter of September 25, 1852, in letters, 1849–52 (MS, Huntington Library, San Marino, Calif.).

"Oh, Matilda . . .": David Dewolf, letter of July 30, 1850, in David Dewolf, "Diary of the Overland Trail . . . and Letters . . . ," *Transactions of the Illinois Historical Society* 32 (1925): 221.

Footnote ("If God will forgive me . . ."): Lucius Fairchild to J. C. Fairchild and family, February 12, 1850, in Fairchild, *California Letters*, 65. ("You can rest assured . . ."): John L. Craven to his wife, May 20, 1850, quoted in Rohrbough, *Days of Gold*, 257.

Twenty to thirty cents per pound: Bancroft, *History of California*, 6:416.

Description of Frémont vein: Herr, *Jessie Benton Frémont*, 205.

page 159

Inset quotation ("I am so lonesome . . . "): Rachael Ann Brown to David Brown, October 18, 1852, and March 4, 1855, in *Gold Rush: A Literary Exploration*, ed. Michael Kowalewski (Berkeley: Heyday Books, 1997), 120–21.

page 160

$50,000 to $100,000 machines: Paul, *California Gold*, 138.

"a sum sufficient . . .": article about Rocky Bar Mining Company, *Michigan Expositor*, November 19, 1850.

90 percent failure rate for early quartz mines: Paul, *California Gold*, 145.

Footnote (wages): Rodman Paul, *Mining Frontiers of the Far West, 1848–1880* (New York: Holt, Rinehart, & Winston, 1963), 35.

page 161

Grass Valley vein, eighteen inches thick: Alonzo Delano, letter of June 11, 1851, in Delano, *Correspondence*, 114–15.

Footnote (rich quartz finds): Bancroft, *History of California*, 6:420–21.

"two hundred wooden houses . . . " and subsequent quotations: Alonzo Delano, letter of June 11, 1851, in Delano, Correspondence, 115–16.

70 to 80 percent waste: Paul, *California Gold*, 139.

"Hope on, Hope ever": Alonzo Delano, letter of June 11, 1851, in Delano, Correspondence, 112.

279 stamp mills, built for $3,270,000: Paul, *California Gold*, 144.

1 percent of 1850s gold production from quartz mining: Paul, *Mining Frontiers*, 32.

page 163

286 sawmills and 284 million board feet in 1858: Eduard Vischer, "A Trip to the Mining Regions in the Spring of 1859," *California Historical Society Quarterly* 11, no. 3 (1932): 228.

"savage struggle with the landscape": Royce, *California*, 172.

"The town is beautifully situated . . .": Borthwick, *Three Years in California*, 151.

East Bay sawmills: Sherwood D. Burgess, "The Forgotten Redwoods of the East Bay," *California Historical Society Quarterly* 30, no. 1 (1951): 7.

A desolation of stumps: ibid., 11.

page 164

Organized violence against Indians: Rawls, *Indians of California*, 171, 175.

Footnote (decline in Indian population): ibid., 171, 176.

"the most common and fatal result . . .": W. Perkins, *Three Years*, 117.

"the greatest drawback . . . ": Lucius Fairchild to J. C. Fairchild and family, December 6, 1851, in Fairchild, *California Letters*, 128–29.

"Five years at most . . .": Prentice Mulford, *Prentice Mulford's Story* (Oakland, Calif.: Biobooks, 1953), 2–3.

Proportion of women to men: Rohrbough, *Days of Gold*, 94.

"neither maids, wives, nor widows": J. S. Hittell, *The Resources of California* (San Francisco: A. Roman, 1863), 440.

page 165

Inset quotation ("The first females to come . . ."): Bancroft, *California Inter Pocula*, 309.

The separation of men from women "back home" is a theme discussed in S. Johnson, "Difference, Domination," 99–101, 208–9; and in Rohrbough, *Days of Gold*, chaps. 3, 6 passim.

Titles of lettersheets: Dorothy Sloan, ed., *Catalogue of the Letter Sheet Collection of Henry H. Clifford* (Austin, Texas: Dorothy Sloan Rare Books, 1994), xv, xvi.

Ninety-seven thousand copies: Gary F. Kurutz, "Images of El Dorado: The California Pictorial Letter Sheet," ibid., x.

Price of newspapers: Orlando J. Hodges, "Prospecting on the Pacific Coast, 1848–1864," transcribed with an introduction by William Frank Zornow, *California Historical Society Quarterly* 33, no. 1 (1954): 54.

"the important and gratifying news . . . ": Parke, *Dreams to Dust*, 93, diary entry for May 4, 1850.

"dealers in liquor and provisions . . . ": Charles Nash, letter of July 10, 1850, in *Columbia (Mo.) Statesman*, September 4, 1850.

"every description of California . . . ": John A. Johnson, diary (MS, Beinecke Rare Book and Manuscript Library, Yale University), entry for September 28, 1849.

page 166

"I really hope . . . ": Lord, *Extremity of Civilization*, 275, diary entry for August 11, 1850.

"a great mistake . . . ": Joseph C. Buffum, diary, (TS, Bancroft Library, University of California, Berkeley), 112–13.

$16,000 potato crop: Franklin A. Buck, letter of September 22, 1852, in Buck, *Yankee Trader*, 108.

$2,100 onion crop: *Sacramento Placer Times*, September 6, 1850, in Boggs, *Playhouse*, 63.

Apples at $1.50 each: Charles H. Carey, *History of Oregon*, vol. 1 (1922), cited in Pomeroy, *Pacific Slope*, 49.

"good frame houses . . .": Borthwick, *Three Years in California*, 149.

Imports from Tahiti, Java, etc.: Lotchin, *San Francisco*, 46–47.

Ice from Boston: *Alta California*, September 29, 1851; *Alta California*, February 23, 1853, in Boggs, *Playhouse*, 151.

Shipment of cats: Charles Plummer, diary (MS, Huntington Library, San Marino, Calif.), entry for May 7, 1851.

Quantities of imports: *Placer Times*, October 10, 1850; *Sacramento Transcript*, December 25, 1850.

page 167

Liquor quantities: Soulé, Gihon, and Nisbet, *Annals of San Francisco*, 495.

"The independence and liberality here . . . ": Charles Plummer, letter of March 14, 1851 (MS, Huntington Library, San Marino, Calif.).

$15,000 in six months: Jackson, *Gold Dust*, 260.

$175,000 gross: Kevin Starr, *Inventing the Dream: California Through the Progressive Era* (New York: Oxford University Press, 1985), 128–29.

$300 a head: Cleland and Hardy, *March of Industry*, 36.

One thousand cattle at $50 a head: Andrew Randall to Abel Stearns, November 5, 1853, in Gates, *California Ranchos and Farms*, 17.

Small calves at $20 to $25 a head: James M. Jensen, "Cattle Drives from the Ranchos to the Gold Fields of California," *Arizona and the West* 2, no. 4 (1960): 350.

page 169

Boom years (1850–56): Cleland, *Cattle,* 110.

25,000 to 30,000 cattle annually: ibid., 107. Cleland applies this number to Los Angeles County alone. I have applied it to all of southern California in view of estimates from other sources, e.g. Gates, *California Ranchos and Farms,* 17.

Large herds and ranchos: Gates, *California Ranchos and Farms,* 5–6.

$10,000 gambling loss: C. R. Johnson to Abel Stearns, n.d., 1851, cited in Cleland, *Cattle,* 333 n. 35.

Bandini debts: Pitt, *Decline of the Californios,* 111.

Monthly/weekly interest rates: ibid, 100. Many specific examples of such interest rates are cited in Cleland, *Cattle,* 111–13.

Sixty-one thousand head of cattle: Gates, *California Ranchos and Farms,* 19 n. 7.

"American Bullocks," $100 to $150 a head: ibid., 19.

"almost every steamer brings an importation . . . ": *Alta California,* April 3, 1860, cited ibid., 24.

Sheep prices/drives: ibid., 32, 34.

"young gentlemen and beautiful and charming young ladies" and "feasting and hilarity": *El Clamor Público,* April 5, 1856, quoted in Cleland, *Cattle,* 84, 83.

page 170

Los Angeles population: Pitt, *Decline of the Californios,* 122.

Array of law enforcement officials: ibid., 153.

"Who can name one instance . . . ": *Los Angeles Star,* September 27, 1851, cited in Cleland, *Cattle,* 308 n. 43.

"homicides averaged one for each day . . .": J. M. Guinn, quoted in Cleland, *Cattle,* 96.

"about as they pleased": C. R. Johnson to Abel Stearns, February 23, 1863, quoted ibid., 71.

"heroic measures": Cleland, *History of California,* 317.

page 171

Population/tax ratios: Carey McWilliams, *Southern California: An Island on the Land* (Salt Lake City: Gibbs-Smith, 1946; reprint, Salt Lake City: Peregrine Smith, 1988), 15; Caughey, *California,* 283–84.

"friendly and peaceful but still complete": McWilliams, *Southern California,* 15.

News/celebration of admission: Bancroft, *History of California,* 6:347–49; Soulé Gihon, and Nisbet, *Annals of San Francisco,* 293–95; *Alta California,* October 31, 1850.

"To read some of the San Francisco papers . . .": John P. Dart to his brother, December 26, 1850; in "A Mississippian in the Gold Fields: The Letters of John Paul Dart, 1849–1856," ed. Howard Mitchum, *California Historical Society Quarterly* 35, no. 3 (1956): 208.

Footnote ("The Union is an exclusive body . . ."): Carey McWilliams, *California: The Great Exception* (New York: A. A. Wyn, 1949), 48.

page 172

Shifting capital site: Joseph A. McGowan, *History of the Sacramento Valley,* vol. 1 (New York: Lewis Historical Publishing, 1961), 111–13; Bancroft, *History of California,* 6:322–23.

"the buying and selling of votes": Bancroft, *History of California,* 6:325.

Projected receipts from Foreign Miners' Tax: Morgan and Scobie, introduction to W. Perkins, *Three Years,* 36.

Footnote (receipts from Foreign Miners' Tax): Bancroft, *History of California,* 6:406.

"Go to Sonora . . .": *Alta California,* May 28, 1850, quoted in Morgan and Scobie, introduction to W. Perkins, *Three Years,* 37.

Confrontation with foreign miners in Sonora: Morgan and Scobie, introduction to W. Perkins, *Three Years,* 38–41.

page 173

"incensed feelings . . . ": William Perkins to the editor of the *Stockton Times,* May 20, 1850, in W. Perkins, *Three Years,* 398–99.

Foreign Miners' Tax: An extensive description and analysis of the racial/ethnic significance of the conflict over this tax is in S. Johnson, "Difference, Domination," 338–51.

Mining population: Soulé, Gihon, and Nisbet, *Annals of San Francisco,* 485.

Monthly gold production: Paul, *California Gold,* 345.

General population: Bancroft, *History of California,* 7:698 n. 6.

1851 statute: Paul, *Mining Frontiers,* 169; Umbeck, "California Gold Rush," 204.

"free mining": Charles Howard Shinn, *Mining Camps: A Study in American Frontier Government* (1885; reprint, New York: Alfred A. Knopf, 1948), 248.

page 174

"the might of the ounce . . .": Peter Decker, *The Diaries of Peter Decker: Overland to California in 1849 and Life in the Mines, 1850–1851,* ed. Helen S. Giffen (Georgetown, Calif.: Talisman Press, 1966), 235, entry for October 2, 1850.

"Brazen chaos": Taylor, *Eldorado,* 205.

"society-cankering rapacity": McGowan, *History,* 130.

Gambling as a cause of conflict: S. Johnson, "Difference, Domination," 278–80.

"nabobs of the land . . .": 1850 letter from Sacramento, quoted in McGowan, *History,* 129.

"there is scarce an officer . . .": Hubert Howe Bancroft, *Popular Tribunals,* 2 vols. (San Francisco: History Co., 1887), 1:130–31.

San Francisco conviction rate, 1850–53: ibid., 1:131.

"criminals of the worst description . . . ": W. Perkins, *Three Years,* 172.

"In a country like this . . .": ibid., 236–37.

"We want a court . . .": ibid., 172.

Lynchings in 1855: Paul, *California Gold Discovery,* 206.

---

page 176

Description of Sonora lynching: W. Perkins, *Three Years,* 233–35.

San Francisco population in 1853: Soulé, Gihon, and Nisbet, *Annals of San Francisco,* 488.

"There is no crime . . .": Bancroft, *History of California,* 7:194.

Fire prevention ordinances: Oscar Lewis, *San Francisco: Mission to Metropolis* (Berkeley: Howell-North, 1966), 65.

Alta California editorial: Royce, *California,* 321–22.

"We are the mayor . . . ": Watkins and Olmstead, *Mirror,* 58.

---

page 177

Lower inset quotation ("I have now only. . . "): Unsigned letter-sheet, December 9, 1850, ibid., 41.

Description of "the great fire": Soulé, Gihon, and Nisbet, *Annals of San Francisco,* 331–32, 604–6.

---

page 178

"Every lover of liberty . . .": Bancroft, *Popular Tribunals,* 1:236.

"the legal tribunals . . .": *San Francisco Evening Picayune,* June 14, 1850, in *San Francisco as It Is: Gleanings from the "Picayune,"* ed. Kenneth M. Johnson (Georgetown, Calif.: Talisman Press, 1964), 158.

"the hungriest, craziest, wildest mob": David P. Barstow, quoted in Bean and Rawls, *California,* 113.

$800,000 embezzlement: Watkins and Olmsted, *Mirror,* 86.

"there is no security . . . ": 1856 Vigilance Committee Constitution, quoted in Bancroft, *Popular Tribunals,* 2:111–12.

---

page 180

"surely enough to kill . . . :" Bancroft, *Popular Tribunals,* 2:50.

"fell about six feet . . . ": ibid., 237.

Editorials from *Evening Journal* and *Alta:* ibid., 213.

"damned pork merchants": David S. Terry, quoted in Sherman, *Memoirs,* 148.

"In point of numbers . . .": *Nevada Journal,* June 27, 1856, quoted in Bancroft, *Popular Tribunals,* 2:366.

---

page 181

"I see no signs of moral reform . . .": William Tecumseh Sherman to Henry S. Turner, April 2, 1857, quoted in Clarke, *Sherman,* 305.

Footnote (Sherman as banker): Clarke, *Sherman,* passim.

Marked monte cards and rigged faro boxes: Henry Chafetz, *Play the Devil: A History of Gambling in the United States from 1492 to 1955* (New York: Bonanza Books, 1960), 81.

---

page 182

1852 seaborne immigration: Wright, "Cosmopolitan California," 341.

1853 imports: Soulé, Gihon, and Nisbet, *Annals of San Francisco,* 495.

Inset quotation ("gambling, drinking, and houses of ill fame . . ."): Lucius Fairchild to John Wilson, June 1, 1850, in Fairchild, *California Letters,* 71.

Sacramento river steamboat competition: McGowan, "Freighting," 37.

---

page 184

1855 shipments to Sacramento and Marysville: Lotchin, *San Francisco,* 54.

Reduced freight rates/passenger fares: McGowan, "Freighting," 84.

Steamboat accidents: ibid., 61.

"soulless and heartless monster": *Sacramento Union,* September 30, 1857, quoted ibid., 142.

"Mammoth Company and Monster Monopoly": ibid., 74.

Marysville opposition steamers, ibid., 82.

---

page 186

Footnote (steamboats to Red Bluff): McGowan, *History,* 80.

Forty thousand men as teamsters, muleteers, wheelrights, etc.: This is a scaled-back estimate from the figure of 187,000 that Lippincott's *Gazetteer* used in 1856 for "drivers and packmen," quoted ibid., 89.

Freight wagons described: McGowan, "Freighting," 270.

Departures from Sacramento in 1852: McGowan, *History,* 89.

Wagonloads to Nevada City in 1857: McGowan, "Freighting," 421.

Loading of stagecoaches: Oscar Winther, *Express and Stagecoach Days in California* (Stanford: Stanford University Press, 1936), 98.

"splendid coaches will pass through . . . ": *Alta California,* May 18, 1852, in Boggs, *Playhouse,* 132.

---

page 187

One thousand mules a day and four thousand mules owned: McGowan, "Freighting," 209.

Profit of Marysville packer: Edward McIlhany, *Recollections of a '49er* (1908), cited ibid., 225.

Inset quotation ("Yesterday a man . . . "): Sallie H. Dryden to her brother and sister, June 27, 1851, in Sloan, *Catalogue,* 68.

Footnote (postal volume): Bancroft, *California Inter Pocula,* 279.

---

page 188

"From our arrangements . . . ": Winther, *Express and Stagecoach Days,* 47–48.

---

page 189

Description of Sacramento: Edith Pitti, "Gold! And All That, 1848–1962" (Sacramento Museum, n.d., photocopy), 15, 17–19.

"anywhere there is a little damp": McGowan, *History,* 77.

1854 freight/bill: McGowan, "Freighting," 345–46, 352.

Footnote (declining freight rates): ibid., 353.

---

page 190

"no calculation can be relied on . . . ": Decker, P. R., *Fortunes and Failures*, 41.

"Luck alone rules his destiny . . . ": William Tecumseh Sherman, letter of June 30, 1853, quoted ibid., 59.

Interest rates: Decker, P. R., *Fortunes and Failures*, 47.

Fires: McGowan, *History*, 119.

Floods of 1850: Morse, *History of Sacramento*, 19–23.

Vote for and cost of earthen dike: Robert Kelley, *Battling the Inland Sea: American Political Culture, Public Policy, and the Sacramento Valley, 1850–1986* (Berkeley: University of California Press, 1989), 15.

---

page 191

"hundreds have lost all they possess . . . ": Mary Cofren to M. Mclain, March 13, 1853, in Sloan, *Catalogue*, 72.

---

page 192

Sacramento's Great Fire: McGowan, *History*, 118.

Huntington's firefighting/losses: Lavender, *Great Persuader*, 42–44.

---

page 193

Inset quotation ("California is the last spot . . . "): *Marysville Herald*, October 21, 1854, quoted in Kelley, *Battling the Inland Sea*, 35.

March 1853 flood: Barbara Lagomarsino, "Early Attempts to Save the Site of Sacramento by Raising Its Business District" (master's thesis, Sacramento State College, 1969), 16.

---

page 194

Elevating Sacramento: Lagomarsino, "Early Attempts," 84.

Newspaper comments on Sacramento flooding and its nature: ibid., 23.

"have been universally more fortunate . . . ": *Sacramento Transcript*, November 1, 1850, quoted in Rodman W. Paul, "The Beginnings of Agriculture in California: Innovation vs. Continuity," *California Historical Society Quarterly* 52, no. 1 (1973): 19.

Horner's farming enterprise and success in 1850–51 : reminiscences of John M. Horner, in *Pacific Rural Press*, June 24, 1899.

---

page 195

Steamboat trade with dairies: Shipley Walters, *West Sacramento: The Roots of a New City* (Woodland, Calif.: Yolo County Historical Society, 1987), 14.

Footnote (butter/egg deliveries by clipper ship): Gates, *California Ranchos and Farms*, 29; T. Hittell, *History of California*, 3:882

Early experience of George Briggs: George G. Briggs, "Fruit Culture," *California State Agricultural Society Transactions* (1881), 182–83.

Transport challenges faced by Briggs/Horner: *Pacific Rural Press*, July 14, 1883; reprint of 1858 *Sacramento Daily Union* article.

Briggs's relay stations: Horace Greeley, *An Overland Journey: From New York to San Francisco in the Summer of 1859*, ed. Charles T. Duncan (New York: Alfred A. Knopf, 1964), 284.

$100,000 gross/$70,000 net: G. G. Briggs to Col. Warren, July 19, 1860 (MS, J.L.L. Warren Papers, Bancroft Library, University of California, Berkeley).

---

page 196

1851 altercation over dam: William Robertson Grimshaw, *Grimshaw's Narrative*, ed. J.R.K. Kantor (Sacramento: Sacramento Book Collectors Club, 1964), ix.

Claims in Grass Valley meadow: Shinn, *Mining Camps*, 251–52.

"hazardous infancy . . . ": Walton Bean, "James Warren and the Beginnings of Agricultural Institutions in California," *Pacific Historical Review* 13, no. 4 (1944): 361.

Influence and success of James Warren: ibid, 361–65.

"The representation from agricultural counties . . . ": ibid., 368.

"the immense sum . . . ": ibid., 368–69.

---

page 197

1853 flour imports: T. Hittell, *History of California*, 3:869.

"the abundance of gold . . . " and other remarks: address of Col. J. B. Crockett, in California State Agricultural Society, *Official Report of the California State Agricultural Society's Third Annual Fair, Cattle Show, and Industrial Exhibit* (San Francisco: California Farmer Office, 1856), 27–28.

Horner's 1853 potato crop: Gates, *California Ranchos and Farms*, 47.

Observations on failing farmers: William Tecumseh Sherman, letter of September 15, 1854, quoted in Clarke, *Sherman*, 59.

Two-thirds of crop rots: *Sacramento Daily Union*, September 3, 1858.

1856 survey of farms: California State Agricultural Society, *Report* (1856), 5, 38–39.

Barley yield: Bancroft, *History of California*, 7:24.

Footnote (wine and alcohol statistics): Gates, *California Ranchos and Farms*, 67–69.

---

page 198

"if now a railroad . . . ": address of E. L. Beard, quoted in California State Agricultural Society, *Report* (1856), 24.

Sale price of flour: McGowan, "Freighting," 338.

"too impatient to plant . . .": *San Francisco Alta California*, August 31, 1855, quoted in Paul, "Beginnings of Agriculture," 20.

Self-sufficiency in wheat: Rodman W. Paul, "The Wheat Trade Between California and the United Kingdom," *Mississippi Valley Historical Review* 45, no. 3 (1958): 394, 401.

1860 wheat exports: Gates, *California Ranchos and Farms*, 56.

550 wheat ships: Rodman W. Paul, "The Great California Grain War: The Grangers Challenge the Wheat King," *Pacific Historical Review* 27, no. 4 (1958): 333.

Footnote (wheat production): Bancroft, *History of California*, 7:28 n; Cleland and Hardy, *March of Industry*, 51.

page 200

Footnote ("first in time, first in right"): Limerick, *Legacy of Conquest*, 66.

Fifteen hundred squatters: Paul W. Gates, "California's Embattled Settlers," *California Historical Society Quarterly* 41, no. 2 (1962): 109.

Thirty-five masked men: ibid.

"litigious misery": Royce, *California*, 385.

"Land pirates": Gates, "California's Embattled Settlers," 121.

page 201

1855 convention: ibid., 11.

"I have no respect . . . ": William Tecumseh Sherman, letter of January 5, 1857, quoted in Clarke, *Sherman*, 278.

Unconstitutional debt: William Tecumseh Sherman, letter quoted in Clarke, *Sherman*, 265.

"that delectable crowd . . . ": *California Daily Times*, quoted in Lavender, *Great Persuader*, 67.

page 202

Class immobility: Charles Sellers, *The Market Revolution in Jacksonian America, 1815–1846* (New York: Oxford University Press, 1991), 442–43.

"among the best paying investments . . .": report of visiting committees, in California State Agricultural Society, *Transactions of the California State Agricultural Society During the Year 1858* (Sacramento: John O' Meara, 1859), 175.

Fossil river beds: *Gold Mines and Mining in California* (Volcano, Calif.: California Traveler, Inc., 1885), 63–82.

page 204

"Our drift is four feet wide . . . ": Bernard Marks, letter of January 1855, in *Publication of the American Jewish Historical Society* 44, no. 1 (1954), reprint (Philadelphia: Maurice Jacobs, n.d.), 54.

Hundreds of drift mines: *Grass Valley Telegraph*, February 12, 1856, in Paul, *California Gold*, 149.

Iowa Hill tunnels: *Sacramento Weekly Union*, July 12, 1856, cited in Paul, *California Gold*, 150.

Spanish Hill mines: Norman Wilson, Charles Blanchard, and Susan Lindstrom, *Spanish Hill, Placerville's Mountain of Gold* (n.p., 1994), 5–26.

Description of "wonders of carpentry": *Hutchings Magazine* 2, no. 3 (1857):105, quoted in, " 'California's Bantam Cock': The Journals of Charles E. De Long, 1854–1863," ed. Carl I. Wheat, *California Historical Society Quarterly* 9, no. 1 (1930): 78 n. 92.

page 206

Tuolumne Water Company canal: Paul, *California Gold*, 162.

Thirty-five-mile delivery network: California State Agricultural Society, *Transactions* (1858), 182.

Thirty cents per miner's inch: ibid.

Footnote (miner's inch): Philip Ross May, *Origins of Hydraulic Mining in California* (Oakland, Calif.: Holmes Book Co., 1970), 10 n.

5,276 miles of ditches/flumes: Paul, *California Gold*, 164.

"the investment of heavy capital . . . ": California State Agricultural Society, *Transactions of the California State Agricultural Society During the Year 1859* (Sacramento: C. T. Botts, 1860), 60.

Description of Eureka Mine: ibid., 82.

page 208

Statement of Alvinza Hayward: ibid., 83.

Cape Claim description/profit: Paul, *California Gold*, 129.

Nevada County ground sluicing operation: May, *Origins*, 39.

page 209

"old drifts and timbers . . .": *Brown and Dallison's Nevada, Grass Valley, and Rough and Ready Directory* (San Francisco: Nat P. Brown and John K. Dallison, 1856), 10–13, cited ibid., 38.

Chabot's hose: May, *Origins*, 43.

"with the hair on the outside": statement of Edward E. Matteson, December 28, 1893, quoted ibid., 65.

Canvas hose: California State Agricultural Society, *Transactions of the California State Agricultural Society During the Year 1860* (Sacramento: C. T. Botts, 1861), 87; *Historical Souvenir of El Dorado County* (Oakland, Calif.: Paolo Sioli, 1883), 218.

"like immensely long, slimy sea serpents": Borthwick, *Three Years in California*, 92.

Matteson's funnel: May, *Origins*, 43.

page 210

"Our water bill was $153 . . .": Matteson statement, quoted ibid., 66.

June 1853 *Daily Alta* report: quoted in May, *Origins*, 46–47.

Hydraulicking at Iowa Hill: *Sacramento Weekly Union*, July 22, 1854, quoted in Paul, *California Gold*, 154–55.

"greatest and most famous contribution . . . ": Paul, *California Gold*, 153.

Increase in water demand: ibid., 163.

175 inches per day: California State Agricultural Society, *Transactions* (1858), 177.

Claim with two large nozzles, profits: ibid., 179.

Three cents of gold per cubic foot: Hittell, *Resources of California*, 255.

Sierra County claim: John S. Hittell, *Mining in the Pacific States of North America* (San Francisco: H. H. Bancroft, 1861), 145.

page 212

Footnote (changing limits on claim size/number): W. Turrentine Jackson, Rand Herbert, and Stephen Wee, *History of the Tahoe National Forest: 1840–1940* (Davis, Calif.: Jackson Research Projects, 1982), 34; Thomas Harsha Pagenhart, "Water Use in the Yuba and Bear River Basins, California" (Ph.D. diss., University of California, Berkeley, 1969), 110.

"Now water is used . . . ": *Nevada Journal,* March 20, 1857, quoted in Paul, *California Gold,* 163.

"At the end of the hose . . .": *Alta California,* March 23, 1856, quoted in Robert L. Kelley, *Gold vs. Grain: The Hydraulic Mining Controversy in California's Sacramento Valley* (Glendale, Calif.: Arthur H. Clark, 1959), 28.

page 213

Inset quotation ("It was the only population . . ."): Mark Twain, *Roughing It* (Hartford, Conn.: American Publishing, 1872), 415.

Chinese immigration/population: There were 7,512 Chinese in California before the 1852 surge in immigration (Bancroft, *History of California,* 7:336). From 1852 through 1859, 47,414 Chinese arrived in San Francisco (Wright, "Cosmopolitan California," 343). By 1854, 10,262 were said to have left California or died (Gunther Barth, *Bitter Strength: A History of the Chinese in the United States, 1850–1870* [Cambridge: Harvard University Press, 1964], 90). It is reasonable to assume the loss of another 10,000 by the end of the decade, which, along with the preceding figures, would account for the remaining population of 35,000 Chinese recorded in the 1860 census, 26,000 of whom resided in the mining region (Paul, *Mining Frontiers,* 35).

page 214

Twenty-one partners shared $140,000 on the Tuolumne River: *San Francisco Bulletin,* April 28, 1856, cited in Bancroft, *History of California,* 6:421 n. 20.

Twenty-three-pound "lump of gold": *Alta California,* September 15, 1856, cited in Bancroft, *History of California,* 6:420 n. 19.

"ready to go anywhere . . .": John S. Hittell, "The Mining Excitements of California," *Overland Monthly* (May 1869), quoted in Paul, Mining Frontiers, 36.

"the mines are much richer . . .": extract from contemporary account, quoted in J. Hittell, *Mining,* 28.

News from the Fraser River: J. Hittell, M*ining,* 29–32.

page 215

24,153 men in 112 ships: *Sierra Democrat,* November 13, 1858, quoted in James J. Sinnott, *History of Sierra County,* 3d ed., vol. 1 (Nevada City, Calif.: Mountain House Books, 1991), 90; Bancroft, *History of California,* 7:683 n. 1.

Gold commissioners: Watkins, *Gold and Silver,* 48.

"the miners are now leaving here very fast": C. O. Phillips to A. D. Merritt, November 12, 1858, in "To the Fraser River! The Diary and Letters of Cyrus Olin Phillips, 1858–1859," ed. F. W. Howay, *California Historical Society Quarterly* 11, no. 2 (1932): 155.

Three thousand remaining miners: J. Hittell, *Mining,* 33.

"Californians are a fast people. . . .": ibid., 35.

CHAPTER 6 *(Astounding Enterprises)*

page 219

"It was a driving, vigorous, restless population . . .": Twain, *Roughing It,* 415.

"devils of the forest": *Oroville Union,* July 25, 1863, quoted in Rawls, *Indians of California,* 181.

page 220

Foreign-born population: Bancroft, *History of California,* 7:700.

175,000 immigrants: ibid., 697 n. 2.

"irrepressible conflict": *San Juan Times,* February 12, 1876, quoted in Pagenhart, "Water Use," 146.

"Our state is a marvel to ourselves . . . ": Nathaniel Bennett, in *Alta California,* October 31, 1850.

page 221

San Francisco Stock and Exchange Board: Bancroft, *History of California,* 7:670 n. 46, 671; George D. Lyman, *Ralston's Ring* (New York: Charles Scribner's Sons, 1937), 1–4.

Richness of Comstock ore: Eliot Lord, *Comstock Mining and Miners* (1883; reprint, Berkeley: Howell-North, 1959), 55.

"Silver—solid, pure SILVER! . . .": J. Ross Browne, *A Peep at Washoe* (1860; reprint, Balboa Island, Calif.: Paisano Press, 1959), 11.

page 222

"bull and bear": Bancroft, *History of California,* 7:182 n.51, 671.

2,467 new mining companies: *Mining and Scientific Press,* January 30, 1864.

"It is within the experience . . .": Report of the 1877–78 California Legislature, quoted in Bancroft, *History of California,* 7:680 n. 55.

"hired liars": Lord, *Comstock Mining and Miners,* 134.

Footnote (San Francisco exchanges): Bancroft, *History of California,* 7:182 n. 51, 669 nn. 43–44.

Yield of Comstock Lode: David Lavender, *Nothing Seemed Impossible: William C. Ralston and Early California* (Palo Alto, Calif.: American West Publishing, 1975), 168; Paul, *Mining Frontiers,* 56.

Size of work force: Paul, *Mining Frontiers,* 68.

Mining jobs: Wells Drury, *An Editor on the Comstock Lode* (New York: Farrar & Rinehart, 1936), 21.

$40,000 salary: Brewer, *Up and Down California,* 559.

page 223

Use of nitroglycerin: Mead B. Kibbey, *The Railroad Photographs of Alfred A. Hart, Artist,* ed. Peter E. Palmquist (Sacramento: California State Library Foundation, 1996), 28 n. 28.

Crown Point mining accident: Mark Wyman, *Hard-Rock Epic: Western Miners and the Industrial Revolution, 1860–1910* (Berkeley: University of California Press, 1979), 99–100.

Footnote (wages): ibid., 35–36.

Investment by miners: Lord, *Comstock Mining and Miners,* 379.

James Galloway's stock trades: Diary of James Galloway, quoted in John Debo Galloway, "Early Engineering Works Contributary to the Comstock," *University of Nevada Bulletin* 41, no. 5 (1947): 19.

Galloway's accident: ibid., 21.

___

page 225

Virginia City fire: Lord, *Comstock Mining and Miners,* 325–28; Dan De Quille, *The Big Bonanza* (1876; reprint, New York: Alfred A. Knopf, 1947), 428–33.

Rush to Idaho: Lord, *Comstock Mining and Miners,* 228.

Gould & Curry mine: ibid., 125, 128.

"California pioneers . . . ": ibid., 125–27.

___

page 226

Receipts on Placerville toll road: ibid., 192.

Animals and teamsters: ibid., 195.

11,103/8,430 passengers: ibid., 194.

Footnote (transportation statistics): ibid., 194–95.

Lumber and cordwood consumption: De Quille, *Big Bonanza,* 174.

Charge for cordwood: Lord, *Comstock Mining and Miners,* 204.

Inset quotation ("sometimes three thousand teams . . ."): Brewer, *Up and Down California,* 552.

600 million feet of timbers: Lord, *Comstock Mining and Miners,* 351.

Wood flumes: ibid., 256–57.

___

page 227

"The Comstock Lode may truthfully be said . . . ": De Quille, *Big Bonanza,* 174.

Confinement of miners: Lord, *Comstock Mining and Miners,* 288–89.

Foreign miners: Paul, M*ining Frontiers,* 69.

"courtroom miners": Limerick, *Legacy of Conquest,* 112.

"icicles in their handshakes": ibid., 113.

Comstock fortunes: George D. Lyman, *The Saga of the Comstock Lode: Boom Days in Virginia City* (New York: Charles Scribner's Sons, 1934), 251.

___

page 228

"The man moved like a cathedral": Idwal Jones, *Ark of Empire* (New York: Doubleday, 1951; New York: Ballantine Books, 1972), 131.

Extravagance of mining magnates: Lyman, *Saga of the Comstock Lode,* 217.

"Not an ounce of gold dug . . . ": Henry George, "What the Railroad Will Bring Us," *Overland Monthly* 1, no. 4 (1868): 300.

"commercial and intellectual centre . . .": James Bryce, *The American Commonwealth,* vol. 2 (1889; reprint, New York: Macmillan, 1914), 429.

___

page 229

"dirty shin-plasters": Alta California, June 21, 1865, quoted in Cross, "Californians and Hard Money," 273.

Californians reclaiming Arizona and New Mexico: Richard H. Dillon, "The California Column," in *California and the Civil War, 1861–1865* (San Francisco: Book Club of California, 1992), n.p.

"shelter for all who may flee the storm": *Los Angeles Star,* quoted in David Lavender, *California: Land of New Beginnings* (New York: Harper & Row, 1972), 258.

Contributions to Sanitary Fund: Zoeth S. Eldridge, *History of California,* vol. 4 (1915), cited in McGowan, *History,* 199.

Footnote (loss of the *Golden Gate*): Lewis, *Sea Routes,* 260; (loss of the *Central America*): Normand E. Klare, *The First Voyage of the Central America* (Spokane, Wash.: Arthur H. Clarke, 1992), 197, 247.

"joining the two oceans with bands of iron": Thomas C. Cochran and William Miller, *The Age of Enterprise: A Social History of Industrial America* (New York: Macmillan, 1949), 54.

___

page 230

$90,000 net from Sacramento Valley Railroad: *Lavender, Nothing Seemed Impossible,* 141.

"the most magnificent project ever conceived": Theodore Judah, *A Practical Plan for Building the Pacific Railroad* (1857), quoted in George Kraus, *High Road to Promontory* (Palo Alto, Calif.: American West Publishing, 1969), 16.

"I shall never talk nor labor . . . ": Lavender, *Great Persuader,* 91.

"Not two years . . . ": Kraus, *High Road,* 27.

___

page 231

Soon—and forever: adapted from Watkins, *California,* 155.

___

page 232

Inset quotation ("The business of California . . . "): Hittell, J., *Resources of California,* 333–34.

"The President has signed the railroad bill . . . ": *Sacramento Union,* July 4, 1862, quoted in Lavender, *Great Persuader,* 113.

"the most brilliant affair of its kind . . . ": *Sacramento Union,* July 12, 1862, quoted in Kraus, *High Road,* 50.

___

page 233

Ames loan: Lavender, *Great Persuader,* 129, 144.

Huntington's requisitions: ibid., 175, 203–204.

"a big row": Theodore Judah, quoted in Kraus, *High Road,* 65.

___

page 234

"shoddy contractors and swarms of official leeches": Salmon P. Chase, quoted in Lavender, *Great Persuader,* 150.

"a maelstrom of political bargaining . . .": Thomas G. and Maria Robins Belden, *So Fell the Angels* (1956), quoted ibid., 151.

"tempest of wildest disorder": Elihu Washburne, in the *Congressional Globe*, 40th Cong., 2d sess., 2135, quoted in Lavender, *Great Persuader*, 156.

"the greatest legislative crime in history": *Congressional Globe*, 38th Cong., June 21, 1864, quoted in Lavender, *Great Persuader*, 156.

Footnote (conversion of bonds to gold): Wesley S. Griswold, *A Work of Giants: Building of the First Transcontinental Railroad* (New York: McGraw-Hill, 1962), 116.

Brannan's investment in CPRR: Lavender, *Great Persuader*, 160–61.

Court approval of bonds: Lavender, *Nothing Seemed Impossible*, 192.

Projected construction costs: Lavender, *Great Persuader*, 162.

page 235

Thirty chartered ships: ibid., 225.

"I am loading iron on ships . . . ": Collis P. Huntington to Mark Hopkins, May 16, 1868, quoted ibid., 204.

CPRR's twenty-five sawmills: Kraus, *High Road*, 183.

"dedicated fury": Griswold, *Work of Giants*, 91.

"the dregs of Asia": Lavender, *Great Persuader*, 161.

Control of Chinese labor: Barth, *Bitter Strength*, 116–17.

Chinese/Irish laborers: Lavender, *Great Persuader*, 168.

"a great army laying seige . . . ": Albert D. Richardson, *Beyond the Mississippi* (Hartford: American Publishing, 1867), quoted in Griswold, *Work of Giants*, 123.

page 236

Sierra snowstorms, 1866–67: Kraus, *High Road*, 145.

Loss of twenty Chinese: ibid., 148.

Tails twisted off: ibid., 146.

Nitroglycerin: Kibbey, *Railroad Photographs*, 28 n. 28.

Five hundred kegs a day: Kraus, *High Road*, 135.

"Work on as though Heaven was before you . . . ": Collis P. Huntington to Charles Crocker, July 1, 1868, quoted in Lavender, *Great Persuader*, 208.

page 238

"a mile of track for every working day . . .": Charles Crocker, "Reminiscences" (MS, Bancroft Library, University of California, Berkeley), quoted in Griswold, *Work of Giants*, 233.

65 million feet of timber: Kraus, *High Road*, 191.

"For the past two weeks . . . ": *Reno Crescent*, August 15, 1868, quoted in Griswold, *Work of Giants*, 248.

Celebration of transcontinental railroad: Kraus, *High Road*, 273, 278–81.

Front page editorial: *Sacramento Union*, May 10, 1869.

page 239

"San Francisco annexes the United States": Watkins and Olmsted, *Mirror*, 119.

"avalanche of goods . . . ": Asbury Harpending, quoted ibid., 120.

Arrivals by rail: Bancroft, *History of California*, 7:697 n. 2.

Footnote (departures by rail): ibid.; (Reed's pear shipment): Walters, *West Sacramento*, 14.

page 240

Hayward's Crown Point stock profits: Bancroft, *History of California*, 7:674.

"body of ore absolutely. . .": *Mining and Scientific Press*, December 26, 1874, quoted in Paul, *Mining Frontiers*, 79.

$105 million from "Big Bonanza": Paul, *Mining Frontiers*, 80.

$610,000 in "legalized blackmail": Lavender, *Great Persuader*, 290; Caughey, *California*, 379.

page 241

"cold-hearted, selfish, sordid men . . .": Editorial from *Baker City (Oregon) Inland Empire*, reprinted in *Sacramento Union*, October 1, 1869, quoted in Lavender, *Great Persuader*, 268.

First law of economics/Nature: Lavender, *Great Persuader*, 269.

"ponderous palaces . . . ," turrets, and granite: ibid., 300–301.

Inset quotation ("in no other region . . ."): Bean and Rawls, *California*, 179.

"The rush to California . . . ": Henry David Thoreau, "Life Without Principle," *Atlantic Monthly* 12 (1863): 488.

page 243

"huddling so closely . . .": Thomas Starr King, quoted in *A Tribute to Thomas Starr King* (Boston, 1865), cited in Starr, *Americans*, 99.

King's observations on hydraulic mining: Thomas Starr King, "A Visit to Nevada County in 1860," *Nevada County Historical Society Bulletin* 49, no. 1 (1995): 4.

"God's fingerprint": source unknown.

"sewn with four seams . . . ": California State Agricultural Society, *Transactions* (1860), 87.

Up to six men a nozzle: Pagenhart, "Water Use," 103.

page 244

"thick as mush": from a song, "Good-bye, Slickens, Good-bye," in Peter J. Delay, *History of Yuba and Sutter Counties* (Los Angeles: Historic Record Company, 1924), 260.

Description of pressure box and distributor: William Irelan Jr., *Ninth Annual Report of the State Mineralogist for the Year Ending December 1, 1889* (Sacramento: J.D. Young, 1890), 127.

Hydraulic accidents: J. Hittell, *Resources of California*, 254.

Diversion of streams: Pagenhart, "Water Use," 79.

page 246

Footnote (Eureka Lake and Yuba Canal Co.): ibid. 130; ("Should much fluming . . . "): Rossiter W. Raymond, *Statistics of Mines and Mining in the States and Territories West of the Rocky Mountains, Being the Fifth Annual Report* (Washington, D.C.: Government Printing Office, 1873), 408.

Sound of sluice boxes: Kelley, *Battling the Inland Sea,* 21.

Description of Yuba River: *Marysville Daily Appeal,* March 31, 1860, quoted ibid., 69.

Floods of 1861–62: McGowan, *History,* 186–87.

page 247

Description of slickens: *Marysville Daily Appeal,* January 27, 30, quoted in Kelley, Battling the Inland Sea, 72.

"where floods and slickens would not reach": George Briggs, "Fruit Culture," 183.

"in a manner as to puzzle . . .": *Marysville Daily Appeal,* October 28, 1862.

Steamer groundings on the Sacramento River: Kelley, *Battling the Inland Sea,* 26–27.

"an evil to be stopped at once . . .": Jones, *Ark of Empire,* 98.

"cash factories": King, "Visit to Nevada County," 3.

page 248

"When you touch the mines . . . ": California State Agricultural Society, *Transactions of the California State Agricultural Society for the Years 1864 and 1865* (Sacramento: O. M. Clayes, 1866), 33.

Footnote (quartz mining percentage): James M. Hill, "Historical Summary of Gold, Silver, Copper, Lead, and Zinc Produced in California, 1848 to 1926," U.S. Bureau of Mines, Economic Paper 3 (1929), cited in Paul, *Mining Frontiers,* 92; (stability of quartz mining): Paul, *California Gold,* 254, 257.

Claude Chana's farm: McGowan, *History,* 294.

"a slimey deposit . . ." and "so deep . . .": *Marysville Daily Appeal,* April 6, 1862.

"scarcely any yield . . .": McGowan, *History,* 294.

"bank-blasting" described: Raymond, *Statistics* (Fifth Annual Report), 404–5; August J. Bowie Jr., *A Practical Treatise on Hydraulic Mining in California,* 11th ed. (New York: D. Van Nostrand, 1910), 206.

Sucker Flat/Forest Hill blasts: Bowie, *Practical Treatise,* 207–9.

page 249

Accepting attitude/observations at Oroville: Kelley, *Battling the Inland Sea,* 82.

Footnote (changing mining laws): Paul, *California Gold,* 231–32; Pagenhart, "Water Use," 110–11.

"this lance-thrust of water . . . ": Raymond, *Statistics* (Fifth Annual Report), 403.

"to fly around in a contrary direction": Henry G. Hanks, *Second Report of the State Mineralogist, from December 1, 1880, to October 1, 1882* (Sacramento: Superintendent of State Printing, 1882), 67.

"tremendous spout": Lavender, *California,* 298.

"as hard to the touch . . .": Raymond, *Statistics* (Fifth Annual Report), 403.

page 251

Directing collapsed banks into sluices: ibid., 404.

Four or five monitors: Irelan, *Ninth Annual Report,* 127.

Crum lawsuit: Kelley, *Gold vs. Grain,* 60.

Defensive arguments in Crum trial: ibid., 63.

"The bed of the Yuba . . .": *Weekly Sutter Banner,* April 1874, quoted ibid., 65.

Poorly attended meeting: Kelley, *Gold vs. Grain,* 66.

page 252

Footnote (reservoir capacity): Irelan, *Ninth Annual Report,* 123, 126; (water use): Bowie, *Practical Treatise,* 95.

Two cents to fifteen dollars: Paul, *California Gold,* 150–51.

"more perfect disintegration . . . ": Hanks, *Second Report,* 82.

Use of sluice blocks: ibid., 84; Irelan, *Ninth Annual Report,* 129; Bowie, *Practical Treatise,* 225–26.

page 253

Grizzlies/undercurrents: Hanks, *Second Report,* 86–87; Bowie, *Practical Treatise,* 231.

Footnote (quicksilver loss): Bowie, *Practical Treatise,* 263–64.

Building levees: Kelley, *Battling the Inland Sea,* 102.

page 254

Background on George Ohleyer: Richard D. Garrison, "Sutter County Opposition to Hydraulic Mining, 1874–1884" (master's thesis, Chico State College, 1967), 25–26; Peter J. Delay, *History of Yuba and Sutter Counties* (Los Angeles: History Record Co., 1924), 258–59.

Ohleyer's letter: *Weekly Sutter Banner,* February 24, 1874, quoted in Kelley, *Battling the Inland Sea,* 104.

Flood of January 1875: *Marysville Daily Appeal,* January 20, 1875 and *Nevada City Daily Transcript,* January 22, 1875; additional details from *Marysville Daily Appeal* "anniversary issues" of January 19–20, 1909.

page 255

"There is no doubt . . . ": *Nevada City Daily Transcript,* January 22, 1975.

Inset quotation ("California state government . . ."): Caughey, *California,* 381–82.

"I have no objection . . . ": James Keyes, quoted in Kelley, *Gold vs. Grain,* 74.

page 256

"Supposing some one . . . ": *Nevada City Daily Transcript,* December 28, 1875.

"Of course there can be no question . . .": *Sacramento Record-Union,* December 24, 1875, quoted in Kelley, *Gold vs. Grain,* 75.

"We confess we do not see . . .": *Mining and Scientific Press,* January 8, 1876, quoted in Kelley, *Gold vs. Grain,* 76.

"there would be riot and bloodshed . . .": Campbell Berry, *Journal of the California Assembly*, 21st sess., 550–51, quoted in Kelley, *Gold vs. Grain*, 83.

Background and quotation on Cadwalader: *San Francisco Daily Evening Bulletin*, March 9, 1878.

---

page 258

Footnote (farmers' lawsuit): *Pacific Rural Press*, July 1, 1876 and February 2, 1877.

"interfere with or embarrass . . .": Hydraulic Miners Association, "Articles of Agreement" (MS, H. P. Davis, Nevada City, Calif.), quoted in Kelley, *Gold vs. Grain*, 90.

---

page 259

"wild waste of waters . . . ": *San Francisco Daily Evening Bulletin*, March 9, 1878, quoted in Kelley, Gold vs. Grain, 93–94.

"All pretense . . . ": *Sacramento Record-Union*, March 9, 1878, quoted in Kelley, *Gold vs. Grain*, 94.

"we say it is a question . . . ": *Marysville Daily Appeal*, February 22, 1878, quoted in Kelley, *Gold vs. Grain*, 94.

"sophistical reasonings" and "long-winded imprecations . . .": *Nevada City Daily Transcript*, February 26, 1878, quoted in Kelley, *Gold vs. Grain*, 103.

Prelude to Keyes trial: Kelley, *Gold vs. Grain*, 107.

James Keyes's testimony ("promiscuously all over . . . "): *Mining and Scientific Press*, August 3, 1878.

---

page 260

"when I saw hundreds . . . ": *Marysville Daily Appeal*, August 8, 1878.

Arguments by miners, quotation and statistics: *San Francisco Daily Alta California*, August 2, 1878.

"The custom of dumping . . . ": *Marysville Daily Appeal*, August 1, 1878.

"the professors who testify ad nauseam": *Marysville Daily Appeal*, August 6, 1878. The *Appeal* published lengthy transcripts from the trial for fourteen days.

"irrepressible conflict": *Sacramento Record-Union*, July 31, 1878.

"it is absolutely necessary . . .": *Pacific Rural Press*, September 7, 1878.

Formation/organization of Anti-Debris Association, with $170,000 subscription: *Mining and Scientific Press*, September 9, 1878.

---

page 262

Judge Keyser's decision and quotations: *Pacific Rural Press*, March 22, 1879.

"Common justice demands . . . ": *Nevada City Daily Transcript*, March 12, 1879.

Marysville suit: Kelley, *Gold vs. Grain*, 119–20.

---

page 263

"Miners will for the present . . .": *Nevada City Daily Transcript*, November 6, 1879, quoted ibid., 120.

"If Marysville were to win her suit . . .": *Nevada City Daily Transcript*, November 13, 1879.

"the decision . . . knocks Marysville's suit . . .": *Nevada City Daily Transcript*, November 26, 1879.

"bombs exploded and steam whistles . . .": *Nevada City Daily Transcript*, November 18, 1879.

"at Little York . . . ": *Nevada City Daily Transcript*, November 19, 1879.

CHAPTER 7 *(Victims of Success)*

---

page 267

700 million cubic yards: official report, U.S. Army Corps of Engineers, quoted in *Sacramento Daily Record-Union*, March 13, 1880.

57 million bushels in 1884: Donald J. Pisani, *From the Family Farm to Agribusiness: The Irrigation Crusade in California and the West, 1850–1931* (Berkeley: University of California Press, 1984), 9.

---

page 268

"to test the right . . . ": *Pacific Rural Press*, May 20, 1882.

---

page 269

Failure/destruction of English Dam: Doris Foley and S. Griswold Morley, "The 1883 Flood on the Middle Yuba River," *California Historical Society Quarterly* 28, no. 3 (1949): 233–36; W. Turrentine Jackson, *Report on the Malakoff Mine, the North Bloomfield Mining District, and the Town of North Bloomfield* (Sacramento: Department of Parks and Recreation, 1967), 84, 85, 87.

"the dam was blown up by powder": H. C. Perkins, interview in *Nevada City Daily Transcript*, June 20, 1883, quoted in W. Jackson, *Report*, 88.

"The *Sacramento Bee* . . . ": *Nevada City Daily Transcript*, June 26, 1883, quoted in Foley and Morley, "1883 Flood": 236.

"Must millions . . . ": *Nevada City Daily Transcript*, July 25, 1883, quoted in Foley and Morley, "1883 Flood": 236.

---

page 270

Capacity of Bowman and three other reservoirs: W. Jackson, *Report*, 25.

Eleven reservoirs/2.2 billion cubic feet: Irelan, *Ninth Annual Report*, 123. 16.5 billion gallons = 2.2 billion cubic feet x 7.48 gallons per cubic foot.

Over $4 million for water works: Rossiter W. Raymond, *Statistics of Mines and Mining in the States and Territories West of the Rocky Mountains, Being the Sixth Annual Report* (Washington, D.C.: Government Printing Office, 1874), 113.

35 to 40 million gallons every twenty-four hours: ibid., 111.

Dimensions of gravel bank: W. Jackson, Report, 8; Chief Engineer's report in *Sacramento Daily Record-Union*, March 13, 1880.

348 million cubic yards: Raymond, *Statistics of Mines and Mining in the States and Territories West of the Rocky Mountains for the Year 1870* (Washington, D.C.: Government Printing Office, 1872), 77.

"Enough gravel to wash . . . ": W. Jackson, *Report*, 35

Footnote (water used/gravel washed): Hanks, *Second Report*, 116. 18.5 billion gallons = 1,086,972 twenty-four-hour-inches x 17,000 gallons per inch.

Yield estimates: Raymond, *Statistics* (1870), 77.

"As an example . . . ": Harry Lauren Wells, *History of Nevada County* (1880; reprint, Berkeley: Howell-North, 1970), 183.

Opinions on North Bloomfield Company: adapted from Pagenhart, "Water Use," 144–45.

---

page 272

Inset quotation ("The operation of washing . . . "): Hanks, *Second Report*, 111.

Depth of gravel/tunnel: Raymond, *Statistics* (Fifth Annual Report), 68.

Seven shafts/175 men: Raymond, *Statistics* (Sixth Annual Report), 110.

Tunnel digging: Raymond, *Statistics* (1870), 59.

One foot a day at each face: W. Jackson, *Report*, 30, 32, 52.

Completion/cost/length of Malakoff tunnel: ibid., 32

"an operation of the most stupendous character": *Nevada City Daily Transcript*, November 30, 1872.

20,000 feet of tunnels: W. Jackson, *Report*, 35.

---

page 274

Sixty-six settlements: Rossiter W. Raymond, *Statistics of Mines and Mining in the States and Territories West of the Rocky Mountains, Being the Eighth Annual Report* (Washington, D.C.: Government Printing Office, 1877), 67.

1879 North Bloomfield year-end review: quoted in W. Jackson, *Report*, 50, 53, 54.

---

page 275

"the great gravel deposits . . . " Taliesin Evans, "Hydraulic Mining in California," *Century Magazine* 25, no. 3 (1883): 338.

"among the greatest marvels . . . "/"In ditches . . . ": *Nevada City Daily Transcript*, September 22, 1882, reprinted in *Mining and Scientific Press*, October 14, 1882, quoted in W. Jackson, *Report*, 62–63.

"There is a real pleasure . . . ": Article reprinted from *San Francisco Daily Evening Bulletin* in *Nevada City Daily Transcript*, July 30, 1879.

"It is an open question . . ." *Nevada City Daily Transcript*, November 8, September 16, 1879, quoted in Kelley, *Gold vs. Grain*, 121.

---

page 277

Over 29 million bushels in 1873: Pisani, *From the Family Farm*, 9 n. 16.

Four million acres, two-thirds of cultivated land: ibid., 286. (Pisani cites 3,750,000 acres rather than 4 million.)

$34 million harvest in 1881, nearly twice the value of gold production: California State Agricultural Society, *Transactions of the California State Agricultural Society for the Year 1881* (Sacramento: J. D. Young, 1881), 154. Bowie, *Practical Treatise*, 288, cites $19,223,000 as the total value of gold production for 1881.

Inset quotation ("had turned from pale yellow . . ."): Frank Norris, *The Octopus* (1901; reprint New York: P.F. Collier & Son, n.d.).

1882 wheat exports (559 ships, $16 million paid for transport): Paul, "Wheat Trade," 403.

---

page 279

"the grain that was waving . . .": C. Daniel Elliot, essay in *Breadbasket of the World: California's Great Wheat Growing Era* (San Francisco: Book Club of California, 1984), n.p.

2,784 sacks in one day: ibid.

1882 exports from Colusa County: McGowan, *History*, 251.

---

page 280

Refrigerated freight cars: Starr, *Inventing the Dream*, 132.

48,000 in farming/36,000 in mining: Pisani, *From the Family Farm*, 102–3.

"The public will soon . . ." *Sacramento Bee*, January 10, 1876, reprinted in *Sacramento Bee*, February, 3, 1958.

Footnote (agricultural press): Starr, *Inventing the Dream*, 137–38.

"the purpose of this new paper . . . ": *Sutter County Farmer*, April 22, 1881, quoted in Richard Dale Garrison, "Sutter County Opposition to Hydraulic Mining, 1874–1884" (master's thesis, Chico State College, January 1967), 26.

---

page 282

Footnote (Kearneyism"): Bryce, *American Commonwealth*, 430–37.

Inaugural address ("the principal sources . . ." and subsequent quotations): George C. Perkins, *Sacramento Record-Union*, January 9, 1880.

---

page 283

"to such depths . . . " William Hamilton Hall, *Report of the State Engineer to the Legislature of California*, pt. 3 (Sacramento: J. D. Young, 1880), 15.

"to convey some conception . . . " and further statements from Hall's report: quoted in *Sacramento Daily Record-Union*, March 13, 1880.

Footnote (volume of debris in rivers): Grove Karl Gilbert, *Hydraulic-Mining Debris in the Sierra Nevada*, United States Geological Survey, Professional Paper 105 (Washington, D.C.: Government Printing Office, 1917), 4.

"still available to be worked . . . ": *Sacramento Daily Record-Union*, March 13, 1880.

Engineer Hall's judgment ("The study of this subject . . ."): quoted in Kelley, *Battling the Inland Sea*, 203.

---

page 284

Reaction to "Act to Promote Drainage": Kelley, *Gold vs. Grain*, 137–39, 208.

"would be just as logical . . . ": *Los Angeles Herald*, March 21, 1880, quoted in Pisani, *From the Family Farm*, 170.

Reporter's description of Yuba River ("demoralized stream"), buried orchard, depth of debris, and brush dam ("downstream face"): *Sacramento Daily Record-Union*, November 11, 1880.

---

page 286

$463,153 for dam/levees: Kelley, *Battling the Inland Sea*, 212.

"Special Message on the Debris Question": quotations by Governor Perkins and his position re: the Drainage Act, *Pacific Rural Press*, January 22, 1881.

Details re. flood of January 1881: John Thompson, *Flood Chronologies and Aftermaths Affecting the Lower Sacramento River* (Urbana: Department of Geography, University of Illinois, 1996), 11–15.

Fate of repeal bill: Kelley, *Gold vs. Grain*, 169, 174, 181; Robert L. Kelley, "The Mining Debris Controversy in the Sacramento Valley," *Pacific Historical Review* 25 (1956): 337–39.

"Things are busted now": William Parks, quoted in Kelley, *Gold vs. Grain*, 186.

---

page 287

"be perpetually enjoined . . . ": *Marysville vs. North Bloomfield*, in *Reports of Cases Determined by the Supreme Court of the State of California at the Sessions of 1881*, vol. 58 (San Francisco: Bancroft-Whitney, 1887), 320.

"a pack of fee-seeking lawyers . . . ": *Nevada City Daily Transcript*, July 3, 1881.

"No more Marysville . . ." and "Send back the fish . . .": *Nevada City Daily Transcript*, June 17, 1881.

Miners' mass meeting, June 18, 1881, described and quotations: *Nevada City Daily Transcript*, June 21, 1881.

Columbia Hill protest meeting: *Nevada City Daily Transcript*, June 20, 1881.

---

page 288

Farmers meetings in various towns: *Marysville Daily Appeal*, June 1, 1881.

"The farmers don't wish . . . ": ibid.

Avoiding sheriffs and defying injunctions: *Mining and Scientific Press*, October 8, 1881.

"at Marysville they cannot find room . . . ": ibid.

A. A. Smith and Knights of Pythias: *Survey of Cultural Resources at Malakoff Diggins State Historical Park* (Sacramento: California Department of Parks and Recreation, 1979), 16.

"When it shall reach the point . . .": *San Francisco Daily Alta California*, October 6, 1881, reprinted in *Nevada City Daily Transcript*, October 8, 1881.

"The people of Nevada County . . . ": *Nevada City Daily Transcript*, October 8, 1881.

---

page 290

Meeting at Western House, main speaker ("the danger from debris . . ."): *Sacramento Daily Record-Union*, October 18, 1881.

"This locality was once . . . ": *Marysville Daily Appeal*, October 23, 1881.

"of sandy desert . . . ": *Marysville Daily Appeal*, October 22, 1881.

San Francisco businessmen's response to Malakoff Mine: *Marysville Daily Appeal*, October 25, 1881.

"wine was brought in": ibid.

Speeches at Grass Valley meeting ("a national issue . . . "): ibid.

---

page 291

"injunction game": *Nevada City Daily Transcript*, November 10, 1881.

San Francisco Board of Trade's advisory report ("render sterile . . ."): *Sacramento Daily Record-Union*, November 11, 1881.

State Attorney General ("injuriously affected . . ."; "wholesale resort to litigation . . . "; "a speedy determination"): *Sacramento Daily Record-Union*, July 30, 1881.

Complaints against Gold Run Company ("filled up some thirty-five feet . . ." and "the debris deposits . . ."): *Sacramento Daily Record-Union*, November 16, 1881.

---

page 293

"no trial in California . . . " and "intricate examinations": ibid.

"The streets are full . . . " and "the working miner . . . ": *Marysville Daily Appeal*, June 13, 1882, quoted in Kelley, *Gold vs. Grain*, 216.

Judge Temple's Gold Run decision and statement, "Perhaps I am . . .": *Sacramento Daily Record-Union*, June 13, 1882. Additional details from *Pacific Rural Press*, June 17, 1882.

"compromise is treason": *Marysville Daily Appeal*, quoted in *Sacramento Daily Record-Union*, July 18, 1882.

June 26, 1881 demand sent by Anti-Debris Association to mines on Yuba River: *Mining and Scientific Press*, July 8, 1882.

"The hell-born and hell-bound wretches . . .": *Nevada City Daily Transcript*, quoted in Kelley, *Gold vs. Grain*, 219.

---

page 294

"The mines are not going to close down . . .": *Forest City Weekly Tribune*, quoted in Kelley, *Gold vs. Grain*, 219.

Formation of Anti-Debris Guard and speech by Cadwalader ("to take up arms . . ."): *Sacramento Daily Record-Union*, August 3, 1882. More information on the Guard from *Sacramento Daily Record-Union*, August 17, 1882.

Marysville meeting of Anti-Debris Guard: *Marysville Daily Appeal*, September 15, 1882.

page 296

Inset quotation ("Certainly by no other means . . . "): Hanks, *Second Report,* 117.

Judge Sawyer viewing the failed debris dams: *Woodruff vs. North Bloomfield,* in *Cases Argued and Determined in the Circuit and District Courts of the United States, November 1883–February 1884,* vol. 18 of *The Federal Reporter* (Saint Paul: West Publishing, 1884), 764.

"I am entirely satisfied . . . ": Lorenzo Sawyer, in *Sacramento Daily Record-Union,* April 10, 1883, quoted in Kelley, *Gold vs. Grain,* 233–34.

page 297

Special commission/two hundred witnesses: *Mining and Scientific Press,* September 1, 1883.

"They won't even let Woodruff . . . ": *Marysville Daily Appeal,* September 11, 1883.

"The boldness with which capitalists . . . ": *Woodruff vs. North Bloomfield,* in *Cases,* 803.

"Deducting liberally . . . ": ibid., 757–58.

page 298

Dr. Teegarden's lands . . .": ibid., 760.

"that now debris . . .": ibid., 764.

Woodruff's damages and costs ("constitute a grievous . . ."): ibid., 764–65, 769.

"After an examination . . ": ibid., 808–9.

"Some of the most sober-minded . . .": *Marysville Daily Appeal,* January 8, 1884.

Description of Marysville celebration: ibid.

"You can have a big time . . .": George Cadwalader, quoted ibid.

page 299

"profound sorrow" and "Most of us will pack our gripsacks": *San Francisco Daily Evening Bulletin,* January 8, 1884. This article is a summary of reactions to the Sawyer decision in different towns in the valley and the foothills.

EPILOGUE

page 301

"an event that . . . "; "retrospection on the gathering . . . "; "that changed the destinies . . . ": *Sacramento Daily Record-Union,* January 24, 1898.

"grand old Argonauts"; "pioneers touched with gray"; "that symbolized the dawn . . . " ; "companions of James Marshall": *San Francisco Daily Evening Bulletin,* January 25, 1898.

"perpetuated the memory . . . ": *Sacramento Bee,* January 24, 1898.

page 302

"There is nothing . . . "; "We lack the associations . . . ": Bancroft, *California Inter Pocula,* 301.

"ought to be gently preserved . . . ": Clarence King, *Mountaineering in the Sierra Nevadas* (1872), quoted in Kowalewski, *Gold Rush,* 381.

page 303

"Recklessness is in the air . . . ": Rudyard Kipling, *American Notes* (Norman, Okla., 1981), 40.

"The independence and liberality . . . ": Charles Plummer, letter of March 14, 1851 (MS, Huntington Library, San Marino, Calif).

page 304.

"America, only more so": first published in the *Overland Monthly* (December 1883): 658.

SOURCES

Throughout the years of my writing and rewriting the text of this book, I have relied on newspapers, official documents, and various other nineteenth century sources—and equally on the writing and more extensive research of the many historians cited in the notes and in this bibliography.

I wish to make particular and respectful mention of several authors to whom I feel most indebted. First, Robert Kelley and Thomas Pagenhart; and Rodman Paul, Neal Harlow, Joseph McGowan, T. H. Watkins, David Lavender, Kevin Starr, James Rawls, and always, Hubert Howe Bancroft.

Atherton, Faxon Dean. *The California Diary of Faxon Dean Atherton.* Edited by Doyce B. Nunis. San Francisco: California Historical Society, 1964.

Bailey, Lynn R. *Supplying the Mining World: The Mining Equipment Manufacturers of San Francisco: 1850–1900.* Tucson, Ariz.: Westernlore Press, 1996.

Bailey, Thomas A. *A Diplomatic History of the American People.* 4th ed. New York: Appleton-Century-Crofts, 1950.

Baker, Issac. Diary, 1850. MS. Bancroft Library, University of California, Berkeley.

Bancroft, Hubert Howe. *California Inter Pocula.* San Francisco: History Co., 1888.

———. *History of California.* 7 vols. San Francisco: History Co., 1886–90.

———. *Popular Tribunals.* 2 vols. San Francisco: History Co., 1887.

Barker, Malcolm E., comp. *San Francisco Memoirs: Eyewitness Accounts of the Birth of a City.* San Francisco: Londonborn Publications, 1994.

Barnard, Frederic W. Letters. MS. Beinecke Rare Book and Manuscript Library, Yale University.

Barnes, James S. Letters, 1849–57. TS. Bancroft Library, University of California, Berkeley.

Barth, Gunther. *Bitter Strength: A History of the Chinese in the United States, 1850–1870.* Cambridge: Harvard University Press, 1964.

Bean, Walton. "James Warren and the Beginnings of Agricultural Institutions in California." *Pacific Historical Review* 13, no. 4 (1944): 361–75.

Bean, Walton, and James J. Rawls. *California: An Interpretive History.* 5th ed. New York: McGraw-Hill, 1988.

Becker, Robert H. *Diseños of California Ranchos: Maps of Thirty-seven Land Grants (1822–1846) from the Records of the United States District Court, San Francisco.* San Francisco: Book Club of California, 1964.

Beecher, Edward. *The Papal Conspiracy Exposed and Protestantism Defended, in the Light of Reason, History, and Scripture.* 1855. Reprint, New York: Arno Press, 1977.

Beilharz, Edwin A., and Carlos U. López, eds. and trans. *We Were 49ers! Chilean Accounts of the California Gold Rush.* Pasadena: Ward Ritchie Press, 1976.

Bidlack, Russell E. *Letters Home: The Story of Ann Arbor's Forty-Niners.* Ann Arbor, 1960.

Billington, Ray Allen. *Westward Expansion.* New York: Macmillan, 1963.

Blake, Stephen Palmer. *The Life of Stephen Palmer Blake from His Journals.* Edited by Elizabeth Hurst Ellwood. Franklin, N.C.: Genealogy Publishing Service, 1995.

Blum, John M., et al. *The National Experience: A History of the United States.* New York: Harcourt, Brace & World, 1963.

Boggs, Mae Hélène Bacon. *My Playhouse Was A Concord Coach.* Oakland, Calif.: Howell-North Press, 1942.

Borthwick, J. D. *Three Years in California.* 1857. Reprint, Oakland, Calif.: Biobooks, 1948.

Bowie, August J. Jr. *A Practical Treatise on Hydraulic Mining in California.* 11th ed. New York: D. Van Nostrand, 1910.

Brandon, William. *The American Heritage Book of Indians.* New York: American Heritage, 1961.

———. *The Last Americans.* New York: McGraw-Hill, 1974.

Breadbasket of the World: California's Great Wheat Growing Era. San Francisco: Book Club of California, 1984.

Brewer, William H. *Up and Down California in 1860–1864: The Journal of William H. Brewer.* Edited by Francis P. Farquhar. New Haven: Yale University Press, 1930.

Briggs, George G. "Fruit Culture." *California State Agricultural Society Transactions* (1881): 181–89.

———. Letter of July 19, 1860. MS. J.L.L. Warren Papers. Bancroft Library, University of California, Berkeley.

Brown and Dallison's Nevada, Grass Valley, and Rough and Ready Directory. San Francisco: Nat P. Brown and John K. Dallison, 1856.

Browne, J. Ross. *A Peep at Washoe.* 1860. Reprint, Balboa Island, Calif.: Paisano Press, 1959.

Browning, Peter, comp. *To the Golden Shore: America Goes to California—1849.* Lafayette, Calif.: Great West Books, 1995.

Bruff, J. Goldsborough. *Gold Rush: The Journals, Drawings, and Other Papers of J. Goldsborough Bruff . . . April 2, 1849– July 20, 1851.* Vol 2: *Bruff's Camp to Washington City.* Edited by Georgia Willis Read and Ruth Gaines. New York: Columbia University Press, 1944.

Bryant, Edwin. *What I Saw in California.* 1848. Reprint, Santa Ana, Calif.: Fine Arts Press, 1936.

Bryce, James. *The American Commonwealth.* Vol 2. 1889. Reprint, New York: Macmillan, 1914.

Buck, Franklin A. *A Yankee Trader in the Gold Rush: The Letters of Franklin A. Buck.* Compiled by Katherine A. White. Boston: Houghton Mifflin, 1930.

Buffum, E. Gould. *Six Months in the Gold Mines: From a Journal of Three Years' Residence in Upper and Lower California, 1847–8–9.* Edited by John W. Caughey. [Los Angeles]: Ward Ritchie Press, 1959.

Buffum, Joseph C. Diary, 1849–51. TS. Bancroft Library, University of California, Berkeley.

Bunje, Emil T. H., and James C. Kean. *Pre-Marshall Gold in California.* Vol. 2: *Discoveries and Near-Discoveries, 1840–1848.* Sacramento: Historic California Press, 1983.

Burgess, Sherwood D. "The Forgotten Redwoods of the East Bay." *California Historical Society Quarterly* 30, no. 1 (1951): 1–14.

California Division of Mines. *The Elephant as They Saw It: A Collection of Contemporary Pictures and Statements on Gold Mining in California.* Sacramento: Office of State Printing, 1949.

California State Agricultural Society. *Official Report of the California State Agricultural Society's Third Annual Fair, Cattle Show, and Industrial Exhibit.* San Francisco: California Farmer Office, 1856.

———. *Transactions of the California State Agricultural Society During the Year 1858.* Sacramento: John O'Meara, 1859.

———. *Transactions of the California State Agricultural Society During the Year 1859.* Sacramento: C. T. Botts, 1860.

———. *Transactions of the California State Agricultural Society During the Year 1860.* Sacramento: C. T. Botts, 1861.

———. *Transactions of the California State Agricultural Society for the Years 1864 and 1865.* Sacramento: O.M. Clayes, 1866.

———. *Transactions of the California State Agricultural Society During the Year 1881.* Sacramento: J. D. Young, 1881.

Canfield, Chauncey L. , ed. *The Diary of a Forty-Niner.* 1906. Reprint, Boston: Houghton Mifflin, 1920.

Carnahan, S.W. Letter of July 29, 1850. TS. Missouri Historical Society.

Cases Argued and Determined in the Circuit and District Courts of the United States, November 1883–February 1884. Vol. 18 of *The Federal Reporter.* Saint Paul: West Publishing, 1884.

Caughey, John Walton. *California.* 2d ed. Englewood Cliffs, N.J.: Prentice-Hall, 1953.

———. *Gold Is the Cornerstone.* Berkeley: University of California Press, 1948.

Caughey, John, and Laree Caughey, eds. *California Heritage: An Anthology of History and Literature.* Los Angeles: Ward Ritchie Press, 1962.

Chafetz, Henry. *Play the Devil: A History of Gambling in the United States from 1492 to 1955.* New York: Bonanza Books, 1960.

Chartkoff, Joseph L., and Kerry Kona Chartkoff. "The Pacific Period." In *New Directions in California History: A Book of Readings,* ed. James L. Rawls. New York: McGraw-Hill, 1988.

Chinard, Gilbert. *When the French Came to California.* San Francisco: California Historical Society, 1944.

Clappe, Louise Amelia Knapp Smith ["Dame Shirley"]. *The Shirley Letters from the California Mines: 1851–1852.* New York: Alfred A. Knopf, 1949.

Clarke, Dwight L. *Stephen Watts Kearny: Soldier of the West.* Norman: University of Oklahoma Press, 1961.

———. *William Tecumseh Sherman: Gold Rush Banker.* San Francisco: California Historical Society, 1969.

Cleland, Robert Glass. *The Cattle on a Thousand Hills: Southern California, 1850–1880.* San Marino, Calif.: Huntington Library, 1951.

———. "The Early Sentiment for the Annexation of California: An Account of the Growth of American Interest in California, 1835–1846." *Southwestern Historical Quarterly* 18, no. 2 (1914): 121–61.

———. *From Wilderness to Empire.* Edited by Glenn S. Dumke. New York: Alfred A. Knopf, 1959.

———. *A History of California.* New York: Macmillan, 1922.

Cleland, Robert Glass, and Osgood Hardy. *March of Industry.* Los Angeles: Powell Publishing, 1929.

Cochran, Thomas C. and William Miller. *The Age of Enterprise: A Social History of Industrial America.* New York: Macmillan, 1949.

Coit, Daniel Wadsworth. *Digging for Gold Without a Shovel: The Letters of Daniel Wadsworth Coit from Mexico City to San Francisco, 1840–1851.* Edited by George P. Hammond. San Francisco: Old West Publishing, 1967.

Colton, Walter. *Three Years in California.* 1850. Reprint, New York: Arno Press, 1976.

Comstock, David Allan. *Gold Diggers and Camp Followers: The Nevada County Chronicles, 1845–1851.* Grass Valley, Calif.: Comstock Bonanza Press, 1982.

Cook, Sherburne F. *Extent and Significance of Disease Among the Indians of Baja California, 1697–1773.* Berkeley: University of California Press, 1937.

———. *The Population of the California Indians, 1769–1970.* Berkeley: University of California Press, 1976.

———. *The Population of Central Mexico in the Sixteenth Century.* Berkeley: University of California Press, 1948.

———. *Population Trends Among the California Indians.* Vol. 17 in *Ibero-Americana,* ed. C. O. Sauer, A. L. Kroeber, and L.B. Simpson. Berkeley: University of California Press, 1940.

Corbett, Winifred. *Following Samuel Plimpton: A Search for My Great Uncle.* N.p., 1994.

Couts, Cave Johnson. *Hepah, California! The Journal of Cave Johnson Couts from Monterey, Nuevo Leon, Mexico, to Los Angeles, California, During the Years 1848–1849.* Edited by Henry F. Dobyns. Tucson: Arizona Pioneers' Historical Society, 1961.

Crandall, Roland D., ed. *Love and Nuggets.* Old Greenwich, Conn.: Stable Books, 1967.

Cronise, Titus F. *The Natural Wealth of California.* San Francisco: H. H. Bancroft, 1868.

Cross, Ira B. "Californians and Hard Money." *California Folklore Quarterly* 4, no. 3 (1945): 270–77.

Dana, Richard Henry. *Two Years Before the Mast.* 1840. Reprint, New York: New American Library, 1964.

Daniels, George G., ed. *The Spanish West.* New York: Time-Life Books, 1976.

Dart, John Paul. "A Mississippian in the Gold Fields: The Letters of John Paul Dart, 1849–1856." Edited by Howard Mitchum. *California Historical Society Quarterly* 35, no. 3 (1956): 205–31.

Decker, Peter. *The Diaries of Peter Decker: Overland to California in 1849 and Life in the Mines, 1850–1851.* Edited by Helen S. Giffen. Georgetown, Calif.: Talisman Press, 1966.

Decker, Peter R. *Fortunes and Failures.* Cambridge: Harvard University Press, 1978.

Delano, Alonzo. *Alonzo Delano's California Correspondence.* Edited by Irving McKee. Sacramento: Sacramento Book Collectors Club, 1952.

Delay, Peter J. *History of Yuba and Sutter Counties.* Los Angeles: Historic Record Company, 1924.

Delgado, James P. "Gold Rush Jail: The Prison Ship *Euphemia.*" *California History* (summer 1981): 134–141.

———. *To California by Sea: A Maritime History of the California Gold Rush.* Columbia: University of South Carolina Press, 1990.

Delmatier, Royce D., Clarence F. McIntosh, and Earl G. Waters, eds. *The Rumble of California Politics.* New York: John Wiley & Sons, 1970.

De Long, Charles E. " 'California's Bantam Cock': The Journal of Charles E. De Long, 1854–1863." Edited by Carl I. Wheat. *California Historical Society Quarterly* 9, no. 1 (1930): 50–80.

de Massey, Ernest. *A Frenchman in the Gold Rush: The Journal of Ernest de Massey, Argonaut of 1849.* Translated by Marguerite Eyer Wilbur. San Francisco: California Historical Society, 1927.

Derbec, Etienne. *A French Journalist in the California Gold Rush.* Edited by Abraham P. Nasatir. Georgetown, Calif.: Talisman Press, 1964.

De Quille, Dan. *The Big Bonanza.* 1876. Reprint, New York: Alfred A. Knopf, 1947.

DeVoto, Bernard. *The Year of Decision: 1846.* Boston: Houghton Mifflin, 1943.

Dewolf, David. "Diary of the Overland Trail . . . and Letters. . . ." *Transactions of the Illinois Historical Society* 32 (1925): 183–223.

Dillon, Richard. "The California Column." In *California and the Civil War, 1861–1865*. San Francisco: Book Club of California, 1992.

———. *Fool's Gold: The Decline and Fall of Captain John Sutter of California*. New York: Coward-McCann, 1967. Reprint, Santa Cruz, Calif.: Western Tanager Press, 1981.

Doble, John. *Journal and Letters from the Mines, 1851–1865*. Edited by Charles L. Camp. Denver: Old West Publishing, 1962.

Doster, Alexis III, Joe Goodwin, and Robert C. Post, eds. *The American Land*. New York: W. W. Norton, 1979.

Doten, Alfred. *The Journals of Alfred Doten, 1849–1903*. 3 vols. Edited by Walter van Tilburg Clark. Reno: University of Nevada Press, 1973.

Doyle, Simon. Letter of January 20, 1849. MS. Beinecke Rare Book and Manuscript Library. Yale University.

Drury, Wells. *An Editor on the Comstock Lode*. New York: Farrar & Rinehart, 1936.

Durham, Walter T. *Volunteer Forty-Niners: Tennesseans and the California Gold Rush*. Nashville: Vanderbilt University Press, 1997.

Egan, Ferol. *The El Dorado Trail: The Story of the Gold Rush Routes Across Mexico*. New York: McGraw-Hill, 1970.

Ellis, George M., ed. *Gold Rush Desert Trails to San Diego and Los Angeles in 1849*. Brand Book Series, no. 9. San Diego: San Diego Corral of the Westerners, 1995.

Ellison, William Henry. *A Self-Governing Dominion: California, 1849–1860*. Berkeley: University of California Press, 1950.

Engelhardt, Zephyrin. *The Missions and Missionaries of California*. Vol. 3. San Francisco: James H. Barry, 1913.

———. *San Francisco or Mission Dolores*. Chicago: Franciscan Herald Press, 1924.

Engstrand, Iris, H. W. "John Sutter: A Biographical Examination." In *John A. Sutter and a Wider West*, ed. Kenneth M. Owens, 76–92. Lincoln: University of Nebraska Press, 1994.

Evans, Taliesin. "Hydraulic Mining in California." *Century Magazine* 25, no. 3 (1883): 323–338.

Fairchild, Lucius. *The California Letters of Lucius Fairchild*. Edited with notes and introduction by Joseph Schafer. Madison: State Historical Society of Wisconsin, 1931.

Farwell, Willard B. "Cape Horn and Cooperative Mining in '49." *Century Magazine* 42 (August 1891): 579–94.

Fender, Stephen. *Plotting the Golden West: American Literature and the Rhetoric of the California Trail*. Cambridge: Cambridge University Press, 1981.

Ferris, Andrew Curtis. "How We Mined Gold in the Early Days of California." *The Pioneer and Historical Review* (November 1898). Photocopy of transcript made from records at the California Historical Society in San Francisco.

Fish, L. I. Diary, October 1849. MS. Huntington Library, San Marino, Calif.

Fitch, John R. Letters, 1849–52. MS. Huntington Library, San Marino, Calif.

Foley, Doris, and S. Griswold Morley. "The 1883 Flood on the Middle Yuba River." *California Historical Society Quarterly* 28, no. 3 (1949): 233–242.

Galloway, John Debo. "Early Engineering Works Contributary to the Comstock." *University of Nevada Bulletin* 41, no. 5 (1947): 1–102.

Gardiner, Howard C. *In Pursuit of the Golden Dream: Reminiscences of San Francisco and the Northern and Southern Mines, 1849–1857*. Stoughton, Mass.: Western Hemisphere, 1970.

Garner, William Robert. *Letters from California, 1846–1847*. Edited by Donald Munro Craig. Berkeley: University of California Press, 1970.

Garr, Daniel J. "A Rare and Desolate Land: Population and Race in Hispanic California." *Western Historical Quarterly* 6, no. 2 (1975): 133–48.

Garrison, Richard D. "Sutter County Opposition to Hydraulic Mining, 1874–1884. Master's thesis, Chico State College, 1967.

Gates, Paul W., ed. *California Ranchos and Farms, 1846–1862*. Madison: State Historical Society of Wisconsin, 1967.

———. "California's Embattled Settlers." *California Historical Society Quarterly* 41, no. 2 (1962): 99–130.

George, Henry. "What the Railroad Will Bring Us." *Overland Monthly* 1, no. 4 (1868): 297–306.

Gilbert, Grove Karl. *Hydraulic-Mining Debris in the Sierra Nevada*. United States Geological Survey, Professional Paper 105. Washington, D.C.: Government Printing Office, 1917.

Gill, William. *California Letters*. Edited by Eva T. Clark. New York, 1922.

Gilmore, N. Ray, and Gladys Gilmore, eds. *Readings in California History*. New York: Thomas Y. Crowell, 1966.

Goetzmann, William H. *Army Exploration in the American West: 1803–1863*. New Haven: Yale University Press, 1959.

Gold Mines and Mining in California. Volcano, Calif.: Traveler, Inc., 1885.

Greeley, Horace. *An Overland Journey: From New York to San Francisco in the Summer of 1859*. Edited by Charles T. Duncan. New York: Alfred A. Knopf, 1964.

Greever, William S. *The Bonanza West: The Story of the Western Mining Rushes, 1848–1900*. Norman: University of Oklahoma Press, 1963.

Griffith, Andrew J. Diary, 1850. MS. David L. Hill, Baltimore.

Grimshaw, William Robinson. *Grimshaw's Narrative*. Edited by J.R.K. Kantor. Sacramento: Sacramento Book Collectors Club, 1964.

Griswold, Wesley S. *A Work of Giants: Building of the First Transcontinental Railroad*. New York: McGraw-Hill, 1962.

Guest, Francis F. "The Franciscan World View." In *New Directions in California History: A Book of Readings*, ed. James L. Rawls. New York: McGraw-Hill, 1988.

Hague, Harlan, and David J. Langum. *Thomas O. Larkin: A Life of Patriotism and Profit in Old California*. Norman: University of Oklahoma Press, 1990.

Hall, Edwin G. Letter of November 25, 1849. TS. California State Library, Sacramento.

Hall, William Hamilton. *Report of the State Engineer to the Legislature of California*. Pt. 3. Sacramento: J. D. Young, 1880.

Hammond, George P. *The Weber Era in Stockton History*. Berkeley: Friends of the Bancroft Library, 1982.

Hanks, Henry G. *Second Report of the State Mineralogist, from December 1, 1880 to October 1, 1882*. Sacramento: Superintendent of State Printing, 1882.

Harlow, Neal. *California Conquered: War and Peace on the Pacific, 1846–1850*. Berkeley: University of California Press, 1982.

Hart, James D. *American Images of Spanish California*. Berkeley: Friends of the University of California, 1960.

———. *A Companion to California*. New York: Oxford University Press, 1978.

Hawgood, John A. "Manifest Destiny." In *British Essays in American History*, ed. H. C. Allen and C. P. Hall. N.p., n.d.

Herr, Pamela. *Jessie Benton Frémont*. New York: Franklin Watts, 1987.

Hittell, John S. *A History of the City of San Francisco and Incidentally of the State of California*. San Francisco: A. L. Bancroft, 1878.

———. *Mining in the Pacific States of North America*. San Francisco: H. H. Bancroft, 1861.

———. *The Resources of California*. San Francisco: A. Roman, 1863.

Hittell, Theodore H. *History of California*. Vol. 3. San Francisco: N. J. Stone, 1898.

Hodges, Orlando J. "Prospecting on the Pacific Coast, 1848–1864." Transcribed with an introduction by William Frank Zornow. *California Historical Society Quarterly* 33, no. 1 (1954): 49–58.

Holliday, J. S. *Introduction to Gold Rush Desert Trails to San Diego and Los Angeles in 1849*, ed. George M. Ellis. Brand Book Series, no. 9. San Diego: San Diego Corral of the Westerners, 1995.

———. *The World Rushed In: The California Gold Rush Experience*. New York: Simon & Schuster, 1981.

Horn, Daniel. "Across the Isthmus in 1850: The Journey of Daniel A. Horn." Edited by James P. Jones and William W. Rogers. *Hispanic American Historical Review* 41 (1961): 533–54.

Hover, Austin A. Letter of November 29, 1849. TS. California State Library, Sacramento.

Howe, Octavius Thorndike. *Argonauts of '49: History and Adventures of the Emigrant Companies from Massachusetts, 1849–1850*. Cambridge: Harvard University Press, 1923.

Hurtado, Albert L. "John A. Sutter and the Indian Business." In *John A. Sutter and a Wider West*, ed. Kenneth M. Owens. Lincoln: University of Nebraska Press, 1994.

Hutchinson, Claude B., ed. *California Agriculture*. Berkeley: University of California Press, 1946.

Hutchinson, W. H. "Man, Land, and Growth in California." Photocopy. A historical continuity prepared for the California Exposition, June 17, 1967.

Hutton, William Rich. *Glances at California, 1847–1853*. San Marino, Calif.: Huntington Library, 1942.

Ingalls, Eleazer. *Journal of a Trip to California by the Overland Route Across the Plains . . .* Waukegan, Ill., 1852.

Irelan, William Jr. *Ninth Annual Report of the State Mineralogist for the Year Ending December 1, 1889*. Sacramento: J. D. Young, 1890.

Jackson, Donald Dale. *Gold Dust*. New York: Alfred A. Knopf, 1980.

Jackson, W. Turrentine. *Report on the Malakoff Mine, the North Bloomfield District, and the Town of North Bloomfield*. Sacramento: Department of Parks and Recreation, 1967.

Jackson, W. Turrentine, Rand Herbert, and Stephen Wee. *History of the Tahoe National Forest, 1840–1940*. Davis, Calif.: Jackson Research Projects, 1982.

Jensen, James M. "Cattle Drives from the Ranchos to the Gold Fields of California." *Arizona and the West* 2, no. 4 (1960): 341–52.

Jewett, William S. "Some Letters of William S. Jewett, California Artist." Edited by Elliot Evans. *California Historical Society Quarterly* 23, no. 3 (1944): 227–246.

Johnson, John A. Diary, 1849. MS. Beinecke Rare Book and Manuscript Library, Yale University.

———. "Letters from the California Gold Mines." In *Pioneering on the Plains*. Kaukauna, Wis.: 1924.

Johnson, Kenneth M., ed. *San Francisco as It Is: Gleanings from the "Picayune."* Georgetown, Calif.: Talisman Press, 1964.

Johnson, Susan Lee. " 'The gold she gathered': Difference, Domination, and California's Southern Mines, 1848–1853." Ph.D. diss., Yale University, 1993.

Jones, Idwal. *Ark of Empire*. New York: Doubleday, 1951; New York: Ballantine Books, 1972.

Kelley, Robert L. *Battling the Inland Sea: American Political Culture, Public Policy, and the Sacramento Valley, 1850–1986*. Berkeley: University of California Press, 1989.

———. "Forgotten Giant: The Hydraulic Gold Mining Industry in California. *Pacific Historical Review* 23, no. 4 (1954): 343–356.

———. *Gold vs. Grain: The Hydraulic Mining Controversy in California's Sacramento Valley*. Glendale, Calif.: Arthur H. Clark, 1959.

———. "The Mining Debris Controversy in the Sacramento Valley." *Pacific Historical Review* 25 (1956): 331–346.

Kemble, John Haskell. *The Panama Route, 1848–1869*. University of California Publications in History, vol. 29. Berkeley: University of California Press, 1943.

Kennedy, Chester Barrett. "Newspapers of the California Northern Mines, 1850–1860: A Record of Life, Letters, and Culture." Ph.D. diss., Stanford University, 1949.

Kibbey, Mead B. *The Railroad Photographs of Alfred B. Hart, Artist*. Edited by Peter E. Palmquist. Sacramento: California State Library Foundation, 1996.

King, Edward A. "List of Passenger Ships Arriving From March to December, 1849," *Quarterly of the Society of California Pioneers* 1, no. 4 (1924): 35–45.

King, Thomas Starr. "A Visit to Nevada County in 1860." *Nevada County Historical Society Bulletin* 49, no. 1 (1995): 1–6.

Kirker, Harold. *California's Architectural Frontier: Style and Tradition in the Nineteenth Century*. San Marino, Calif.: Huntington Library, 1960. Reprint, Santa Barbara, Calif.: Peregrine Smith, 1973.

Klare, Normand E. *The First Voyage of the Central America*. Spokane, Wash.: Arthur H. Clarke, 1992.

Kowalewski, Michael, ed. *Gold Rush: A Literary Exploration*. Berkeley: Heyday Books, 1997.

Kraus, George. *High Road to Promontory*. Palo Alto.: American West Publishing, 1969.

Kurutz, Gary F. "Images of El Dorado: The California Pictorial Letter Sheet." In *Catalogue of the Letter Sheet Collection of Henry H. Clifford*, ed. Dorothy Sloan. Austin, Texas: Dorothy Sloan Rare Books, 1994.

Lagomarsino, Barbara. "Early Attempts to Save the Site of Sacramento by Raising Its Business District." Master's thesis, Sacramento State College, 1969.

Lamar, Howard R., ed. *The Reader's Encyclopedia of the American West*. New York: Thomas Y. Crowell, 1977.

Lanyon, Milton, and Laurence Bulmore. Cinnabar Hills: *The Quicksilver Days of New Almaden*. Los Gatos, Calif.: Village Printers, 1967.

Larkin, Thomas Oliver. *The Larkin Papers: Personal, Business, and Official Correspondence of Thomas Oliver Larkin, Merchant and United States Consul in California*. Edited by George P. Hammond. 10 vols. Berkeley: University of California Press, 1951–64.

Lavender, David. *California: Land of New Beginnings*. New York: Harper & Row, 1972.

———. *The Great Persuader.* New York: Doubleday, 1970.

———. *Nothing Seemed Impossible: William C. Ralston and Early San Francisco.* Palo Alto, Calif.: American West Publishing, 1975.

Leighly, John. *California as an Island.* San Francisco: Book Club of California, 1972.

Lewis, Oscar. *The Big Four: The Story of Huntington, Stanford, Hopkins, and Crocker, and of the Building of the Central Pacific.* New York: Alfred A. Knopf, 1938.

———. *San Francisco: Mission to Metropolis.* Berkeley: Howell-North, 1966.

———. *Sea Routes to the Gold Fields: The Migration by Water to California in 1849–1852.* New York: Alfred A. Knopf, 1949.

———. *Sutter's Fort: Gateway to the Gold Fields.* Englewood Cliffs, N.J.: Prentice-Hall, 1966.

Limerick, Patricia Nelson. *The Legacy of Conquest: The Unbroken Past of the American West.* New York: W. W. Norton, 1987.

Lord, Eliot. *Comstock Mining and Miners.* 1883. Reprint, Berkeley: Howell-North, 1959.

Lord, Isaac. Diary and Letters. MS. Huntington Library, San Marino, Calif.

Lord, Israel Shipman Pelton. *"At the Extremity of Civilization": An Illinois Physician's Journey to California in 1849.* Edited by Necia Dixon Liles. Jefferson, N.C.: McFarland, 1985.

Lorton, William B. Diary, 1849–50. MS. Bancroft Library, University of California, Berkeley.

Lotchin, Roger W. *San Francisco, 1846–1856: From Hamlet to City.* New York: Oxford University Press, 1974; Lincoln: University of Nebraska Press, 1979.

Lyman, George D. *Ralston's Ring.* New York: Charles Scribner's Sons, 1937.

———. *The Saga of the Comstock Lode: Boom Days in Virginia City.* New York: Charles Scribner's Sons, 1934.

MacMullen, Jerry. *Paddle-wheel Days in California.* Stanford University: Stanford University Press, 1944.

Magee, David, ed. *Eliza Farnham's Bride-Ship: An 1849 Circular Inviting Young Women of the East to Go to California.* No. 3 in *Attention Pioneers!* series. San Francisco: Book Club of California, 1952.

Main, Charles. Diary, 1849–51. MS. Bancroft Library, University of California, Berkeley.

Marks, Bernard. Letter of January 1855. Publication of the American Jewish Historical Society 44, no. 1 (1954). Reprint; Philadelphia: Maurice Jacobs, n.d.

Marryat, Frank. *Mountains and Molehills.* 1855. Reprint, New York: J. B. Lippincott, 1962.

May, Philip Ross. *Origins of Hydraulic Mining in California.* Oakland, Calif.: Holmes Book Co., 1970.

McCullough, David. *The Path Between the Seas: The Creation of the Panama Canal, 1870–1914.* New York: Simon & Schuster, 1977.

McGowan, Joseph Aloysius. "Freighting to the Mines in California, 1849–1859." Ph.D. diss., University of California, Berkeley, 1949.

———. *History of the Sacramento Valley.* Vol. 1. New York: Lewis Historical Publishing, 1961.

McKinstry, Byron N. *The California Gold Rush Overland Diary. . . .* Edited by Bruce L. McKinstry. Glendale, Calif., 1975.

M'Collum, William. *California as I Saw It: Pencillings by the Way of Its Gold and Gold Diggers! And Incidents of Travel by Land and Water.* Edited by Dale L. Morgan. Los Gatos, Calif.: Talisman Press, 1960.

McWilliams, Carey. *California: The Great Exception.* New York: A. A. Wyn, 1949.

———. *Southern California: An Island on the Land.* Salt Lake City: Gibbs-Smith, 1946. Reprint, Salt Lake City: Peregrine Smith, 1988.

Miller, Robert Ryal. *Captain Richardson.* Berkeley: La Loma Press, 1995.

Milner, John T. "John T. Milner's Trip to California, Letters to the Family." *Alabama Historical Quarterly* 20, no. 3 (1958): 523–56.

Moerenhout, Jacques Antoine. *The Inside Story of the Gold Rush.* Translated and edited by Abraham P. Nasatir. San Francisco: California Historical Society, 1935.

Monaghan, Jay. *Australians and the Gold Rush.* Berkeley: University of California Press, 1966.

Morgan, Dale L. Introduction to William M'Collum, *California as I Saw It: Pencillings by the Way of Its Gold and Diggers! And Incidents of Travel by Land and Water,* ed. Dale L. Morgan. Los Gatos, Calif.: Talisman Press, 1960.

———, ed. *Overland in 1846: Diaries and Letters of the California-Oregon Trail.* 2 vols. Georgetown, Calif.: Talisman Press, 1963.

Morgan, Theodore. *Hawaii: A Century of Economic Change, 1778–1876.* Cambridge: Harvard University Press, 1948.

Morrell, W. P. *The Gold Rushes.* London: Adam and Charles Black, 1940. New York: Macmillan, 1941.

Morse, John F. *The Sacramento Directory for the Year 1853–54 . . . Together with a History of Sacramento.* Sacramento: Samuel Colville, 1853. Reprint, Sacramento: California State Library Foundation, 1997.

Mulford, Prentice. *California Sketches.* Edited by Franklin Walker. San Francisco: Book Club of California, 1935.

———. *Prentice Mulford's Story.* Oakland, Calif.: Biobooks, 1953.

Nasatir, A. P., trans. "Alexander Dumas fils and the Lottery of the Golden Ingots." *California Historical Society Quarterly* 33, no. 2 (1954): 125–42.

Norris, Frank. *The Octopus, A Story of California.* 1901. New York: P. F. Collier & Son, n.d.

Ogden, Adele. *The California Sea Otter Trade, 1784–1848.* Berkeley: University of California Press, 1941.

———. "Alfred Robinson: New England Merchant in Mexican California." *California Historical Society Quarterly* 23, no. 3 (1944): 193–218.

Olmsted, R. R., ed. *Scenes of Wonder and Curiosity from Hutchings' California Magazine, 1856–1861.* Berkeley: Howell-North Press, 1962.

Owens, Kenneth M., ed. *John A. Sutter and a Wider West.* Lincoln: University of Nebraska Press, 1994.

Owens, Ken, et al. "Research Document." 4 vols. Sacramento, Calif.: Sacramento History Center.

Pagenhart, Thomas Harsha. "Water Use in the Yuba and Bear River Basins, California." Ph.D. diss., University of California, Berkeley, 1969.

Parke, Charles Ross. *Dreams to Dust: A Diary of the California Gold Rush, 1849–1850.* Edited by James E. Davis. Lincoln: University of Nebraska Press, 1989.

Patterson, E.H.N. Diary, October 1850–January 1851. Published in *Oquawka (Ill.) Spectator,* March–July 1851.

Paul, Rodman W. "The Beginnings of Agriculture in Califiornia: Innovation vs. Continuity." *California Historical Society Quarterly* 52, no. 1 (1973): 16–27.

———. *California Gold: The Beginning of Mining in the Far West.* Cambridge: Harvard University Press, 1947.

———, ed. *The California Gold Discovery: Sources, Documents, Accounts, and Memoirs Relating to the Discovery of Gold at Sutter's Mill.* Georgetown, Calif.: Talisman Press, 1966.

———. "The Great California Grain War: The Grangers Challenge the Wheat King." *Pacific Historical Review* 27, no. 4 (1958): 331–39.

———. *Mining Frontiers of the Far West, 1848–1880.* New York: Holt, Rinehart & Winston, 1963.

———. "The Wheat Trade Between California and the United Kingdom." *Mississippi Valley Historical Review* 45, no. 3 (1958): 391–412.

Perkins, Elisha. *Gold Rush Diary: Being the Journal . . . on the Overland Trail.* Edited by Thomas D. Clark. Lexington: University of Kentucky Press, 1967.

Perkins, William. *Three Years in California: William Perkins' Journal of Life at Sonora, 1849–1852.* With an introduction and annotation by Dale L. Morgan and James R. Scobie. Berkeley: University of California Press, 1964.

Perlot, Jean-Nicolas. *Gold Seeker: Adventures of a Belgian Argonaut During the Gold Rush Years.* Translated by Helen Harding Bretnor; edited by Howard R. Lamar. Yale Western American Series, vol. 31. New Haven: Yale University Press, 1985.

Peterson, Richard H. *Manifest Destiny in the Mines: A Cultural Interpretation of Anti-Mexican Nativism in California, 1848–1853.* Saratoga, Calif.: R & E Research Associates, 1975.

Phillips, Cyrus Olin. "To the Fraser River! The Diary and Letters of Cyrus Olin Phillips, 1858–1859." Edited by F. W. Howay. *California Historical Society Quarterly* 11, no. 2 (1932): 150–156.

Pisani, Donald J. *From the Family Farm to Agribusiness: The Irrigation Crusade in California and the West, 1850–1931.* Berkeley: University of California Press, 1984.

Pitt, Leonard. *The Decline of the Californios: A Social History of the Spanish-Speaking Californians, 1846–1890.* Berkeley: University of California Press, 1970.

Pitti, Edith. "Earthmaker's People." Photocopy. Sacramento, Calif.: Sacramento Museum, n.d.

———. "Gold! And All That, 1848–1962." Photocopy. Sacramento, Calif.: Sacramento Museum.

Pitti, Joe, et al. "Research Document." Pt. 1. Photocopy. Sacramento, Calif.: Sacramento History Center, n.d.

Plummer, Charles. Diary, 1850–51. MS. Huntington Library, San Marino, Calif.

———. Letter of March 14, 1851. MS. Huntington Library. San Marino, Calif.

Polk, Dora Beale. *The Island of California: A History of the Myth.* Lincoln: University of Nebraska Press, 1991.

Polk, James K. Message to Congress, December 5, 1848. H. Ex. Doc. 1, serial 537, 30th Cong., 2d Sess.

Pomeroy, Earl. "California, 1846–1860: Politics of a Representative Frontier State." *California Historical Society Quarterly* 32, no. 4 (1953): 291–301.

———. *The Pacific Slope: A History of California, Oregon, Washington, Idaho, Utah, and Nevada.* New York: Alfred A. Knopf, 1965.

Porter, Rufus. *Aerial Navigation: The Practicability of Traveling Pleasantly and Safely from New York to California in Three Days.* 1849. Reprint, San Francisco: Lawton R. Kennedy, 1935.

Ramey, Earl. "The Beginnings of Marysville." *California Historical Society Quarterly* 14, no. 3 (1935): 195–229 and no. 4 (1935): 375–407.

Rawls, James L. *Indians of California: The Changing Image.* Norman. University of Oklahoma Press, 1984.

Rawls, James L., ed. *New Directions in California History: A Book of Readings.* New York: McGraw-Hill, 1988.

Raymond, Rossiter. *Statistics of Mines and Mining in the States and Territories West of the Rocky Mountains for the Year 1870.* Washington, D.C.: Government Printing Office, 1872.

———. *Statistics of Mines and Mining in the States and Territories West of the Rocky Mountains, Being the Fifth Annual Report.* Washington, D.C.: Government Printing Office, 1873.

———. *Statistics of Mines and Mining in the States and Territories West of the Rocky Mountains, Being the Sixth Annual Report.* Washington, D.C.: Government Printing Office, 1874.

———. *Statistics of Mines and Mining in the States and Territories West of the Rocky Mountains, Being the Eighth Annual Report.* Washington, D.C.: Government Printing Office, 1877.

Reid, John Phillip. *Law for the Elephant: Property and Social Behavior on the Overland Trail.* San Marino, Calif.: Huntington Library, 1980.

Reports of Cases Determined by the Supreme Court of the State of California at the Sessions of 1881. Vol. 58. San Francisco: Bancroft Whitney, 1887.

Richman, Irving Berdine. *California Under Spain and Mexico.* Boston: Houghton Mifflin, 1911.

Robinson, Alfred. *Life in California: During a Residence of Several Years in That Territory.* 1846. Reprint, New York: Da Capo Press, 1969.

Robinson, W. W. *Land in California: The Story of Mission Lands, Ranchos, Squatters, Mining Claims, Railroad Grants, Land Script, Homesteads.* Berkeley: University of California Press, 1948.

Rohe, Randall. "Man and the Land: Mining's Impact in the Far West." *Arizona and the West* 28, no. 4 (1986): 299–338.

Rohrbough, Malcolm J. *Days of Gold: The California Gold Rush and the American Nation.* Berkeley: University of California Press, 1997.

Rojas, Lauro de, ed. "California in 1844 as Hartnell Saw It." *California Historical Society Quarterly* 17, no. 1 (1938): 21–27.

Rolle, Andrew J. *California: A History.* New York: Thomas Y. Crowell, 1963.

Roske, Ralph J. "The World Impact of the California Gold Rush, 1849–1857." *Arizona and the West* 5, no. 3 (1963): 187–232.

Royce, Josiah. *California: From the Conquest in 1846 to the Second Vigilance Committee in San Francisco: A Study in American Character.* 1886. Reprint, New York: Alfred A. Knopf, 1948.

Salley, H. E. *History of California Post Offices.* 2d ed. Edited by Edward L. Patera. Lake Grove, Ore.: Depot, 1991.

San Joaquin Diving Bell Mining Company stock certificate. Henry Clifford Collection. Huntington Library, San Marino, Calif.

Scamehorn, Howard L., ed. *The Buckeye Rovers*. Athens: Ohio University Press, 1965.

Schafer, Joseph, ed. *California Letters*. Madison, Wis., 1931.

Scherer, James A. B. *The Lion of the Vigilantes: William T. Coleman and the Life of Old San Francisco*. New York: Bobbs-Merrill, 1939.

Scott, Reva. *Samuel Brannan and the Golden Fleece*. New York: Macmillan, 1944.

Sellers, Charles. *The Market Revolution in Jacksonian America, 1815–1846*. New York: Oxford University Press, 1991.

Severson, Thor. *Sacramento: An Illustrated History, 1839–1874*. San Francisco: California Historical Society, 1973.

Sherman, William Tecumseh. *The California Gold Fields in 1848: Two Letters from Lt. W. T. Sherman, U.S.A.* Privately published for Frederick W. Beinecke, 1964.

———. *Memoirs*. New York: Literary Classics of the United States, 1990.

Shinn, Charles Howard. *Mining Camps: A Study in American Frontier Government*. 1885. Reprint, New York: Alfred A. Knopf, 1948.

Simpson, George. "Letters of Sir George Simpson, 1841–1843." Edited by Joseph Schafer. *American Historical Review* 14, no. 1 (1908): 70–94.

Sinnot, James J. *History of Sierra County*. 3d ed. Vol. 1. Nevada City, Calif.: Mountain House Books, 1991.

Sloan, Dorothy, ed. *Catalogue of the Letter Sheet Collection of Henry H. Clifford*. Austin, Texas: Dorothy Sloan Rare Books, 1994.

Soares, Celestino. *California and the Portuguese: How the Portuguese Helped to Build Up California*. Lisbon: S P N Books, 1939.

Soulé, Frank, John H. Gihon, and James Nisbet. *The Annals of San Francisco*. New York: D. Appleton, 1855.

Starr, Kevin. *Americans and the California Dream, 1850–1915*. New York: Oxford University Press, 1973.

———. *Inventing the Dream: California Through the Progressive Era*. New York: Oxford University Press, 1985.

———. "Sam Brannan, A Flawed Founder." TS. Author's photocopy.

Stevens, Moreland L. *Charles Christian Nahl: Artist of the Gold Rush, 1818–1878*. Sacramento: E. B. Crocker Art Gallery, 1976.

Stillman, Jacob D. B. *The Gold Rush Letters . . .* Edited by Kenneth Johnson. Palo Alto, Calif., 1967.

Stuart, Joseph A. *My Roving Life*. Vol. 1. Auburn, Calif., 1895.

Survey of Cultural Resources at Malakoff Diggins State Historical Park. Sacramento: California Department of Parks and Recreation, 1979.

Sutter, John A. *The Diary of Johann August Sutter*. San Francisco: Grabhorn Press, 1932.

———. *New Helvetia Diary: A Record of Events Kept by John A. Sutter and His Clerks at New Helvetia, California, from September 9, 1845, to May 25, 1848*. San Francisco: Grabhorn Press, 1939.

Swain, William. *Diary and Letters*. MS. Beinecke Rare Book and Manuscript Library, Yale University.

Sylva, Seville. "Foreigners in the California Gold Rush." Master's thesis, University of Southern California, 1932.

Taylor, Bayard. *Eldorado or Adventures in the Path of Empire, Comprising a Voyage to California, via Panama; Life in San Francisco and Monterey; Pictures of the Gold Region; and Experiences of Mexican Travel*. 1850. Reprint, New York: Alfred A. Knopf, 1949.

Thompson, John. *Flood Chronologies and Aftermath Affecting the Lower Sacramento River*. Urbana: Department of Geography, University of Illinois, 1996.

Thoreau, Henry David. "Life Without Principle." *Atlantic Monthly* 12 (1863): 484–495.

Turner, Frederick. *Rediscovering America: John Muir in His Time and Ours*. San Francisco: Sierra Club Books, 1987.

Twain, Mark. *Roughing It*. Hartford, Conn.: American Publishing, 1872.

Umbeck, John. "The California Gold Rush: A Study of Emerging Property Rights." *Explorations in Economic History* 14, no. 3 (1977): 197–226.

Underhill, Reuben L. *From Cowhides to Golden Fleece*. Stanford: Stanford University Press, 1939.

Unruh, John D. *The Plains Across: The Overland Emigrants and the Trans-Mississippi West, 1840–60*. Urbana: University of Illinois Press, 1979.

Vischer Eduard. "A Trip to the Mining Regions in the Spring of 1859." *California Historical Society Quarterly* 11, nos. 3–4 (1932): 224–46, 321–38.

Walker, Franklin D. *San Francisco's Literary Frontier*. New York: Alfred A. Knopf, 1939.

Walters, Shipley. *West Sacramento: The Roots of a New City*. Woodland, Calif.: Yolo County Historical Society, 1987.

Watkins, T. H. *Gold and Silver in the West*. Palo Alto, Calif.: American West Publishing, 1971.

———. *California: An Illustrated History*. New York: American Legacy Press, 1983.

———. "Outline of Contents for Docent Training Program, California History." TS, n.d.

Watkins, T. H., and R. R. Olmsted. *Mirror of the Dream: An Illustrated History of San Francisco*. San Francisco: Scrimshaw Press, 1976.

Watson, Douglas S. "The Great Express Extra of the *California Star* of April 1, 1848." *California Historical Society Quarterly* 11, no. 2 (1932): 129–37.

Weber, David J. "The Collapse of the Missions." In *New Directions in California History: A Book of Readings,* ed. James L. Rawls. New York: McGraw-Hill, 1988.

Wells, Harry Lauren. *History of Nevada County*. 1880. Reprint, Berkeley: Howell-North, 1970.

Wilkes, Charles. *Narrative of the United States Exploring Expedition During the Years 1838, 1839, 1840, 1841, 1842*. Vol. 5. Philadelphia: C. Sherman, 1844.

Williamson, R. S. *Report of Exploration in California for Railroad Routes. . .* Vol. 5. Washington, D.C., 1853.

Wilson, Eugene B. *Hydraulic and Placer Mining*. New York: John Wiley & Sons, 1898.

Wilson, Norman, Charles Blanchard, and Susan Lindstrom. *Spanish Hill, Placerville's Mountain of Gold*. N.p., 1994.

Wilson, William. Letters. MS. Beinecke Rare Book and Manuscript Library, Yale University.

Wiltsee, Ernest A. *The Pioneer Miner and the Pack Mule Express*. San Francisco, 1931.

Winchester, Jonas. Letters. MS. California State Library, Sacramento.

Winther, Oscar. *Express and Stagecoach Days in California*. Stanford: Stanford University Press, 1936.

Woods, Daniel B. *Sixteen Months at the Gold Diggings*. New York: Harper & Bros., 1851.

Wortley, Emmeline Stuart. *Travels in the United States, 1849–1850*. Vol. 2. London, 1851.

Wright, Doris. "The Making of Cosmopolitan California: An Analysis of Immigration, 1848–1870." *California Historical Society Quarterly* 19, no. 4 (1940): 323–42.

————. "The Making of Cosmopolitan California: An Analysis of Immigration, 1848–1870. Pt. 2: Immigration from European Countries." *California Historical Society Quarterly* 20, no. 1 (1941): 65–79.

Wyman, Mark. *Hard-Rock Epic: Western Miners and the Industrial Revolution, 1860–1910.* Berkeley: University of California Press, 1979.

Wyman, Walker D., ed. *California Emigrant Letters.* New York: Bookman Associates, 1952.

Young, Otis E., Jr. *Western Mining: An Informal Account of the Precious-Metals Prospecting, Placering, Lode Mining, and Milling on the American Frontier from Spanish Times to 1893.* With the technical assistance of Robert Lenon. Norman: University of Oklahoma Press, 1970.

Zinn, Howard. *A People's History of the United States, 1492– Present.* Rev. and updated ed. New York: Harper Perennial, 1995.

The following newspapers were used as primary sources:

Alta California (San Francisco)
Buffalo Morning Express
Columbia (Mo.) Statesman
Detroit Daily Advertiser
Ithaca (N.Y.) Journal
Kalamazoo (Mich.) Gazette
Marysville (Calif.) Daily Appeal
Michigan Expositor (Adrian)
Mining and Scientific Press (San Francisco)
Nevada City (Calif.) Daily Transcript
New York Herald
Pacific Rural Press (San Francisco)
Placer Times (Sacramento)
Oquawka (Ill.) Spectator
Oregon Spectator (Oregon City)
Polynesian (Honolulu)
Sacramento Daily Union
Sacramento Daily Record-Union
Sacramento Transcript
San Francisco Daily Alta California
San Francisco Daily Evening Bulletin
Times (London)

ILLUSTRATION ACKNOWLEDGMENTS

The process of gathering images to illustrate historical text is a rewarding one that requires the expertise of many individuals. Image research for this publication was conducted throughout California and on the East Coast to locate never before or rarely published pictures.

Many people at over fifty institutions assisted in gathering the illustrations. They are too numerous to mention individually, but without them this publication would not be as richly illustrated. They all deserve our gratitude.

Because of their dedication to the project and perseverance in finding the proverbial needle in a haystack, the following individuals merit special mention: Susan Snyder, Bancroft Library; Emily Wolff, California Historical Society; Gary Kurutz and Ellen Harding, California History Room, California State Library; Peter Blodgett and Jennifer Martinez, Huntington Library; Susan Haas and Bill McMorris, Society of California Pioneers; and Marcia Eymann, Drew Johnson, Diane Curry, Sandy Wong, and Marianne Germann, Oakland Museum of California. Finally many thanks to Jim Henley, Manager, Sacramento Archives and Museum Collection Center. You answered every question. I could not have done it without you.

Cherie Newell
Illustration Researcher

ABBREVIATIONS FOR INSTITUTIONS AND COLLECTORS:

AC	The Anschutz Collection, Denver
AG	Archivo General de Indias, Seville, Spain
AMON	Amon Carter Museum, Fort Worth, Texas
AMWH	Autry Museum of Western Heritage, Los Angeles
BL	The Bancroft Library, University of California, Berkeley
BRBL	Yale Collection of Western Americana, Beinecke Rare Book and Manuscript Library
CHM	Colton Hall Museum, Monterey, CA
CHS	California Historical Society, San Francisco
CM	Carmel Mission, Carmel, CA
CSA	California State Archives, Sacramento
CSL	California State Library, California History Room, Sacramento
CSP	California State Parks, State Museum Resource Center, Sacramento
CSRR	California State Railroad Museum, Sacramento
DFL	Doris Foley Historical Research Library, Nevada City, CA
DV	Mr. Daniel G. Volkman, Jr. Collection
FAM	Fine Arts Museums of San Francisco
FDR	Franklin D. Roosevelt Library, Hyde Park, NY
FG	Fraenkel Gallery, San Francisco
GDM	Gold Discovery Museum, Marshall Gold Discovery State Park, Coloma, CA
GP	Gilman Paper Company Collection, New York
HAG	Hirschl and Adler Galleries, New York
HL	The Huntington Library, San Marino, CA
HPC	Hallmark Photographic Collection, Hallmark Cards, Inc., Kansas City, MO
HSYC	Historical Society of York County Pennsylvania
JL	James Lenhoff Collection
JM	John McWilliams Collection
JS	Joseph T. Silva Collection
MCNY	Museum of the City of New York
MI	Matthew R. Isenburg Collection
MK	Mead Kibbey Collection
MM	The Mariners' Museum, Newport News, VA
MN	Museo Naval, Madrid, Spain
NL	The Newberry Library, Chicago
NMAA	National Museum of American Art, Smithsonian Institution
NMAH	National Museum of American History, Smithsonian Institution
NYPL	The New York Public Library
OMCA	Oakland Museum of California, History Department
OPL	Oakland Public Library
OSU	Ohio State University Cartoon Research Library
PP	Peter E. Palmquist Collection
SA	Stephen Raul Anaya Collection
SAMCC	Sacramento Archives and Museum Collection Center

SC	Seaver Center for Western History and Research, Los Angeles County Museum of Natural History
SCP	The Society of California Pioneers
SFM	San Francisco Maritime National Historic Park
SL	Searls Library, Nevada City, CA
SMC	San Mateo County Historical Association
SPH	Security Pacific Historical Photograph Collection, Los Angeles Public Library
SRM	Scientific Research Museum of the Academy of Arts, USSR
SUL	Department of Special Collections, Stanford University Libraries
SWM	The Southwest Museum, Los Angeles
UCD	Department of Special Collections, University of California Library, Davis, CA
UPM	Union Pacific Museum Collection, Omaha, NE
WBL	W. Bruce Lundberg Collection
WFB	Wells Fargo Bank Historical Services, San Francisco
YCL	Yuba County Library, Marysville, CA

ABBREVIATIONS FOR REPRODUCTION PHOTOGRAPHERS:

ap	Action Photo, Concord, CA
cb	Catherine Buchanan, Oakland Museum of California
cc	Cali Color, Sacramento
cck	Chip Clark, National Museum of American History
cp	Custom Process, Berkeley
dhj	Drew Heath Johnson, Oakland Museum of California
dj&rb	Dan Johnston and Robert Bain, The Bancroft Library
dl	Deborah Lohrke, Oakland Museum of California
fc	Ferrari Color, Sacramento
gg	General Graphics, San Francisco
hc	Hackercolor, Sacramento
hp	Helga Photo Studio, Upper Montclair, NJ
jh	John Hartz, Camera Corner, Oakland
jm	James O. Milmoe, The Anschutz Collection
kc	Kaufman's Cameras and Custom Photo Lab, San Bruno, CA
kk	Kathryn Kowalewski, California Historical Society
mi	Matthew R. Isenburg
mk	Mead Kibbey, Sacramento
mlf	M. Lee Fatherree, Emeryville, CA
nl	The New Lab, San Francisco
pp	Peter E. Palmquist, Arcata, CA
pps	Palmer's Photography, Sacramento
pt	Patrick Tregenza, Monterey, CA
sr	Stephen Rahn, Oakland Museum of California
sw	Sam Woo, Creative Communication Services, University of California, Davis
th	Thomas Hegre, Sacramento Archives and Museum Collection Center
tm	Tony Molatore, Oakland

Illustrations are listed in the order they appear on each page, from top left to lower right. Each citation includes: title or description—institution/accession number, if available/artist, if known/date/reproduction photographer, if known.

CHAPTER 1

1.
The Mission of San Carlos, Monterey — AMWH/Richard Beechey/c.1821.

2.
astrolabe — OMCA/H72.63.1/18-19th century/sr.
Spanish galleon, detail — HL/n.d.
western hemisphere: California as an island — BL/#21696C/Carolus Allard/1700/dl.

5.
Juan Rodriguez Cabrillo — SPH/n.d.

7.
Balthazar, Resident of California — SRM/Mikhail T. Tikhanov/1818.
Savages of San Francisco — BL/fG420K84C6/Louis Choris/c.1816/dl.
cooking basket, Maidu tribe — OMCA/late 19th century/cb.
Indian rancheria — public domain/1852/cb.

14.
cavalryman — AG/MP Uniformes, 81/17th century.
leather shield — CM/c.1835/pt.

97.
passenger ticket from Harnden & Company — SAMCC, Mrs. John
  Matthew Collection/82.64.80/1849/dl.

99.
"Gordon's California Association" broadside — SAMCC, The Eleanor
  McClatchy Collection/82.04(MC8:6)/c.1849/dl.
The California Company — HSYC/Lewis Miller 1796-1882/Lewis
  Miller/c.1849.

100.
Chagres — SMC/Book 1528/William H. Dougal/December 1850/kc.
Crossing the Isthmus — BL/C-F53v.1/Isaac Wallace Baker/1849/jh.
Incident on the Chagres River — BL/1963:002.1361/Charles
  Nahl/1867/nl.

106.
Overland Miner Laden with Weapons — JM/c.1850.
bowie knife — OMCA/c.1849/sr.
rifle — OMCA/c.1848/cb.
Woman with Child — OMCA/H74.427.3a/c.1850/dhj.

108.
Ferriage of the Platte... — HL/hm8044#50/J. Goldsborough Bruff/July
  20, 1849.
Wagons on the Plains... — HL/hm8044#18/J. Goldsborough Bruff/1849.

110.
Camp Cooking Equipment — HL/hm8044#19/J. Goldsborough
  Bruff/c.1849.
iron pot — OMCA/H26.481/c.1849/cb.
Wagon Train at Independence Rock — HL/hm8044#60/J. Goldsborough
  Bruff/1849.

CHAPTER 4

112.-113.
Hawkins Bar — SWM/22.G.978C/John Woodhouse Audubon/1849.

114.
James Galway — CHS, Gift of Miss Rose Sullivan/FN-25775/c.1852/kk.
San Francisco in '49 — CHS, Ralph H. Cross Collection/FN-
  13113/c.1849/kk.
Portsmouth Square — BL/1899.001:9/Daniel Wadsworth Coit/c.1850/dl.

118.
Miner with Gold Pan and Nuggets — WBL/c.1850.
gold nuggets and poke bag — OMCA/n.d./cb.

119.
California Forty-Niner, detail — AMON/P1983.20/c.1850.

121.
Panning Out — HAG/APG8004.037/Adolph Schwartz/n.d./hp.

123.
Bayard Taylor — MI/n.d./mi.

125.
San Francisco from Rincon Point — NYPL, Print Collection, Miriam
  and Ira D. Wallach Division of Art, Prints and Photographs/Deale
  581/c.1850.
"100 laborers wanted" broadside — OMCA/Roach &
  Woodworth/c.1849/dk.
Prison brig *Euphemia & storeship* Apollo — SAMCC, Adrianna Saltonstall Collection/97.84.32/1849/th.

127.
Saint Francis Hotel... — CHS, Gift of Templeton Crocker/Harrison
  Eastman/1849/kk.
gambling tools — OMCA/c.1850/sr.
bill of fare — CHS, North Baker Research Library/FN-31365/December
  27, 1849/kk.
lettersheet depicting a monte game — CSL/John D. Borthwick/n.d./dl.

130.
Post Office in San Francisco — HL/print box #1011-21/H.F.
  Cox/c.1850.
Pacific Mail Steamship, Oregon — MM, Elwin M. Eldredge
  Collection/1848.
letter from home to William Swain — BRBL/WAMss96:Box 2/George
  Swain/ February 9, 1850.
envelope addressed to William Swain — BRBL/WAMss96:Box 1/Sabrina
  Swain/November 7, 1849.

132.
General Bennett Riley — BL/P-1/n.d./tm.

134.
great seal of California — CSA/n.d./pps.

135.
Sunday at Forbes Diggings... — CHS, C. Templeton Crocker Collection/
  FN-19210/A. Chappel/c.1848/mlf.

137.
Steamship Senator — MM, Elwin M. Eldredge Collection/
  1941.0879.000001/James and John Bard/c.1849.

143.
"Good news for miners" broadside — BL/xfZ209C25E13#38x/1849/dl.
Miners' Tent Store — MI/c.1852/cb.
Sacramento in '49 — CSL/E. Wittenbach/n.d./dl.

145.
Gold Miners with Sluice — HPC/c.1850.
Mining Scene with Flume — BL/1905.16242(85)/c.1853/dj&rb.

CHAPTER 5

148.-149.
Bidwell's Bar — HAG/Henry Rust Mighels/1853.

150.
Two Men Outside a Cabin, detail — MI/n.d./mi.
Group of Miners — CHS/FN-25814/c.1850/kk.
Miners in Rocky Stream Bed — SA/1850s.

157.
Miners at Taylorsville — HL/Phot DAG 55/c.1850.
Moving Boulders with Crane — BL/1905.16242(79)/c.1850/dj&rb.
Mechanized Mining View — BL/1905.16242(81)/1850s/dj&rb.
Mining the Bed of the American River — BL/1958:024:12-ffALB/
  Charles Leander Weed/c.1859/tm.

159.
New York Daily Times newspaper — MI/November 3, 1851/mi.

160.
Stamps of the first Quartz Crushing Mill Erected in California —
  SAMCC, The Ernest W. Myers Collection/89.41.856/Edward J.
  Muybridge/1851/th.

162.
Hotel de Paris advertisement — public domain/n.d./dl.
Hotel de Paris — SL/1853/jh.
Hangtown — SAMCC, The Edwin Beach Collection/85.152.280/
  1849/th.

168.
California Vaqueros — AC/James Walker/n.d./jm.
The Lugo Family — SC/#4670/n.d.

175.
Great Fire in San Francisco — BL/19xx.097.16-A/June 14, 1850/tm.
San Francisco Fire Brigade No. 2 — BL/1905.16242(105)/1850s/dhj.
San Francisco Fire — WFB, *Gleason's Pictorial Drawing Room
  Companion*/July 12, 1851.

176.
great seal of San Francisco — SAMCC, Adrianna Saltonstall Collection/
  97.84.32/c.1850/dl.

179.
Hanging of Casey and Cora — JS/G.R. Fardon/May 22, 1856/cp.
vigilante certificate — BL/1963.002.647C/1856/dl.
The Revolution of the People — BL/1963.002.115A/c.1856/tm.
First Trial and Execution in San Francisco... — BL/1963.002.38B/
  June 1851/tm.

180.
William T. Coleman — SCP/C010917/Taber/c.1852/gg.

183.
San Francisco in 1850 — BL/Oliver 71-72/William Shew/c.1851/dj&rb.
"California Steam Navigation Company" broadside — SAMCC, Mrs.
  Joel S. Gardner Collection/86.108.03/1856/dl.
steamer *New World* — SAMCC, The Setzer Foundation and Mead
  Kibbey Collection/84.199.01/c.1851/dl.
Senator deck passage ticket — SAMCC, California State Archives
  Collection/80.132.08/c.1853/dl.
Governor Dana — SCP/C001003/Norton Bush/1857/cb.

185.
Teams on the Summit, Dutch Flat... — SCP/LH 780/Lawrence &
  Houseworth/c.1860s/gg.
"California Stage Company" broadside — YCL/1858/dl.
Sierra Nevada House, Coloma — SCP/C035140/1850s/gg.
stagecoach with passengers — JS/Charles Savage/c. 1875/ap.
A Ferry on the Tuolumne River — CSL/n.d./dl.

191.
City of the Plain — SAMCC/82.x-01.04/George H. Baker/1857/fc.
Sacramento State Journal Extra — SAMCC, The Eleanor McClatchy Collection/82.04.63/1852/dl.
The Great Conflagration of Sacramento — SAMCC, The Eleanor McClatchy Collection/82.05.5645/1852/th.
Sacramento Flooded — SAMCC/82.05.5987/January 1850/fc.

196.
Warren and Company... — SAMCC, *The Sacramento Bee* Collection/70.210.01/1851/th.

199.
View of Forbestown — JS/n.d./pp.
Gold Mining Camp, Jamestown, CA — OSU, Floyd and Marion Rinhart Collection/c.1851.
Downieville, detail — CSL/1998-0018 Neg.#25,092/Mrs. M.N. Horton/1852/dl.

201.
Agricultural Society ribbon — SAMCC, The Eleanor McClatchy Collection/82.06.449/1855/fc.

204.
Miners in a Bucket — OPL, Magazine and Newspaper Room, *Harper's Monthly*/August 1857/dl.

205.
Uncle Bill and Others at Mining — OMCA, The S.H. Cowell Foundation/H75.177.3A/1850s/cb.
Flume on the Ophir Ditch... — CHS/x57-695-18/Joseph Lamson/1857/kk.
Coyote Diggings — CHS, C. Templeton Crocker Collection/FN-19213/William Pearson/c.1848/kk.

209.
Ground Sluicing, detail — OPL, Magazine and Newspaper Room, *Hutchings California Magazine*/September 1860/dl.

211.
Hydraulic Mining Scene — MI/B-23/n.d./mi.
The Diggins at Michigan Bluff — WFB/1854.
Near Nevada City — CSL/1852/dl.

CHAPTER 6
216.–217.
Hydraulic Mining, North Bloomfield, Nevada County — CSL/Carleton E. Watkins/c.1860s.

218.
Train on Newcastle Trestle — MK/Kibbey#P-13.22/Alfred A. Hart/1865/tm.
River Steamers at the Broadway Wharf, San Francisco — SCP/LH 293/Lawrence & Houseworth/1866/gg.
California Pan Mill — BL/1905.17175.71/Carleton E. Watkins/1860-70/tm.
Elevated Flume Crossing a Valley — SUL/RBC:917.94W335ff/Carleton E. Watkins/c.1880.

221.
Interior Ophir Hoisting Works, detail — CHS/FN-02552/Carleton E. Watkins/1870s/kk.

224.
Miners at the Ophir Mine in Virginia City — OMCA/H4282.1153/1875/tm.
Mining on the Comstock... — BL/1963.002.761-E/T.L. Dawes/1876/dj&rb.
Cars coming out of shaft, Comstock Mine... — BL/1957.027v.1:35/Timothy O'Sullivan/c.1867/jh.

227.
Oxen Team Logging on Plank Road — SAMCC, Louis L. Stein, Jr. Collection/74.04/1870s/dl.

230.
Theodore D. Judah — BL/P-2/n.d./jh.

233.
C.P. Huntington — CSRR/n.d.

235.
Charles Crocker — CSRR/n.d.

236.
Snow Plow (headed West) at Cisco — SCP/Co26819/Alfred A. Hart/1860s/gg.

237.
Huntington & Hopkins Hardware Store — SAMCC, The Eleanor McClatchy Collection/82.05.1692/n.d./th.
Summit Tunnel... — SCP/Co16964/Alfred A. Hart/1860s/gg.
Snow Gallery, Crested Pk... — SCP/Co16993/Alfred A. Hart/1860s/tm.
CPRR advertisment — UPM/X-6239/August 1869.
CPRR Locomotive on Trestle — SUL/PC16:#135/Lawrence & Houseworth/1860s.

241.
Stanford's San Francisco House: India Room — SUL/PC6: Muybridge/Edward Muybridge/1880.

242.
Maine Bar from the East — SCP/Co35610/E.P. Vollum, M.D., U.S. Army/1859/gg.
Sacramento Waterfront at Foot of 'K' Street... — MK/Kibbey#311.26/Alfred A. Hart/c.1867/mk.
Residence of Charles Crocker... — CHS, Luke Fay Collection/FN-22572/Carleton E. Watkins/n.d./kk.
View of San Francisco, Towards the Palace Hotel... — CHS/FN-19908/Carleton E. Watkins/1884-85/kk.

245.
Feeding the Teams..., detail — SCP/LH 621/Lawrence & Houseworth/1860s/gg.
Hydraulic Mining: The Pressure Box... — SCP/LH 793/Lawrence & Houseworth/1860s/gg.

250.
Three Men and a Monitor... — MK/Kibbey#182.04/A.J. Everett/1870-78/mk.
Cherokee Flat, Butte County — CSL/n.d./dl.
Hydraulic Mining: The Pipe and Tank — SCP/LH 803/Lawrence & Houseworth/1860s/gg.
Hydraulic Mining in the Michigan Bar District — CSL/1860s/dl.

257.
Hydraulic Mining: The Tail Sluices... — SCP/LH 807/Lawrence & Houseworth/1866/gg.
Pacific Mine Near Dutch Flat — MK/Kibbey#179/J. M. Jacobs/1875-80/mk.

259.
Hydraulic Mining: The Dump and Tailings — SCP/LH 806/Lawrence & Houseworth/1860s/gg.

261.
Mill Street, Grass Valley — MK/Kibbey#B234.16/Thomas Houseworth/c.1868/mk.
Marysville... — MK/Kibbey#237.1/Oliver Denny/c.1870/mk.
Dutch Flat... — SCP/LH 823/Lawrence & Houseworth/1860s/gg.

263.
The Daily Transcipt, Nevada City — DFL/November 18, 1879/dl.

CHAPTER 7
264.–265.
Harvest Time — FAM, Gift of Mrs. Harold R. McKinnon and Mrs. Harry L. Brown/1962.21/William Hahn/1875.
266.
English Dam — FG/Carleton E. Watkins/c.1871/dl.
Gold Run — BL/1983.166.8—Ster/James Monroe Jacobs/1870s/dl.
Flumes Running Into North San Juan — SL/c.1857.
Stacking Hay in the Diablo Valley — BL/1968.012.833/c.1890/dj&rb.

271.
Bowman Dam — BL/1905.17175.90/Carleton E. Watkins/n.d./tm.
Miocene Mining Company Flume — JL/c.1884/dl.
Malakoff Mining Operations — SAMCC/98.x01.04/n.d./th.

276.
Malakoff Diggins, North Bloomfield Gravel Mines — FG/Carleton E. Watkins/c.1871/dl.
Spring Valley Hydraulic Gold Mine at Cherokee — JL/c.1880/dl.

278.
Old Method Harvesting... — CHS, Ralph H. Cross Collection/FN-19019/n.d./kk.
John M. Benson's Outfit, San Joaquin County — CHS/FN-01025/B.P. Batchelder/n.d./kk.
Mayflower Steam Rig, detail — UCD, F. Hal Higgins Collection/Dr. Hogan/January 1868/sw.
Empire Iron and Brass Foundry, Marysville — MK/Kibbey#237.46/Amos Woods/c.1872/mk.

280.

George Ohleyer — YCL, *Marysville Daily News*/August 16, 1896/dl.

281.

Steamer Varuna *and Barge* Nevada... — CHS/FN-27156/c.1890/kk.

Potato Farmers — PP/n.d./pp.

Table of Fruit — PP/Hayward and Muzzall/n.d./pp.

Vineyard and residence of Mr. Mel, Vine Hill — PP/Carleton E. Watkins/
n.d./pp.

283.

William Hammond Hall — CSL/Neg.#21,215/n.d./tm.

285.

Log Dam — CHS/FN-29933/From #2900 U.S. Circuit Court District of
California, Edwards Woodruff vs. North Bloomfield Gravel Mining
Company, et. al./J. A. Todd/1882/kk.

Deposit from the Tail Flumes, Yuba River — MK/Kibbey#169.14/
Lawrence & Houseworth/1865/mk.

George Ohleyer Residence... — CSL/Neg.#21,216/n.d./tm.

287.

George Cadwalader — CSL/Neg.#1455/n.d./tm.

289.

Hydraulic Mining Scene — CHS/FN-29935/From #2900 U.S. Circuit
Court.../J. A. Todd/1882/kk.

Overrun Dam — CHS/FN-29931/From #2900 U.S. Circuit Court.../J. A.
Todd/1882/kk.

Clearing Up Under-Currents — OPL, Magazine and Newspaper Room,
Century Magazine/January 1883/dl.

292.

Dam Site — CHS/FN-29930/From #2900 U.S. Circuit Court.../J. A.
Todd/1882/kk.

South end of Yuba River Bridge, Marysville — CHS/FN-29938/From
#2900 U.S. Circuit Court.../J. A. Todd/1882/kk.

Lands (on right) formerly known as Briggs Orchard — CHS/FN29940/
From #2900 U.S. Circuit Court .../J. A. Todd/1883/kk.

293.

Marysville Daily Appeal newspaper — YCL/June 13, 1882/dl.

296.

Judge Lorenzo Sawyer — CHS/Monroe & Potter/c.1870/mlf.

299.

What Hydraulic Mining is Doing for the Country — SAMCC, The
Eleanor McClatchy Collection/82.04(MC8:14)/G.F. Keller/n.d./dl.

APPENDIX:

MONEY CONVERSION (TO 1998 DOLLARS)

To convert prior-year dollars to 1998 dollars, multiply by the conversion factor shown

Year	Conversion Factor	Year	Conversion Factor	Year	Conversion Factor
1848	18.49	1866	10.93	1884	17.81
1849	19.23	1867	11.45	1885	17.81
1850	19.23	1868	12.02	1886	17.81
1851	19.23	1869	12.02	1887	17.81
1852	19.23	1870	12.65	1888	17.81
1853	19.23	1871	13.36	1889	17.81
1854	17.81	1872	13.36	1890	17.81
1855	17.17	1873	13.36	1891	17.81
1856	17.81	1874	14.14	1892	17.81
1857	17.17	1875	14.57	1893	17.81
1858	18.49	1876	15.03	1894	18.49
1859	17.81	1877	15.03	1895	19.23
1860	17.81	1878	16.58	1896	19.23
1861	17.81	1879	17.17	1897	19.23
1862	16.03	1880	16.58	1898	19.23
1863	12.99	1881	16.58	1899	19.23
1864	10.23	1882	16.58		
1865	10.45	1883	17.17		

NOTE: The Bureau of Labor Statistics did not begin tabulating the Consumer Price Index (CPI) until 1913, but the Bureau of the Census has used various historical sources to estimate a comparable index for prior years (Bureau of the Census, *Historical Statistics of the United States, Colonial Times to 1970*, Part 1 [Washington, D.C., 1975], 210–11). To obtain the conversion factors used in this appendix, this historical index (on a scale with 1967=100) has been divided into 480.8 (the CPI for 1997, also on a scale with 1967=100) for each of the years shown.

Prepared by Steven Thayer